Escrow 1
An Introduction

3ʳᵈ Edition

Walt Huber
Glendale College

Joe Newton
Bakersfield College

Copyright 1985, 1996, 2005, Third Edition
Educational Textbook Company, Inc.
P.O. Box 3597
Covina, California 91722
(626) 339-7733
(626) 332-4744 (Fax)
www.etcbooks.com

Library of Congress Cataloging-in-Publication Data

Escrow 1: An Introduction - Walt Huber and Joe Newton

ISBN 0-916772-51-9

This publication is designed to provide accurate and authoritative information in regard to the subject matter covered. It is sold with the understanding that the publisher is not engaged in rendering legal or other professional services. If legal or other expert assistance is required, the services of a competent professional person should be sought. All advice is given as purely anecdotal, and reflects the opinions and experiences of the authors, but is not held out as standard operating procedure. Practice varies throughout the state and brokerage by brokerage.

Preface

New and Improved 3rd Edition!

This text was originally designed to answer the needs of the escrow profession for a college-level introductory Escrow course. It has been widely recognized as one of the most comprehensive, yet easy-to-follow, textbooks available on this subject.

This text includes several sample escrow procedures, and their corresponding forms. You will notice we use the year 2050-2051 on these documents. That's because this book is meant to be kept by students long after their college days are over. It will serve as a helpful reference guide for many many years to come. It's that timeless.

This new and improved edition also includes a new vocabulary section at the end of each chapter. If you know what the words mean, you have won half the battle. The second half consists of learning how to work through the escrow process step-by-step and form-by-form. This text is written in such a way that it walks you through those steps, so your progress is steady and smooth from beginning to end.

Escrow can be a very complex subject, but this text really does make it less difficult. Together, Joe Newton and Walt Huber have over 60 years experience teaching college-level courses and have authored over 20 books between them. Who better to have created a textbook this complete, this straightforward, and learner-friendly?

Let the authors take you on this interesting journey into escrow. And have no fear, you couldn't ask for more experienced guides!

The authors wish to thank Dr. Elliot J. Dixon from East Los Angeles College for his assistance in the preparation of this book.

Also, a special thanks for the valuable assistance given by the people who helped design and produce this book: Philip Dockter, art director; Melinda Winters, cover design; Colleen Taber, executive editor; Linda Serra and Andrea Adkins, editors; and Rick Lee, pre-press editor and layout.

Table of Contents

Chapter 9 – Sample Three, Part One   229

Chapter 10 – Sampe Three, Part Two   253

Chapter 11 – Exchange Escrow Sample   273

Chapter 12 – Processing the Exchange Escrow   *313*

Chapter 13 – Note and Trust Deed Escrow Sample 353

Chapter 14 – Processing the Note and Trust Deed Escrow — 383

Chapter 15 – Laws, Regulations, and Sale of a Business — 413

NORTH AMERICAN TITLE COMPANY

Escrow Services | Buying / Selling a House | Property Information |
Office Locations | Site Index | Related Links | Home

an Ti... | CDMENU - CDIN | Xcel 2000 Comps |

TROGON

What is Escrow?

Escrow is a process by which a complex sale, exchange, or loan transaction involving real property is brought to completion.

I. History of Escrow

Transferring title to real property was a simple process at one time. The buyer would hand over consideration (money or something else of value) in exchange for a deed to the desired property. With the advent of community property laws, environmental impact reports, joint tenancy grant deeds and disclosure laws, transferring property became a much more involved process.

Small communities might still be able to operate this way. In larger areas, however, where parties to a transaction may not know each other, a process was needed to allow strangers to transfer property for consideration. The process is called escrow.

An **ESCROW** *is created when a separate written agreement instructs a neutral third party to hold funds and only proceed when all the agreed to conditions have been performed.* In California, an escrow is usually a requirement for the sale of a home or other real estate. Although it is not always required by law, it is an indispensable process by which an independent third party handles the legal paperwork of a real estate sale.

CHAPTER OUTLINE

A. ESCROWS TAKE TIME

There are several reasons why most real property transactions must have a period of time between the agreement and the final handing over of the money to the seller and the deed to the buyer:

1. Buyers or borrowers usually need time to gather funds, or to apply and qualify for loans.

2. Buyers want sellers to provide proof or guarantee that the deed is good: that there are no unknown legal owners or financial obligations against the property. Such guarantee is usually provided in the form of a policy of title insurance, which gives the buyer protection against a wide variety of problems arising from faulty deeds.

3. Other persons who hold loans for which the property is already pledged as collateral may want to be paid off when the property changes hands.

4. New lenders need enough time to examine the credit scores and financial backgrounds of potential borrowers, and to ascertain the value of the property before agreeing to lend.

5. Some buyers, such as ranchers or developers, must be reassured that the land can be used for their intended purposes; such things as water percolation testing and geological examination or preparation of environmental impact studies can take considerable time.

This very sensible plan of depositing funds and documents with a trustworthy third person until completion became accepted practice in feudal times, and the concept was adopted in early English Common Law. *Black's Law Dictionary* repeats the ancient precedent: *"… and deliver the deed unto a stranger, an escrow."* The word derives from the Middle French *escroue* (scroll), the form of most documents in those early times. *Webster's Collegiate Dictionary* defines it this way: *"escrow (1) a deed, a bond, money, or a piece of property delivered to a third person to be delivered by him to the grantee only upon the fulfillment of a condition (2) a fund or deposit designed to serve as an escrow."* The word escrow can also be used as a verb, "to place in escrow." A simplified definition is commonly used in the escrow industry:

Escrow is a deposit of money and instruments by two or more persons with a neutral third person, which are held by that person until certain conditions are met.

B. THE THIRD PERSON (Stakeholder)

The third person is the escrow officer, called the "stakeholder."

A *STAKEHOLDER is the agent of the respective parties until the escrow closes.* At this point the stakeholder becomes a trustee for the money and documents until their distribution

in accordance with the escrow instructions. Although the main function of escrow is to provide a safe place for the stake—the collection of documents and funds—until the deal can be concluded, it is also the place where many arrangements and accounting details are cleared up. The escrow officer does these things, but first he or she writes down the exact instruction of the principals (who usually are buyers and sellers, but who may also be others), making a new instrument called the escrow instructions. *ESCROW INSTRUCTIONS advise the escrow officer how to make the arrangements for completing the transaction, and he or she must not deviate from them.*

An escrow allows the buyer and seller to deal with each other without risk because the responsibility for handling all funds and documents lies with the escrow holder.

C. ESCROWS NOT REQUIRED BY LAW

Contrary to popular belief, escrows are NOT required by law for most residential sales. They are, however, required by state law for transactions involving the court-ordered sale or transfer of property which is being probated in court. It must also be used in sales or transfers of liquor licenses, negotiable securities, and impound accounts. These all make up a small percentage of escrow business, and all require compliance with legal guidelines, which are far more sophisticated than you will need for this course.

Escrows are **highly recommended** and nearly always used in the sale or transfer of land and businesses in California. This course will be devoted to the most common types of simple real property sales, the home sales that are the backbone of the escrow industry in this state. First, we should clarify the difference between real property and personal property. (See **Figures 1-1** and **1-2**.)

Figure 1-1

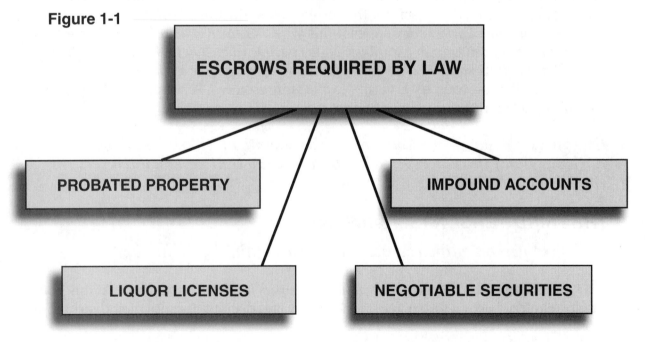

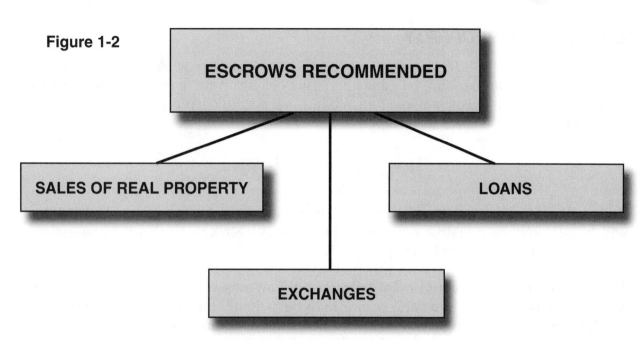

Figure 1-2

Escrows are highly recommended and nearly always used in the sale or transfer of land and businesses in California.

D. REAL PROPERTY

REAL PROPERTY is land and those things affixed to it. The California Civil Code, Section 660, says that a thing is affixed to land if:

1. it is attached to the land by roots;
2. it is imbedded in it, such as a retaining wall, a basement, well, or septic system;
3. it is permanently resting on it, such as a building or a parking lot;
4. it is attached in any way to (1), (2), (3), by way of mortar, nails, bolts, or screws. This is usually called a fixture, and includes anything which contributes in a basic way to the proper intended use of the property, such as built-in store equipment or bathroom fixtures.

The way judges determine if something is affixed to land in disputes is to decide if the property would be lessened in value or harmed if the supposedly affixed things were removed. There are many exceptions, particularly concerning farm property and growing crops, but they do not concern us here.

Also included in the definition of real property are things incidental or appurtenant to land, such as easements, covenants, restrictions, conditions, and water and mineral rights. These will be described more fully in a later chapter.

E. PERSONAL PROPERTY

PERSONAL PROPERTY is anything which can be owned or possessed that is not real property. This can be solid, tangible goods such as furniture (a synonym for tangible goods is chattels). Less tangible things like stock portfolios, money, and evidences of debt are also called personal property.

II. Contract Law

Escrows are legal processes, and their operative documents are the escrow instructions, which are companion instruments to the Purchase Agreement—if there is one—which has previously been signed by the principals.

Therefore, escrows must conform to contract law. If an escrow dispute is be brought into court for solution, despite whatever else may be at issue, the escrow will be deemed invalid from the beginning if it does not meet the basic requirements of a legal contract. An escrow will not be valid unless the following conditions are met. (See **Figure 1-3**.)

A. ALL PARTIES ARE LEGALLY ABLE TO MAKE CONTRACTS

In order to legally enter escrow as third parties, escrow holders must be licensed or otherwise permitted to hold escrows by the State of California. **Principals** must be legally capable of entering into contracts. **Minors** may obtain title alone, but they may not convey title (unless they are **emancipated minors**) except through their guardians and only if the action is first given court approval. They must not be persons legally judged to be *INCOMPETENT (not of sound mind, legally insane, or non compos mentis)*, but incompetent persons may also contract through their guardians if the action is approved by the court.

They must not be **convicts** who are serving their sentences either by incarceration or by parole. Convicts are, during their sentences, wards of the California Adult Authority. They may enter into contracts only with the prior approval of this Authority. Both convicts and incompetents may become owners of property by gift or inheritance. Persons who are not citizens of the United States are not limited in their ability to buy, sell, or transfer property: citizenship is not a factor in making escrow contracts. Entities other than persons may enter into escrow contracts; legally chartered corporations and partnerships, and other entities permitted to act as individuals may also make escrow contracts.

The escrow officer has no authority to inquire into the ability of parties who come to put transactions into escrow, or to make judgments in the matter.

It is the responsibility of the parties themselves to satisfy this requirement. The most an escrow officer can do if confronted by persons who may not qualify is to very

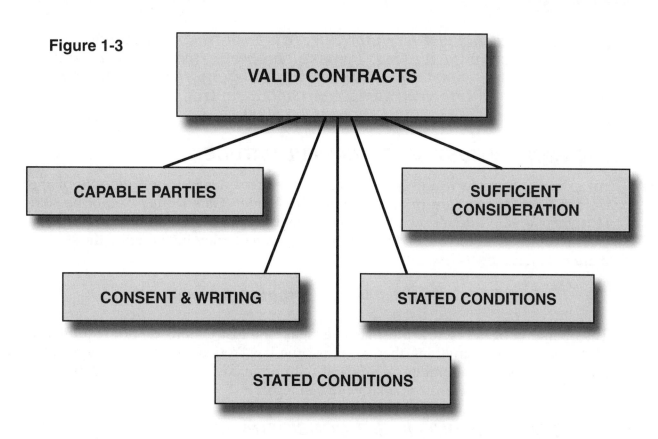

Figure 1-3

VALID CONTRACTS

CAPABLE PARTIES

SUFFICIENT CONSIDERATION

CONSENT & WRITING

STATED CONDITIONS

STATED CONDITIONS

discreetly place the question before a superior or the legal department of his/her firm. In any case, the officer should take the escrow, and not indicate to the parties that there is a problem.

B. THERE MUST BE MUTUAL CONSENT AND PROPER WRITING

These elements of a valid contract are satisfied by signed, written escrow instructions.

When the principals sign the instructions, they indicate that they consent to what is written therein, that is, they show their willingness to enter into a contract and their willingness to be bound by the conditions they have agreed upon. *If it is discovered in litigation that one party has knowingly lied about a material fact (FRAUD)*, or that parties are **mistaken** as to the matter of the agreement, or that one party is acting under **duress** or **threat of duress**, or that a party is acting under the **undue influence** of another, the escrow may be declared invalid.

Escrow personnel need to be aware of these things so they can perform their service properly, but they do not make decisions about the validity of the agreements brought to them for escrow. The validity of an escrow is seldom questioned unless legal action is brought, but good escrow officers will discreetly discuss any obviously questionable escrows with superiors before closing.

Not all contracts must be in writing. Most contracts involving real property must be in writing. Personal property items such as and refrigerators are transferred with a bill of sale. A written contract is not necessary for enforcement in a court of law for transfers of personal property where the amount paid is under $500.

C. THE ESCROW MUST HAVE A LAWFUL NATURE

An extreme example would be an attempted escrow dealing with the sale of the Golden Gate Bridge by a private citizen. The Golden Gate Bridge cannot be sold by someone who doesn't own it. It might seem flippant to quote such an obvious example, but, as an escrow officer, you have no way of knowing whether the subject matter of an escrow is lawful.

You should refuse to accept any escrow that is obviously illegal.

The operation of the escrow must also be legal. The instructions cannot require any of the parties to do anything that is against the law. You are on slightly more solid ground here: you can familiarize yourself with basic law well enough to determine whether to refuse an escrow you know to be illegal.

D. THERE MUST BE SUFFICIENT CONSIDERATION

Consideration is typically seen as payment, although consideration need not be money.

Consideration can be stocks and bonds, some form of service, other property, even love and affection. The important thing is that there be some consideration in exchange for the real property and that it be agreed upon beforehand by the parties making the deal. When the consideration is only love and affection, the transfer falls into the category of a gift, which action is governed by other laws than those which usually govern escrows. It is a good idea to ask parties who bring a "gift" transfer to escrow if they have consulted legal counsel in the matter.

Often, counsel would recommend that some money change hands, even if only a dollar or two. Escrow personnel should venture no opinion as to whether the consideration is sufficient.

E. THERE MUST BE STATED CONDITIONS

As we have said before, escrow holders do one unique thing in addition to all the accounting, sorting, and sending which is the largest physical part of their work. They write escrow instructions. They do not actually create these documents, since they follow the directions of the principals, but it is their interpretation of such directions that is written down and will be seen by others later—possibly including judges, if there is a dispute between the parties that must be resolved by litigation. These documents are binding contracts.

The purchase agreement that parties sign before coming to escrow is also a binding contract, and the escrow instructions work together with it to explain exactly when and how the sale agreement will be worked out. The escrow instructions more fully explain the **conditions** of the sale or transfer. Examples of conditions are:

1. Buyer will give XXXXX dollars to seller.
2. Seller will give a Grant Deed to buyer.
3. Seller will obtain a Policy of Title Insurance for buyer.
4. Seller will pay for termite work.
5. Escrow officer will prorate property taxes.
6. Escrow officer will see that the transaction is recorded with the County.

These are just a few of the kinds of promises that parties to an escrow make. There are numerous ways that conditions can be placed upon transactions, limited only by lawfulness under contract law. The instructions are tangible evidence that an escrow exists, and they demonstrate the stated conditions.

If an uncompleted (not closed) escrow is taken into court to try to specifically enforce its completion, the courts will probably halt its completion if any one of the above necessary elements is missing.

The last page of the purchase agreement contains an acknowledgement for receipt of the completed agreement (see **Figure 1-4**). Escrow companies often write a disclaimer regarding any discrepancies between the Purchase Agreement and the escrow instructions, stating that it's not the parties' intention to supersede the original terms of the Purchase Agreement. To avoid any discrepancies, always double check for mistakes and file addendums for changes.

Figure 1-4

ESCROW HOLDER ACKNOWLEDGMENT:
Escrow Holder acknowledges receipt of a Copy of this Agreement, (if checked, ☐ a deposit in the amount of $ _____), counter offer numbers _____ and _____
_____ , and agrees to act as Escrow Holder subject to paragraph 28 of this Agreement, any supplemental escrow instructions and the terms of Escrow Holder's general provisions.

Escrow Holder is advised that the date of Confirmation of Acceptance of the Agreement as between Buyer and Seller is _____

Escrow Holder _____ Escrow # _____
By _____ Date _____
Address _____
Phone/Fax/E-mail _____
Escrow Holder is licensed by the California Department of ☐ Corporations, ☐ Insurance, ☐ Real Estate. License # _____

Courts have provided that the "Doctrine of Substantial Performance" does not apply to escrows. In an escrow, all of the instructions must be carried out in accordance with those instructions given to the escrow holder.

If you are ever a principal in an escrow where you know there is a violation of the preceding requirements, do not sign the escrow instructions.

F. FORGERY PREVENTION

An escrow officer should always be alert to the possibility of a forged instrument. Forgery is the production of something counterfeit or fraudulent. Some suspicions may be raised by the following:

　1. Grantor/Borrower:

　　a. Is unavailable or has third party representing him or her.

　　b. Has no previous title insurance, escrow, or consideration.

　　c. Only recently took title or held title for a long time with no liens.

　　d. Is part of a dissolution of marriage.

　2. Buyer/Seller:

　　a. Demands quick close or other extreme processing by escrow.

　　b. Is using a witness for an acknowledgement.

　　c. Is an individual acting as a trustee.

　　d. Has unusual reconveyance form.

　　e. Uses Power of Attorney.

　　f. Requires transaction(s) outside of escrow.

　　g. Has incomplete Statement of Identity.

　　h. Is buying/selling vacant property.

　　i. Is using funds transferred to or from another escrow.

　　j. Is recording outside of escrow.

　　k. Has handwriting differences from other samples.

III. Who May Be an Escrow Holder?

A. ESCROW HOLDERS ARE AGENTS

To understand what an escrow agent is, it's necessary to understand the idea of agency. An *AGENT is anyone who is properly authorized to act for another.* This is very general, and there are many kinds of agents, including entities other than persons.

Corporations may be escrow agents too, since corporations are legally recognized entities with many of the same rights and responsibilities as individual persons. We will primarily discuss the special "limited" agency employed by escrow holders.

When a principal authorizes an escrow officer to deliver funds or documents to others, the principal is authorizing that officer to act for him. An ***ESCROW OFFICER*** *is agent to both principals (buyers and sellers)*. Actually, the principals usually authorize the escrow company or the escrow department to take care of their transaction. Although the escrow officer, who is an employee, has the role of agent and exercises agency, the actual legally licensed escrow agent is the company. Individual persons do not hold licenses as escrow agents in California.

The relationship of an escrow agent with the parties to an escrow is a ***FIDUCIARY RELATIONSHIP***; *that is, the agent has a duty to act in the highest faith, and to protect the trust and confidence of his principals*. This fiduciary role is absolutely basic to the escrow industry. Most rules concerning the ethical behavior of escrow personnel revolve around a code of ethics, which will be discussed later.

Individual persons do not hold licenses as escrow agents in California.

Escrow may be conducted by a variety of professionals in California. Each category of escrow holder is supervised differently under State Law, and only those firms which are organized solely for the processing of escrows and nothing else are required to have escrow licenses. (See **Figure 1-5**.)

1. Independent Escrow Agent Corporations

As commonly used in the escrow industry, the term "Escrow Agent" refers only to corporations which are devoted entirely to the processing of escrows.

Escrow agents must be licensed by the State of California to be qualified agents.

When they apply for licensing they must post a bond of at least $25,000, as stated in the part of the California Financial Code known as **Escrow Regulations, Section 17202**. Agent companies must also see that each employee who has access to money, negotiable securities, checking or trust accounts of the firm or its clients is bondable (Fin.C. Section 17203.1).

Escrow agents must at all times maintain a tangible net worth of at least $50,000, including liquid assets which are at least $25,000 more than current liabilities (Section 17210). The first branch office of the corporation must show a tangible net worth of 50% of the above and each subsequent branch office must show 25% of that amount in net worth (Fin.C Sec. 17210).

Figure 1-5

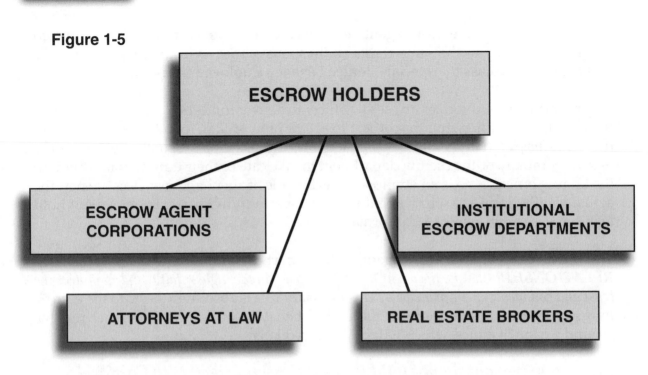

In addition to this surety bonding and proof of net worth, the Financial Code also requires certain experience.

Within the organization of each escrow agent corporation (either as an owner, officer, or employee), there must be one or more persons possessing a minimum of five (5) years of responsible escrow experience.

At least one such qualified person must be stationed on duty at each licensed business location during the time the location is open for business (Fin.C. Sec. 17200.8). Escrow licenses are issued by the California Commissioner of Corporations, who with his Commission is the officer who oversees the escrow industry in the State.

www.corp.ca.gov
California Department of Corporations

2. Escrow Departments of Title Companies

Most title insurance companies have escrow departments. This a natural extension of title insurance because title insurance companies understand the real estate business. Title insurance companies are regulated by the publicly elected insurance commissioner. Most title insurance escrow departments are in northern California, though they are becoming increasingly popular in southern California.

3. Escrow Departments of Financial Institutions

Most commercial banks, savings banks, and insurance companies operate escrow departments as a service to their customers. They provide all-in-one-place service to people and businesses whose loans, accounts or estate executors are in the same institution. The commercial banks are regulated and supervised by various bodies, depending on whether they are nationally-chartered or state-chartered institutions. They may or may not be members of the Federal Reserve Bank (The Fed), with automatic inclusion in the Federal Deposit Insurance Corporation (FDIC). If they are members, as most banks in California are, they are supervised by The Fed. In turn, The Fed and the other national banks, whether members of The Fed or not, are issued their charters and are supervised by the Comptroller of the Currency.

www.occ.treas.gov
Office of the Comptroller of the Currency

Savings banks may also be either nationally or state chartered, and thus are regulated by appropriate bodies, usually the Federal Home Loan Bank Board. They make the majority of loans for the purchase of real property in California. Insurance companies also make loans for real property purchases, and their escrow departments are overseen by the Insurance Commissioner of the state in which their companies are chartered, although like the Savings and Loan Institutions they may not conduct escrows (or other business) in ways that are contrary to the laws of the other states in which they do business.

4. Attorneys-at-Law

Lawyers may conduct escrows for their clients as part of their usual legal practice. They are not directly regulated by a Commissioner but they must adhere to all the laws and regulations set forth in the Law of their own states. Indeed, in many portions of the United States, lawyers are the *only* agents legally permitted to conduct escrows.

California's difference in this area is a result of action taken by Title Insurance companies shortly after this state's admission to the Union in 1850. During this time, there was a massive sorting-out of tangled ownership records resulting from Spain's and Mexico's conflicting Land Grant practices. There were two large coalitions of title companies, north and south, who established customary escrow practices for their areas, and the differences we see today between north and south date from that time. Back then, there was a shortage of lawyers experienced in land-ownership history, and theory was being newly written into law. They permitted the title companies and other specialists to assume the legal responsibility for conducting escrows, and made agreements with them as to the exact amount of legal work that escrow practitioners could do. These agreements became the State Bar Treaty, which we will discuss later in the section devoted to ethical behavior.

5. Real Estate Brokers

Real estate brokers may conduct escrows if the escrows are directly connected to transactions in which they are agent for buyer or seller. They must process their escrows at the address which is listed on their brokers's license, which is issued by the State Department of Real Estate. The Department of Real Estate supervises and regulates the escrow business of real estate brokers, but like all the rest they must follow the law.

IV. What Associations Help Escrow Agents in Their Work?

A. CALIFORNIA ESCROW ASSOCIATION (CEA)

Founded in 1956, this is the largest and most active group devoted to improving escrow service in this state. Its members are escrow officers and agents who work for all the escrow-processing entities, mostly the independent agents and the larger financial institutions. The organization holds monthly meetings in 30 regions of the state and presents conferences and seminars several times each year. Its education committee works toward improving the training of new escrow employees and increasing the expertise of those already working in the field. It also has an influential committee which proposes and promotes legislation designed for the betterment of the escrow industry and its practitioners.

CEA offers the only statewide program for professional designation of escrow officers based on comprehensive examination. The designations include:

1. Certified Senior Escrow Officer (CSEO)
2. Certified Escrow Officer (CEO)
3. Certified Mobile Home Specialist (CMHS)
4. Certified Bulk sales Specialist (CBSS)
5. Certified Escrow Instructor (CEI)
6. Certified Escrow Technician (CET)

CEA also publishes a monthly newsletter which may be subscribed to by any interested person, membership in CEA notwithstanding.

www.ceaescrow.org
California Escrow Association (CEA)

B. ESCROW INSTITUTE OF CALIFORNIA

This is an organization of the owners of independent escrow companies. Since its beginning in 1947 (with the addition in 1978 of the title "dba Independent Escrow Licensees of California") it has devoted itself to all the aims listed above for CEA, with special emphasis on the problems of the independent agents. This group helps solve corporate problems for its members, and maintains active relationships with many related industries in the state—such as the California Association of Realtors®. It is committed to the development of cooperation and goodwill among the myriad groups connected with the real property business in California.

www.escrowinstitute.org
Escrow Institute of California

C. CALIFORNIA LAND TITLE ASSOCIATION (CLTA)

All the title companies in California, whether independents or subsidiaries of larger companies, are members of CLTA. This organization sets standards and preferred procedure for the state's title companies. It works closely with current and pending action in the Legislature by helping to guide beneficial bills and keeping its members informed of changes relating to title work. It issues periodic bulletins and publishes an annual summary of legislative action. CLTA was instrumental in standardizing the types of policies offered by title insurance companies.

www.clta.org
California Land Title Association (CLTA)

V. How Should Escrow Officers Behave?

A. THEY MUST SERVE THE PUBLIC

Escrow is a service occupation. The only product is the fast, efficient, *correctly done*, and courteous processing of the customer's transaction. Every employee who meets the customer is the direct representative of the company and as such has control of the customer's feeling about the company. Each must strive to give the impression that he or she wants only to serve the customer to the very best of his or her ability.

This helpful service attitude is crucial to the good name of the firm and must be kept in mind always.

B. THEIR INFORMATION IS STRICTLY CONFIDENTIAL

Theoretically there are *no* circumstances under which any employee may reveal to anyone any fact about any escrow in progress, past or present. Persons such as bill

collectors or lawyers are extremely curious to find out if escrows in progress may affect their interests, but the duty of loyalty under the fiduciary relationship of the escrow officer to his or her principals requires that he or she protect the principal's confidence.

The parties to an escrow are not entitled to know elements of their own escrows which are not their concern—for instance, if a buyer intends to sell the property immediately upon close of escrow, it is not the business of escrow to tell the original seller of the buyer's plans. It is not the buyer's business what the seller intends to do with money realized from the sale. This is a delicate area, and actual practice varies: some theorists feel that parties should never be told the other party's side of the escrow, and some feel that there are extenuating circumstances when it would be right to do so.

Real estate brokers for the parties need to be kept informed of escrow facts, but they are operating under fiduciary restrictions too. Sometimes parties are represented by legal counsel—which must be stated in writing by the party using counsel—and in such cases the attorney must be kept informed. Both brokers and counsel should be told only what pertains to the matter at hand, though, and not given all the chatty details.

Teachers of escrow, too, may discuss past escrows in their classes but must take care not to divulge any giveaways like exact names or addresses. Whether the company holds a conservative or a liberal view on the matter of confidentiality, escrow employees must be extremely circumspect on the *telephone*; never divulging any information to callers unless they know for absolute fact who the caller is, and that the caller is entitled to information.

C. THEIR POSITION IS STRICTLY NEUTRAL

Because of their expertise, escrow officers are often tempted to advise clients in matters pertinent to their escrows, but the act of imparting certain kinds of advice can sway the course of an escrow in ways unforeseen by the officer.

It is extremely dangerous to attempt to advise clients, but it is quite permissible to explain things to clients.

The dividing line between advice and education is very fine. Neutrality becomes an issue when the officer, who knows both sides of the escrow, unwittingly reacts to his or her knowledge by giving slanted explanations: this can lead to collapsed escrows and litigation against the company for ruining a transaction. Therefore, escrow officers must use great caution in discussing escrow matters with their customers. These guidelines may be helpful:

1. If you find yourself unable to maintain neutrality (if, for instance, you strongly suspect that one party is taking advantage of another), find a way to back out before you get involved: give the escrow to another officer.

2. When parties ask leading questions ("Which do you think is better, vesting this way or that way ... ?") always refer them to their broker or attorney. Beware of "clever" ploys to get you to commit yourself.

3. You may explain the extent and nature of various title insurance policies, and the approval requirements of some policies; and you should discuss unusual items that may appear in title searches with affected parties, but guard against giving advice about what their reaction to your explanation should be. Here, trouble could result from withholding information from parties.

4. Never suggest that a pest control inspection report be made. When an institutional lender is involved, there is usually a requirement for a report on a 1-to-4 unit family dwelling sale—then you must make it known (the lender usually does) so the seller can make arrangements.

5. Sometimes principals or even brokers are obviously uninformed. **You have a responsibility to inform them of matters directly pertinent to them.** Be guided by your common sense and your superiors—beginning escrow personnel are expected to worry about going too far in these delicate areas. Superiors may sigh at having many questions from cautious beginners, but they would rather answer questions than see employees be too liberal with information.

D. THEIR EMPLOYERS ARE IN BUSINESS TO MAKE MONEY

Escrow agents or departments cannot show expected profits at the end of the year if their employees have been careless or ignorant. This can involve the company in lawsuits. They do not gain high standing in the community if their employees are rude and unkempt, or lose valuable documents, or cause good customers to go elsewhere for better service. In other words, they are in business to make money. The ideal employee will have the attributes of a saint—personal integrity, patience, tact, foresight, and honesty.

E. THEY MAY NOT PRACTICE LAW

Escrow officers should become familiar with the legal aspects of real estate and escrow procedures, and they must keep up with changes in the law, but they must never advise clients about legal matters.

They are also strictly limited in the types of legal documents (synonym: *instruments*) they may prepare during the course of an escrow. The first formal arrangement between the legal community in California and the escrow industry was made in 1936 between the State Bar of California and the California Land Title Association (CLTA). Since then, several other agreements have been made, culminating in 1966 with the State Bar Treaty between the Escrow Institute and the State Bar. This agreement spells out what an escrow officer may do and may not do, in order to prevent problems resulting from possible unauthorized practice of law. The Treaty provides a guide for the entire escrow industry. In very simplified form it states:

1. Escrow may not make wills or living trusts under any circumstances.

2. Escrow may not presume expertise in legal matters.

3. Escrow may not recommend specific attorneys to its clients.

4. Escrow may not attempt to interpret any contract, including agreements of sale or escrow instructions for customers, but escrow may make statements as to its own duties and may give factual information about the general nature and procedure of escrows.

5. Escrow may not offer the services of its own legal counsel to clients.

6. Escrow may not suggest that legal advice is unnecessary and may not suggest that such advice is relatively unimportant.

7. Escrow may neither choose nor draw (design) legal instruments, except certain generally accepted pre-printed forms used in normal escrow transactions. These may be filled in only, and they may not be leases, subleases, or agreements for the sale of real property.

F. THEY SHOULD LEARN CEA'S CODE OF ETHICS

This code was adopted by the California Escrow Association Escrow Association in 1969. It is reproduced here.

CALIFORNIA ESCROW ASSOCIATION (CEA) CODE OF ETHICS

The Escrow Holder is the instrumentality through which, ideally, most real estate transactions are carried on, the responsibility and obligations undertaken in escrow being of the utmost importance. The Escrow Officer, therefore, is zealous to maintain and improve the standards of his or her calling and shares with his or her fellow escrow officers a common responsibility for its integrity and honor. Wherever the word Escrow Officer is used within the context hereof and hereinafter; such designation shall be deemed to refer to all persons who are practicing any type of escrow activity who are members of the California Escrow Association.

Every person engaged in the processing of escrow work who holds such membership in the California Escrow Association pledges himself or herself to observe the spirit of and conduct his or her business in accordance with the following Code of Ethics:

(continued)

ARTICLE I: An Escrow Officer shall keep himself or herself informed as to legislation and laws affecting the escrow profession in order to contribute to the public thinking on matters relating to escrows, real estate, financing and other matters and questions relative to the escrow profession.

ARTICLE II: Protection of public against fraud, misrepresentation and unethical practices in the escrow profession shall be uppermost in the mind of the Escrow Officer and he or she shall, at all times, be ready to expose such offenses.

ARTICLE III: An Escrow Officer should expose, without fear or favor, before the proper tribunal, corrupt or dishonest conduct in the profession.

ARTICLE IV: It is the duty of an Escrow Officer to preserve his or her clients' confidence, including all matters surrounding an escrow, either opened or closed; he or she should never reveal the contents of any file to any person not entitled to such contents except where a subpoena has been issued, or to expose corrupt or dishonest practice.

ARTICLE V: An Escrow Officer shall not be a party to the naming of a false consideration in an escrow.

ARTICLE VI: An Escrow Officer shall not engage in activities that constitute the practice of law and should never hesitate recommending that a party seek legal counsel in connection with an escrow.

ARTICLE VII: An Escrow Officer shall accept escrow instructions only in writing; acceptance of instructions verbally does a disservice to the public.

ARTICLE VIII: An Escrow Officer shall deliver copies of all instructions to all parties who are affected by such instructions.

ARTICLE IX: An Escrow Officer must maintain strict neutrality as an "Unbiased Third Party" to each transaction.

ARTICLE X: An Escrow Officer should not accept an escrow which he or she knows is outside of his or her scope of knowledge unless he or she makes such fact first known to his or her principals.

ARTICLE XI: An Escrow Officer should not seek unfair advantage over his or her fellow Escrow Officers and should willingly share with them lessons of his or her study and experiences.

ARTICLE XII: An Escrow Officer shall conduct his or her profession so as to avoid controversies with fellow Escrow Officers. In the event of a controversy between Escrow Officers, such controversy shall be arbitrated at the level of the Regional Association.

ARTICLE XIII: In the event of controversy between Escrow Officers of different Regional Associations, such controversy should be arbitrated by a board comprised of two members from each Association of members so involved.

(continued)

ARTICLE XIV: An Escrow Officer shall cooperate with his or her fellow Escrow Officers in escrow matters which affect each mutually.

ARTICLE XV: When an Escrow Officer is charged with unethical practices, he or she should place all pertinent facts before the proper tribunal of Regional Association to which he or she belongs, for investigation and judgement.

ARTICLE XVI: An Escrow Officer shall never disparage the professional practice of a competitor, nor volunteer an opinion of a competitor's transaction. If his or her opinion is sought, it should be rendered with strict professional integrity and courtesy.

ARTICLE XVII: An Escrow Officer should not solicit the service of an employee in the organization of a fellow Escrow Officer without the knowledge of the employer.

ARTICLE XVIII: It is the duty of an Escrow Officer, at the outset of an escrow, to disclose to the clients all circumstances, if any, of his relationship to the parties, and any interest in or connection with the escrow which might influence one or both clients in the selection of an escrow holder.

ARTICLE XIX: It is the duty of an Escrow Officer to his or her clients and the public in general to be punctual and direct in the closing of his or her escrows.

ARTICLE XX: In the best interests of society, his or her associates and his or her own profession, an Escrow Officer shall be loyal to the California Escrow Association and the Escrow Association of his or her local vicinity and be active in its work, and conform to this Code of Ethics and the By-Laws of this Association.

VI. CHAPTER SUMMARY

An ESCROW is conducted to insure completion of a sale, exchange, or loan as it involves real property. It is a deposit of money and instruments whereby a third person or STAKEHOLDER holds these funds and documents according to ESCROW INSTRUCTIONS.

The escrow involves REAL PROPERTY, which is land and those things which are affixed to it. PERSONAL PROPERTY is anything that can be owned or possessed and is not real property.

Escrow is a legal process and must include certain essentials. The requirements include MUTUAL CONSENT, IN WRITING, LEGAL PURPOSE, SUFFICIENT CONSIDERATION, and CAPABLE OR COMPETENT PARTIES.

An escrow is a dual AGENT that is authorized to act for both parties in a transaction. Such agents may be independent or employed by a financial institution. Brokers and attorneys may also act as an escrow in those transactions pertinent to their normal course of business.

The CALIFORNIA ESCROW ASSOCIATION (CEA) is devoted to the betterment of escrow services in the state. Members include escrow officers and agents that work either independently or for institutions. Various designations are given by the CEA to qualified members.

The ESCROW INSTITUTE of California is made up of members who are employed by the independent escrow companies that are licensed by the California Department of Corporations. It is the DOC that regulates the procedures and practices of the independent companies and subjects them to stringent requirements designed to protect consumers.

All title companies in California are members of the California Land Title Association (CLTA), who sets standards and procedures for the state's title companies. The AMERICAN ESCROW ASSOCIATION is a national association that represents members at the federal level.

VII. TERMS

Agent: One who represents a principal in contracts with third persons.

American Escrow Association: A group of title and escrow representatives that meet to further goals in education and professionalism for the escrow industry as a whole.

California Escrow Association (CEA): An association dedicated to the professionalism of escrow personnel through education and legislation.

California Land Title Association: An organization of title companies in California that sets standards and procedures for title companies.

Capable Parties: Principals must legally be able to enter into a contract.

Escrow: Neutral depository whereby funds and documents are deposited with a third person for the purpose of completing a real estate transaction.

Escrow Institute: An organization of independent escrow companies.

Escrow Instructions: When signed, they become a binding contract that tells the parties to an escrow what they are required to perform.

Independent Escrow Agent: An escrow company licensed by the California Department of Corporations.

Lawful Nature: Subject matter of an escrow must able to be legally bought or sold.

Mutual Consent: In a contract it is the meeting of the minds with a proper offer and acceptance.

Personal Property: Anything that can be owned or possessed that is not real property.

Proper Writing: Refers to the requirements of law that states certain contracts must be in writing to be enforceable.

Real Estate Licensees: A licensee by the Department of Real Estate capable of representing buyers or sellers in a real estate transaction.

Real Property: Land and those things affixed to it.

Stakeholder: Refers to the role of an escrow holder.

Sufficient Consideration: Contractual requirement that value must be exchanged for value.

VIII. CHAPTER QUIZ

1. Escrow is a:

   a. legal requirement.
   b. process.
   c. both a and b.
   d. neither a nor b.

2. How many parties, other than neutral escrow, are usually involved in escrow?

   a. 1
   b. 2
   c. 3
   d. 4

3. The escrow officer is considered:

   a. an attorney.
   b. a stakeholder.
   c. a gambler.
   d. an agent of the buyer.

4. Escrows in California are:

   a. sometimes recommended.
   b. seldom recommended.
   c. highly recommended.
   d. never recommended.

5. The years of experience an escrow agent must have before opening a business is:

   a. 3 years.
   b. 5 years.
   c. 7 years.
   d. 10 years.

6. Real estate brokers may conduct escrows if the escrows are:

   a. authorized by the state.
   b. transactions in which the broker is not an agent.
   c. agreed to by buyer and seller.
   d. transactions where the broker is an agent for buyer or seller.

7. One association that helps escrow agents in their work is the:

    a. U.S. Real Estate Co.
    b. United Escrow Association.
    c. California Escrow Association.
    d. California Real Estate Association.

8. The California Escrow Association was founded in:

    a. 1900.
    b. 1956.
    c. 1960.
    d. 1965.

9. It is dangerous for an escrow agent to give:

    a. advice.
    b. explanations.
    c. restrictions.
    d. all of the above.

10. Under any circumstance, escrow may NOT make:

    a. wills
    b. living trusts
    c. both a and b
    d. neither a nor b

ANSWERS: 1. b; 2. b; 3. b; 4. c; 5. b; 6. d; 7. d; 8. b; 9. b; 10. c

Basic Escrow Processes

I. Introduction

The average escrow (this is fiction, for there is no "average" escrow) is not particularly complicated or difficult. You, as an escrow officer, have these main tasks to perform:

1. Obtain the instructions of the parties
2. Draw the instruments of transfer
3. Obtain a policy of title insurance
4. Collect the funds
5. See that the transfer is recorded in the county records
6. Give the money to the seller and give the deed to the buyer.

There are several steps involved with each of these tasks. Each step must be properly done, or there is a risk that the transaction will fall through. This chapter will show a general overview of the steps commonly taken to process an average single-family residence sale. You'll see most of the common terms and phrases used in the escrow industry. When you begin to process sample escrows yourself, the terms and procedures will be used, but with more variety and detail.

CHAPTER OUTLINE

A. PROCESS BASICALLY THE SAME THROUGHOUT CALIFORNIA

It is very important to realize that the escrow process is essentially the same throughout California, no matter who is doing the processing or where it is done. Other states vary slightly.

There are considerable differences in the timing of the steps; some areas insist on getting signed escrow instructions before doing anything else, while others do that much later and get the title search right away. These variations can be said to be methodological, since the closing of the escrow shows that all the same steps will have been done. Some escrow experts say the dividing line lies roughly at Bakersfield, and refer to "north" procedure and "south" procedure. However, many statewide escrow agents insist on uniform practice throughout their territories. Remember, the main difference is in the timing of the steps and not different practice.

1. Slight Escrow Differences Between North and South

A very slight philosophical difference exists that is more of a favorite topic of escrow experts' arguments than an actual problem (see **Figure 2-1**). Apparently the further north one goes, the more concerned escrow is with protecting the parties' privacy of information (emphasis on confidentiality). Further south, there is more concern for making sure that pertinent facts are not withheld (emphasis on the impartial third party nature of escrow). *This slight difference in priorities generally results in separate instructions for buyers and sellers in the north (**UNILATERAL INSTRUCTIONS**)*

Figure 2-1

California Customs (North vs. South)
for Escrow Services and Title Insurance

When are signed escrow instructions delivered?

Customarily in Southern California, the (bilateral) escrow instructions are signed by both the buyer and seller just after the **start of escrow**.

Customarily in Northern California, the (unilateral) escrow instructions are given to the escrow officer just before the **close of escrow**.

Who performs the escrow services?

Escrow services in Southern California are traditionally performed by **independent escrow companies (corporations) or financial institutions**.

Escrow services in Northern California are traditionally performed by **title insurance companies**.

Who pays the escrow fees?

Escrow service fees in Southern California are usually split **50-50 between the buyer and the seller**.

Escrow service fees in Northern California are usually **paid for by the buyer**.

Who traditionally pays title insurance fees?

Customarily in Southern California, **the seller pays for the California Land Title Association (CLTA) policy (standard policy)**.

Customarily in Northern California, **the buyer pays for the California Land Title Association (CLTA) policy (standard policy)**.

In both the North and the South, **the buyers pay for any coverage above the California Standard Title Insurance policy**.

and a single instruction signed by both buyers and sellers in the south (BILATERAL INSTRUCTIONS). These are broad generalizations, and are given as an explanation. Arguments as to the relative merits of one view or another have no place in an introductory course such as this. See the end of the chapter for more details.

Figure 2-2 shows the general plan of the escrow process. It demonstrates that there are several lines of endeavor which move along concurrently. Some escrows may have fewer tasks. For instance, there may be no existing loans that need to be settled. Some escrows have many different new loans to coordinate. But we are dealing with an example of an escrow here, and will discuss the six basic escrows tasks. The word "tasks" is used to avoid confusion, in that the terms "escrow duties" and "escrow processes" are a slightly different matter, as explained further.

II. Six Main Escrow Tasks

A. OBTAIN THE INSTRUCTIONS OF THE PARTIES

1. Taking an Escrow

When buyers and sellers come to an agreement, they or their broker will suggest an escrow holder. When all agree as to whom the escrow holder will be, they or one of the brokers will telephone, fax, e-mail, or will go in person to "open the escrow." This is an important time for the escrow officer, for the smoothness with which the escrow will proceed is greatly helped by the skillful way the officer elicits the necessary information.

It is an escrow officer's duty to ascertain the essence of the transaction and see that it is implemented according to the intentions of all parties.

Each officer will have his or her own style. But an effective escrow officers make a continuing effort to be pleasant, calm, and reassuring to the client. He or she may find it difficult to believe the depth of the clients' ignorance in matters so familiar to themselves. The escrow officer may be offended by apparent rudeness. He or she may even be amused by what seems to be totally unnecessary terror. But the escrow officer must keep in mind that, for many home buyers, the transaction may be the greatest investment of their lives and could well mean financial disaster for them if something goes wrong.

It cannot be repeated too often that the escrow officer must be sensitive to the clients' needs, all the while remaining strictly impartial as to the actual matters at hand.

A friendly but not "chummy" manner and an efficient but not "fussy" way of handling the business is the best way to inspire the confidence of the client.

Figure 2-2

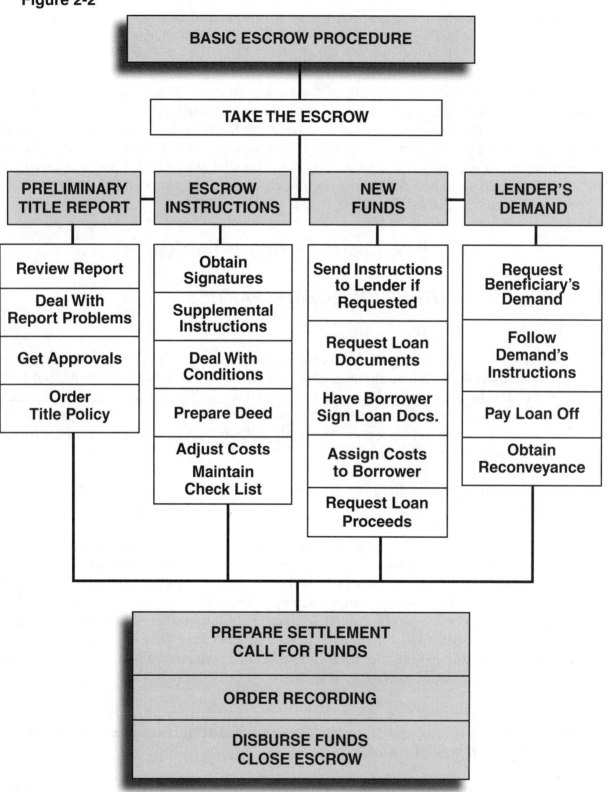

BASIC ESCROW PROCEDURE

TAKE THE ESCROW

PRELIMINARY TITLE REPORT	ESCROW INSTRUCTIONS	NEW FUNDS	LENDER'S DEMAND
Review Report	Obtain Signatures	Send Instructions to Lender if Requested	Request Beneficiary's Demand
Deal With Report Problems	Supplemental Instructions	Request Loan Documents	Follow Demand's Instructions
Get Approvals	Deal With Conditions	Have Borrower Sign Loan Docs.	Pay Loan Off
Order Title Policy	Prepare Deed	Assign Costs to Borrower	Obtain Reconveyance
	Adjust Costs / Maintain Check List	Request Loan Proceeds	

PREPARE SETTLEMENT CALL FOR FUNDS

ORDER RECORDING

DISBURSE FUNDS CLOSE ESCROW

Remember that the "client" is the principal to the escrow, who will pay the escrow fees. They may or may not be represented by a broker, and you may or may not ever meet them. But they, and not the broker, are the "client." The officer needs to work well with brokers, to insure that future escrows might result from the pleasant experience, but must first and foremost serve the client.

It cannot be repeated too often that the escrow officer must be sensitive to the clients' needs, all the while remaining strictly impartial as to the actual matters at hand.

2. The Escrow Memo (Escrow Order)

In order to have a complete picture of the transaction, there are a number of facts you must know. This is true whether the escrow instructions are to be drawn immediately or much later. (See **Figure 2-3**.)

Figure 2-3   **The Escrow Memo**

1. Date escrow is opened.
2. Your in-house code number for this escrow.
3. The type of escrow: loan, sale, exchange, etc.
4. The price, and its breakdown:
    a. Full price of the property.
    b. Money paid outside (before) escrow and to whom paid.
    c. Money paid outside escrow and to be deposited into escrow.
    d. Money paid into escrow as down payment.
    e. Money paid into escrow as the proceeds of new loans.
    f. Money not converted into cash in escrow, such as loans from seller to buyer.
5. Street address of property.
6. Full legal description of the property.
7. Full names of all who hold title to property, addresses, phone, and e-mail address.
8. Full names of all buyers and the manner in which they intend to hold title, present address, phone, and e-mail address.
9. Amounts and types of loans sought. If private loans rather than institutional, all details as specified by buyers and sellers.
10. Amounts and data on loans to be settled in escrow.
11. Expenses to be adjusted for buyers and sellers.
12. Commission data.
13. Other directions about the transaction given by buyers and sellers.
14. Length of time or suggested closing date for the escrow.

As you can see, there are quite a few items to accomplish. In actual practice, most escrow officers are happy to let some of the items go until a little later. Even when the instructions are to be drawn right away, it is permissible to type in place of the missing information something like "as per additional information to be deposited in escrow" for items like the full legal description. This call, fax, e-mail, or visit is also a good time to let the broker or client know which documents might be required by you for the escrow, such as the present grant deed and the present title insurance policy.

This opening interview is a time when questions are likely. If, for example, the client, or his or her salesperson or broker, should ask for your opinion about some matters relating to the transaction, you may be placed in the position of possibly giving legal advice. Whenever your opinion is requested about the manner of vesting or funding, it is necessary that you suggest they seek the advice of their attorney or other counsel of choice.

The parties, on the **CAR® California Residential Purchase Agreement and Joint Escrow Instructions** (see **Figure 2-13**), will specify other details of their transaction, such as whether there will be an approved building inspection or a pest control inspection. They will probably be very specific about what things are requirements, the failure of which prevents the deal from being concluded. The duties of an escrow officer include handling those things which pertain to the proper funding, obtaining of clear title for the new owner, and arranging for the division of ongoing expenses (proration).

Whenever your opinion is requested about the manner of vesting or funding, you must suggest they seek the advice of their attorney or other counsel of choice. Do not give legal or financial advice.

They may want to exchange personal property as part of the deal, arrange for the possession date, or assure that various things on the property are in working order. These things are not the duties of escrow, since they aren't directly connected with the transfer of legal title to real property and cannot be guaranteed through the transmission of correct documents. You may tell the parties this, and ask that they take care of "extraneous" matters by other agreement outside of escrow, or you may explain that you can't actually see that such things are performed, but will note they agreed to arrangements as memoranda in your typing of escrow instructions.

You must see that those elements of the transaction that can be assured by the property transmission of documents are fulfilled.

3. Escrow Instructions

ESCROW INSTRUCTIONS are usually computer-generated forms that permit the listing of all the funds and documents that will move through escrow, and specify the conditions under which they may be transmitted. They then set forth the proper recipients of all funds and documents.

Written escrow instructions (or a signed purchase agreement and joint escrow instructions) to an escrow holder constitute a contract.

A simple metaphor serves to show the importance of the instructions. The transaction is the actual event—ownership or indebtedness changes hands. It is the territory, and the escrow instruction is the map—a written explanation of the nature and direction of the transaction. The parties describe the territory to you, the escrow officer, and then you make the map and follow it.

Regardless of the type of escrow used, escrow holders can only act on written instructions. Each and every aspect of an escrow must be initiated by written, signed instructions.

See **Figure 2-4** for a list of the essential duties of an escrow.

Figure 2-4

Essential Escrow Duties

Conditional	Confidentiality	Deposit Holder
Delivery of all funds and documents when the conditions of the escrow have been met.	All escrow instructions are confidential, and disclosure can be authorized only by the buyer or seller.	The escrow company can disburse funds and documents only when all conditions have been met and both parties have reached an agreement.

The California Residential Purchase Agreement (and Joint Escrow Instructions)

The California Association of Realtors® has changed the language in their "purchase agreement form" to allow an escrow company to start the escrow process by accepting a faxed copy and simply approving the "escrow holder acknowledgment" section on the last page. The escrow company fills out that that part of the form, issues an Escrow Number, and sends it (page 8 acceptance) back to the Salesperson/Broker's office. It is simple and straight forward, but most escrow company's will wait until they actually get the deposit in their hands before proceeding.

(continued)

The California Residential Purchase Agreement and Joint Escrow Instructions (CAR Form RPA-CA) has allowed salespeople and brokers to make a smooth transition from the Purchase Agreement to the start of escrow. Since most details are taken directly from the Purchase Agreement, the escrow process starts faster. Some details of the escrow process must be clarified, answered, and signatures received before the escrow is advanced and closed. In addition, most escrow companies also want their specific provisions approved and signed by the parties as they proceed.

This has revolutionized the escrow industry for starting a normal salesperson-assisted sale. But all too quickly the salesperson will realize that he or she must help coordinate the escrow officer's need for specific documents from the client in a timely manner, to make sure the escrow closes on schedule.

B. DRAW THE INSTRUMENTS OF TRANSFER

Throughout the world, the most common method of acquiring ownership (title) to real property is by deed transfer.

In California, all real property transfers must be in writing. A **DEED** *is a written instrument which transfers the title to real property from one owner to another.* While it is now a pre-printed document that is completed with the proper information, it can actually be any object of any permanent material, size, shape, or workmanship which conveys its intent and is agreed to be a deed by its native society. The world's museums contain many ancient and lovely objects of ivory, pottery, cloth and precious metal that are in fact deeds. Currently, when a deed becomes lost or destroyed, serious complications arise when the owner attempts to transfer the property.

The deed is possibly the most valuable evidence of title (artifact) that can be associated with land.

1. Kinds of Deeds

There are several kinds of deeds, each denoting certain warranties to the deed's owner and the one to whom the deed is given in a transfer. They can be divided into several types, either by the kinds of warranties they offer, by the identification of the grantors, or by their operative words. But it is most correct to classify them in two major categories: grant deeds or quitclaim deeds. (See **Figure 2-5**.)

The grant deed uses the word "grant" to convey title. There are three main types of grant deeds, listed here in the descending power of their warranties:

1. The land patent or land grant
2. The warranty deed
3. The grant deed

Figure 2-5

```
                    ┌─────────────────────┐
                    │        DEEDS        │
                    └─────────────────────┘
                       /               \
                      /                 \
    ┌───────────────────────┐   ┌──────────────────────────┐
    │      GRANT-TYPE        │   │      QUITCLAIM-TYPE      │
    │ Conveys Freehold Estate│   │         Conveys          │
    │                        │   │ Less-Than-Freehold Estate│
    └───────────────────────┘   └──────────────────────────┘
```

a. Land Patents or Land Grants

Land patents or land grants are seldom seen today, but they are still a legally accepted method of conveying title. *LAND PATENTS or LAND GRANTS are given by a monarch or a government to a citizen in return for, or as a reward for, faithful and meritorious service.* They carry the highest form of warranty, since their words of conveyance are backed by the full power of the government. Their only drawback is that their validity comes into question when the government's power is removed. Much of California's land was distributed by means of land patents from the Spanish Crown during the time when California was Spain's colonial possession. Except for a promise to support the Crown, the grantee, or ranchero, had absolute control of his or her land and everything and everyone on it. The patents were voided when Mexico took over from Spain, and ownership became increasingly muddled through the Gold Rush when vast numbers of settlers acquired land.

When California joined the United States, one of the first duties of the new legislature was to reorganize rightful title to the land. As a result of these efforts, many of the original patents were reinstated and new grant deeds were issued. There is now an orderly record of title (called a chain of title) for most of California's real estate dating back to 1850, when statehood was declared.

b. Warranty Deed

Warranty deeds are also seldom seen in California but are widely used in Eastern and Midwestern states. *WARRANTY DEEDS spell out in specific wording exactly what they warrant; usually that the grantor has lawful authority to sell or transfer title, and that he or she will defend the title against the claims of others.* Escrow officers occasionally deal with warranty deeds in interstate transfers, and most seek the advice of their company attorneys to draw them correctly. Whenever a

deed in escrow is more complicated than a simple grant deed, it is best to have an attorney draw it or at least advise on its proper drawing.

c. Grant Deed

*The **GRANT DEED** is a document that transfers title (evidence of property ownership), with the key word being "grant."*

The grant deed is the usual form of deed in California and the western states.

A grant deed's warranties are "implied" by law. That is, laws have been enacted that specify what the word "grant" means in this state, although they are not actually written into the deed. These implied warranties are:

1. that the grantor has not already conveyed the property to another; and

2. that the property is free from encumbrances except those which are disclosed by the grantor.

A grant deed conveys all after-acquired title in addition to the extent of title written into the original deed. ***AFTER-ACQUIRED TITLE*** *is title to property acquired after the owner attempts to sell or transfer the title to another person before he/she actually got legal title.* An example of after-acquired title would be the acquisition of mineral rights to the property sometime after the original purchase of the land by the grantor. Its major difference from the warranty deed is that it does not warrant that the grantor has the lawful right to convey title.

> Whenever you see words ending in -or and -ee, remember that the suffix -or roughly means "one who gives" and the suffix -ee means "one who receives."

d. Sub-Types of Grant Deeds

There are many sub-types of grant deeds, which are given their names by identifying the grantors.

1. **Gift Deeds.** Granted as a gift of love and affection. No other consideration is necessary, but is void if given to defraud creditors.

2. **Tax Deeds.** Given if property is sold as payment of past-due property taxes ("tax sale").

3. **Sheriff's Deeds.** Granted to the purchaser at a court-ordered sale.

4. **Administrator's Deeds or Executor's Deeds.** Given to the purchaser of the deceased person's real property.

5. **Trustee's Deeds.** Given to the purchaser of property at a trust deed foreclosure sale.

6. **Guardian's Deeds.** Used by a guardian to transfer the real property of minors or incompetents.

A "trust deed" is not a deed, it is a financial instrument (security device). Do not confuse trustee's deed with trust deed.

All the above grant deeds, warranty deeds, and land patents are used in cases where the full ownership of real property is being conveyed. They provide that ownership shall be fee, fee simple, or fee absolute. *These kinds of ownership, indicated by the word fee, are called* **FREEHOLD ESTATES**. Although ownership may be limited by conditions and requirements of use, they are essentially full estates, capable of complete transfer. The **LIFE ESTATE**, *where title is given for the lifetime of the grantee*, can be created by grant deed also, but it is not usually drawn by an escrow officer.

e. Quitclaim Deeds (Carry No Warranty)

QUITCLAIM DEEDS *are used to convey less than full ownership in real property, such as part ownership or mineral rights.* They use different words of conveyance than grant deeds: "Remise, release, and forever quitclaim" or in some cases merely "quitclaim." They offer no warranty to the grantee.

2. Requisites of a Valid Deed

All deeds must satisfy the law to be held valid. They must have these elements (see **Figure 2-6**):

1. They must be written instruments containing the names of the grantor and grantee, operative words of conveyance, and sufficient description of the property to unmistakably identify the property. The legal description may be in several accepted forms: lot, block and tract, metes and bounds, or section map.

2. The parties must be capable of contracting, satisfying the same capability requirements mentioned for contracts in Chapter 1.

3. The property must be legally transferred. The title must be truly owned by the grantor at the time of transfer and not be "promised," even if a will is very specific, an heir may not transfer title to property he or she expects to inherit.

4. The deed must be property executed (signed). Although slight defects in the making of a deed will probably not endanger its validity, they could cause problems. Your professional standards should permit no defects in any instrument you draw, and you must see that they are properly signed in ink exactly as the names are typed.

Figure 2-6

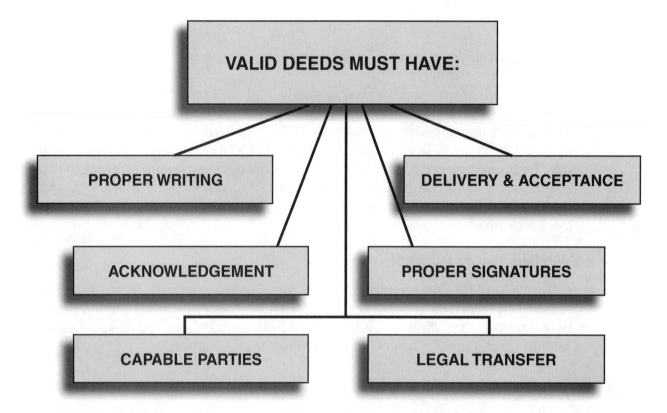

5. The deed must be delivered and accepted. It is a duty of escrow to deliver instruments at the end of a transaction. Usually, delivery to the Recorder in the county where the property is located will satisfy this duty, although it is a good practice to follow through later (if there is some question or problem brought by the client) and make sure the actual document gets into the hands of the grantee.

6. The deed must be acknowledged. Before the county Recorder will accept a deed, it must be proved that the signatures are genuine. This is done by having the grantees appear before a commissioned Notary Public to sign the deed. The Notary Public will acknowledge that they are truly the people whose names are on the deed, and he or she will affix his or her stamp or seal affirming it.

Your professional standards should permit no defects in any instrument you draw, and you must see that they are properly signed in ink exactly as the names are typed.

3. Vesting (Ways to Hold Title)

The names of the grantees must be followed by the manner in which they plan to take (invest) title.

The different ways title can be possessed have important legal ramifications for the grantees and their heirs, making vesting a matter to be considered with their counsel before coming to escrow. Since you have no knowledge of their personal affairs other than the transaction they bring to escrow, you should not assume how they should take title. If parties express doubt or confusion about vesting, suggest they consult their counsel and tell them you will finish drawing the deed when they return with their decision.

Deeds should contain the status of both grantors and the grantees. In the case of individual persons, type their marital status after their names, i.e., "husband and wife," "a single man," etc. When the grantor or grantee is a business entity, type which kind, i.e., "a corporation, formed under the laws of _____," "a joint venture," etc.

The vesting is required after the names and status of the grantee only (we already know the status of the grantor). Some common kinds of vesting are discussed next.

a. Severalty

SEVERALTY is ownership by one person or corporation. If the status is the same, it is not necessary to repeat the phrase, and the complete name on the deed would read:

**"John Doe,
a single (or an unmarried) man"**

**"Urbanalysis, Inc.,
a corporation formed under the laws of California"**

In other cases, you must type both the status and the vesting:

**"Mary Doe, a married woman,
as her sole and separate property"**

b. Tenancy in Common

TENANCY IN COMMON can be the vesting when two or more persons own property together. They each own a share of the income, expenses and value of the property. Each may sell, lease, or will, to his or her heirs, his or her own share of the property. All tenants in common have the right to occupy the property together. A sample reads:

**"John Doe, Mary Smith and William Jones, all single persons,
as tenants in common"**

c. Joint Tenancy

JOINT TENANCY contains the right of survivorship without probate. Most often used by married couples, it conveys a deceased person's estate in the property to the surviving spouse immediately. It is not limited to married couples. A joint tenancy recital would read:

**"John Doe and Mary Doe, husband and wife,
as joint tenants"**

d. Community Property

COMMUNITY PROPERTY refers to property acquired during marriage. All such property in California is shared equally, therefore husbands and wives must both sign all agreements and documents of transfer. Debts acquired after marriage are also community property. Title is automatically conveyed to a surviving spouse only if there is no will, otherwise either spouse can convey title by will to whomever he or she wishes. Such an heir or devisee would then be a tenant in common with the surviving spouse. Married persons can inherit or receive property and keep it separate, but must not mingle income from separate property with income from community property, which would cause the separately held property to become community property. This is the only manner of vesting which depends exclusively upon marital status: it can only be used by persons married to each other:

**"John Doe and Mary Doe,
husband and wife, as their community property"**

Community property is the only manner of vesting which depends exclusively upon marital status.

e. Community Property With Right of Survivorship

The California legislature enacted legislation which allows married couples in California to hold title to real and personal property as "community property with right of survivorship." *COMMUNITY PROPERTY WITH RIGHT OF SURVIVORSHIP transfers ownership to the spouse at death, with income tax benefits.* The goal of the legislation was to combine the right of survivorship benefit of joint tenancy with the favorable tax status of community property under federal tax law. The survivorship benefit allows title to pass to the surviving spouse at the death of one spouse. The surviving spouse also gets the benefit of a stepped up basis for 100% of the property upon the death of a spouse. The surviving spouse may use an affidavit of death of spouse to satisfy title company underwriting requirements to convey or encumber title. Probate proceedings are not necessary to transfer title to the surviving spouse.

4. Documentary Transfer Tax

Grant deeds must show, in addition to the filled-in data of names and legal description, the amount of Documentary Transfer Tax. The ***DOCUMENTARY TRANSFER TAX** is a tax applied to the actual money consideration in a transaction involving a recordable deed (may vary from one escrow to another).* It is not applied to existing loans or liens remaining on the property through the sale. (Actual money consideration = cash + all new loans except loans in favor of seller; "paper consideration" = old loans and liens transferred to new owners + new loans in favor of seller.) An easy way to remember the application is "compute on cash through escrow." This will become clear as you progress through the sample escrow in this book.

The Tax is paid to the county in which the deed is recorded. In most counties, half of the tax is then rebated to the city in which the property is located. The amount of Documentary Transfer Tax must be written on the deed before it can be recorded.

Tax Rate is $0.55 cents per $500 in California.

The Tax applies to all real property transfers that involve actual money consideration over $100.00, and is figured at the rate of $0.55 per each $500.00 of consideration and an additional $0.55 for any portion of $500.00 remaining. If the consideration happens to be in even thousands, for instance $37,000.00, the Tax can be conveniently figured at $1.10 per thousand.

FORMULA:

$$\frac{\text{Taxable consideration}}{\$500.00} = \text{base units} \times \$.55 = \text{amount of Tax}$$

EXAMPLES:

1. $250,000 sale, all cash

$$\frac{\$250,000.00}{\$500.00} = 500 \text{ base units} \times .55 = \$275.00 \text{ (Tax)}$$

or since the amount is in even thousands:

$$\frac{\$250,000.00}{\$1,000.00} = 25 \text{ base units} \times \$1.10 = \$275.00 \text{ (Tax)}$$

2. $207,750.00 sale, cash down payment of $8,500.00 and buyer assuming the existing loan for the rest. Since the balance of the price will not be converted into actual cash in escrow but represents "paper consideration," its amount is not taxed.

$\underline{\$8,500.00}$ = 17 base units x .55 = \$9.35 (Tax)
  \$500.00

3. \$185,950.00 sale; cash down payment of \$18,595.00, new loan of \$148,760.00 from a savings bank, and new "second" loan in favor of the seller for \$18,595.00. The tax will be computed on the down payment and the institutional loan, since the second loan is also "paper consideration" and its cash does not move through escrow.

\$18,595.00 + \$148,760.00 = \$167,355.00

$\underline{\$167,355.00}$ = 334.71 = 335 base units x .55 = \$184.25 (Tax)
  \$500.00

C. OBTAIN A POLICY OF TITLE INSURANCE

Long before the original Colonies became the Untied States, they began to enact laws governing the validity of property ownership. The Massachusetts Registry Act of 1640 first required that all documents of ownership be recorded in governmental archives, and the practice spread throughout the states as they joined the Union. That way, the history of ownership could be traced, and challengers to title could be verified or disallowed in the courts. Usually, the attorney assisting in the transfer of real property would go to the archives and "search the title" to assure that his or her clients were making a valid transfer.

Gradually, as the records multiplied, specialists in title search began to keep copies of records in their own files, developing huge files which speeded the search process. They could then build upon already prepared chains of title rather than starting over each time. As records and specialists proliferated, some pooled their resources and formed the first "title companies." In some states, such as California, title companies have garnered virtually the whole field of title abstraction (which is the process of searching the chain of title), while in many others, title abstractors and lawyers in private practice continue to do so as well.

A policy of title insurance insures against imperfection in the "title" largely through examination of the public records.

The title companies began to issue certificates of title, which assured customers that the title search and titles were valid according to records. Eventually they established cash funds to reimburse customers who suffered losses as a result of faulty title searching.

There were, however, defective or forged documents that found their way into recorded archives before the recording process became as standardized and careful as it is today. To protect customers from these and "off the record" defects in true title (such as deeds that were never properly recorded), the California title companies, beginning in 1876, organized and incorporated themselves as title insurance companies to issue policies that indemnified against both on- and off-record risks. Title insurance policies are now considered nearly indispensable in the legal transfer or real property, giving new owners solid protection for their titles. If, after new owners take title to real property under a grant deed, someone comes forth from the past challenging their right to the land, the title insurance company will defend the new title—through the courts if necessary—and will pay the policyholder if losses are incurred.

1. Kinds of Title Insurance Policies

a. California Land Title Association (CLTA)

The most commonly issued policy of title insurance in California is the CALIFORNIA LAND TITLE ASSOCIATION (CLTA) STANDARD COVERED POLICY. It can be written in various ways to cover owners, lenders and many types of less-than-freehold estates such as leasehold, life estate, or owners of easements. If issued as a *CLTA JOINT PROTECTION POLICY, it covers both owner and lender at once.* The policy is usually written to cover the amount of **purchase price** for **owners** and the amount of the **loan for lenders**. Generally, a CLTA policy insures against all the defects in title that can be revealed by examination of public records (records that give **constructive notice** according to law), against forgeries, and against defects of competency and capacity under contract law. Not covered are off-record matters such as encroachment, discrepancies in boundary lines, and unrecorded easements.

The California Land Title Association was founded in 1907.

The *CLTA EXTENDED COVERAGE POLICY can cover, in addition to all the above risks, defects that are discoverable by **actual inspection** of the land, or risks resulting from encumbrances against the property which may or may not be recorded but which are not required to give constructive notice.* These can include, but are not limited to, special local assessments, violations of original subdivision restrictions, and claims for access to minerals brought forward by previous owners.

b. American Land Title Association (ALTA)

The *AMERICAN LAND TITLE ASSOCIATION (ALTA) LENDER'S POLICY is designed for the protection of real property loans, both institutional and private.* There is also a short-term CLTA policy, at a lower premium rate, which can be requested for properties that have been transferred, and give title insurance policies within two years of the new escrow. All these policies may be amended with extra indorsements of many kinds. Such indorsements can be for the protection of condominium owners (who are tenants in common with other owners) and for upward adjustments of coverage in the event of inflationary pressure. All title insurance policies have preprinted **exceptions** listing those

things not ever covered, and spaces for the title officer to type in exceptions (such as taxes, loans, and adjustments against owners) that appear upon inspection of individual records.

The title officer is your source for all questions about title insurance, whether general or for problems arising in individual title searches.

Since most purchasers know very little about title insurance, you should be prepared to describe the different kinds of coverage for them. You should be aware of the policies that can or cannot be obtained for various transactions. The title officer at the title insurance company with which you do business will gladly answer all your questions in this area. Most companies will send educational material and fee schedules that you can keep on hand. Always call the title officer, whose name will appear on individual title searches (called Preliminary Reports), first if you see a discrepancy between the parties' instructions and the report, before you contact the parties.

A buyer should have a title insurance policy for the full amount of the purchase price. A lender need only be covered for the amount of the loan.

Superior escrow officers attempt to initiate the title search as early as possible in escrow and usually can call the title company to order a report as soon as there is evidence that the transaction will indeed be fulfilled. Such evidence can be the depositing of binding money into escrow or the commitment of a lender that a funding loan will eventually be made.

This early start gives the title company time to make a complete report, since there are still early records that have not been transferred to the instant-recall computer banks and that may have to be searched by hand in the county records. It also gives the escrow officer time to help parties clear away any questions or defects brought forth by the title search, preventing delays in the closing date of the escrow.

The CLTA standard coverage policy provides joint protection for both lender and owner. The standard ALTA policy is for the protection of the lender.

D. COLLECT THE FUNDS

Added to the proper preparation of the instruments of title, a very important duty of escrow is the proper gathering and transmission of the funds. The officer will receive cash from the principals, proceeds of the loan from institutions, and orders to transfer indebtedness from one party to another. The officer must see that the parties receive the correct amount at the end of escrow. These also include all the taxing agencies and the various companies who provide services to escrow.

1. Cash Received into Escrow

All actual money received by escrow must be deposited into a trust account within 24 hours of receipt. It must be kept separate from the company's general funds.

If parties so specify, the money can be deposited into an interest-bearing savings account at a local savings institution. This a recent development, and is carefully regulated by statute. Receipts must be given to all parties who bring cash, checks, money orders or other negotiable instruments to escrow.

2. Deeds of Trust and Notes

The common form of loans for real property in California is the Deed of Trust and Note.

This method of **HYPOTHECATION**, *which is the putting up of a property as collateral for a loan without giving up possession of it*, uses two documents, the deed of trust and note. The **PROMISSORY NOTE** *is the promise to pay, according to stated conditions, a sum of money.* The note, whether **FULLY AMORTIZED** *(equal monthly payments including principal and interest)*, or an **INSTALLMENT NOTE WITH A BALLOON PAYMENT** *(periodic payments with a larger payment at the end)*, or a **STRAIGHT NOTE** *(all paid at once at the end)*, is held by the lender, who is called the **beneficiary**.

The **DEED OF TRUST** *is a device that secures the property as collateral for the note. The* **TRUSTEE** *holds naked legal title to the property, but only in so far as the trustee may have to sell the property for the* **BENEFICIARY** *(lender), should the* **TRUSTOR** *(borrower) default.*

In the event of a default, the beneficiary will instruct the trustee to begin the default period, during which time the borrower can pay all the back payments, taxes and fees, and reinstate the note. If he or she fails to do so, the property will be sold at auction in a public **trustee's sale**. There have been distressing instances where valuable property has been sold for a few hundred dollars without the knowledge of the borrower, who may be unaware that it is his or her responsibility to find out if a default and foreclosure has been started against him or her. The three party arrangement is shown in **Figure 2-7**.

When the note is paid in full, the beneficiary notifies the trustee of the fact and the trustee then reconveys his or her interest in the title back to the trustor.

In everyday usage, the term "trust deed" refers to both the deed of trust and the note. It is a short way of identifying the instruments of indebtedness.

Figure 2-7

THREE-PARTY HYPOTHECATION

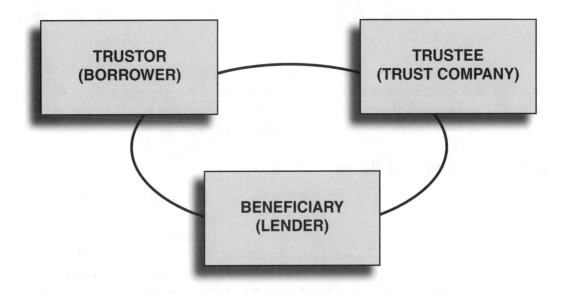

3. Terms Associated with Deeds of Trust and Notes

a. Acceleration, Alienation, and Due-on-sale clauses

An *ACCELERATION CLAUSE* in an installment note provides that when the trustor fails to perform a required act, such as paying the property taxes, the lender has the right to demand the entire payment of the loan. An *ALIENATION CLAUSE* permits the lender to require that the entire amount be paid whenever the original trustor sells or otherwise transfers the property, or allows the lender to change the terms of the agreement by increasing the interest rate or charging new fees to private lenders. The *DUE-ON-SALE CLAUSE* is regarded as synonymous with the alienation clause.

b. Assignment

The names of the three parties involved in the funding arrangement—trustor, trustee and beneficiary—may be changed during the term of the loan. The note may be sold by the beneficiary to another, thereby resulting in the assignment of the note to a new beneficiary. The trustor may sell the property, with the new owner taking over payments under the existing deed of trust; resulting in the assignment of the deed of trust to a new trustor. Preprinted deeds of trust (the only kind you will deal with as an escrow officer) contain assignment sections, which are filled in if needed and recorded at the close of escrow.

c. Beneficiary's Statement, Demand, and Reconveyance

These are documents associated with already existing loans. When you inform a beneficiary that you intend to pay off his or her note, he or she sends you a **Demand** telling how much is left to pay. After he or she has been paid off at the close of escrow, he or she will issue a **Full or Partial Reconveyance**, depending on whether the note was paid in full or partially paid off. When a buyer is taking over an existing loan, the beneficiary sends a **Statement**, telling how much is left on the loan and giving necessary information about the loan.

d. Land Contracts

These are instruments used sometime in the transfer of unimproved (raw) land. In a *LAND CONTRACT, the seller retains full title to the property until the final payment has been made. The contract is usually made between the buyer and seller rather than introducing third parties.* These agreements for financing are extremely complex and should be negotiated by real estate attorneys familiar with your state laws.

e. Liens

LIENS are documents using property to secure the payment of a debt. They can be *VOLUNTARY (applied to property by owners)* or *INVOLUNTARY (applied to property by others to obtain payment of debts).*

Deeds of trust and other loans secured by property are examples of voluntary liens. Property taxes, special assessments for sewers or sidewalks, judgments, and mechanics liens are involuntary liens.

Lien holders have the legal right to force the sale of the property if they cannot obtain payment any other way, but ordinarily property cannot be sold until liens have been paid or transferred to new owners. Generally, the priority rights of lien holds to be paid off depends upon the time of **recording the lien**—first recorded, first paid. This is why it is essential that new first deeds of trust and notes be recorded first, followed immediately by junior deeds of trust and notes.

f. Other Private Money

Anybody can make a loan secured by real property. Buyers may seek funds from private individuals or from mortgage loan brokers whose business is to "match up" private lenders with borrowers. Such loans are usually secured by deeds of trust, the same as other real property loans and may be purchase money deeds of trust or not, depending on their timing. They may be for most of the purchase price or for only a small portion of the price.

g. Points

This refers to a basis for the charge made to a borrower by a lender when granting a loan. A *POINT equals 1% of the amount of the loan.* Lenders may charge one or more points as loan origination fees. The exact amount varies from time to time

49

and from lender to lender. The party borrowing the money usually pays this fee, but with Federal Housing Administration (FHA) and Veteran's Administration (VA) loans, who pays the points is negotiated between the buyer and seller.

h. Prepayment Penalty

Most first deeds of trust allow for a lender to recover some of the interest that would have accrued if the loan payments had been made for a longer time. Within the first five years of a loan, the institutions add a charge of several months' interest when a loan is being paid off sooner than its due date. There is seldom a prepayment penalty after five years or if there is a new loan replacing the one being paid off.

i. Purchase Money Deed of Trust

This is always a loan that is obtained for the purchase of real property at the time of purchase. A refinancing loan would not be called a purchase money trust deed. Although a loan taken with a lending institution can be technically a purchase money instrument, the term is almost exclusively used to denote a forbearance on the part of a seller to take part of the selling price in later payments rather than all at once at the time of the sale. Such arrangements are also called private loans and "back to the seller" loans. Loans designated as purchase money instruments have a protection built into them by law that is not present in ordinary loans. *If the property must be sold at the foreclosure sale and the selling amount is less than is owned on the loans, the beneficiary cannot get a judgment, called a* **DEFICIENCY JUDGMENT**, requiring the trustor to pay the difference.

This protection extends to the owner of 1-to-4 residential units where the owner lives in one of the units.

j. Second Trust Deeds and Junior Trust Deeds

These are smaller loans, taken in addition to first trust deeds, that secure funds for the major portion of the purchase price. They are usually purchase money instruments and may be obtained from sellers, private individuals, and institutions devoted to junior trust deeds. They are almost never given by institutions such as savings bank organizations who make first trust deed loans. They may be fully amortized or straight notes. **All junior trust deeds involved in a transaction must be recorded after the first trust deed and note is recorded, and holders of junior trust deeds are advised to file a "request for notice" when their deeds of trust are recorded**. This way, they will be notified if the trustee fails to pay the "first" and can prepare to buy the property themselves at a trustee's sale or to reinstate the "first" and start default actions of their own against the trustor.

k. Subordination Clause

This is a clause included in many deeds of trust that allow for a future change in the **priority of liens** against the property. The first deed of trust is recorded first and, as a result, its holder has first rights in cases of default. If, for instance, a buyer intends at some later date to add more buildings to his or her land, he or she may ask that a clause be drawn giving the future financing institution first rights.

Subordination clauses must be very carefully written and should not be attempted unless the escrow officer is very experienced.

4. ADJUSTMENTS AND PRORATIONS

Property ownership involves the responsibility for ongoing expenses other than loan payments. The day escrow closes (or any day to which the parties agree) these expenses cease to be the responsibility of the seller and become the responsibility of the buyer. The same is true for property's income, such as rents. You will compute the amounts due to, or due from, the parties as part of your duties.

Prorations apply to charges incurred by either party prior to the transfer of property.

These computations usually involve finding out the per day cost of each item to be adjusted, then assigning the costs between the parties. The exact arithmetical ways of computing adjustments and prorations are shown in the sample escrows later in this book.

a. California Property Taxes

Property taxes are the most common adjustment in escrow.

When you receive the preliminary report from the title company, it will show whether taxes were or were not paid by the owner. It will usually show the half-year figure—the amount for the half-year in which the escrow begins. **Figure 2-9** shows the California property tax time table.

The property tax time table follows the "fiscal," not the "calendar," year.

The tax year runs from July 1 through June 30 of the next calendar year (see **Figure 2-8**). It is divided in half at December 31, the first half being July 1 through December 31, and the second half being January 1 through June 30. Remember it this way:

first half due in the Fall
second half due in the Spring

Figure 2-8

TAX CALENDAR

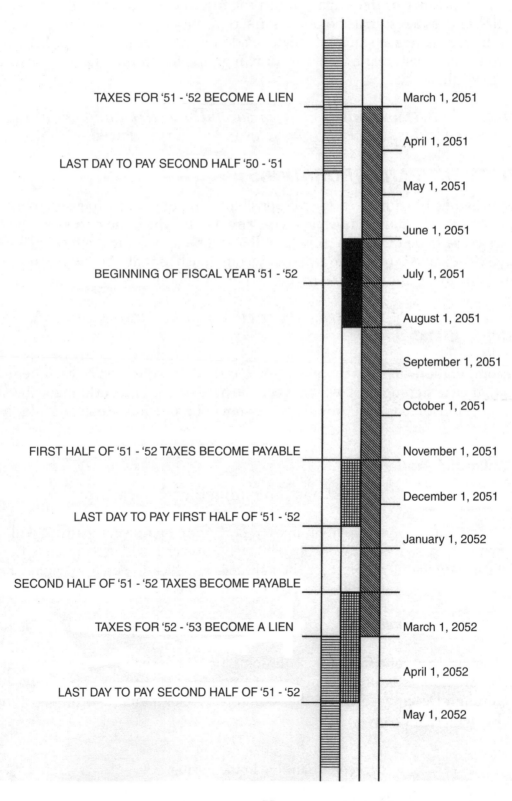

TAXES FOR '51 - '52 BECOME A LIEN — March 1, 2051

April 1, 2051

LAST DAY TO PAY SECOND HALF '50 - '51 — May 1, 2051

June 1, 2051

BEGINNING OF FISCAL YEAR '51 - '52 — July 1, 2051

August 1, 2051

September 1, 2051

October 1, 2051

FIRST HALF OF '51 - '52 TAXES BECOME PAYABLE — November 1, 2051

December 1, 2051

LAST DAY TO PAY FIRST HALF OF '51 - '52 — January 1, 2052

SECOND HALF OF '51 - '52 TAXES BECOME PAYABLE

TAXES FOR '52 - '53 BECOME A LIEN — March 1, 2052

April 1, 2052

LAST DAY TO PAY SECOND HALF OF '51 - '52 — May 1, 2052

Figure 2-9

CALIFORNIA PROPERTY TAX TIME TABLE

January 1	July 1	November 1	February 1
Property tax becomes a lien on real property	Fiscal year starts	1st installment is due and delinquent after December 10 at 5:00pm	2nd installment is due and delinquent after April 10 at 5:00pm

Payment for the whole taxable year may be made in the Fall, but normally only the first half is paid in the Fall payment period, between November 1 and December 10, at which time the first half taxes become delinquent. The second half payment period is February 1 to April 10. Taxes may not be paid before November 1, even though they are levied against the property on March 1, and are recorded as liens against the property at that time.

b. Interest on Loans

After property taxes, interest on loans is the next most common adjustment you will make in escrow.

Lenders, whether they are involved in new financing, the assignment of loans to new trustors, or will be paid in full through escrow, insist on being paid daily interest for the full time their loans are in effect. Institutional lenders will be quite specific, stating the daily dollar amount of interest. When you adjust for an institutional lender, you need only multiply this rate by the number of days which lie outside the regular monthly payment.

Different institutional lenders follow different practices. They show their interest prorating practices in their loan origination documents or, in the case of already existing loans, their beneficiary statements, and you must follow their instructions to the letter. Some want interest to the day escrow closes and some want it to the day they receive their money. Private lenders usually want interest to the date they receive their money, and with some private lenders you may have to determine the per-day interest. Although there are books and tables to calculate interest rates, the use of a pocket calculator, using programs such as Excel®, simplify the calculation process.

c. Fire Insurance

Since it is important that **fire insurance** coverage not be interrupted, you will usually be asked to oversee the assignment of the policy to the new owners or

to obtain a new policy at the time escrow closes. Premiums are often prepaid for one to three years, making a refund to the seller necessary. You will see different methods of handling fire insurance coverage in the sample escrows.

d. Rents

Rental revenue is monthly income that requires adjustment so that the days of the closing month are prorated properly to both the seller and the buyer. For example, if escrow closes on April 15, the seller receives fifteen days revenue, and the buyer receives the remaining revenue for the month.

e. Other Adjustments

There are other adjustments and prorations that are seen less often in escrow. These can be **water or irrigation district assessments, special bond issue assessments** and *impound accounts* held by lenders, **mortgage insurance** policies being transferred to new owners, and many others. Each has its own exact requirements for adjustment, supplied by the lien holder. Adjusting these generally follows the same arithmetical style of "*daily rate x days*" as is used for other adjustments.

The escrow officer has a printed sheet on which to record all these adjustments, called a **SETTLEMENT SHEET.** *This sheet has spaces for recording the disposal of all funds in escrow, and is set up with debit and credit columns so that the accounts may be easily balanced to the closing date (or other date specified by parties).* Escrow officers usually make an estimate of escrow costs in pencil as escrow progresses, then fill in a fresh final settlement in ink when escrow closes (See **Figure 2-10**).

Many escrow forms are now available online and may be filled out on the computer, although signatures must still be written by hand in ink.

Figure 2-10

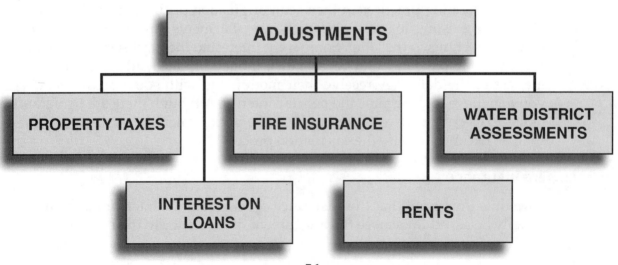

E. SEE THE TRANSFER DISCLOSURE IS RECORDED IN THE COUNTY RECORDS

Any acknowledged document of transfer (or, for that matter, any other acknowledged legal document) can be recorded in county records. This recording becomes, in effect, a public notice in that it announces to all that a transaction has been made. The timing of the recording is especially important for real property transfers, since if a property is sold twice, the deed recorded first will be deemed the legal title.

Real property transfers must be recorded in the county where the property is located.

If a piece of property crosses a county line, duplicate documents must be recorded in both counties. Although title companies perform the recording service for most real property transfers in California, recordings may be made by any citizen who has an acknowledged document he or she wants to record.

The timing of the recording is especially important for real property transfers, since if a property is sold twice, the deed recorded first will be deemed the legal title.

1. Electronic Escrow Services

With wire transfers, electronic signatures, and electronic delivery of documents that are printed at the agent's or principal's location, the escrow company is being forced to increase online services. With computer electronic handling, the escrow firm can be located anywhere. Hence, E-escrows, such as www.escrow.com, are becoming more common. Internet escrows are expected to greatly increase during the next decade as a means to reduce costs and to allow access 24/7 from any Internet location. As more international transactions occur, the need for international Internet escrows has become common and the business market is filling those needs by offering these services. Because computers can now translate between languages and with the easy access to the information, a buyer or a seller, as well as you, the agent, lender, title company, and appraiser, can check the status of the escrow at any time. **Figure 2-11** shows various e-commerce escrows.

2. Ready to Close Escrow

Once the **funds** have been gathered and costs have been listed for the parties, once the **instruments of title** have been drawn, **acknowledged** and **signed**, and the other **conditions** of escrow have been satisfied, escrow can close.

The last thing an escrow officer should do before closing is review the instructions carefully, comparing them with all the other sheets in the escrow file to make sure everything has been done correctly.

Figure 2-11

Escrow Company Information

Escrow Company	Geography	Services
Aliso Escrow, Inc. www.alisoescrow.com	California	Independent Escrow. All types of property
E-Escrow, Inc. www.e-escrow.com	California	Resident and business.
Escrow by Bankers Escrow	Nationwide	Loan servicing. e-commerce escrow. Holding escrow.
Diversified Title and Escrow Co. www.todiversified.com	Nationwide	Forms library and escrow order entry and tracking.
I-Escrow www.i-escrow.com	Nationwide	Business agreements. Third-party intermediary.

Then he or she should check all the math and balance the accounts before making a final settlement statement in ink, and run a check of the figures through a calculator or program like Excel® just to be sure that the figures were typed or penned correctly.

Computers do most of the work, but the inputting is still the responsibility of the escrow officer.

3. Recording

Some escrow or title companies provide printed recording orders for escrow officers to use, some use a standard in-house form letter, and some title companies will accept an order to record over the telephone or fax (always, however, followed by a written request). The documents to be recorded (the grant deed, deeds of trust, etc.) must first be sent to the title company. If the escrow holder is outside the title company, the documents will usually be picked up by a messenger service, or they can be mailed.

The actual times of recording vary from county to county. It is necessary that you familiarize yourself with customary recording times in your own and nearby counties.

They may accept documents all day, then record them all at exactly 8:00 a.m. the following business day. They may have several designated recording times each business day, say 8:00 a.m. and 2:00 p.m., or they may record each document as it comes in to the County Recorder's office. When a document is recorded, it is stamped with the date, time, and a document number, important in determining priority of recordings. It is also assigned a book and page number for easy future reference. The original documents then will usually be mailed to the recipients listed on their faces, or sometimes they will come back to you for transmittal.

F. COUNTY RECORDER MAILS DEED TO THE SELLER - MONEY GOES TO THE SELLER

Since the County Recorder will mail the deed to the buyer, you are mostly concerned with paying creditors, including the seller, of the escrow.

1. Transmitting Funds

Your final settlement will state exactly how much is owing each creditor. Not only do you give the seller his or her proceeds after deducting his or her expenses, but you also pay for title insurance, escrow fees, recording fees, pest control operators, beneficiaries of loans being discharged—the list can be very long. Most of these charges will come out of the seller's funds, but the buyer will pay some also. You simply make out the checks and enclose them with a form letter stating the escrow number, the property address, and other pertinent data.

2. Closing Escrow (Day of Recording)

Once the recording has been made and all the bills paid, escrow is closed.

Your file will contain unsigned copies of all the sheets and documents you've used, plus adding machine tapes, computer files, or other evidence of your calculations. You should place the file in safe storage. Your last duty to your clients involves confidentiality. Do not leave their file laying about where others can read it, and do not dispose of any part in a way that others can get it. The file will stay in storage for a period of time required by law or company policy, for reference, and it remains confidential during the entire time.

You are not any more free to discuss escrows after they have closed than you were during their active life.

3. Cancelling an Escrow

There are three ways to end an escrow. One is through closing where it can be said the contract has been performed. The majority of escrows are ended in this manner. (See **Figure 2-12**).

The second way is **cancellation by mutual agreement**. When parties sign escrow instructions, they agree to conditions that, if not met, are grounds for the deal to

Figure 2-12

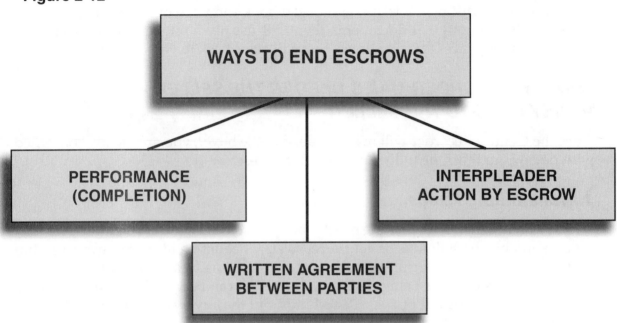

fall through and for the escrow to be possibly canceled. For example, parties may specify, either in their original agreement or in their escrow instructions, that there is a certain time wherein escrow must be closed or canceled. This would not just be the time limit asked for at the opening, but would have to be written out as a condition of escrow.

Cancellation is never automatic, even when there is such a specification.

Another example is a condition in instructions that the buyer must obtain a new institutional loan. The seller will be aware of this condition from the beginning, and may well agree to drop the escrow if the buyer can't get a loan, but he or she could agree to finance the purchase price himself or herself by taking a purchase money deed of trust and note, thus allowing escrow to go through.

If the parties agree to drop an escrow, they must notify you in writing to cancel it.

Otherwise you must keep it open despite whatever closing date may be suggested in the memo or typed in the instructions.

Sometimes one party wants to cancel and the other does not, or they cannot resolve a difference that has appeared during the processing of the escrow. In order to keep escrows from being open and "on the books" for years at a time, the escrow holder's attorney can file a suit in **interpleader** with the court, asking that the court require the parties to litigate their differences.

The interpleader action permits escrow fees and escrow's attorney's fees to be paid right away.

The escrow holder then transfers all remaining funds in the escrow to the court's trust account, and is legally "out" of the escrow.

When parties file suit against one another during escrow (without escrow filing an interpleader action), the escrow remains open pending the court's decision and the outcome of appeals.

Then it follows the order of the judge in either completing or canceling the escrow. If court action drags on too long, escrow can file an interpleader action to get "out" and recover escrow fees.

Figure 2-13

RESIDENTIAL PURCAHSE AGREEMENT (1)

CALIFORNIA
ASSOCIATION
OF REALTORS®

**CALIFORNIA
RESIDENTIAL PURCHASE AGREEMENT
AND JOINT ESCROW INSTRUCTIONS**
For Use With Single Family Residential Property — Attached or Detached
(C.A.R. Form RPA-CA, Revised 10/02)

Date _June 14, 2051_ , at _Costa Mesa_ , California.

1. **OFFER:**
   A. THIS IS AN OFFER FROM _Walter and Debbie Buyer_ ("Buyer").
   B. THE REAL PROPERTY TO BE ACQUIRED is described as _264 Beach Lane_ , Assessor's Parcel No. _____ , situated in _Costa Mesa,_ County of _Orange_ , California, ("Property").
   C. THE PURCHASE PRICE offered is _Eight Hundred Thousand✓_ _no/100_ Dollars $ _800,000.✓_ .
   D. CLOSE OF ESCROW shall occur on _____ (date)(or X _90_ Days After Acceptance).

2. **FINANCE TERMS:** Obtaining the loans below **is a contingency** of this Agreement unless: **(i)** either 2K or 2L is checked below; or **(ii)** otherwise agreed in writing. Buyer shall act diligently and in good faith to obtain the designated loans. Obtaining deposit, down payment and closing costs **is not a contingency.** Buyer represents that funds will be good when deposited with Escrow Holder.
   A. **INITIAL DEPOSIT:** Buyer has given a deposit in the amount of .... $ _10,000_
      to the agent submitting the offer (or to ☐ _____), by personal check
      (or ☐ _____), made payable to _ABC Escrow_
      which shall be held uncashed until Acceptance and then deposited within **3 business days** after
      Acceptance (or ☐ _____), with
      Escrow Holder, (or ☐ into Broker's trust account).
   B. **INCREASED DEPOSIT:** Buyer shall deposit with Escrow Holder an increased deposit in the amount of ...$ _____
      within ____ **Days** After Acceptance, or ☐ _____ ...$ _640,000_
   C. **FIRST LOAN IN THE AMOUNT OF** .... $ _640,000_
      (1) NEW First Deed of Trust in favor of lender, encumbering the Property, securing a note payable at
      maximum interest of ____ _8_ % fixed rate, or ____ % initial adjustable rate with a maximum
      interest rate of ____%, balance due in ____ years, amortized over _30_ years. Buyer
      shall pay loan fees/points not to exceed _2_ . (These terms apply whether the designated loan
      is conventional, FHA or VA.)
      (2) ☐ FHA ☐ VA: (The following terms only apply to the FHA or VA loan that is checked.)
      Seller shall pay ____% discount points. Seller shall pay other fees not allowed to be paid by
      Buyer, ☐ not to exceed $_____ . Seller shall pay the cost of lender required Repairs
      (including those for wood destroying pest) not otherwise provided for in this Agreement, ☐ not to
      exceed $ _____ . (Actual loan amount may increase if mortgage insurance premiums,
      funding fees or closing costs are financed.)
   D. **ADDITIONAL FINANCING TERMS:** ☐ Seller financing, (C.A.R. Form SFA); ☐ secondary financing, ...$ _____
      (C.A.R. Form PAA, paragraph 4A); ☐ assumed financing (C.A.R. Form PAA, paragraph 4B)

   E. **BALANCE OF PURCHASE PRICE** (not including costs of obtaining loans and other closing costs) in the amount of ...$ _150,000_
      to be deposited with Escrow Holder within sufficient time to close escrow.
   F. **PURCHASE PRICE (TOTAL):** .... $ _800,000_
   G. **LOAN APPLICATIONS:** Within **7 (or** ☐ _____ **) Days** After Acceptance, Buyer shall provide Seller a letter from lender or
      mortgage loan broker stating that, based on a review of Buyer's written application and credit report, Buyer is prequalified or
      preapproved for the NEW loan specified in 2C above.
   H. **VERIFICATION OF DOWN PAYMENT AND CLOSING COSTS:** Buyer (or Buyer's lender or loan broker pursuant to 2G) shall, within
      7 (or ☐ _____ **) Days** After Acceptance, provide Seller written verification of Buyer's down payment and closing costs.
   I. **LOAN CONTINGENCY REMOVAL: (i)** Within **17 (or** ☐ _____ **) Days** After Acceptance, Buyer shall, as specified in paragraph
      14, remove the loan contingency or cancel this Agreement; **OR (ii)** (if checked) ☐ the loan contingency shall remain in effect
      until the designated loans are funded.
   J. **APPRAISAL CONTINGENCY AND REMOVAL:** This Agreement is **(OR,** if checked, ☐ is NOT) contingent upon the Property
      appraising at no less than the specified purchase price. Buyer shall, as specified in paragraph 14, remove the appraisal
      contingency or cancel this Agreement when the loan contingency is removed (or, if checked, ☐ within **17 (or** ☐ _____ **) Days**
      After Acceptance).
   K. ☐ **NO LOAN CONTINGENCY** (If checked): Obtaining any loan in paragraphs 2C, 2D or elsewhere in this Agreement is NOT
      a contingency of this Agreement. If Buyer does not obtain the loan and as a result Buyer does not purchase the Property, Seller
      may be entitled to Buyer's deposit or other legal remedies.
   L. ☐ **ALL CASH OFFER** (If checked): No loan is needed to purchase the Property. Buyer shall, within **7 (or** ☐ _____ **) Days** After Acceptance,
      provide Seller written verification of sufficient funds to close this transaction.

3. **CLOSING AND OCCUPANCY:**
   A. Buyer intends (or ☐ does not intend) to occupy the Property as Buyer's primary residence.
   B. **Seller-occupied or vacant property:** Occupancy shall be delivered to Buyer at _11_ AM/PM, X on the date of Close Of
      Escrow; ☐ on _____ ; or ☐ no later than _____ **Days** After Close Of Escrow. (C.A.R. Form PAA, paragraph 2.) If
      transfer of title and occupancy do not occur at the same time, Buyer and Seller are advised to: **(i)** enter into a written occupancy
      agreement; and **(ii)** consult with their insurance and legal advisors.

RPA-CA REVISED 10/02 (PAGE 1 OF 8) Print Date

Buyer's Initials (_WB_)(_DB_)
Seller's Initials (_TP._)(_mp._)
Reviewed by _JR_ Date _6/14/51_

EQUAL HOUSING OPPORTUNITY

CALIFORNIA RESIDENTIAL PURCHASE AGREEMENT (RPA-CA PAGE 1 OF 8)

RESIDENTIAL PURCAHSE AGREEMENT (2)

Property Address: _264 Beach Lane, Costa Mesa, CA 92627_   Date: _June 14, 2051_

    C. **Tenant-occupied property: (i) Property shall be vacant** at least **5** (or ☐ _____) **Days** Prior to Close Of Escrow, unless otherwise agreed in writing. **Note to Seller: If you are unable to deliver Property vacant in accordance with rent control and other applicable Law, you may be in breach of this Agreement.**

    OR (ii) (if checked) ☐ **Tenant to remain in possession.** The attached addendum is incorporated into this Agreement (C.A.R. Form PAA, paragraph 3.);

    OR (iii) (if checked) ☐ **This Agreement is contingent** upon Buyer and Seller entering into a written agreement regarding occupancy of the Property within the time specified in paragraph 14. If no written agreement is reached within this time, either Buyer or Seller may cancel this Agreement in writing.

    D. At Close Of Escrow, Seller assigns to Buyer any assignable warranty rights for items included in the sale and shall provide any available Copies of such warranties. Brokers cannot and will not determine the assignability of any warranties.

    E. At Close Of Escrow, unless otherwise agreed in writing, Seller shall provide keys and/or means to operate all locks, mailboxes, security systems, alarms and garage door openers. If Property is a condominium or located in a common interest subdivision, Buyer may be required to pay a deposit to the Homeowners' Association ("HOA") to obtain keys to accessible HOA facilities.

4. **ALLOCATION OF COSTS** (If checked): Unless otherwise specified here, this paragraph only determines who is to pay for the report, inspection, test or service mentioned. If not specified here or elsewhere in this Agreement, the determination of who is to pay for any work recommended or identified by any such report, inspection, test or service shall be by the method specified in paragraph 14.

    A. **WOOD DESTROYING PEST INSPECTION:**

       (1) ☐ Buyer ☒ Seller shall pay for an inspection and report for wood destroying pests and organisms ("Report") which shall be prepared by ___BUG-R-GONE___, a registered structural pest control company. The Report shall cover the accessible areas of the main building and attached structures and, if checked: ☐ detached garages and carports, ☐ detached decks, ☐ the following other structures or areas _____. The Report shall not include roof coverings. If Property is a condominium or located in a common interest subdivision, the Report shall include only the separate interest and any exclusive-use areas being transferred and shall not include common areas, unless otherwise agreed. Water tests of shower pans on upper level units may not be performed without consent of the owners of property below the shower.

       OR (2) ☐ (If checked) The attached addendum (C.A.R. Form WPA) regarding wood destroying pest inspection and allocation of cost is incorporated into this Agreement.

    B. **OTHER INSPECTIONS AND REPORTS:**

       (1) ☐ Buyer ☐ Seller shall pay to have septic or private sewage disposal systems inspected _____.

       (2) ☐ Buyer ☐ Seller shall pay to have domestic wells tested for water potability and productivity _____.

       (3) ☐ Buyer ☐ Seller shall pay for a natural hazard zone disclosure report prepared by _____.

       (4) ☐ Buyer ☐ Seller shall pay for the following inspection or report _____.

       (5) ☐ Buyer ☐ Seller shall pay for the following inspection or report _____.

    C. **GOVERNMENT REQUIREMENTS AND RETROFIT:**

       (1) ☐ Buyer ☒ Seller shall pay for smoke detector installation and/or water heater bracing, if required by Law. Prior to Close Of Escrow, Seller shall provide Buyer a written statement of compliance in accordance with state and local Law, unless exempt.

       (2) ☐ Buyer ☐ Seller shall pay the cost of compliance with any other minimum mandatory government retrofit standards, inspections and reports if required as a condition of closing escrow under any Law. _____.

    D. **ESCROW AND TITLE:**

       (1) ☒ Buyer ☒ Seller shall pay escrow fee _50%/50%_ _____.
           Escrow Holder shall be _ABC Escrow_ _____.

       (2) ☒ Buyer ☐ Seller shall pay for **owner's** title insurance policy specified in paragraph 12 _____.
           Owner's title policy to be issued by _____.
           (Buyer shall pay for any title insurance policy insuring Buyer's **lender**, unless otherwise agreed in writing.)

    E. **OTHER COSTS:**

       (1) ☐ Buyer ☐ Seller shall pay County transfer tax or transfer fee _____.

       (2) ☐ Buyer ☐ Seller shall pay City transfer tax or transfer fee _____.

       (3) ☐ Buyer ☐ Seller shall pay HOA transfer fee _____.

       (4) ☐ Buyer ☐ Seller shall pay HOA document preparation fees _____.

       (5) ☐ Buyer ☐ Seller shall pay the cost, not to exceed $ _____, of a one-year home warranty plan, issued by _____ with the following optional coverage: _____.

       (6) ☐ Buyer ☐ Seller shall pay for _____.

       (7) ☐ Buyer ☐ Seller shall pay for _____.

5. **STATUTORY DISCLOSURES (INCLUDING LEAD-BASED PAINT HAZARD DISCLOSURES) AND CANCELLATION RIGHTS:**

    A. **(1)** Seller shall, within the time specified in paragraph 14, deliver to Buyer, if required by Law: **(i)** Federal Lead-Based Paint Disclosures and pamphlet ("Lead Disclosures"); and **(ii)** disclosures or notices required by sections 1102 et. seq. and 1103 et. seq. of the California Civil Code ("Statutory Disclosures"). Statutory Disclosures include, but are not limited to, a Real Estate Transfer Disclosure Statement ("TDS"), Natural Hazard Disclosure Statement ("NHD"), notice or actual knowledge of release of illegal controlled substance, notice of special tax and/or assessments (or, if allowed, substantially equivalent notice regarding the Mello-Roos Community Facilities Act and Improvement Bond Act of 1915) and, if Seller has actual knowledge, an industrial use and military ordnance location disclosure (C.A.R. Form SSD).

       (2) Buyer shall, within the time specified in paragraph 14, return Signed Copies of the Statutory and Lead Disclosures to Seller.

       (3) In the event Seller, prior to Close Of Escrow, becomes aware of adverse conditions materially affecting the Property, or any material inaccuracy in disclosures, information or representations previously provided to Buyer of which Buyer is otherwise unaware, Seller shall promptly provide a subsequent or amended disclosure or notice, in writing, covering those items. **However, a subsequent or amended disclosure shall not be required for conditions and material inaccuracies disclosed in reports ordered and paid for by Buyer.**

Buyer's Initials (_WB_)(_DB_)
Seller's Initials (_TP._)(_up._)

RPA-CA REVISED 10/02 (PAGE 2 OF 8)

Reviewed by _____ Date _6/14/51_

CALIFORNIA RESIDENTIAL PURCHASE AGREEMENT (RPA-CA PAGE 2 OF 8)

Property Address: _264 Beach Lane, Costa Mesa, CA 92627_ Date: _June 14, 2051_

    (4) If any disclosure or notice specified in 5A(1), or subsequent or amended disclosure or notice is delivered to Buyer after the offer is Signed, Buyer shall have the right to cancel this Agreement within **3 Days** After delivery in person, or **5 Days** After delivery by deposit in the mail, by giving written notice of cancellation to Seller or Seller's agent. (Lead Disclosures sent by mail must be sent certified mail or better.)

    (5) Note to Buyer and Seller: Waiver of Statutory and Lead Disclosures is prohibited by Law.

  B. **NATURAL AND ENVIRONMENTAL HAZARDS:** Within the time specified in paragraph 14, Seller shall, if required by Law: **(i)** deliver to Buyer earthquake guides (and questionnaire) and environmental hazards booklet; **(ii)** even if exempt from the obligation to provide a NHD, disclose if the Property is located in a Special Flood Hazard Area; Potential Flooding (Inundation) Area; Very High Fire Hazard Zone; State Fire Responsibility Area; Earthquake Fault Zone; Seismic Hazard Zone; and **(iii)** disclose any other zone as required by Law and provide any other information required for those zones.

  C. **DATA BASE DISCLOSURE:** NOTICE: The California Department of Justice, sheriff's departments, police departments serving jurisdictions of 200,000 or more and many other local law enforcement authorities maintain for public access a data base of the locations of persons required to register pursuant to paragraph (1) of subdivision (a) of Section 290.4 of the Penal Code. The data base is updated on a quarterly basis and a source of information about the presence of these individuals in any neighborhood. The Department of Justice also maintains a Sex Offender Identification Line through which inquiries about individuals may be made. This is a "900" telephone service. Callers must have specific information about individuals they are checking. Information regarding neighborhoods is not available through the "900" telephone service.

6. CONDOMINIUM/PLANNED UNIT DEVELOPMENT DISCLOSURES:

  A. **SELLER HAS: 7 (or ☐ _____) Days** After Acceptance to disclose to Buyer whether the Property is a condominium, or is located in a planned unit development or other common interest subdivision.

  B. If the Property is a condominium or is located in a planned unit development or other common interest subdivision, Seller has **3 (or ☐ _____) Days** After Acceptance to request from the HOA (C.A.R. Form HOA): **(i)** Copies of any documents required by Law; **(ii)** disclosure of any pending or anticipated claim or litigation by or against the HOA; **(iii)** a statement containing the location and number of designated parking and storage spaces; **(iv)** Copies of the most recent 12 months of HOA minutes for regular and special meetings; and **(v)** the names and contact information of all HOAs governing the Property (collectively, "CI Disclosures"). Seller shall itemize and deliver to Buyer all CI Disclosures received from the HOA and any CI Disclosures in Seller's possession. Buyer's approval of CI Disclosures is a contingency of this Agreement as specified in paragraph 14.

7. CONDITIONS AFFECTING PROPERTY:

  A. Unless otherwise agreed: **(i) the Property is sold (a) in its PRESENT physical condition as of the date of Acceptance and (b) subject to Buyer's Investigation rights; (ii)** the Property, including pool, spa, landscaping and grounds, is to be maintained in substantially the same condition as on the date of Acceptance; and **(iii)** all debris and personal property not included in the sale shall be removed by Close Of Escrow.

  B. **SELLER SHALL, within the time specified in paragraph 14, DISCLOSE KNOWN MATERIAL FACTS AND DEFECTS** affecting the Property, including known insurance claims within the past five years, **AND MAKE OTHER DISCLOSURES REQUIRED BY LAW.**

  C. **NOTE TO BUYER: You are strongly advised to conduct investigations of the entire Property in order to determine its present condition since Seller may not be aware of all defects affecting the Property or other factors that you consider important. Property improvements may not be built according to code, in compliance with current Law, or have had permits issued.**

  D. **NOTE TO SELLER: Buyer has the right to inspect the Property and, as specified in paragraph 14, based upon information discovered in those inspections: (i) cancel this Agreement; or (ii) request that you make Repairs or take other action.**

8. ITEMS INCLUDED AND EXCLUDED:

  A. **NOTE TO BUYER AND SELLER:** Items listed as included or excluded in the MLS, flyers or marketing materials are **not** included in the purchase price or excluded from the sale unless specified in 8B or C.

  B. **ITEMS INCLUDED IN SALE:**

    (1) All EXISTING fixtures and fittings that are attached to the Property;

    (2) Existing electrical, mechanical, lighting, plumbing and heating fixtures, ceiling fans, fireplace inserts, gas logs and grates, solar systems, built-in appliances, window and door screens, awnings, shutters, window coverings, attached floor coverings, television antennas, satellite dishes, private integrated telephone systems, air coolers/conditioners, pool/spa equipment, garage door openers/remote controls, mailbox, in-ground landscaping, trees/shrubs, water softeners, water purifiers, security systems/alarms;

    (3) The following items: _____

    _____ .

    (4) Seller represents that all items included in the purchase price, unless otherwise specified, are owned by Seller.

    (5) All items included shall be transferred free of liens and without Seller warranty.

  C. **ITEMS EXCLUDED FROM SALE:** _____

    _____ .

9. BUYER'S INVESTIGATION OF PROPERTY AND MATTERS AFFECTING PROPERTY:

  A. Buyer's acceptance of the condition of, and any other matter affecting the Property, is a contingency of this Agreement as specified in this paragraph and paragraph 14. Within the time specified in paragraph 14, Buyer shall have the right, at Buyer's expense unless otherwise agreed, to conduct inspections, investigations, tests, surveys and other studies ("Buyer Investigations"), including, but not limited to, the right to: **(i)** inspect for lead-based paint and other lead-based paint hazards; **(ii)** inspect for wood destroying pests and organisms; **(iii)** review the registered sex offender database; **(iv)** confirm the insurability of Buyer and the Property; and **(v)** satisfy Buyer as to any matter specified in the attached Buyer's Inspection Advisory (C.A.R. Form BIA). Without Seller's prior written consent, Buyer shall neither make nor cause to be made: **(i)** invasive or destructive Buyer's Investigations; or **(ii)** inspections by any governmental building or zoning inspector or government employee, unless required by Law.

  B. Buyer shall complete Buyer Investigations and, as specified in paragraph 14, remove the contingency or cancel the Agreement. Buyer shall give Seller, at no cost, complete Copies of all Buyer Investigation reports obtained by Buyer. Seller shall make the Property available for all Buyer Investigations. Seller shall have water, gas, electricity and all operable pilot lights on for Buyer's Investigations and through the date possession is made available to Buyer.

Buyer's Initials (_WB_)(_DB_)
Seller's Initials (_TP._)(_yp._)

Reviewed by _SR_ Date _6/14/51_

RPA-CA REVISED 10/02 (PAGE 3 OF 8)

EQUAL HOUSING OPPORTUNITY

CALIFORNIA RESIDENTIAL PURCHASE AGREEMENT (RPA-CA PAGE 3 OF 8)

RESIDENTIAL PURCAHSE AGREEMENT (4)

Property Address: _264 Beach Lane, Costa Mesa, CA 92627_   Date: _June 14, 2051_

10. **REPAIRS:** Repairs shall be completed prior to final verification of condition unless otherwise agreed in writing. Repairs to be performed at Seller's expense may be performed by Seller or through others, provided that the work complies with applicable Law, including governmental permit, inspection and approval requirements. Repairs shall be performed in a good, skillful manner with materials of quality and appearance comparable to existing materials. It is understood that exact restoration of appearance or cosmetic items following all Repairs may not be possible. Seller shall: **(i)** obtain receipts for Repairs performed by others; **(ii)** prepare a written statement indicating the Repairs performed by Seller and the date of such Repairs; and **(iii)** provide Copies of receipts and statements to Buyer prior to final verification of condition.

11. **BUYER INDEMNITY AND SELLER PROTECTION FOR ENTRY UPON PROPERTY:** Buyer shall: **(i)** keep the Property free and clear of liens; **(ii)** Repair all damage arising from Buyer Investigations; and **(iii)** indemnify and hold Seller harmless from all resulting liability, claims, demands, damages and costs. Buyer shall carry, or Buyer shall require anyone acting on Buyer's behalf to carry, policies of liability, workers' compensation and other applicable insurance, defending and protecting Seller from liability for any injuries to persons or property occurring during any Buyer Investigations or work done on the Property at Buyer's direction prior to Close Of Escrow. Seller is advised that certain protections may be afforded Seller by recording a "Notice of Non-responsibility" (C.A.R. Form NNR) for Buyer Investigations and work done on the Property at Buyer's direction. Buyer's obligations under this paragraph shall survive the termination of this Agreement.

12. **TITLE AND VESTING:**
    A. Within the time specified in paragraph 14, Buyer shall be provided a current preliminary (title) report, which is only an offer by the title insurer to issue a policy of title insurance and may not contain every item affecting title. Buyer's review of the preliminary report and any other matters which may affect title are a contingency of this Agreement as specified in paragraph 14.
    B. Title is taken in its present condition subject to all encumbrances, easements, covenants, conditions, restrictions, rights and other matters, whether of record or not, as of the date of Acceptance except: **(i)** monetary liens of record unless Buyer is assuming those obligations or taking the Property subject to those obligations; and **(ii)** those matters which Seller has agreed to remove in writing.
    C. Within the time specified in paragraph 14, Seller has a duty to disclose to Buyer all matters known to Seller affecting title, whether of record or not.
    D. At Close Of Escrow, Buyer shall receive a grant deed conveying title (or, for stock cooperative or long-term lease, an assignment of stock certificate or of Seller's leasehold interest), including oil, mineral and water rights if currently owned by Seller. Title shall vest as designated in Buyer's supplemental escrow instructions. THE MANNER OF TAKING TITLE MAY HAVE SIGNIFICANT LEGAL AND TAX CONSEQUENCES. CONSULT AN APPROPRIATE PROFESSIONAL.
    E. Buyer shall receive a CLTA/ALTA Homeowner's Policy of Title Insurance. A title company, at Buyer's request, can provide information about the availability, desirability, coverage, and cost of various title insurance coverages and endorsements. If Buyer desires title coverage other than that required by this paragraph, Buyer shall instruct Escrow Holder in writing and pay any increase in cost.

13. **SALE OF BUYER'S PROPERTY:**
    A. This Agreement is NOT contingent upon the sale of any property owned by Buyer.

OR B. ☐ (If checked): The attached addendum (C.A.R. Form COP) regarding the contingency for the sale of property owned by Buyer is incorporated into this Agreement.

14. **TIME PERIODS; REMOVAL OF CONTINGENCIES; CANCELLATION RIGHTS: The following time periods may only be extended, altered, modified or changed by mutual written agreement. Any removal of contingencies or cancellation under this paragraph must be in writing (C.A.R. Form RRCR).**
    A. **SELLER HAS: 7 (or ☐ _____) Days** After Acceptance to deliver to Buyer all reports, disclosures and information for which Seller is responsible under paragraphs 4, 5A and B, 6A, 7B and 12.
    B. **(1) BUYER HAS: 17 (or ☐ _____) Days** After Acceptance, unless otherwise agreed in writing, to:
        (i) complete all Buyer Investigations; approve all disclosures, reports and other applicable information, which Buyer receives from Seller; and approve all matters affecting the Property (including lead-based paint and lead-based paint hazards as well as other information specified in paragraph 5 and insurability of Buyer and the Property); and
        (ii) return to Seller Signed Copies of Statutory and Lead Disclosures delivered by Seller in accordance with paragraph 5A.
        (2) Within the time specified in 14B(1), Buyer may request that Seller make repairs or take any other action regarding the Property. Seller has no obligation to agree to or respond to Buyer's requests. (C.A.R. Form RR)
        (3) By the end of the time specified in 14B(1) (or 2I for loan contingency or 2J for appraisal contingency), Buyer shall, in writing, remove the applicable contingency (C.A.R. Form RRCR) or cancel this Agreement. However, if the following inspections, reports or disclosures are not made within the time specified in 14A, then Buyer has **5 (or ☐ _____) Days** after receipt of any such items, or the time specified in 14B(1), whichever is later, to remove the applicable contingency or cancel this Agreement in writing: **(i)** government-mandated inspections or reports required as a condition of closing; or **(ii)** Common Interest Disclosures pursuant to paragraph 6B.
    C. **CONTINUATION OF CONTINGENCY OR CONTRACTUAL OBLIGATION; SELLER RIGHT TO CANCEL:**
        (1) **Seller right to Cancel; Buyer Contingencies:** Seller, after first giving Buyer a Notice to Buyer to Perform (as specified below), may cancel this Agreement in writing and authorize return of Buyer's deposit if, by the time specified in this Agreement, Buyer does not remove in writing the applicable contingency or cancel this Agreement. Once all contingencies have been removed, failure of either Buyer or Seller to close escrow on time may be a breach of this Agreement.
        (2) **Continuation of Contingency:** Even after the expiration of the time specified in 14B(1), Buyer retains the right to make requests to Seller, remove in writing the applicable contingency or cancel this Agreement until Seller cancels pursuant to 14C(1). Once Seller receives Buyer's written removal of all contingencies, Seller may not cancel this Agreement pursuant to 14C(1).
        (3) **Seller right to Cancel; Buyer Contract Obligations:** Seller, after first giving Buyer a Notice to Buyer to Perform (as specified below), may cancel this Agreement in writing and authorize return of Buyer's deposit for any of the following reasons: **(i)** if Buyer fails to deposit funds as required by 2A or 2B; **(ii)** if the funds deposited pursuant to 2A or 2B are not good when deposited; **(iii)** if Buyer fails to provide a letter as required by 2G; **(iv)** if Buyer fails to provide verification as required by 2H or 2L; **(v)** if Seller reasonably disapproves of the verification provided by 2H or 2L; **(vi)** if Buyer fails to return Statutory and Lead Disclosures as required by paragraph 5A(2); or **(vii)** if Buyer fails to sign or initial a separate liquidated damage form for an increased deposit as required by paragraph 16. **Seller is not required to give Buyer a Notice to Perform regarding Close of Escrow.**
        (4) **Notice To Buyer To Perform:** The Notice to Buyer to Perform (C.A.R. Form NBP) shall: **(i)** be in writing; **(ii)** be signed by Seller; and **(iii)** give Buyer at least **24 (or ☐ _____)** hours (or until the time specified in the applicable paragraph, whichever occurs last) to take the applicable action. A Notice to Buyer to Perform may not be given any earlier than **2 Days** Prior to the expiration of the applicable time for Buyer to remove a contingency or cancel this Agreement or meet a 14C(3) obligation.

Buyer's Initials (_WB_)(_OB_)
Seller's Initials (_T.P._)(_yp._)

RPA-CA REVISED 10/02 (PAGE 4 OF 8)

Reviewed by _JR_ Date _6/14/51_

CALIFORNIA RESIDENTIAL PURCHASE AGREEMENT (RPA-CA PAGE 4 OF 8)

Property Address: _264 Beach Lane, Costa Mesa, CA 92627_　　　　Date: _June 14, 2051_

D. EFFECT OF BUYER'S REMOVAL OF CONTINGENCIES : If Buyer removes, in writing, any contingency or cancellation rights, unless otherwise specified in a separate written agreement between Buyer and Seller, Buyer shall conclusively be deemed to have: **(i)** completed all Buyer Investigations, and review of reports and other applicable information and disclosures pertaining to that contingency or cancellation right; **(ii)** elected to proceed with the transaction; and **(iii)** assumed all liability, responsibility and expense for Repairs or corrections pertaining to that contingency or cancellation right, or for inability to obtain financing.

E. EFFECT OF CANCELLATION ON DEPOSITS: If Buyer or Seller gives written notice of cancellation pursuant to rights duly exercised under the terms of this Agreement, Buyer and Seller agree to Sign mutual instructions to cancel the sale and escrow and release deposits, less fees and costs, to the party entitled to the funds. Fees and costs may be payable to service providers and vendors for services and products provided during escrow. **Release of funds will require mutual Signed release instructions from Buyer and Seller, judicial decision or arbitration award. A party may be subject to a civil penalty of up to $1,000 for refusal to sign such instructions if no good faith dispute exists as to who is entitled to the deposited funds (Civil Code §1057.3).**

15. FINAL VERIFICATION OF CONDITION: Buyer shall have the right to make a final inspection of the Property within **5 (or _____) Days** Prior to Close Of Escrow, NOT AS A CONTINGENCY OF THE SALE, but solely to confirm: **(i)** the Property is maintained pursuant to paragraph 7A; **(ii)** Repairs have been completed as agreed; and **(iii)** Seller has complied with Seller's other obligations under this Agreement.

16. LIQUIDATED DAMAGES: If Buyer fails to complete this purchase because of Buyer's default, Seller shall retain, as liquidated damages, the deposit actually paid. If the Property is a dwelling with no more than four units, one of which Buyer intends to occupy, then the amount retained shall be no more than 3% of the purchase price. Any excess shall be returned to Buyer. Release of funds will require mutual, Signed release instructions from both Buyer and Seller, judicial decision or arbitration award.
BUYER AND SELLER SHALL SIGN A SEPARATE LIQUIDATED DAMAGES PROVISION FOR ANY INCREASED DEPOSIT. (C.A.R. FORM RID)

Buyer's Initials _wB_ _DB_	Seller's Initials _TA_ _up_

17. DISPUTE RESOLUTION:

A. MEDIATION: Buyer and Seller agree to mediate any dispute or claim arising between them out of this Agreement, or any resulting transaction, before resorting to arbitration or court action. Paragraphs 17B(2) and (3) below apply whether or not the Arbitration provision is initialed. Mediation fees, if any, shall be divided equally among the parties involved. If, for any dispute or claim to which this paragraph applies, any party commences an action without first attempting to resolve the matter through mediation, or refuses to mediate after a request has been made, then that party shall not be entitled to recover attorney fees, even if they would otherwise be available to that party in any such action. THIS MEDIATION PROVISION APPLIES WHETHER OR NOT THE ARBITRATION PROVISION IS INITIALED.

B. ARBITRATION OF DISPUTES: (1) Buyer and Seller agree that any dispute or claim in Law or equity arising between them out of this Agreement or any resulting transaction, which is not settled through mediation, shall be decided by neutral, binding arbitration, including and subject to paragraphs 17B(2) and (3) below. The arbitrator shall be a retired judge or justice, or an attorney with at least 5 years of residential real estate Law experience, unless the parties mutually agree to a different arbitrator, who shall render an award in accordance with substantive California Law. The parties shall have the right to discovery in accordance with California Code of Civil Procedure §1283.05. In all other respects, the arbitration shall be conducted in accordance with Title 9 of Part III of the California Code of Civil Procedure. Judgment upon the award of the arbitrator(s) may be entered into any court having jurisdiction. Interpretation of this agreement to arbitrate shall be governed by the Federal Arbitration Act.
(2) EXCLUSIONS FROM MEDIATION AND ARBITRATION: The following matters are excluded from mediation and arbitration: **(i)** a judicial or non-judicial foreclosure or other action or proceeding to enforce a deed of trust, mortgage or installment land sale contract as defined in California Civil Code §2985; **(ii)** an unlawful detainer action; **(iii)** the filing or enforcement of a mechanic's lien; and **(iv)** any matter that is within the jurisdiction of a probate, small claims or bankruptcy court. The filing of a court action to enable the recording of a notice of pending action, for order of attachment, receivership, injunction, or other provisional remedies, shall not constitute a waiver of the mediation and arbitration provisions.
(3) BROKERS: Buyer and Seller agree to mediate and arbitrate disputes or claims involving either or both Brokers, consistent with 17 A and B, provided either or both Brokers shall have agreed to such mediation or arbitration prior to, or within a reasonable time after, the dispute or claim is presented to Brokers. Any election by either or both Brokers to participate in mediation or arbitration shall not result in Brokers being deemed parties to the Agreement.

"**NOTICE: BY INITIALING IN THE SPACE BELOW YOU ARE AGREEING TO HAVE ANY DISPUTE ARISING OUT OF THE MATTERS INCLUDED IN THE 'ARBITRATION OF DISPUTES' PROVISION DECIDED BY NEUTRAL ARBITRATION AS PROVIDED BY CALIFORNIA LAW AND YOU ARE GIVING UP ANY RIGHTS YOU MIGHT POSSESS TO HAVE THE DISPUTE LITIGATED IN A COURT OR JURY TRIAL. BY INITIALING IN THE SPACE BELOW YOU ARE GIVING UP YOUR JUDICIAL RIGHTS TO DISCOVERY AND APPEAL, UNLESS THOSE RIGHTS ARE SPECIFICALLY INCLUDED IN THE 'ARBITRATION OF DISPUTES' PROVISION. IF YOU REFUSE TO SUBMIT TO ARBITRATION AFTER AGREEING TO THIS PROVISION, YOU MAY BE COMPELLED TO ARBITRATE UNDER THE AUTHORITY OF THE CALIFORNIA CODE OF CIVIL PROCEDURE. YOUR AGREEMENT TO THIS ARBITRATION PROVISION IS VOLUNTARY.**"
"**WE HAVE READ AND UNDERSTAND THE FOREGOING AND AGREE TO SUBMIT DISPUTES ARISING OUT OF THE MATTERS INCLUDED IN THE 'ARBITRATION OF DISPUTES' PROVISION TO NEUTRAL ARBITRATION.**"

Buyer's Initials _wB_ _DB_	Seller's Initials _TA_ _up_

Buyer's Initials (_wB_)(_DB_)
Seller's Initials (_TA_)(_up._)

Reviewed by _____ Date _6/14/51_

RPA-CA REVISED 10/02 (PAGE 5 OF 8)

CALIFORNIA RESIDENTIAL PURCHASE AGREEMENT (RPA-CA PAGE 5 OF 8)

Property Address: _264 Beach Lane, Costa Mesa, CA 92627_ Date: _June 14, 2051_

18. PRORATIONS OF PROPERTY TAXES AND OTHER ITEMS: Unless otherwise agreed in writing, the following items shall be PAID CURRENT and prorated between Buyer and Seller as of Close Of Escrow: real property taxes and assessments, interest, rents, HOA regular, special, and emergency dues and assessments imposed prior to Close Of Escrow, premiums on insurance assumed by Buyer, payments on bonds and assessments assumed by Buyer, and payments on Mello-Roos and other Special Assessment District bonds and assessments that are now a lien. The following items shall be assumed by Buyer WITHOUT CREDIT toward the purchase price: prorated payments on Mello-Roos and other Special Assessment District bonds and assessments and HOA special assessments that are now a lien but not yet due. Property will be reassessed upon change of ownership. Any supplemental tax bills shall be paid as follows: **(i)** for periods after Close Of Escrow, by Buyer; and **(ii)** for periods prior to Close Of Escrow, by Seller. TAX BILLS ISSUED AFTER CLOSE OF ESCROW SHALL BE HANDLED DIRECTLY BETWEEN BUYER AND SELLER. Prorations shall be made based on a 30-day month.

19. WITHHOLDING TAXES: Seller and Buyer agree to execute any instrument, affidavit, statement or instruction reasonably necessary to comply with federal (FIRPTA) and California withholding Law, if required (C.A.R. Forms AS and AB).

20. MULTIPLE LISTING SERVICE ("MLS"): Brokers are authorized to report to the MLS a pending sale and, upon Close Of Escrow, the terms of this transaction to be published and disseminated to persons and entities authorized to use the information on terms approved by the MLS.

21. EQUAL HOUSING OPPORTUNITY: The Property is sold in compliance with federal, state and local anti-discrimination Laws.

22. ATTORNEY FEES: In any action, proceeding, or arbitration between Buyer and Seller arising out of this Agreement, the prevailing Buyer or Seller shall be entitled to reasonable attorney fees and costs from the non-prevailing Buyer or Seller, except as provided in paragraph 17A.

23. SELECTION OF SERVICE PROVIDERS: If Brokers refer Buyer or Seller to persons, vendors, or service or product providers ("Providers"), Brokers do not guarantee the performance of any Providers. Buyer and Seller may select ANY Providers of their own choosing.

24. TIME OF ESSENCE; ENTIRE CONTRACT; CHANGES: Time is of the essence. All understandings between the parties are incorporated in this Agreement. Its terms are intended by the parties as a final, complete and exclusive expression of their Agreement with respect to its subject matter, and may not be contradicted by evidence of any prior agreement or contemporaneous oral agreement. If any provision of this Agreement is held to be ineffective or invalid, the remaining provisions will nevertheless be given full force and effect. **Neither this Agreement nor any provision in it may be extended, amended, modified, altered or changed, except in writing Signed by Buyer and Seller.**

25. OTHER TERMS AND CONDITIONS, including attached supplements:
   A. ☑ Buyer's Inspection Advisory (C.A.R. Form BIA)
   B. ☐ Purchase Agreement Addendum (C.A.R. Form PAA paragraph numbers: _____)
   C. _____
   _____
   _____

26. DEFINITIONS: As used in this Agreement:
   A. **"Acceptance"** means the time the offer or final counter offer is accepted in writing by a party and is delivered to and personally received by the other party or that party's authorized agent in accordance with the terms of this offer or a final counter offer.
   B. **"Agreement"** means the terms and conditions of this accepted California Residential Purchase Agreement and any accepted counter offers and addenda.
   C. **"C.A.R. Form"** means the specific form referenced or another comparable form agreed to by the parties.
   D. **"Close Of Escrow"** means the date the grant deed, or other evidence of transfer of title, is recorded. If the scheduled close of escrow falls on a Saturday, Sunday or legal holiday, then close of escrow shall be the next business day after the scheduled close of escrow date.
   E. **"Copy"** means copy by any means including photocopy, NCR, facsimile and electronic.
   F. **"Days"** means calendar days, unless otherwise required by Law.
   G. **"Days After"** means the specified number of calendar days after the occurrence of the event specified, not counting the calendar date on which the specified event occurs, and ending at 11:59PM on the final day.
   H. **"Days Prior"** means the specified number of calendar days before the occurrence of the event specified, not counting the calendar date on which the specified event is scheduled to occur.
   I. **"Electronic Copy" or "Electronic Signature"** means, as applicable, an electronic copy or signature complying with California Law. Buyer and Seller agree that electronic means will not be used by either party to modify or alter the content or integrity of this Agreement without the knowledge and consent of the other.
   J. **"Law"** means any law, code, statute, ordinance, regulation, rule or order, which is adopted by a controlling city, county, state or federal legislative, judicial or executive body or agency.
   K. **"Notice to Buyer to Perform"** means a document (C.A.R. Form NBP), which shall be in writing and Signed by Seller and shall give Buyer at least 24 hours **(or as otherwise specified in paragraph 14C(4))** to remove a contingency or perform as applicable.
   L. **"Repairs"** means any repairs (including pest control), alterations, replacements, modifications or retrofitting of the Property provided for under this Agreement.
   M. **"Signed"** means either a handwritten or electronic signature on an original document, Copy or any counterpart.
   N. **Singular and Plural** terms each include the other, when appropriate.

Buyer's Initials (WB)(DB)
Seller's Initials (T.P.)(yp.)

Reviewed by _____ Date 6/14/51

RPA-CA REVISED 10/02 (PAGE 6 OF 8)

EQUAL HOUSING OPPORTUNITY

CALIFORNIA RESIDENTIAL PURCHASE AGREEMENT (RPA-CA PAGE 6 OF 8)

Property Address: _264 Beach Lane, Costa Mesa, CA 92627_   Date: _June 14, 2051_

27. AGENCY:

A. DISCLOSURE: Buyer and Seller each acknowledge prior receipt of C.A.R. Form AD "Disclosure Regarding Real Estate Agency Relationships."

B. POTENTIALLY COMPETING BUYERS AND SELLERS: Buyer and Seller each acknowledge receipt of a disclosure of the possibility of multiple representation by the Broker representing that principal. This disclosure may be part of a listing agreement, buyer-broker agreement or separate document (C.A.R. Form DA). Buyer understands that Broker representing Buyer may also represent other potential buyers, who may consider, make offers on or ultimately acquire the Property. Seller understands that Broker representing Seller may also represent other sellers with competing properties of interest to this Buyer.

C. CONFIRMATION: The following agency relationships are hereby confirmed for this transaction:
Listing Agent _Sail Realty_ (Print Firm Name) is the agent of (check one): ☒ the Seller exclusively; or ☐ both the Buyer and Seller.
Selling Agent _Ramos Realty_ (Print Firm Name) (if not same as Listing Agent) is the agent of (check one): ☒ the Buyer exclusively; or ☐ the Seller exclusively; or ☐ both the Buyer and Seller. Real Estate Brokers are not parties to the Agreement between Buyer and Seller.

28. JOINT ESCROW INSTRUCTIONS TO ESCROW HOLDER:

A. **The following paragraphs, or applicable portions thereof, of this Agreement constitute the joint escrow instructions of Buyer and Seller to Escrow Holder,** which Escrow Holder is to use along with any related counter offers and addenda, and any additional mutual instructions to close the escrow: 1, 2, 4, 12, 13B, 14E, 18, 19, 24, 25B and C, 26, 28, 29, 32A, 33 and paragraph D of the section titled Real Estate Brokers on page 8. If a Copy of the separate compensation agreement(s) provided for in paragraph 29 or 32A, or paragraph D of the section titled Real Estate Brokers on page 8 is deposited with Escrow Holder by Broker, Escrow Holder shall accept such agreement(s) and pay out from Buyer's or Seller's funds, or both, as applicable, the Broker's compensation provided for in such agreement(s). The terms and conditions of this Agreement not set forth in the specified paragraphs are additional matters for the information of Escrow Holder, but about which Escrow Holder need not be concerned. Buyer and Seller will receive Escrow Holder's general provisions directly from Escrow Holder and will execute such provisions upon Escrow Holder's request. To the extent the general provisions are inconsistent or conflict with this Agreement, the general provisions will control as to the duties and obligations of Escrow Holder only. Buyer and Seller will execute additional instructions, documents and forms provided by Escrow Holder that are reasonably necessary to close escrow.

B. A Copy of this Agreement shall be delivered to Escrow Holder within **3** business days after Acceptance (or ☐ _____). Buyer and Seller authorize Escrow Holder to accept and rely on Copies and Signatures as defined in this Agreement as originals, to open escrow and for other purposes of escrow. The validity of this Agreement as between Buyer and Seller is not affected by whether or when Escrow Holder Signs this Agreement.

C. Brokers are a party to the escrow for the sole purpose of compensation pursuant to paragraphs 29, 32A and paragraph D of the section titled Real Estate Brokers on page 8. Buyer and Seller irrevocably assign to Brokers compensation specified in paragraphs 29 and 32A, respectively, and irrevocably instruct Escrow Holder to disburse those funds to Brokers at Close Of Escrow or pursuant to any other mutually executed cancellation agreement. Compensation instructions can be amended or revoked only with the written consent of Brokers. Escrow Holder shall immediately notify Brokers: **(i)** if Buyer's initial or any additional deposit is not made pursuant to this Agreement, or is not good at time of deposit with Escrow Holder; or **(ii)** if Buyer and Seller instruct Escrow Holder to cancel escrow.

D. A Copy of any amendment that affects any paragraph of this Agreement for which Escrow Holder is responsible shall be delivered to Escrow Holder within **2** business days after mutual execution of the amendment.

29. BROKER COMPENSATION FROM BUYER: If applicable, upon Close Of Escrow, **Buyer** agrees to pay compensation to Broker as specified in a separate written agreement between Buyer and Broker.

30. TERMS AND CONDITIONS OF OFFER:
This is an offer to purchase the Property on the above terms and conditions. All paragraphs with spaces for initials by Buyer and Seller are incorporated in this Agreement only if initialed by all parties. If at least one but not all parties initial, a counter offer is required until agreement is reached. Seller has the right to continue to offer the Property for sale and to accept any other offer at any time prior to notification of Acceptance. Buyer has read and acknowledges receipt of a Copy of the offer and agrees to the above confirmation of agency relationships. If this offer is accepted and Buyer subsequently defaults, Buyer may be responsible for payment of Brokers' compensation. This Agreement and any supplement, addendum or modification, including any Copy, may be Signed in two or more counterparts, all of which shall constitute one and the same writing.

Buyer's Initials (WB)(QB)
Seller's Initials (TA)(yp)

RPA-CA REVISED 10/02 (PAGE 7 OF 8)

Reviewed by _JR_ Date 6/14/51

☖ EQUAL HOUSING OPPORTUNITY

CALIFORNIA RESIDENTIAL PURCHASE AGREEMENT (RPA-CA PAGE 7 OF 8)

RESIDENTIAL PURCAHSE AGREEMENT (8)

Property Address: _264 Beach Lane, Costa Mesa, CA 92627_   Date: _June 14, 2051_

31. EXPIRATION OF OFFER: This offer shall be deemed revoked and the deposit shall be returned unless the offer is Signed by Seller and a Copy of the Signed offer is personally received by Buyer, or by _____, who is authorized to receive it by 5:00 PM on the third calendar day after this offer is signed by Buyer (or, if checked) ☐ by _____ (date), at _____ AM/PM).

Date _June 14, 2051_   Date _June 14, 2051_

BUYER _Walter Buyer_   BUYER _Debbie Buyer_

Walter Buyer   _Debbie Buyer_
(Print name)   (Print name)

100 Boat Lane, Marina del Rey, CA 90292
(Address)

32. BROKER COMPENSATION FROM SELLER:
   A. Upon Close Of Escrow, **Seller** agrees to pay compensation to Broker as specified in a separate written agreement between Seller and Broker.
   B. If escrow does not close, compensation is payable as specified in that separate written agreement.
33. ACCEPTANCE OF OFFER: Seller warrants that Seller is the owner of the Property, or has the authority to execute this Agreement. Seller accepts the above offer, agrees to sell the Property on the above terms and conditions, and agrees to the above confirmation of agency relationships. Seller has read and acknowledges receipt of a Copy of this Agreement, and authorizes Broker to deliver a Signed Copy to Buyer.
   ☐ (If checked) **SUBJECT TO ATTACHED COUNTER OFFER, DATED** _____.

Date _June 15, 2051_   Date _June 15, 2051_

SELLER _Tony Seller_   SELLER _Yolanda Seller_

TONY SELLER   _YOLANDA SELLER_
(Print name)   (Print name)

264 Beach Lane, Costa Mesa, CA 92627
(Address)

CONFIRMATION OF ACCEPTANCE: A Copy of Signed Acceptance was personally received by Buyer or Buyer's authorized
_(WB DB)_ agent on (date) _6/15/51_ at _3_ AM/PM. A binding Agreement is created when
(Initials) a Copy of Signed Acceptance is personally received by Buyer or Buyer's authorized agent whether or not confirmed in this document. Completion of this confirmation is not legally required in order to create a binding Agreement; it is solely intended to evidence the date that Confirmation of Acceptance has occurred.

REAL ESTATE BROKERS:
A. Real Estate Brokers are not parties to the Agreement between Buyer and Seller.
B. Agency relationships are confirmed as stated in paragraph 27.
C. If specified in paragraph 2A, Agent who submitted the offer for Buyer acknowledges receipt of deposit.
D. **COOPERATING BROKER COMPENSATION:** Listing Broker agrees to pay Cooperating Broker (**Selling Firm**) and Cooperating Broker agrees to accept, out of Listing Broker's proceeds in escrow. **(i)** the amount specified in the MLS, provided Cooperating Broker is a Participant of the MLS in which the Property is offered for sale or a reciprocal MLS; or **(ii)** ☐ (If checked) the amount specified in a separate written agreement (C.A.R. Form CBC) between Listing Broker and Cooperating Broker.

Real Estate Broker (Selling Firm) _Ramos Realty_
By _Joseph Ramos_   Date _6/14/51_
Address _777 Newport Blvd._   City _Newport Beach_   State _CA_ Zip _92663_
Telephone _714-647-0000_   Fax _714-647-0001_   E-mail _jr@ramosrealty.com_

Real Estate Broker (Listing Firm) _Sail Realty_
By _Carmen Caro_   Date _6/15/51_
Address _227 Harbor Blvd._   City _Costa Mesa_   State _CA_ Zip _92627_
Telephone _714-626-2828_   Fax _714-646-2829_   E-mail _carmen@sailreal.com_

ESCROW HOLDER ACKNOWLEDGMENT:
Escrow Holder acknowledges receipt of a Copy of this Agreement, (if checked, ☐ a deposit in the amount of $_____),
counter offer numbers _____ and _____
_____, and agrees to act as Escrow Holder subject to paragraph 28 of this Agreement, any supplemental escrow instructions and the terms of Escrow Holder's general provisions.

Escrow Holder is advised that the date of Confirmation of Acceptance of the Agreement as between Buyer and Seller is _____

Escrow Holder _____   Escrow # _____
By _____   Date _____
Address _____
Phone/Fax/E-mail _____
Escrow Holder is licensed by the California Department of ☐ Corporations, ☐ Insurance, ☐ Real Estate. License # _____

THIS FORM HAS BEEN APPROVED BY THE CALIFORNIA ASSOCIATION OF REALTORS® (C.A.R.). NO REPRESENTATION IS MADE AS TO THE LEGAL VALIDITY OR ADEQUACY OF ANY PROVISION IN ANY SPECIFIC TRANSACTION. A REAL ESTATE BROKER IS THE PERSON QUALIFIED TO ADVISE ON REAL ESTATE TRANSACTIONS. IF YOU DESIRE LEGAL OR TAX ADVICE, CONSULT AN APPROPRIATE PROFESSIONAL.
This form is available for use by the entire real estate industry. It is not intended to identify the user as a REALTOR®. REALTOR® is a registered collective membership mark which may be used only by members of the NATIONAL ASSOCIATION OF REALTORS® who subscribe to its Code of Ethics.

SURE TRAC
The System for Success™

Published by the
California Association of REALTORS®

Reviewed by _____ Date _6/14/51_

EQUAL HOUSING OPPORTUNITY

RPA-CA REVISED 10/02 (PAGE 8 OF 8)

CALIFORNIA RESIDENTIAL PURCHASE AGREEMENT (RPA-CA PAGE 8 OF 8)

III. CHAPTER SUMMARY

When an escrow is opened, it will begin with a MEMO or ORDER which will be the results of the opening interview with the broker or principal parties. It will be from this that the ESCROW INSTRUCTIONS will be drawn.

A DEED for transfer will be prepared. There are many kinds of deeds such as the LAND PATENT, GRANT; QUITCLAIM, WARRANTY, GIFT, TAX, SHERIFF, ADMINISTRATORIEXECUTOR DEED. All have their particular purpose but all are capable of moving title to another person. A TRUSTEE DEED and INTERSPOUSAL DEED are also used in particular cases.

VESTING has to do with how the person(s) will hold title. The various choices are SEVERALTY, that is alone; TENANCY IN COMMON, with other people; and JOINT TENANCY, with the right of suvivorship. COMMUNITY PROPERTY is between husband and wife. DOCUMENTARY TAX is paid at the time a deed is recorded.

TITLE INSURANCE is normally a part of any escrow and certain policies may be issued. A CLTA is a standard owner's policy while the ALTA is normally reserved for a lender who wants additional protection.

A DEED OF TRUST is a lien instrument recorded with a new loan. A PROMISSORY NOTE is executed and is evidence of the debt with the agreement to repay. HYPOTHECATION is the borrowing of money without giving up possession of the security such as real estate.

There may be provisions included such as ACCELERATION, ALIENATION, or DUE ON SALE CLAUSES that are designed to protect the lender in cases of transfer of property without the lender's consent.

A BENEFICIARY STATEMENT shows the amount of loan due and its terms and is sent to escrow upon a DEMAND from the parties. If the loan is repaid in escrow, there will be a RECONVEYANCE. Special contracts, such as LAND CONTRACTS, are financing tools where the seller retains title while the buyer is purchasing the property. It is a LIEN that protects the lender and allows a foreclosure in the event of a default.

POINTS are paid to the lender for the granting of the loan. One point represents one per cent of the loan. A PREPAYMENT PENALTY is paid on loans that are paid early. A PURCHASE MONEY DEED OF TRUST is a loan made as payment of the purchase price of the real property. The SUBORDINATION agreement allows the changing of loan priorities previously recorded.

At the close of escrow there will be PRORATIONS which charge buyers and seller individually for costs. This will be shown in the SETTLEMENT SHEET given to each party. The escrow documents are RECORDED to insure public notice.

In the event of a CANCELLATION, both parties must sign a statement insuring that there would be no further liability to either party. In the event of a conflict, the escrow may ask for a legal proceeding called an INTERPLEADER, where the funds and papers are distributed by the courts.

IV. TERMS

Acceleration: A provision that allows the lender under stated conditions to accelerate the loan for early prepayment.

Administrator/Executor Deed: A deed given as a result of transfer of decedent's property.

Alienation: The act of transferring ownership, title or an interest in real property to another person.

ALTA: American Land Title Association title policy designed for private and institutional lenders.

Assignment: The act of transferring a contractual right to another in the example of a promissory note assigned to another individual.

Beneficiary Statement: A statement by a lender or beneficiary as to the amount required to pay the entire indebtedness.

Cancellation: Specific agreement by parties to cancel or terminate a contract or escrow.

CLTA: California Land Title Association title policy that covers owners, lenders and leaseholds in various ways.

Community Property: Ownership by married persons of property acquired after or during marriage.

Deed: A written instrument which gives over the title to real property from one owner to another.

Deed of Trust: A device which secures the property as collateral for the note. When recorded, it becomes a lien.

Demand: A letter from a creditor/beneficiary stating the amount needed to pay off an existing loan.

Documentary Transfer Tax: Tax applied and collected at recording applied to the money consideration in a transaction.

Due on Sale: Permits the lender to require the owner pay the entire mortgage debt in the event title is transferred. It is the same as an alienation clause.

Escrow Instructions: Preprinted forms that permit the listing of all the funds and documents which will move through escrow. Conditions of escrow are also stated.

Escrow Memo/Order: Record of the transaction details taken at the initial interview of the parties to an escrow.

Gift Deed: A deed in which the consideration is "love and affection."

Hypothecation: To pledge property as security without surrendering possession of the property.

Interpleader: A legal proceeding whereby escrow deposits with the court funds and papers to be properly distributed.

Interspousal Deed: A deed executed between married couples to transfer or otherwise correct title.

Joint Tenancy: Ownership by two or more persons with the right of survivorship.

Land Contract: A real property seller financed contract where the seller retains title until the loan is fully repaid.

Land Patent/Grant: An original conveyance from the government to a private owner.

Lien: A recorded document that secures real property for an obligation or debt.

Points: Charges usually percentages that lenders charge for making a loan.

Prepayment Penalty: A charge by lenders for early prepayment of a loan.

Promissory Note: A written promise to repay a sum of money with certain stated conditions. It is evidence of a debt.

Prorations: Computations in escrow of charges to each party for various items usually based on calendar days.

Purchase Money Deed of Trust: A deed of trust given as part of the purchase price.

Quitclaim Deed: A deed that releases whatever interest the grantor has in the property.

Reconveyance: Either full or partial that indicates a recorded release of the indebtedness against real property.

Recording: The process of entering into the public record any written instruments affecting the title to real property.

Settlement Sheet: A detailed cash accounting of a real estate transaction that shows charges and credits with cash paid out.

Severalty: Ownership by one person or corporation.

Sheriff's Deed: Deed given by a court to effect the sale of property to satisfy a judgment.

Status: Refers to the legal character or condition of how a person holds title, i.e., Married, Single, etc.

Subordination: A clause in a trust deed that allows for the future change of priority of a loan.

Tax Deed: A deed that conveys title sold by a governmental agency for nonpayment of taxes.

Tenancy in Common: Ownership by two or more persons without the right of survivorship.

Title Insurance: An indemnity contract where a title company warrants good marketable title.

Trustee Deed: A deed given at a foreclosure sale. Not to be confused with a trust deed.

Vesting: To place ownership and control in the name of specific parties.

Warranty Deed: A deed that warrants good clear title with a guarantee to defend title.

V. CHAPTER QUIZ

1. Which of the following is NOT an escrow job?

    a. Use only deposit receipt
    b. Collect funds
    c. Obtain title insurance
    d. All of the above

2. The last job in a sale sequence is:

    a. give money to seller.
    b. give deed to buyer.
    c. both a and b.
    d. neither a nor b.

3. The escrow process is essentially the same throughout California; the differences are:

    a. timing of the steps.
    b. signing of escrow instructions.
    c. start of title search.
    d. all of the above.

4. The first step in the escrow procedure, without a doubt, is:

    a. make adjustments.

    b. take the escrow.

    c. disburse funds.

    d. close escrow.

5. Which of the following is NOT a basic process in the escrow procedure?

    a. Escrow instructions

    b. Pay old loans

    c. Return funds

    d. Order title search

6. The escrow memo is to:

    a. obtain all information about.

    b. amend escrow.

    c. both a and b transaction.

    d. neither a nor b.

7. The main transfer of real property in California is:

    a. a deed.

    b. a trust deed.

    c. both a and b.

    d. neither a nor b.

8. The grant deed has which implied warranties:

    a. free of encumbrances (unless stated).

    b. after-acquired title.

    c. seller has not conveyed property before.

    d. all of the above.

9. A valid deed must have:

    a. proper writing.

    b. proper signatures.

    c. delivery and acceptance.

    d. all of the above.

10. Which of the following vestings requires individuals to be married?

    a. Community property

    b. Severalty

    c. Joint tenancy

    d. Tenancy in common

ANSWERS: 1. a; 2. c; 3. d; 4. b; 5. c; 6. a; 7. a; 8. d; 9. d; 10. a

Sample One,
Part One

We will now begin to process an actual sale escrow, a simple sale that contains the elements presented in many single-family residential transactions: cash down to a new 80% loan, and the pay-off of the seller's old loan. You'll follow this sample escrow in exact detail from start to finish. You've made the acquaintance of the major processes in Chapter Two, and now you'll be putting the escrow theory to work.

We'll assume that you are working in the escrow department at Glendale Federal Savings Bank. (Later on, you'll be working for a title insurance company and an independent escrow agent.) Right now, you are about to receive a real estate agent, Mr. Thomas Broker, who called your company because the sellers suggested it and the buyer agreed.

You place on your desk an Escrow File that contains a number of preprinted sheets and documents. **For the purpose of this example, we will discuss filling out all escrow forms manually, but many forms in the escrow world today are available to use with a computer.**

When Mr. Broker comes to your desk, he brings with him the Purchase Agreement and Joint Escrow Instructions, which has been signed by both the sellers and the buyer. He attempts to hand it to you, but you politely decline and tell him you'd much rather have him explain the details of the transaction himself.

CHAPTER OUTLINE

Mr. Broker also tells you that he wants to "take out" the escrow instructions and other documents, so he can get the necessary signatures on them and return them to you quickly. Although it is a reasonably long escrow (60 days), he wants to get it smoothly underway. You will have to make up these forms now, while he waits. Be extra sure to read them all very carefully before you hand them over, since you may feel slightly pressured with him sitting there.

I. Taking an Escrow

A. THE MEMO SHEET

Now take the "Sale Escrow Memo Sheet" out of the escrow file, and begin work. (See **Figures 3-1** and **3-2**).

The memo sheet, when completed, will contain all the information necessary to begin an escrow.

Never trust your memory to help you with an escrow. As an escrow officer, you'll have many escrows open at the same time—write it down! There are two other important reasons:

1. any other escrow officer must be able to pick up your file and complete the escrow in case you are called away, go on vacation, or move to another job; and

2. your work must be available and understandable to members of auditing teams or bank examiners who periodically and without prior notice come in to review the financial status of your company.

The **MEMO SHEET**, *or escrow work sheet, or escrow order sheet, is a printed form supplied by your company that contains spaces to write down all the elements of the transaction.* Sometimes it is printed directly on the file folder, but it is usually a separate sheet. You will frequently be asked to use blank paper to write down the escrow specifics. Fill it out quickly, recording points of the transaction as they are given. The broker usually presents the facts without any prompting from you, but sometimes you must ask questions.

Your questions should be short and direct. (Extra words have a way of becoming suggestions in the minds of others.) Do not ask such things as "Will this be joint tenancy or community property?" Only ask questions such as "How do you want the vesting?" or "What is the vesting to be?" At the end of your memo-taking session, check to see that you have everything you need. Add up the monies. Do they equal the price? See that the names and addresses are correct.

Figure 3-1

BLANK SALE ESCROW MEMO

SALE ESCROW MEMO ⑦ ⑧ **Escrow No.**

A Nature of Transaction ① Time Limit ②

Seller Borrower ③

Buyer Lender ④

Legal Description ⑤

⑥

B
Paid out of Escrow $ ⑨
Cash through Escrow ⑩
Encumbrances of Record ⑪
New Encumbrances ⑫
Total Consideration ⑬
From Agent ⑭

C ENCUMBRANCE To Remain in favor of ⑮

With Interest @ ⑯ % Monthly Payments$ ⑰ Present Unpaid Balance ⑱

D DESCRIPTION OF NEW ENCUMBRANCE ⑲

⑳ Trust Deed on your usual form securing Note for $ ㉑, dated during escrow, due (if straight note) ㉒

in favor of ㉓ or order

payable at ㉔

interest from ㉕ at rate of ㉖ per cent per annum, payable ㉗

principal and interest payable $ ㉘ or more on the ㉙ day

of each ㉚ month, beginning on the ㉛ day of ㉜, 19 ㉝;

㉞ and continuing until said principal and interest have been paid;

executed by above named Grantee(s) and ㉟

Bonus for prepayment ㊱

E ENCUMBRANCE To Pay ㊲ ㊳ ㊴

Commission $ ㊵ To: ㊶

F Commission $ ㊷ To: ㊸

㊹

G Adjustments Through Escrow: Interest ㊺ Taxes ㊻ Rents ㊼

Fire Insurance ㊽ Other ㊾

H Instruments To Draw: ㊿ Revenue Stamps $ (51)

I Miscellaneous (52)

J (53)

K (54)

332 R 4/72

Figure 3-2

SALE ESCROW MEMO

A. PARTIES AND PROPERTY IN THIS ESCROW
1. Sale, loan or exchange escrow
2. Number of days for escrow to be accomplished
3. Full names of sellers
4. Full names of buyer and how he wishes to take title
5. Legal description of property, if available
6. Street address of property

B. CASH SUMMARY
7. Today's date
8. In-house escrow number
9. Amount already paid to seller, if any
10. Total of all monies through escrow, or total or all cash through escrow
11. Remaining amount of existing loan, if it is to be assumed by the buyer
12. Amount of new loan or list of new loans
13. Total price of property
14. Amount given as deposit by buyer to broker, if any

C. DETAILS OF ASSUMED FIRST TRUST DEED, IF THAT IS THE CASE
15-18. Name and address of beneficiary, amount and other details

D. DETAILS OF NEW LOAN, IF ANY ARE SPECIFIED BY BUYERS
19. Amout of new institutional trust deed
20-36. Describe trust deed and note to be drawn by escrow (non-institutional), if any

E. EXISTING LOAN TO PAY OFF IN ESCROW, IF ANY
37-39. Name of beneficiary, loan number and approximate remaining balance

F. COMMISSION, IF ANY
40. Amount of commission, in dollars not percentage
41. Name of broker and his or her license number
42-44. Spaces for other brokers as needed

G. ADJUSTMENTS
45-49. Dates upon which prorations are to be based (usually close of escrow)

H. INSTRUMENTS
50. List of legal forms which will be used in this escrow.
51. Amount of Documentary Transfer Tax to be affixed to the Deed

I. MISCELLANEOUS
52. Additional **requirements** of this escrow, or items this transaction is **"subject to."** To be typed under "Instructions" section of escrow instructions

J. ADDITIONAL LINES
53. Other matters included in the transaction that aren't duties of the escrow holder. To be typed under "Memorandum" section of instructions

K. ADDITIONAL LINES
54. Other information given by principals that is not given as part of the transaction, but is mentioned; this for your reference and use, such as the name of the title company they approve or the lender they plan to see

Strive for accuracy from the start. Never assume that you know the spelling of any name. John could be spelled Jon, Mary could be spelled Merry. Verify all spellings and figures with whomever you are meeting, and check each time you receive or draw up a document.

Another duty in taking an escrow involves a personal decision. You often must decide which items on your memo sheet are **conditions of the escrow** and which are **memoranda**. Be guided by common sense: you cannot go out to see that the refrigerator has been left for the new owner, but you can generally see that funds are gathered and the necessary instruments are delivered. Extreme patience, tact, and creativity are required for these latter two functions. Negotiating such things as patio furniture is outside of your job responsibility, unless the principals state that it is a condition of escrow. You'll review that situation in another sample escrow.

Figure 3-1 shows the blank memo sheet, which is divided into general sections (lettered A, B, C, etc. and boxed) to indicate different categories of information. Each blank space is indicated with an encircled number, and the accompanying list (Figure 3-2) shows you how to fill it out.

1. Notes on Memo

Full names of seller(s). . . . . **Section A, Number 3**

One of the best ways to get their correct names is to ask to see their deed or title insurance policy. If they do not come in for the opening interview in person, you may verify the correct names with the Title Company.

The names for this escrow are John Sellers and Mary Sellers.

You do not usually need to have their vesting, but if they are "taking back" a loan on the property, be sure to get it.

Full names of buyers and how they wish to take title. . . . **Section A, Number 4**

This time you must get the vesting as well as the buyer's full name, correctly spelled, since you will be preparing the new deed right away.

Our buyer's name is Bruce Buyer and he will take title as a single man.

Legal description of property. . . . . **Section A, Number 5**

You may be given a legal description of the property that has been taken from the seller's property tax bill. Write it down, but be sure to compare it to the seller's deed or policy of title insurance in escrow. Tax bills' descriptions are not always correct; they are taken from tax assessor's records, which are different from County Records.

Figure 3-5
CONTENTS OF THE ESCROW INSTRUCTIONS

A. The Salutation
1. If a branch office, fill in which
2. In-house escrow number
3. City in which escrow is being taken
4. Date escrow is being opened

B. Consideration (Cash) Summary
5. *"Paid outside of escrow"* is all money paid to seller by buyer prior to escrow
   "Cash through escrow" is all money that will pass through escrow
   "Encumbrances of Record" is the total of remaining balances of all loans which will be assumed by the buyer
   "New Encumbrances" is the listing of all new loans
   "Total Consideration" is the total selling price of the property

C. Explanation of Consideration
6. Closing date of escrow
7. Sentence explaining where all the money is coming from

D. Title Insurance Liability
8. Indication of type of coverage
9. County in which property is located
10. Complete legal description if available
11. Street address of property
12. Complete name and vesting of buyer
13. That portion of property tax which will be paid by buyer
14. Date of fiscal year in which escrow occurs
15. Other information which must appear on the face of the title insurance policy
16. Details of existing first deed of trust if it is to be assumed by buyer
17. Details of new first or second deed of trust to be drawn by escrow officer.

E. Instructions — This blank section is for other conditions of escrow not already printed
18. Details of new loans as given by principals, pest control reports or other matters specified as *conditions* of escrow.

F. Memorandum — items included in the transaction but not duties of escrow
19. Possession date, personal property, etc., as mentioned by principals

G. Adjustments and Prorations
20-23. Dates upon which to base adjustments

H. Buyer's Signature
24-27. Buyer's signature, present address and telephone number

I. Seller's Instructions
28. Selling price of property *minus total of loans carried by seller*
29. Other instructions. *In this escrow, escrow is to pay off the existing loan*

J. Seller's Signature
30. Amount of Documentary Transfer Tax
31-34. Seller's signature, present address and telephone number

blank instructions, note that the major portion of the sheet is under the title BUYER; about 3/4 down the page is a section under the title SELLER. Glendale Federal Savings Bank puts both on the same sheet, while other companies may have separate sheets for buyers and sellers. There is no rule on this practice. It is a matter of individual or regional choice. In any case, the signatures "cover" all that is written above them. Here Mr. Buyer agrees to the upper 3/4 of the page, the Sellers agree to the entire page.

B. NOTES ON WRITING ESCROW INSTRUCTIONS

Explanation of Consideration . . . . **Section C, Number 7**

When you are composing your sentence of explanation, be certain that all the funds are described as having been converted into cash. For instance, if the buyers are obtaining a loan or loans to help pay the full amount, write *"...and $XXX, which will be derived from a new loan"* or write *"...and will cause to be handed you loan proceeds of $XXX."* Sometimes a negotiable instrument such as a stock certificate or a personal note will be used as a down payment. In such cases, you describe how it will be converted into cash. For instance, you write *"...and a promissory note in the amount of $XXX, to be redeemed within five working days and said funds to be deposited in escrow."*

Title Insurance Liability, type of policy. . . . . **Section D, Number 8**

The transaction dictates the type of policy; for a single family home sale, the choice is nearly always the CLTA Owner's Standard Coverage Policy.

**Title Insurance Liability,
legal description** . . . .**Section D, Number 10**

If the complete legal description is not available at the time you draw up the instructions, it is permissible to write "as per complete legal description to be deposited in escrow and approved by buyer and seller."

Title Insurance Liability, tax liability. . . . . **Section D, Number 13**

This line begins that list of encumbrances that will be permitted under the title insurance policy. The policy ensures that there are no other encumbrances of record. In this escrow the line will be filled in to read "all" general and special taxes, because the escrow is begun and ended before the first payment can be made (November 1).

**Title Insurance Liability,
other encumbrances** . . . . **Section D, Number 15**

This line is for the listing of new loans against the property. For this escrow, the loan is in the form of a deed of trust in the amount of $64,000.00. That is all you need to say. All other details will be set down later in the instructions. The use of the phrase "to file" indicates that its a new loan rather than an existing one.

Instructions . . . . **Section E, Number 18**

Write here the details of the loan or loans to be obtained, as specified by the principals. If they specify a pest control inspection report, write it here also. This item in the filled out instructions (**Figure 3-6**) reads *"(B) Seller at his or her expense is to furnish a pest control report by a state licensed operator showing the accessible portion of the house and garage to be free of visible evidence of infestation caused by wood-destroying insects, fungi and/or dry rot. Seller is to pay for corrective work; no preventive work will be required. Copy of pest control report and completion certificate, if any, is to be furnished to buyer for buyer's signature prior to close of escrow."*

This is a standard clause, used often in escrow instructions. It contains many key words and phrases, which you should also use when writing other instructions. You must, of course, use the directions given by principals and noted in your memo sheet. The following is a list of the key words you should include when writing instructions:

1. **Pest control report.** Don't write "termite" unless principals make a very definite point that they are concerned only with termites.
2. **State licensed operator.** This helps assure proper work and helps prevent future lawsuits.
3. **Accessible portion.** No inspector is willing to knock down walls to see inside. If termites are found later, this phrase helps prevent suits.
4. **House and Garage.** Fences, sheds, etc. can be termite ridden, too; expenses can be great in treating everything. Unless they specify "all improvements" write only house and garage.
5. **Visible evidence.** this backs up "accessible portion."
6. **Wood destroying insects, fungi and/or dry rot.** This further clarifies the term pest.

Memorandum . . . . **Section F**

Escrow companies and departments differ in the way they handle extraneous matters, but they agree that it is done as a courtesy to the principals. They often insist on an exculpatory clause in their typing of extraneous material in escrow instruments. **EXCULPATORY** *means, "We do not intend to assume any blame or guilt if the matters set out here are not resolved as written."* There are several ways of noting memoranda. Follow your company policy in actual practice.

When you have finished typing the escrow instructions, read them carefully, comparing the information with your memo sheet. Try to image that you are a stranger to this escrow, and ask yourself *"Are the instructions clear? Do they express the essence of this transaction exactly as it was originally given? Can any other meaning be put to these statements?"* Check spelling, addresses, and all numbers.

Figure 3-6

ESCROW INSTRUCTIONS

ESCROW INSTRUCTIONS   **BUYER**   M E M O

Paid outside of Escrow		
Cash through Escrow	16,000	00
Encumbrances of Record		
new loan New Encumbrances	64,000	00
Total consideration	80,000	00

TO: GLENDALE FEDERAL SAVINGS AND LOAN ASSOCIATION
Sherman Oaks.............OFFICE. ESCROW NO.2000
Sherman Oaks........................California.......June 1, 2051
On or before. August 1, 2051.................I will hand you.$80,000.00; $1,000.00 of
which has been handed to the broker for deposit in escrow, $64,000.00 of which will be derived from a new loan,
and the balance of $15,000.00 will be handed you prior to the close of escrow;

and any additional funds and instruments, required from me to enable you to comply with these instructions which you are to use provided instruments have been
filed for record entitling you to procure.................standard..................Owners or Joint Protection policy of title insurance with title company liability
for the amount of total consideration on real property in the County of.................Los Angeles.................State of California
Described as:..Lot 8 and the southwesterly 4.9 feet of Lot 9 of Tract 9985 in the city of Noetown, as per map recorded
in Book 541, page 62, of Maps in the office of the County Recorder of said county.

Also known as:..1234 Noway Way, Noetown, CA 92328
Showing title vested in:..Bruce Buyer, a single man
Free of encumbrances except:
(1) All.................General and Special Taxes for fiscal year 2051 2052 /a lien not yet payable

INSTRUCTIONS:
(A) This escrow is subject to buyer qualifying for and obtaining a new loan securing a note in the amount of $64,000.00 with interest rate not to exceed 9.5% per annum for 30 years. Said loan is to be at buyer's expense, and buyer's signature on the loan documents will constitute his approval of the terms and conditions contained therein.

(B) Seller at his expense is to furnish a pest control report by a state licensed operator showing the accessible portion of the house and garage to be free of visible evidence of infestation caused by wood destroying insects, fungi and/or dry rot. Seller is to pay for any corrective work; no preventive work will be required. Copy of termite report and completion certificate, if any, is to be furnished to buyer for buyer's signature prior to close of escrow.

MEMO: AGREEMENTS BETWEEN BUYER AND SELLER WITH WHICH ESCROW IS NOT TO BE CONCERNED
(1) Possession to be at close of escrow.
(2) Personal property included as follows: window treatments, fireplace equipment including grate, screen and tools, and patio furniture.

Buyer's Signature: Bruce Buyer
Address 900 West A Street, apt. 12, Noetown, CA 92329   Phone 841-1892

SELLER
Pay demand of Glendale Federal Savings and Loan Association, loan number 4400-70000 in an amount sufficient to obtain full reconveyance. Pay cost of termite inspection report, and work to be completed, if any

Affix Documentary stamps in the amount of $ 88.00 to my deed.
Seller's Signature: John Sellers / Mary Sellers
Address 1234 Noway Way, Noetown, CA 92328

While you are a beginner, it is a good idea to practice writing the "explanation of consideration," "subject to," and "pest control report" sections of the instructions. Since you won't often be required to type the instructions on the spot, you'll have a chance to write the sentences on scratch paper as you understand them, then edit and refine until you have clear, succinct statements.

Now, as a practice exercise, fill out the blank instructions (Figure 3-4), using the filled out memo sheet (Figure 3-3) as your guide. Even if you must copy directly from the already prepared instructions (Figure 3-6), you will find the exercise useful.

The instructions for this escrow are provided by Glendale Federal Savings Bank. In its original form, the packet is a seven-part form. When the instructions are typed and checked for accuracy, the escrow officer customarily gives two copies to the buyer (one to sign and return, one to keep), two copies to the seller (one to sign and return, one to keep), one to the broker (just as a courtesy; it is not required), one will be certified to be true and sent to the lender.

Whatever your company policy is, take care that you always have at least one copy in your file. Make as many photocopies as necessary to ensure it.

It is a nice touch to mark with an "X" and highlight the lines upon which the principals must sign, before sending their copies out.

Now it is time to draw up the grant deed for the sellers to sign, and make up the other papers which the broker wants to take with him when he leaves.

III. The Grant Deed

There are several companies that print recognized legal forms, but the forms are essentially the same. For this escrow we will use the deed printed by SAFECO.

Remember that, of all the documents you will prepare in escrow, the deed is the instrument that will be recorded and seen most often in years to come. Make no mistakes!

It is far better to tear up several in the effort rather than allow a deed to go out with erasures, and it could be disastrous if one goes out with the wrong names and addresses. Call upon your professional pride: let this always be your best work.

Figure 3-7 shows the completed grant deed, and its explanatory list can be found opposite in **Figure 3-8**. Study both.

Figure 3-7

COMPLETED GRANT DEED

RECORDING REQUESTED BY

③ Glendale Federal Savings and Loan
Association

AND WHEN RECORDED MAIL THIS DEED AND. UNLESS OTHER-
WISE SHOWN BELOW, MAIL TAX STATEMENTS TO:

④ ⑤

NAME

ADDRESS Bruce Buyer
CITY & 1234 Noway Way
STATE Noetown, CA 92328
ZIP

Title Order No. ⑰   Escrow No. **2000**

① ②

——— SPACE ABOVE THIS LINE FOR RECORDER'S USE ———

GRANT DEED

⑥ The undersigned declares that the documentary transfer tax is $**88.00** .... and is

☒ computed on the full value of the interest or property conveyed, or is
☐ computed on the full value less the value of liens or encumbrances remaining thereon at the time of sale. The land, tenements or realty is located in
☐ unincorporated area   ☒ city of ..**Noetown**.. and

⑦ FOR A VALUABLE CONSIDERATION, receipt of which is hereby acknowledged,

⑧   John Sellers and Mary Sellers, husband and wife

⑨ hereby GRANT(S) to

⑩ Bruce Buyer, a single man

⑪ the following described real property in the
county of   **Los Angeles**   state of California:

Lot 8 and the southwesterly 4.9 feet of Lot 9 of Tract 9985 in the city of Noetown, as per map recorded in Book 541, page 62 of Maps in the office of the County Recorder of said county.

⑫ Dated__June 1, 2051_____

⑬
       John Sellers
       Mary Sellers

⑭ STATE OF CALIFORNIA
COUNTY OF_____ } SS.

On _____ before me, the under-
signed, a Notary Public in and for said County and State, personally
appeared **John Sellers and Mary Sellers**

⑮ _____

_____, known to me
to be the person **s**_____whose name **s**_____subscribed to the within
instrument and acknowledged that **they**___executed the same.

_____
Signature of Notary

FOR NOTARY SEAL OR STAMP

⑯

Assessor's Parcel No. ....

MAIL TAX STATEMENTS TO PARTY SHOWN ON FOLLOWING LINE: IF NO PARTY SO SHOWN, MAIL AS DIRECTED ABOVE

Name   Street Address   City & State

L-1 (G.S.) (Rev. 4-75) **8 pt.**

Figure 3-8

CONTENTS OF A GRANT DEED

1. **DOCUMENT NUMBER:** This is assigned to the document by the County Recorder's office. Later, the book and page of the County Recorder's index books where the document is entered will be added adjacent to the document number.

2. **COUNTY RECORDER STAMPS:** A large stamp reflects the time and date of recording of the document as well as reference to names of the county and the County Recorder himself. A small stamp refers to the fee paid for recording. These stamps are placed on the document by the clerk in the Recorder's office.

3. **RECORDING REQUESTED BY:** This identifies the party requesting that the document be recorded and often shows the names of title companies when they submit groups of documents to the county for recording.

4. **AND WHEN RECORDED MAIL TO:** After recording, the county will mail the document to the addressee shown in this section. (Usually the new owner.)

5. **MAIL TAX STATEMENTS TO:** This is usually the same party mentioned in the **"and when recorded mail to"** section, and if so, "Same as above" would be shown in the space, although if preferred a different name or address may be given.

6. **DOCUMENTARY TRANSFER TAX:** This is a tax levied on the sale of the property by the county (and sometimes the city) where the property is located.

7. **FOR A VALUABLE CONSIDERATION:** A statement which reflects the fact that money or some legal consideration is being given in exchange for the property. (A hold-over from earlier times and no longer necessary in a voluntary conveyance.)

8. **GRANTOR:** In this area the name of the party selling or transferring the property is shown, and this party is called the grantor.

9. **OPERATIVE WORDS OF CONVEYANCE:** There must be wording to show an intent to transfer title to the property. With a grant deed, the word **GRANT(S)** fulfills this requirement.

10 **GRANTEE:** The name of the party buying or receiving the property is shown and this party is referred to as the grantee. The status and type of tenancy should also be set out, and is shown in the sample as Bruce Buyer, *a single man.*

11. **LEGAL DESCRIPTION:** This identifies the property conveyed which is usually by lot, block, and tract; or by metes and bounds, or by government survey.

12. **DATE OF EXECUTION:** This should be the date of the signing of the deed by the grantor, but can also be the date the deed is drawn.

13. **SIGNATURE(S) OF THE GRANTOR(S):** The signatures of the grantors will appear on the line in this section. Always type the name or names beneath the lines where they must sign.

14. **VENUE:** State and county where the acknowledgment (notarization) is taken.

15. **ACKNOWLEDGMENT:** In this area a formal declaration is personally made in the presence of a notary public by the seller who has executed (signed) the document, that such execution is his act and deed. (The document will not be accepted for recording without an acknowledgment.)

16. **NOTARY SEAL OR STAMP:** In this section the official seal of the notary public must be affixed or stamped. The stamp must be clear and readable or it may be sent back by the Recorder's office to be done over since deeds are usually microfilmed and indistinct stamps do not reproduce well.

17. **TITLE ORDER NUMBER AND ESCROW NUMBER:** On this line the title company order number will appear, along with the customer escrow number, if the document was recorded as part of a title order which culminated in the closing of an escrow.

A. NOTES ON PREPARING THE DEED

Grantor(s) . . . . **Number 8**

When the grantor is a person or persons, rather than corporation or other entity, all you usually need to do is check the spelling of the name. If there is more than one name, each person must execute the deed (that is, sign it). You do not have to list their vesting, but if they are married write "husband and wife" after their names. Do not write "Mr. and Mrs." Use their full names. If there are several persons listed they all must sign unless some convey their interest to one grantor by quitclaim deed first.

There are some instances where the right of the grantor to convey the title may be questioned or limited under the law. You should seek the advice of your superiors if you know that any of these conditions are present:

1. Any person listed as grantor is deceased.
2. Any person listed is divorced or involved in divorce proceedings.
3. Any person listed is younger than eighteen years old.
4. Any person listed is recorded incompetent, or appears to be incompetent, whether recorded or not.
5. Any person listed acquired title "As trustee."
6. Any person listed is acting as attorney-in-fact.

Grantee(s) . . . . **Number 10**

Vesting is absolutely necessary when typing the name of the grantee.

IV. Statement of Information

The **STATEMENT OF INFORMATION** *is a strictly confidential method of assurance against mistaken title reports.* Various companies print these statements and supply them to escrow holders—they are all similar. They are usually requested by title companies before they begin a title search, to save time and confusion in the processing of escrows.

> *It should be noted that the statement of information form is not used in all escrow offices or counties in California.*

A good time to hand the buyers and sellers the statement of information for completion is while the escrow instructions are being typed.

The title company's computers will search for any and all documents recorded against the name requested. In addition to the grant deeds, these can include recordation of judgments, divorce, insanity commitment, and death. It is crucial that the computer locate information relating only to the person(s) involved and not other persons with the same or similar names. Also, since the title company keeps the signed statements of information, signatures can be compared with future statements to protect the parties against possible forgery of future recordable documents. **Figure 3-9** shows a sample statement. You do not have to fill in anything. Mr. Broker will see that the principals fill them out and sign them.

Preliminary Change of Ownership Report

In accordance with the California Revenue and Taxation code, a preliminary change of ownership report must be filed when a conveyance is submitted for recording. The report is required for deeds of any type.

V. Commission Instructions

The **COMMISSION INSTRUCTIONS** *is a simple printed form that gives escrow permission to pay the broker his or her commission.*

> *Under no circumstances may escrow pay the commission or any part of it before the closing of escrow.*

It must be signed by the party or parties from whose funds the commission is to be paid (usually the seller). **Figure 3-10** shows an example. Sometimes the commission instructions are printed directly on the escrow instructions. Some companies require their escrow officers to write a commission instruction recital into the escrow instructions. In any case, it is to be approved by the seller(s).

Now you have completed all the documents you need to give to Mr. Broker. Look them over again before turning them over to him. In the next chapter, you'll finish up the opening segment of escrow and get it solidly underway.

Figure 3-9

STATEMENT OF INFORMATION

Confidential Information Statement to be Used in Searching the Records in Connection with its Order No._____

NAME			NAME		
FIRST	MIDDLE	LAST	FIRST	MIDDLE	LAST

BIRTHPLACE _____ YEAR OF BIRTH _____ | BIRTHPLACE _____ YEAR OF BIRTH _____

SOCIAL SECURITY NO._____ | SOCIAL SECURITY NO._____

I HAVE LIVED IN CALIFORNIA SINCE_____ | I HAVE LIVED IN CALIFORNIA SINCE_____

WE WERE MARRIED ON _____ AT _____ WIFE'S MAIDEN NAME _____

——— RESIDENCE(S) FOR LAST 10 YEARS ———

NUMBER AND STREET	CITY	FROM DATE	TO DATE
NUMBER AND STREET	CITY	FROM DATE	TO DATE
NUMBER AND STREET	CITY	FROM DATE	TO DATE

——— OCCUPATION(S) FOR LAST 10 YEARS ———

HUSBAND_____

PRESENT OCCUPATION	FIRM NAME	ADDRESS	NO. YEARS
PRIOR OCCUPATION	FIRM NAME	ADDRESS	NO. YEARS
PRIOR OCCUPATION	FIRM NAME	ADDRESS	NO. YEARS

WIFE_____

PRESENT OCCUPATION	FIRM NAME	ADDRESS	NO. YEARS
PRIOR OCCUPATION	FIRM NAME	ADDRESS	NO. YEARS

——— FORMER MARRIAGES ———

IF NO FORMER MARRIAGES, WRITE "NONE"_____

NAME OF FORMER WIFE_____

DECEASED_____ DIVORCED_____ WHEN_____ WHERE_____

NAME OF FORMER HUSBAND_____

DECEASED_____ DIVORCED_____ WHEN_____ WHERE_____

THE STREET ADDRESS OF THE PROPERTY IN THIS TRANSACTION IS:_____

OCCUPIED BY: ☐ OWNER ☐ TENANTS ☐ LESSEE

IMPROVEMENTS: ☐ SINGLE RESIDENCE ☐ MULTIPLE RESIDENCE ☐ COMMERCIAL

IS ANY PORTION OF THE NEW LOANS FUND TO BE USED FOR IMPROVEMENTS ☐ YES ☐ NO

DATE_____

SIGNATURE_____

HOME PHONE_____ BUSINESS PHONE_____

SIGNATURE_____
(IF MARRIED, BOTH HUSBAND AND WIFE SHOULD SIGN)

Figure 3-10

COMMISSION INSTRUCTIONS

GLENDALE FEDERAL SAVINGS
AND LOAN ASSOCIATION

COMMISSION INSTRUCTIONS.

ESCROW NO. 2000

DATE June 1, 2051

From the funds due my (our) account at the close of this escrow you are authorized to pay the following commissions:

(1) $ 4,800.00   TO: Thomas Broker

LICENSE NO. XYO339   ADDRESS 919 Sherlock Drive, Burbank CA 90511

(2) $ _____   TO: _____

LICENSE NO. _____   ADDRESS _____

(3) $ _____   TO: _____

LICENSE NO. _____   ADDRESS _____

John Sellers   (SELLER)   Mary Sellers   (SELLER)

VI. CHAPTER SUMMARY

The information taken by the escrow officer from the buyer and seller is written on a MEMO or work sheet. It is a preprinted form supplied by the company. If some point comes up regarding something not being in the escrow, the memo sheet will verify whether it did get included.

Ask only questions necessary to prepare your escrow. Ask whether there is anything else after the parties have given the initial facts about the transaction. Always be the disinterested third neutral participant that is required.

The ESCROW INSTRUCTIONS are printed forms or computer generated forms. No escrow exists until the instructions are signed by both parties. When you have completed the instructions, read them carefully while comparing the information with your memo sheet. Be sure they are clear and express the meaning of the parties.

A STATEMENT OF INFORMATION is a confidential form used to insure against mistaken identities. It will reveal any information that may affect the issuing of a title policy.

VII. TERMS

Escrow File: A desk file that contains the documents and preprinted sheets relevant to a specific escrow.

Escrow Instructions: A writing signed by buyer and seller that details the procedures necessary to close a transaction and directs the escrow agent how to proceed.

Sale Escrow Memo Sheet: A memo sheet when completed will contain all the information necessary to start an escrow.

Statement of Information: A confidential form prepared for the title and escrow company to insure against mistaken identity.

VIII. CHAPTER QUIZ

1. A simple sale escrow usually has the following:

   a. cash down.
   b. a new loan.
   c. a pay-off of the old loan.
   d. all of the above.

2. The reasonable length of time for an escrow is:

   a. 60 days.
   b. 6 days.
   c. 6 months.
   d. 1 year.

3. The escrow officer should be sure if items on the memo sheet are:

   a. conditions of escrow.
   b. memoranda.
   c. both a and b.
   d. neither a nor b.

4. Patio furniture is usually NOT a direct part of an escrow unless it is a:

   a. condition.
   b. memoranda.
   c. both a and b.
   d. neither a nor b

5. Escrow instructions usually express funds as:

   a. dollar amounts.
   b. percentages.
   c. both a and b.
   d. neither a nor b.

6. Legal advice should be obtained by the escrow officer if he knows:

   a. grantor is a minor.
   b. grantor is deceased.
   c. grantor is incompetent.
   d. all of the above.

7. Vesting is absolutely necessary when typing the name of the:

    a. grantee.

    b. buyer.

    c. both a and b.

    d. neither a nor b.

8. A Statement of Information is requested by title companies because:

    a. it saves time.

    b. it reduces confusion.

    c. both a and b.

    d. neither a nor b.

9. What must all grant deeds have to be recorded?

    a. Acknowledgment

    b. Notary seal

    c. Both a and b

    d. Neither a nor b

10. A Statement of Information requires:

    a. social security numbers.

    b. addressed.

    c. occupations.

    d. all of the above.

ANSWERS: 1. d; 2. a; 3. c; 4. c; 5. a; 6. d; 7. c; 8. c; 9. c; 10. d

Sample One, Part Two

You have completed the taking of the escrow, the first phase of the escrow process. Mr. Broker comes back in about a week, bringing back the papers he took out at the end of the opening interview. They are signed by the principals and ready for you. To recap, he brings:

1. **The deposit,** a check drawn on the real estate agent's trust account. (He received a personal check for $1,000.00 made out to him, from Mr. Buyer, then deposited it immediately in his firm's trust account.)
2. **Escrow instructions,** which have been signed by both buyer and seller.
3. **The grant deed,** signed by the sellers and acknowledged.
4. **Statement of Information,** filled out by both buyer and seller.
5. **Commission instructions,** signed by the seller.

You are ready to begin the processing phase of the escrow.

> *The purpose of this phase is to take all actions necessary to see that the escrow conforms to the buyer's and seller's instructions so that closing occurs in a timely and efficient manner.*

You've received the documents and checked them over. They have all been correctly signed and dated. It is important at this point to get organized. With the number of documents you already have, and the number that will be coming in during the escrow process (often more than 50), there has to be file system created to keep things in order.

CHAPTER OUTLINE

An escrow file system takes different forms. The most common is file folders organized in advance with the escrow number on each one and all forms that will be needed during the escrow in each folder.

With the file system set up, the next step is to record the fact that you have received the papers from Mr. Broker on your check list.

Nothing undermines the confidence of a customer more than a lost document.

I. Escrow Check List

The **CHECK LIST**, *or escrow requirements sheet, is a preprinted sheet used for keeping track of the escrow's progress.* It is usually part of the prepared escrow file. The check list used here is printed on the back of the memo sheet. After you have drawn the instructions, turn the memo sheet over, since it will no longer be needed, and use the check list.

Whenever you send documents out, or perform other duties for your escrow, mark the date on the check list. Also mark the date you get anything back.

If another person has to pick up your escrow and carry it through to closing, he or she can see exactly where you are in your process and will know where all the important papers are.

Fill in the date you sent the documents out, and with whom. **Figure 4-1** is the check list for this escrow, as it would appear after the escrow is finished.

II. Accepting Money Into Escrow

You will now accept the deposit for $1,000.00 from Mr. Broker, since it will be part of the down payment.

For all monies received, you must make receipts.

There are many kinds of computer-printed forms in use. You will use whatever your office provides. There will be three copies of the receipt:

1. Give one to the recipient.
2. Put one in your file.
3. There is usually someone designated to receive money and place it in your company's escrow account. Clip the check and one receipt together and give it to that person.

Figure 4-1

ESCROW CHECK LIST

SALE ESCROW REQUIREMENT SHEET

Seller: *John Sellers and Mary Sellers* Escrow No. *2000*

Address *1234 Noway Way* Date Opened *6-1-2051*

Phone *841-1892* Time Limit *60 days*

Address after C/E *?*

✓ Instructions *out 6-1. in 6-8. amend out 6-22. in 6-26*

✓ Commission Instructions *out 6-1. in 6-8*

✓ Stmt. of Identity *out 6-1. in 6-8*

✓ Deed *out 6-1. in 6-8*

✓ Fire Insurance

✓ Termite Report *in 6-22*

Bill of Sale

Rent Statement

Assignment of Leases

Approve

✓ 1st Beneficiary Ordered *Glen. Fed.* Buyer: *Bruce Buyer*

✓ Demand/Benf's. Stmt. Address

✓ Fire Insurance Phone

Deed of Trust Address after C/E *1234 Noway Way ---*

Recon Ordered ✓ Instructions *out 6-1 in 6-8 AMEND 6-22, 6-26*

✓ Stmt. of Identity *out 6-1 in 6-8*

2nd Beneficiary Ordered ✓ Deed of Trust *in 7-21 Glen Fed $5,000*

Demand/Benf's Stmt. Deed of Trust 2nd

Fire Insurance ✓ Fire Insurance *increase to 64,700*

Deed of Trust ✓ Approve Termite Report

Recon Ordered Approve Beneficiary Statement

Approve Bill of Sale

Approve Rent Statement

Approve Leases/Assignment of Leases

Approve

Approve

Money $ *1,000 deposit 6-8*

Agent for Seller *Thomas Broker* Title Search Ord { ✓ phone
{ letter

Phone Title Ord. No.

Agent for Buyer Title Officer

Phone Report Received

Filing Ord { } phone
{ } letter

332 R 4/72

Remember to follow through. As you may recall, all funds must be officially converted to cash. When you receive a check (or other negotiable instrument) into escrow, find out if it has been negotiated.

If there's plenty of time, you can afford to wait for the bank upon which the check has been drawn to call you or write you—and they will if they cannot honor the check. If you receive no call or letter within ten days, you can be pretty sure the check has cleared. It is considered proper to call the bank after three days or so, if you wish, to ask if it has cleared. You'll save the teller time if you mention the account number, which should be recorded on the receipt.

When you get checks very late in escrow, you may call the bank to inquire if they can honor the check and ask them to let you know the moment they do honor it. You'll probably be advised as to which action your company prefers. Many now insist on cashier's checks for money coming in near an escrow's closing date.

III. Accepting Documents Into Escrow

Now that the deposit has been taken care of, turn your attention to the instructions. Examine the signatures. If they are correct, mark today's date on your check list and place the instructions in your file.

Do the same with the grant deed, inspecting the acknowledgment, especially the notary public's stamp, with extra care. Many county recorder's offices are extremely particular about these stamps in order to ensure against forgeries. The stamp's impression should be clear and every part must be readable. If it is smudged or not easily read, it may be refused recordation and you may have to make a new deed at the last minute. When you get a deed back from the seller where notarization is obviously messy, take it to your superiors for a judgment as to whether it will need to be replaced.

Look at the Commission instructions and Statements of Information, record them on the check list and place them in the file.

IV. Escrow Settlement Sheet (Introduction)

There is another very important piece of paper in your file, the Escrow Settlement Sheet (sometimes called Estimated Charges Sheet). *The **ESCROW SETTLEMENT SHEET** is the accounting report for escrow.* Every penny that passes through escrow must be carefully recorded. All fees and charges must be listed against whom they will be debited or to whom they will be credited.

The sequence of entries in the settlement sheet is about the same for all escrows:

1. The total consideration to be paid and how it's paid.

2. Prorations and adjustments, if any.

3. Payoff figures.

4. Miscellaneous charges for loan fees, escrow and title fees, processing fees, commission fees, utility bills, and demand fees.

You'll be seeing much more of the settlement sheet later, but for now, just fill in the top with names, dates, etc., and enter the "$1,000" in the buyer's credit column opposite the line that says "deposit." This column will record all the funds that the buyer will "put in" to this transaction, including the proceeds of the new loan. It could total more than the purchase price.

Always use pencil for this!

The first line, "total consideration," can be filled in also. Write "$80,000" in the seller's credit column (this column will not reflect "put ins" as in buyer's credits, but reflects "seller gets"). Also write "$80,000" in the buyer debits column on the same line. The two debit columns mean "buyer/seller pays this." **Figure 4-2** shows only the top of the settlement sheet, the portion you are using today.

Figure 4-2

SETTLEMENT SHEET

GLENDALE FEDERAL
ESCROW SETTLEMENT
J&M Sellers

ESCROW NUMBER *Bruce Buyer* **2000**

SELLER DEBITS		SELLER CREDITS		DESCRIPTION	BUYER DEBITS		BUYER CREDITS	
		80	000 —	Total Consideration	80	000 —		
				Paid Outside of Escrow				
				Amount of New Loan				
				Trust Deed in Favor of Seller				
				Balance of Existing Loan				
				Deposit			1	000 —
				Deposit				

Make it a practice to add all new information to check lists and settlement sheets the moment you get it.

These chores will take much less time than you spent reading and understanding the foregoing material. This is how most escrow meetings run: a substantial amount of time is required for the opening interview, then its just quick visits by brokers or principals as the escrow proceeds.

Since you have received signed escrow instructions from both parties, you should take a copy of instructions from your file (without signatures), certify it to be a true and correct copy of the original by stamping it with a "certified" stamp, and send it to the lender. Before Mr. Broker leaves, you might ask him if he would like to deliver it to the lender, or in this case, the loan officer.

V. Amendments to Escrow Instructions

A week later, Mr. Broker drops in to see you again. He tells you that Glendale Federal has made the loan commitment, but they are asking for a higher interest rate than 9.5%. He says that Mr. Buyer has given verbal approval of this change. He also says that the lender wants a policy of title insurance—an ALTA extended coverage policy on the amount of the loan.

You must not have any conflicting instructions in your escrow.

Since the buyer had agreed in writing to only 9.5% interest and the best interest rate the lender could give him was 9.75%, you must have an amendment in your file showing that he has agreed to it. Rather than redrawing the entire instructions, you will draw an **amendment to instructions**, setting forth the terms of the new loan as approved and stating that the interest rate will be 9.75%.

Figure 4-3 shows the amendment for this escrow. Note that the monthly payment is now included, and the *LOAN COST (loan origination fee)* is written in. This amendment must be signed by all the principals, so their names are typed beneath the signature lines. Make the same number of copies as you did for the instructions and distribute them as you did before, certifying one copy before sending it to the lender. As soon as you get the copies back with signatures, you can consider the escrow "well and truly opened," since you now have a pretty good idea that Mr. Buyer will be able to pay for the Sellers' house.

VI. Order for Title Insurance

The next step is to begin the title search. There is a note at the bottom of the memo sheet that specifies the A.B.C. Title Insurance Company, so you call A.B.C. to request a title

Figure 4-3

AMENDMENT TO INSTRUCTIONS

GLENDALE FEDERAL
SAVINGS AND LOAN ASSOCIATION

ADDITIONAL INSTRUCTION

ESCROW NO. __2000__

DATE __June 15, 2051__

My previous instructions in the above numbered escrow are hereby modified in the following particulars only.

The terms of the new first trust deed loan will be as follows: Loan in the amount of $64,000.00, payable $550.00 per month including interest at 9.75% per annum instead of 9.50% as set forth in original escrow instructions, for thirty years, in favor of Glendale Federal Savings and Loan Association. Loan cost is 1 point plus $100.00

ALL OTHER TERMS AND CONDITIONS TO REMAIN THE SAME.

_____
John Sellers

_____
Mary Sellers

_____

_____
Bruce Buyer

_____

_____

112 R 4/72

search. The title officer will ask you the necessary questions, and will probably assign an "order number." This is enough to get the search underway, but follow up your call with a written **Title Order**. This will result in your receiving a **Preliminary Report**.

Among the myriad of preprinted forms to which you have access is one called an **Order for Title Insurance**. Fill it in as fully as possible in order to expedite A.B.C.'s issuance of the policy. **Figure 4-4** shows the completed title order for this escrow. Directions for filling it out are as follows:

1. Fill in the name and address (if you have the address) of the title insurance company. Use today's date. The order number is the one you were given over the phone. If you didn't call first, fill in "new order."

2. Fill in that you want a standard CLTA policy covering the total price, $80,000.00, as written in the instructions. Also fill in the lender's desire for an ALTA Lender's policy covering the new loan amount, $64,000.00. Give the street address and type of property.

3. Copy the legal description from the instructions.

4. Copy the seller's name from the grant deed, and tell whose statements of information will be sent. Write in the amount of documentary transfer tax, $88.00.

5. Copy the buyer's name from the deed, with vesting.

6. Copy numbers 13, 14, and 15 from instructions. This is the part of the Title Insurance Liability section which designates the encumbrances permitted in the policy of title insurance.

7. Fill in the customary requirements of your company, then give your name, escrow's address and your escrow number.

Notice where it says "Upon further authorization" in Section 5 of the Title Order. This statement is important, in that it makes clear that you are only asking for a report on the condition of the title, and do not want anything recorded until you give later permission.

The title company assumes responsibility for insuring the marketability of the title, and careful examination of all pertinent documents for accuracy is part of their process. When you send your order to A.B.C., also send the **Statement of Information** for buyer and seller and the **Grant Deed**. These may be clipped together and mailed in the special envelope provided by A.B.C., or they may be placed in a designated container to be picked up by A.B.C.'s messenger. With this done, it is time to turn your attention to paying off the Sellers' old loan.

The title company assumes responsibility for insuring the marketability of the title, and careful examination of all pertinent documents for accuracy is part of their process.

Figure 4-4

ORDER FOR TITLE INSURANCE

To: (1) A. B. C. Title Company
        (NAME OF TITLE COMPANY)

GLENDALE FEDERAL SAVINGS
AND LOAN ASSOCIATION

(ADDRESS)

TITLE OFFICER:

DATE: June 15, 2051

ORDER NO. ___65432___

ORDER FOR TITLE INSURANCE

Please enter ☐
THIS CONFIRMS ☐ } (2) order for policy or policies of title insurance as checked below:

CLTA OWNER'S/LENDER'S...Standard Coverage Form.................... ☒ with liability in the amount of...........$ 80,000.00
CLTA JOINT PROTECTION...Standard Coverage Form..................... ☐ with liability in the amount of...........$ _____
ALTA LENDER'S.................... American Land Title Association Form............ ☒ with liability in the amount of...........$ 64,000.00
CLTA INDORSEMENT .... ☐
➝ IF ALTA POLICY IS REQUESTED ☒ SINGLE RESIDENCE ☐ MULTIPLE RESIDENCE ☐ COMMERCIAL
THIS INFORMATION WILL EXPEDITE YOUR REPORT ➝ ☐ STREET ADDRESS 1234 Noway Way, Noetown, CA 92328

The property to be covered is described as

(3) (4) Lot 8 and the southwesterly 4.9 feet of Lot 9 of Tract 9985 in the city of Noetown,
as per map recorded in Book 541, page 62, of Maps in the office of the County Recorder
of the county of Los Angeles.

Present Owner's Name John Sellers and Mary Sellers, husband and wife

We Enclose the Following: ☐ Our Deed of Trust will be forwarded to you by _____
                         ☐ Our Deed of Trust is enclosed

Statements of Information by Sellerses and Buyer
Affix $88.00   D.T.T. on Deed From Sellers   to Buyer

Upon Further Authorization From _____ the undersigned _____ you will record all instruments without collection when you can issue
said form of Policy showing Title vested in:

(5) Bruce Buyer, a single man

Free from Encumbrances except: 1. All   General and special Taxes for fiscal year 20 51 /a lien not yet payable 52
(6) 2. C. C. & R's of record
       3. Deed of Trust to file in the amount of $64,000.00 in favor of Glendale Federal Savings and Loan Assn.

IF THERE IS A NEW GLENDALE FEDERAL SAVINGS LOAN TO BE RECORDED, YOU MUST ACCEPT THE FOLLOWING ADDITIONAL INSTRUCTIONS: The policy of Title Insurance to be issued must comply with these instructions exactly. PRIOR TO RECORDING YOU MUST EXAMINE ALL FOUR PAGES OF OUR DEED OF TRUST. IF THERE ARE ANY CHANGES, ALTERATIONS, AND/OR DELETIONS, OR IF THE DEED OF TRUST IS NOT EXECUTED PROPERLY, DO NOT RECORD OUR DEED OF TRUST, BUT CONTACT THE UNDERSIGNED IMMEDIATELY FOR FURTHER INSTRUCTIONS. DO NOT ATTEMPT TO ALTER OUR DOCUMENTS.

☒ Lender will order tax service
☐ Please order tax service (Type _____ for _____ years thru _____) (7)
☐ No tax service required

SECONDARY FINANCING IS NOT TO EXCEED none
Send 3 copies of report to escrow

Street _____   Street 13730 Riverside Drive
City _____ Zip _____   City Sherman Oaks   Zip 91423

Please Forward: (check items requested, if any.)   By Jo-An Winslow
    1. _____ copies of covenants and restrictions.
    2. _____ copies of plat map.   Telephone _____
    3. Amount of _____ taxes for proration purposes.
                                                       Escrow No. 2000 _____ Loan No. _____

GFS FORM 438 (R12-76)

VII. The Reconveyance

There is a formal process to be followed in paying off loans of record. Although it may seem unduly strict, its process helps to prevent disastrous mistakes, such as the accidental recording of payment-in-full before any money changes hands. The process is as follows.

Escrow, as **agent** for the **trustor**, writes to the **beneficiary**, saying that the loan is soon to be paid in full.

The beneficiary replies to escrow, "demanding" from the trustor and saying that the trustee will be asked to release his hold on the property as soon as the beneficiary receives payment from the trustor via escrow.

When the trustee has been told by the beneficiary that the loan is paid, the trustee issues a full reconveyance to the trustor, which means that he or she has relinquished his or her interest in the property.

> *The full reconveyance must be recorded in the county records, and the trustee must keep it as proof that he or she no longer owes money to the beneficiary.*

Mr. and Mrs. Sellers want you to pay off their old loan with part of the purchase price given by Mr. Buyer. You write to the beneficiary (in this case, another form letter that you will fill out) asserting your intention to pay off the loan and asking for several documents. You want:

1. The **Deed of Trust and Note** that they hold. This direction is usually for a private lender who has personal possession of the document. Institutional lenders keep theirs in vaults and do not relinquish them.
2. The **Beneficiary's Demand**, filled out by them, which is their permission for you to start the recording process as soon as you have enough money to pay off the loan (they fill in the exact amount they will "demand").
3. The signed (executed) **Request for Full Reconveyance**, which is printed on the back of the deed of trust. It asks the trustee to convey back to the trustor all interest he or she has had in the property as holder of the deed of trust.

The three party arrangement for the loan you are now paying off has been:

1. **Trustor** – John Sellers and Mary Sellers
2. **Trustee** – Verdugo Service Corporation
3. **Beneficiary** – Glendale Federal Savings Bank

Although Verdugo Service Corporation is a trust institution, closely allied with Glendale Federal, it doesn't matter—the trustee and beneficiary can be the same person or company, but the trustor can never be either trustee or beneficiary. Remember it this way: two "e's" in trustee, two "e's" in beneficiary, two "e's" in together, no "e's" in trustor.

Figure 4-6 is the escrow departments **Letter to the Beneficiary**. Also printed on it is the Beneficiary's Demand, which can be filled out by the beneficiary. This would probably be done if the beneficiary were a private person or a small lender. Institutional lenders have their own form that they naturally prefer to use.

Figure 4-5 is a reproduction of the section on the back of the Deed of Trust which asks the trustee to reconvey the trustee's estate in the property.

Figure 4-5

REQUEST FOR FULL RECONVEYANCE

REQUEST FOR FULL RECONVEYANCE

To VERDUGO SERVICE CORPORATION, Glendale Federal Building, 401 N. Brand Blvd., Glendale, Calif. 91209 DATE ....

The undersigned is the legal owner and holder of all indebtedness secured by the within Deed of Trust. All sums secured by said Deed of Trust have been fully paid and satisfied; and you are hereby requested and directed on payment to you of any sums owing to you under the terms of said Deed of Trust, to cancel all evidences of indebtedness secured by said Deed of Trust, delivered to you herewith together with the said Deed of Trust, and to reconvey, without warranty, to the parties designated by the terms of said Deed of Trust, the estate now held by you under same.

When Recorded Mail To: ....

GLENDALE FEDERAL SAVINGS AND LOAN ASSOCIATION

By ....

GFS FORM 227 (R8-76)

When you make these requests, whether by letter or by preprinted form, remember that this pay-off has no actual connection with the purchase of the property by Mr. Buyer. Do not mention any names or the selling price, or any other details of our current escrow except what is needed. The information needed is the borrower's name, address of the property and the loan number. If your escrow includes the assumption of an existing fire insurance policy held by the beneficiary, you must ask that it be sent along with the other documents, but you need not deal with the matter now since, in this case, the policy is held by the seller.

VIII. The Pest Control Inspection Report

As it happens, today's mail brings the pest control inspection report. Although the phrase "termite report" is universally used by both customers and escrow personnel, it is somewhat misleading. It actually covers a range of pests that damage and destroy wood.

Figure 4-6

LETTER TO THE BENEFICIARY

GLENDALE FEDERAL SAVINGS

Glendale Federal Savings and Loan Assoc.

401 North Brand Blvd.

Glendale, California 91209

Date ...... June 16, 2051 ....
Escrow No. ...... 2000 ....
Office ...... Sherman Oaks ....
Your Loan No. 4400-70000 ....

An escrow has been opened at this Association by...John Sellers and Mary Sellers...............
which includes the **payment** of an encumbrance held by you covering.Lot 8+SW 4.9'of Lot 9..Block...........
Tract.9985 in the city of Noetown, as per map recorded in Book 541, page 62 of Maps in the
office of the County Recorder of ....Los Angeles County, California.
.....AkA: 1234 Noway Way, Noetown CA 92328.....
You are requested to fill in and sign the original of the **Beneficiary's Demand** below and return this entire
page, together with the Note, Trust Deed securing same, Request for Reconveyance thereof signed by all of
the owners of the Note, and any fire insurance policies or other papers which you hold in connection with said
loan. (Request for Reconveyance Form is generally printed on back of Trust Deed.)

Please send me a copy of the demand which you
have forwarded to:

GLENDALE FEDERAL SAVINGS AND LOAN ASSOCIATION

Address 13730 Riverside Drive, Sherman Oaks, CA 91423 ....

By Jo-An Winslow, Escrow Officer

(DO NOT DETACH)

BENEFICIARY'S DEMAND

Escrow No.................................

Glendale Federal Savings & Loan Association
   I hand you herewith:

Date...

1. Note for $...........................
2. Trust Deed securing same covering above described property and recorded in Book..............Page.............
of Official Records.
3. Request for Reconveyance thereof executed by..
....
4. Fire Insurance Policy described as..
....
....

   You are authorized to use all of the above described documents provided on or before.........................20 .....
you hold for the account of the parties executing said Request for Reconveyance the sum of $..............................
with interest on the sum of $....................at the rate of...........per cent per annum from...........................
............20......... to date of issuance of your check, together with.............days unearned interest on
$.........................as a bonus.
   Make disbursement by check mailed to address given below.
   You will, as my agent, waive my interest in any fire or other insurance policies handed you.
   In the event that the conditions of this demand have not been met within the time provided herein, you are
authorized, nevertheless, to use said documents at any time thereafter as soon as the conditions (except as to
time) have been met, unless I shall have made written demand upon you for their return to me. No supplemental instructions extending the time by which your demand shall be complied with or completed shall be
deemed to limit the provisions of this paragraph.

Street
Address... Signature...

City &
Zone... Signature...
                    Telephone

GFS FORM 192 · R. 12-75'

Termite (or pest control) reports are not required by law in California, and you should make sure to avoid mentioning anything about them during the course of any escrow.

> *Controversies arising from pest control reports and other types of inspections have probably caused the collapse of more escrows (and escrow officers) than any other element of escrow.*

Principals very often include pest control reports in their instructions to you, since termites are extremely common in most areas of the state and can do major damage to valuable structures.

Although there are many kinds and species of wood damaging pests, the most common are:

1. **Subterranean termites**, which breed in the ground and tunnel to nearby wood to feed. These will affect any wood on or near the earth such as foundation pillars, mud sills, fence posts and wood piles. From there they can travel upwards to affect all parts of a structure.

2. **Dry wood termites**, which usually migrate from nearby trees and structures to roof areas, eating through shingles and joists to nest in upper, dry parts of a building.

3. **Dry rot**, a fungus, which usually affects wood that has been subjected to continuing dampness. It is most often seen in floors of bathrooms or service areas, or anywhere water may have seeped into wood unnoticed for long periods of time.

Two documents are usually needed in dealing with the termite inspection:

1. The **Structural Pest Control Inspection Report** (required for recommended repairs), and

2. The **Notice of Work Complete and Not Completed**.

The "Report" is the sheet on which the pest control inspector lists all damage seen, its location in the structure, the planned method of treatment, and the cost of such treatment. Inspectors also list areas that, because of their condition or location, may dispose them to future infestation. The report lists recommended ways of preventing future infestations.

Who pays for the (1) pest control inspection report and (2) any required or recommended repair work is up to the buyer and seller, although they are usually paid for by the seller. There may sometimes be a local custom that dictates who will pay, while in other instances financial institutions or financing agencies will decide which one of the parties will pay.

> *A report does not certify in any way that anything has been done; it is only the result of the inspection.*

www.pestboard.ca.gov

The "Notice of Completion" will be given by the pest control operator after the work ordered by the customer has been done. The company will usually provide several copies of each to the customer (usually the seller), one which he or she should keep and the rest that should be given to escrow. Escrow does not hire pest control operators or make any of the arrangements. This document is also called the "Certificate of Completion." Whether there is work to be done or not, it is good practice to obtain the buyer's approval of either the report or the Notice of Completion. Remember, discretion and impartiality must be exercised.

A. RECEIVING PEST CONTROL REPORTS INTO ESCROW

Agents should suggest that buyers or sellers obtain to two or more inspection reports if one or both of the principals feels the estimates are excessive or insufficient.

When you receive the report, compare it with the escrow instructions to make sure the necessary structures have been inspected and that the charges are noted to the proper party. You'll need to make several copies.

IX. Obtaining the Buyer's Approval

Compare the completion notice with the report and escrow instructions to see that the required work has been done, and type or stamp an **Approval Recital** on the copy that must be signed by the buyers. The report you receive from Bugs Away Pest Control

Company states that the property is free from any infestation, and gives the inspection fee of $40.00. You list this charge as a debit to the seller in your Settlement Sheet. Also note the date on your check list, and remember to have Mr. Buyer read and sign it when he comes in to sign documents later when the escrow is further along. If reports from several operators come into escrow, ask the seller to specify which is to be used. The buyer must be given copies of the reports when escrow closes. The seller must be shown copies of all reports before escrow closes. A standard recital reads as follows:

WE ACKNOWLEDGE HAVING READ A COPY OF THE WITHIN REPORT AND/OR COMPLETION CERTIFICATE, AND BY SIGNATURE HERETO APPROVED SAME, AND STATE THAT WE HAVE RECEIVED A COPY OF SAID REPORT AND/OR COMPLETION CERTIFICATE.

_____
(Buyer)

_____
(Buyer)

_____
Date

X. CHAPTER SUMMARY

When the principals to the transaction return the documents to escrow. it will be important to use an ESCROW CHECK LIST for keeping track of the escrow's progress. The check list is a summary of the various activities that take place.

At this time. you will be accepting money and other documents into escrow. Handling money in a proper way is one of the most important tasks for the escrow. You will receive the money, record it, and determine if the funds are good before disbursement.

When documents are received, check the signatures and acknowledgement. If the document is messy or smudged, you may have to redo it.

Next, a SETTLEMENT SHEET will be used. Sometimes called an estimated charges sheet, it will show the different credits and debits to the buyer and seller accounts. Every penny that passes through escrow must be accounted for.

Sometimes an amendment must be made to change one of the original terms of the escrow. You must not have any conflicting instructions in your escrow. You will also order title insurance which will result in receiving a PRELIMINARY REPORT OF TITLE. This will be a report on the condition of the title which may have to be changed due to liens and other encumbrances.

One of the essential duties is to request from the BENEFICIARY by demand what is owing on the existing loans. The TRUSTOR or borrower requests from the TRUSTEE a DEED OF RECONVEYANCE. Once signed and recorded, this will relieve the property of the pre-existing lien.

The PEST CONTROL REPORT often is ordered at the request of the parties or new lender. It will show whether there are any visible signs of termites or other related damage. The NOTICE OF WORK COMPLETED AND NOT COMPLETED will be the statement of what work is done or isn't done. Then a NOTICE OF COMPLETION will be given by the pest control operator when the work is officially completed. The buyer should sign an APPROVAL RECITAL showing their acceptance of the work completed.

XI. TERMS

Amendment to Instructions: A change to either correct or alter or add to the escrow instructions to avoid any conflict in the instructions.

Approval Recital: Signed by the buyer showing they have seen and approved the pest control report.

Beneficiary: The lender in a trust deed loan transaction.

Beneficiary's Demand: The lender's written statement that gives the amount needed to pay off an existing loan.

Buyer Credit: An increase to the buyer's side as deposit, loans, and prorations.

Buyer Debit: A charge against the buyer's side as in the purchase price and other expenses.

Certificate of Completion: Given by the pest control operator after the work ordered by the customer has been done.

Deed of Trust: When recorded, it creates a lien against specific property to secure performance of a loan.

Deposit: Money received from the buyer used as partial payment towards the down payment and demonstrating good faith.

Dry Rot: A fungus which affects damp or wet wood.

Dry Wood Termites: Termites that migrate from tree and wood structures to roof areas.

Escrow Check List: A pre-printed sheet used for keeping track of an escrow's status or progress.

Escrow Settlement Sheet: Called Estimated Charges Sheet; the accounting report for escrow where all funds are accounted for and all fees and charges are listed.

Notice of Work Completed/Not Completed: A report that states any termite work completed or not completed on specific property.

Pest Control Inspection Report: A report from a licensed operator showing a range of pests that damage and destroy wood.

Reconveyance: When the debt is paid off, the property is reconveyed by the trustee to the trustor by means of a reconeyance deed.

Report: Refers to a structural pest control report that lists all the damage seen, its location in the structure, and the planned method of treatment with the cost.

Request for Full Reconveyance: Written to the trustee of record requesting that the trustee execute the reconveyance.

Seller Credit: An increase to the sellers side such as sales price and other increases as prorations.

Seller Debit: An offset or charge against the seller's credits.

Subterranean Termites: A specific breed of termites which breed in the ground and tunnel to nearby to eat.

Title Order: A request to the title officer to begin preparation of the Preliminary Report of Title.

Trustee: Usually a Corporation that holds title in trust to secure performance of an obligation.

Trustor: The borrower in a trust deed loan transaction.

XII. CHAPTER QUIZ

1. The initial money put into the escrow is called:

    a. a trust fund.

    b. a deposit.

    c. both a and b.

    d. neither a nor b.

2. The escrow check list:

    a. is a list of check numbers.

    b. checks escrow's progress.

    c. both a and b.

    d. neither a nor b.

3. Although the escrow check list is pre-printed, most of the entries are:

    a. typed.

    b. hand written.

    c. pre-printed.

    d. none of the above.

4. The Escrow Settlement Sheet is:

    a. typed.

    b. written in ink.

    c. written pencil.

    d. none of the above.

5. After receiving signed amendments from both parties:

    a. put a copy in the file.

    b. send "certified" copy to.

    c. both a and b.

    d. neither a nor b lender.

6. The reconveyance is a polite way to:

    a. order title.

    b. order a new loan.

    c. pay off a loan of record.

    d. none of the above.

7. The Title Order with the words "upon further authorization" is:

    a. a condition of title.
    b. a preliminary report.
    c. both a and b.
    d. neither a nor b.

8. A full reconveyance is completed by the trustee when:

    a. trustor makes payment.
    b. beneficiary receives payment.
    c. both a and b.
    d. neither a nor b.

9. A request for full reconveyance is usually printed on the back of the:

    a. deed of trust.
    b. note.
    c. both a and b.
    d. neither a nor b.

10. The pest control "Notice of Completion" should be approved by:

    a. the buyer.
    b. the seller.
    c. the beneficiary.
    d. none of the above.

ANSWERS: 1. b; 2. b; 3. b; 4. c; 5. c; 6. c; 7. c; 8. c; 9. a; 10. a

Sample One, Part Three

I. Preliminary Report of Title

It is now July 5, and you receive the preliminary report of title. (Synonyms are prelim and title report. Henceforth, we will call it the prelim.) **YOU MUST EXAMINE IT CAREFULLY.** The first page, after identifying your escrow, contains two statements of importance. First, it tells whether A.B.C. Title Insurance Company is or is not prepared to issue a policy of title insurance on the property. Second, it restates that there should be no misunderstanding that A.B.C. is assuming no liability at this time, only revealing how things stand with the people and property in question.

> *Compare the statements given in the prelim with your instructions to see that there are no conflicting facts.*

If you find conflicts, call your principals and tactfully report the discrepancy. They will probably clarify matters for you.

The first page will contain the recorded owners' names and the nature of their estate in the property you described in your title order. See that the names are correct and that their interest in the land is described as a **fee, fee simple,** or **fee absolute**. This means that they have full ownership and can convey title without anybody else's prior approval if they can also satisfy other contract requirements.

CHAPTER OUTLINE

Agents and their principals, in trying to save costs, cannot use the preliminary report to transfer title.

A. ENCUMBRANCES

There will also be a list of preexisting encumbrances. In the title insurance industry, the word encumbrance means more than loans against the property. It covers all the following, since any of them could affect clear title:

1. Liens such as taxes, trust deeds, and involuntary liens
2. Covenants, Conditions, and Restrictions (CC&Rs)
3. Easements

1. Liens

LIENS are financial obligations against the property. Every year property taxes become a new lien. First trust deeds and junior trust deeds are voluntary liens; mechanic's liens and judgments against owners are examples of involuntary liens. These are the encumbrances that immediately come to mind for most escrow officers.

2. Covenants, Conditions, and Restrictions (CC&Rs)

COVENANTS, CONDITIONS, and RESTRICTIONS (CC&Rs) are rules that apply to the land and buildings, such as zoning regulations and restrictions on building height or architectural style. Note that title reports and title policies contain this phrase or a similar one: "Restrictions if any, based on race, color, religion, or national origin are deleted." Whatever CC&Rs may have been placed on real property, subsequent law changes may void them.

Restrictions are not usually printed on grant deeds, nor are they usually spelled out in prelims or policies.

They are most often recorded at the time of the original development of the land, and may be referred to by repeating their location in the county records by book and page. When a buyer wants to examine the full list of CC&Rs for approval, the title company will provide it.

Most residential area property is subject to restrictions, most often through the general plan for the entire tract.

3. Easements

EASEMENTS grant persons, entities, or properties other than recorded owners the right to use portions of the property for their own (stated) purposes. Easements will be discussed at greater length in the next sample escrow.

Bruce Buyer signed the instructions, which state that he accepts the property with all normal encumbrances, so you have no problem. If, however, in reading a prelim you see a peculiar easement, such as one giving a right-of-way through the middle of the lot or one that covers a large portion of the lot, you should call this to the attention of the buyer. You would write him or her a letter (make several copies) describing the unusual easement and type an approval recital at the bottom for him or her to sign and send back to you. Keep a copy, send one to his or her broker and one to his or her attorney if the buyer is represented by counsel in the transaction.

Having read the prelim sent by A.B.C., you find it contains no surprises, so you can put it away in your escrow file. There are further steps in clearing the old loan, which should be done as soon as the demand comes in from the beneficiary.

II. The Demand

You receive the Demand from the beneficiary, Glendale Federal Savings Bank. Usually with a private lender, or even an institutional lender that is not the escrow agent's parent company, the Demand comes back accompanied by a number of other documents, such as the deed of trust and note, the policy of title insurance, and a fire insurance policy. (Refer to the illustrated Letter to the Beneficiary, **Figure 4-6**, with a printed Demand below it).

However, the in-house situation greatly simplifies things with large institutions using computers and money-flow is a matter of data-flow within the company's electronic accountant. The beneficiary will hold onto the documents until all other requirements for the escrow have been met, and you will receive a Demand from their Loan Records Department (on their own preprinted form) that gives the necessary figures and costs. (See **Figure 5-1**.) Then, on the day before recording, you call the loan processor to inform him or her that you will record the next day. He or she will then *FREEZE THE LOAN, permitting no further action on the account so that it will be in the condition you expect when it is recorded.*

Freezing the account prevents sudden changes, such as unexpected large loan payments totally outside escrow, that could foul up your accounting for escrow.

When the new grant deed and deed of trust are recorded, the loan department will issue a full reconveyance, which will be recorded a few days after the closing of escrow. This is called a DELAYED RECORDING and is perfectly proper in a reconveyance, while it can be an appalling mistake in recording the deed and new loans. The full reconveyance will be mailed to the seller.

You are always charged with the responsibility for recording the fees, charges, and adjustments correctly in your settlement, but the lender will save you the trouble of

Figure 5-1

BENEFICIARY'S DEMAND

GLENDALE FEDERAL SAVINGS

401 NORTH BRAND BOULEVARD, GLENDALE, CALIFORNIA 91209

7/3/51		
DATE	YOUR NUMBER	OUR NUMBER
	2000	4400-70000

┌   ┐

Glendale Federal Savings
13730 Riverside Drive
Sherman Oaks, California 91423

└ ATTEN. Jo-An Winslow ┘

BENEFICIARY'S DEMAND

In connection with the proposed payment in full of this loan, and on receipt of pay off remittance, the following described documents will be forwarded, all of which affect the property held as security under deed of trust recorded __2/11/48__ in Book __T19240__ Page __410__ County of __Los Angeles__, California.

( ) 1. Note dated _____ for $ _____ signed by _____
( ) 2. Trust Deed securing same together with Request for Full Reconveyance.
(X) 3. Full Reconveyance.
( ) 4. Fire Policy issued by __(Held by Borrower)__
        # _____ for $ _____ expiring _____
( ) 5.

☐ Items 4 and 5 enclosed:
☐ Items 4 and 5 sent with copy of this demand to:
    Glendale Federal Savings
    _____

Attention: _____ Escrow # _____

The following sums are required to complete satisfaction of the loan in full: **WE WILL DEDUCT THE AMOUNT OF THIS DEMAND FROM OUR NEW LOAN PROCEEDS IF GLENDALE FEDERAL MAKES A NEW LOAN ON SUBJECT PROPERTY.**

1. Unpaid Principal Balance $ __19,437.00__
2. Interest at __8.0__ % from __July 1, 2051 (365 Day Year)__
    to date funds are received in this office
    at $ __4.260__ per day on a 365 day year. $ _____
3. Forwarding Fee $ __15.00__
4. Prepayment Fee — Waived if we make new __CONVENTIONAL__ $ _____
    loan on same property.
5. Less Impound credit $ _____
6. Send US separate check payable to __VERDUGO SERVICE__ $ __25.00__
    __CORPORATION__ for Reconveyance Fee.
7. Please hold $ __N/A__ until _____ pending clearance of customer's check.

We certify that the _____ installment of the 20_____ Real Estate Tax in the amount of $ _____ has been paid.

It is understood:
1. In the event this escrow is not closed within 30 days from date, you are, without further notice, to return all of the above documents.
2. If escrow is cancelled, all documents are to be returned promptly together with our forwarding fee. This fee is due and payable REGARDLESS of disposition of the escrow.
3. All payments maturing during course of escrow must be paid when due.
4. We do not guarantee that premium on the enclosed insurance policy has been paid. Please check with agent.

    Kindly acknowledge receipt of the above on the enclosed copy of this demand.

Receipt acknowledged:

Date _____

By _____

GLENDALE FEDERAL SAVINGS AND LOAN ASSOCIATION

By _____
        Loan Records Department

(213) 956— _____

GFS FORM 149 (R 3-78)

writing several disbursement checks. They will deduct their fees, charges, adjustments, and the amount of the old loan to be paid off from the proceeds of the new loan, then send you a check for the remainder.

The Demand also states exactly how much is needed to pay off the loan ($19,437.00), the rate of interest (8%), and the date upon which to base your adjustment (July 1, 2051). As a courtesy, you are given the daily interest cost (4.260). There are two additional fees, a document forwarding fee of $15.00 and a reconveyance fee of $25.00. These fees can be noted on your settlement sheet now. Record the two fees as debits to the seller on their respective lines. This stand to reason. The seller is the one who is having this loan paid off in escrow.

Record the loan figures in the center section of the settlement sheet under "disbursements." You can assume that escrow will close August 1, 2051, since that is 60 days from the opening and all is going well.

The date given in the demand is the time to which monthly interest is already paid.

The seller will have to pay interest every day up to the day escrow closes because of the in-house situation instead of to the usual to-and-including-receipt-of-funds adjustment date.

When you do actually send a check to pay off a loan of record, you must be sure to add enough days of interest to cover mailing time. In all reconveyances, except the completely in-house transaction, the seller pays interest up to and including the day lender receives final payment, or as per the instructions written in the demand. Six days is usually plenty of time unless the lender is in a far distant state or country, or unless weekends or holidays interfere with normal postage delivery.

In all reconveyances, except the completely in-house transaction, the seller pays interest up to and including the day lender receives final payment, or as per the instructions written in the demand.

III. Adjusting Interest

You must find out how many days' interest are due. To do so, simply subtract the demand's date from the escrow closing date.

> August 1 - July 1 = one month exactly
> July is a month with 31 days, so:
> 31 days x daily interest cost (4.260) = $132.06

On the Settlement Sheet, write the adjusted interest for this escrow ($132.06) in the seller's debit column on the same line where you recorded the interest rate and adjustment dates.

Remember: do not adjust interest until you know the rate basis that the lender requires. There are no hard and fast rules to go by.

IV. Obtaining the Reconveyance

The instrument that discharges the debt and ends the tripartite borrower-lender-trustholder (trustor-beneficiary-trustee) agreement is called the **FULL RECONVEYANCE***.* This will be ordered after you have checked all the documents forwarded to you by the bank, including the proper new deed of trust (recorded), and credited the correct portion of its proceeds to the seller in the loan department's internal accounts.

In many instances where there is to be the reconveyance of a loan of record, you request the Demand from the beneficiary, who then sends the Demand directly to the title company with a copy going to you. The title company is charged with obtaining the full reconveyance from the trustee. There are several other ways a full reconveyance is obtained, some of which you will be using in later escrows in this book. The seller is eventually sent the full reconveyance, after it is recorded and the tripartite arrangement is dissolved. That's true in this instance; you will not be receiving the full reconveyance into escrow, but will be notified by the title company that it was recorded. Add such notification to your escrow file, even if the escrow has been closed for some time.

Any note and deed of trust that is sent through the mail to the trustee should be sent certified or registered.

A. MORTGAGES

Paying a mortgage is a slightly different process since there are only two parties involved, the *MORTGAGOR (borrower)* and the *MORTGAGEE (lender)*. The necessary instrument is called a **Full Release of Mortgage**, executed and *acknowledged (NOTARIZED)* by the mortgagee. It may be obtained by any of the above methods and treated the same way in escrow.

V. Fire Insurance

When one party agrees to indemnify another for loss in return for periodic premium payments, it is called "insurance."

A. FIRE INSURANCE . . . A MUST!

Fire insurance is very inexpensive compared to the possible dollar loss due to fire, and all property owners should have this financial protection. A lending institution will require coverage for the amount of its loan. However, it is in the owner's best interest to carry sufficient fire insurance to replace the structure if it is totally destroyed. It is only necessary to insure the current replacement value of the dwelling, since the land itself cannot be destroyed by fire.

The ***CALIFORNIA STANDARD FORM FIRE INSURANCE POLICY*** *insures the dwelling against (1) fire and (2) lightning.* If you so desire, you may procure an ***EXTENDED COVERAGE ENDORSEMENT*** *that will insure you against the additional perils of windstorm, explosion, hail, aircraft, smoke, riot, and vehicles not attributed to a strike or civil commotion.* Other types of endorsements may insure you against vandalism, malicious mischief, floods, and other damage. Coverage depends on your needs and the perils common to your area.

B. FIRE INSURANCE PRORATION

If the old policy is canceled, the seller is charged a higher rate. It is said to be "short-rated."

When purchasing property, a buyer usually obtains a new policy. **If the seller/owner has filed an insurance claim during the previous three years, he or she must disclose this to the buyer in writing**. This may cause some hardship to the new owner/buyer in obtaining his or her own insurance. Cancellation of the seller's insurance must be initiated by the seller after close of escrow, with any unused premium to be prorated and reimbursed to the seller. It is always the buyer's choice to select his or her own house insurance. Condo insurance is chosen by the association.

Whenever you are buying insurance, review the policy carefully to determine if you have the correct type of coverage and are carrying an adequate amount of insurance, particularly when your property value has increased.

Debit the buyer's account for $80.00 on the settlement sheet. Follow your phone call with a filled-out form called an Insurance Order, stating the increased liability amount, and asking that the new loan number be substituted in the policy. You may add a request that the bill be sent to escrow. If the bill does not come in time to be paid before escrow closes, hold the $80.00 in the escrow's account for later payment.

The lender requires that fire insurance be at least as great as the amount of the loan.

Meanwhile, Mr. Sellers has paid for insurance he is not going to need. Its stated on the face of the policy that the annual premium is $150.00. **You will determine exactly how much of this should be credited to his account in the settlement sheet.** Whenever you're dealing with insurance policies in escrow, notice whether a premium is quoted for three years, one year, or a portion of a year, since all three billing practices are commonly used. When you prorate, it's simplest to base adjustments on the one year rate, which you may have to determine yourself if it is not given. Simply divide a three year premium by three, or multiply a quarterly premium by four, etc., to get an annual rate.

Use the 360-day year, the 30-day month. If you are calculating with pencil and paper, carry your answer out to at least three decimal places. If using a mechanical or electronic calculator, it's a good idea to carry it out five places and round if off to four. You already know the yearly rate, $150.00. Now adjust the premium:

1. Find the monthly and daily rates of coverage:

   $150 ÷ 12 = $12.50 (monthly rate)
   $12.50 ÷ 30 = .4166 (daily rate)

2. Find the adjustment time by subtracting August 1, 2051 from March 13, 2052. Using pencil and paper, set up a simple problem, making sure it's in the following order:

YEAR	MONTH	DAY
	+12	
52	3	13
51	8	01
7		12

   You have 7 months and 12 days remaining. Now:

   7 x $12.50 = $87.50 = months
   12 x .4166 = 4.9992 (round this off to $5.00) = days
   $87.50 + $5.00 = $92.50

The premium overpayment is $92.50. Enter this amount in the settlement sheet as a credit to Mr. Sellers and a debit to Mr. Buyer. The proper place for it is just below the taxes line in the "Adjustment" section.

VI. Property Taxes

The adjustment and payment of property taxes is extremely important in escrow. A slip up here could result in the property being forcible held for public sale by the state.

The least of the problems brought on by that eventuality would be sizable litigation against your company, and yourself looking for gainful employment—in another field of endeavor.

The property tax reported in the prelim is $778.30 for the fiscal year of July 1, 2051 to July 1, 2052. The Sellers have not yet received their tax bill, but this year's taxes become a lien against the property March 1, 2051, and therefore were present in the records that A.B.C.'s computers examined. The prelim showed that the previous year's taxes were paid; that is, taxes are paid up to July 1, 2051.

The Sellers are responsible for property taxes up to the day escrow closes.

The Sellers will pay a portion of the '51-'52 tax, for the time between July 1, to the close of escrow, August 1. (See **Figure 5-2.**)

Always apply a bit of common sense when adjusting taxes. You may find it is useful in other escrow processes too. Note that the yearly tax bill is approximately $800.00. Naturally, the tax for one month will be around $75.00. If, when making adjustments, you get a figure that is far different than common sense allows, go back and try it again— you're doing something wrong.

When taxes for one year are quoted, it is easiest to divide the annual bill in half before adjusting.

1/2 of $778.30 = $389.15 = the first half

You need not deal with the second half of taxes, since you can see in Figure 5-2 that they fall entirely within the buyer's scope and escrow will have long been closed. Even if the buyer wanted you pay the first installment of next year's taxes in escrow, you couldn't. Even though they became a lien against the property last March 1, they won't be payable until November 1 at the earliest. Mr. Buyer will be paying the tax in November, but he must be credited with the portion of taxes during which the Sellers still own the property.

Taxes are adjusted on the basis of the 30-day month, the 360-day year.

You'll need to find the amount of tax for the period between July 1, the beginning of the fiscal year, and August 1, the closing day of escrow. July 1 to August 1 is one month, but you don't have to be concerned with how many days in July, as you did in prorating interest on the loan pay-off.

$389.15 ÷ 6 = $64.86 = tax for one month

You will frequently need to use daily tax computations in adjusting taxes in escrow. To get it, simply divide the monthly rate by 30, or divide the half-year taxes by 180.

Figure 5-2

PROPERTY TAX CALENDAR FOR THIS ESCROW
TAX YEARS 2051-2052

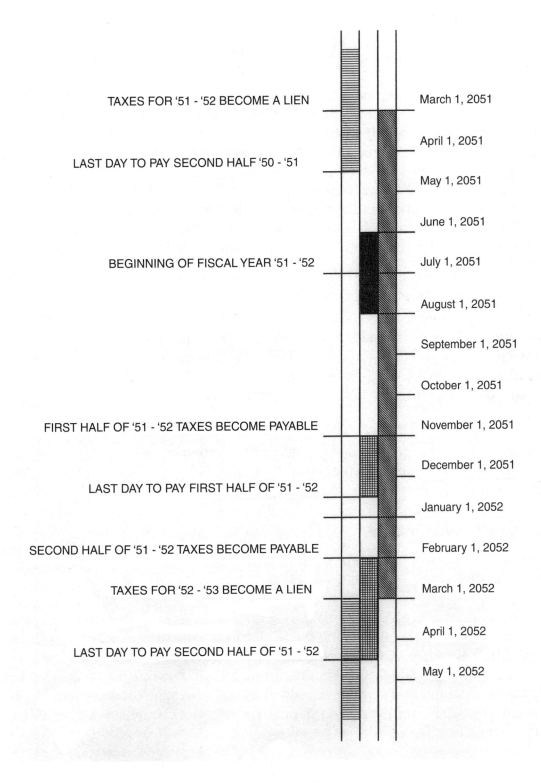

TAXES FOR '51 - '52 BECOME A LIEN	March 1, 2051
	April 1, 2051
LAST DAY TO PAY SECOND HALF '50 - '51	May 1, 2051
	June 1, 2051
BEGINNING OF FISCAL YEAR '51 - '52	July 1, 2051
	August 1, 2051
	September 1, 2051
	October 1, 2051
FIRST HALF OF '51 - '52 TAXES BECOME PAYABLE	November 1, 2051
	December 1, 2051
LAST DAY TO PAY FIRST HALF OF '51 - '52	January 1, 2052
SECOND HALF OF '51 - '52 TAXES BECOME PAYABLE	February 1, 2052
TAXES FOR '52 - '53 BECOME A LIEN	March 1, 2052
	April 1, 2052
LAST DAY TO PAY SECOND HALF OF '51 - '52	May 1, 2052

$64.86 \div 30 = 2.1619 =$ tax for one day

Now enter $64.86 in the settlement sheet, as a credit to the buyer and a debit to the seller, under the section heading "Adjustments."

VII. Finishing the Settlement Sheet

The closing phase of escrow begins as soon as the documents for the new loan arrive. These documents, known as the "loan docs," will include a letter to escrow setting forth the various loan charges and giving instructions for recording the deed of trust. They will also include Federal Reserve Regulation Z Notice, required of all institutional lenders, when making loans on 1-to-4 residential units in which the borrower intends to reside, under the "Truth in Lending" law. It gives the complete itemized statement of all loan costs, interest costs, and total expenditures over the life of the loan. It is rather interesting to note that the $64,000.00 loan will cost $197,697.02, including principal and interest, if all payments are made for thirty years. This "Reg. Z" statement is shown in **Figure 5-3**. It is to be given to the buyer at close of escrow.

A. LOAN FEES

The loan documents indicate that, in addition to the principal and interest, forwarding fee and reconveyance fee, Mr. buyer is going to pay a loan origination fee of $640.00, a loan processing fee of $100.00, a credit report fee of $10.00 and a tax service fee of $16.50. The loan processing fee and loan origination fee are usually listed together as one fee, the loan fee.

These newly set out charges should be noted in the settlement sheet in the "payment for new loan" section as debits to the buyer. You should also record receipt of the loan docs in your check list.

B. TITLE INSURANCE FEES

Title insurance has a one time premium, or policy fee, paid when the policy is issued.

The title companies furnish escrow holders with schedules of policy premiums that can be consulted to quickly determine the fee for each type of policy and amount of coverage. Mr. Sellers has agreed to obtain a CLTA policy with a liability of $80,000. The chart furnished by A.B.C. gives a premium of $352. Put this figure in his debit column, in the "paid to title company" section. Across the page on the same line, fill in the premium ($70.90) for the ALTA policy that the lender requires as a condition of Mr. Buyer's new loan.

Figure 5-3

REGULATION "Z" STATEMENT

NOTICE TO CUSTOMER REQUIRED BY FEDERAL LAW
FEDERAL RESERVE REGULATION Z
(To Be Executed in Duplicate)

GLENDALE FEDERAL
SAVINGS AND LOAN ASSOCIATION

REAL PROPERTY TRANSACTION SECURED BY FIRST LIEN ON A DWELLING   LOAN NO. 5500–125000

NAME OF BORROWER(S)   BRUCE BUYER
The undersigned association agrees to make a loan to the borrower listed hereon in the amount and on the terms set forth hereon and in the borrower's application for loan on condition that the loan be first approved by the association's loan committee and be consumated prior to   8-15-51   and that the association be furnished by borrower with the following: (1) **ALTA** policy of title insurance insuring the association's deed of trust described below to be a first lien. (2) **APPROVED** policy of fire and hazard insurance with coverage not less than the amount of the note and with Lender's Loss Payable Endorsement written with BFU 438.
Payments for principal and interest exclusive of mortage insurance premium on this transaction shall be @ 9.75   % in 360   monthly installments of $ 550.00   each, beginning on the   1st   day of September, 2051   and due on the same day of each month thereafter. In addition, all payments will include additional amounts for mortgage insurance premiums. These additional amounts will range from $ N/A   in the first payment due   N/A   19   to $ N/A   in the payment due   N/A   19   which is the last payment due.

The FINANCE CHARGE on this transaction will begin to accrue on the date funds are disbursed or the date of recording, whichever occurs first.

The AMOUNT OF THE LOAN in this transaction is $64,000.00
Less the PREPAID FINANCE CHARGE on this transaction which includes:

Loan Fee $640.00	*Prepaid Interest (7 days) . . . . $	121.31	
Processing Fee $100.00	Tax Service Contract . . . . $	16.50	
Private Mortgage Ins. Premium . . . . $ .00	Commitment Fee . . . . $	.00	
Discount Fee . . . . $ .00	. . . .		
	TOTALS	$	877.81

Equals the AMOUNT FINANCED in this transaction . . . . $ 63,122.19
This amount includes:

Title Insurance Premium . . . . $ 70.90	*Impounded Funds . . . . $	
Revenue Stamps . . . . $	Construction Funds . . . . $	
*Recordings . . . . $ 9.00	Payoff Demand . . . . $	
*Escrow Fee $173.50	Inspection Fee . . . . $	
Drawing Documents . . . . $	Repair Hold . . . . $	
New Fire Ins. Premium . . . . $	Present Loan Balance . . . . $	
Reconveyance Fee . . . . $	. . . . $	
Credit Report . . . . $ 10.00	To Escrow Holder: . . . . $	
Appraisal Fee . . . . $	BALANCE DUE YOU . . . . $	62,858.79
Flood Insurance Premium . . . . $		
	NET PROCEEDS . . . . $	63,122.19

The FINANCE CHARGE on this transaction totals $ 134,574.02   This amount includes the PREPAID FINANCE CHARGE
shown above, $ 133,697.02   interest, and $ Private Mortgage Insurance Premiums.
The Total of Payments is $ 197,697.02
The ANNUAL PERCENTAGE RATE on this transaction is   10.0   %.

*Amount is estimated

SECURITY INTEREST. This loan is secured by a Deed of Trust on property located at

which is specifically described in the documents for this loan. The Deed of Trust also covers all after acquired property located on or attached to the described real property together with any approved additional advances and other indebtedness, the terms of which are described in the documents . . . you are provided copies of all such documents.

INSURANCE. Fire and other hazard insurance protecting the property, if written in connection with this loan, may be obtained by the borrower through any person of his choice, provided, however, the Association may, for reasonable cause, refuse to accept an insurer on any such insurance which is required.

LATE CHARGE. Any payment that is not paid when due is subject to a late charge of 5% of such late installment past due.

PREPAYMENT PRIVILEGE. This loan may be paid prior to maturity in whole or in part upon payment of an additional sum equal to 6 months' interest on the amount so paid in any year in excess of 20% of the original amount of this note.

GLENDALE FEDERAL SAVINGS AND LOAN ASSOCIATION

I (we) hereby acknowledge receipt of the disclosures made in this notice. I (we) hereby agree to accept and enter into the loan transaction as recited above.

BY_____

_____JO- AN WINSLOW_____
(ESCROW OFFICER)

Bruce Buyer
_____
_____
_____

(DATE)
GFS FORM 653 (8-77)

C. RECORDING FEES

Though the county will eventually receive them, send the documentary transfer tax and document recording fees to the title company.

When they record the documents, they will pay the fees. Who pays which fee? This is an area where escrow practice differs widely from place to place and certainly can vary from transaction to transaction. In Los Angeles county, the DTT and the $3.00 reconveyance fee (this is fee for recording the full reconveyance, not the same as the fee charged by the beneficiary) are paid by the seller. The buyer pays the $6.00 deed of trust recording fee and the $3.00 grant deed recording fee. These notations are to be made in the "Title Company" section of the settlement sheet.

D. PEST CONTROL INSPECTION FEES

When Bugs Away Pest Control Company sent their report, they included a bill for the inspection, amounting to $40.00. The seller agreed to furnish the report, therefore debit his account $40.00. The proper line can be found in the "Disbursement" section.

E. COMMISSION

You have a commission instruction in your file stating that Thomas Broker is to be paid $4,800.00. Mr. Sellers has agree to pay this, in accordance with custom. Record the commission in his debit column.

F. ESCROW FEES

Escrow holders set their fees in accordance with local practice. Usually the fee is a small percentage of the property's selling price plus a set figure.

Payment of the fee—not whether but who—is also a matter of regional custom, but can be agreed upon between the parties. In this case they have agreed to split the escrow fee, which is the usual practice in Los Angeles county. It works out to a total of $346.00. You record $173.50 as a debit to the seller and $173.50 as a debit to the buyer under the heading "Paid to escrow holder."

VIII. Calling for the Buyer's Funds

All the charges are now listed in your settlement sheet. The loan is ready: all the conditions set forth in your instructions have been prepared. You have:

1. drawn escrow instructions;
2. drawn a new deed;

3. arranged for a Policy of Title Insurance to be issued;

4. received a pest control report;

5. arranged to reconvey the loan of record;

6. arranged for the fire insurance policy; and

7. adjusted taxes, interest on the loan of record and fire insurance.

It is time to decide how much money you want Mr. Buyer to bring with him when he comes in to sign documents—his down payment is the last major necessity for this escrow. Turn your full attention now to the settlement sheet, **Figure 5-4**. For now, don't be concerned with the seller's side, but concentrate on the buyer's side of the sheet.

1. Add together all the debits

   They total $81,192.40

2. Add together all the credits (lines 3, 6, 10)

   They total $65,064.86

   Enter this as a subtotal near the bottom of the credit column.

3. Subtract credits from debits

   The difference is $16,127.54—**the amount you will need from Mr. Buyer.**

What if, by some chance, your escrow cannot close on August 1? For every added day, the seller's charges become larger and the buyer's become smaller on the items that you have so carefully adjusted to August 1. If you were to close escrow a few days before August 1, the buyer's adjusted charges would increase. It is best to remember that people don't like to be asked for more money (especially if they have handed you a very large check only a few days before), but they don't usually mind getting some back. If you were to ask Mr. Buyer for slightly more than your settlement figure, the problem wouldn't arise.

> *There is a rule for escrow officers: Do not close escrow short of funds. Always add enough to your settlement figure to cover changes in the closing date.*

There are several ways to compute a reasonable "leeway." Most escrow officers have their own favorite methods, but personal judgment is always required. Some escrows seem likely to close early, either because of singularly agreeable circumstances or inordinately cooperative parties. For such escrows, a conservative decision to allow for up to a week's worth of adjustment leeway is a good practice. Other times it is all right to tack on a few dollars "just in case." Some ways of arriving at a good estimate for buyer's funds are:

1. Add $25 or so.

2. Using the daily rates, add a few days' worth of each adjustment to the settlement figure.

3. Add a small percentage of the buyer's debit subtotal, say .002%.

Figure 5-4

COMPLETED SETTLEMENT SHEET

GLENDALE FEDERAL
ESCROW SETTLEMENT

close : 8-1-51

ESCROW NUMBER **2000**

SELLER DEBITS	SELLER CREDITS	DESCRIPTION	BUYER DEBITS	BUYER CREDITS
	80 000 —	Total Consideration	80 000 —	
		Paid Outside of Escrow		
		Amount of New Loan		64 000 —
		Trust Deed in Favor of Seller		
		Balance of Existing Loan		
		Deposit		1 000 —
		Deposit		16 150 —
		ADJUSTMENTS		
64 86		Taxes on $ 389.15 From 7-1-51 To 8-1-51		64 86
	92 50	Ins. on $ 150 — Prem. For 1 yr. Mo. F 8-1-51 o 3-13-52	92 50	
		increase insurance to $64,000 —	20 —	
		Int. on $ @ % Fr. To		
		Rents on $ @ Fr. To		
		Adjustment of Impounded Funds		
		DISBURSEMENTS		
19 437 —		Payment of Demand From Glendale Federal		
132 06		Int. @ 8.0% (4.26) Per Day From 7-1-51 To 8-1-51		
		Prepayment Charge		
15 —		Forwarding Fee		
25 —		Reconveyance Fee		
		Payment of Demand From		
		Int. @ Per Day From To		
		Payment of Ins. Prem. on $ Policy		
40 —		Payment to Termite Company Bugs Away		
4 800 —		Payment of Commission Thomas Brokers		
		PAID TO TITLE COMPANY		
352 50		Title Policy/Alta Title Policy	70 90	
		Endorsements to Title Policy		
		Documentary Stamps on Deed		
3 —		Recording: X Deed X T/D X Recon.	9 —	
		Reconveyance Fee		
		Sub Escrow Fee Paid to Title Company		
		Payment of Taxes $ Payment of Bonds $		
		PAID TO ESCROW HOLDER		
173 50		Escrow Fee $ 346 Loan Tie-in Fee $	173 50	
		PAYMENT FOR NEW LOAN		
		Loan Fee $ 640 — Disc. Fee $ Proc. Fee $ 100 —	740 —	
		Int. From To @ %		
		Imp. Funds Taxes $ Fire Ins. $		
		Tax Service Contract	16 50	
		Credit Report	10	
		Appraisal Fee		
		Construction Funds		
25 042 92	80 092 50	subtotal subtotal	81 192 40	65 064 86
		Balance Due From You — Please Remit		
55 049 58		Balance Due You		22 46
80 092 50	80 092 50	TOTAL	81 214 86	81 214 86

437 R 8/74

Escrow officers should be prepared to discuss the estimated settlement sheet with the principals.

The sheet should be clear, but you should also be able to sit with a buyer or seller to explain the various charges and your methods of arriving at adjustments.

Bruce Buyer still needs to hand you $16,127.54. The figure $16,150.00 seems to give an appropriate leeway, since there are relatively few adjustments and their daily rates are moderate. Enter $16,150.00 beneath the other deposit—the $1,000.00 he put in at the start of escrow. If his account balances correctly and escrow closes on August 1, he should be getting a refund after escrow closes. Be sure to check your math before turning to the seller's side of the page. You've previously determined that the debits add up to $81,192.40. The credit column should, with the added $16,150.00, total $81,214.86. If this number is ever less than the debits total, you face the possibility of **CLOSING ESCROW SHORT OF FUNDS**. Should it ever be less, you must increase the amount you will ask from the buyer. You can see why these calculations must be done before you call the buyer to ask for funds.

Now, balance Mr. Buyer's account. Subtract the credit total from the debits total as you did before. The difference should be $22.46. Enter this amount at the point indicated near the bottom of the sheet that reads "Balance Due You." Enter the total of debits ($81,192.40) near the bottom of the column as a subtotal. Enter the total of credits **plus the $22.46** at the bottom of the credits column. The two columns' totals should be the same.

Balancing the seller's account is neither as critical nor as troublesome as balancing the buyer's account.

After all, you will usually have a large amount of money from which to subtract the various debits. There is one situation that could prove difficult on the seller's side. Sometimes the old loans to be paid off in escrow plus the fees and charges will amount to more than the amount the seller is to receive from the buyer, resulting in a net loss for the seller. In such cases you need to arrange for the seller to put in the amount needed in order to avoid delays in closing. To determine if there's enough, add the credits together, then subtract the total of debits from total of credits. The remainder will be disbursed to the seller when escrow closes. To balance the account, add the seller's money to the debits. It should equal the total of credits. If there is a discrepancy, adjust the seller's money to fit.

IX. Meeting With the Buyer

Now that you know how much to ask for, call Mr. Buyer to tell him that you are ready to begin closing escrow. Let him know how much money you will need from him in the form of a cashier's check, and tell him that the loan docs are ready for his signature. Mr. Broker should be advised of all this, also.

Later, when he does come in to hand you the check, get him to approve the pest control report that you've been holding in your file. Now, the last conditions have been met, except for the recording.

Some offices write a note to the buyer requesting funds to close escrow. If your office has such a practice, keep the note short and to the point.

X. Closing the Escrow

As soon as Mr. Buyer's check has been deposited in your escrow account, you may notify the title company and the lender that you are ready to record. Request them to record the documents they hold on August 1.

Many title companies offer daily pick-up and delivery messenger service.

The actual recording process in California varies from county to county. In many counties, including Los Angeles county, documents are recorded at 8:00 a.m. each day, just before the office is opened to the public. Other county recorders may allow recordings to be made at several specific times during the day. Still others have no set time— it's first-come, first-served. Every escrow officer should familiarize himself or herself with the procedure used in his or her county, and act according to local rule. Here, a telephone call to the title company and lender will be enough to effect the recordation, but be sure to follow the call with written instructions for recording. It is essential that the deed of trust and the grant deed be recorded at the same time!

After the recording has been made, the title officer will call to inform you of that fact (and also send you written notice). The moment (usually 8:00 a.m.) that the documents are recorded, the transaction is officially made, and:

1. John and Mary Sellers have a legal right to that portion of the purchase monies left after deducting their various obligations.
2. Title passes into the ownership of Bruce Buyer.
3. There is a new encumbrance against the property, for $64,000.00, in favor of Glendale Federal Savings Bank.
4. Verdugo Service Corporation has (once again) a trustee's interest in the property.

XI. Final Escrow Settlement

The deal may be made—the deed, policy of title insurance and full reconveyance may be started on their journeys to their new owners— but nobody has received any money yet. You still have plenty of work to do today.

You've been penciling figures onto your settlement sheet for two months, but only **after recording** can you be sure of the date upon which to base adjustments. If there is any difference between the estimated closing date and the actual recording date, you must now re-compute all the adjustments and re-balance the two accounts.

The final settlement will be typed (or computer-generated) on a different sheet, the **U.S. Department of Housing and Urban Development Settlement Statement**. (**Figures 5-5** and **5-6**) For obvious reasons it is referred to as the **HUD Statement**, or sometimes the **RESPA Statement**.

The HUD Settlement Statement is required by law in all escrows of this type, and must be used even if an escrow holder also uses a different final statement.

The form is multilevel, as the escrow instruction was, but there are two pages and both must be used. Each page has four copies: for buyer, seller, escrow and lender. Each page has cutouts in various places, so that while escrow and the lender see all the charges, buyer and seller see only that information which is pertinent to them.

Since you have no changes in closing date, enter the various figures in the places provided. **Complete page two first**. When you have finished, clip the adding machine tape or other paper that you used in arriving at the adjustments and reconciliation to escrow's copy and place them in your file. Use page two as a list for disbursements, and make cashier's checks, drawn on your escrow trust account, for the following amounts:

1. $4,800.00, to Thomas Broker, his commission.
2. $80,00, to the insurance agent, for the increased in liability, telling him also that escrow has close on August 1. He will see that the policy coverage is reassigned.
3. $347.00, to your own company, for the escrow fee.
4. $523.40, to A.B.C. Title Company, for title insurance and county fees.
5. $40.00, to Bugs Away Termite Company, for the inspection report.
6. $22.46 to Bruce Buyer.
7. $55,042.92, to John Sellers and Mary Sellers. Call them and ask if they'd like to come in to pick it up.

Send each check with an appropriate form letter.

X. Escrow is Closed

Record the disbursements and the recording date on the check list. Put away the escrow file. Your assistant has made an appointment for Mr. and Mrs. Arthur Miller for today, and you see they are waiting. You take out a fresh escrow file...

Figure 5-5

HUD SETTLEMENT STATEMENT – PAGE 1

Form Approved OMB NO. 63-R-1501

A.	U.S. DEPARTMENT OF HOUSING AND URBAN DEVELOPMENT SETTLEMENT STATEMENT	B. TYPE OF LOAN

GLENDALE FEDERAL SAVINGS AND LOAN ASSOCIATION

1. ☐ FHA 2. ☐ FMHA 3. ☒ CONV. UNINS.	
4. ☐ VA 5. ☐ CONV. INS.	
6. FILE NUMBER:	7. LOAN NUMBER: 4400-987567
8. MORT. INS. CASE NO.:	

C. NOTE: This form is furnished to give you a statement of actual settlement costs. Amounts paid to and by the settlement agent are shown. Items marked "(p.o.c.)" were paid outside the closing; they are shown here for informational purposes and are not included in the totals.

D. NAME OF BORROWER:	E. NAME OF SELLER:	F. NAME OF LENDER:
BRUCE BUYER	JOHN SELLERS and MARY SELLERS	GLENDALE FEDERAL SAVINGS AND LOAN ASSOCIATION 13730 Riverside Drive Sherman Oaks, CA 91423

G. PROPERTY LOCATION:	H. SETTLEMENT AGENT:	I. SETTLEMENT DATE:
1234 Noway Way Noetown, CA 92329	GLENDALE FEDERAL SAVINGS AND LOAN ASSOCIATION PLACE OF SETTLEMENT: 13730 Riverside Drive Sherman Oaks, CA 91423	August 1, 2051

	J. SUMMARY OF BORROWER'S TRANSACTION:			K. SUMMARY OF SELLER'S TRANSACTION:	
100.	GROSS AMOUNT DUE FROM BORROWER		400.	GROSS AMOUNT DUE TO SELLER	
101.	Contract sales price	80,000.00	401.	Contract sales price	80,000.00
102.	Personal property		402.	Personal property	
103.	Settlement charges to borrower (line 1400)	1,099.90	403.		
104.	Hazard Ins. @ $150.00 per year		404.	Hazard Ins. @ $150.00 per year	
105.	from 8-1-51 to 3-13-52	92.50	405.	from 8-1-51 to 3-13-52	92.50
	Adjustments for items paid by seller in advance			Adjustments for items paid by seller in advance	
106.	City/town taxes to		406.	City/town taxes to	
107.	County taxes to		407.	County taxes to	
108.	Assessments to		408.	Assessments to	
109.	Hazard Ins. @ $150.00 per year		409.	Hazard Ins. @ $150.00 per year	
110.	from 8-1-51 to 3-13-52	92.50	410.	from 8-1-51 to 3-13-52	92.50
111.			411.		
112.			412.		
120.	GROSS AMOUNT DUE FROM BORROWER	81,192.40	420.	GROSS AMOUNT DUE TO SELLER	80,092.50
200.	AMOUNTS PAID BY OR IN BEHALF OF BORROWER		500.	REDUCTIONS IN AMOUNT DUE TO SELLER	
201.	Deposit or earnest money	17,214.86	501.	Excess deposit (see instructions)	
202.	Principal amount of new loan(s)	64,000.00	502.	Settlement charges to seller (line 1400)	5,457.00
203.	Existing loan(s) taken subject to		503.	Existing loan(s) taken subject to	
204.			504.	Payoff of first mortgage loan Glendale Fed.	19,437.00
205.			505.	Payoff of second mortgage loan	
206.			506.	Int. @ 4.260 per day fr. 7-1-51 to 8-1-51	132.06
207.			507.	Forwarding Fee	15.00
208.			508.	Reconveyance Fee	25.00
209.			509.		
	Adjustments for items unpaid by seller			Adjustments for items unpaid by seller	
210.	City/town taxes to		510.	City/town taxes to	
211.	County taxes 7-1-51 to 8-1-51	64.86	511.	County taxes 7-1-51 to 8-1-51	
212.	Assessments to		512.	Assessments to	
213.			513.		
214.			514.		
215.			515.		
216.			516.		
217.			517.		
218.			518.		
219.			519.		
220.	TOTAL PAID BY/FOR BORROWER		520.	TOTAL REDUCTION AMOUNT DUE SELLER	25,042.92
300.	CASH AT SETTLEMENT FROM OR TO BORROWER		600.	CASH AT SETTLEMENT TO OR FROM SELLER	
301.	Gross amount due from borrower (line 120)	81,192.40	601.	Gross amount due to seller (line 420)	80,092.50
302.	Less amounts paid by/for borrower (line 220)	(81,214.40)	602.	Less reduction amount due seller (line 520)	(25,042.92)
303.	CASH (☐ FROM) (☒ TO) BORROWER	22.46	603.	CASH (☒ TO) (☐ FROM) SELLER	55,049.58

HUD 1A REV. 5/76 AS & AS (1323)   LENDER'S COPY

Figure 5-6

HUD SETTLEMENT STATEMENT – PAGE 2

GLENDALE FEDERAL SAVINGS AND LOAN ASSOCIATION

U.S. DEPARTMENT OF HOUSING AND URBAN DEVELOPMENT
SETTLEMENT STATEMENT
PAGE 2

L. SETTLEMENT CHARGES		PAID FROM BORROWER'S FUNDS AT SETTLEMENT	PAID FROM SELLER'S FUNDS AT SETTLEMENT
700.	TOTAL SALES/BROKER'S COMMISSION based on price $80,000.00 @ 6% = $4,800.00		
	Division of commission (line 700) as follows:		
701.	$ to		
702.	$ to		
703.	Commission paid at Settlement Thomas Broker		4,800.00
704.			
800.	ITEMS PAYABLE IN CONNECTION WITH LOAN		
801.	Loan Origination Fee 1% + $100.00	740.00	
802.	Loan Discount %		
803.	Appraisal Fee to		
804.	Credit Report to	10.00	
805.	Lender's Inspection Fee		
806.	Mortgage Insurance Application Fee to		
807.	Assumption Fee		
808.	Tax Service	16.50	
809.			
810.			
811.			
900.	ITEMS REQUIRED BY LENDER TO BE PAID IN ADVANCE		
901.	Interest from to @ $ /day		
902.	Mortgage Insurance Premium for mo. to		
903.	Hazard Insurance Premium for (increase) yrs. to 3-13-52	80.00	
904.	yrs. to		
905.			
1000.	RESERVES DEPOSITED WITH LENDER FOR		
1001.	Hazard insurance mo. @ $ /mo.		
1002.	Mortgage insurance mo. @ $ /mo.		
1003.	City property taxes mo. @ $ /mo.		
1004.	County property taxes mo. @ $ /mo.		
1005.	Annual assessments mo. @ $ /mo.		
1006.	mo. @ $ /mo.		
1007.	mo. @ $ /mo.		
1008.	mo. @ $ /mo.		
1100.	TITLE CHARGES		
1101.	Settlement or closing fee to Glendale Federal Savings (Escrow)	173.50	173.50
1102.	Abstract or title search to		
1103.	Title examination to		
1104.	Title insurance binder to		
1105.	Document preparation to		
1106.	Notary fees to		
1107.	Attorney's fees to		
	(includes above items No.:)		
1108.	Title insurance to	70.90	352.50
	(includes above items No.:)		
1109.	Lender's coverage $		
1110.	Owner's coverage $		
1111.			
1112.			
1113.			
1200.	GOVERNMENT RECORDING AND TRANSFER CHARGES		
1201.	Recording fees: Deed $3.00 ; Mortgage $6.00 ; Releases $3.00	9.00	3.00
1202.	City/county tax/stamps: Deed $ 88.00 ; Mortgage $		88.00
1203.	State tax/stamps: Deed $; Mortgage $		
1204.			
1205.			
1300.	ADDITIONAL SETTLEMENT CHARGES		
1301.	Survey to		
1302.	Pest inspection to Bugs Away		40.00
1303.			
1304.			
1305.			
1400.	TOTAL SETTLEMENT CHARGES (enter on lines 103 and 502, Sections J and K)	1,099.90	5,457.00

The Undersigned Acknowledges Receipt of This Settlement Statement and Agrees to the Correctness Thereof.

_____
Buyer

_____
Seller

HUD 1B REV. 5/76 AS & AS (1324)   **LENDER'S COPY**

XII. CHAPTER SUMMARY

A PRELIMINARY REPORT of title is an offer by the title company to issue title insurance. It will contain the names of the owners and their FEE SIMPLE interest. There will also be a list of ENCUMBRANCES which affect the use of property. There may be LIENS, CC&Rs, or EASEMENTS that load or burden the use of property. The purpose of the PRELIM is to avoid surprises when the parties discuss the condition of title.

There will be a DEMAND from the beneficiary, or lender, which will set forth exactly how much is needed to pay off the loan. Miscellaneous fees will be included by the lender. You will be asked to ADJUST INTEREST to find out how many days' interest is due.

A FULL RECONVEYANCE that ends the lender's lien against the property will be executed. It will be recorded after the new Deed of Trust is recorded. If a MORTGAGE is involved, there will be a FULL RELEASE OF MORTGAGE executed and recorded. It too removes the lender's lien against the property.

FIRE INSURANCE will also be a requirement of the escrow. Generally a new policy will be issued by an insurance company.

An adjustment and proration of PROPERTY TAXES will occur. As with other prorations, the escrow must be accurate in these amounts.

The Federal Reserve has a REGULATION Z that insures truth in lending through loan transactions. It gives the complete itemized statement of all loan costs, interest costs, and total cost over the life of the loan. LOAN FEES, TITLE INSURANCE FEES, PEST CONTROL FEES, RECORDING FEES, COMMISSION FEES, and ESCROW FEES will be carefully listed in the FINAL ESCROW SETTLEMENT. When there is a new loan, the HUD STATEMENT will be used to satisfy law.

XIII. TERMS

Adjusting Interest: The calculation of how much interest is due usually based on the number of days interest is earned or will be prepaid.

CC&Rs: Covenants, conditions, and restrictions, which are private limits on the use of property.

Demand: From a beneficiary, it sets forth exactly how much is needed to pay of the existing loan balance.

Easements: A nonpossessory property interest that one person has in the land owned by another.

Encumbrances: Anything that loads or burdens title and restricts the owner rights in the property.

Federal Reserve Regulation Z: Also known as Truth in Lending with a purpose of insuring borrower' are given disclosure of the cost of credit.

Fees: Various charges in escrow for items as loans fees, title insurance, recording etc.

Fee Simple/Fee Absolute: Indicates full ownership with power to transfer without others approval.

Final Escrow Settlement: A detailed cash accounting of a real estate transaction prepared by escrow. Shows all cash received, all charges and credits made and all cash paid out in the transaction.

Fire Insurance: Property insurance required when escrow closes covering losses due to fire, and other specific perils.

Full Reconveyance: The instrument which discharges the debt and ends the borrower and lender relationship.

Full Release of Mortgage: The formal release of a mortgage lien when the lender is satisfied to complete the release.

HUD Statement: A required loan statement by the Housing and Urban Development allocating the appropriate charges and credits.

Liens: A type of encumbrance that arises from a charge that one has on specific property. It may be voluntary or involuntary.

Mortgage: A lien that created when money is loaned on real property.

Mortgagor: The borrower in a mortgage contract

Mortgagee: The lender in a mortgage contract

Preliminary Report of Title: A report that is issued before a title insurance policy generally at the time an escrow is opened.

Property Taxes: Tax levied against real property by local agencies and municipalities. They are levied for the general support of government.

XIV. CHAPTER QUIZ

1. A preliminary report of title is synonymous with:

    a. the prelim.
    b. the title report.
    c. both a and b.
    d. neither a nor b.

2. Easements grant the right to use portions of the property to whom:

    a. persons.
    b. entities.
    c. properties.
    d. all of the above.

3. When the escrow officer sends a check to pay off a loan it must include:

    a. principal.
    b. interest.
    c. interest to cover mailing time.
    d. all of the above.

4. The reconveyance discharges the relationship between:

    a. trustor.
    b. trustee.
    c. beneficiary.
    d. all of the above.

5. When determining the prorating of a three-year insurance policy:

    a. divide by 3.
    b. divide by 3, then 12.
    c. divide by 3, then 360.
    d. divide by 360.

6. Loan fees include:

    a. loan origination fee.
    b. loan processing fee.
    c. credit report.
    d. all of the above.

7. Commission for the real estate salesperson is paid:

    a. only if escrow is instructed.

    b. no matter what.

    c. both a and b.

    d. neither a nor b.

8. Calling for the buyer's funds comes:

    a. at start of escrow.

    b. near end of escrow.

    c. both a and b.

    d. neither a nor b.

9. Calling for the buyer's funds comes after you have:

    a. drawn a new deed.

    b. received pest control report.

    c. arranged for a fire policy.

    d. all of the above.

10. The final closing statements must be on a form approved by:

    a. HUD.

    b. FHA.

    c. VA.

    d. Cal-Vet.

ANSWERS: 1. c; 2. d; 3. d; 4. d; 5. d; 6. c; 7. a; 8. b; 9. d; 10. a

Sample Two, Part One

This sample escrow, also a single-family home sale, is a type of sale quite common in California, particularly for small houses and those that provide rental income to their owners: **a small down payment (here, less than 7% of the price) and the seller taking back a deed of trust and note for the balance of the purchase price**.

The escrow will be processed by the escrow department of **Safeco Title Insurance Company, a division of the Safeco Insurance Company**. You are, as in the last sample escrow, the escrow officer. In this instance, the principals come into your office with their agreement. It differs from the previous transaction in several important ways:

1. There is only an oral agreement, they have no real estate agent and, as yet, no written contract.
2. The seller will take most of the purchase price in the form of a deed of trust and note.
3. The seller's wife is ill and cannot sign the grant deed.
4. The property is located in an area served by a private water company, where property owners hold shares of stock entitling them to water service.

After introductions, the elder Mr. Miller (he asks to be called Ollie) begins to explain the transaction. A year ago, he and his wife attempted to sell the back part of their large lot, and the guest cottage on it, to their favorite nephew, Arthur. Their attorney informed them

CHAPTER OUTLINE

that recent law changes made it more complicated than it used to be, and he helped them through the process of officially subdividing the land. They got approved surveys, field subdivision requests, and maps from municipal offices, and did all that was necessary to divide their one lot into two. So that the new lot could have access to the street, they created an easement along one side of their new smaller lot. These changes were duly recorded in the county recorder's office, and the taxing bodies assigned property taxes to the two lots. Now at last they are ready to make the change in ownership.

I. Taking the Escrow

We will not show **Safeco's** escrow worksheet, since it is essentially the same as other worksheets, memo sheets, escrow order sheets, and "take" sheets, having spaces for the parts of the transaction. Instead, we will describe the transaction in a list.

A. BASIC ITEMS OF THE TRANSACTION

1. Seller

Oliver Flatt Miller and his wife Edith Vernon Miller. Ollie tells you that Edith is very ill, in a hospital, and that he will act for her under a power of attorney.

2. Buyer

Arthur V. Miller and his wife Margaret C. Miller.

3. Price

$42,950.00. Arthur has already given $2,000.00 to Ollie, and they have agreed to a first trust deed and note for $40,000.00, payable to Ollie. They ask you if you want the $2,000.00 placed in escrow. There is still $950.00 of the price not accounted for. This amount might be enough cash in escrow to cover ordinary expenses, but you need more information. Inform them that it probably won't be necessary, but you'll return to it later when you know more about the transaction. You do inform them that some cash in escrow is essential.

4. Taxes

Ollie has recently paid the first half taxes. Escrow needs to prorate the second half taxes. The two men (Ollie and Arthur) suggest an escrow closing date of February 1.

Remember: the second-half of the tax year begins January 1.

5. Title Insurance

Ollie wants the loan he's making to be insured under an ALTA Lender's Policy, if possible. It is possible: both private and institutional lenders can obtain ALTA

policies, but the premium is somewhat higher than for standard policies. Arthur wants "regular" title insurance. Since there's no real estate salesperson to explain things to him, you explain the various policies to him. It turns out he wants a CLTA Owner's Standard Coverage Policy.

6. Pest Control

They don't want a pest control inspection. Ollie says he has the property (both houses) inspected each year as part of his regular upkeep. Arthur agrees that the inspection is unnecessary. These statements are voluntary. Although the officer must ask questions to get the necessary information, in the absence of a prior written agreement, the prohibitions against asking about matters not directly concerned with the transaction are still in force. Since there is no institutional lender's requirements to follow here, the pest control question is not essential.

7. Tenant

Mr. A. Wrenter. He has a five-year lease on the guest cottage that still has two years to run. Ollie will assign the lease to Arthur, and Mr. Wrenter has verbally agreed to it. The Millers want to get the agreement in writing—an offset statement.

8. Old Loans to Pay Off

None. Ollie says the property has been unencumbered (clear) for many years.

9. Fire Insurance

Ollie, the lender, requires a new fire insurance policy on the guest cottage. He wants the policy coverage to be set for the amount of the loan he is making, $40,000.00.

10. Water Stock

There are five shares of stock in the Flowing Water Company that were appurtenant to the original large lot owned by Ollie and Edith. At the time of the lot split, two shares were deemed appurtenant to the new small lot now being sold to Arthur, but ownership was not yet transferred (naturally, since Ollie still owned the lot). You will have to write to Flowing Water to determine whether there are any outstanding bills, etc..., so be sure to get the company's address. It's a good idea to get the owner's stock certificate, or a copy, in order to refer correctly to the certificate number in your letter. Ollie agrees to bring it in soon.

11. Property Description and Addresses of the Parties

Ollie has brought the legal description, issued at the time of the lot split, with him. It reads *"PARCEL 1: Lot 'A' of Blackacre tract, as per Map recorded in Book 100, Pages 1 and 2 of Maps, in the office of the County Recorder of said County, EXCEPT the South*

140 feet thereof, (and) PARCEL 2: An easement of ingress and egress over the East 15 feet of the South 140 feet of Lot 'A' of said Blackacre Tract." (Now the property that Ollie retains will be referred to as "the South 140 feet of Lot "A", etc." instead of its older description "Lot 'A', etc.")

The street address of the property being sold is:

2553 Hollywood Way
Burbank, CA 91502

The address of the sellers is:

2551 Hollywood Way
Burbank, CA 91502

The address of the buyers is:

2711 Runway Rd.
Burbank, CA 91503

Now that you have the essence of the transaction written in your memo sheet, you can see that there are no outstanding loans to be paid off and no institutional loan origination fees—two of the most expensive items for the parties in an escrow. It looks like the $950.00 will be more than sufficient for the other fees and charges, so you inform the two men that they will not be required to deposit the $2,000.00 into escrow. You may suggest that you write into the escrow instructions this wording:

"I have handed seller, outside of this escrow, as a portion of the total consideration, the sum of $2,000.00, receipt of which is hereby acknowledged by Oliver Flatt Miller and Edith Vernon Miller."

You mention that it is advantageous to have everything specified carefully, since the escrow instructions will be the only written contract in this transaction. They agree that it is a good way to account for all the money without having to put it through escrow. They have with them a cashier's check made payable to **Safeco**. You accept it, filling out a receipt to Arthur Miller, the maker of the check.

B. POWER OF ATTORNEY – ATTORNEY-IN-FACT

All deeds and deeds of trust, or any other documents to be recorded, must be acknowledged by a notary public before being accepted by the office of the Recorder.

The fact that Ollie said he had power of attorney for his wife, to enable him to sign the documents for her, cannot be accepted at face value. Ollie cannot act for her in the transfer unless her legal granting of permission is present in county records.

When one person (called the **principal**) authorizes another person (called the **attorney-in-fact**) to act as agent for him or her, there must be a properly drawn and executed document, called a **POWER OF ATTORNEY**, to that effect. This form may be purchased at any stationary store, and may be filled out by an attorney at law, the principal, or the person to be named attorney-in-fact. **It may not** be filled out by an escrow officer. Although a power of attorney does not have to be recorded in all cases, it must be notarized in all cases, **and must be notarized and recorded in cases where it is used to transfer title**. There are general and special powers of attorney. The general form has a long list of permitted duties printed on its face, while a special power of attorney is drawn by a lawyer on blank paper or letter head with the particular duty clearly set out.

As attorney-in-fact transactions are quite common in escrow work, you must be familiar with the basic law relating to these instruments, the authority they grant, and their limitations.

A person must be legally competent to contract in order to grant a power of attorney to another. If the principal is either unconscious or incompetent, the person who would act as attorney-in-fact must petition the courts to be appointed guardian (in the cases of minor principals) or conservator (in the case of adults). An escrow officer should not accept the signature of any attorney-in-fact, guardian, or conservator, without first checking to see that the document is present in county records. This is most easily done by examining the **prelim**. This is done by asking the title officer to examine the "general index," that part of the title company's fund of information which is keyed to names rather than descriptions of property. It has records of deaths, declarations of bankruptcy, marriages, dissolutions of marriages, etc. Also, since the power of attorney must be recorded in cases of title transfer, the escrow officer frequently will need to get it recorded before the close of escrow.

An attorney-in-fact is prohibited from making a deed or mortgage without valuable consideration or from dealing with a principal's property for his or her own benefit.

Mrs. Edith Miller, while ill, is both conscious and competent. She could, if she chose, sign the grant deed, escrow instructions, etc., if they were brought to the hospital and a notary public were present to witness the signing. In this case, she felt that it would be more convenient for her husband to execute all the necessary documents, so she signed only the power of attorney, in the presence of the notary public whom her husband brought to the hospital. Mr. Miller then had a choice. He could take the document to the County Recorder's officer, pay the fee himself and have it recorded, or he could take it to escrow and have it recorded, then pay the fee as part of the regular escrow expenses. He chose the latter. **Figure 6-1** shows the power of attorney executed by Ollie and Edith duly notarized by their lawyer-notary public, Francis McKenna. Ollie now gives the document to you. You accept it, making a note to yourself to get it recorded immediately.

Figure 6-1

POWER OF ATTORNEY

RECORDING REQUESTED BY

WHEN RECORDED MAIL TO

Name / Street Address / City & State
Oliver F. Miller
2551 Hollywood Way
Burbank, CA 91502

———— (SPACE ABOVE THIS LINE FOR RECORDER'S USE) ————

POWER OF ATTORNEY

GENERAL

Know All Men by These Presents: That I, _____ EDITH VERNON MILLER _____

the undersigned (jointly and severally, if more than one) hereby make, constitute and appoint_____
OLIVER FLATT MILLER

my true and lawful Attorney for me and in my name, place and stead and for my use and benefit:

(a)   To ask, demand, sue for, recover, collect and receive each and every sum of money, debt, account, legacy, bequest, interest, dividend, annuity and demand (which now is or hereafter shall become due, owing or payable) belonging to or claimed by me, and to use and take any lawful means for the recovery thereof by legal process or otherwise, and to execute and deliver a satisfaction or release therefor, together with the right and power to compromise or compound any claim or demand;

(b)   To exercise any or all of the following powers as to real property, any interest therein and/or any building thereon: To contract for, purchase, receive and take possession thereof and of evidence of title thereto; to lease the same for any term or purpose, including leases for business, residence, and oil and/or mineral development; to sell, exchange, grant or convey the same with or without warranty; and to mortgage, transfer in trust, or otherwise encumber or hypothecate the same to secure payment of a negotiable or non-negotiable note or performance of any obligation or agreement;

(c)   To exercise any or all of the following powers as to all kinds of personal property and goods, wares and merchandise, choses in action and other property in possession or in action: To contract for, buy, sell, exchange, transfer and in any legal manner deal in and with the same; and to mortgage, transfer in trust, or otherwise encumber or hypothecate the same to secure payment of a negotiable or non-negotiable note or performance of any obligation or agreement;

(d)   To borrow money and to execute and deliver negotiable or non-negotiable notes therefor with or without security; and to loan money and receive negotiable or non-negotiable notes therefor with such security as he shall deem proper;

(e)   To create, amend, supplement and terminate any trust and to instruct and advise the trustee of any trust wherein I am or may be trustor or beneficiary; to represent and vote stock, exercise stock rights, accept and deal with any dividend, distribution or bonus, join in any corporate financing, reorganization, merger, liquidation, consolidation or other action and the extension, compromise, conversion, adjustment, enforcement or foreclosure, singly or in conjunction with others of any corporate stock, bond, note, debenture or other security; to compound, compromise, adjust, settle and satisfy any obligation, secured or unsecured, owing by or to me and to give or accept any property and/or money whether or not equal to or less in value than the amount owing in payment, settlement or satisfaction thereof;

(f)   To transact business of any kind or class and as my act and deed to sign, execute, acknowledge and deliver any deed, lease, assignment of lease, covenant, indenture, indemnity, agreement, mortgage, deed of trust, assignment of mortgage or of the beneficial interest under deed of trust, extension or renewal of any obligation, subordination or waiver of priority, hypothecation, bottomry, charter-party, bill of lading, bill of sale, bill, bond, note, whether negotiable or non-negotiable, receipt, evidence of debt, full or partial release or satisfaction of mortgage, judgment and other debt, request for partial or full reconveyance of deed of trust and such other instruments in writing of any kind or class as may be necessary or proper in the premises.

Giving and Granting unto my said Attorney full power and authority to do and perform all and every act and thing whatsoever requisite, necessary or appropriate to be done in and about the premises as fully to all intents and purposes as I might or could do if personally present, hereby ratifying all that my said Attorney shall lawfully do or cause to be done by virtue of these presents. The powers and authority hereby conferred upon my said Attorney shall be applicable to all real and personal property or interests therein now owned or hereafter acquired by me and wherever situate.

My said Attorney is empowered hereby to determine in his sole discretion the time when, purpose for and manner in which any power herein conferred upon him shall be exercised, and the conditions, provisions and covenants of any instrument or document which may be executed by him pursuant hereto; and in the acquisition or disposition of real or personal property, my said Attorney shall have exclusive power to fix the terms thereof for cash, credit and/or property, and if on credit with or without security.

The undersigned, if a married woman, hereby further authorizes and empowers my said Attorney, as my duly authorized agent, to join in my behalf, in the execution of any instrument by which any community real property or any interest therein, now owned or hereafter acquired by my spouse and myself, or either of us, is sold, leased, encumbered, or conveyed.

When the context so requires, the masculine gender includes the feminine and/or neuter, and the singular number includes the plural.

WITNESS my hand this _____15th_____ day of ____November_____, 2051

___Edith Vernon Miller___

State of California,

County of ___Los Angeles___ } SS.

On____November 15, 2051_____, before me, the undersigned, a Notary Public in and for said
State, personally appeared_____ Edith Vernon Miller _____

known to me to be the person___ whose name ___is___ subscribed to the within instrument and acknowledged that___she____
executed the same.

Witness my hand and official seal.

_____ (Seal)_____

OFFICIAL SEAL
FRANCIS G. McKENNA
NOTARY PUBLIC · CALIFORNIA
...
My Commission Expires OCT 14, 1979

POWER OF ATTORNEY—GENERAL
WOLCOTTS FORM 1400—REV. 10-62

This standard form covers most usual problems in the field indicated. Before you sign, read it, fill in all blanks, and make changes proper to your transaction. Consult a lawyer if you doubt the form's fitness for your purpose.

155

Documents using a power of attorney must show that the principal, not the attorney-in-fact, is conveying or receiving title. Also, an attorney-in-fact must always act in the best interests of the principal.

C. RECITATIONS FOR FUNDING

At this point you might ask the terms of the trust deed and note which the seller is taking back. They tell you that interest on the $40,000.00 loan is to be 9.25% per annum. They want the payments to be the amount specified for an amortization over a term of 30 years, but they want the actual term of the loan to be 15 years, at which time the entire unpaid principal and interest will be due. Their description of the loan tells you that you will choose an installment note from your selection of notes.

There is no standard note form for an installment note with balloon payment. It isn't necessary, since the term must be indicated on all notes whether installment or straight.

You look in your **amortization book** or on a financial calculator (essential equipment for all escrow officers) and see that a monthly payment on a 30-year, 9.25%, $40,000.00 loan is $329.08. Make sure this is agreeable to the parties.

CALCULATOR USE

A calculator is used to determine the qualifying ratios, the down payment, the estimated closing costs, and the monthly loan payment. A calculator may be found online at **www.bankrate.com/brm/rate/calc_home.asp**. Another calculator to use when trying to figure a borrower's loan payment is in the "Calculator and Tools" section of the "Homeownership resources" section of the Freddie Mac website (**www.freddiemac. com/calculators**). Also note that Microsoft's EXCEL® can be set up for amortizing.

You also need to find out if this is an "or more" or "only" note. The seller agrees that the payments may be larger than $329.08. Now ask how the sellers want the beneficial interest in the note to read. *BENEFICIAL INTEREST tells who actually owns the note— in whom the interest is "vested."* The seller says the deed of trust and note are to read "Oliver Flatt Miller and Edith Vernon Miller, husband and wife as Joint Tenants" In addition, ask how the buyers want the grant deed vested. Arthur says "Arthur V. Miller and Margaret C. Miller, husband and wife as joint tenants."

They do not mention any clauses, such as an acceleration clause, to be inserted in the deed of trust or note, and **you should not ask if there are to be any**. This would be putting ideas into the sellers' heads, and the buyers might not appreciate your "helpfulness."

If the buyers were to ask for an acceleration clause, you must ask what wording they want. If they don't know, suggest that they seek counsel and get back to you with their wording.

There are some questions you **should ask** in addition to the amount and terms of the note and deed of trust. You may ask if a **Request for Notice** is to be prepared for the benefit of the sellers. Ask if the note and deed of trust is to contain a prepayment penalty. Ask also if the note is to contain a **late charge**, and if so, how many days after payment is due. Find out **when the payments are to begin**. Although the first payment 30 days after close of escrow is usual, the first payment can be any time specified by the seller. These questions do not always have to be answered in specific recitations in escrow instructions, but since this escrow has no prior contract, it is best to get it all spelled out. If the seller does not know when he or she wants payments to begin, or if the payment date depends on the date of closing, the following wording in instructions will cover the situation:

"Escrow holder is instructed to endorse the reverse of the Note, at the close of escrow, to indicate the date interest to accrue, date of the first payment of principal and interest and the maturity date."

II. Completing the Escrow Order

You now have all the major items needed for the transaction, but your company has a section of its instruction sheet that is not present in many others: a space where all fees and charges are to be typed by the escrow officer with the parties who pay for them identified. This is particularly helpful in transactions where there is no previous written agreement, since it specifies fee payment details that often depend only on local custom. Principals are often unfamiliar with these payment customs, and misunderstandings can be fertile ground for contention and difficulties in escrow.

Ask about the fees you see will have to be paid. You may use phrases like "Do you agree that seller and buyer each pay half of the escrow fee?" If they seem confused, it is permissible to say (impartially, of course) something like: "When there are government backed loans involved, such as VA or FHA loans, certain parties must pay certain fees. But there are no laws that say who must pay fees in this kind of escrow. However, it is the custom here that the seller pays the documentary transfer tax."

These are the fees for which you should ascertain payment:

1. Escrow fee. They each agree to pay half.
2. ALTA Lender's Title Insurance. Ollie will pay this.
3. CLTA Owner's Title Insurance. Arthur will pay this.
4. Document drawing fees, customary in your company.

a. Grand deed. Arthur pays.

b. Deed of trust. Arthur pays.

c. Note. Arthur pays.

d. Assignment of the lease. Arthur pays.

e. Offset statement. Ollie pays.

f. Rental statement. Ollie pays.

5. Recording fees, as required by county recorder:

a. Grant deed. Arthur pays.

b. Deed of trust. Arthur pays.

c. Power of attorney. Ollie pays.

6. Documentary transfer tax. Ollie pays.

7. Prorations. They each agree to pay their share.

a. Property taxes.

b. Rents.

c. Water stock assessments.

8. Charges arising from any defects found in the preliminary report of title. Before Ollie agrees to pay, you reassure him that if any defects or problems do appear in the prelim, you will call him at once to discuss the matter and will not simply add costs to his settlement estimates. He is agreeable to this and agrees to pay such costs if any do become necessary.

III. The Escrow Instructions

The escrow instructions for this transaction are reproduced for you on the next three pages. Read them thoroughly and note the differences from the preprinted forms used in the previous escrow. **Safeco** provides a standard first and last sheet, and additional blank center sheets for writing as many items as may be necessary for the complete instructions (some complicated escrows may require twenty-five or more pages). The instructions are shown in **Figures 6-2, 6-3,** and **6-4.**

The escrow officer is expected to demonstrate each item of the transaction in a clear and complete manner, and has reference material at hand showing the company's preferred wording for each type of escrow item. If you work for a large company, always familiarize yourself with your own firm's preferred wording. We will discuss each section of the instructions.

Remember, as with all escrow instructions, they take the form of a letter to you from the parties.

Figure 6-2

ESCROW INSTRUCTIONS - PAGE 1

ESCROW INSTRUCTIONS

SAFECO **TO:** SAFECO TITLE INSURANCE COMPANY

Los Angeles .... California

Escrow No. 3000 .... Escrow Officer .... Date December 1, 2051

1. I have handed Seller, OUTSIDE OF THIS ESCROW, as a portion of
2. the total consideration, the sum of . . . . $ 2,000.00
3. receipt of which is hereby acknowledged by Oliver Flatt Miller
4. and Edith Vernon Miller, sellers
5.
6. I hand you herewith a Cashier's Check made payable to Safeco Title
7. Insurance Company, in the amount of . . . . $ 950.00
8. which represents the total cash deposit in this escrow
9.
10. I will execute and deliver a new first Deed of Trust securing one
11. promissory note in favor of Seller, as hereinafter described, in
12. the amount of . . . . $ 40,000.00
13.
14.
15. TO EFFECT A TOTAL CONSIDERATION IN THE AMOUNT OF . . . . $ 42,950.00
16.
17.
18.
19.
20. which you are instructed to use when you can obtain a CLTA standard coverage **Owner's and ALTA Loan**
21.
22. form policy of title insurance containing the insuring clauses, exceptions, exclusions, provisions and stipulations
23. customarily contained in the printed provisions of such form with liability not less than $ 42,950.00 and $40,000.00
24. describing the land in the ..... **city of Los Angeles** .... respectively,
25. County of ....**Los Angeles**........................., State of California described as:
26.
27. PARCEL 1:   Lot "A" of Blackacre Tract, as per Map recorded in Book 100, Pages 1 and 2
28.   of Maps, in the office of the County Recorder of said County,
29.
30.   EXCEPT the South 140 feet thereof.
31. PARCEL 2:   An easement for ingress and egress over the East 15 feet of the South 140
32.   feet of said Blackacre Tract.
33.
34.
35. showing the   **fee title**
36.
37. in said land vested in ARTHUR V. MILLER and MARGARET C. MILLER, husband and wife as
38.   JOINT TENANTS,
39.
40. Subject to:
41.
42. 1. Second installment general and special taxes for the fiscal year 2051/2052 ,
43.   not delinquent.
44.
45. 2. Covenants, conditions, restrictions, reservations, rights, rights-of-way and
46.   easements of record, if any, as disclosed by preliminary title report from
47.   Safeco Title Insurance Company.
48.
49. 3. First Deed of Trust, to file in your form, executed by above Vestee in favor of
50.   OLIVER FLATT MILLER and EDITH VERNON MILLER, husband and wife AS JOINT TENANTS,
51.   to secure one promissory Note in the principal amount of $40,000.00 bearing interest
52.   at the rate of 9 1/4% per annum on the unpaid principal. Principal and interest
53.   payable in installments of $329.08 OR MORE per month commencing on the 30th day
54.   after the close of escrow and continuing on the same day of each calendar month
55.   thereafter for a term of fifteen (15) years, at which time the entire unpaid
56.   balance of principal and accrued interest will be all due and payable.
57.   Escrow holder is instructed to endorse the reverse of the Note, at the close of
58.   escrow, to indicate the date interest to accrue, date of the first payment of
59.   principal and interest and the maturity date.
60.
61.   * * * * *
62.
63.
64.
65.
66.
67.
68. (CONTINUED ON PAGE 2)

Figure 6-3

ESCROW INSTRUCTIONS - PAGE 2

ESCROW INSTRUCTIONS (CONTINUED)

TO: SAFECO TITLE INSURANCE COMPANY

(CONTINUED FROM PAGE 1)

Escrow No. 3000

Date: December 1, 2051

1.
2. Buyer to cause to have delivered into escrow an Extended Coverage Fire Insurance
3. Policy covering property which is the subject of this escrow, insuring improvements
4. for at least $40,000.00, with first loss payable clause in the name of OLIVER FLATT
5. MILLER and EDITH VERNON MILLER, husband and wife as Joint Tenants. Policy to be
6. effective prior to the close of escrow for a term of at least one year. Premium,
7. as required, to be paid by Buyer from funds deposited into escrow. Escrow holder
8. is instructed to forward the original policy to Seller, with a copy to Buyer, at
9. the close of escrow.
10.
11. Oliver Flatt Miller to deposit into escrow, for recording at Seller's expense, a
12. Power of Attorney executed by Edith Vernon Miller, his wife, as required, to enable
13. him to execute documents as the Attorney-in-Fact of Edith Vernon Miller.
14.
15. Seller to deposit Rental Statement into escrow, for approval of Buyer and prorations
16. of rent at the close of escrow. Security Deposits, if any, per Statement, to be
17. credited to Buyer and charged to Seller, at the close of escrow.
18.
19. Seller to execute an Assignment of the unrecorded Lease, on property which is the
20. subject of this escrow, in favor of Arthur V. Miller and Margaret C. Miller, husband
21. and wife as Joint Tenants. You are instructed to deliver said executed Assignment
22. to Buyer at the close of escrow.
23.
24. Escrow holder is instructed to forward an Offset Statement to Lessee (Tenant) covering
25. property which is the subject of this escrow, for completion by said Lessee. Prior to
26. the close of escrow said Statement to be executed by Seller and approved by Buyer.
27. You are to deliver a copy of said executed Statement to Buyer, at the close of escrow.
28.
29. You are instructed to obtain a statement from Flowing Water Company, P. O. Box X,
30. Los Angeles, California, relative to the two (2) shares of water stock, Certificate
31. #X274, issued in the name of seller Oliver Flatt Miller and Edith Vernon Miller, to
32. ascertain the amount of any unpaid charges, taxes, assessments or any other matters
33. pertaining to said water stock. Upon receipt of same, prior to the close of escrow,
34. you are instructed to forward a copy of said statement to Seller for approval. At
35. the close of escrow you are instructed to prorate assessment, per statement, and
36. transfer ownership of said stock to Buyer, Arthur V. Miller and Margaret C. Miller.
37.
38. The closing of this escrow is not conditioned upon receipt of a Structural Pest
39. Control Report on property which is the subject of this escrow.
40.
41.
42.
43.   * * * * *
44.
45.
46. These escrow instructions are not intended to amend, modify or supersede any prior
47. agreements between the parties as to the following:
48.
49.   a. Possession of subject property.
50.
51.   b. Personal property included in the purchase price.
52.
53.
54. Escrow is to be concerned only with provisions specifically set forth in these
55. instructions, and is not concerned in effecting the above agreements.
56.
57.   * * * * *
58.
59.
60.
61.
62.
63.
64.
65.
66.
67.
68.
69. (CONTINUED ON PAGE 3)
70.
71.
72.   (Page   2   )

E-325 (G.S.)

Figure 6-4

ESCROW INSTRUCTIONS - PAGE 3

TO: SAFECO TITLE INSURANCE COMPANY

1. PRORATE as of **date of recording deed** the following **taxes, rentals per statement and**
2. **water stock assessments pursuant to statement from Flowing Water Company.**
3. Assume a 30 day month in any prorate herein provided, and unless the parties otherwise instruct you, you are to
4. use the information contained in the last available tax statement, rental statement as provided by the seller, beneficiary's
5. statement, and fire insurance policies delivered into escrow for the prorates provided above. In the event any beneficiary's
6. statement reveals a deposit, account or funds for a future payment of taxes, insurance or other future payment obligations of the
7. loan, you are to **not applicable**
8. Your agency as escrow holder shall terminate six months following the date set forth next below, and shall be subject to
9. earlier revocation by receipt by you prior to close of escrow of written notice signed, (1) in case this escrow has not been
10. placed in a condition to close by **February 1, 2052** by any party hereto, or (2) if received prior
11. to said date, but after (there shall have been) a failure of a condition or performance to be complied with or performed on
12. or before a date, or within a period, stated herein, then by any party other than a party responsible for such compliance or
13. performance. Any such revocation shall be effective upon receipt of such notice, but you shall not return the documents or
14. deposits of the revoking party prior to ten days after you have mailed a copy of such notice to each of the other parties.
15. Your knowledge of matters affecting the property, provided such facts do not prevent compliance with these instructions,
16. does not create any liability or duty in addition to your responsibility under these instructions. No notice, demand or change
17. of instructions, except a demand for revocation made in accordance with the foregoing paragraph, shall be of any effect in
18. this escrow unless given in writing by all parties affected thereby.
19. Proceeds of this escrow may be disbursed by your check payable to the parties as their names are signed hereon, and your
20. checks and documents may be mailed to the addresses set forth in these instructions.
21. You are instructed to furnish to any broker or lender identified with this transaction or anyone acting on behalf of such lender,
22. any information concerning this escrow, copies of all instructions, amendments and statements upon request.
23. Indicate on the deed to file, all future tax statements are to be mailed to **Buyer at address below**
24.
25. I agree to pay:
26.
27. **One-half of the escrow fee.**
28. **Drawing fee for Deed of Trust and Note.**
29. **Recording fee for Grant Deed and Deed of Trust.**
30. **Prorations as required, if any.**
31. **Premium for ALTA Lender's Policy of Title Insurance, as required.**
32. **Premium for Extended Coverage Fire Insurance Policy, per Page 2, lines 2 thru 9.**
33. **Drawing fee for Assignment of unrecorded Lease.**
34. **Fee for transfer of water stock, as required.**
35.
36. **BUYER:**
37.
38. **Arthur V. Miller**   ADDRESS **2711 Runway Road**
39.   **Burbank, CA 91503**
40.
41.
42. **Margaret C. Miller**
43.   Phone No.
44.
45. I will hand you the instruments, documents and money required to comply with these instructions, which you may use, and
46. pay such costs, taxes, assessments and demands to insure title as set forth herein when you can comply with these
47. instructions and deliver the net proceeds to the order of the undersigned.
48.
49. Pay Documentary Transfer Tax. If the documentary tax declaration has not been furnished in connection with the Deed from
50. **Grantor** to **Grantee** you are instructed to complete and sign the
51. declaration on such Deed as follows: Documentary Transfer Tax $ **47.30** **XX** Computed on full value of property
52. conveyed, or ☐ Computed on full value less liens and encumbrances remaining thereon at time of sale.
53. I agree to pay:
54.
55. **One-half of the escrow fee.**
56. **Premium for Owner's Policy of Title Insurance.**
57. **Prorations, as required.**
58. **Drawing fee for Grant Deed, Offset Statement and Rental Statement.**
59. **Documentary transfer tax, per above.**
60. **Demands, if any, for release of encumbrances and/or liens of record applicable to Seller,**
61. **together with charges and expenses in connection with releases thereof.**
62. **Recording fee for Power of Attorney, if applicable.**
63. **SELLER:**
64.
65.   ADDRESS **2551 Hollywood Way**
66. **Oliver Flatt Miller**
67.   **Burbank, CA 91502**
68. **Edith Vernon Miller, by**
69.
70. **Oliver Flatt Miller, her Attorney-in-Fact**
71.   Phone No.
72.   Page (3)   Escrow No. **3000**

E-324 (G.S.)

PAGE ONE . . . . **LINES 1 THROUGH 15**

This section is the explanation of consideration. You see that each separate amount is described completely. You have already seen the statement for the $2,000.00 deposit. The second statement, *"I hand you herewith a Cashier's check made payable to Safeco Title Insurance Company, in the amount of $950.00, which represents the total cash deposit in this escrow,"* shows very clearly the amount of cash with which you will have to deal.

The third statement, *"I will execute and deliver a new first deed of trust securing one promissory note in favor of Seller, as hereinafter described, in the amount of $40,000.00,"* indicates the amount and intended beneficiary of the new loan.

These are followed by, "TO EFFECT A TOTAL CONSIDERATION IN THE AMOUNT OF $42,950.00." This point could not be illustrated more obviously. Although you may be somewhat intimidated by having to write so much, you can see the advantage in having plenty of space in which to describe your transaction.

PAGE ONE. . . . . **LINES 40 THROUGH 60**

There are three items to which this escrow is subject: taxes, the standard CC&Rs, and the first deed of trust. These have already been discussed under the memo.

PAGE TWO . . . . **LINES 15 THROUGH 27**

These items deal with the **tenant** and **the terms of the lease or rental agreement**. The seller must provide escrow with a **Rental Statement**, noting the monthly rent and the date to which it is paid. He must reveal any amounts held as security deposits or portions of "first and last month's rent," or amounts owed by the tenant, so they can be credited to the buyer at the close of escrow (or debited, in the case of monies owed by the tenant).

The lease must be **assigned to the buyer**. For this, you ask the seller to supply escrow with an **Assignment of Unrecorded Lease** (if the lease has not been recorded in county records). If he does not have an Assignment recitation typed on the back of the lease or on a separate sheet, you may show him a selection of Assignment recitations that are considered acceptable by your company. **You should not improvise an assignment.** If the seller is unsure about the wording, have him ask his attorney to draft an Assignment. You may fill the Assignment out, preparing it for the signatures of the sellers. Following is one frequently used recitation for this document:

> *"KNOW ALL MEN BY THESE PRESENTS: That I/We, the undersigned, for value received, hereby sell, assign, transfer and set over unto (buyer) _____all of my/our right, title and interest as Lessor(s) in and to that*

*certain LEASE, dated_____by and between (seller)_____as Lessor(s)
and (tenant)_____as Lessor(s), covering the property described in said
LEASE AS: (Address)_____*

*IN WITNESS THEREOF: I/We have hereunto set my/our hand(s) this day
of (Date)_____.*

The names of buyer and seller should be accompanied by their full vesting. Ask the buyers how they want the vesting to read. The name of the tenant should have his status. In this case, his name would read **"A. Wrenter, an unmarried man."** This is not the same as a **single man**. It is used for any person who is not presently married.

The single status is reserved for persons who have never been married.

The tenant has certain rights also. Among them is the right to be informed that the property is changing hands, and the right to demonstrate his understanding of the leasehold agreement. The **Offset Statement**, signed by both the tenant (lessee) and the landlord (lessor), shows the status of payments and any agreements between them that may not appear in the original lease. Such agreements could be for reduction in monthly payments in exchange for garden work, prepaid rents, promises to pay for decorating done by the tenant and many others. It sets forth that the tenant does indeed occupy the property and reveals his understanding of the terms of the lease.

Offset Statements, like Assignments, should not be wholly drawn by escrow, but can be supplied by the seller or chosen by him.

You are not to ask about Offset Statements, as they are not required. After execution by both tenant and landlord, it is to be signed (formally approved) by the buyer and given to him at close of escrow. See the Rent Statement and the Offset Statement in **Figures 6-5** and **6-6**, respectively.

PAGE THREE. . . . . LINES 1 THROUGH 24

This area is the instruction to escrow as to which adjustment and proration's are to be made. It has, starting on line eight, a recitation about escrow's duties as agent: escrow's agency continues for as long as the escrow remains open, up to six months.

PAGE THREE . . . . LINES 25 THROUGH 43

Here, the escrow officer is to type the list of fees that the buyer agrees to pay. Under it, the escrow officer types the names of the buyers for their signatures.

Figure 6-5

RENT STATEMENT

SAFECO

ESCROW INSTRUCTIONS - RENT STATEMENT

SAFECO TITLE
INSURANCE COMPANY

Los Angeles .... Office

Date 1-16-52 .... Escrow No. 3000

I make the following statement of rentals of the property I am conveying so that said rents may be adjusted in escrow based on said statement:

HOUSE OR APT. NO.	NAME OF TENANT	RATE PER MONTH	DATE PAID TO	SECURITY MONEY
2553 Hollywood Way Burbank, CA 91502	A. WRENTER	$200.00	2-15-52	$200.00

Unless prior to date of recording documents in this escrow I have notified you in writing of some change in the above statement, you are to consider that I will collect all rents which fall due according to the foregoing statement prior to the close of escrow, and you will make all adjustments of rents accordingly. You will also pay my grantee the above security money (if any) charging my account therefor.

ss(Oliver Flatt Miller)
Seller Oliver Flatt Miller

ss(Edith Vernon Miller)
Seller Edith Vernon Miller
ss(Oliver Flatt Miller)

BY:

Oliver Flatt Miller, her Attorney-in-Fact

SAFECO Title Insurance Company

The above statement of rents is hereby approved and you will prorate accordingly.

Dated January 20, 2052

ss(Arthur V. Miller)
Buyer Arthur V. Miller

ss(Margaret C. Miller)
Buyer Margaret C. Miller

E-106 2-4-64

® SAFECO Insurance Company of America, registered trademark owner.

Figure 6-5

OFFSET STATEMENT

DATE OF UNRECORDED LEASE January 15, 2049

LESSOR: **OLIVER FLATT MILLER and EDITH VERNON MILLER**

LESSEE: **A. WRENTER**

PROPERTY ADDRESS: 2553 Hollywood Way, Burbank, CA 91502

UNDERSIGNED HEREBY CONFIRM THE FOLLOWING:

That Lessee has accepted possession and is in occupancy of the premises pursuant to the terms of the aforesaid unrecorded LEASE, which Lease is in full force and effect.

That the improvements and space required to be furnished according to the aforesaid Lease have been completed in all respects.

That the Lessor has fullfilled all of its duties of an inducement nature.

That the aforesaid unrecorded Lease has not been modified, altered or amended,

except   **no exceptions**

That there are no offsets or credits against rentals and no claims or defenses to endorcement of the lease, nor have rentals been prepaid, except as provided by the lease terms.

That Lessee has no notice of a prior assignment or pledge of rents or the lease.

The terms of the unrecorded Lease is **five (5)** years. The primary Lease term expires December 15, 2054.

The monthly rental is $ **200.00** and rent has been paid to February 15, 2052

Amount of Security deposit is $ **200.00**.

Buyer in Escrow Number **3000** with Safeco Title Insurance Company Escrow Department is relying materially upon the truth, correctness and accuracy of all statements made herein in agreeing to consummate said escrow.

EXECUTED THIS **16th** day of January, 2052

BY: LESSEE (TENANT)   BY: LESSOR (LANDLORD)

ss(A. Wrenter)   ss(Oliver Flatt Miller)

                                       ss(Edith Vernon Miller)

                                       BY: ss(Oliver Flatt Miller, her
                                           attorney-in-fact

APPROVED:

ss(Arthur V. Miller)   (BUYER IN ESCROW NO. 3000)

ss(Margaret C. Miller)

PAGE THREE . . . . **LINES 45 THROUGH 72**

This is the seller's section of instructions, setting out the fees he pays. Notice (Figure 6-4) the way in which the signature lines are typed for the seller, taking into account Ollie's attorney-in-fact status.

IV. Receiving Cash Into Escrow

Now you have all the information for proper drawing of escrow instructions. Whether you do them now or after the two Mr. Millers leave depends on whether they want to sign them promptly. It isn't necessary that they sign them at this point, of course. You can deal with the check for $950.00 right now. Fill out a receipt that includes this information:

1. Name of escrow holder and branch, escrow number and date of receipt.
2. Name of party who is to receive credit in escrow. If more than one, include all names.
3. Type of check: whether cashier's, personal, certified, etc.
4. Amount of check.
5. Bank, branch number and customer's account number.
6. Total deposit (most receipts allow for more than one check).
7. Your signature.

This receipt is in triplicate form, giving one copy for the buyer, one for your file, and one for the escrow bookkeeper who accepts the check from you.

Occasionally the deposit check will be made by a broker or someone other than the buyer. In such cases, consult your company manual or your superiors for directions as to whom the receipt should be made out.

V. Check List and Settlement Sheet

This company has a preprinted file folder with the check list on the front and the estimated settlement sheet inside. It provides spaces for recording the persons and companies to whom disbursements will later be made and a place to clip receipts and record them as they come in. The back has another check list, naming items that would presumably be dealt with somewhat later in escrow. We will show the settlement sheet section later (in Chapter 8) when you will be near to closing. For now, the escrow officer should be noting items and figures on both the check list and settlement sheet as they become known.

VI. Ending the Interview

You will need several documents form Ollie before you can proceed much further. Ask him to bring the **water stock certificate**, his **fire insurance policy**, the **power of attorney**, and the **lease** with its two companion documents, the **assignment of lease** and the **offset statement**. While the Messers Miller are still in your office, you ask them to fill out **statements of information**. If they agree to do so, it will speed the title search. After they fill out their statements of information, Ollie promises to return with the various papers within the week. Ask Ollie to leave his grant deed with you.

VII. Ordering the Preliminary Report of Title

Call the T.O. (*TITLE OFFICER—almost everyone in the escrow and title insurance industry refers to title officers as T.O.*), obtaining an order number and mentioning that you have the statements, which you'll send right over. Also send Ollie's grant deed for the T. O. to examine.

VIII. The Power of Attorney

Ollie brings back the papers for which you asked, and now you must get the power of attorney recorded. Simply call the T. O., who will take it from there. Note the recording fee ($3.00) in the settlement sheet as a debit to the seller.

IX. Assignment of Water Stock

A *MUTUAL WATER COMPANY is a company organized by or for water users in a given district with the object of securing an ample water supply at a reasonable rate. Stock is issued to users.* In many cases the water company considers the stock as appurtenant to the land, and automatically transferred to new owners. In other cases the stock is considered separate from the land, and if a separate transfer is not made of the stock, the new buyer will not receive water. Our property in question lies within the scope of Flowing Water Company, which considers the stock separate from the land. You must obtain a statement from Flowing Water, ascertaining the amount of all charges and whether there are any unpaid bills. When the property was divided, two shares were tentatively "assigned" to the new property, but since there was no new owner, transfer was not made. You must also check that the certificate numbers are correct—that the number identifies the property in question. It would be a major blunder if you transferred water stock to or from the wrong owner or property by accident.

Lenders will often require that the water stock be assigned to them as additional security for payment of the loan, holding the stock in their possession until the loan is paid in full.

This escrow holder has specific wording to be typed into instructions in the event of water stock transfers. Although less specific recitations are acceptable to many escrow holders, the absence of a prior contract makes the very detailed recitation most sensible. (You may feel it redundant to keep reminding you of the lack of a previous written contract, but whenever you have this type of transaction you must be extremely careful in writing complete instructions.) (See Figure 6-3, lines 29-37).

You will fax or e-mail a letter to the Flowing Water Company, informing them of the escrow, the certificate number with which you are dealing, and asking them to transfer ownership when you later send the stock certificate. See **Figure 6-7** for the letter to the water company. Note hat it has a statement typed at the bottom, and is filled out as if by the Secretary of the company. When you receive the statement back, write the amount of assessment ($42.00) into the settlement sheet but do not adjust yet. Write the charge of sending the statement ($5.00) as a debit to the buyer. You will send Ollie's stock certificate, with its endorsement section properly filled out, at the close of escrow. Then the water company will issue new shares to Arthur and send Ollie's certificate back to him.

Sometimes you will have to deal with public utility bills in escrow. Although the regular maintenance bills of a property are not the proper subject of an escrow and do not create a lien on property when unpaid, there are some areas of California where a government agency provides water and garbage collection. In these areas, you will have to prorate expenses and the collection of past due payments through escrow.

X. The Grant Deed

As soon as you hear from the title officer that the power of attorney is of record, you may prepare the grant deed. It is prepared like the grant deed for the first sample escrow, with one exception: this escrow holder recommends that when a power of attorney is exercised, *a* **special notarization is to be attached with staples**, covering the original acknowledgment recitation. First, complete the deed as usual, typing a space for Edith to sign. Then under it, type another signature line for Oliver, identifying him as her attorney-in-fact. When you type the acknowledgment section, use his name only. The deed will show notarization for **his** name.

Then, to show notarization for Edith's name, attached the special acknowledgment for Ollie's signature as **Edith Vernon Miller**. The completed deed is shown in **Figure 6.8 with the special acknowledgment attached**. The documentary transfer tax is computed at the full value ($42,950 ÷ $500 = 85.9, which, when rounded up to the next whole number, gives 86 base units x .55 = documentary transfer tax of $47.30) because there are no existing loans to be assumed by the buyer.

Figure 6-7

LETTER TO WATER COMPANY

SAFECO

HOME OFFICE   SAFECO TITLE INSURANCE COMPANY
13640 ROSCOE BOULEVARD
PANORAMA CITY, CALIFORNIA 91402

P.O. BOX 2233
LOS ANGELES, CALIFORNIA 90051

(213) 873-7788

Flowing Water Company
Post Office Box 2345
Blue Jay, California   92411

Date: ___January 18, 2052___

Escrow No. ___3000___

Gentlemen:

Our above numbered escrow involves the transfer of two (2)
shares of stock of your Company, represented by Certificate
No. X 274 issued in the names of Oliver Flatt Miller and
Edith Vernon Miller.

The escrow instructions provide that we obtain a statement
from you that there are no encumbrances of assessments
against said stock and that you will transfer ownership of
said stock when presented with the stock certificate endorsed in blank.

We therefore, request that you please complete the information
requested on the bottom of this letter and return one copy to
us in the enclosed envelope.

Very truly yours,

BY: _____
    Sr. Escrow Officer

Amount of unpaid assessment: $_____ period from _____ to_____
Amount of unpaid water bills: $_____ period from _____ to_____
Assessments in the amount of $ _42.00_ have been prepaid for the
period from _7-1-51_   to _7-1-52_ .
Our charges for transfer of said stock: $ _5.00_ .

Dated: February 10, 2052

FLOWING WATER COMPANY

BY: _____
        Secretary

169

Figure 6-8

GRANT DEED

RECORDING REQUESTED BY

AND WHEN RECORDED MAIL THIS DEED AND, UNLESS OTHER-
WISE SHOWN BELOW, MAIL TAX STATEMENTS TO:

NAME ⌐ Arthur V. Miller and
ADDRESS Margaret C. Miller
CITY &
STATE 2711 Runway Road
ZIP ⌐ Burbank, CA 91503

Title Order No.   Escrow No.   **3000**

_____ SPACE ABOVE THIS LINE FOR RECORDER'S USE _____

GRANT DEED

The undersigned declares that the documentary transfer tax is $ **47.30** .... and is
☒ computed on the full value of the interest or property conveyed, or is
☐ computed on the full value less the value of liens or encumbrances remaining thereon at the time of sale. The land,
tenements or realty is located in
☐ unincorporated area   ☒ city of ....**Los Angeles**.. and

FOR A VALUABLE CONSIDERATION, receipt of which is hereby acknowledged,

OLIVER FLATT MILLER and EDITH VERNON MILLER, husband and wife

hereby GRANT(S) to

ARTHUR V. MILLER and MARGARET C. MILLER, husband and wife as Joint Tenants

the following described real property in the   **city of Los Angeles**
county of **Los Angeles**   . state of California:

> PARCEL 1:   Lot "A" of Blackacre Tract, as per Map recorded in Book 100,
> Pages 1 and 2 of Maps, in the office of the County Recorder
> of said County,
>
> EXCEPT the South 140 feet thereof.
>
> PARCEL 2:   An easement for ingress and egress over the East 15 feet
> of the South 140 feet of Lot "A" of said Blackacre Tract.

Dated **December 1st, 2051**

     ss(Oliver Flatt Miller)
     Oliver Flatt Miller

     SS(Edith Vernon Miller)
     Edith Vernon Miller by
     ss(Oliver Flatt Miller)
     Oliver Flatt Miller, her Attorney-in-Fact

STATE OF CALIFORNIA
COUNTY OF. **Los Angeles**   } SS.
On **December 1st, 2051**   before me, the under-

STATE OF CALIFORNIA
COUNTY OF **Los Angeles**   } SS.
On **December 1st, 2051**   before me,
the undersigned, a Notary Public in and for said County and State,
personally appeared **Oliver Flatt Miller**
known to me to be the person__ whose name__ **is**
subscribed to the within instrument, as the Attorney__ in fact of
__**Edith Vernon Miller**__,
and acknowledged to me that__**he**__ subscribed the name__
of __**Edith Vernon Miller**__ thereto as
principal__ and __**his**__ own name__ as Attorney__ in fact.

Signature__ **ss(notary public)**

FOR NOTARY SEAL OR STAMP

SAFECO

SEAL

Name   Street Address   City & State

L-1 (G.S.) (Rev. 4-75) **8 pt.**

XI. CHAPTER SUMMARY

Sometimes in an escrow it will be necessary to authorize another person (called an ATTORNEY IN FACT) to act as agent for the parties. A properly drafted POWER OF ATTORNEY may be filled out by an attorney, or either party to the document. It is not to be filled out by the escrow. A NOTARY must witness the signature as it will be recorded.

When a seller carries back a loan on the property, the escrow will need to know the terms and conditions of the transaction. The parties should volunteer the terms they want to agree to. Some questions are appropriate as to whether there should be a REQUEST FOR NOTICE, PREPAYMENT PENALTY, LATE CHARGES, and when the payments are to begin. You will also need to ascertain who will be responsible for various fees, such as ESCROW, DRAWING DOCUMENTS, and RECORDING FEES. Parties will also agree as to the PRORATIONS which is a share of property taxes and other charges.

It is normal to receive money from the buyer in the form of a CASHIER'S CHECK, which is a promise by the bank to pay the money and is an instrument of unimpeachable integrity that insures the money is good. If there is a rental agreement involved, the seller will provide a RENTAL STATEMENT listing the date monthly rent and deposits that have been made by tenants.

If there are leases, the seller will provide escrow with an ASSIGNMENT that will transfer the rights to the buyer of the lease. Ask the buyers how they want the VESTING to read.

Sometimes there will be an OFFSET STATEMENT signed by the tenant and landlord that shows the status of payments and any agreements between them which may not appear in the original lease. When there is issued stock in a water company, the seller will execute an assignment in favor of the buyer.

XII. TERMS

Assignment: The transfer of the right, title, and interest in the property of one person (assignor) to another (assignee).

Cashier's Check: A check drawn by a bank upon itself and payable on demand. It is considered by escrow to be "good" funds in preference to a personal check.

Drawing Fee: Charges made in escrow for preparation of documents as the deed, deed of trust note, etc.

Escrow Fee: The fee normally split by buyer and seller for the services of the escrow company.

Late Charge: An added charge to a borrower for failure to pay a regular installment when it is due.

Notary: A public officer who functions as an official witness to attest and certify documents by their official seal and signature.

Offset Statement: May be a statement of an owner or lienholder to the buyer as to the balance of existing loans. Or, a statement by a tenant to a buyer setting forth the terms of the rental agreement including the rent and amount of security deposit.

Power of Attorney/Attorney in Fact: Written authorization giving a person (attorney in fact) authority to act as the agent to the extent indicated in the instrument.

Prepayment Penalty: The amount set by a lender as a penalty for paying off a debt before it matures.

Prorations: Calculations in escrow that charge buyer and sellers their share of taxes, interest, rents, etc.

Recording Fee: Required by the County Recorder for recording deeds, etc. The fee will vary by county.

Rental Agreement: Agreement between landlord and tenant specifying the terms and conditions of the residential agreement.

Rent Statement: Prepared by the owner that shows the status of tenants and the amounts of rent paid to certain dates.

Request for Notice: When recorded, a trustee in a foreclosure is required to notify all persons requesting notice if a notice of default is recorded on a specific property.

Vesting: Refers to the manner of holding title selected by the buyers in escrow. Escrow should not recommend how to hold title.

Water Stock Certificate: Evidence of water stock issued to an owner of real property that entitles them to use of water. It is considered to be appurtenant to the property therefore transfers with the land.

XIII. CHAPTER QUIZ

1. In order to start an escrow there must be:

    a. a deposit receipt.
    b. oral agreement.
    c. either a or b.
    d. neither a nor b.

2. Private water companies divide their ownership:

    a. through shares of stock.
    b. there are NO agreements.
    c. both a and b.
    d. neither a nor b.

3. If a person is ill in the hospital, someone may act in their behalf if they:

    a. are an employee.
    b. have power of attorney.
    c. both a and b.
    d. neither a nor b.

4. If tenants occupy a property, what escrow document shows their interest in the property?

    a. Offset statement
    b. Income statement
    c. Both a and b
    d. Neither a nor b

5. A power of attorney form may NOT be filled out by an:

    a. escrow officer.
    b. attorney.
    c. both a and b.
    d. neither a nor b.

6. The escrow officer may endorse the back of the note to indicate:

    a. date interest is to start.
    b. date of first payment.
    c. maturity date.
    d. all of the above.

7. If a buyer and seller do NOT mention how fees are to be paid, you should:

    a. mention the local custom.
    b. let the buyer decide.
    c. let the seller decide.
    d. none of the above.

8. The seller must provide escrow with a rental statement telling:

    a. monthly rent.
    b. date rent is due.
    c. security and 1st and last.
    d. all of the above.

9. A recitation is:

    a. how an item is to be worded.
    b. dictated by state law.
    c. dictated by federal law.
    d. none of the above.

10. Sometimes an escrow officer may have to pro-rate:

    a. water bills.
    b. garbage collection bills.
    c. both a and b.
    d. neither a nor b.

ANSWERS: *1. c; 2. a; 3. b; 4. a; 5. a; 6. d; 7. a; 8. d; 9. a; 10. c*

Sample Two,
Part Two

I. Preliminary Report of Title

The prelim arrives and states that Safeco is prepared to issue a policy of title insurance with certain exceptions, which it will list in Schedule B. The report contains five pages, including the cover notice, which are stapled together in a light "legal-type" cover. We will show each page, which you must read carefully. **Figure 7-1** shows the cover notice, giving the escrow and title order number and the date. At the bottom, it clearly states that it is a report as to the condition of title at present, and no liability is assumed hereby. The last sentence reads, *"If it is desired that liability be assumed prior to issuance of a policy of title insurance, a Binder or Commitment should be requested."* Let's examine this more closely.

A. BINDERS

A **BINDER** *(also called an **INTERIM BINDER**) is a written agreement by the title insurance company to issue a policy, but at a later date.* Regular policies are issued after the escrow has closed, and they show the new vestees and any new encumbrances on the property. Sometimes the new vestee's name will not be known, or a new encumbrance will not be recorded at the time of closing escrow. While the coverage is equal to the coverage promised in the actual policy to follow, the binder is not a policy of title insurance. A binder always shows the exact date within which the policy must be issued, and always states that, if new exceptions appear after the binder is issued and before the

CHAPTER OUTLINE

Figure 7-1

COVER PAGE, PRELIMINARY REPORT

PRELIMINARY REPORT

 **SAFECO**

P-118

SAFECO TITLE INSURANCE COMPANY

13640 ROSCOE BOULEVARD
P. O. BOX 7741
PANORAMA CITY, CALIFORNIA 91409
(213) 781-3650

SAFECO TITLE INSURANCE CO.
13640 ROSCOE BOULEVARD
PANORAMA CITY, CALIFORNIA 91409

Attention: ALMA CONOVER

Your No: 3000
Our No: 7812345

Dated as of   December 14, 2051   at 7:30 a.m.

In response to the above referenced application for a policy of title
insurance,

SAFECO TITLE INSURANCE COMPANY

hereby reports that it is prepared to issue, as of the date hereof, a
California Land Title Association Standard Coverage Form Policy of
Title Insurance describing the land and the estate or interest therein
hereinafter set forth in Schedule A, insuring against loss which may be
sustained by reason of any defect, lien or encumbrance not shown or
referred to as an Exception in Schedule B or not excluded from coverage
pursuant to the printed Schedules, Conditions and Stipulations of said
policy form.

This report (and any supplements or amendments thereto) is issued
solely for the purpose of facilitating the issuance of a policy of
title insurance and no liability is assumed hereby. If it is desired
that liability be assumed prior to the issuance of a policy of title
insurance, a Binder or Commitment should be requested.

Title Officer J. BROWN

actual policy is issued, they will be added (as exceptions to title) to the policy. Most binders have a time limit of 24 months, but some may be extended from one more year (36 months).

The cost of a binder policy is ten percent of the basic title insurance rate.

One type of binder is often used when a buyer intends to resell the property quickly. The buyer obtains a commitment from the title insurance company to insure the title when the property is subsequently sold.

Another type of binder is used when a transfer of title is intended at a later date and the owner wants to deal specifically with mechanic's liens. This binder may not be extended.

Binders are ordered the same way policies of title insurance are ordered, but the escrow officer must make it very clear that it is a binder being requested.

Sometimes a title insurance company will receive a request for a title search from persons who are not involved in escrows. They have reason to inquire into the condition of title, but title insurance companies are somewhat reluctant to issue preliminary reports of title unless a title insurance policy is sought. Such interested parties can be attorneys, lenders, land developers, governmental bodies, engineers, real estate brokers, even the county recorder. With a few exceptions, any customer who has reason to require title indemnification can get a title report, but it will be limited to matters pertinent to that customer. Although they may not obtain a policy of title insurance as new owners and lenders of record do, they can obtain a **Guarantee of Title**, which has stated liabilities (and fees which vary accordingly).

Each title company has established rules for how much information is granted to different kinds of special request customers.

The **second page** of the prelim, called **Schedule A**, **(Figure 7-2)** is reserved for identification of the recorded owner and the property in question. You have already seen the legal description and the sellers' vesting in their grant deed and have written it into instructions. Fortunately, your examination of this page shows no difference.

The **third page, Schedule B, (Figure 7-3)** shows the encumbrances of record. Item 1, property taxes, shows that Ollie did pay the first half year. Notice (b), Amounts that may hereafter be assessed. This recitation is the result of Proposition 13, and is an attempt to deal with the chaos in reporting property taxes during the year in which Prop. 13 was enacted. It will be dropped when the counties have completed their adjustments in assessments, and tax rolls are once again regularized.

Figure 7-2

SCHEDULE A, PRELIMINARY REPORT

Order No. 7812345

SCHEDULE A

The estate or interest in the land described or referred to in this schedule covered by this report is:

A fee, as to Parcel 1
An easement as more fully described below, as to Parcel 2

Title to said estate or interest at the date hereof is vested in:

OLIVER FLATT MILLER AND EDITH VERNON MILLER,
husband and wife

The land referred to in this report is situated in the State of California, County of Los Angeles, and is described as follows:

PARCEL 1:

Lot "A" of Blackacre Tract, as per map recorded in Book 100, Pages 1 and 2 of Maps, in the office of the County Recorder of said County.

EXCEPT therefrom the South 140 feet thereof.

PARCEL 2:

An easement for ingress and egress over the East 15 feet of the South 140 feet of Lot "A" of Blackacre Tract, as per map recorded in Book 100, Pages 1 and 2 of Maps, in the office of the County Recorder of said County.

Figure 7-3

SCHEDULE B, PRELIMINARY REPORT

Order No. 7812345

SCHEDULE B

At the date hereof Exceptions to coverage in addition to the printed exceptions and exclusions contained in said policy form would be as follows:

1. General and special County and City taxes for the fiscal year 2051-2052 including personal property taxes, if any:

a. Amounts currently assessed:

Total   : $500.00
First Installment   :   250.00   PAID
Personal Property Taxes   :   None
Second Installment   :   250.00

b. Amounts that may hereafter be assessed:

(1) Upon a determination that property on the 2048 tax bill was not assessed to the 2048-2049 tax levels.

(2) Upon a determination that a change of ownership, purchase, or new construction has occurred after March 1, 2048 and prior to March 1, 2051.

(3) Upon a final judgment that Article XIIIA of the California Constitution (PROPOSITION 13 approved at the primary election held June 6, 1978) has been improperly applied.

2. Covenants, conditions and restrictions, (deleting therefrom any restrictions based on race, color, or creed), as provided in a Declaration recorded January 10, 2031 as Instrument No. 1024.

Said covenants, conditions and restrictions provide that a violation thereof shall not defeat nor render invalid the lien of any mortgage or deed of trust made in good faith and for value.

3. A judgment for $400.00 against Oliver Flatt Miller, in favor of Jim's Saloon entered October 1, 2042 in Municipal Court, Los Angeles Judicial District, Case No. 45623, an abstract of which judgment was recorded October 5, 2042 as Instrument No. 2143.

4. A lease, affecting the premises herein stated, executed by and between the parties named herein, for the term and upon the terms and provisions therein provided,

Item 3 reveals a nasty little surprise—a judgment against Ollie that created an involuntary lien against the property. When checking, make a note of this, and go on to the rest of the prelim. You will want to take steps to get this cloud on the title cleared away as soon as possible.

The **fourth page**, page 2 of **Schedule B**, (**Figure 7-4**) has two notes for informational purposes. It states that the legal description for the property being sold has not yet been recorded, since this is the first time it will appear on a grant deed. Hereafter it will be the description of record and the prelim note will not appear in subsequent sales or transfers.

The second prelim note sets forth what information the title plant has about the recent division of Ollie's lot. Although Ollie has said that the subdivision is taken care of and recorded, the title plant's computers do not show it. You must ask Ollie to bring his records in for examination by the title officer, who will then inquire further. Perhaps the recording was made in another county, or mistakenly made under the attorney's name (if the attorney failed to properly specify some of the information). If no record can be found after further search, one of the documents named in the prelim note will need to be recorded before the close of escrow. This is another matter which should be discussed with Ollie very soon.

The **last page** of the prelim (**Figure 7-5**) deals with the request for an **ALTA Lender's Policy** for Ollie. Its note at the bottom states that a **CLTA Indorsement Form 100** will be issued with the ALTA policy.

B. EASEMENTS

This indorsement, one of many possible indorsements, is usually attached to lender's policies, and modifies the coverage of the policy in the areas of CC&Rs, encroachments, and mineral rights. These are usually covered under the Owner's policy.

Many prelims come with a copy of the *PLAT MAP, showing the location of the property in relation to neighboring properties.* We do not show the plat map, but **Figure 7-6** is the plan of Ollie's lot, showing the lot being deeded to Arthur and how the easement affects Ollie's lot.

This easement is being "created" just as the new lot is being "created" by recording it at the end of escrow. Until now, all the property has been in Ollie's name. It is the deeding of part of it to another that will officially create the dominant and servient tenements.

When conveying an easement, as with other interests in real property, a clear and precise description is essential.

Figure 7-4

SCHEDULE B, continued

7812345
page 2

NOTE NO. 1:   The legal discription shown as Parcels 1 and 2 has not been created of record and is shown for conveyancing purposes only.

NOTE NO. 2:   Information in possession of this Company indicates that a division of land, as defined in Government Code Section 66424, is contemplated in the current transaction involving the land described in this report.   Such contemplated division of land would appear to fall within the purview of the Subdivision Map Act (commencing with Government Code Section 66410) and as a prerequisite to the issuance of final title evidence at least one of the following requirements must be accomplished to this Company's satisfaction:

(1)   That a Final (Tract) Map has been recorded in compliance with the Subdivision Map Act and related ordinances;

(2)   That a Parcel Map has been recorded in compliance with the Subdivision Map Act and related ordinances; or

(3)   That a Certificate of Compliance as provided for in the Subdivision Map Act has been recorded; or that other satisfactory evidence indicating compliance or non-violation be furnished.

da

Figure 7-5

PRELIMINARY REPORT, last page

SAFECO TITLE INSURANCE COMPANY, 13640 ROSCOE BOULEVARD, P. O. BOX 7741
PANORAMA CITY, CALIFORNIA 91409
(213) 781-3650

LENDERS SUPPLEMENTAL REPORT

SAFECO TITLE INSURANCE CO.
13640 ROSCOE BOULEVARD
PANORAMA CITY, CALIFORNIA 91409

Attention: ALMA CONOVER

Your No: 3000
Our No: 7812345

Gentlemen:

The above numbered report (including any supplements or amendments thereto) is hereby modified and/or supplemented in order to reflect the following additional items relating to the issuance of an American Land Title Association Loan Form Policy of Title Insurance.

Dated as of   December 14, 2051   at 7:30 a.m.

Title Officer J. BROWN

NOTE NO. 1:   None of the items shown herein will cause the company to decline to attach CLTA Indorsement Form 100 to an ALTA Loan Policy when issued.

Said land is also known as 2551 Hollywood Way, Burbank, CA 91502

Figure 7-6

LOT PLAN

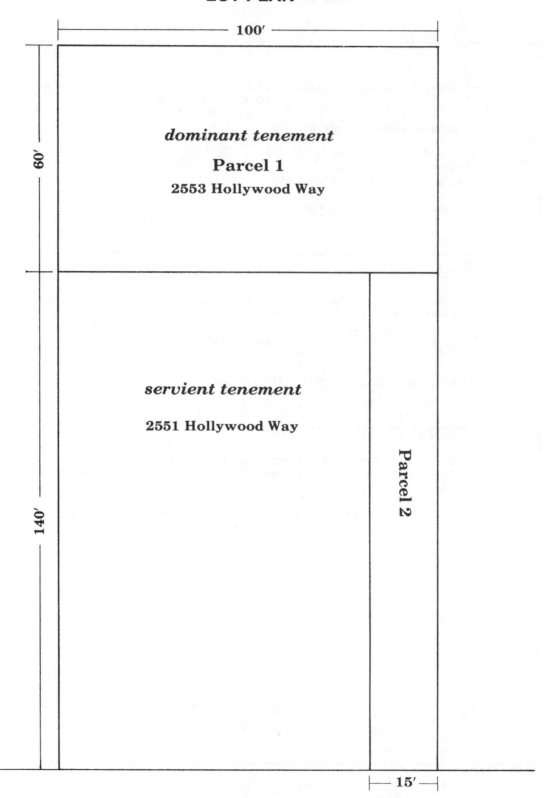

There are many kinds of easements. The most common kind is the *PUBLIC UTILITY EASEMENT (EASEMENT IN GROSS)*, *which gives utilities the right to construct and maintain pipes and power lines through property*. Owners also grant easements that allow others to take water, wood, minerals, to conduct business or sports activities, to receive light, air or heat from the owner's land, or to use a wall as a common party wall. *In this case, the easement is created specifically to benefit the owner of adjacent land. It is an EASEMENT APPURTENANT*.

In easements appurtenant, there is always a *DOMINANT TENEMENT*, *the land, the owner of which gains the benefit*, and a *SERVIENT TENEMENT*, *the land, the owner of which grants the easement to the dominant tenement*. An easement appurtenant becomes a part of the dominant tenement's land and cannot be transferred separately from it.

To pass with the title, an easement in gross must be described in the deed.

II. Clearing Clouds on the Title

Call Ollie to discuss the two items you need to clear up. Whenever you see that an *ABSTRACT OF JUDGMENT* (*an order from a judge to place a lien on a property*) has been filed, use the utmost tact in mentioning it to your principal. It is possibly an error. First, find out, gently, if it is true that a judgment affects him. Ollie says yes and that he was ashamed to mention it because it was the result of a rather boisterous St. Patrick's Day celebration at the local pub, and some new decoration was necessary. He had hoped that, since it was quite long ago, it would have been erased from the records. He paid it all off, and has a **satisfaction of judgment** from the judge to prove it.

You tell him it's no problem—it was just under the ten-year statute of limitations for judgment liens. If he brings his satisfaction of judgment in, you will have it recorded right away, and everyone can forget about it.

If you have an escrow where a principal has not paid the judgment, these are the steps you should take it get it cleared from title:

1. Find out if the principal would like it paid through escrow. If not, he should pay the lien and bring a satisfaction of judgment to escrow.
2. If he or she wants to handle it through escrow, find out the name of the creditor (and that person's lawyer, if the creditor is represented by a lawyer, as is usually the case).
3. Write to the lawyer, identifying your escrow by number and name of the principals against whom the judgment is charged. Write that you have instructions calling for payment of the lien and ask that he or she send a satisfaction of judgment and a demand for its use.

4. You should receive the satisfaction of judgment and instructions to record it as soon as you have the payment amount held for the creditor.

5. Prepare an amendment to instructions, directing you to pay the judgment. State the amount and interest rate (if the creditor wants interest), the creditor's name and the case number. Have the seller(s) sign it.

6. Have the title officer examine the satisfaction of judgment, to be sure it is correct and sufficient to remove the cloud from the title.

7. Record the payment and the recording fee in the settlement sheet as a debit to the seller.

Sometimes it is possible to get a creditor to agree to release a particular piece of property from the judgment. This is frequently done if the lien is applied to several parcels of property and the creditor wants to pay off only part of the lien. It can only be done, of course, with an agreement between the creditor and the principal, and the instrument used is called a partial release of judgment.

Both satisfactions of judgments and partial releases of judgments should be recorded in the county where the property lies before closing your escrow. They, like all recordable instruments, must be acknowledged.

III. The Policy of Title Insurance

As an escrow officer, you will probably not see the actual policy or policies of title insurance, since they will most often be sent directly to the principals who requested them, sometime after the close of escrow. However, for your information, we will show the two policies to be issued in this escrow.

A policy of title insurance should be carefully compared with the escrow instructions to be certain the condition of title stated is in accordance with the instructions.

A. CLTA OWNER'S STANDARD COVERAGE POLICY

The cover, **Figure 7-7**, states that the company will pay losses, damages, costs, attorney's fees, and expenses up to the amount of coverage for items 1 through 4. Items listed as 5 through 7 also cover possible losses, damages, costs, attorney's fees, and expenses for lenders, since the CLTA Owner's policy is often issued as a Joint Protection Policy, covering owners and lenders immediately.

Schedule A (**Figure 7-8**) shows the new titleholders and their interest (estate) in the land as a fee for Parcel 1 and an easement for Parcel 2. The complete legal description is not reproduced since it is exactly the same as Figure 7-2.

Figure 7-7

CLTA POLICY, COVER PAGE

CLTA - 1973

SAFECO

STANDARD COVERAGE

POLICY OF TITLE INSURANCE

SAFECO TITLE INSURANCE COMPANY

SUBJECT TO SCHEDULE B AND THE CONDITIONS AND STIPULATIONS HEREOF, SAFECO TITLE INSURANCE COMPANY, a California corporation, herein called the Company, insures the insured, as of Date of Policy shown in Schedule A, against loss or damage, not exceeding the amount of insurance stated in Schedule A, and costs, attorneys' fees and expenses which the Company may become obligated to pay hereunder, sustained or incurred by said insured by reason of:

1. Title to the estate or interest described in Schedule A being vested other than as stated therein;

2. Any defect in or lien or encumbrance on such title;

3. Unmarketability of such title; or

4. Any lack of the ordinary right of an abutting owner for access to at least one physically open street or highway if the land, in fact, abuts upon one or more such streets or highways;

and in addition, as to an insured lender only:

5. Invalidity of the lien of the insured mortgage upon said estate or interest except to the extent that such invalidity, or claim thereof, arises out of the transaction evidenced by the insured mortgage and is based upon

   a. usury, or

   b. any consumer credit protection or truth in lending law;

6. Priority of any lien or encumbrance over the lien of the insured mortgage, said mortgage being shown in Schedule B in the order of its priority; or

7. Invalidity of any assignment of the insured mortgage, provided such assignment is shown in Schedule B.

Secretary

President

P-218 (Area 1) (Rev. 5-78)

Figure 7-8

SCHEDULE A, CLTA POLICY

```
                          SCHEDULE A

                                        Policy No. 7812345
                                        Charge    $232.00
   Amount of Insurance:  $42,950.00
   Date of Policy: January 1, 2052        at 8.00 a.m.


   1.   Name of Insured:


        ARTHUR V. MILLER AND MARGARET C. MILLER

   2.   The estate or interest in the land described herein and which is
        covered by this policy is:

        A fee, as to Parcel 1
        An easement as more fully described below, as to Parcel 2


   3.   The estate or interest referred to herein is at Date of Policy
        vested in:


        ARTHUR V. MILLER AND MARGARET C. MILLER,
        husband and wife as joint tenants


   4.   The land referred to in this policy is situated in the State of
        California, County of Los Angeles, and described as follows:


             SEE EXHIBIT I ATTACHED HERETO AND MADE A PART HEREOF
```

Schedule B (**Figure 7-9**) shows those things against which the policy does not protect. Its first part is preprinted and is the same for all policies of this type. The second part is for things particular to this property: taxes, CC&Rs, and the new deed of trust and note in favor of Ollie and Edith.

The parties to escrow make the determination of what type of title insurance will be ordered, not the escrow holder.

The policy also contains general stipulations and conditions, which are reproduced for you in **Figures 7-10** and **7-11**.

B. ALTA LOAN POLICY WITH ALTA INDORSEMENT, FORM 1

This policy, for which Ollie pays a slightly higher premium than if he had chosen to be named in a CLTA Joint Protection policy, is designed to protect lenders (usually institutional Lenders) against defects in title that might render the land which is offered as collateral less valuable than the loan that is secures. (It shows again how all business procedure is based ultimately upon common sense: The solidity of the entire transaction is greatly weakened if a property cannot be sold to satisfy a defaulted loan because of defects in title).

The ALTA policy follows the same general plan as the CLTA policy, with Schedule A naming the insured party and giving a complete legal description, Schedule B showing encumbrances against the property (ALTA Schedule B does not have a preprinted "part 1" page), etc. We have reproduced all the parts of the ALTA policy, that differ from the CLTA policy, in **Figures 7-12 through 7-16**.

An Owner's policy of title insurance remains in effect until the property is conveyed to another, even if the owner dies.

In that case, the persons named under a will to inherit the property are protected under the policy. The same is true if the policyholder is a corporation—it covers the successors of the corporation whether by merger or dissolution. Lender's policies remain in effect until the loan is paid off and a reconveyance issued, even if the loan is assigned to new beneficiaries or trustees.

An Owner's policy of title insurance remains in effect until the property is conveyed to another, even if the owner dies.

California law requires that all title companies publish schedules of fees for commonly issued types of policies, and that the actual fees conform to the published fee schedules.

191

Figure 7-9

SCHEDULE B, CLTA POLICY

P-218-B (G.S.) Rev. 8-73
California Land Title Association
Standard Coverage Policy—1973

SCHEDULE B

This policy does not insure against loss or damage, nor against costs, attorneys' fees or expenses, any or all of which arise by reason of the following:

PART I

1. Taxes or assessments which are not shown as existing liens by the records of any taxing authority that levies taxes or assessments on real property or by the public records.

   Proceedings by a public agency which may result in taxes or assessments, or notices of such proceedings, whether or not shown by the records of such agency or by the public records.

2. Any facts, rights, interests or claims which are not shown by the public records but which could be ascertained by an inspection of the land or by making inquiry of persons in possession thereof.

3. Easements, liens or encumbrances, or claims thereof, which are not shown by the public records.

4. Discrepancies, conflicts in boundary lines, shortage in area, encroachments, or any other facts which a correct survey would disclose, and which are not shown by the public records.

5. (a) Unpatented mining claims; (b) reservations or exceptions in patents or in Acts authorizing the issuance thereof; (c) water rights, claims or title to water.

6. Any right, title, interest, estate or easement in land beyond the lines of the area specifically described or referred to in Schedule A, or in abutting streets, roads, avenues, alleys, lanes, ways or waterways, but nothing in this paragraph shall modify or limit the extent to which the ordinary right of an abutting owner for access to a physically open street or highway is insured by this policy.

7. Any law, ordinance or governmental regulation (including but not limited to building and zoning ordinances) restricting or regulating or prohibiting the occupancy, use or enjoyment of the land, or regulating the character, dimensions or location of any improvement now or hereafter erected on the land, or prohibiting a separation in ownership or a reduction in the dimensions or area of the land, or the effect of any violation of any such law, ordinance or governmental regulation.

8. Rights of eminent domain or governmental rights of police power unless notice of the exercise of such rights appears in the public records.

9. Defects, liens, encumbrances, adverse claims, or other matters (a) created, suffered, assumed or agreed to by the insured claimant; (b) not shown by the public records and not otherwise excluded from coverage but known to the insured claimant either at Date of Policy or at the date such claimant acquired an estate or interest insured by this policy or acquired the insured mortgage and not disclosed in writing by the insured claimant to the Company prior to the date such insured claimant became an insured hereunder; (c) resulting in no loss or damage to the insured claimant; (d) attaching or created subsequent to Date of Policy; or (e) resulting in loss or damage which would not have been sustained if the insured claimant had been a purchaser or encumbrancer for value without knowledge.

(Schedule B continued on next page of this Policy)

Figure 7-10

CLTA CONDITIONS AND STIPULATIONS, part 1

CONDITIONS AND STIPULATIONS

1. Definition of Terms

The following terms when used in this policy mean:

(a) "insured": the insured named in Schedule A, and, subject to any rights or defense the Company may have had against the named insured, those who succeed to the interest of such insured by operation of law as distinguished from purchase including, but not limited to, heirs, distributees, devisees, survivors, personal representatives, next of kin, or corporate or fiduciary successor. The term "insured" also includes (i) the owner of the indebtedness secured by the insured mortgage and each successor in ownership of such indebtedness (reserving, however, all rights and defenses as to any such successor who acquires the indebtedness by operation of law as described in the first sentence of this subparagraph (a) that the Company would have had against the successor's transferor), and further includes (ii) any governmental agency or instrumentality which is an insurer or guarantor under an insurance contract or guaranty insuring or guaranteeing said indebtedness, or any part thereof, whether named as an insured herein or not, and (iii) the parties designated in paragraph 2(a) of these Conditions and Stipulations.

(b) "insured claimant": an insured claiming loss or damage hereunder.

(c) "insured lender": the owner of an insured mortgage.

(d) "insured mortgage": a mortgage shown in Schedule B, the owner of which is named as an insured in Schedule A.

(e) "knowledge": actual knowledge, not constructive knowledge or notice which may be imputed to an insured by reason of any public records.

(f) "land": the land described, specifically or by reference in Schedule A, and improvements affixed thereto which by law constitute real property; provided, however, the term "land" does not include any area excluded by Paragraph No. 6 of Part I of Schedule B of this Policy.

(g) "mortgage": mortgage, deed of trust, trust deed, or other security instrument.

(h) "public records": those records which by law impart constructive notice of matters relating to the land.

2. (a) Continuation of Insurance after Acquisition of Title by Insured Lender

If this policy insures the owner of the indebtedness secured by the insured mortgage, this policy shall continue in force as of Date of Policy in favor of such insured who acquires all or any part of the estate or interest in the land described in Schedule A by foreclosure, trustee's sale, conveyance in lieu of foreclosure, or other legal manner which discharges the lien of the insured mortgage, and if such insured is a corporation, its transferee of the estate or interest so acquired, provided the transferee is the parent or wholly owned subsidiary of such insured; and in favor of any governmental agency or instrumentality which acquires all or any part of the estate or interest pursuant to a contract of insurance or guaranty insuring or guaranteeing the indebtedness secured by the insured mortgage. After any such acquisition the amount of insurance hereunder, exclusive of costs, attorneys' fees and expenses which the Company may be obligated to pay, shall not exceed the least of:

(i) the amount of insurance stated in Schedule A:

(ii) the amount of the unpaid principal of the indebtedness plus interest thereon, as determined under paragraph 6(a) (iii) hereof, expenses of foreclosure and amounts advanced to protect the lien of the insured mortgage and secured by said insured mortgage at the time of acquisition of such estate or interest in the land; or

(iii) the amount paid by any governmental agency or instrumentality, if such agency or instrumentality is the insured claimant in acquisition of such estate or interest in satisfaction of its insurance contract or guaranty.

(b) **Continuation of Insurance after Conveyance of Title**

The coverage of this policy shall continue in force as of Date of Policy, in favor of an insured so long as such insured retains an estate or interest in the land, or owns an indebtedness secured by a purchase money mortgage given by a purchaser from such insured, or so long as such insured shall have liability by reason of covenants of warranty made by such insured in any transfer or conveyance of such estate or interest; provided, however, this policy shall not continue in force in favor of any purchaser from such insured of either said estate or interest or the indebtedness secured by a purchase money mortgage given to such insured.

3. Defense and Prosecution of Actions - Notice of Claim to be Given by an Insured Claimant

(a) The Company at its own cost and without undue delay, shall provide for the defense of an insured in litigation to the extent that such litigation involves an alleged defect, lien, encumbrance or other matter insured against by this policy.

(b) The insured shall notify the Company promptly in writing (i) in case of any litigation as set forth in (a) above, (ii) in case knowledge shall come to an insured hereunder of any claim of title or interest which is adverse to the title to the estate or interest or the lien of the insured mortgage, as insured, and which might cause loss or damage for which the Company may be liable by virtue of this policy, or (iii) if title to the estate or interest or the lien of the insured mortgage, as insured, is rejected as unmarketable. If such prompt notice shall not be given to the Company, then as to such insured all liability of the Company shall cease and terminate in regard to the matter or matters for which prompt notice is required; provided, however, that failure to notify shall in no case prejudice the rights of any such insured under this policy unless the Company shall be prejudiced by such failure and then only to the extent of such prejudice.

(c) The Company shall have the right at its own cost to institute and without undue delay prosecute any action or proceeding or to do any other act which in its opinion may be necessary or desirable to establish the title to the estate or interest or the lien of the insured mortgage, as insured; and the Company may take any appropriate action, whether or it shall be liable under the terms of this policy, and shall not thereby concede liability or waive any provision of this policy.

(d) Whenever the Company shall have brought any action or interposed a defense as required or permitted by the provisions of this policy, the Company may pursue any such litigation to final determination by a court of competent jurisdiction and expressly reserves the right, in its sole discretion, to appeal from any adverse judgment or order.

(e) In all cases where this policy permits or requires the Company to prosecute or provide for the defense of any action or proceeding, the insured hereunder shall secure to the Company the right to so prosecute or provide defense in such action or proceeding, and all appeals therein, and permit the Company to use, at its own option, the name of such insured for such purpose. Whenever requested by the Company, such insured shall give the Company, at the Company's expense, all reasonable aid (1) in any such action or proceeding in effecting settlement, securing evidence, or prosecuting or defending such action or proceeding, and (2) in any other act which in the opinion of the Company may be necessary or desirable to establish the title to the estate or interest or the lien of the insured mortgage, as insured, including but not limited to executing corrective or other documents.

4. Proof of Loss or Damage - Limitation of Action

In addition to the notices required under Paragraph 3(b) of these Conditions and Stipulations, a proof of loss or damage, signed and sworn to by the insured claimant shall be furnished to the Company within 90 days after the insured claimant shall ascertain or determine the fact giving rise to such loss or damage. Such proof of loss or damage shall describe the defect in, or lien or encumbrances on the title, or other matter insured against by this policy which constitutes the basis of loss or damage and, when appropriate, state the basis of calculating the amount of such loss or damage.

Should such proof of loss or damage fail to state fact sufficient to enable the Company to determine its liability hereunder, insured claimant, at the written request of the Company, shall furnish such additional information as may reasonably be necessary to make such determination.

No right of action shall accrue to insured claimant until 30 days after such proof of loss or damage shall have been furnished.

Failure to furnish such proof of loss or damage shall terminate any liability of the Company under this policy as to such loss or damage.

(Conditions and Stipulations Continued and Concluded on Last Page of this Policy)

Figure 7-11

CLTA CONDITIONS AND STIPULATIONS, part 2

CONDITIONS AND STIPULATIONS (Continued and Concluded From Reverse Side of Policy Face)

5. Options to Pay or Otherwise Settle Claims and Options to Purchase Indebtedness

The Company shall have the option to pay or otherwise settle for or in the name of an insured claimant any claim insured against, or to terminate all liability and obligations of the Company hereunder by paying or tendering payment of the amount of insurance under this policy together with any costs, attorneys' fees and expenses incurred up to the time of such payment or tender of payment by the insured claimant and authorized by the Company. In case loss or damage is claimed under this policy by the owner of the indebtedness secured by the insured mortgage, the Company shall have the further option to purchase such indebtedness for the amount owing thereon together with all costs, attorneys' fees and expenses which the Company is obligated hereunder to pay. If the Company offers to purchase said indebtedness as herein provided, the owner of such indebtedness shall transfer and assign said indebtedness and the mortgage and any collateral securing the same to the Company upon payment therefor as herein provided. Upon such offer being made by the Company, all liability and obligations of the Company hereunder to the owner of the indebtedness secured by said insured mortgage, other than the obligation to purchase said indebtedness pursuant to this paragraph, are terminated.

6. Determination and Payment of Loss

(a) The liability of the Company under this policy shall in no case exceed the least of:

(i) the actual loss of the insured claimant; or

(ii) the amount of insurance stated in Schedule A, or, if applicable, the amount of insurance as defined in paragraph 2(a) hereof; or

(iii) If this policy insures the owner of the indebtedness secured by the insured mortgage, and provided said owner is the insured claimant, the amount of the unpaid principal of said indebtedness, plus interest thereon, provided such amount shall not include any additional principal indebtedness created subsequent to Date of Policy, except as to amounts advanced to protect the lien of the insured mortgage and secured thereby.

(b) The Company will pay, in addition to any loss insured against by this policy, all costs imposed upon an insured in litigation carried on by the Company for such insured, and all costs, attorneys' fees and expenses in litigation carried on by such insured with the written authorization of the Company.

(c) When the amount of loss or damage has been definitely fixed in accordance with the conditions of this policy, the loss or damage shall be payable within 30 days thereafter.

7. Limitation of Liability

No claim shall arise or be maintainable under this policy (a) if the Company, after having received notice of an alleged defect, lien or encumbrance insured against hereunder, by litigation or otherwise, removes such defect, lien or encumbrance or establishes the title, or the lien of the insured mortgage, as insured, within a reasonable time after receipt of such notice; (b) in the event of litigation until there has been a final determination by a court of competent jurisdiction, and disposition of all appeals therefrom, adverse to the title or to the lien of the insured mortgage, as insured, as provided in paragraph 3 hereof; or (c) for liability voluntarily admitted or assumed by an insured without written consent of the Company.

8. Reduction of Insurance; Termination of Liability

All payments under this policy, except payment made for costs, attorneys' fees and expenses, shall reduce the amount of the insurance pro tanto; provided, however, if the owner of the indebtedness secured by the insured mortgage is an insured hereunder, then such payments, prior to the acquisition of title to said estate or interest as provided in paragraph 2(a) of these Conditions and Stipulations, shall not reduce pro tanto the amount of the insurance afforded hereunder as to any such insured, except to the extent that such payments reduce the amount of the indebtedness secured by such mortgage,

Payment in full by any person or voluntary satisfaction or release of the insured mortgage shall terminate all liability of the Company to an insured owner of the indebtedness secured by the insured mortgage, except as provided in paragraph 2(a) hereof.

9. Liability Noncumulative

It is expressly understood that the amount of insurance under this policy, as to the insured owner of the estate or interest or interest covered by this policy, shall be reduced by any amount the Company may pay under any policy insuring (a) a mortgage shown or referred to in Schedule B hereof which is a lien on the estate or interest covered by this policy, or (b) a mortgage hereafter executed by an insured which is a charge or lien on the estate or interest described or referred to in Schedule A, and the amount so paid shall be deemed a payment under this policy. The Company shall have the option to apply to the payment of any such mortgage any amount that otherwise would be payable hereunder to the insured owner of the estate or interest covered by this policy and the amount so paid shall be deemed a payment under this policy to said insured owner.

The provisions of this paragraph 9 shall not apply to an owner of the indebtedness secured by the insured mortgage, unless such insured acquires title to said estate or interest in satisfaction of said indebtedness or any part thereof.

10. Subrogation Upon Payment or Settlement

Whenever the Company shall have paid or settled a claim under this policy, all right of subrogation shall vest in the Company unaffected by any act of the insured claimant, except that the owner of the indebtedness secured by the insured mortgage may release or substitute the personal liability of any debtor or guarantor, or extend or otherwise modify the terms of payment, or release a portion of the estate or interest from the lien of the insured mortgage, or release any collateral security for the indebtedness, provided such act occurs prior to receipt by such insured of notice of any claim of title or interest adverse to the title to the estate or interest or the priority of the lien of the insured mortgage and does not result in any loss of priority of the lien of the insured mortgage. The Company shall be subrogated to and be entitled to all rights and remedies which such insured claimant would have had against any person or property in respect to such claim had this policy not been issued, and the Company is hereby authorized and empowered to sue, compromise or settle in its name or in the name of the insured to the full extent of the loss sustained by the Company. If requested by the Company, the insured shall execute any and all documents to evidence the within subrogation. If the payment does not cover the loss of such insured claimant, the Company shall be subrogated to such rights and remedies in the proportion which said payment bears to the amount of said loss, but such subrogation shall be in subordination to an insured mortgage. If loss should result from any act of such insured claimant, such act shall not void this policy, but the Company, in that event, shall as to such insured claimant be required to pay only that part of the losses insured against hereunder which shall exceed the amount, if any, lost to the Company by reason of the impairment of the right of subrogation.

11. Liability Limited to this Policy

This instrument together with all endorsements and other instruments, if any, attached hereto by the Company is the entire policy and contract between the insured and the Company.

Any claim of loss or damage, whether or not based on negligence, and which arises out of the status of the lien of the insured mortgage or of the title to the estate or interest covered hereby, or any action asserting such claim, shall be restricted to the provisions and conditions and stipulations of this policy.

No amendment of or endorsement to this policy can be made except by writing endorsed hereon or attached hereto signed by either the President, a Vice President, the Secretary, an Assistant Secretary, or validating officer or authorized signatory of the Company.

No payment shall be made without producing this policy for endorsement of such payment unless the policy be lost or destroyed, in which case proof of such loss or destruction shall be furnished to the satisfaction of the Company.

12. Notices, Where Sent

All notices required to be given the Company and any statement in writing required to be furnished the Company shall be addressed to it at the office which issued this policy or to its Home Office, 13640 Roscoe Blvd., Panorama City, California 91409.

13. THE CHARGE SPECIFIED IN SCHEDULE A IS THE ENTIRE CHARGE FOR TITLE SEARCH, TITLE EXAMINATION AND TITLE INSURANCE.

P-218 (Area 1) (Rev. 5-78)

Figure 7-12

ALTA LOAN POLICY, COVER PAGE

ALTA LOAN POLICY - 1970
WITH ALTA ENDORSEMENT
FORM 1 COVERAGE
(Amended 10-17-70)

POLICY OF TITLE INSURANCE

SAFECO TITLE INSURANCE COMPANY

SUBJECT TO THE EXCLUSIONS FROM COVERAGE, THE EXCEPTIONS CONTAINED IN SCHEDULE B AND THE PROVISIONS OF THE CONDITIONS AND STIPULATIONS HEREOF, SAFECO TITLE INSURANCE COMPANY, a California corporation, herein called the Company, insures, as of Date of Policy shown in Schedule A, against loss or damage, not exceeding the amount of insurance stated in Schedule A, and costs, attorneys' fees and expenses which the Company may become obligated to pay hereunder, sustained or incurred by the insured by reason of:

1. Title to the estate or interest described in Schedule A being vested otherwise than as stated therein;

2. Any defect in or lien or encumbrance on such title;

3. Lack of a right of access to and from the land;

4. Unmarketability of such title;

5. The invalidity or unenforceability of the lien of the insured mortgage upon said estate or interest except to the extent that such invalidity or unenforceability, or claim thereof, arises out of the transaction evidenced by the insured mortgage and is based upon

    a. usury, or
    b. any consumer credit protection or truth in lending law;

6. The priority of any lien or encumbrance over the lien of the insured mortgage;

7. Any statutory lien for labor or material which now has gained or hereafter may gain priority over the lien of the insured mortgage, except any such lien arising from an improvement on the land contracted for and commenced subsequent to Date of Policy not financed in whole or in part by proceeds of the indebtedness secured by the insured mortgage which at Date of Policy the insured has advanced or is obligated to advance;

8. Any assessments for street improvements under construction or completed at Date of Policy which now have gained or hereafter may gain priority over the insured mortgage; or

9. The invalidity or unenforceability of any assignment, shown in Schedule A, of the insured mortgage or the failure of said assignment to vest title to the insured mortgage in the named insured assignee free and clear of all liens

In Witness Whereof, SAFECO Title Insurance Company has caused its corporate name and seal to be hereunto affixed by its duly authorized officers as of Date of Policy shown in Schedule A.

Secretary

W H Little
President

P-204 (Area 1) 1-78

Figure 7-13

ALTA LOAN POLICY, INDORSEMENT 100

100

INDORSEMENT

The Company hereby insures against loss which said Insured shall sustain by reason of any of the following matters:

1. Any incorrectness in the assurance which the Company hereby gives:
   (a) That there are no covenants, conditions, or restrictions under which the lien of the mortgage referred to in Schedule A can be cut off, subordinated, or otherwise impaired;
   (b) That there are no present violations on said land of any enforceable covenants, conditions, or restrictions;
   (c) That, except as shown in Schedule B, there are no encroachments of buildings, structures, or improvements located on said land onto adjoining lands, nor any encroachments onto said land of buildings, structures, or improvements located on adjoining lands.

2. (a) Any future violations on said land of any covenants, conditions, or restrictions occurring prior to acquisition of title to said estate or interest by the Insured, provided such violations result in impairment or loss of the lien of the mortgage referred to in Schedule A, or result in impairment or loss of the title to said estate or interest if the Insured shall acquire such title in satisfaction of the indebtedness secured by such mortgage;
   (b) Unmarketability of the title to said estate or interest by reason of any violations on said land, occurring prior to acquisition of title to said estate or interest by the Insured, of any covenants, conditions, or restrictions.

3. Damage to existing improvements, including lawns, shrubbery or trees,
   (a) which are located or encroach upon that portion of the land subject to any easement shown in Schedule B, which damage results from the exercise of the right to use or maintain such easement for the purposes for which the same was granted or reserved;
   (b) resulting from the exercise of any right to use the surface of said land for the extraction or development of the minerals excepted from the description of said land or shown as a reservation in Schedule B.

4. Any final court order or judgment requiring removal from any land adjoining said land of any encroachment shown in Schedule B.

Wherever in this indorsement any or all of the words, "covenants, conditions, or restrictions" appear, they shall not be deemed to refer to or include the terms, covenants and conditions contained in any lease referred to in Schedule A.

The total liability of the Company under said policy and any indorsements therein shall not exceed, in the aggregate, the face amount of said policy and costs which the Company is obligated under the conditions and stipulations thereof to pay.

This indorsement is made a part of said policy and is subject to the schedules, conditions, and stipulations therein, except as modified by the provisions hereof.

Dated: January 1, 2052

Policy No. 7812345

SAFECO TITLE INSURANCE COMPANY

By ....
Authorized Signature

100
CLTA Form (L.A.) (Rev. 12-4-69)
ALTA Restrictions etc.

Figure 7-14

ALTA LOAN POLICY, INDORSEMENT 116

116

INDORSEMENT

The Company assures the Insured that at the date of this policy there is located on said land

.... **single family residence** ....

known as .... 2553 Hollywood Way, Burbank California ....

and that the map attached to this policy shows the correct location and dimensions of said land according to those records which under the recording laws impart constructive notice as to said land.

The Company hereby insures the Insured against loss which said Insured shall sustain in the event that the assurance herein shall prove to be incorrect.

The total liability of the Company under said policy and any indorsements therein shall not exceed, in the aggregate, the face amount of said policy and costs which the Company is obligated under the conditions and stipulations thereof to pay.

This indorsement is made a part of said policy and is subject to the schedules, conditions and stipulations therein, except as modified by the provisions hereof.

Dated: January 1, 2052

Policy No.   **7812345**

SAFECO TITLE INSURANCE COMPANY

By..
                             Authorized Signature

116

CLTA Form (LA.) (Rev. 2-20-61)

Figure 7-15

ALTA CONDITIONS AND STIPULATIONS, part 1

SCHEDULE OF EXCLUSIONS FROM COVERAGE

The following matters are expressly excluded from the coverage of this policy:

1. Any law, ordinance or governmental regulation (including but not limited to building and zoning ordinances) restricting or regulating or prohibiting the occupancy, use or enjoyment of the land, or regulating the character, dimensions or location of any improvement now or hereafter erected on the land, or prohibiting a separation in ownership or a reduction in the dimensions or area of the land, or the effect of any violation of any such law, ordinance or governmental regulation.

2. Rights of eminent domain or governmental rights of police power unless notice of the exercise of such rights appears in the in the public records at Date of Policy.

3. Defects, liens, encumbrances, adverse claims, or other matters (a) created, suffered, assumed or agreed to by the insured claimant; (b) not known to the Company and not shown by the public records but known to the insured claimant either at Date of Policy or at the date such claimant acquired an estate or interest insured by this policy or acquired the insured mortgage and not disclosed in writing by the insured claimant to the Company prior to the date such insured claimant became an insured hereunder; (c) resulting in no loss or damage to the insured claimant; (d) attaching or created subsequent to Date of Policy (except to the extent insurance is afforded herein as to any statutory lien for labor or material).

4. Unenforceability of the lien of the insured mortgage because of failure of the insured at Date of Policy or of any subsequent owner of the indebtedness to comply with applicable "doing business" laws of the state in which the land is situated.

CONDITIONS AND STIPULATIONS

1. Definition of Terms

The following terms when used in this policy mean:

(a) "insured": the insured named in Schedule A. The term "insured" also includes (i) the owner of the indebtedness secured by the insured mortgage and each successor in ownership of such indebtedness (reserving, however, all rights and defenses as to any such successor who acquires the indebtedness by operation of law as distinguished from purchase including, but not limited to, heirs, distributees, devisees, survivors, personal representatives, next of kin or corporate or fiduciary successors that the Company would have had against the successor's transferor), and further includes (ii) any governmental agency or instrumentality which is an insurer or guarantor under an insurance contract or guaranty insuring or guaranteeing said indebtedness, or any part thereof, whether named as an insured herein or not, and (iii) the parties designated in paragraph 2 (a) of these Conditions and Stipulations.

(b) "insured claimant": an insured claiming loss or damage hereunder.

(c) "knowledge": actual knowledge, not constructive knowledge or notice which may be imputed to an insured by reason of any public records.

(d) "land": the land described, specifically or by reference in Schedule A, and improvements affixed thereto which by law constitute real property; provided, however, the term "land" does not include any property beyond the lines of the area specifically described or referred to in Schedule A, nor any right, title, interest, estate or easement in abutting streets, roads, avenues, alleys, lanes, ways or waterways, but nothing herein shall modify or limit the extent to which a right of access to and from the land is insured by this policy.

(e) "mortgage": mortgage, deed of trust, trust deed, or other security instrument.

(f) "public records": those records which by law impart constructive notice of matters relating to said land.

2. (a) Continuation of Insurance after Acquisition of Title

This policy shall continue in force as of Date of Policy in favor of an insured who acquires all or any part of the estate or interest in the land described in Schedule A by foreclosure, trustee's sale, conveyance in lieu of foreclosure, or other legal manner which discharges the lien of the insured mortgage, and if the insured is a corporation, its transferee of the estate or interest so acquired, provided the transferee is the parent or wholly owner subsidiary of the insured; and in favor of any governmental agency or instrumentality which acquires all or any part of the estate or interest pursuant to a contract of insurance or guaranty insuring or guaranteeing the indebtedness secured by the insured mortgage; provided that the amount of insurance hereunder after such acquisition, exclusive of costs, attorneys' fees and expenses which the Company may become obligated to pay, shall not exceed the least of:

(i) the amount of insurance stated in Schedule A;

(ii) the amount of the unpaid principal of the indebtedness as defined in paragraph 8 hereof, plus interest thereon, expenses of foreclosure and amounts advanced to protect the lien of the insured mortgage and secured by said insured mortgage at the time of acqustion of such estate or interest in the land; or

(iii) the amount paid by any governmental agency or instrumentality, if such agency or instrumentality is the insured claimant, in the acquisition of such estate or interest in satisfaction of its insurance contract or guaranty.

(b) **Continuation of Insurance after Conveyance of Title**

The coverage of this policy shall continue in force as of Date of Policy in favor of an insured so long as such insured retains an estate or interest in the land, or holds an indebtedness secured by a purchase money mortgage given by a purchaser from such insured, or so long as such insured shall have liability by reason of covenants of warranty made by such insured in any transfer or conveyance of such estate or interest; provided, however, this policy shall not continue in force in favor of any purchaser from such insured of either said estate or interest or the indebtedness secured by a purchase money mortgage given to such insured.

3. Defense and Prosecution of Actions - Notice of Claim to be given by an Insured Claimant

(a) The Company, at its own cost and without undue delay, shall provide for the defense of an insured in all litigation consisting of actions or proceedings commenced against such insured, or defenses, restraining orders or injunctions interposed against a foreclosure of the insured mortgage or a defense interposed against an insured in an action to enforce a contract for a sale of the indebtedness secured by the insured mortgage, or a sale of the estate or interest in said land, to the extent that such litigation is founded upon an alleged defect, lien, encumbrance, or other matter insured against by this policy.

(b) The insured shall notify the Company promptly in writing (i) in case any action or proceeding is begun or defense or restraining order or injunction is interposed as set forth in (a) above, (ii) in case knowledge shall come to an insured hereunder of any claim of title or interest which is adverse to the title to the estate or interest or the lien of the insured mortgage, as insured, and which might cause loss or damage for which the Company may be liable by virtue of this policy, or (iii) if title to the estate or interest or the lien of the insured mortgage, as insured, is rejected as unmarketable. If such prompt notice shall not be given to the Company, then as to such insured all liability of the Company shall cease and terminate in regard to the matter or matters for which such prompt notice is required; provided, however, that failure to notify shall in no case prejudice the rights of any such insured under this policy unless the Company shall be prejudiced by such failure and then only to the extent of such prejudice.

(c) The Company shall have the right at its own cost to institute and without undue delay prosecute any action or proceeding or to do any other act which in its opinion may be necessary or desirable to establish the title to the estate or interest or the lien of the insured mortgage, as insured, and the Company may take any appropriate action under the terms of this policy, whether or not it shall be liable thereunder, and shall not thereby concede liability or waive any provision of this policy.

(d) Whenever the Company shall have brought any action or interposed a defense as required or permitted by the provisions of this policy, the Company may pursue any such litigation to the final determination by a court of competent jurisdiction and expressly reserves the right, in its sole discretion, to appeal from any adverse judgment or order.

(Conditions and Stipulations Continued and Concluded on Last Page of this Policy)

Figure 7-16
ALTA CONDITIONS AND STIPULATIONS, part 2

CONDITIONS AND STIPULATIONS (Continued and Concluded From Reverse Side of Policy Face)

(e) In all cases where this policy permits or requires the Company to prosecute or provide for the defense of any action or proceeding, the insured hereunder shall secure to the Company the right to so prosecute or provide defense in such action or proceeding, and all appeals therein, and permit the Company to use, at its option, the name of such insured for such purpose. Whenever requested by the Company, such insured shall give the Company all reasonable aid in any such action or proceeding, in effecting settlement, securing evidence, obtaining witnesses, or prosecuting or defending such action or proceeding, and the Company shall reimburse such insured for any expense so incurred.

4. Notice of Loss - Limitation of Action

In addition to the notices required under paragraph 3(b) of these Conditions and Stipulations, a statement in writing of any loss or damage for which it is claimed the Company is liable under this policy shall be furnished to the Company within 90 days after such loss or damage shall have been determined and no right of action shall accrue to an insured claimant until 30 days after such statement shall have been furnished. Failure to furnish such statement of loss or damage shall terminate any liability of the Company under this policy as to such loss or damage

5. Options to Pay or Otherwise Settle Claims

The Company shall have the option to pay or otherwise settle for or in the name of an insured claimant any claim insured against or to terminate all liability and obligations of the Company hereunder by paying or tendering payment of the amount of insurance under this policy together with any costs, attorneys' fees and expenses incurred up to the time of such payment or tender of payment by the insured claimant and authorized by the Company. In case loss or damage is claimed under this policy by an insured, the Company shall have the further option to purchase such indebtedness for the amount owing thereon together with all costs, attorneys' fees and expenses which the Company is obligated hereunder to pay. If the Company offers to purchase said indebtedness as herein provided, the owner of such indebtedness shall transfer and assign said indebtedness and the mortgage and any collateral securing the same to the Company upon payment therefor as herein provided.

6. Determination and Payment of Loss

(a) The liability of the Company under this policy shall in no case exceed the least of:

    (i) the actual loss of the insured claimant; or

    (ii) the amount of insurance stated in Schedule A, or, if applicable, the amount of insurance as defined in paragraph 2(a) hereof; or

    (iii) the amount of the indebtedness secured by the insured mortgage as determined under paragraph 8 hereof, at the time the loss or damage insured against hereunder occurs, together with interest thereon.

(b) The Company will pay, in addition to any loss insured against by this policy, all costs imposed upon an insured in litigation carried on by the Company for such insured, and all costs, attorneys' fees and expenses in litigation carried on by such insured with the written authorization of the Company.

(c) When liability has been definitely fixed in accordance with the conditions of this policy, the loss or damage shall be payable within 30 days thereafter.

7. Limitation of Liability

No claim shall arise or be maintainable under this policy (a) if the Company, after having received notice of an alleged defect, lien or encumbrance insured against hereunder, by litigation or otherwise, removes such defect, lien or encumbrance or establishes the title, or the lien of the insured mortgage, as insured, within a reasonable time after receipt of such notice; (b) in the event of litigation until there has been a final determination by a court of competent jurisdiction, and disposition of all appeals therefrom, adverse to the title or to the lien of the insured mortgage, as insured, as provided in paragraph 3 hereof; or (c) for liability voluntarily assumed by an insured in settling any claim or suit without prior written consent of the Company.

8. Reduction of Liability

(a) All payments under this policy, except payments made for costs, attorneys' fees and expenses, shall reduce the amount of the insurance pro tanto; provided, however, such payments, prior to the acquisition of title to said estate or interest as provided in paragraph 2(a) of these Conditions and Stipulations, shall not reduce pro tanto the amount of the insurance afforded hereunder except to the extent that such payments reduce the amount of the indebtedness secured by the insured mortgage.

Payment in full by any person or voluntary satisfaction or release of the insured mortgage shall terminate all liability of the Company except as provided in paragraph 2 (a) hereof.

(b) The liability of the Company shall not be increased by additional principal indebtedness created subsequent to Date of Policy, except as to amounts advanced to protect the lien of the insured mortgage and secured thereby.

No payment shall be made without producing this policy for endorsement of such payment unless the policy be lost or destroyed, in which case proof of loss or destruction shall be furnished to the satisfaction of the Company.

9. Liability Noncumulative

If the insured acquires title to the estate or interest in satisfaction of the indebtedness secured by the insured mortgage, or any part thereof, it is expressly understood that the amount of insurance under this policy shall be reduced by any amount the Company may pay under any policy insuring a mortgage hereafter executed by an insured which is a charge or lien on the estate or interest described or referred to in Schedule A, and the amount so paid shall be deemed a payment under this policy

10. Subrogation Upon Payment or Settlement

Whenever the Company shall have settled a claim under this policy, all right of subrogation shall vest in the Company unaffected by any act of the insured claimant, except that the owner of the indebtedness secured by the insured mortgage may release or substitute the personal liability of any debtor or guarantor, or extend or otherwise modify the terms of payment, or release a portion of the estate or interest from the lien of the insured mortgage, or release any collateral security for the indebtedness, provided such act occurs prior to receipt by the insured of notice of any claim of title or interest adverse to the title to the estate or interest or the priority of the lien of the insured mortgage and does not result in any loss of priority of the lien of the insured mortgage. The Company shall be subrogated to and be entitled to all rights and remedies which such insured claimant would have had against any person or property in respect to such claim had this policy not been issued, and if requested by the Company, such insured claimant shall transfer to the Company all rights and remedies against any person or property necessary in order to perfect such right of subrogation and shall permit the Company to use the name of such insured claimant in any transaction or litigation involving such rights or remedies. If the payment does not cover the loss of such insured claimant, the Company shall be subrogated to such rights and remedies in the proportion which said payment bears to the amount of said loss, but such subrogation shall be in subordination to the insured mortgage. If loss of priority should result from any act of such insured claimant, such act shall not void this policy, but the Company, in that event, shall be required to pay only that part of any losses insured against hereunder which shall exceed the amount, if any, lost to the Company by reason of the impairment of the right of subrogation.

11. Liability Limited to this Policy

This instrument together with all endorsements and other instruments, if any, attached hereto by the Company is the entire policy and contract between the insured and the Company.

Any claim of loss or damage, whether or not based on negligence, and which arises out of the status of the lien of the insured mortgage or of the title to the estate or interest covered hereby or by any action asserting such claim, shall be restricted to the provisions and conditions and stipulations of this policy.

No amendment of or endorsement to this policy can be made except by writing endorsed hereon or attached hereto signed by either the President, a Vice President, the Secretary, an Assistant Secretary, or validating officer or authorized signatory of the Company.

12. Notices, Where Sent

All notices required to be given the Company and any statement in writing required to be furnished the Company shall be addressed to it at the office which issued this policy or to its Home Office, 13640 Roscoe Blvd., Panorama City, California 91409.

13. THE PREMIUM SPECIFIED IN SCHEDULE A IS THE ENTIRE CHARGE FOR TITLE SEARCH, EXAMINATION AND TITLE INSURANCE.

P-204 (Area 1) 1-78

When making estimated settlement sheets, you may refer to these schedules, which are supplied to your company by title insurance companies.

Lender's policies remain in effect until the loan is paid off and a reconveyance issued, even if the loan is assigned to new beneficiaries or trustees.

It is possible to obtain policies of title insurance for leasehold estates, sub-leasehold estates, easement owners, timber rights owners, life estates, condominium owners, and several others, none of which should be attempted by beginners in escrow.

In addition to Standard, Joint Protection, and Lender's policies, an extended policy of title insurance is available to all the above customers. An extended policy covers the items listed in basic policies, plus several matters that cannot be determined from examination of public records. For more information, refer to Chapter Two, page 34.

Another common indorsement (or rider) to Lender's policies is Form 116, which sets out the kind of improvements on the land being insured and the street address. This indorsement and Form 100, when attached to a policy at the time it is issued, does not increase the premium cost.

Many title insurance companies publish booklets that define and explain the uses for all their policies and indorsements. These helpful guides should become part of every escrow professional's office library, along with the fee schedules.

IV. CHAPTER SUMMARY

When a preliminary report (prelim) of title is received, it is a statement that the title company is prepared to issue a policy of title insurance. If a BINDER or INTERIM BINDER is issued, it will be a written agreement to issue a title policy at a future date. The binder is not a policy of title insurance but will show the exact date when the policy will be issued. When a GUARANTEE OF TITLE is issued, it will be given to an individual who is not involved in an escrow but is requesting title information regarding a certain property.

SCHEDULE A and SCHEDULE B are reserved for specific information. Schedule A is reserved for the recorded owner and the property in question. SCHEDULE B shows the encumbrances of record.

The ALTA LENDER'S POLICY is designed specifically to meet the needs of lenders who are seeking extended coverage on the property.

Many preliminary title reports come with a PLAT MAP that shows the location of the property in relation to other properties. Sometimes PUBLIC UTILITY EASEMENTS will be shown that give utility companies the right to construct and maintain lines through the property. An EASEMENT APPURTENANT is an easement that runs with the land regardless of who the owner is. There will be a DOMINANT TENEMENT who *is* one holding the benefit and the SERVIENT TENEMENT who is the one subject to the easement.

When there are CLOUDS ON THE TITLE, it will important to clear those conditions that affect title to the property. An ABSTRACT OF JUDGMENT is an order by a court to place a lien on a property. When the judgment is paid, there will be a SATISFACTION OF JUDGMENT, which will be recorded to remove the judgment lien.

A CLTA OWNER'S STANDARD POLICY is issued to the owner to insure their interest against loss or damage that the insured may sustain due to unmarketability of title. If an EXTENDED POLICY is issued, it will cover additional matter that cannot be determined by simple examination of public records.

V. TERMS

Abstract of Judgment: An order from a court to place a lien on a property.

ALTA Lender's Policy: Extended title coverage given to lenders that provides coverage beyond the standard policy.

CLTA Owner's Standard Policy: The usual policy issued to a owner that protects against matters of record and certain off record hazards.

Dominant Tenement: The owner of property whose property gains the benefit of the easement.

Easement Appurtenant: An easement created to benefit the owner of adjacent land.

Extended Policy: Additional protection at added cost that protects against risks limited in the standard policy.

Guarantee of Title: Title company assurances about the title to real property however no title policy is issued.

Interim Binder: Written agreement by a title company to issue a title policy at a later date. It is not a title policy and will normally have a time limit to be issued.

Plat Map: The public record of maps of subdivided land showing the division of the land into blocks, lots, and parcels indicating the dimensions of various parcels.

Public Utility Easement: An easement that gives utility companies the right to construct and maintain pipes and power lines through property.

Satisfaction of Judgment: A legal document when filed with the record will release a previous judgment lien.

Schedule A: Part of the preliminary title report that is reserved for the identification of the recorded owner and the property in question.

Schedule B: Part of the preliminary title report that shows the encumbrances of record.

Servient Tenement: The owner of land whose property is subject to an easement for the benefit of adjoining land.

VI. CHAPTER QUIZ

1. An agreement by the title company to issue a policy of title, at a later date, may be referred to as:

    a. a binder.
    b. an interim binder.
    c. a commitment.
    d. all of the above.

2. A binder is NOT:

    a. a policy of title insurance.
    b. temporary.
    c. both a and b.
    d. neither a nor b.

3. A "Guarantee of Title" will indemnify, but:

    a. means new owners do NOT want a policy.
    b. has only stated liability.
    c. means lenders do NOT want a policy.
    d. all of the above.

4. Judgments which are involuntary appear on the:

    a. title policy.
    b. preliminary title.
    c. both a and b.
    d. neither a nor b.

5. An easement is created for the benefit of the:

    a. dominant tenement.
    b. servient tenement.
    c. title company.
    d. none of the above.

6. When a judgment is paid off, what is filed:

    a. abstract of judgment.
    b. satisfaction of judgment.
    c. both a and b.
    d. neither a nor b.

7. Satisfactions of judgment and partial releases of judgment should both be:
   a. acknowledged.
   b. recorded.
   c. both a and b.
   d. neither a nor b.

8. The escrow officer will probably NOT see the actual policy of title because it is:
   a. only on film.
   b. sent to principals.
   c. both a and b.
   d. neither a nor b.

9. An ALTA lender's policy remains in effect until:
   a. the loan is paid off.
   b. a reconveyance is issued.
   c. both a and b.
   d. neither a nor b.

10. A CLTA policy remains in effect until:
   a. the property is conveyed.
   b. for five years.
   c. both a and b.
   d. neither a nor b.

ANSWERS: 1. d; 2. a; 3. d; 4. b; 5. a; 6. b; 7. c; 8. c; 9. b; 10. a

Sample Two,
Part Three

When Ollie brings his satisfaction of judgment to be examined by the title officer and recorded, he also brings the *Certificate of Compliance*, issued to him upon completing the process of dividing his lot. He informs you that his lawyer was going to record it, but he forgot to give it to his lawyer. You fax the certificate with the satisfaction of judgment to the title officer.

A few hours later, the title officer calls you to say that the two documents are sufficient, and can be recorded. Remember to note the $6.00 recording fee in your settlement sheet as a debit to the seller.

I. The Deed of Trust

You have instructions to prepare a deed of trust and note in favor of the sellers in the amount of $40,000.00, and you have obtained all the information you need to do so in your memo sheet.

As you have seen earlier, **a deed of trust creates a lien on a piece of property, securing it for payment of a financial obligation or the performance of some other condition**. When the deed of trust and note are private rather than institutional, you are to fill in the blank forms as you do with a grant deed. (**See Figure 8-1**.)

CHAPTER OUTLINE

Figure 8-1

SHORT FORM DEED OF TRUST

RECORDING REQUESTED BY

AND WHEN RECORDED MAIL TO

NAME Oliver Flatt Miller and
ADDRESS Edith Vernon Miller
CITY & 2551 Hollywood Way
STATE
ZIP Burbank, CA 91503

Title Order No._____ Escrow No. **3000**

SPACE ABOVE THIS LINE FOR RECORDER'S USE

DEED OF TRUST AND ASSIGNMENT OF RENTS

BY THIS DEED OF TRUST, made this **1st** day of December 2051 between

ARTHUR V. MILLER and MARGARET C. MILLER, husband and wife

herein called **Trustor**, whose address is

2711 Runway Road, **Burbank** **California** **91502**
(number and street) (city) (state) (zip)

and SAFECO TITLE INSURANCE COMPANY, a California corporation, herein called **Trustee**, and **OLIVER FLATT MILLER and EDITH VERNON MILLER, husband and wife as Joint Tenants,**

herein called **Beneficiary**.

Trustor grants, transfers, and assigns to trustee, in trust, with power of sale, that property in

Los Angeles County, California, described as:

PARCEL 1: Lot "A" of Blackacre Tract, as per Map recorded in Book 100, Pages 1 and 2 of Maps, in the office of the County Recorder of said County,

EXCEPT the South 140 feet thereof.

PARCEL 2: An easement for ingress and egress over the East 15 feet of the South 140 feet of Lot "A" of said Blackacre Tract.

Trustor also assigns to Beneficiary all rents, issues and profits of said realty reserving the right to collect and use the same except during continuance of default hereunder and during continuance of such default authorizing Beneficiary to collect and enforce the same by any lawful means in the name of any party hereto.

For the purpose of securing:
(1) Payment of the indebtedness by one promissory note in the principal sum of $ **40,000.00** of even date herewith, payable to Beneficiary, and any extensions or renewals thereof; (2) the payment of any money that may be advanced by the Beneficiary to Trustor, or his successors, with interest thereon, evidenced by additional notes (indicating they are so secured) or by endorsement on the original note, executed by Trustor or his successor; (3) performance of each agreement of Trustor incorporated by reference or contained herein.

On October 25, 1973, identical fictitious Deeds of Trust were recorded in the offices of the County Recorders of the Counties of the State of California, the first page thereof appearing in the book and at the page of the records of the respective County Recorder as follows:

COUNTY	Book	Page	COUNTY	Book	Page	COUNTY	Book	Page	COUNTY	Book	Page
Alameda	3540	89	Kings	1018	394	Placer	1528	440	Siskiyou	697	407
Alpine	18	753	Lake	743	552	Plumas	227	443	Solano	1860	581
Amador	250	243	Lassen	271	367	Riverside	1973	139405	Sonoma	2810	975
Butte	1870	678	Los Angeles	T8512	751	Sacramento	731025	59	Stanislaus	2587	332
Calaveras	368	92	Madera	1176	234	San Benito	386	94	Sutter	817	182
Colusa	409	347	Marin	2736	463	San Bernardino	8294	877	Tehama	630	522
Contra Costa	7077	178	Mariposa	143	717	San Francisco	B820	585	Trinity	161	393
Del Norte	174	526	Mendocino	942	242	San Joaquin	3813	6	Tulare	3137	567
El Dorado	1229	594	Merced	1940	361	San Luis Obispo	1750	491	Tuolumne	396	309
Fresno	6227	411	Modoc	225	668	San Mateo	6491	600	Ventura	4182	662
Glenn	565	290	Mono	160	215	Santa Barbara	2486	1244	Yolo	1081	335
Humboldt	1213	31	Monterey	877	24?	Santa Clara	0623	713	Yuba	564	153
Imperial	1155	801	Napa	922	96	Santa Cruz	2358	744			
Inyo	205	660	Nevada	665	303	Shasta	1195	293	San Diego	File No.	
Kern	4809	2351	Orange	10961	398	Sierra	59	439		73-299568	

The provisions contained in Section A, including paragraphs 1 through 5, and the provisions contained in Section B, including paragraphs 1 through 9 of said fictitious Deeds of Trust are incorporated herein as fully as though set forth at length and in full herein.

The undersigned Trustor requests that a copy of any notice of default and any notice of sale hereunder be mailed to Trustor at the address hereinabove set forth, being the address designated for the purpose of receiving such notice.

ss (Arthur V. Miller)
Arthur V. Miller
ss (Margaret C. Miller)
Margaret C. Miller

STATE OF CALIFORNIA.
COUNTY OF **Los Angeles** } ss.
On December 1, 2051 before me, the undersigned, a Notary Public in and for said County and State, personally appeared **Arthur V. Miller and Margaret C. Miller *** known to me to be the person(s) whose name(s) is (are) subscribed to the within instrument and acknowledged that **they** executed the same.

ss (notary public)

FOR NOTARY SEAL OR STAMP

SEAL

L-92 (G.S.) (Rev. 10-73) (8 pt.)

You must not use any information not supplied by the principals, and you should not prepare any unusual types of notes or deeds of trust.

If in doubt, consult your superiors. If your superiors tell you not to prepare the document, recommend that your principals have their attorney prepare the deed of trust and note.

This escrow does not require any unusual document, so you will fill out **the Deed of Trust and Assignment of Rents (Individual)**. There are forms for corporations and partnerships also. This type of deed of trust is available in two versions: **Short Form and Long Form**.

The Short Form Deed of Trust and Assignment of Rents is by far the most often used.

There are many general provisions in a deed of trust that are identical, no matter who the named parties are or how much the deed of trust secures. *To save time and recording fees (counties usually charge a per-page fee for each recording), title companies have recorded all the deed of trust general provisions in each county where they do business. These are known as* **FICTITIOUS DEEDS OF TRUST**, *and are seen as continuations of the Short Form.* Each Short Form has printed on its face a list of the counties where the rest of the general provisions are recorded. The Long Form contains all the general provisions, and each page must be recorded.

First, check your information. Do the principals agree on the type of deed of trust to be used? Who shall be named trustee? (**Safeco**) Is the monthly payment enough to cover the borrowed amount in the time specified? This applies to most loans which are fully amortized and allow equal payments over the life of the loan. In this case it doesn't matter, since there will be a balloon payment at the end of fifteen years.

1. In the upper left-hand corner, type the names and the address of the beneficiary.
2. When typing the names of the trustor, use their marital status but not their full vesting, and their address.
3. When typing the names of the beneficiary, use both their marital status and their vesting.
4. Use the complete legal description: copy it from the title report, if you have it, or the grant deed.
5. Type the amount of the loan in the space provided at the center of the document.
6. Prepare signature lines for the trustors.
7. Prepare the document for notarization by filling in as much as you can of the acknowledgment.

II. The Note

There are three general kinds of notes, each with its own printed form. They are:

1. **The installment note-interest included**. Usually fully amortized and the payments include principal and interest.

2. **The straight note**. The entire sum, both principal and interest, due at once on a specified date.

3. **The installment note-interest extra**. Payments of interest are made at regular intervals, then the remaining amount of interest plus all the principal is due at once on a specified date.

Fill out the note, writing the full amount, in numerals, in the upper left-hand corner. Then fill in the name of the beneficiaries and the full amount, this time spelled out. The rest of the space is reserved for the terms of the note. (See **Figure 8-2**.)

Since the date from which interest accrues is usually the last day of escrow, and the day of the first payment is usually 30 days after close of escrow, it is sometimes difficult to fill in this part of the note. If escrow were to close on a day different from the suggested date, the note might have to be written over. You can take care of this eventuality by filling in *date indorsed* in sections provided for payment dates, and then typing this indorsement (or one like it) on the back of the note when escrow does close:

"Per instructions in Escrow No. 3000

Interest to accrue from February 1, 2052. First monthly payment of principal and interest to commence on March 1, 2052, and continue on the 1st calendar day of each month to and including February 1, 2067, at which time the entire remaining unpaid balance of principal and accrued interest to be all due and payable.

NAME OF HOLDER OF DEED OF TRUST (TRUSTEE) *as signature of escrow officer."*

This way, you can prepare the note earlier in escrow, and even get it signed if you wish. Closing is always a busy time, and it is nice to get as much done ahead of time as possible. However, when you are typing a recitation on the back of a note on closing day, **TAKE EXTRA CARE:** your principals will certainly be most interested to see that their financial arrangement has been set out properly.

A. NOTES ON NOTES

Whenever you fill out a note, be sure that the amount of the loan and the amount of the monthly payments is listed both in numerals and in words.

If you are writing a fully amortized note, you may change the wording of the terms. After setting out the terms of payment you could write *"...and continuing until said principal and interest have been paid."*

Figure 8-2

PROMISSORY NOTE

DO NOT DESTROY THIS NOTE: When paid, this note, with Deed of Trust securing same, must be surrendered to Trustee for cancellation before reconveyance will be made.

NOTE SECURED BY DEED OF TRUST
(INSTALLMENT - INTEREST INCLUDED)

$ __40,000.00__ _____ **Los Angeles** _____ California, _____ December 1st __ 2051

In installments as herein stated, for value received, I promise to pay to __OLIVER FLATT MILLER and__ _____

__EDITH VERNON MILLER, husband and wife as JOINT TENANTS__ _____

_____ or order

at _____ **Los Angeles, California** __ the principal sum of

__FORTY THOUSAND AND NO/100__ * __ dollars

with interest from **date endorsed** _____ on unpaid principal at the rate of __ 9 1/4 _____ per cent

per annum; principal and interest payable in installments of **THREE HUNDRED TWENTY-NINE and 08/100** * * * * *

* * * * * * **($329.08)** * * * * * * * * __ dollars or more on the **(date endorsed)** _____ day of

each __ **calendar** _____ month, beginning on the **(date endorsed)** day of **(date endorsed)** __ 20 __

and continue on the 1st calendar day of each month to and including February 1,

2067 , at which time the entire remaining unpaid balance of principal and accrued

interest to be all due and payable. _____

_____

_____

_____

~~xxxxxxxxxxxxxxxxxxxxxxxxxxxxxxxxxxxxxxx~~

Each payment shall be credited first on interest then due; and the remainder on principal, and the interest shall thereupon cease upon the principal so credited. Should default be made in payment of any installment of principal and interest, the whole sum of principal and interest shall, at the option of the holder of this note, become immediately due. Principal and interest payable in lawful money of the United States. If action be instituted on this note, the undersigned promise_ _ _to pay such sum as the Court may adjudge as attorney s fees. This note is secured by a DEED OF TRUST to SAFECO TITLE INSURANCE COMPANY, a corporation.

Arthur V. Miller _____   **Margaret C. Miller** _____

_____   _____

L-78-NL (GS) 12-74   THIS FORM FURNISHED BY SAFECO TITLE INSURANCE COMPANY

Per instructions in Escrow No. 3000

Interest to accrue from   February 1, 2052 .
First monthly payment of principal and interest to commence on March 1, 2052
and continue on the 1st calendar day of each month to and including
   February 1, 2067 , at which time the entire remaining unpaid balance
of principal and accrued interest to be all due and payable.

SAFECO TITLE INSURANCE COMPANY

_____
(ss) Escrow Officer

It is not absolutely essential that the name of the trustee appear on the indorsement, but it is good practice. The note must be associated with its deed of trust at the time of its reconveyance or use in a foreclosure action, and the extra recitation helps clarify the connection.

The note will not be recorded, but the deed of trust will. These and the grant deed are the three most important documents in any sale of property. **Never attempt to get them signed without first checking them carefully for accuracy.**

The note, deed of trust, and the grant deed are the three most important documents in any sale of property.

The note is a negotiable instrument, and extremely valuable to its holder. Every note has printed somewhere on its face these words: "DO NOT DESTROY THIS NOTE: *When paid, this note, with Deed of Trust securing same, must be surrendered to Trustee for cancellation before reconveyance will be made.*" Sometimes a note will be lost. If you are processing an escrow where the note cannot be found, here are some suggestions for solving the problem:

1. Get a **certified copy of the deed of trust** (which is still of record since the note has not been surrender for reconveyance).
2. Then locate the beneficiary and ask him (them) to execute the **request for reconveyance** using the recital on the back of the deed of trust.
3. Then obtain a **lost instrument bond** for double the face value of the note and ask the beneficiary and trustee to accept that in lieu of the note. They usually will accept it, and will execute the reconveyance. This can be expensive for the trustor, since the cost of the bond usually amounts to 4% of the face amount of the note, but it is less expensive and time consuming than the other possible courses of action:

   a. Instead of obtaining the bond, obtain an **affidavit and indemnity** (to be prepared by an attorney). The beneficiary will probably charge an "extra hazard" fee, which could be as much as 75% of the cost of a bond. This together with attorney's fees might be very costly.
   b. Go through a **quiet title** action. Quiet title means a court action to prove title. As you know, any court action can be a very lengthy process and the escrow would almost certainly extend long after the suggested closing date.

Do not take any of the above actions without consulting your superiors and possibly your company's attorney.

The deed of trust must be kept also, and surrendered at the time of reconveyance. But since it is recorded, a copy can easily be obtained from the county recorder. Don't forget to note the document drawing fees in the settlement sheet, a total of $15.00 as a debit to the buyer. This figure varies with different companies.

III. Assignment of Water Stock

We return, once again, to the necessity for very explicit instructions because there is no prior contract. You should prepare a supplement to escrow instructions to clearly set out the method in which you are to assign the water stock to Arthur and Margaret. The supplement demonstrates receipt into escrow of Ollie's certificate, and specifies that you will send it to Flowing Water Company.

You have already type instructions as to the water stock in your original escrow instructions. This supplement, prepared after receipt of the stock certificate and the water company's statement, serves as an approval recital. It is to be signed by both the sellers and the buyers. See the supplement in **Figure 8-3**. Make special note of the signature areas.

IV. Ready to Close Escrow

Now that you have arranged for all the conditions of escrow to be met, escrow is ready to close. All that is left to do is to prepare these last items before calling for recording.

1. Write a cover letter for enclosure with the water stock certificate, identifying again your escrow and escrow number.
2. See that all documents are properly executed and acknowledged (if necessary).
3. Prepare an Order for Title Insurance, and include the grant deed and the deed of trust for recording. (The power of attorney, satisfaction of judgment and Certificate of Compliance will have already been recorded).
4. Prorate taxes, water stock, fire insurance, and rents. Add the escrow fee and title insurance premiums to the settlement sheet. Check figures.

V. Adjustments and Prorations

A. PROPERTY TAXES

The buyer has paid the first half, which runs from July 1 to January 1. He will be responsible for taxes up to but not including the closing day; he must pay taxes up to and including January 31. In other words, all of the month of January. (See the tax calendar, **Figure 8-4**). The half-year taxes are $250.00. Remember, use the 30-day monthly if you need to find a daily tax rate, which you don't need to do here.

$250 ÷ 6 = $41.67 = taxes for one month

DEBIT THE SELLER AND CREDIT THE BUYER $41.67.

Figure 8-3

AMENDMENT TO INSTRUCTIONS

ESCROW INSTRUCTIONS (CONTINUED)

TO: SAFECO TITLE INSURANCE COMPANY
13640 Roscoe Boulevard, Panorama City, Ca. 91409

Escrow No. 3000

Date January 28, 2052

1.
2.
3. The previous instructions in the above numbered escrow are hereby
4. modified/supplemented in the following particular (s) only:
5.
6.
7. Undersigned has received a copy of statement from Flowing Water
8. Company, pertaining to transfer of water stock and hereby approves
9. same.
10.
11. I hand you herewith Certificate No. X274 representing two shares
12. of water stock of Flowing Water Company endorsed in blank by the
13. undersigned. At the close of escrow forward said certificate to
14. Flowing Water Company, requesting that stock be reissued in the
15. names of Arthur V. Miller and Margaret C. Miller.
16.
17.
18. SELLER:
19.
20.
21. _____
22. Oliver Flatt Miller
23.
24.
25. _____   _____
26. Edith Vernon Miller   Oliver Flatt Miller, her attorney-
27.   in-fact.
28.
29. BUYER HAS READ ABOVE STATEMENT AND HEREBY APPROVES SAME.
30.
31.
32. BUYER:
33.
34.
35.
36. _____
37. Arthur V. Miller
38.
39.
40. _____
41. Margaret C. Miller
42.
43.
44.
45.
46.
47.
48.
49.
50.
51.
52.
53.
54.
55.
56.
57.
58.
59.
60.   (Page

E-325 (G.S.)

215

Figure 8-4

TAX CALENDAR

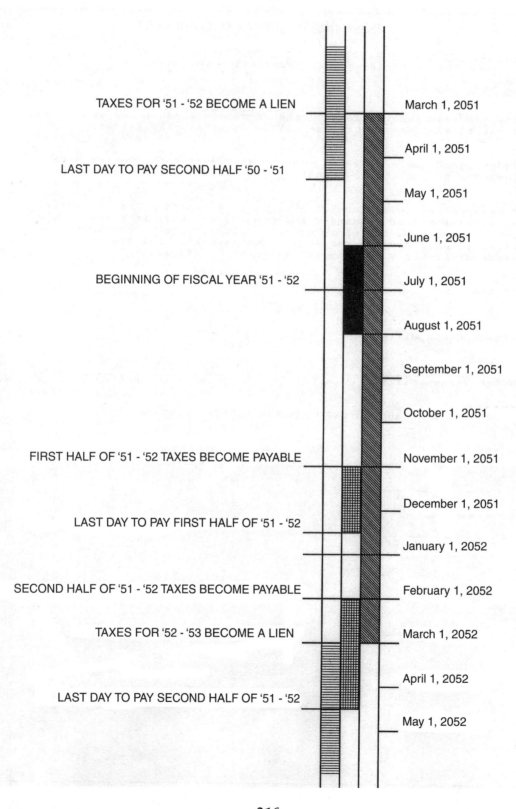

TAXES FOR '51 - '52 BECOME A LIEN	March 1, 2051
	April 1, 2051
LAST DAY TO PAY SECOND HALF '50 - '51	May 1, 2051
	June 1, 2051
BEGINNING OF FISCAL YEAR '51 - '52	July 1, 2051
	August 1, 2051
	September 1, 2051
	October 1, 2051
FIRST HALF OF '51 - '52 TAXES BECOME PAYABLE	November 1, 2051
	December 1, 2051
LAST DAY TO PAY FIRST HALF OF '51 - '52	January 1, 2052
SECOND HALF OF '51 - '52 TAXES BECOME PAYABLE	February 1, 2052
TAXES FOR '52 - '53 BECOME A LIEN	March 1, 2052
	April 1, 2052
LAST DAY TO PAY SECOND HALF OF '51 - '52	May 1, 2052

B. WATER STOCK

The water stock statement tells you that the assessment has been paid until July 1, 2052. You will need to credit the seller for the amount he has paid in advance. The statement tells that the assessment is for one year, so you know that the figure is $42.00 per year for the two shares.

First: $42.00 ÷ 12 = $3.50 = monthly assessment

then:

YEAR	MONTH	DAY
52	07	01
52	02	01
0	5	0

then: $3.50 x 5 = $17.50

CREDIT THE SELLER AND DEBIT THE BUYER $17.50.

C. FIRE INSURANCE

Ollie wants a new policy of fire insurance, in the amount of the loan with the premiums to be paid by Arthur. He asks you to arrange for it with **Safeco Insurance Company**. You discuss it with the agent, and ask that a policy be prepared for a tentative beginning date of February 1. He prepares a one-year policy with an annual premium of $110.00.

DEBIT THE BUYER $110.00.

D. RENTS

The rent statement discloses that the rent is paid until February 15, so the rent days from February 1 to February 15, already paid to Ollie, will "belong" to Arthur. Mr. Wrenter paid a $200.00 security deposit when he moved in. This will be credited to Arthur. When prorating rents, use the 30-day month.

First: $200.00 ÷ 30 = 6.667 = daily rent

then: 15 rent days x 6.667 = $100.00

DEBIT THE SELLER AND CREDIT THE BUYER $100.00.

VI. Balancing the Accounts

The estimated settlement sheet is shown in **Figure 8-5**. Add up the buyer's debits and credits, as you did in the last sample escrow, but **you do not have to call for down payment funds, so do not subtract credits from debits.**

Chapter 8

Figure 8-5

SETTLEMENT SHEET

CHARGES		CREDIT		PROPERTY: 2553 Hollywood Way, Burbank	CHARGES		CREDIT	
		42	950 —	TOTAL CONSIDERATION	42	950 —		
2 000	—			PAID OUTSIDE OF ESCROW TO SELLER			2 000	—
				DEPOSITS DEPOSITS 12-1-51			950	—
				DEPOSITS DEPOSITS				
40 000	—			BY FIRST TRUST DEED FAVOR OF SELLER			40 000	—
				BY SECOND TRUST DEED				
				PRO-RATIONS MADE AS OF C/E 2-1-52				
41	67			TAXES FOR ONE-HALF YEAR $250.00 PAID TO 1-1-52			41	67
				Safeco Ins. Co.				
				$40,000 INSURANCE EXPIRES 2-1-53 PREMIUM $ 110	110	—		
				INTEREST ON $ @ PAID TO				
100	—			RENT @ $200 PER MO. PAID TO 2-15-52 (6.667 day)			100	—
200	—			SECURITY MONEY			200	—
		17	50	FLOWING WATER COMPANY - 2 shares @ $21.00 ea.	17	50		
				COMMISSION PAID TO 2 paid to 7-1-52				
232	—			TITLE POLICY FEE OWNERS - ALTA	54	45		
47	30			TRANSFER TAX STAMPS				
3				RECORDING POWER OF ATTY RECORDING DEED ✓	3			
3				SATISFACTION OF JUDGM. RECORDING TRUST DEED ✓	3			
3				CERTIFICATE OF COMPLIANCE RECORDING				
				RECONVEYANCE FEE				
				TAXES PAID				
80	50			ea (½) ESCROW FEE 161 —	80	50		
10	—			DRAWING DEED ✓ DRAWING TRUST DEED ✓ NOTE	15	—		
5	—			DRAWING OFFSET STATEMENT DRAWING ASSIGN. OF LEASE	5	—		
5	—			RENTAL STATEMENT				
				TRANSFER WATER STOCK	5	—		
				PRINCIPAL OF ENCUMBRANCE PAID TO				
				INTEREST @ % FROM TO				
				PREPAYMENT PENALTY NEW LOAN CHARGE $				
				RECON. FEE TAX RESERVES				
				INS. RESERVES				
				INT. @ FROM TO				
				M.M.I. PREMIUM				
				TOTAL LENDERS CHARGES & RESERVES				
42 730 47				← SUBTOTALS →	43 243 45			
				BALANCE DUE THIS ESCROW				
237	03			BALANCE DUE YOU FOR WHICH OUR CHECK IS ENCLOSED	48	22		
42 967 50		42 967 50		TOTALS	43 291 67		43 291 67	
INDEXED		TITLE CO. ORDER NO.		OPENED	FILED			

MILLER, OLIVER FLATT & EDITH VERNON — STREET 2551 Hollywood Way — TELEPHONE — BURBANK CITY 91503

2 MILLER, ARTHUR V. & MARGARET C. — STREET 2711 Runway Road — TELEPHONE — BURBANK CITY 91503

218

Instead, see that the buyer must pay $43,243.45 (from the buyer's debit column). He is entitled to credits of $43,291.67 (from the buyer's credit column). Subtract debits from credits to get $48.22. You will write Arthur and Margaret a check for that amount. Do exactly the same for the seller's account. You will be writing a check for $237.03 to Ollie and Edith.

Note, that we did not "upholster" the buyer's debits in this escrow. It wasn't necessary, because we did not call for funds from the buyer—all the funds were already in escrow. Sometimes, even when all the funds are in escrow early, the buyer's debits may be heavy, and you would have to call for funds. In that case, do add a few days worth of daily rent and interest, just to cover the possibility of escrow closing on a different date than originally specified.

Now, balance the accounts once more, and check to see that all expenses are listed in the sheet.

VII. Calling for Recording

Phone the title officer and tell her you are ready to record. Prepare a written order for recording. Place it with the grant deed, the deed of trust and the order for title insurance, and send the package over to the title officer. When she calls to tell you that recording has been accomplished, you may prepare closing letters.

A. SELLER'S CLOSING LETTER

On your company's form letter, or on the letterhead, write to the seller and list the items you are enclosing. In this escrow, the list includes:

1. A check for $237.03 for proceeds of the sale.
2. Original policy for fire insurance.
3. A copy of the deed of trust and the original note, properly endorsed.
4. Seller's Statement, listing all the items for his account. (See **Figure 8-6**).
5. Return the documents brought to you, the old grant deed, power of attorney, etc., that have been examined by the title officer and returned to you.

B. BUYER'S CLOSING LETTER

Do the same for the buyer, enclosing these items:

1. A check for $48.22, refund.
2. A copy of the deed of trust and note.
3. A copy of the authorization for fire insurance policy.
4. Buyer's Statement, listing all items for his account. (See **Figure 8-7**).
5. The original lease brought in by Ollie, and the Assignment of lease.

Figure 8-6

SELLER'S SETTLEMENT

SAFECO

SAFECO TITLE
INSURANCE COMPANY

Office Panorama City, Ca.

STATEMENT OF ESCROW NO.
TO Oliver Flatt Miller and Edith Vernon Miller

DATE February 1, 2052

PROPERTY: 2553 Hollywood Way, Burbank, Ca.	CHARGES	CREDITS
CONSIDERATION OR SALES PRICE	$	$ 42,950.00
Paid outside of Escrow	2,000.00	
Deposits		
By First Trust Deed in favor of seller	40,000.00	
By Second Trust Deed		
PRO-RATIONS MADE AS OF close of escrow 2-1-52		
Taxes for one-half year $250.00 paid to 1-1-52	41.67	
Rent @ $200.00 per month, paid to 2-15-52	100.00	
Security money	200.00	
Water assessment, 2 shares @ $21.00 per share		
paid to 7-1-52		17.50
COMMISSION PAID TO		
POLICY OF TITLE INSURANCE Owner's	232.00	
Transfer Tax Stamps	47.30	
Recording Deed		
Recording Trust Deed		
Recording Power of Attorney	3.00	
Recording Satisfaction of Judgment	3.00	
Recording Certificate of Compliance	3.00	
Reconveyance Fee		
ESCROW FEE one-half of $161.50	80.50	
Drawing Deed	10.00	
Drawing Trust Deed		
Drawing Offset Statement	5.00	
Drawing Rental Statement	5.00	
Balance due		
Balance due you for which our check is enclosed	237.03	
TOTALS	$ 42,967.50	$ 42,967.50

E-312 (GS)

Figure 8-7

BUYER'S SETTLEMENT

 SAFECO

SAFECO TITLE INSURANCE COMPANY

Office Panorama City

STATEMENT OF ESCROW NO. 3000
TO Arthur V. Miller and Margaret C. Miller

DATE February 1, 2052

PROPERTY: 2553 Hollywood Way, Burbank, Ca.	CHARGES	CREDITS
Consideration or Sales Price	$ 42,950.00	$
Paid outside of Escrow		2,000.00
Deposits		950.00
By First Trust Deed in favor of seller		40,000.00
By Second Trust Deed		
Pro-rations made as of close of escrow 2-1-52		
Taxes for one-half year $250.00 paid to 1-1-52		41.67
$40,000.00 Insurance (Safeco) expires 2-1-53	110.00	
Rent @ $200.00 per month, paid to 2-15-52		100.00
Security money		200.00
Water assessment, 2 shares @ $21.00 per share paid to 7-1-52	17.50	
Commission Paid to		
Policy of Title Insurance ALTA	54.45	
Transfer Tax Stamps		
Recording Deed	3.00	
Recording Trust Deed	3.00	
Recording		
Reconveyance Fee		
Escrow Fee one-half of $161.00	80.50	
Drawing Deed		
Drawing Trust Deed and note	15.00	
Drawing Lease Assignment	5.00	
Transfer of water stock	5.00	
Balance due		
Balance due you for which our check is enclosed	48.22	
TOTALS	$ 43,291.67	$ 43,291.67

E-312 (GS)

There will be no Regulation Z Statement or HUD Statement necessary, since the lender is a private individual, and the property in question is the residence of fewer than four families.

C. OTHER DISBURSEMENTS

Each company sets its own policy in the matter of internal disbursements. Here, you will issue separate checks to the various entities within the parent company. Send $348.95 to the title company (for policies, DTT and recording) and $110.00 to the insurance company (fire).

You will send a check for $5.00 to the Flowing Water Company, their charge for forwarding the Statement.

Now review your check list to be sure that the principals have received copies of their instructions. ESCROW IS CLOSED.

VIII. CHAPTER SUMMARY

A CERTIFICATE OF COMPLIANCE will be necessary for the title company to be satisfied that a project or other public approval has occurred. When a DEED OF TRUST is prepared simply fill in the blank forms as you do with a grant deed. Do not prepare any unusual notes or deeds. Remember a deed trust creates a lien on specific real property.

An ASSIGNMENT OF RENTS CLAUSE is used to secure the lender with additional security in the event there is a default on the terms of the note. A deed of trust can be a SHORT FORM or a LONG FORM. A short form is used frequently and eliminates the necessity of repeating the many general provisions in a long form deed of trust. It saves time and recording fees but must be recorded in the county to be effective. The LONG FORM is a complete recital of all of the terms and conditions and can include many pages of recitals. The FICTITIOUS DEED OF TRUST is a continuation of the short form to complete all of the many provisions. It is not an actual deed of trust.

Promissory notes can be of various kinds. They may be an INSTALLMENT NOTE, which is usually amortized with principal and interest or they may be a STRAIGHT NOTE where the entire principal and interest is due at a future date. An INSTALLMENT NOTE-INTEREST INCLUDED requires payments of interest at regular intervals with a future due date of principal. Take extra care in preparing the promissory note. Sometimes you will need to obtain a CERTIFIED COPY of one of the documents. A certified copy assures that the document is authentic and true. If a particular instrument is lost. you may have to obtain a LOST INSTRUMENT BOND. This is an insurance company willing to indemnify someone in case of a financial loss. Sometimes a promissory note has been lost and the parties affected will accept the bond in order to reconvey a deed of trust of record.

When a QUIET TITLE ACTION occurs, there is a legal action to establish title to property. It will most often occur in Superior Court and will extend the closing time for escrow.

A closing letter to both buyer and seller notifies that the escrow has closed and enclosed is a listing of documents and other pertinent information due each party. The closing is the most important part of a transaction and it is a time to slow down and think while letting another person double check the file.

IX. TERMS

Affidavit: A sworn statement before a notary public or other public official stating that the facts contained are true and correct.

Assignment of Rents: An agreement in the deed of trust that grants the right to the lender to collect rents even though title is held by the trustor.

Certificate of Compliance: Issued by a governmental authority indicating that the owner has completed the requirements mandated by the government.

Certified Copy: A copy of a document, such as a deed, signed by the person having possession of the original and declaring it to be a true copy.

Closing Letter: Escrow company letter to either buyer or seller listing items enclosed after the escrow is closed.

Deed of Trust: Creates a lien on real property securing it for repayment of a financial obligation or the performance of some other condition.

Fictitious Deed of Trust: After recording, any provision of a fictitious mortgage or trust deed may be incorporated by reference to another trust deed affecting real property in the same county.

Indemnity: An agreement to reimburse or compensate someone for a loss.

Installment Note: Usually fully amortized where the payment includes both principal and interest.

Installment Note – Interest Extra: Interest payments are at interval times and the remaining amount plus interest owing comes due at a specified date.

Long Form: A recital of all of the terms and conditions related to a deed of trust with its general provisions.

Lost Instrument Bond: In the event of lost instruments, an insurance bond may be issued to serve as indemnity in the event of a claim.

Quiet Title Action: A court action intended to establish or settle the title to a particular property such as when there is a cloud.

Short Form: A recordable document such as a trust deed that simply recites the fact that a contract has been made between the parties covering certain described property.

Straight Note: Written so that the entire sum of principal and interest come due and payable on a specified date usually in a lump sum.

Sample Three, Part One

This escrow comes in to the Van Nuys office of **Southland Escrow,** an independent licensed escrow agent corporation. As before, we will treat you as a beginning escrow officer there.

The transaction, which is for the sale of a single family home set on 10 acres of rural land, has these new elements: **the buyer will take over payments on the existing deed of trust and note, there is a new second trust deed and note, and the seller wants to retain ownership of mineral rights to the land.**

I. Taking the Escrow

A broker calls to explain the deal, and you start your memo sheet right away, while on the phone. The preprinted memo sheet for **Southland Escrow** is entitled "Transaction Memo Data" and is shown in **Figure 9-1**. The items for this transaction are as follows:

1. SELLER: Timothy Smythe and Marylou Smythe
   6947 Calle Los Robles, Green Valley, California 91503

2. BUYER: Jacob Snell and Martha Snell
   5451 Hobbs Drive, La Canada Flintridge, California 91011

229

CHAPTER OUTLINE

Figure 9-1

ESCROW MEMO SHEET

10 acres ±
6947 Calle Los Robles
Green Valley Ca 91503
PROPERTY ADDRESS

TRANSACTION MEMO DATA

PERIOD OF ESCROW 30 days

SELLER Timothy Smythe
LENDER Marylou Smythe

PAID OUTSIDE ESCROW TO
DEPOSIT $5,000.00 ck to broker

ADDRESS: On the property
805 786 3402
PHONE:

CASH THROUGH ESCROW BY BROKER
CASH THROUGH ESCROW BY BUYER 36,000.00
TRUST DEED OF RECORD (BALANCE) 100,000.00
TRUST DEED OF RECORD (BALANCE)

LEGAL: SE 1/4 NE 1/4 NE 1/4
Sec 12 T 6 N R 15 W
S B B M

TRUST DEED TO FILE 2nd TD 43,500.00
TRUST DEED TO FILE

TOTAL CONSIDERATION $179,500.00

BUYER Jacob Snell
BORROWER Martha Snell
H/w comm psty

SUBJECT TO 2nd 1/2 TAXES FOR FISCAL YEAR 51-52

BONDS OF RECORD UNPAID BALANCE $

ADDRESS: 5451 Hobbs Dr
La Canada Ca PHONE: 213 342
91011 9321

TRUST DEED OF RECORD UNPAID BALANCE $100,000.00
MONTHLY PRIN. & INT. INSTALL $ 775.36
INCLUDING INTEREST AT 7 % PER ANNUM
UNTIL paid

BENEFICIARY: Anne B. Johnson
17754 Elizabeth Road
ADDRESS: Lancaster, Cal 91604

DELIVER THRU ESCROW:
LEASES:
BILL OF SALE:
WATER STOCK: ✓ T. REPORT: ✓
ADJUSTMENTS AND DATE OF PRORATIONS: c/e
TAXES: c/e BONDS: c/e
RENTS: c/e INTEREST: c/e
ADJUST PRINCIPAL OF T.D. OF RECORD IN:
_____ (CASH) (T.D. TO FILE) ✓
INSURANCE c/e
PAYMENT OF COMMISSION 6% of S.P.
50% TO: Green Valley Realty
7270 Calle Manzanita, Green Valley
ADDRESS:
50% TO Antelope Hills Realty
23700 Sierra Highway, Canyon Country
ADDRESS:
BOARD LISTING NO: _____ AMT: $ _____

TRUST DEED OF RECORD UNPAID BALANCE $
MONTHLY PRIN. & INT. INSTALL. $
INCLUDING INTEREST AT _____ % PER ANNUM
UNTIL

BENEFICIARY:

ADDRESS: 2nd
TRUST DEED TO FILE AMOUNT $ difference
PRIN. & INT. PAY IN MONTHLY INSTALL OF $ 10%
OR MORE, INCLUDING INT. AT 9 % PER ANNUM
BEGINNING 30 days UNTIL 5 years
BENEFICIARY: Sellers h/w jttns

ADDRESS:
TRUST DEED TO FILE AMOUNT $
PRIN. & INT. PAY IN MONTHLY INSTALL. OF $
OR MORE, INCLUDING INT. AT _____ % PER ANNUM
BEGINNING _____ UNTIL _____

Seller warrants that septic
system, water well and
water softener are in good
working order.

Termite report, dwelling
and garage only. Not
including stables, out-
buildings and fence

BENEFICIARY:

ADDRESS:

PAY OFF OF EXISTING TRUST DEED OF RECORD:
AMOUNT $ _____ (PLUS INT. @ _____ % PER ANNUM
FROM _____ TO _____) (PLUS INT. AND
BONUS, IF ANY.)
NAME OF HOLDER:
ADDRESS:

Except all oil, gas, hydrocarbon substances, minerals,
gold etc below 500 feet, without the rt of surf
entry

SIGNATURES: SELLER mail BUYER mail
Antelope Hills Rlty
BROKER Antelope Hills Rlty SALESMAN Peggy Miller PHONE 805 842 1796

3. LEGAL DESCRIPTION OF PROPERTY: SE 1/4 of the NE 1/4 of the NE 1/4 of Section 12, T. 6N, R. 15W, S.B.B.M. (This will be translated for you later in the chapter.)

4. PRICE: $179,500.00 to be composed of:

5. DEPOSIT TO BROKER: $5,000.00 to be deposited in escrow.

6. DOWN PAYMENT: $36,000.00, made up of the above $5,000.00 and $31,000.00 cash to be deposited in escrow.

7. FIRST TRUST DEED AND NOTE: Held by Anne B. Johnson, 17754 Elizabeth Road, Lancaster, California 91604. Approximate remaining balance, $100,000.00. Monthly payments are $775.30 at 7% interest. The escrow is subject to this note, the broker tells you.

8. SECOND TRUST DEED AND NOTE: $43,500.00 at 9% interest, monthly payments 1% ($435.00) or more for 5 years, all remaining principal and interest then due. The exact amount of this loan is to be adjusted if the actual balance of the first deed of trust and note varies from $100,000.00.

9. PEST CONTROL: Yes. Seller will pay for report and corrections. Buyer and seller agree that the report is for house and garage only, not to include the stables and other outbuildings.

10. MINERAL RIGHTS: Seller will retain with no right of surface entry. The recitation is to be typed on the grant deed. (Seller owns nearby property and can obtain the minerals by slant drilling or mining from that property). This exception is already printed on the instructions under "Free From Encumbrances Except," but should be restated for clarity, and the necessity of typing the recitation on the grant deed should be set forth.

11. FIRE INSURANCE: Terminate seller's policy at close of escrow.

12. MEMO: Buyer wants seller to assure that the water well and pump, septic system and water softener/conditioner are in good working order. You tell her that you cannot handle this in escrow, but that she may make arrangements between the parties for an inspection or some other way that the buyer can be assured by the seller. She agrees to this, but asks that you type the statement into the instructions anyway, as a memo. (She knows that if there is a future problem resulting in litigation, the fact that it is written down will help prove that there was such an agreement).

13. COMMISSION: Yes. There are two brokers involved. The commission (6% of the selling price) is to be split half and half between them. They are Green Valley Realty, 7270 Calle Manzanita, Green Valley; and Antelope Hills Realty, 23700 Sierra Highway, Canyon Country. Don't forget to get their broker's license numbers.

14. MAILING ADDRESSES: Ask the broker where to mail the grant deed and other documents. She says the buyers, Mr. and Mrs. Snell, will be living in the p.i.q. (a very common abbreviation in escrow, meaning property in question) and the street address has been given. The sellers will be living at 1791 Folsom Lake View, Placerville, CA 95667. The holder of the first deed of trust and note, Mrs. Johnson, wants her mail addressed to her home in Lancaster, already given.

15. TIME FRAME: Thirty days, dating from January 2, 2052.

II. The Escrow Instructions

This escrow holder has a slightly different rule for instructions than you have seen, but this rule is common in the industry. All items that are to appear on the title insurance policy are set out first, as in your previous experience, but a separate category is reserved for other conditions of escrow, which are not to appear on the title policy. These are listed under the heading "MEMORANDA OF AGREEMENT." This is different from MEMO headings you have seen, and indicates that the items are part of the agreement. The other items asked for by the principals that escrow cannot attend to are listed under a separate "MEMORANDA OF AGREEMENT, with which escrow is not to be concerned" heading. For clarity, this holder asks that the first heading be typed all in capital letters and the second heading be typed in lower case.

While these instructions (see **Figure 9-2**) appear identical to the forms used by Glendale Federal in the first sample escrow, there is one small variation we should note. There appeared (in the small print) on the face of Glendale Federal's instructions a recitation as to who pays fees and charges, just above the areas for principals' signatures. This recitation is absent from the face of Southland's instructions. Instead, the following is printed above the principals' signature lines: "The foregoing terms, conditions and instructions, as well as the "GENERAL PROVISIONS" and paragraph captioned 'BUYER (or SELLER)' as set forth on the reverse hereof, have been read and are understood and agreed to by each of the undersigned."

This "general provisions" section of instructions is a somewhat delicate area to deal with in the escrow industry. Many escrow instructions have general provisions on their reverse sides, usually in very small type and pale gray ink. They are part of the contract that principals sign. While they usually simple spell out who will pay for what, and give escrow directions as to the accepted procedure for implementing the items (e.g., paying off old loans, etc.) shown on the front, it is not often that an escrow officer makes a strong point of insisting that principals actually read the general provisions. The responsibility for doing so rests with the principals, as common sense on their part would indicate. There are two reasons why escrow would rather not mention the back side of the instructions: (1) although the payors of fees are stipulated, no law enforces such stipulation except where government insured loans are involved, and it could cause endless and unnecessary wrangling over details; and (2) many principals would be more or less forced to ask questions about terms

Figure 9-2

COMPLETED ESCROW INSTRUCTIONS

ESCROW INSTRUCTIONS **Southland** ESCROW CORPORATION

☐ 2320 WEST MAGNOLIA BLVD., BURBANK   (213) 842-2121 • 849-1161
☒ 7309 VAN NUYS BLVD., VAN NUYS   (213) 786-7960 • 873-3112

Escrow No. __3000__
Escrow Officer _____
Date ____January 2, 2052____

BUYER
on or before __30 days_____, I will hand you
__$31,000.00 on demand, having handed the broker__
__my deposit of $5,000.00__ which broker will
__deposit into escrow upon the opening of escrow.__
---   ----
---   ----

M E M O		
Paid outside of escrow....................	$	
Cash through escrow		36,000.00
Encumbrances of record..................		100,000.00
New encumbrances...**Second T. D.**		43,500.00
TOTAL CONSIDERATION	$	179,500.00

and any additional funds and documents required from me to enable you to comply with these instructions, all of which you are authorized to use provided on or before the time or date set forth above you hold instruments, duly executed, upon recordation of which you can obtain a Standard Owner's or Joint Protection Policy of Title Insurance with the usual title company's exceptions with liability for $__179,500.00__, the amount of total consideration, on real property in the County of __Los Angeles__, State of California, viz: __The Southeast 1/4 of__ __the Northeast 1/4 of the Northeast 1/4 of Section 12, Township 6 North, Range 15 West, San__ __Bernardino Base and Meridian,__

as per map recorded in Book __- - - -__, Page/s __- - - -__, of __Official__ records of said County.
Property address __6947 Calle Los Robles, Green Valley, Calif. 91503__ (Not Verified)
TITLE TO APPEAR VESTED IN __JACOB SNELL and MARTHA SNELL, husband and wife as community property.__

FREE FROM ENCUMBRANCES EXCEPT: __1. 2nd ½__ General and Special Taxes for the fiscal year __2051, 2052__, including Personal Property Taxes, if any, of any former owner and also including any special district levies, payment of which are included therein. All taxes and assessments levied or assessed subsequent to date of these instructions; conditions, restrictions, reservations, covenants, easements, rights and rights of way, now of record, if any. Also exception or reservation of oil, gas, or mineral rights, if any, providing there is no right of entry on the surface thereof;

(__2.__) Trust Deed, securing an indebtedness with approximate unpaid balance of $__100,000.00__, now of record, but if same should show to be more or less than said amount then you are to keep the total consideration the same as shown above, by accordingly adjusting the cash through ~~of total~~ __second trust deed to the difference. First trust deed payable $775.30, or more, per month__ (~~A trust deed is held and in an indebtedness with approximate unpaid of s~~ __including principal and interest at__ __7% per annum and continuing until paid.__

(__3.__) Trust Deed on your usual form executed by ABOVE VESTEES, in favor of __sellers, Timothy Smythe and Marylou__ __Smythe, husband and wife as joint tenants,__
securing Note for $__43,500.00__, dated __during escrow__, with interest at the rate of __nine (9%)__ per cent per annum, from __close of escrow__, payable __monthly__ at __place to be designated by beneficiary__
Principal and interest payable $__One %__ OR MORE, on the __same__ day of each __- - - -__ month, beginning __30__ __days after close of escrow and continuing for five years after date of close of escrow when the__ __full amount of principal and interest then remaining unpaid shall be all due and payable. You__ __are authorized and instructed to insert the first and final payment dates in the note above the__ __trustor's signatures when said dates become known at close of escrow. The original principal__ __amount of this note and deed of trust shall be adjusted at the close of escrow to equal the__ __difference between the total consideration and the cash down payment plus the unpaid balance of__ __the first loan. The monthly payment shall be adjusted to equal one percent, or more, of the__ __original amount of the second trust deed as adjusted at the close of escrow.__
0-0-0-0

MEMORANDA OF AGREEMENT:
1. Seller will deposit into escrow for buyer a termite report of recent date from a licensed
   pest control operator, showing the accessible portions of the dwelling and garage to be free
   of visible evidence of infestation caused by wood destroying insects, fungi, and/or dry rot.
   If any infestation is found, seller agrees to have all damage caused by said infestation
   repaired at his expense, and furnish an operator's certificate of completion. Other recommended work may be done at the buyer's option and expense. Inspection and report shall include only the dwelling and garage and shall not include stables, outbuildings or fences.

In accordance with the manner specified under General Provisions, the following are to be adjusted or pro-rated to __close of escrow:__
(__1.__) Taxes   (__3.__) Interest on encumbrances (of record) (new)
(__2.__) Fire Insurance   (__none__) Rentals

The foregoing terms, conditions and instructions, as well as the "GENERAL PROVISIONS" and paragraph captioned " BUYER " as set forth on the reverse hereof, have been read and are understood and agreed to by each of the undersigned.

Buyer __JACOB SNELL__   Buyer __MARTHA SNELL__
Address __5451 Hobbs Drive, La Canada, Calif. 91011__   Phone __213 342 9321__

SELLER

The foregoing terms, conditions and instructions, as well as the "GENERAL PROVISIONS" and paragraph captioned "SELLER" as set forth on the reverse hereof, are hereby concurred in, approved and accepted.
I will hand you all instruments and money necessary of me to enable you to comply therewith, including a deed to the property described, executed in favor of the vestees, which you are authorized to use and deliver when you hold in the escrow for my account the sum of $__36,000.00__ and any pro-rata adjustments and instruments deliverable to me under these instructions. Pay at the close of escrow any encumbrances necessary to place title in condition called for under these instructions, my portion of pro-rata or other adjustments and the following _____
__see supplemental instructions.__

Seller __TIMOTHY SMYTHE__   Seller __MARYLOU SMYTHE__
Address __6947 Calle Los Robles, Green Valley, Calif. 91503__   Phone __805 786 3402__

and processes with which they are unfamiliar. To be quite candid, escrow officers do not have the time to give a complete course in basic escrow processes to clients.

These instructions do not have enough space to list all the items necessary for this transaction, so a supplement to instructions will be required. A supplement to instructions is not the same as an amendment to instructions (such as you had to make in the first sample escrow). A *SUPPLEMENT is only an extra page, while an AMENDMENT modifies the original typing of instructions so that the transaction can proceed.* Note that neither an original instruction, a supplement, or an amendment may modify or change the original agreement between the parties for the transfer of the property without their written consent. The supplement is shown in **Figure 9-3**.

Figure 9-3

SUPPLEMENT TO INSTRUCTIONS

SUPPLEMENT TO INSTRUCTIONS
AMENDMENT

Escrow No. 3000

Date January 2, 2052

Southland ESCROW CORPORATION

7309 VAN NUYS BLVD. P.O. BOX 3176, VAN NUYS, CALIF. 91407
STATE 6-7960 (213) TRIANGLE 3-3112

The previous instructions in this Escrow are hereby modified or amended in the following particulars only:

1. Grant deed to recite: "EXCEPTING AND RESERVING UNTO THE GRANTORS all oil, gas, hydrocarbon substances, minerals, and gold in and under said land, lying below a depth of 500 feet measured vertically from the surface of said land, but without the right to enter upon the surface of said land for the purpose of drilling, mining, excavating or extracting any of the aforementioned substances.

Memoranda of Agreement, with which escrow is not to be concerned:
1. Seller warrants that septic system, water well and water pump, and water softener/conditioner are in good working order.

2. Seller will give possession of the premises to buyer at the close of escrow.

The undersigned, by their signatures hereto, acknowledge receipt of a copy of these instructions.

JACOB SNELL   TIMOTHY SMYTHE

MARTHA SNELL   MARYLOU SMYTHE

III. Preparing the Broker's Mailing

Now type the instructions, making sure you are sending out five copies. Remember to type the buyers' and sellers' names below their signature lines.

Prepare the commission instructions. (See **Figure 9-4**).

Gather statements of information, and add them to the papers.

Figure 9-4

COMMISSION INSTRUCTIONS

COMMISSION AUTHORIZATION

Southland **ESCROW** CORPORATION

Escrow No. 3000

Date January 2, 2052

You are hereby authorized and instructed to pay commission as follows:

(6% of sales price, divided equally between listing and selling brokers)

$ 5,385.00 ....to the order of: Green Valley Realty, 7270 Calle Manzanita, Green Valley, Calif. (Broker's license No. 528967)

$ 5,385.00 ....to the order of: Antelope Hills Realty, 23700 Sierra Highway, Canyon Country, Calif. (Broker's license No. 479683)

$............ ....to the order of:

$ 10,770.00 ....TOTAL

TIMOTHY SMYTHE

MARYLOU S MYTHE

Prepare the grant deed, using any of a number of generally used recitations for a mineral rights reservation without surface entry rights. It is shown in **Figure 9-5**. Make copies of documents for your files, then send the package to the broker.

IV. Check List

This company uses a preprinted file folder check list. You fill it out with as much information as you have. Be sure to place copies inside of all documents you've sent out. You can start your penciled settlement sheet now, also, with the figures you have.

Figure 9-5

GRANT DEED

RECORDING REQUESTED BY

A.B.C. Title Co.

AND WHEN RECORDED MAIL TO

Name
Street Address
City & State

⌜ JACOB SNELL and MARTHA SNELL, ⌝
6947 Calle Los Robles
Green Valley, Calif. 91503
⌞ ⌟

MAIL TAX STATEMENTS TO

Name
Street Address
City & State

Same as above

SPACE ABOVE THIS LINE FOR RECORDER'S USE

Grant Deed

THIS FORM FURNISHED BY SOUTHLAND ESCROW CORPORATION

The undersigned grantor(s) declare(s):
Documentary transfer tax is $ 87.45 _____.
( ) computed on full value of property conveyed, or
XXX computed on full value less value of liens and encumbrances remaining at time of sale.
XXX Unincorporated area: ( ) City of _____, and

FOR A VALUABLE CONSIDERATION, receipt of which is hereby acknowledged,

TIMOTHY SMYTHE and MARYLOU SMYTHE, husband and wife,

hereby GRANT(S) to JACOB SNELL and MARTHA SNELL, husband and wife as community property

the following described real property in the
County of   Los Angeles   , State of California:

The Southeast ¼ of the Northeast ¼ of the Northeast ¼ of Section 12, Township 6
North, Range 15 West, San Bernardino Baseline and Meridian.

EXCEPTING AND RESERVING UNTO THE GRANTORS all oil, gas, hydrocarbon substances,
minerals, and gold in and under said land, lying below a depth of 500 feet
measured vertically from the surface of said land, but without the right of
entering upon the surface of said land for the purpose of drilling, mining,
excavating or extracting any of the aforementioned substances.

Dated _____

STATE OF CALIFORNIA
COUNTY OF Los Angeles _____ ⎰SS.
On _____ before me, the under-
signed, a Notary Public in and for said State, personally appeared
TIMOTHY SMYTHE and MARYLOU SMYTHE
_____
_____ known to me
to be the person s whose name s are subscribed to the within
instrument and acknowledged that they executed the same.
WITNESS my hand and official seal.

Signature _____

_____
Name (Typed or Printed)

TIMOTHY SMYTHE
_____
MARYLOU SMYTHE
_____

_____

(This area for official notarial seal)

Title Order No. _____   Escrow or Loan No. 3000 _____

MAIL TAX STATEMENTS AS DIRECTED ABOVE

237

V. Order for Title Report

You do not have to await lender's commitments or appraisals, but you may run into a time problem getting the title insurance policy within the short 30 day escrow. This would not be much of a problem in the North, where title officers may often go forward with title searches on a phone call only, but company policy of most companies in the South requires that there be some way to pay for the prelim before it can be ordered. Therefore, you should institute the title search right after you have a deposit into escrow or signed escrow instructions, which contain the agreement for payment of the prelim fee. (Remember, this escrow takes place in Southern California). In this case, open the title search as soon as you receive the $5,000.00 deposit from the broker.

As soon as you receive the statements of information, send them to the title officer with the written title report order along with the seller's grant deed.

VI. Obtaining the Beneficiary's Statement

You will not be receiving a Demand this time, since the holder of the note will not be paid off, but you need a statement as to the exact amount left to pay. You must notify the beneficiary that the property which secures the note is being sold. The response of the beneficiary about the amount, interest rate, and monthly payment should be carefully compared with your escrow instructions.

> *Any variation in any of the facts presented by the beneficiary will require an immediate call to the broker so that discrepancies can be cleared up at once, usually by obtaining signatures of approval from the buyer and seller.*

Look at the letter you send in **Figure 9-6** and read it carefully. Note that it does not say anything about whether the note is to be assumed or whether the sale is subject to the note and deed of trust. It says nothing about the buyers or the purchase price. It only asks for the facts of the loan and serves notice that the property is in escrow.

Although the beneficiary may be unhappy that the borrower/trustor wants to sell the property with the loan attached, and may take an unduly long time returning the Beneficiary's Statement, law requires that it be returned within 21 business days. There is actually little you can do if the beneficiary refuses to send the statement, other than follow-up letters. If you ever have such a reluctant beneficiary, an approved action would be to call the broker (or the seller, if there is no broker) and suggest that legal counsel be sought in the matter. Fortunately, most lenders return their statements promptly. They don't really care who makes the payments as long as they are made. And, beneficiaries cannot refuse to permit the loan to be attached to the sale of property in cases where the buyer cannot (or will not) obtain outside funding. Such a refusal would prohibit the sale, which would be illegal interference in the title holder's right to sell.

Figure 9-6

BENEFICIARY'S STATEMENT

Southland ESCROW CORPORATION

BENEFICIARY'S STATEMENT

7309 VAN NUYS BLVD. • P.O. BOX 3176 • VAN NUYS, CALIFORNIA 91407 • LOCAL 786-7960 • FROM L.A. (213) 873-3112

Ms. Anne B. Johnson,

17754 Elizabeth Road,

Lancaster, Calif. 91604

Escrow No. **(fill in)**

Date **(fill in)**

Dear Ms. Johnson:

An escrow has been opened with us by **Timothy Smythe and Marylou Smythe** covering the sale of the premises commonly known as **6947 Calle Los Robles, Green Valley, Cal. 91503** which property we understand is encumbered by a Trust Deed held by you.

At the request of the parties in interest please fill in and sign the original of the beneficiary's statement below and return this entire page, together with any insurance policies which you may hold in connection with your loan. Insurance policies which you send us, together with the name and address of new owner, will be mailed to you at completion of escrow.

SOUTHLAND ESCROW CORPORATION

By **(fill in)**
　　　　Escrow Officer

(DO NOT DETACH)

BENEFICIARY'S STATEMENT

Escrow No.

Date

SOUTHLAND ESCROW CORPORATION

I hereby certify as follows: I am the legal holder of that certain promissory note dated **January 5, 2045** executed by **TIMOTHY SMYTHE and MARYLOU SMYTHE** in favor of **ANNE B. JOHNSON** and secured by a Trust Deed **Recorded in book 17963 page 428** of Official Records of Los Angeles County, California, and covering the property described as follows: **SE 1/4 NE 1/4 NE 1/4 Section 12 Township 6 North, Range 15 West SBBM**

The original principal of said note was $ **115,000.00**
I have made no advances under the terms of said encumbrance except $ **None**
The unpaid balance of said note, plus advances, if any, is $ **100,000.00**
The rate of interest is **7** percent per annum and is fully paid to **Jan. 1, 2052**
The PRINCIPAL AND INTEREST is payable in installments of $ **775.30** OR MORE, on the **1st** day of each **- -** month,
The balance of principal and interest is due and payable on **until paid.**

No default now exists in the terms of said note or encumbrance, except **none**

All of the consideration for said note actually passed to the makers thereof.

I make this statement for the benefit of the Southland Escrow Corporation and all parties in interest, including buyer of said real property, and I understand that it is being relied upon by all of said parties. I understand that said property has been sold and that you will furnish me with new owner's name and address. Upon completion of your escrow any insurance policies deposited by me are to be mailed to me at the address shown below.

17754 Elizabeth Road,
　　　　(Address)

Lancaster, Cal. 91604

805 942 6588

/s/ANNE B. JOHNSON
　　　　(Signature)

C-202　　　　(Telephone)

　　　　(Signature)

239

A. "ASSUMED" VS. "SUBJECT TO"

There is a difference between an existing note secured by a deed of trust being assumed, and a sale subject to a note and deed of trust.

When a buyer assumes an existing loan, he or she signs an assumption agreement with the lender.

In this agreement, the buyer agrees to assume the responsibility for paying the remaining balance of payments, and to comply with all the other terms and conditions of the loan. The lender may then choose to:

1. RELEASE the previous trustor from all responsibility to pay;
2. RETAIN the former payor responsible, so that he or she must make payments if the new trustor fails to pay; or
3. ACTIVATE the acceleration clause in the deed of trust, if there is one, by either demanding payment in full or by changing the interest rate.

If the sale is designated "subject to" the note and deed of trust in escrow instructions, the buyer rarely signs any sort of agreement with the lender making himself or herself responsible or liable for the payments or to perform any other contractual obligations after escrow closes. This is based on the buyer's knowledge that the lender will have no objections to this arrangement so long as payments and other obligations are met regularly and without loss to the lender (you have this knowledge because if the lender did object, you would have been notified in no uncertain terms by the lender).

If the buyer fails to perform in meeting the obligations under the loan, the lender will probably file a Notice of Default and cause the trustee under the deed of trust to start foreclosure action.

This is a funding area that causes confusion because actual practice seems to be rather at odds with legal reality. When a buyer takes a loan under a subject to arrangement, the seller is not legally released from responsibility. The new payor is simply making payments instead of the old payor. The situation is, legally, almost identical to the assumption arrangement. The main difference is that a lender cannot activate an acceleration agreement under the subject to arrangement—a very important consideration for a buyer. In actual practice, a beneficiary very seldom goes back to the original payor in either type of arrangement. Instead, the trustee files a Request for Notice of Default (asks escrow to ask the title company to record the Request for Notice at the same time as the new deed is recorded).

It is a very good idea for the sellers to also file a Request for Notice, since they are legally still liable for the note and will surely want to know if payments are not being made.

In this escrow, the sellers are the holders of a junior note secured by deed of trust also. In the event of nonpayment on the first, they will want to take steps to protect their interest.

B. "WRAPAROUND" OR "ALL INCLUSIVE" DEED OF TRUST

These terms are often heard in the escrow industry, and although we are not using one in this sample escrow, it is appropriate to mention them here. The two terms mean the same thing, and they are used to designate second or other junior trust deeds and notes in favor of the seller. They act in escrow exactly like purchase money deeds of trust—which is what they are, technically. They are always given in lieu of part of the purchase price of the property, usually the down payment. They are drawn by escrow, using a form entitled ALL INCLUSIVE DEED OF TRUST, and a note appropriate to the terms.

Although newly drawn by escrow, they are not new loans, but are "connected" to existing loans upon which the seller is already paying.

The buyer makes payments to the seller and the seller makes payments to the already designated beneficiary.

When making this document, proceed the same as for a "subject to" arrangement, obtaining a Beneficiary's Statement, and comparing the received figures and data with memo and instructions. Then fill out the note, stating the original terms of the existing loan, the size of payments, amount of impounds if any, and the present balance. Then type the following information:

1. If the seller defaults in any senior loans, the buyer may make payments and they may be credited to the note secured by the all inclusive deed of trust.
2. The equity of the payee shall be the difference between the unpaid balance of the new note and the unpaid balance of the old note secured by recorded deed of trust.

The statement illustrated looks very much like the Demand that you use for private lenders. Like the Demand, it is not usually filled out by an institutional lender, who has statements that he or she prefers to use. (Loans may be either assumed or "subject to" with institutional lenders, also). Both private individuals and institutional lenders will send their statements along with a letter to you that states the amount they are charging for sending the statement. There may not be any, but if there is a charge, it may not legally be more than $15. Your statement will also instruct the lender to send any insurance policies held for the p.i.q. In this escrow, the seller has the insurance policy, which is to be concluded, so you get only a notification of the $15 fee. Record it on the settlement sheet as a debit to the seller.

The prompt return from Mrs. Johnson reveals the following facts:

1. The legal description is exactly the same as you have in the instructions.
2. The original balance of the loan was $115,000.00 when it began in 2045.
3. The balance is now $100,000, with interest at 7%, paid until January 1, 2052, with payments of $775.30 OR MORE.
4. There are no back payments or other expenses due on the note.

It appears that the January payment has been made. If escrow closes on the scheduled date, the buyer will be making the February payment, with most of it credited to the seller, since payments are retroactive rather than in advance.

There isn't much to do until the prelim comes in, but fortunately it arrives within a few days.

VII. Preliminary Report of Title

The first page after the cover declaration, which states that A.B.C. is willing to issue a policy of title insurance, gives the recorded vestees and legal description of the p.i.q., as you have seen before. It sets forth:

Timothy Smythe and Marylou Smythe, husband and wife, as joint tenants, subject to the effect of a declaration of homestead by Timothy Smythe and Marylou Smythe, recorded February 15, 2045.

This will cause you no problems in this escrow, since the declaration will automatically become inactive when the property passes to new owners and the Smythes have not asked that it be transferred to a new property.

A. DECLARATION OF HOMESTEAD

A *DECLARATION OF HOMESTEAD, after acknowledgment and recording, protects a residence from judgments that become liens.* This protects you for $75,000 if you are the head of a family. Persons who are mentally or physically disabled, over the age of 65, or 55 or older with a specific low income, are entitled to protection for up to $150,000. Any resident who does not qualify under one of these conditions has a homestead valued at $50,000. If the equity exceeds the exemption, the home may be sold to satisfy creditors, but the exemption amount is protected for six months for reinvestment in another home. When a person files a homestead, it does not protect that person against trust deeds, mechanic's liens, or liens owed prior to homestead filing.

A homestead is NOT an encumbrance.

There is some confusion about the "Homestead" concept. Under California law, homeowners can declare a homestead to protect part of the equity in their home (the house and its outbuildings, condominium, townhouse, or other cooperative unit, in which they reside) from forced sale to satisfy creditors who hold involuntary liens against them. This is not the same as the government land homestead, where a settler can obtain title by satisfying certain specified improvement and time of residence requirements. Note that a declaration of homestead only protects against "outside" creditors. It does not protect against sale to satisfy defaults on deeds of trust, mechanic's liens, or liens recorded prior to recording the declaration of homestead.

For married persons, the homestead affects title in several ways other than protecting it from involuntary liens. Upon the death of one partner, the homestead transfer automatically (in its full amount) to the surviving spouse. It tends to create joint tenancy in the title even if they did not seek joint tenancy when they created the homestead. The law regarding homesteads, Section 1242 of the California Civil Code, requires that "The homestead of a married person cannot be conveyed or encumbered unless the instrument by which it is conveyed or encumbered is executed and acknowledged by both husband and wife, or unless each spouse executes and acknowledges a separate instrument so conveying or encumbering the homestead in favor of the same party or his or her successor in interest." This means that, if one partner wants to sell the property and transfer the homestead to a new property, offer the property as security for a loan, or formally abandon the homestead, all the documents must be personally signed, notarized and recorded exactly as the homestead was drawn. A power of attorney may not be used.

A homestead may only be held on one property at a time.

A homestead may be automatically terminated by sale, or it may be formally terminated by the recording of a DECLARATION OF ABANDONMENT. Although it is designed to protect the dwelling place, it is applied to the property. If a house or apartment building (co-op or condo) burns down or is otherwise destroyed, the homestead is still valid.

VIII. Legal Description by Section Map

The first page of the prelim also gives the legal description:

> The Southeast 1/4 of the Northeast 1/4 of the Northwest 1/4 of Section 12, T. 6N, R. 15W, San Bernardino Base and Meridian.

This is a **U.S. Government Survey description**, also called a **section map description**. Most of California's land was surveyed and designated into sections (not including recognized Mexican and Spanish ranchos and settled pueblos) shortly after California became a State.

Three reference points were established in California, at San Bernardino, Mt. Diablo and Humboldt.

From these points, lines were extended running north-to-south, every six miles, dividing the state into longitudinal strips called ranges. East-to-west lines also crossed the points and more were drawn, every six miles, creating bands running parallel to the equator called tiers. The squares created by the intersections of these lines, each six miles on a side and enclosing 36 square miles, are called townships.

The measurements are fairly accurate, but there is no guarantee that each township measures exactly six miles on a side.

The lines do not take into account the sometimes drastic irregularities of the land, nor do they accurately reflect the slight narrowing of the ranges as they go north (remember, longitudinal lines meet at one point near the North pole). Look at **Figure 9-7** to locate California's three reference points. The enlarged segment shows the range and tier bands.

Each township is divided into 36 sections, and the sections are identified by number; the same order in each township, starting at the northeast corner. Each section, one mile on a side, is further divided into 640 acres. **Figure 9-8** shows a township with our escrow's section identified.

Section descriptions are divided into quarter containing 160 acres, with each quarter divided into quarters, containing 40 acres.

When describing lots of less than 40 acres, it is common to speak of acreage, but a proper legal description should not use the term acres, since the division and subdivision into acres is based on possibly faulty township descriptions. Use fractions instead.

The description need not be entirely in quarters. You may describe, for instance, a property as E 1/2 SE 1/4 Section XX. This would be a strip of land located in the far southeast corner of the section. It would contain 20 acres, an eighth-mile wide by one-fourth-mile deep.

It's a good idea to try to place the property with which you are dealing on the Section Maps available in your office, just to be sure that common sense jibes with written material. When locating a property on a Section Map, you proceed backwards, starting at the end of the description. The legal description for our Green Valley property reads, in its most condensed form, *SE 1/4 NE 1/4 NE 1/4 SEC. 12 T6N R15W SBM*. See the Section Map, Figure 9-7, and follow this list:

Figure 9-7

DESCRIPTION BY U.S. GOVERNMENT SURVEY

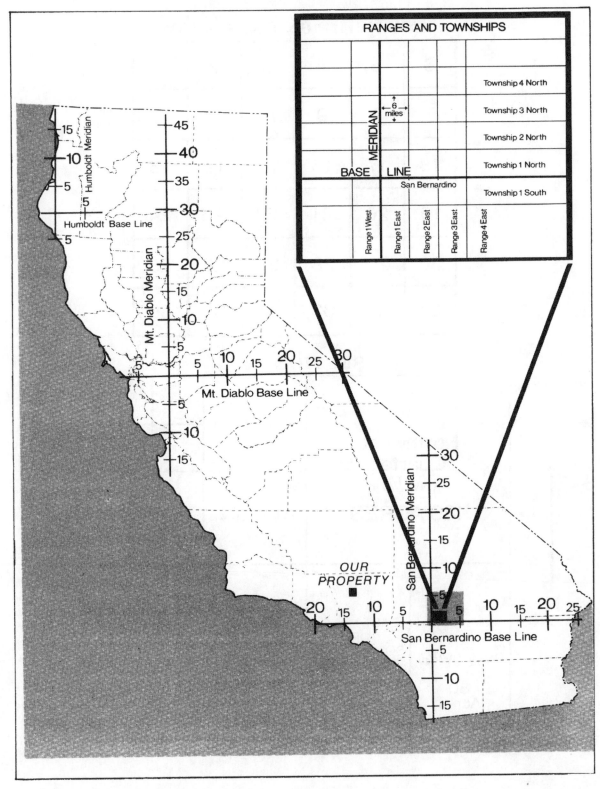

Figure 9-8

TOWNSHIP AND SECTION

TOWNSHIP 6N RANGE 15W

6	5	4	3	2	1
7	8	9	10	11	12 ← Our Property
18	17	16	15	14	13
19	20	21	22	23	24
30	29	28	27	26	25
31	32	33	34	35	36

SECTION 12

Northwest Quarter (NW ¼) 160 ACRES

(NW¼ NE¼)

Our Escrow's Property

(SW¼ NE¼)

(SE¼ NE¼)

N

(W½ SW¼) 80 Acres

EAST HALF OF SOUTHWEST QUARTER (E½ SW¼) 80 Acres

40 Acres

10 Acres

2½ Acres | 2½ Acres

2½ Acres | 2½ Acres

10 Acres | 10 Acres

40 Acres

40 Acres

1. SBM: locate the San Bernardino Base and Meridian.
2. R15W: move 15 ranges west (to the left).
3. T6N: now move up 6 tiers from there. This is the township.
4. NE 1/4: now find the northeast quarter of Section 12 of this township.
5. NE 1/4: now find the northeast quarter of that quarter.
6. SE 1/4: now find the southeast quarter of that quarter.

Once you have located the township on your large Section Map, you should locate the property within the township using a section sheet, which is usually available in abundance at your office. If your client is actually in your office, it's nice to show him or her the maps and how to read the description, if any confusion is expressed.

IX. CHAPTER SUMMARY

Land includes ores, metals, coal, and other MINERAL RIGHTS on or in the land to the center of the earth. The owner may convey the minerals to another person and retain ownership of the land, or vice versa.

In the title policy there will be a separate category reserved for conditions of the escrow and is headed MEMORANDA OF AGREEMENT. These are usually items that the escrow is not to be concerned. GENERAL PROVISIONS are small type provisions that the principals agree and sign. A SUPPLEMENT TO INSTRUCTIONS is an extra page to the instructions and is necessary when there is not enough space to list all the items in the instructions. COMMISSION INSTRUCTIONS will be an authorization and instruction to pay a commission. The BENEFICIARY STATEMENT is the exact amount left to pay on the existing loan and notifies the lender that the property is being sold. When a buyer ASSUMES a loan, they agree to take over the responsibility and liability of the seller. If the loan is taken SUBJECT TO, the buyer only agrees to make the payments on the loan but does not assume contractual liability. The ASSUMPTION AGREEMENT is the formal agreement between lender and buyer.

If there is an ACCELERATION CLAUSE, the lender under certain conditions may call the loan due and payable. Commonly, when the property is sold, the acceleration, also called alienation clause, grants the lender the right to accelerate the loan.

A WRAPAROUND or ALL-INCLUSIVE DEED OF TRUST loans are not new loans but instead wraparound existing loans that the seller is paying. It will be a junior loan with a face value of both the new amount of seller equity and the balance due under the existing loans. A PURCHASE MONEY DEED OF TRUST is a new loan given as part of the purchase price for the property.

A HOMESTEAD EXEMPTION is filed by the homeowner as a statutory protection against unsecured debts. It does not defeat any secured liens against the property. A DECLARATION OF ABANDONMENT removes the homestead from the property.

A LEGAL DESCRIPTION describes the property being transferred. It will include TOWNSHIPS that are areas 36 square miles and SECTIONS that are areas 1 mile square. U.S. GOVERNMENT SURVEY is one of three methods for describing real property. RANGES are imaginary lines running north and south while TIERS are lines running east to west.

X. TERMS

Acceleration Clause: A provision in the deed of trust that allows the lender to call the loan due and payable upon the occurrence of a specified event. I.E. sale of property without lender's consent.

Assumed: The written act of agreeing to be personally liable for the terms and conditions of an existing loan thereby relieving the previous borrower of that liability.

Assumption Agreement: An agreement prepared by a lender that outlines the new buyer's responsibility for assuming the existing loan.

Beneficiary's Statement: A statement of the unpaid balance of a loan and the condition of the indebtedness, as it relates to a deed of trust transaction.

Commission Instructions: An order signed by parties to the escrow that authorizes and instructs to pay commissions as stated through escrow.

Declaration of Abandonment: The termination of a previously recorded Declaration of Homestead that will terminate the homestead when recorded.

Homestead Exemption: A protection for homeowners that exempts a portion of the equity from general judgment creditors.

Legal Description: A description of real property acceptable by the courts and recorders for use in conveyance documents. Description is complete enough so that it is locatable by an independent surveyor.

Memoranda of Agreement: Items asked for by the principals that escrow cannot attend are listed under a separate memoranda of agreement. A heading stating that the escrow is not to be concerned will be included.

Mineral Rights: Rights to subsurface land and profits; usually passes to the new owner unless reserved to a previous grantor.

Purchase Money Deed of Trust: A loan granted by a lender to represent part of the total consideration of the purchase price. It may also be a loan taken back by a seller.

Ranges: Refers to the government survey system consisting of a strip of land six miles wide running in a north-south direction.

Section: As used in the government survey method, an area of one square mile or 640 acres which equals 1/36 of a township.

Standard Provisions: Standard escrow provisions usually on the reverse side which are part of the contract. They state who will pay for what and gives escrow directions as to the accepted procedure for implementing the items.

Subject To: Taking title to property with an existing loan without assuming personal liability for payment of the loan.

Supplement to Instructions: When there is limited space to list all items in an escrow, a supplement is prepared (not an amendment) as an extra page that does not modify the original instruction.

Tiers: A row of townships extending east and west.

Township: In the rectangular government survey method, it describes an area six miles square and contains 36 sections each of which is one mile square.

U.S. Government Survey: One of three legal description methods that rely on principal meridian and base lines that survey designated areas into checkerboard squares.

Wraparound/All Inclusive Deed of Trust: A new deed of trust that combines the existing loan(s) with the seller's equity to equal a total indebtedness that the buyer agrees to pay. Seller continues to pay on the existing loans.

XI. CHAPTER QUIZ

1. In short escrows, what should the escrow officer do first?

    a. Get ready for closing
    b. Start title search
    c. Both a and b
    d. Neither a nor b

2. "Assumed" and "subject to":

    a. are the same.
    b. are different.
    c. do NOT involve loans.
    d. none of the above.

3. In a "wraparound" of "all-inclusive" deed of trust, the buyer makes payments to the:

    a. seller.
    b. financial institution.
    c. both a and b.
    d. neither a nor b.

4. "Wraparound" or "all-inclusive" deeds of trust are connected to:

    a. existing loans.
    b. seller generated loans.
    c. both a and b.
    d. neither a nor b.

5. Homesteading protects against:

   a. voluntary liens.
   b. involuntary liens.
   c. both a and b.
   d. neither a nor b.

6. What is filed to start a homestead?

   a. Statement of Homestead
   b. Declaration of Homestead
   c. Nothing is required
   d. None of the above

7. What terminates a homestead?

   a. Declaration of Abandonment
   b. Abandonment of Homestead
   c. Both a and b
   d. Neither a nor b

8. Which is NOT one of the three reference points for the U. S. Government Survey System?

   a. San Diego B & M
   b. San Bernardino B & M
   c. Mt. Diablo
   d. Humboldt

9. The difference between ranges and tiers is:

   a. East and West.
   b. North and South.
   c. both a and b.
   d. neither a nor b.

10. When reading a U.S. Government Survey (section and township), read from:

   a. right to left.
   b. left to right.
   c. both a and b.
   d. neither a nor b.

ANSWERS: *1. b; 2. b; 3. a; 4. c; 5. b; 6. b; 7. a; 8. a; 9. c; 10. a*

Sample Three, Part Two

I. Preliminary Report of Title (Continued)

A. THE SECOND PAGE OF THE PRELIM

The second page of the prelim contains, as you recall from Sample Two, a list of the encumbrances against the property. This page sets forth the following:

1. Property taxes of $1,795.00 the first half ($897.50) paid and second half ($897.50) not paid.

2. Deed of trust securing a note in favor of Anne B. Johnson, for the original amount of $115,000.00, recorded January 5, 2045.

3. An easement affecting the property: an undivided one fourth interest in the water well and water produced there from, as reserved in the deed from John Tinwoodie, recorded on September 16, 1992.

While the first two items listed against the property are normal, the discovery of such an easement can be enough to induce palpitations in even a veteran escrow officer. This appears to be an old riparian rights easement, dating from early farming or ranching in the area. Although successive changes of ownership should have dealt with this old easement, it is still of record. It could mean that all the previous owners felt that

253

CHAPTER OUTLINE

it was of little importance, or it could mean that the rights are still being exercised by Mr. Tinwoodie, his heirs or successors in interest.

In either case, the buyers must be informed, and the escrow officer must hope that they will not see this as a major hindrance to completion of escrow. There is one hint to go on: if the rights were still being exercised, the sellers would have not (hopefully) withheld mention of it, since water rights have been and still are of great importance in rural areas. The matter could be cleared up with a single phone call to the broker; but even if it is that simple, you will probably have to obtain the approval of the buyers, Mr. and Mrs. Snell. First, let us discuss riparian rights.

A *RIPARIAN RIGHT is the right of a landowner to use the water on, under and adjacent to his or her land, providing that his or her use does not infringe on the rights of neighboring landowners.* This water can include a fair share of water in steams, lakes, and rivers bordering on or flowing through the land, including water in underground watercourses and in the water table. Users are not supposed to deprive downstream owners of their fair share, but this infringement is extremely hard to prove and obtain redress.

The water is actually considered public property, under the stewardship of the California Water Resources Agency, to be used for the greater public benefit.

The right to the use of water is of such primary importance that it (the riparian right) is considered real property in itself, and able to be transferred by deed separately from the land through which it flows.

Ordinarily the right is assumed to be a part of land title and is rarely mentioned in a deed for real property.

The title report states that Mr. Tinwoodie was given an easement in 2019 to use one-fourth of the output of the well on the p.i.q. He is possibly no longer alive, but in any case there is no recorded transfer of the rights by deed or quitclaim deed to any successors in interest, nor any recorded abolishment of the easement.

In this case, the call to the broker elicits this response, "Oh, yes, the sellers forgot to mention it. When they bought the property Mrs. Johnson said something about some ancient cattle watering agreement, but that nobody had run cattle on the land for over forty years, the length of time she had lived there. The Smythes remembered that their broker had, at the time, asked if they wanted to find out more about it and possibly get it cleared from the title, but they never bothered". The broker went on to say that she had spoken to the buyers, Mr. and Mrs. Snell, and that they didn't mind leaving it alone for now and would take title subject to the easement. This is exactly the kind of solution which causes escrow officers to sigh in relief. The buyers could have chosen to require that the titles of Mr. Tinwoodie be searched and that he, his heirs of successors of interest deed the easement back, before proceeding with escrow.

You can do several things. You can draw an amendment to escrow, for the signatures of the buyers; or you can type or stamp an approval recital on the preliminary report of title and have it signed by the buyers.

Either way, there is written approval in escrow, an absolute necessity in cases like this.

Now that you have the prelim problems worked out, there are no foreseeable hindrances to escrow closing on time. You may safely draw the deed of trust and the note for the second trust deed, using the agreed upon closing date as a base for adjustments.

II. The Second Deed of Trust and Note

Preparing a second deed of trust and note is exactly like preparing a "first." The **size** of the note has nothing whatever to do with the name first, second, third, or even fourth deed of trust. It is the **time of recording**, as specified by the parties involved, which is the determining factor.

Take out a short-form deed of trust and its companion note. Since the instructions do not specify **interest only** or **principal only** as part of the terms, use an "Installment - Interest Included" note. This company uses a multi-level packet for these instruments, which give two copies when typed or printed. Each copy clearly states "copy" on its face, to prevent possible misuse. (Note: Many escrow forms are now computer-generated.)

The deed of trust is essentially the same as the one used in the last sample, except that it lists Southland Escrow Corporation as trustee and the list of counties where the complete provisions are recorded is considerably smaller. While it is unlikely that you will be provided documents unsuitable to your area, some statewide companies may stock several different deeds of trust for different areas.

Always check to make sure that the county in which the property is located is listed on the deed of trust you use.

The note has printed at the end of its terms recitation this phrase "...and continuing until said principal and interest have been paid." This phrase contradicts the five-year time limit you will have just typed above it, and should be unmistakably obliterated.

You should cross out any printed statement which conflicts with the instructions of parties to escrow, not only on notes but also on any other instrument you fill out.

Study both for proper phraseology (**Figures 10-1** and **10-2**).

Figure 10-1

SHORT FORM DEED OF TRUST

RECORDING REQUESTED BY

A.B.C. Title Co.

AND WHEN RECORDED MAIL TO

TIMOTHY SMYTHE and MARYLOU SMYTHE
1791 Folsom Lake View,
Placerville, Calif. 95667

————SPACE ABOVE THIS LINE FOR RECORDER'S USE————
SHORT FORM DEED OF TRUST AND ASSIGNMENT OF RENTS

This Deed of Trust, made this 15th day of January, 2052 , between

JACOB SNELL and MARTHA SNELL, husband and wife
, herein called TRUSTOR,

whose address is 6947 Calle Los Robles, Green Valley, California 91503 ,
(number and street) (city) (state) (zip code)

SOUTHLAND ESCROW CORPORATION, a California corporation, herein called TRUSTEE, and

TIMOTHY SMYTHE and MARYLOU SMYTHE, husband and wife as joint tenants,
, herein called BENEFICIARY.

Witnesseth: That Trustor IRREVOCABLY GRANTS, TRANSFERS AND ASSIGNS to TRUSTEE IN TRUST, WITH POWER OF SALE, that property in Los Angeles County, California, described as:

The Southeast ¼ of the Northeast ¼ of the Northeast ¼ of Section 12, Township 6 North,

Range 15 West, San Bernardino Baseline and Meridian.

TOGETHER WITH the rents, issues and profits thereof, SUBJECT, HOWEVER, to the right, power and authority given to and conferred upon Beneficiary by paragraph (10) of the provisions incorporated herein by reference to collect and apply such rents, issues and profits.
For the Purpose of Securing: 1. Performance of each agreement of Trustor incorporated by reference or contained herein. 2. Payment of the indebtedness evidenced by one promissory note of even date herewith, and any extension or renewal thereof, in the principal sum of $ 43,500.00 executed by Trustor in favor of Beneficiary or order.
To Protect the Security of This Deed of Trust, Trustor Agrees: By the execution and delivery of this Deed of Trust and the note secured hereby, that provisions (1) to (14), inclusive, of the fictitious deed of trust recorded in Santa Barbara County and Sonoma County October 18, 1961, and in all other counties October 23, 1961, in the book and at the page of Official Records in the office of the county recorder of the county where said property is located, noted below opposite the name of such county, viz.:

COUNTY	BOOK	PAGE	COUNTY	BOOK	PAGE	COUNTY	BOOK	PAGE
Imperial	1091	501	Orange	5889	611	Santa Barbara	1878	860
Kern	3427	60	Riverside	3006	523	San Diego	Series 2 Book 1961, Page 183887		
Los Angeles	12066	899	San Bernardino	5567	61	Ventura	2062	386

(which provisions, identical in all counties, are printed on the reverse hereof) hereby are adopted and incorporated herein and made a part hereof as fully as though set forth herein at length; that he will observe and perform said provisions; and that the references to property, obligations, and parties in said provisions shall be construed to refer to the property, obligations, and parties set forth in this Deed of Trust.
The undersigned Trustor requests that a copy of any Notice of Default and of any Notice of Sale hereunder be mailed to him at his address hereinbefore set forth.

STATE OF CALIFORNIA, } SS.
COUNTY OF Los Angeles
On before me, the undersigned, a Notary Public in and for said State, personally appeared
JACOB SNELL
MARTHA SNELL
known to me to be the person S whose name S are subscribed to the within instrument and acknowledged that they executed the same.
WITNESS my hand and official seal.

Signature
Name (Typed or Printed)

Signature of Trustor

JACOB SNELL

MARTHA SNELL

Title Order No.
Escrow or Loan No. 3000

(This area for official notarial seal)

FORM 140

Figure 4-2

SETTLEMENT SHEET

Do Not Destroy The Original Note: When paid, said Original Note, together with the Deed of Trust securing same, must be surrendered to Trustee for Cancellation and retention before reconveyance will be made.

NOTE SECURED BY DEED OF TRUST
(INSTALLMENT—INTEREST INCLUDED)

$43,500.00   Van Nuys   , California,   January 26, 2052

In installments as herein stated, for value received, I promise to pay to TIMOTHY SMYTHE and MARYLOU SMYTHE, husband and wife as joint tenants

at place to be designated by beneficiary   , or order,

the sum of FORTY THREE THOUSAND FIVE HUNDRED & NO/100 - - - - - - - - - DOLLARS, with interest from January 30, 2052 on unpaid principal at the rate of nine (9%) per cent per annum; principal and interest payable in installments of FOUR HUNDRED THIRTY-FIVE & NO/100 ($435.00) - - - - - - - - - - - - - - Dollars or more on the 30th day of each - - - - - - month, beginning on the last day of February, 2052, and then continuing until on the 30th day of each month, or the last day of February of each year, until the last day of February, 2057, when the full amount of principal and interest then remaining unpaid shall be all due and payable. - - - - - - - and continuing until said principal and interest have been paid.

Each payment shall be credited first on interest then due and the remainder on principal; and interest shall thereupon cease upon the principal so credited. Should default be made in payment of any installment when due the whole sum of principal and interest shall become immediately due at the option of the holder of this note. Principal and interest payable in lawful money of the United States. If action be instituted on this note I promise to pay such sum as the Court may fix as attorney's fees. This note is secured by a DEED OF TRUST to SOUTHLAND ESCROW CORPORATION, a California corporation, as trustee.

JACOB SNELL   MARTHA SNELL

FORM 141 REV. 3/72   **DO NOT DESTROY THIS NOTE**

III. Pest Control Report

When the pest control report arrives, it shows that there is termite damage to portions of the house and garage requiring correction. The estimated costs of repairs is $390.00. The normal occurrence in dealing with correctional work in escrow is to:

1. Receive several copies of the pest control report into escrow.

2. Send one copy of the report to the buyers for approval.

3. When approval is received from the buyers, notify the sellers that approval has been received, so they may authorize work to begin.

4. When work is done, receive a Standard Notice of Work Completed and Not Completed form the pest control operator, with his or her statement of charges.

5. Debit the seller's account for the costs of the work.

6. Be sure to give a copy of the report to the sellers at close of escrow, and give a copy of the report and the Notice of Completion to the buyers.

If the pest control operator sends only one report, you may make copies of it but be sure to copy the backs of the pages too, since important material is contained there.

Sometimes, there is not enough time to get the work done before escrow closes. When that happens, three things can be done:

1. Delay closing until the Notice of Completion is received.

2. Prepare an instruction stating that the funds are to be paid to the buyer from the seller's account, in the amount stated by the report, so that the buyer may pay for the work when it is actually completed.

3. Prepare an instruction which allows funds to be held in escrow after closing to pay for the work when the Notice of completion is received.

Escrow is near to closing, so there is a good chance that the work won't be finished in time. Another call to the broker is required. He or she discusses the alternatives with his or her clients and returns with a direction that the costs is to be credited to the buyer, so that escrow can close on time without money left in escrow. Type an amendment to instructions, stating (in these general terms) that:

"Buyer has examined and approves the pest control inspection report furnished by _____and dated _____ 20 _____. Buyer is allowed a credit of $ _____ by the seller at close of escrow."

If they had decided otherwise, and wanted to hold funds in escrow after closing, your amendment would read:

"Buyer has examined and approves the pest control inspection report furnished by _____and dated _____20 _____. You are authorized to proceed with the closing of this escrow and hold from the seller's account the sum of $ _____. You are authorized to pay upon presentation of the bill from _____ together with a Notice of Completion. This escrow holder shall be held in no way responsible for payment of any sums in excess of the amount held."

These amendments must, of course, be signed by both buyers and sellers. You may add the pest control figure, $390, to your settlement sheet as a **debit to the seller** and a **credit to the buyer**.

IV. Adjustments and Prorations

A. PROPERTY TAXES

The prelim state that the second half of taxes ($897.50) are not yet paid (while the entire year's taxes may be paid during the first payment period, it is done very rarely). You must apportion the taxes as you have done before, and will do in 99% of all escrows you process. The seller will be making the next tax payment, which covers the time between January 1, 2052 until July 1, 2052. When escrow closes on January 30, about one month's worth will "belong to" the seller, so you'll **credit the buyer** and **debit her seller** for that amount.

    1. $897.50 ÷ 180 = 4.986 = tax base for one day

    2. January 30 - January 2 = 28 days =

       number of days for which seller pays taxes

    3. 28 x 4.986 = $139.61

    4. Record this figure in the settlement, debiting the seller and crediting the buyer.

B. ADJUSTING THE NOTE OF RECORD

There will be no monthly payments to be made by the sellers during this escrow. You will adjust the amount of interest for which the sellers will be responsible. The buyers will make the February payment, as they have indicated through the broker. In other cases, you may have to discreetly inquire about who will be making payments, in order to issue proper debits and credits. Remember this is an estimate since you do not know exactly when escrow will close. Interest adjustments are a good spot to make slight increases, to provide that enough funds are called for. Simply make your calculations as if escrow were to close several days later than indicated. We will use a supposed closing date of February 2, allowing 3 extra days of interest.

Remember the current principal balance is $100,000.00, the monthly payments are $775.30, and the interest rate is 7%.

    1. $100,000.00 x .07 = $7,000.00 (1 year's interest)

    2. $7,000.00 ÷ 12 = $583.33 (1 month's interest)

    3. $583.33 ÷ 30 = $19.44 (1 day's interest)

    4. To find the number of interest days, use the 30 day month: All of January (31 days) + 1 day of February = 31 interest days.

       *Remember, prorate interest **to** the closing day, not **through** it.*

    5. $19.44 x 31 = $602.64

    6. CREDIT THE BUYER AND DEBIT THE SELLER on your estimated settlement.

If, perhaps, the seller were to make a payment during escrow, you'll need to change the current principal balance. If the escrow closes after the seller makes another payment, you will need to get an amended Statement from the beneficiary, before escrow closes, in order to make the final settlement. Disregard the fact that there is no set figure for principal and interest over the life of the loan. You are working with the figures arrived at with the balance base of $100,000.00. When making the estimate, work with the already determined 1 month interest amount to determine the amount that the principal balance would be reduced:

1. Monthly payment - monthly interest = monthly principal
   $775.30 - $583.33 = $191.97

2. Current loan balance - this month's principal = new loan balance
   $100,000.00 - $191.97 = $99,808.03

   INSERT THE NEW BALANCE IN YOUR SETTLEMENT SHEET, AND DEBIT THE BUYER $191.97. If you don't charge this to the seller, you would be, in effect, reducing the selling price by $191.97.

3. Then, compute the daily interest rate on the new loan balance, and adjust, from the new date to which interest is paid, to your chosen estimate date. It won't be needed for our sample escrow, but just for practice, do it right now: see if you can follow this pattern:

   New balance x interest rate ÷ 12 ÷ divided by 30 = ?
   How many days of interest?
   Who pays?
   Do you get $19.41 as a debit to the seller and a credit to the buyer?

Our escrow instructions read *"Trust Deed, securing an indebtedness with approximate unpaid balance of $100,000.00, now of record, but if same should show to be more or less than said amount then you are to keep the total consideration the same as shown above, by accordingly adjusting the second trust deed to the difference."* (Item 2 under encumbrances, Figure 9-2)

This is another way of handling it. If the Beneficiary's Statement, whether the original or an amended one, is **less** than the suggested note balance, find the difference and **subtract** it from the total balance of the second deed of trust and note. If the actual balance is **more** than the suggested balance, **add** the difference to the original balance of the second deed of trust and note. If you've already prepared those instruments, they'll have to be done over. If the principals don't specify what is to be done if there is a variance between suggested and actual figures, ask them.

V. Fire Insurance

Your memo sheet indicates that you are to terminate the seller's policy at close of escrow. The buyers have indicated that they will start new coverage as soon as escrow closes and

have already arranged for a new policy with their insurance agent, Jacob Snell, Jr. They will inform him of the closing date themselves. You will write to the insurance company that holds the existing fire insurance policy, asking them to terminate the policy as of the closing date. They will rebate the prepaid amount to the sellers. **Do this as soon as you know that the transfer has been recorded, but not before**. The buyers may want to activate their policy a day or two before escrow closes. The resulting overlapping coverage can be clarified if they tell the insurance company something like "Start coverage on January 26 or as per date of escrow closing, whichever comes first." Then, a call to their agent followed by written authorization to him on the day of closing will get their coverage started.

The effective date for the insurance must be on or before the new loan will fund.

VI. Finishing the Settlement Sheet

Your settlement sheet has, up to this point, these figures recorded on it:

DEBITS TO THE SELLER

Trust deed in favor of Anne B. Johnson	$100,000.00
Trust deed in favor of seller	43,500.00
Property tax adjustment	139.61
Interest on exiting trust deed	602.64
Commission of	10,770.00
Pest control	390.00

CREDITS TO THE SELLER

Full purchase price	$179,500.00

DEBITS TO THE BUYER

Full purchase price	$179,500.00

CREDITS TO THE BUYER

Cash deposited in escrow	$ 5,000.00

Trust deed in favor of Anne B. Johnson 100,000.00

Trust deed in favor of seller 43,500.00

Property tax adjustment 139.61

Interest on existing trust deed 602.64

Pest control 390.00

There are still the additional fees and charges:

DEBITS TO THE SELLER

Title insurance policy .... $ 607.25

Documentary transfer stamps 87.45

One-half the escrow fee 330.00

Document preparation fee (deed of trust, note) 10.00

Notary fee (deed of trust) 4.00

Beneficiary's fee for forwarding Statement 15.00

Recording fees (grant deed, deed of trust) 6.00

DEBITS TO THE BUYER

One-half the escrow fee $330.00

Document preparation fee (grant deed) ....

Document preparation fee (grant deed,

Beneficiary's Statement) 10.00

Notary fee (grant deed) 4.00

Reconcile the buyer's account by subtracting total credits from total debits. The difference is $30,211.75. Since you have over estimated the interest by a few days, this is more than will actually be needed if escrow closes on January 30 as suggested. It is safe to call for this amount, along with $25.00 or so "extra," from the buyer. Write to the buyer, stating

that you are ready to close escrow pending receipt from him of the amount $30,236.00, and of its subsequent clearance through the bank.

When you receive the funds from the buyer and they clear the bank, notify the title company that you wish to record. Send the deed and deed of trust, together with an order for the policy of title insurance.

A. FINAL SETTLEMENT, BUYER

The recording took place on January 30. The total buyer credits are $179,868.25. Now, to determine the refund to the buyer, subtract total buyer's debits from this figure. The check to the buyer should be for $24.25.

Now make out the FINAL ESCROW SETTLEMENT STATEMENT for the buyer, using ink. It is illustrated in **Figure 10-3**. Don't forget to run another adding machine tape to check all figures. Photocopy it and place the copy in your file with the tape.

Make up the buyer's package. Include:

1. Your company's check for $24.25.
2. The final settlement statement.
3. A copy of the pest control report.
4. Complete escrow instructions, if they do not have them already.
5. The buyer's closing letter (See **Figure 10-4**).
6. A copy of the grant deed and the second deed of trust and note.

B. FINAL SETTLEMENT, SELLER

The previous pages reported the debits and credits for the seller, both the preliminary notations and pre-closing additions. Total credits for the seller are $179, 500.00. Total debits for the seller are $156,461.95. The seller's net amount will be $23,038.05. Now, make the seller's FINAL ESCROW SETTLEMENT STATEMENT, just as you did for the buyer (See **Figure 10-5**). There will be no HUD Statement in this escrow, since it does not involve an institutional lender. Prepare the seller's package, including:

1. Your company's check for $23, 038.05.
2. Seller's statement.
3. A copy of the pest control report.
4. Complete escrow instructions, if they do not have them already.
5. The original note for the "second."
6. A policy of title insurance "to follow," since the title company will send it later.
7. The seller's closing letter.

Figure 10-3

BUYER'S SETTLEMENT

ESCROW STATEMENT

Southland ESCROW CORPORATION

7309 VAN NUYS BLVD. P.O. BOX 3176, VAN NUYS, CALIF. 91407
STATE 6-7960 (213) TRIANGLE 3-3112

Date: January 30, 2052

Escrow No. 3000

Statement of: BUYER   Jacob Snell and Martha Snell

Recorded:

PROPERTY: 6947 Calle Los Robles, Green Valley, CA

ITEMS	DEBITS		CREDITS	
CONSIDERATION: Sale (xxx) Loan ( )	$179,500	00		
Deposited 1-2-52 $5,000.00 1-26-52 $30,236.00			35,236	00
Paid Outside of Escrow				
Balance of Encumbrance of Record				
Trust Deed in favor of: Anne B. Johnson			100,000	00
Trust Deed in favor of Seller			43,500	00
ADJUSTMENTS as of close of escrow 1-30-52				
Taxes on $ 897.50 for 6 Months Paid to 1-1-52			139	61
Insurance Premium $ yr's				
Interest on $ 100,000.00 @ 7 % paid to 1-1-52			602	64
Impounded Funds Held By Lender				
Rents				
PAID TO TITLE COMPANY:				
Title Policy				
Revenue Stamps on Deed				
Recording: Deed ( ), Trust Deed ( ), Reconveyance ( ),				
Commission				
Escrow Fee one-half of $660.00	330	00		
Drawing Documents	10	00		
Notary Fees	4			
Insurance Endorsements				
Service Fee: Beneficiary's Statement ( ) Demand ( )				
LENDER'S LOAN CHARGES:				
Loan Fee $ Appraisal Fee $ Tax Service $				
Interest @ %				
Lender's Forwarding Fee — Beneficiary's Statement				
PAYMENT OF ENCUMBRANCES:				
Demand of Principal $				
Interest @ % from to $				
Reconveyance Fee $				
Prepayment Charge $				
Forwarding Fee $				
Pest Control			390	00
Balance Due This Company				
Our Check To Balance	24	25		
TOTALS	179,868	25	179,868	25

Figure 10-4

BUYER'S CLOSING LETTER

Southland **ESCROW** CORPORATION

7309 VAN NUYS BLVD. • P.O. BOX 3176 • VAN NUYS, CALIFORNIA 91407 • LOCAL 786-7980 • FROM L.A. (213) 873-3112

BUYERS CLOSING LETTER

Mr. and Mrs. Jacob Snell,
6947 Calle Los Robles,
Green Valley, Cal. 91503

Date January 30, 2052

Escrow No. 3000

Dear Mr. and Mrs. Snell :

The above numbered escrow has been completed in accordance with your instructions and you are now record owner of the property as described in the Escrow Instructions.

Your first lender is: **Mrs. Anne B. Johnson, 17754 Elizabeth Road, Lancaster, Cal. 91604**

Unpaid principal balance of Note:	$ 100,000.00
Monthly payment - principal and interest (7 %)	$ 775.30
Monthly payment - impounds	$ none
Total:	$ 775.30

Your first payment is due: February 1, 2052 .

Your second lender is: **Mr. and Mrs. Timothy Smythe, 1791 Folsom Lake View, Placerville, Cal. 95667**

Unpaid principal balance of Note:	$ 43,500.00
Monthly payment - principal and interest (9 %)	$ 435.00

Your first payment is due: February 28, 2052 .

Enclosed are the following:
(X) Refund check for $ 24.25 .
(X) Escrow Statement.
(   )
(X) Copy of the Trust Deed and Note (   ) 1st (X) 2nd
(X) Policy of Title Insurance.   (to follow)
(   ) Copy of new fire insurance policy.
(X) Copy of our letter of instructions to Insurance Agent.
(X) Copy of Termite Inspection Report.
(X) Copy of Certificate of Completion issued by Termite Company.
(   )
(   )
(   )
(   )
(   )
(   )
(   )
(   )
(   )
(   )
(   )
(   )

Your recorded deed will come to you direct from the office of the County Recorder. We suggest that you list your property with the County Tax Collector, **Los Angeles** County, California, so that you will receive future tax notices promptly. The first installment of taxes is due November 1st and is delinquent if not paid by December 10th of each year; the second installment is due January 1st and is delinquent if not paid by April 10th of each year. It is imperative that you register with the tax office. If the loan on your property is an FHA or GI loan, the lending institution will receive the tax bill each year.

We wish to thank you for this opportunity of serving you, and trust that you will find everything in order. Please do not hesitate to call upon us at any time in the future when you feel we may be of assistance to you.

Sincerely yours,

_____
Escrow Officer

Figure 10-5

SELLER'S SETTLEMENT

ESCROW STATEMENT.

Southland ESCROW CORPORATION

7309 VAN NUYS BLVD. P.O. BOX 3176, VAN NUYS, CALIF. 91407
STATE 6-7960 (213) TRIANGLE 3-3112

Date: January 30, 2052

Escrow No. 3000

Statement of: SELLER   Timothy Smythe and Marylow Smythe   Recorded:

PROPERTY: 6947 Calle Los Robles, Green Valley, CA

ITEMS	DEBITS		CREDITS	
CONSIDERATION: Sale (xxx) Loan ( )			$ 179,500	00
Deposited				
Paid Outside of Escrow				
Balance of Encumbrance of Record				
Trust Deed in favor of: Anne B. Johnson	100,000	00		
Trust Deed in favor of Seller	43,500	00		
ADJUSTMENTS as of close of escrow 1-30-52				
Taxes on $ 897.50 for 6 Months Paid to 1-1-52	139	61		
Insurance on $ Premium $ yr's				
Interest on $ 100,000 @ 7 % paid to 1-1-52	602	64		
Impounded Funds Held By Lender				
Rents				
PAID TO TITLE COMPANY.				
Title Policy	607	25		
Revenue Stamps on Deed	87	45		
Recording: Deed (X), Trust Deed (X), Reconveyance ( ),	6	00		
Commission Green Valley Realty	5,385	00		
Antelope Hills Realty	5,385	00		
Escrow Fee one-half of $660.00	330	00		
Drawing Documents	10	00		
Notary Fees	4			
Insurance Endorsements				
Service Fee: Beneficiary's Statement (xxx) Demand ( )	15			
LENDER'S LOAN CHARGES:				
Loan Fee $ Appraisal Fee $ Tax Service $				
Interest @ %				
Lender's Forwarding Fee — Beneficiary's Statement				
PAYMENT OF ENCUMBRANCES:				
Demand of Principal $				
Interest @ % from to $				
Reconveyance Fee $				
Prepayment Charge $				
Forwarding Fee $				
Pest Control	390	00		
Balance Due This Company				
Our Check To Balance	23,038	05		
TOTALS	179,500	00	179,500	00

C. OTHER DISBURSEMENTS

These checks are to be accompanied by letters stating their purpose and the escrow number. The commission check should be accompanied by a personal note, in handwriting, telling how you enjoyed working with them and hope to work with them in the future. If you are very pleased with the performance of the particular broker with whom you had the most contact, it's nice to mention that to his or her boss, also. Do this even if you customarily send a form letter with the check. It reminds everybody that you're all involved in a personal service, which can best be done in the spirit of mutual cooperation and friendship. Once escrow has closed, you can relax your required strictly business attitude a little. (**NEVER to the point of disclosing confidential facts around town or bad-mouthing anybody involved, OF COURSE!**) It could only be helpful for all the people with whom you deal to know that you are cheerful and friendly, as well as a consummate professional.

Disburse these amounts:

1. A.B.C. Title Company. . . . . $ 700.70
2. Green Valley Realty 5,385.00
3. Antelope Hills Realty 5,385.00
4. Anne B. Johnson 15.00

ESCROW IS CLOSED.

VII. CHAPTER SUMMARY

An EASEMENT is a legal nonpossessory property interest that one person (the benefited party) has in land owned by another (the burdened party) entitling the holder to use for a specific purpose. When there are RIPARIAN RIGHTS, it will refer to the right to use the water on and under or adjacent to the owner's land.

In escrow there will be an APPROVAL RECITAL to indicate approval by either the buyer or seller of a specific document. A SECOND TRUST DEED is a junior lien to other liens recorded earlier.

Most escrows will have a PEST CONTROL REPORT which is the visible inspection of the property to determine what problems exist. A STANDARD NOTICE OF WORK COMPLETED and NOT COMPLETED indicates the work of the pest control operator completed or not and will have the charges included. Escrow should immediately contact the parties to the escrow to obtain their approval.

A PROMISSORY NOTE represents an unconditional promise to repay a debt. It is a negotiable instrument that can be transferred to another person.

ADJUSTMENTS, PRORATIONS, and the SETTLEMENT SHEET are involved in determining and showing how the various charges are distributed in the escrow.

VIII. TERMS

Adjustments: In escrow it is the credits and debits of a settlement sheet such as property taxes, insurance, rent prorations etc.

Approval Recital: A stamped or typed statement when signed by a buyer or seller indicates acceptance or approval of the document.

Easement: A right of use in the property of another.

Pest Control Report: The written results of a visible inspection of real property by a licensed operator. Parties should address the problem of what responsibility, if any, the seller has to correct existing damage to the structure.

Promissory Note: The unconditional written promise of one person to pay a certain sum of money to another at a future specified time.

Prorations: Refers to dividing or distributing proportionately according to the agreement of the buyers and sellers various charges and expenses in escrow. Common prorations include sewer charges, interest on loans, insurance premiums, rent, mortgage impounds, utilities and real property taxes.

Riparian Rights: A right of a landowner to use the water on, under and adjacent to his land, providing his use does not infringe on the rights of neighboring landowners.

Second Trust Deed: A junior trust deed to other loans having priority.

Settlement Sheet: Also called a closing statement or adjustment sheet. The statement shows how all closing and adjustment costs plus prepaid and unpaid expenses are allocated between buyer and seller. Separate closing statements are prepared for the buyer showing credits, charges and the balance due at closing; for the seller it shows credits, charges and the proceeds they will receive at closing.

Standard Notice of Work Completed and Not Completed: The written report of the pest control operator with a clearance of work completed or not completed together with the statement of charges.

IX. CHAPTER QUIZ

1. A riparian right easement concerns:

    a. water rights.
    b. earthquake.
    c. electric power lines.
    d. natural gas lines.

2. Water and streams are actually considered:

    a. private property.
    b. public property.
    c. real property.
    d. none of the above.

3. If an easement problem is NOT covered in the escrow instructions there must be:

    a. automatic escrow cancellation.
    b. escrow amendment.
    c. both a and b.
    d. neither a nor b.

4. A first trust deed means it was:

    a. typed first.
    b. the largest amount.
    c. recorded first.
    d. none of the above.

5. The county in which the property is located should be listed on the:
    a. trust deed.
    b. escrow memo.
    c. both a and b.
    d. neither a nor b.

6. If pest control work is NOT completed before escrow closes:
    a. delay closing.
    b. never close.
    c. both a and b.
    d. neither a nor b.

7. When adjusting for property taxes NOT paid by seller:
    a. determine amount owed.
    b. charge seller.
    c. credit buyer.
    d. all of the above.

8. When adjusting for interest on the existing loan, prorate until:
    a. the day before closing.
    b. closing.
    c. the day after closing.
    d. none of the above.

9. If the monthly interest payment on the loan is NOT made before closing:
    a. charge the seller.
    b. charge the buyer.
    c. both a and b.
    d. neither a nor b.

10. Checks disbursed by the escrow company should be accompanied by a:
    a. letter.
    b. note.
    c. phone call.
    d. any of the above.

ANSWERS: 1. a; 2. b; 3. b; 4. c; 5. c; 6. a; 7. d; 8. b; 9. a; 10. d

Exchange Escrow Sample

I. Real Property Exchanges

The first section of this book has concerned itself with real property sales escrows. From the detailed handling of these transactions and from our general discussion of the role of escrow, it is apparent that an escrow holder is essential to the proper closing of an escrow where real property is sold.

In California, very few sales transactions are handled outside of escrow and without the services of an escrow agent.

However, escrow companies are not limited to handling the sales of real estate. Escrows are also applied to a number of other real estate related transactions. We will now concentrate on the basics of real estate exchanges.

A. WHY AN EXCHANGE?

In Chapters 11 and 12, we will take a look at another important type of escrow transaction that is frequently encountered; an escrow where one property is traded, or "exchanged," for another.

CHAPTER OUTLINE

I. **REAL PROPERTY EXCHANGES (p. 273)**
   A. Why an Exchange? (p. 273)
   B. Tax Considerations (p. 275)
   C. Buying and Selling in One Transaction (p. 275)

II. **DIFFERENT APPROACHES (p. 276)**

III. **PARTIES TO THE EXCHANGE (p. 277)**
   A. Property One (p. 277)
   B. Property Two (p. 277)

IV. **REASON FOR THE EXCHANGE (p. 277)**

V. **THE EXCHANGE MEMO (p. 278)**

VI. **BOOT (p. 278)**

VII. **VALUATIONS OF PROPERTY (p. 279)**

VIII. **TWO OR MORE DEEDS (p. 280)**

IX. **THE EXCHANGE DEPOSIT RECEIPT (p. 280)**

X. **SAMPLE AGREEMENT (p. 283)**
   A. Determining the Consideration (p. 283)
   B. Determining Boot (p. 284)

XI. **FILLING OUT THE MEMOS (p. 285)**
   A. Party Number Two Memo (p. 285)
      1. Assumption of the Deed (p. 288)
      2. Adjustments (p. 288)
      3. Payments (p. 288)
      4. Miscellaneous (p. 289)
   B. Party Number One Memo (p. 290)
      1. Adjustments and Payments (p. 290)
      2. Tax Redemption of Real Property (p. 290)
      3. Miscellaneous (p. 291)

XII. **PROBATE (p. 291)**

XIII. **YOU ARE NOW READY TO PREPARE THE ESCROW INSTRUCTIONS (p. 292)**
   A. Escrow Instructions (p. 292)
   B. Exchange Instruction Form (p. 292)
   C. First and Second Party (p. 298)
   D. First Party Instructions (p. 299)
      1. The Beneficiary's Staterment (p. 299)
      2. Structural Pest Control Report (p. 300)
      3. Probate and Commission (p. 300)
      4. Adjustments to the Date of Closing (p. 301)
      5. Payments (p. 301)
      6. Charge's Check List (p. 302)
      7. Other Instructions of the First Party (p. 303)

To start with, we'll examine some of the basic reasons why such a transaction might take place. After all, would it not be easier for the parties just to sell the properties to each other in the standard manner? Wouldn't that be simpler for everyone involved— the real estate broker, the escrow holder and, especially, the two parties?

There must be a very good reason for this unusual kind of transaction. Actually, there are several good reasons, all of them important and valid. The main one can be summed-up in two words … income taxes!

B. TAX CONSIDERATIONS

Tax considerations are most commonly the motivating reason behind real property exchanges.

Think about the person who owns income generating property such as an apartment house. In selling this building such a person is bound to pay income taxes on any gain or profit realized in the sale. This is true even if the proceeds are immediately reinvested in another property acquired simultaneously and both deals close at the same time. The government will take its portion, but an exchange can be tax-free. If the owner exchanges the apartment house for one of equal or greater value, it is very possible that no income tax would be owed. This is the beauty of the tax-free exchange. As with all important tax planning, an accountant or tax attorney should be consulted.

C. BUYING AND SELLING IN ONE TRANSACTION

There are also other nice advantages to this procedure. For example, suppose the owner of a residence must suddenly move to another location for business reasons. He or she may have no trouble selling the present home but might not be able to find a new home in the new location. Perhaps a new home is located right away but it takes several months to close the sale on the old house. Somewhere in here our property owner is either sitting on two properties (and paying expenses and taxes on both) or is out in the street with nowhere to go for an indefinite period of time. A real estate exchange might circumvent these problems.

Because of these advantages the number of real estate exchanges has increased in recent years. This statement is especially true of residential properties. For example, very often land developers and subdividers will now accept "trade-ins." They encourage new buyers to use their old properties as part of the purchase price on a new home or condominium.

This increase is not limited to residential property exchanges. Income, commercial, and industrial properties are also commonly exchanged for one another.

These transactions are often financing strategies and can become extremely complex. There is a whole specialized field of professional commercial property exchangers who deal exclusively with this complicated kind of operation. Often, for example, numerous properties spread across several counties or even several states may be involved. The first step in dealing with these very complex exchange problems is to learn the basics. In this and the next two chapters we will outline the basic approaches, terminology and procedures for the real property exchange escrow.

II. Different Approaches

There are as many different approaches to such an escrow as there are escrow agents.

The essentials, as in any other escrow, are that you properly take the instructions of the parties, set up the instructions, and complete the processing.

For now, we will take you step by step through one approach, offering additional suggestions along the way that you may find helpful. As you acquire experience, you will no doubt develop your own methods and find a personal approach that works best for you.

Back when exchanges weren't as standardized as they are today, the escrow officer would prepare the paperwork as if dealing with two separate sales and set up two sets of escrow sales instructions. Now that exchanges are more common, there are printed forms designed specifically for that purpose and, of course, these should be used. We have selected one such form of printed instructions for our purposes here. It should be kept in mind, however, that this is only one of many such exchange forms that have been developed. The different forms have their own characteristics and will have a big impact on the procedures to be followed in taking the instructions and processing the escrow.

III. Parties to the Exchange

At this point, it is time to meet the parties to our exchange. We need to learn some of the background to the transaction before getting started taking the instructions.

A. PROPERTY ONE

Richard Hornbussel, a single man, lives in an apartment in Hollywood. Richard's mother, Matilda Hornbussel, owned a single-family residence in Los Angeles in which she resided up to the time of her death in January of this year. She left this property to Richard in her will. Richard decided that he didn't want to live in the house and would rather sell it and reinvest the money in other income property. To do this he engaged Tim Doyle, a real estate broker, and gave Tim an Exclusive Right To Sell listing. Probate proceedings are currently pending in the estate of Matilda Hornbussel. Stephen Tischler, an attorney, is handling the estate.

B. PROPERTY TWO

Pedro Gonzales has owned a duplex in San Francisco for the past six years. Title to the property is vested under the names of Pedro Gonzales and his wife, Angela Gonzales. Angela died earlier this year. Pedro has decided that he wants to live in Southern California where he was born. He arranged with his company to be transferred to their Pasadena office. He wants to acquire a home near his new office. He does not have sufficient cash for such a purchase and, as a result, must sell his San Francisco property. Dave Bentley, a real estate broker in San Francisco, has been given an Exclusive Agency listing on the property. Pedro's attorney, Sam Black, is handling Angela's estate.

IV. Reason for the Exchange

Pedro decided that he would like to live in the Los Angeles area and, because of this, stopped in to see Tim Doyle at his L.A. office. Doyle showed him the Hornbussel house and Pedro expressed interest, but indicated his need to sell the San Francisco duplex before he could come up with any cash. This gave Broker Doyle the idea for a property exchange and he suggested the idea to Pedro. Doyle then discussed this possibility with Richard Hornbussel. Richard made an offer to exchange based upon certain conditions. This offer was submitted to Pedro who accepted it immediately. Since Dave Bentley has the listing on the San Francisco property, he and Doyle worked out an agreement as to the commission on this transaction. Doyle now brings Gonzales and Hornbussel to you to open up the escrow.

V. The Exchange Memo

In a normal sales escrow it is generally possible to begin writing the escrow instructions as soon as you can get the parties to sit down with you and explain the terms.

You simply note them on your memo pad (or PDA or computer) and the escrow instructions are constructed.

With an exchange escrow it is a good idea to make sure you have a complete grasp of the agreement as both parties see it before attempting to commit it to paper.

If it makes it clearer in your head, you might find it a good idea to continue thinking of the transaction as two separate sales. After all each party is, in effect, selling his property to the other. In the case of an exchange, however, all or part of the consideration paid in each of the two sales will be represented by the parcel of real property presently owned by the other party.

Neither party need own the property outright. More often the property will be at least partially subject to a mortgage or trust deed. In this case what the parties actually exchange is their "equities" in the property—that portion which they have paid off. The owner of one property exchanges the equity held in that property for the equity held by the owner of the other property. All outstanding loans must be either assumed or paid off.

It is unlikely, for example, that the market values will be equal. Even if one party owns a property free and clear and it is worth $50,000, he may exchange it equally for a property worth $70,000 which is subject to a loan secured by a trust deed for the unpaid balance of $20,000. The equities in these two properties are equal at $50,000.

An even exchange can be effected in spite of the fact that the actual market values are different.

VI. Boot

In actual practice, of course, it is extremely unlikely to find such an even match-up of equities. They are almost inevitably different. In the above example, perhaps the second party's unpaid balance is $25,000. This would leave them with only $45,000 in equity to exchange. In order to create an even exchange the second party would have to pay the first party an additional $5,000 to make up for the difference in equities. In this way both sides are throwing $50,000 into the pot. The first party offers a $50,000 home. The second party offers $45,000 in equity plus $5,000 cash. *In exchange terminology this additional $5,000 is called **BOOT.***

Boot can be cash or any other valuable consideration agreeable to both parties.

Often, boot is promissory notes, stock certificates, or even another piece of land. Most exchanges will involve the payment of boot by one or more of the parties.

VII. Valuations of Property

It is generally the intention of the parties to try and create an even exchange if possible. Every effort will be made to balance the equities in some manner. Before you can prepare the escrow instructions you will need to know how this balance is intended to be achieved. Examine all the elements. **What valuations have been placed on the properties for the purposes of this exchange? What, if any, existing encumbrances are to remain on the properties? If boot is to be paid, who is receiving it and what is the amount? What form will it take? Is it to be paid as a function of escrow?** A valuation form (**Figure 11-1**) is often filled out before attempting to begin the escrow memo. Such a form is not essential, but is a very good way to be sure the elements of the exchange balance out and are understood by the escrow officer before the escrow instructions are prepared.

Figure 11-1

VALUATION FORM

First Party _____	Second Party _____
First Property _____	Second Property _____

	First Party	Second Party
Grantor's valuation	$ _____	$ _____
Less encumbrances totalling	$ _____	$ _____
Total equity conveyed	$ _____	$ _____
Boot (to balance equities)		
Cash through escrow		
Payable now	$ _____	$ _____
Payable later	$ _____	$ _____
Cash outside escrow	$ _____	$ _____
New deed of trust	$ _____	$ _____
Other _____	$ _____	$ _____
TOTAL	$ _____	$ _____

VIII. Two or More Deeds

You will note that on this form we identify the parties as **first party** and **second party**. This really doesn't indicate any kind of priority. Rather it is almost a necessity when dealing with two or more deeds to keep them distinct in this manner. After all, each party is both a "grantor" and a "grantee." These more customary titles are therefore rendered useless as a method of discriminating between the people involved. Similarly, the properties may simply be referred to as the "first" property and the "second" property. **As long as you identify them more fully early on and are consistent with the titles throughout, this should actually help eliminate confusion.**

There is no hard and fast rule about who should be made first and who should be made second. Often escrow officers like to refer to the party paying out boot as first. However, many others do the opposite.

A good policy is to start with the property of greatest value or perhaps the one requiring the greatest amount of detail in setting up the escrow instructions.

It is likely that this all may be decided for you based upon which preprinted form you use in noting the escrow instructions. Depending on how this form is set up, either party and either property may be first or second.

IX. The Exchange Deposit Receipt

If the parties followed the normal procedure, the exchange will have been put together with the help of a broker.

The broker will have seen to it that the agreement was formalized in a type of a deposit receipt called an "exchange agreement."

An exchange agreement is a binding contract executed by both parties. In the case of our example, such an agreement was prepared by Broker Doyle. Any exchange form may be used (see **Figure 11-2**).

Study this form carefully. It will give you a better understanding of the nature of exchanges. Like the normal deposit receipt, this form is the initial contract between the two parties. When properly filled in and signed it is **fully binding**. The parties may, however, by subsequent agreement, amend, expand, change, or add new provisions as they see fit. This is done at any time through the execution of an amended contract or by the execution of a new contract, such as the escrow instructions.

Figure 11-2

EXCHANGE AGREEMENT, page 1

EXCHANGE AGREEMENT

Richard Hornbussel, a single man

hereinafter called first party, hereby offers to exchange the following described property, situated in

city of Los Angeles _____, County of ___ Los Angeles _____, California:

The south 100 feet of the northeast quarter of the southeast quarter of the northwest quarter of Section 55, Township 9 North, Range 20 West, San Bernardino Meridian, also known as 2120 Carson Street, Los Angeles, hereinafter referred to as
first property.

Subject to: (1) Taxes for the fiscal year 20XX-XX, a lien not yet payable
             (2) Covenants, conditions, restrictions, and easements of record

For the following described property of Pedro Gonzales, an unmarried man _____

_____ hereinafter called second party, situated in

the city of San Francisco ___, County of ___ San Francisco _____, California:

Lots 23 and 24 of SUMMER VIEW TRACT, as per map recorded in Book 20, page 28 of
Maps in the office of the county recorder of said county, also known as 1019 Maine
Road, San Francisco, hereinafter referred to as second property.

Subject to: (1) Taxes for the fiscal year 20XX-XX a lien not yet payable
             (2) Covenants, conditions, restrictions, and easements of record
             (3) A deed of trust of record in favor of Premiere Financial Company
                 to secure a note in the original amount of $100,000 with an approxi-
                 mate unpaid balance of $76,000, the payments on said note to be
                 current to August 1, 20XX.

TERMS AND CONDITIONS OF EXCHANGE:

For the purposes of this exchange, the properties are valued as follows:
      First property: $55,000
      Second property: $136,000

First party will assume the unpaid balance of the loan of record on second property
and pay the difference in cash to second party to balance the equities.

This offer to exchange and acceptance are contingent upon American Financial Company approving the assumption of the above loan by first party and the release of
second party from further liability as the maker of the note.

First party will furnish termite report showing no visible infestation of wood-
destroying pests or organisms, and will pay for all corrective (but not preventitive)
work.

All delinquent taxes, bonds, assessments (if any) will be paid by each party on
the property which he is transferring.

EHCHANGE AGREEMENT, page 2

The parties hereto shall execute and deliver, within ___60___ days from the date this offer is accepted, all instruments, in writing, necessary to transfer title to said properties and complete and consummate this exchange. Each party shall supply Preliminary Title Reports for their respective properties. Evidences of title shall be California Land Title Association standard coverage form policies of title insurance showing titles to be merchantable and free of all liens and encumbrances, except taxes and those liens and encumbrances as otherwise set forth herein. Each party shall pay for the policies of Title Insurance for the property to be acquired ☐ conveyed ☒.

If either party is unable to convey a marketable title, except as herein provided, within three months after acceptance hereof by second party, or if the improvements on any of the herein named properties be destroyed or materially damaged prior to transfer of title or delivery of agreement of sale, then this agreement shall be of no further effect, except as to payment of commissions and expenses incurred in connection with examination of title, unless the party acquiring the property so affected elects to accept the title the other party can convey or subject to the conditions of the improvements.

Taxes, insurance premiums (if policies be satisfactory to party acquiring the property affected thereby), rents, interest and other expenses of said properties shall be pro-rated as of the date of transfer of title or delivery of agreement of sale, unless otherwise provided herein.

___Tim Doyle___	of ___4216 Figueroa St., Los Angeles___	CA ___(213) 662-3134___
Broker # 411	Address	Phone No.

is hereby authorized to act as broker for all parties hereto and may accept commission therefrom. Should second party accept this offer, first party agrees to pay said broker commission for services rendered as follows:

___Three thousand three hunderd and no/100 ($3,300.00) dollars to be paid at close of___
___escrow.___

Should second party be unable to convey a marketable title to his property then first shall be released from payment of any commission, unless he elects to accept the property subject thereto. First party agrees that broker may cooperate with other brokers and divide commissions in any manner satisfactory to them.

This offer shall be deemed revoked unless accepted in writing within ___10___ days after date hereof, and such acceptance is communicated to first party within said period. Broker is hereby given the exclusive and irrevocable right to obtain acceptance of second party within said period.

All words used herein in the singular shall include the plural and the present tense shall include the future and the masculine gender shall include the feminine and neuter.

Richard Hornbussel, 1551 Sunset Ave., L.A., CA
(213) 662-1917   90030

Dated ___June 26___ 20 __XX__   *Richard Hornbussel*

ACCEPTANCE

Second party hereby accepts the foregoing offer upon the terms and conditions stated and agrees to pay commission for services rendered to:

___David Bentley___	of ___663 First St., San Francisco___	CA ___(415) 555-1820___
Broker #	Address	Phone No.

as follows: ___each one-half of Eight Thousand One Hundred and Sixty and no/100 ($8,160.00)___
___dollars, to be paid at close of escrow.___

Second party agrees that broker may act as broker for all parties hereto and may accept commissions therefrom, and may co-operate with other brokers and divide commissions in any manner satisfactory to them.

Should first party be unable to convey a marketable title to his property then second party shall be released from payment of any commission, unless he elects to accept the property of first party subject thereto.

Pedro Gonzales

Pedro Gonzales, 1019 Maine Road, San Francisco, CA
(818) 247-2223   94102

Dated ___July 1___ 20 __XX__   _____

Such a contract automatically supersedes the original agreement.

This is often the intent of the parties as they open escrow.

Like the normal deposit receipt, this form is the initial contract between the two parties.

X. Sample Agreement

Take the time now to study closely our sample agreement (Figure 11-2). It is essential that you be very familiar with the content of this form as we will be referring back to it constantly as we take the instructions of the parties into escrow.

Right from the top you can see that the printed form immediately identifies the parties as "first" and "second." The form also shows the matters to which each of the properties is **subject to**. The Hornbussel property appears to be unencumbered except for the usual taxes, covenants, conditions, restrictions, and normal easements of record. The Gonzales property, however, is to be exchanged subject to an existing deed of trust. The specific conditions concerning this deed of trust and other matters to which the parties have agreed are then detailed under that part of the exchange agreement called **Terms and Conditions of Exchange**. Each of these is very important. Note them well because, with a few modifications, all of these must appear in the escrow instructions.

Take a look at the printed provisions on the backside of the form. The first and third paragraphs are of particular interest to the escrow holder. The first **sets a time limit for the completion of the transaction** and also indicates the type of title insurance to be purchased and whether the acquiring or conveying party pays. The third paragraph **lists the various adjustments which will need to be prorated**. You will also note that the specifics of the commissions to be paid to Broker Doyle and Broker Bentley are spelled out on the second page of the form.

A. DETERMINING THE CONSIDERATION

As the first step in taking the instructions from the parties to the escrow, it is a good idea to establish clearly the amount and nature of the considerations involved.

Let's assume Doyle has the exchange agreement. The consideration form can be completed from the information he gives you.

Let's take a close look at this form (**Figure 11-3**) and compare it with the exchange agreement. Who is listed as first party and which property is "first property"? Hornbussel and his property are designated as such. Gonzales will be the second party and his San Francisco home is the second property.

Figure 11-3

CONSIDERATION FORM

First Party _HORnBUSSEL_ Second Party _GonzALES_

First Property _Los AngELES_ Second Property _San FRanCisco_

	First Party	Second Party
Grantor's valuation	$ _55,000.00_	$ _136,000.00_
Less encumbrances totalling	$ _0_	$ _76,000.00_
Total equity conveyed	$ _55,000.00_	$ _60,000.00_
Boot (to balance equities)		
Cash through escrow		
Payable now	$ _2,000.00_	$
Payable later	$ _3,000.00_	$
Cash outside escrow	$	$
New deed of trust	$	$
Other _____	$	$
TOTAL	$ _60,000.00_	$ _60,000.00_

What are the **Grantor's Valuations** in each case? Look under Terms and Conditions in the exchange agreement. The first property is valued at $55,000 while the second property is worth $136,000. However you will note that under the description of the second property, the exchange agreement requires that it be transferred subject to a trust deed of record with an unpaid balance of approximately $76,000. This amount is entered on your form and then **subtracted** from the total valuation to find the equity ($60,000). The Hornbussel property (property one) has no such encumbrance, so the **Total Equity Conveyed** is the entire valuation of $55,000.

B. DETERMINING BOOT

What is the difference between the two equities? Hornbussel's is $55,000 while Gonzales' is $60.000. This leaves a difference of $5,000. **The agreement clearly states** that the first party will pay this amount in cash to balance the two equities. You must find out if this boot will be paid through escrow or on the outside. You speak with Hornbussel who agrees to pay $2,000 into escrow now and promises the remaining $3,000 before the close. No money will be paid outside of escrow.

If you enter all these amounts and total the figures, they should balance out to $60,000 from both parties. Each is bringing an equal amount to the transaction.

XI. Filling Out the Memos

The rest of the instructions are first carefully noted on escrow memos (**Figures 11-4** and **11-5**)—one for each property—just as if you were processing two separate sales transactions. Distinguish between the two by designating one "first property" and the other "second property." **Cross out Sale and Loan** and leave the word **Exchange** to help identify the type of transaction.

The property descriptions can be copied exactly from the exchange agreement. Attach a copy of the consideration form and write **see attached** in the space provided for this information. Names, addresses, and telephone numbers are all on the agreement. Also on the agreement is the **Time Limit** on escrow. The form says 60 days from the date of acceptance. Gonzales accepted the offer on July 1. A 60-day time limit sets the close of escrow on August 30. This can, of course, be extended by mutual agreement.

This basic information aside, the rest of the terms should be gathered in specific detail from each of the parties. We'll start with party number two because property number two is encumbered by that existing trust deed and so this part of the transaction looks to be the more complicated.

A. PARTY NUMBER TWO MEMO

The exchange agreement requires each party to provide a **CLTA title insurance policy** on the property being conveyed. The second property is valued at $136,000. This should be the amount of the policy. The loan of record is insured by a previous policy so this will be a CLTA owner's policy.

Title is to be vested to **Richard Hornbussel, a single man**. This is how he is identified in the exchange agreement.

Let's say that this escrow is opened on July 12. As of this date the taxes for the current fiscal year are a lien but are not yet payable. According to the exchange agreement, the second property will be subject to these taxes and no others. As far as other encumbrances go, there are the covenants, conditions, restrictions, and easements of record. There is also the trust deed owed to Premiere Financial company of San Francisco.

Figure 11-4

PROPERTY MEMO – Property #1

Property #1

SALE - LOAN - EXCHANGE

CASH THROUGH ESCROW   NOW $ _See Attached_

     LATER $

MTG-TRUST DEED $

MTG-TRUST DEED $

CASH OUTSIDE OF ESCROW $

     TOTAL CONSIDERATION $

TIME LIMIT

FIRST PARTY

ADDRESS

SECOND PARTY

ADDRESS

ISSUE (CLTA) JT PRO OWNER'S LOAN ALTA LEASEHOLD: FOR $

ON _S. 100' of NE 1/4 of SE 1/4 of NW 1/4 Sec. 55_
Twnshp. 9 n Rng 20W SBM Co Los Angeles

VEST IN _Pedro Gonzales, a widower_

SUBJECT TO _all_ GENERAL AND SPECIAL TAX 20XX 20XX _a lien not yet payable_ BONDS AND ASSESSMENTS

COVENANTS, CONDITIONS, RESTRICTIONS AND EASEMENTS OF RECORD

MORTGAGE-TRUST DEED (OF RECORD)   FORM EXECUTED BY

TO SECURE A NOTE FOR $ PAYABLE IN INSTALLMENTS TO

AT   WITH INTEREST FROM   ON UNPAID PRINCIPAL AT   % PER ANNUM (PAYABLE)

PRINCIPAL (AND INTEREST) PAYABLE IN INSTALLMENTS OF $ OR MORE ON THE   DAY OF EACH   MONTH

BEGINNING   MATURITY DATE   PREPAYMENT PRIVILEGE

PRESENT UNPAID BALANCE $

MORTGAGE-TRUST DEED (OF RECORD)   FORM EXECUTED BY

TO SECURE A NOTE FOR $ PAYABLE IN INSTALLMENTS TO

AT   WITH INTEREST FROM   ON UNPAID PRINCIPAL AT   % PER ANNUM (PAYABLE)

PRINCIPAL (AND INTEREST) PAYABLE IN INSTALLMENTS OF $ OR MORE ON THE   DAY OF EACH   MONTH

BEGINNING   MATURITY DATE   PREPAYMENT PRIVILEGE

PRESENT UNPAID BALANCE $

ADJUSTMENTS

TAXES AS OF _C/E_

   BASIS _latest tax bill_

INSURANCE AS OF _C/E as handled_

INTEREST AS OF

   BASIS

RENTS AS OF

   BASIS

WATER STOCK & SEC'Y STATEMENT

PAYMENT

CHARGES PAID BY _usual_

TRANSFER TAX $ _18-15_   TAX SERVICE

COMM $ _3,300_ TO _Jim Doyle_

ADDRESS _4216 Figueroa St_   BROKER No _411_

TAXES   TAX SALES   ASSESSMENTS

PAY THE FOLLOWING AT CLOSE OF ESCROW _Tax Sale 2nd 1/2_

_20XX-XX_ _taxes_

ESCROW OPENED AND
CHARGES GUARANTEED BY

WE DRAW _Deed. Deliver termite report - 1st party's expense_

REMARKS _Title to be acquired by dec/dist in est of Matilda Hernandez_
case # 96741 certif copy decree to come from atty. Stephen Tuchler

Figure 11-5

PROPERTY MEMO – Property #2

Property #2

SALE - LOAN - EXCHANGE

TIME LIMIT *August 30, 20XX*

CASH THROUGH ESCROW NOW $
LATER $

FIRST PARTY *Richard Hornbussel*
ADDRESS *1551 Sunset Ave. LA 90039*
telephone (213) 662-1917

MTG TRUST DEED
MTG TRUST DEED
CASH OUTSIDE OF ESCROW $ *see attached sheet*

SECOND PARTY *Pedro Gonzales*
ADDRESS *1019 Maine Rd. San Francisco*
CA 94102
telephone (415) 247-2223

TOTAL CONSIDERATION $

ON *Lots 23 and 24 of Summer View Tract*
cy & co of San Francisco @ 20/28 maps
VEST IN *Richard Hornbussel, a single man*

ISSUE (CLTA) JT PRO OWNER'S LOAN ATA LEASEHOLD FOR $ *136,000*
use pending order 5209
Confidential of San Francisco
obtain 110.5

SUBJECT TO *all* GENERAL AND SPECIAL TAX 20XX 20XX *a lien not yet payable*
BONDS AND ASSESSMENTS *in dorgement for lender*

COVENANTS, CONDITIONS, RESTRICTIONS AND EASEMENTS OF RECORD

MORTGAGE-TRUST DEED (OF RECORD) FORM EXECUTED BY *Pedro Gonzales & Angela Gonzales*

TO SECURE A NOTE FOR $ *100,000* PAYABLE IN INSTALLMENTS TO *Cremiere Financial Company*

AT *SF* WITH INTEREST FROM ON UNPAID PRINCIPAL AT *12* % PER ANNUM (PAYABLE)

PRINCIPAL (AND INTEREST) PAYABLE IN INSTALLMENTS OF $ *1277.77* OR MORE ON THE *1st* DAY OF EACH *calendar* MONTH

BEGINNING *approx $76,000 is shown by bfcy stmt* MATURITY DATE PREPAYMENT PRIVILEGE

PRESENT UNPAID BALANCE $ *Loan to be assumed by first pty. 2nd pty to be released note to be modified to provide for*

MORTGAGE TRUST DEED (OF RECORD) FORM EXECUTED BY

TO SECURE A NOTE FOR $ PAYABLE IN INSTALLMENTS TO

AT WITH INTEREST FROM *9-1* ON UNPAID PRINCIPAL AT *12.5* PER ANNUM (PAYABLE)

PRINCIPAL (AND INTEREST) PAYABLE IN INSTALLMENTS OF $ *1319.44* OR MORE ON THE *1st* DAY OF EACH *calendar* MONTH *assump & modif agmt to come from lender; to be exec by 1st & 2nd parties*

BEGINNING MATURITY DATE PREPAYMENT PRIVILEGE *1st party to pay assump fee of 1% & $50 incid charges*

PRESENT UNPAID BALANCE $ *on recording of assumption agreement.*

A
D
J
U
S
T
M
E
N
T
S

TAXES AS OF *Close of escrow*
BASIS *2nd install latest tax bill*
INSURANCE AS OF *C/E is headed by Cremiere*
INTEREST AS OF *C/E*
BASIS *benef stmt*
RENTS AS OF *C/E - basis $600 monthly paid to 8/15 payments to be collected as due*
BASIS
WATER STOCK & SEC'Y STATEMENT *Credit 1st party*
$300 for cleaning deposit

WE DRAW *deed*

REMARKS *Attorney Sam Black to provide doc to term jttncy with Angela Gonzales and inheritance tax release*

P
A
Y
M
E
N
T
S

CHARGES PAID BY *1/2 each party*
TRANSFER TAX $ *as reqd* TAX SERVICE
COMM $ *8,160 1/2 to David Bentley*
ADDRESS *663 First St S.F.* BROKER NO. *831*
1/2 to Jim Doyle Broker #411
TAXES SALES ASSESSMENTS
PAY THE FOLLOWING AT CLOSE OF ESCROW *sewer bond in full Sept installment on loan - chg to 1st party*

ESCROW OPENED AND CHARGES GUARANTEED BY
Escrow contingent upon lender's approval of assumption

1. Assumption of the Trust Deed

The original note was for $100,000 but the unpaid balance will be around $76,000 after the August 1 payment is made. These payments are $1,277.77 a month. Hornbussel will assume this loan and payments while Gonzales is to be released from any further liability as maker of the note. The entire exchange agreement, however, **is contingent upon Premiere Financial's approval of this assumption and release**.

Upon questioning the parties, you find that they have already made preliminary arrangements with the lender. Premiere intends to supply a beneficiary's statement after the August 1 payment is made by Gonzales. They have conditionally approved the assumption and release provided they are permitted to increase the interest rate to **12.5%** and the monthly payments as of September 1 to **$1,319.44**. The first party (Hornbussel) will pay an assumption fee of 1% of the unpaid balance plus a charge of $50 for the beneficiary's statement and other paperwork. Premiere will send you an agreement modifying the note and providing for the assumption and release. Both parties must sign this and it is to be recorded, Hornbussel agrees to pay for recording. Premiere also requires a **CLTA 110.5 Indorsement** insuring the modification of the note. This will be attached to their present ALTA policy. Escrow is contingent upon final approval of all these arrangements by the loan committee at Premiere.

All this information is filled in on the second property memo form. Notice how the 110.5 Indorsement is added in with the other title insurance information and how the contingency is included at the bottom of the page.

2. Adjustments

The adjustments are all listed to take effect **C/E (as of the close of escrow)**. Taxes will switch over as of that date and Premiere will turn over the Fire insurance policy. Interest on the loan also adjusts as of the close of escrow. This adjustment will be based on the figures contained in the beneficiary's statement.

As you may recall, the Gonzales property is a duplex. The Gonzales family currently lives in one part, but the other part is inhabited by a tenant. This is a **month-to-month tenancy** with rent of $600. Rent is collected in advance, due on the 15th each month. The tenant is paid up until August 15, but Gonzales will continue to collect until the close of escrow. He also received a $300 cleaning deposit from the tenant that may need to be refunded when the unit is vacated. For this reason **Hornbussel must receive a credit for $300 from Gonzales** to cover this deposit.

3. Payments

If you look in the payment section you can see that the parties have agreed to split the escrow charges. **As far as transfer tax goes, it is owed on the total value of**

the property minus the amount of the unpaid trust deed balance. The property is valued at $136,000 and the balance owed is approximately $76,000. This transfer tax will be based upon a transfer amount of around $60,000. We won't know the exact figure until the beneficiary's statement arrives from the lender. However, Gonzales agrees to pay the required tax when it has been ascertained. We fill in as required and wait to compute the exact amount.

With the commission it must be remembered that two brokers are involved in this transaction—Bentley in San Francisco and Doyle in Los Angeles. These two have negotiated a split where each is to receive one-half the commission for the sale of this property. Doyle included this provision in the exchange agreement and Gonzales agreed to it when he signed. Doyle will also receive a commission from Hornbussel for the sale of the first property. Both parties should be aware of this fact and must agree to it **in writing**. This consent should be reflected in the escrow instructions.

It is important also that each of the brokers give you their license number issued by the Department of Real Estate.

You will also note that there is a sewer bond lien against the property. Several years ago the City of San Francisco levied a special assessment against this property because it benefited from improvements made in the local sewer system. Gonzales has agreed to pay this bond in full as a condition of the transaction. We note this fact so that a provision arranging this payment will be included in the escrow instructions.

4. Miscellaneous

Escrow is scheduled to close August 30 and Hornbussel is supposed to assume loan payments as of September 1. For Hornbussel this is calling it close. He doesn't want to send out money to Premiere before knowing for sure if escrow has closed successfully. If he waits until after the 30th, though, his first payment will almost certainly be late. **The best suggestion is for him to include this payment with the funds delivered to Premiere at closing**. In this way the payment will arrive on time, but only if escrow has closed to everyone's satisfaction.

Another potential problem is the fact that title to the second property is vested in **joint tenancy** to Gonzales and his deceased wife. Before the transfer of this property can be insured this joint tenancy must be terminated in the record and the state must release the inheritance estate tax. Gonzales' attorney, Sam Black, is currently arranging the tax matter with the state and will provide documents terminating the joint tenancy. This is noted under **Remarks**.

Gonzales has gone ahead and opened title order No. 5209 with **Confidential Title Insurance and Trust of San Francisco** to use in gaining the tax release. Since this

order is still open and pending, it can be used to save time and money in obtaining the title report. This information is noted with the other title insurance materials.

B. PARTY NUMBER ONE MEMO

The memo sheet on the first property part of the transaction is a bit simpler to map out. Information here is largely taken from the agreement, but conversations with Gonzales and, especially, Hornbussel will reconfirm and fill in details.

Gonzales will take title as **a widower**. The stated value of the property is $55,000, so he will need CLTA owner's title insurance for the full amount. There is no deed of trust encumbering this parcel. Gonzales will take title subject only **to current taxes, easements, and CC&Rs**.

1. Adjustments and Payments

As with the San Francisco property, all adjustments operate as of the close of escrow. The taxes and fire insurance will be prorated as of that date. Hornbussel will deliver the fire insurance policy into escrow.

As we already discussed, each party has agreed to pay half of the escrow fee. This can be indicated by noting that they are following the "usual" arrangement in the matter. **Look to the exchange agreement for details on the payment of the commission** (Figure 11-2). In this case there is no split since Doyle is both the "listing" and "selling" agent. Hornbussel has already agreed to pay him $3,300.

2. Tax Redemption of Real Property

There is a slight complication regarding tax payments to the state. Hornbussel neglected to pay the second installment of property taxes for the last fiscal year and the property has been "sold" to the state. This is not as serious as it sounds, as we will see when we examine the property tax time table.

NOVEMBER 1	FIRST INSTALLMENT DUE and PAYABLE
DECEMBER 10	FIRST INSTALLMENT DELINQUENT as of 5pm
FEBRUARY 1	SECOND INSTALLMENT DUE and PAYABLE
APRIL 10	SECOND INSTALLMENT DELINQUENT as of 5pm
JUNE 30	END FISCAL YEAR (PROPERTY SOLD to STATE)
JULY 1	BEGINNING NEW FISCAL YEAR

Since we said that today is July 12, we are already in the new fiscal year and the Hornbussel property has already been sold to the state for nonpayment of the second installment. But this is not a sale in the conventional sense. **It is a book transaction to initiate the beginning of a redemption period at the end of which title actually does pass to the state**. This is a long way off, however. Hornbussel, the legal owner, still holds full title to the property and has five years to pay off the delinquent taxes and penalties.

If, for some reason, he were not to redeem the property by the end of the fifth year following this "sale" to the state, there would be a second sale. **This would be an actual sale and the state would acquire legal title**. The state could in turn offer it to the public at an auction and the highest bidder would gain fee title to the property.

Most title insurance companies will insure a property from a tax sale after a year has elapsed and no one has found defects in the tax sale proceedings.

Hornbussel, of course, wants to redeem the property in this case and instructs you to do so. You must wait for the title report to find out how much is owed to affect this redemption. It will show the tax sale as an exception to title and will indicate the taxes and penalties payable. You will instruct the title company to handle the actual payment, but all this information needs to be in the escrow instructions and so you **make note of it on your memo for the first property**.

3. Miscellaneous

You may recall that Hornbussel agreed to furnish a **pest control report** and to pay for all corrective work in the event of infestation. You should remind him of this and get his assurance that he will have this report delivered to escrow.

Title of record on the first property is actually still vested in the name of Hornbussel's deceased mother, Matilda Hornbussel. Title passed immediately to Richard upon her death as he was the devisee of her will, but title still must be properly administered through a probate proceeding. The **Superior Court of California** must judicially establish his fee ownership.

XII. Probate

The main purpose of probate is to gather the assets of the decedent, pay any debts or taxes which may be due on the estate, and to appropriately distribute whatever is left.

The transfer of these assets is evidenced by a probate court order called a **DECREE OF DISTRIBUTION**. *In the case of the Hornbussel estate, Richard must obtain a decree establishing his ownership of the real property in question. You must record this decree with the county recorder's office in Los Angeles County, where the property is located. As soon as this decree comes through, Richard's attorney, Stephen Tischler, will send you a certified copy. Note the case number in the* **remarks column**.

XIII. You Are Now Ready to Prepare the Escrow Instructions

Assuming all of this information was gathered correctly, you now have the exchange agreement, your consideration detail and two memo sheets completely filled out. You have a great deal of important information to assimilate. All of this must be woven clearly into your comprehensive escrow instructions.

Let's say that all of this has been achieved in one office visit from Hornbussel, Gonzales and Doyle on the morning of July 12. You can suggest several alternatives to them with regard to the completed instructions. They may go their separate ways now and you will mail copies to each of the principals in a few days for their approval. You could prepare the instructions and deliver them to Doyle so that he may arrange for them to be signed. Or, you could set up an appointment on a later date for them to return to your office.

Gonzales, however, made a special trip down from San Francisco for the day and must return tomorrow. He wishes to settle the instructions today. You agree to complete them as quickly as possible to accommodate this problem and invite them to return at 4 PM.

A. ESCROW INSTRUCTIONS

Your two memo sheets, the exchange agreement and the consideration form are all laid out in front of you. The parties have left and now you can concentrate on properly preparing the escrow instructions.

The key thing here is to write out the instructions in such a way that both parties will have a good understanding of their role in the transaction and you will have a comprehensive guide in the performance of your job.

Rather than making out two separate sales instructions, we will use a form specifically designed for exchange transactions. This form differs somewhat from the instructions we have used thus far in this book. Let's take a look at it and discuss some of the unique features.

B. EXCHANGE INSTRUCTION FORM

As you can see, the form we are using here (**Figure 11-6**) consists of three pages of instruction plus a sheet of **General Provisions. These provisions are normally printed on the back of the last page**, but for convenience here we are making it a separate sheet. We have also inserted an additional page between one and two in order to include all of the detailed instructions of this rather complicated sample transaction. **Generally, the three printed pages will be sufficient**. Often, however, you may want the option of an additional page or pages. Do not hesitate to insert them if it helps you draw

Figure 11-6

EXCHANGE ESCROW INSTRUCTIONS, page 1

EXCHANGE
ESCROW INSTRUCTIONS

ESCROW NO. 243279
ESCROW NO. 243280

To:
Address: Your Escrow Company
          111 N. Business Street
          Anytown, California 94321

DATE July 12, 20XX

On or before   August 30, 20XX   I/we   will   hand you the sum of $3,000.00
and you are handed herewith $2,000.00
and a deed executed by   RICHARD HORNBUSSEL, a single man, hereinafter referred to
as First Party, to PEDRO GONZALES, a widower, hereinafter referred to as Second Party,

on the property described (herein referred to as FIRST property)
   the South 100 feet of the northeast quarter of the southeast quarter of the northwest
   quarter of Section 55, Township 9 North, Range 20 West, San Bernardino Meridian, in the
   County of Los Angeles, State of California

which you will deliver when you can issue yur current form of CLTA Standard
Coverage Owner's policy of title insurance on said land, with liability
in the amount of $ 55,000.00   showing title vested in PEDRO GONZALES, a widower

SUBJECT ONLY TO: All   taxes for the fiscal year 20XX   - 20XX
           A Lien not yet payable.
Covenants, conditions, restrictions, and easements of record.

providing you obtain for me a deed to the property described (herein referred
to as SECOND property)
   Lots 23 and 24 of Summer View Tract, in the City and County of San Francisco, State of
   California, as per map recorded in Book 20, page 28 of Maps in the office of the County
   Recorder of said County.

and when you can issue your current form of CLTA Standard Coverage Owner's   policy
of title insurance on said property with liability in the amount of $ 136,000.00
showing title vested in   RICHARD HORNBUSSEL, a single man

SUBJECT ONLY TO: All   taxes for the fiscal year 20XX   - 20XX
           A Lien not yet payable.
Covenants, conditions, restrictions, and easements of record.

A deed of trust of record securing an indebtedness of $100,000.00 in favor of Premiere
Financial Company.

You will be handed a beneficiary's statement by Premiere Financial Company showing the
unpaid balance of the note secured by said trust deed to be approximately $76,000.00, payable
in installments of $1272.77 on the first day of each month, including interest at 12% per
annum, principal and interest paid to August 1, 20XX (.

See next page

EXCHANGE ESCROW INSTRUCTIONS, page 2

The final consummation of this escrow is contingent upon Premiere Financial Company approving my assumption of the indebtedness on second property and releasing second party from further personal liability thereon. Execution of the hereinafter mentioned agreement by the first and second parties shall constitute approval of all terms and conditions thereof and shall satisfy this contingency.

You will be handed an agreement by Premiere Financial Company providing for the foregoing assumption and release. Said agreement shall further provide for a modification of the terms of payment of said indebtedness to change the interest rate to 12.5% per annum and to increase the monthly payments of principal and interest to $1319.44.

You are to have said agreement recorded at close of escrow, and obtain a CLTA 110.5 indorsement on the lender's policy of title insurance, insuring the modification of the trust deed in accordance with instructions of Premiere Financial Company.

****

First party will cause to be handed you a current termite report by a structural pest control operator, describing the house and garage located at 2120 Carson Street, Los Angeles, Ca., showing free from visible evidence of wood destroying pests or organisms. If any infestation is found, first party agrees to have said infestation and damage repaired at his expense, and to furnish an operator's certificate of completion. Other recommended work, if any, is to be done at second party's option and expense.

****

First party will acquire title to first property by decree of distribution in the Estate of Matilda Hornbussel, deceased, probate #96741, Los Angeles County Superior Court. A certified dopy of said decree will be handed you by Stephen Tischler, attorney, for recording at first party's expense.

****

It has been disclosed that Tim Doyle, realtor, is receiving a commission from both parties in this exchange; both parties approve payment of such commission.

****

Adjust the following to date of close of escrow:

On both properties:

      1. Taxes for the current fiscal year based on latest issued tax bill.

      2. Premiums on fire insurance policies as handed you.

On second property only:

      1. Rents based on $600 per month, payable monthly in advance and now paid to August 15, 20XX . You are to assume that further rents will be collected by second party as they fall due unless notified to the contrary in writing prior to the close of escrow.

      2. Credit first party and charge second party $300 cleaning deposit paid by tenant of second property.

      3. Interest on loan of record on second property based on the Beneficiary's statement to be handed you by Premiere Financial Company. In the event said statement shows the unpaid principal balance to be more or less than $76,000.000, you are to adjust the difference in cash.

****

EXCHANGE ESCROW INSTRUCTIONS, page 3

EXCHANGE
ESCROW INSTRUCTIONS

ESCROW NO. 243279
ESCROW NO. 243280

To:
Address: Your Escrow Company
             111 N. Business Street
             Anytown, CA 94321

DATE July 12, 20XX

we have read and approve the foregoing instructions. On or before August 30, 19XX
we will hand you a deed to said SECOND property to the vestee shown,
executed by   Pedro Gonzales, a widower

which you will deliver when you obtain for me a deed to said FIRST property
and when you can issue your title insurance policy as provided on page 1
hereof,   and hold for my account $5,000.00 less charges and adjustments herein authorized
and other documents deliverable to me, if any, as above provided for.

Take all adjustments and deliver fire insurance as provided in the foregoing
instructions.

ADDITIONAL INSTRUCTIONS

Title order No. 5209 has been opened with Confidential Title Insurance and Trust Company
of San Francisco. You are to obtain a title report and title policy under this order as
herein provided. All charges in connection with said title order are to be paid by me through
this escrow.

****

Sam Black, attorney, will deposit in escrow for recording without collection documents required
to enable the title company to determine that the joint tenancy with Angela Gonzales had
been terminated by reason of her death, together with a release of any California Inheritance
Tax Lien or Consent to Transfer.

****

From funds accruing to my account herein, you are to pay the following at close of escrow:
1. Bond for sewer installation on second property, including penalties & interest, if any.
2. Commission in the amount of $8,160.00 payable as follows:
   ½ to David Bentley, 663 First Street, San Francisco, CA (License No. 831)
   ½ to Tim Doyle, 4216 Figueroa Street, Los Angeles, CA (License No. 411)
3. Title and escrow charges as provided below.

The GENERAL PROVISIONS printed on the reverse side of this page of these
instructions are by reference thereto incorporated herein and made a part
hereof and have been read and are hereby approved by the undersigned.
          Time is of the essence of these instructions. If this escrow is
not in condition to close by the "time limit date: of   , and
demand for cancellation is made, you will proceed to close this escrow
when the principals have complied with the escrow instructions.

Any amendments of or supplements to any instructions affecting this
escrow must be in writing. I will hand you any funds and instruments
required to complete this escrow.

All documents, balances and statements due the undersigned are to be
mailed to the address shown below.

Signature_____Address_____Tel._____

Signature_____Address_____Tel._____

EXCHANGE ESCROW INSTRUCTIONS, page 4

EXCHANGE
ESCROW INSTRUCTIONS
(continued)

ESCROW NO. 243279
ESCROW NO. 243280

DATE July 12, 20XX

You are to pay the following at close of escrow from funds to be deposited
by first party:

1. Tax sale on 1st property for 2nd installment 20XX-XX taxes plus penalties
   and delinquencies.

2. Payment due 9/1/XX on note on 2nd property in the amount of $1319.44.

3. Assumption Fee of 1% on unpaid balance of said note, plus $50 for bene-
   ficiary's statement and incidental costs, to Premiere Financial Company.

4. Commission in the amount of $3,300.00 to Time Doyle, Realtor,
   4216 Figueroa Street, Los Angeles, CA (Broker No. 411)

****

A RECAPITULATION OF THIS ESCROW IS AS FOLLOWS:

	First Property	Second Property
Grantor's valuation	$55,000.00	$136,000.00
Encumbrance of Record		76,000.00
Equity Conveyed	55,000.00	60,000.00
Cash to balance equities	5,000.00	
Totals	$60,000.00	$ 60,000.00

****

These escrows must close, and all necessary documents be recorded, concurrently. The
closing of the escrow on each property is contingent upon concurrent closing and recording
as to the other property.

The GENERAL PROVISIONS printed on the reverse side of this page of these
instructions are by reference there, incorporated herein and made a part
hereof and have been read and are hereby approved by the undersigned.
    Time is of the essence of these instructions. If this escrow is not
in condition to close by the "time limit date" of   8/30/XX   , and demand
for cancellation is received by you from any principal to this escrow
after said date , you shall act in accordance with Paragraph 7 of the
General Provisions printed on the reverse side hereof. If no demand for
cancellation is made, you will proceed to close this escrow when the
principals have complied with the escrow instructions.

Any amendments of or supplements to any instructions affecting this
escrow must be in writing. I will hand you any funds and instruments
required to complete this escrow.   I pay ½ escrow fee, title policy premium, drawing
deeds, transfer tax of $18.15 & recording decree on 1st property; CLTA 110.5 indorsement,
recording deeds and assumption agreement on 2nd property.
All documents, balances and statements due the undersigned are to be
mailed to the address shown below.

Signature _____ Address 1551 Sunset Avenue   Tel. (818) 662-1917
         Richard Hornbussel   Los Angeles, CA 90039
Signature _____ Address _____   Tel. _____

Page 2

EXCHANGE ESCROW INSTRUCTIONS, General Provisions

GENERAL PROVISIONS

1. Deposit of Funds

All funds received in this escrow shall be deposited with other escrow funds in a general escrow account or accounts of Title Insurance and Trust Company, with any state or national bank, and may be transferred to any other such general escrow account or accounts. All disbursements shall be made by check of Title Insurance and Trust Company.

Any commitment made in writing to Title Insurance and Trust Company by a bank, trust company, insurance company, or savings and loan association to deliver its check or funds into this escrow may, in the sole discretion of Title Insurance and Trust Company, be treated as the equivalent of a deposit in this escrow of the amount thereof.

2. Prorations and Adjustments

All prorations and/or adjustments called for in this escrow are to be made on the basis of a thirty (30) day month unless otherwise instructed in writing.

The phrase "close of escrow" (COE or CE) as used in this escrow means the date on which documents are recorded and relates only to proration and/or adjustments unless otherwise specified.

3. Recordation of Instruments

Recordation of any instruments delivered through this escrow, if necessary or proper for the issuance of the policy of title insurance called for, is authorized.

4. Authorization to Furnish Copies

You are authorized to furnish copies of these instructions, supplements, amendments, or notices of cancellation and closing statements in this escrow, to the real estate broker(s) and lender(s) named in this escrow.

5. Authorization to Execute Assignment of Hazard Insurance Policies

You are to execute, on behalf of the principals hereto, form assignments of interest in any insurance policy (other than title insurance) called for in this escrow, forward assignment and policy to the agent requesting that insurer consent to such transfer and/or attach a loss payable clause and/or such other indorsements as may be required, and, forward such policy(s) to the principals entitled thereto.

6. Personal Property Taxes

No examination or insurance as to the amount or payment of personal property taxes is required unless specifically requested.

7. Right of Cancellation

Any principal instructing you to cancel this escrow shall file notice of cancellation in your office, in writing. You shall within two (2) working days thereafter mail, by certified mail, one copy of such notice to each of the other principals at the address stated in this escrow. Unless written objection to cancellation is filed in your office by a principal within ten (10) days after date of such mailing, you are authorized to comply with such notice and demand payment of your cancellation charges as provided in this agreement. If written objection is filed, you are authorized to hold all money and instruments in this escrow and take no futher action until otherwise directed, either by the principals' mutual written instructions, or final order of a court of competent jurisdiction.

The principals hereto expressly agree that you, as escrow holder, have the absolute right at your election to file an action in interpleader requiring the principals to answer and litigate their several claims and rights among themselves and you are authorized to deposit with the clerk of the court all documents and funds held in this escrow. In the event such action is filed, the principals jointly and severally agree to pay your cancellation charges and costs, expenses and reasonable attorney's fees which you are required to expend or incur in such interpleader action, the amount thereof to be fixed and judgment therefor to be rendered by the court. Upon the filing of such action, you shall thereupon be fully released and discharged from all obligations to further perform any duties or obligations otherwise imposed by the terms of this escrow.

8. Termination of Agency Obligation

If there is no action taken on this escrow within six (6) months after the "time limit date" as set forth in the escrow instructions or written extension thereof, your agency obligation shall terminate at your option and all documents, monies or other items held by you shall be returned to the parties depositing same.

In the event of cancellation of this escrow, whether it be at the request of any of the principals or otherwise, the fees and charges due Title Insurance and Trust Company, including expenditures incurred and/or authorized shall be borne equally by the parties hereto (unless otherwise agreed to specifically).

9. Conflicting Instructions

Upon receipt of any conflicting instructions other than cancellation instructions, you are no longer obligated to take any further action in connection with this escrow until further consistent instructions are received from the principals to this escrow except as provided in Paragraph 7 of these General Provisions.

out the terms and provisions more fully to your own and the principals' satisfaction. Just remember to **number the pages consecutively**. In this case, our additional page becomes page two and the original page two is bumped to page three.

As you can see on the first page of the form, we have begun with Hornbussel's instructions. These begin on page one and continue over two and three. **He is to sign on the bottom of page three. Gonzales will sign at the bottom of page four.**

Gonzales's instructions are all on page four. These begin with a statement that he has read Hornbussel's instructions and approves of them. After this comes the balance of his (the second party's) instructions in detail. He signs these instructions at the bottom of the page. The last sheet of "General Provisions" is quite similar to the type of provisions included in any sales transaction. **It provides a clear explanation for everyone involved of the normal rights, responsibilities and practices of escrow.**

C. FIRST AND SECOND PARTY

You will recall that from the start we have referred to Hornbussel as the "first party" and his Los Angeles parcel as the "first property" or "property number one." The reason for this is made much more apparent if you look at the first few lines of the instruction form. This section is very similar to the wording in the buyer's portion of a sales escrow instructions. The fact that he is to pay in additional consideration (or boot) makes him the first party. The main difference is that in addition to handing in cash he will also supply the title deed to his first property.

If you look at the fourth page instructions for the second property, you will note that Gonzales is only bringing property into escrow. He pays Hornbussel no additional consideration. **This distinction defines who is the first and second property**.

In the case of an absolutely even exchange, one where there is no cash or other consideration in addition to the deeds, it would make no difference which party's instructions came first.

It is our preference here, and the obvious preference of this form, to draw the distinction in this manner. Other forms reverse this and refer to the party paying boot as the second party.

The important thing to remember is that the parties must be clearly distinguishable in the wording of the instructions. At no time should there be any confusion regarding which party or which property is being discussed.

D. FIRST PARTY INSTRUCTIONS

Take a look at the first page of the instructions. As you can see, these are written as a letter to your escrow company from the parties of the exchange.

The first provision is that Hornbussel will come up with $3,000.00 in cash (in addition to the $2,000.00 deposit) and the deed to his mother's property. This deed will be conveyed to Pedro Gonzales, the second party. He authorizes you to deliver this money and the deed to Gonzales as soon as two things have happened: A CLTA owner's policy must be issued insuring Gonzales title to the first property and the title deed for the second property must be obtained for Hornbussel with an owner's policy of title insurance protecting his claim.

In each case clear title is "subject only to" the agreed upon encumbrances. The first property has the tax lien and the recorded CC&Rs. The second property has the tax lien, CC&Rs and the debt to Premiere Financial.

There are other conditions to the exchange of deeds and consideration, such as the delivery of the beneficiary's statement as set out on the bottom of page one. Still, the basic transaction is clearly outlined on this first page. Hornbussel will provide a deed and boot while Gonzales will provide a deed.

1. The Beneficiary's Statement

The importance of the beneficiary's statement is that it provides authoritative verification of the current status of the loan on the second property.

Gonzales has estimated that he still owes $76,000.00. The beneficiary, Premiere Financial Company, will send you a statement giving the exact amount. The parties already ordered it. This information is rather important to Hornbussel as he wants to assume the debt on this trust deed.

On the top of page two are three separate, but closely related, instructions regarding this deed of trust on property number two. As you will recall, all of this information came out of the instructions given you earlier by the two parties. Hornbussel makes the escrow contingent on Premiere Financial's approving his assumption of Gonzales' note. He also provides that Premiere will do so in exchange for a hike in the interest rate and monthly payments.

At the end of the first paragraph is a very important statement: **"Execution of the hereinafter mentioned agreement by first and second parties shall constitute approval of all terms and conditions thereof and shall satisfy this contingency."** This sentence does two things. Firstly, as you probably realize by now, whenever the closing of an escrow is made **subject to a contingency**, it is essential that you

299

clarify what constitutes compliance. Otherwise it may later be difficult to prove that the contingency was ever satisfied. Secondly, the next paragraph supplies the new loan terms upon which Premiere and Hornbussel have tentatively agreed.

These terms, however, are still subject to further modification during negotiation. The new agreement might very well contain other and differing provisions when it finally comes to you from the lender for execution by the two parties. This would normally necessitate your preparing a supplemental escrow instructions for Hornbussel's signature. In this case, however, you have anticipated the problem and probably saved yourself the extra work.

2. Structural Pest Control Report

In the next section of the instructions, the first party promises to supply you with a pest control report from a structural pest control operator who will inspect the first property. The phrasing here is quite standard, reflecting accurately the specific agreement of the parties to this escrow. By this time you should have a pretty good understanding of this kind of report from our discussions in previous chapters.

3. Probate and Commission

Hornbussel here explains to escrow how he expects to establish his right to title in the first property. The title report will probably show title vested in the heirs or devisees of Matilda Hornbussel, deceased. Here, in the instructions, it is important to indicate that a decree of distribution is anticipated from the probate court and that when this decree is issued a certified copy will be delivered to you, for recording, by Hornbussel's attorney, Tischler.

If someone were to take over this escrow from you in your absence, this sort of information could save a good deal of confusion.

The next part of the instructions is one of several references to the brokers' commissions involved in this transfer. This particular passage is an effort to establish clear approval in the minds of both parties that Broker Doyle is receiving a commission from both.

It is entirely proper for a broker to be paid by both parties to a transaction, whether it be an exchange or even a simple sale, provided both are informed and express approval of the arrangement.

If this is not made expressly clear, in writing, Doyle might be found guilty of dual agency and be subject to discipline or prosecution under the Real Estate Law. Later in the instructions are more specific authorizations regarding the amount of commissions and who is to receive them.

4. Adjustments to the Date of Closing

The adjustments all follow closely the notations made in the memos and are fixed as of the date escrow closes.

These adjustments are similar in nature to those made in sales escrows that we have already examined earlier in this book. They should present no particular difficulty, but one fact should, perhaps, be examined a bit.

The adjustments for both properties are presented together.

Despite the fact that this section of the instructions deals almost exclusively with the first property, it is important that the adjustments be presented in this manner. This is done primarily because it simply makes them easier to understand and to work with.

Instructions should be as concise as possible so long as the information is complete and understandable.

In this case the material will be more easily understood by the two parties because it is so concise. The adjustments that will affect both parties in the same way are grouped and listed first. These are then followed by those which refer only to the second property. In truth, of course, all adjustments affect both parties equally in that each will constitute either a debit or a credit to their escrow account.

5. Payments

Despite the fact that adjustments are grouped together, the payments of the two parties must be outlined separately.

The respective charges must be segregated and listed in different parts of the instructions. **Here on page three** are those of the first party. You will find the charges for the second party with the bulk of his instructions on **page four**.

As you can see on page three, the fifth item charged to Hornbussel is listed **"Title and escrow charges as provided below."** If you look below, right above his signature space, you will see the charges to which this notation refers. The same thing is done on page four with the title, escrow and recording charges made to Gonzales.

This is a problem inherent in the particular form we are using. There is nothing improper or unacceptable about this method, but it does give rise to possible errors and confusion. After all, even in a relatively simple real property exchange like this one, there are bound to be numerous separate items that are to be paid by one or the other party. On this form we have various charges set out in four different locations in the instructions. It is conceivable, under these circumstances, that an item might be left out or that some other serious error might be made.

301

6. Charge's Check List

The conscientious escrow officer is always looking for new and better ways to eliminate the possibility of error.

In this case we have revised a plan of considering all the charges at once by listing them out on a separate sheet of paper—a sort of charges checklist (**Figure 11-7**).

Figure 11-7

CHARGES CHECK LIST

1st Party Pays:	**2nd Party Pays:**
<u>1st Property</u>	<u>1st Property</u>
tax sale	recording deed
commission	<u>2nd Property</u>
1/2 escrow fees	sewer bond
title policy	commission
draw deed	1/2 escrow fees
transfer tax	draw deed
record dec. of dist.	transfer tax
<u>2nd Property</u>	title policy
Sept. note payment	record termin. jnt. tenancy
assumption charges	
110.5 indorsement	
record deed & assump.	

This is not an official part of the escrow instructions. It is for your eyes only. It just provides an easy strategy for minimizing the chances of forgetting a payment to escrow.

If a payment is not listed in the instructions, there is a good chance that it might end up being a loss to you or your escrow company.

As you can see, there is no need to go into a lot of detail. You already have all the specific information in your memos. This is just a way of laying them out in front of you so you can be sure you list every expense and payment to be made. As you write out the formal instructions, you can simply check off each item as you include it in the proper section.

Hold on to this sheet of paper for later. It will prove useful again when you are filling out the settlement sheet.

In the same manner, that consideration detail we used earlier to balance out the equities and calculate the necessary boot comes in handy again here. Take a look at the middle of **page three**. There you see the summary once again written out in the form of an escrow recapitulation. This kind of summary is standard practice at some escrow companies and we think it is a good idea, again, in the interest of greater clarity. The printed form we are using in this case has no provision for such a recap, so we put it in here where space allows. It is a good policy and easy to do in that all the necessary calculations have already been made.

7. Other Instructions of the First Party

The next section under the recapitulation is a passage added to require **concurrent recording of title for both properties**. In an exchange such as this, part of the consideration tendered by each party is the delivery of the respective deeds.

This consideration is not truly "delivered" until each deed is properly recorded by the county recorder's office of the county in which the property is located.

So, in order that both parties' consideration passes to the other party at the same time and both properties may be issued title insurance at the same time, all the necessary documents must be recorded at the same time. A brief instruction regarding concurrent recording is incorporated at this point. Concurrent recording is especially involved if the properties which are subject to the exchange are located **in different states or counties**, as in this case. Pre-planning will be necessary to coordinate the elements in both counties needed to bring about this concurrent recording.

The final portion of the first party instructions are pretty much supplied by the preprinted form. There is a reference to the general escrow provisions on the reverse side of the sheet. As indicated before, we have reprinted these on a separate sheet for greater convenience.

We have filled in the time limit date as established by the 60-day provision in the exchange agreement. We have also filled in the title and escrow charges as previously discussed. This portion of the instructions reads pretty much like the buyer's section in the sales form of escrow instructions. While, obviously, it should be carefully studied and considered as with any other part of the form, it is rather unlikely to generate any questions among the principals that you could not easily answer and explain. Fill in the specifics of the first party's name, address, and telephone number and you have completed Richard Hornbussel's section of the exchange escrow instructions.

E. SECOND PARTY INSTRUCTIONS

Look at the **fourth page** of the form and you see the instructions for the second party to this exchange escrow, Pedro Gonzales. Much, however, of the material on the first three pages was also second party instructions and it is important that he read and understand this material fully. In fact, the first section on this page requires him to acknowledge having read and approved of the foregoing material.

On page two, for example, the first paragraph addresses the assumption of Gonzales's trust deed by Hornbussel and in part provides that the closing of escrow is contingent upon Premiere Financial's releasing Gonzales from "further personal liability" regarding the repayment of the loan. It also provides that Gonzales must join with Hornbussel in executing the instrument that modifies the trust deed.

Further down the page, the second party must join with the first party in acknowledging and approving the fact that both are paying a commission to Broker Doyle.

The adjustment section also involves instructions from Gonzales. There is a list of three items that refer only to the second property involving rents, the tenant's security deposit and the estimated amount of the unpaid principal balance on his loan from Premiere Financial.

On page three the recapitulation of considerations and the passage outlining the concurrent recording provision are also, at least in part, instructions from the second party. Gonzales must read and, of course, approve them before escrow may continue.

1. Additional Instructions

The first paragraph of this section instructs you to obtain a title report and title policy using the title order that Gonzales already opened. He has promised to hand to you the necessary deed to be given to Hornbussel and authorizes you to deliver it under the specified conditions. Gonzales has also instructed you to **"make all adjustments and deliver fire insurance as provided in the foregoing instructions."**

Attorney Black will provide you with documents to terminate the joint tenancy of record and a waiver or release of inheritance taxes on the second property. This is duly noted in the instructions. In the next section we list the charges Gonzales is to pay. You can take these directly from your checklist. Remember that the title and escrow charges are not detailed at this point, but at the bottom of the page above the signature.

Once again, the instructions of the second party set in the final preprinted paragraph are very similar to those of the seller in a normal sales escrow. They should be fairly simple to fill in and explain to the principals, just as were those of the first party. Make these final entries and the escrow instructions are complete and ready for signatures.

XIV. Executing the Instructions

If you have time before your principals return to execute the instructions, you can next **draw the deeds for the two properties** so that these, too, are ready for signatures. We have discussed this procedure in detail before, so there is no reason to run through it again here.

The return appointment is for 4pm. This is not the best time being as how afternoons will probably be your busiest work period. In this case, however, it was probably unavoidable so the best thing to do is make good use of the visit. You should accomplish as much as possible toward the successful closing of escrow at this time. Your two principals live quite a distance apart and it is likely to be quite difficult to arrange any future meetings.

When they arrive make certain that they **take the time to read the instructions over carefully before signing**. This, of course, should go without saying. The way we have drawn up these forms, the complexities of this transaction are not difficult to follow. Even someone with a limited understanding of real estate should see clearly in these completed instructions the nature of the exchange that is about to take place. If they appear uncertain, you must explain the logic behind the approach the form takes in laying out the transaction.

> *As you know, however, you must be careful to not go beyond describing the organization of the form itself.*

XV. Other Business to Complete

There are other business matters that can be completed at this time. For example, if the deeds are drawn, these also can be executed. They must be acknowledged before a notary public, but in all likelihood you or someone in your office will be able to notarize them. If necessary the parties may, of course, take the deeds with them to be signed and acknowledged elsewhere. If this is the case, you can speed matters a bit by supplying the principals with stamped envelopes printed with your address. This will assure the prompt return of the acknowledged documents.

Now is also the time when any boot should be provided for the escrow account. On the top of the **first page** of the escrow instructions the first party promises to turn in $2,000.00 of the $5,000.00 owed at the opening of escrow. Escrow is open and Hornbussel should have brought his money.

If he is prepared to do so, he can pay in the entire amount owed at this time. In addition to the $5,000.00, he should pay in for all his charges, fees, and the broker's commission. It is unlikely that you can be extremely precise at this point as to how much he will owe. However, it is possible for you to estimate intelligently, based upon your experience and the information provided by the parties. In any event, getting the money from him now will save both of you the trouble of bringing it in later. Remember to overestimate his debits somewhat to provide a margin for under anticipated costs.

In some counties, statements of information are requested from both parties.

If this practice is followed in your county, these should be obtained at this time. If, as in this case, properties located in two different counties are being exchanged, you should find out if such statements are required in either county or simply cover yourself by having them completed and signed as a precaution. Even if doing so proves unnecessary, taking care of this now will only take a few moments and could easily avert several days of delay later.

As a final step, before the parties leave your office, be sure to thank them and offer a special thanks to Broker Doyle for bringing this transaction to you.

Remember, you are never too busy to be gracious.

Indeed, your prompt and careful handling of this escrow will bring their business back to you, but a few appropriate words can mean a great deal to people. Let them know you appreciate their business, especially Broker Doyle who, if all proceeds well, you are likely to see again and again.

XVI. The Escrow File

The actual processing of the escrow file need not proceed immediately from the signing of the escrow instructions.

With any luck at all you will have other, more immediately pressing matters to conduct—perhaps another set of escrow instructions for the next day!

The important thing to remember is that before you put this escrow aside, **you absolutely must have the file organized**. Don't take the risk of losing anything. If you haven't had the chance to do so earlier you must now gather all the forms and documents relating to the Hornbussel/Gonzales escrow (**Escrow Numbers 243279 and 243280**) together and arrange them into an escrow file according to the systems and procedures followed in your office. Then go ahead and put it aside until time allows you to devote your full attention. The file will be waiting for you, ready when you are to proceed with confidence and efficiency.

XVII. CHAPTER SUMMARY

This chapter introduces the tax-deferred EXCHANGE which is a trade of properties instead of a sale. TAX-FREE EXCHANGE means taxes are not immediately paid on the capital but may be taxable in a later transaction. TRADE-INS are popular with new home builders and subdividers and will be determined by how the EQUITIES balance after all liens and charges are deducted.

BOOT refers to anything received in addition to the subject property such as cash, promissory notes or other personal property. A VALUATION FORM will assist the escrow in calculating the exchange of properties to balance out the equities exchanged.

Designating parties as FIRST or SECOND party helps to separate the individuals in the transaction. There is no requirement as to how these parties are selected as first or second party.

The EXCHANGE AGREEMENT is the formal agreement filled out by a licensee to create a binding contract. ADJUSTMENTS will be made to show charges and credits for items such as taxes, insurance, or rent and deposits.

When property is SOLD to THE STATE, it means taxes are delinquent and the redemption time begins running for a five-year period.

A PROBATE is the court proceeding to determine the validity of a will. It will include a DECREE OF DISTRIBUTION which orders a distribution to certain parties after expenses are paid.

The escrow will find helpful a CHARGES CHECK LIST that is not part of escrow but helps consider all the charges to the escrow to minimize leaving out any items.

It will be followed by an ESCROW RECAPITULATION in the instructions that form the details of the exchange.

XVIII. TERMS

Adjustments: As in any escrow, there will be prorations that show credits and debits such as property taxes, insurance, rent etc.

Boot: Money or other property that is considered "not like-kind" which is given to make up any difference in value or equity between exchanged property.

Charges Check list: A separate sheet not part of escrow where the escrow considers all the charges to the escrow to minimize the chances of forgetting any items.

Decree of Distribution: A court order to distribute the decedent's estate to certain ones.

Equities: The interest or value remaining in property after all liens and charges on the property. Normally it is the monetary interest over and above the indebtedness.

Escrow Recapitulation: A printed summary form of the details in the exchange that appears in the instructions.

Exchange: A real estate transaction where one property is traded for another.

Exchange Agreement: A type of deposit receipt prepared by a broker to become a binding agreement in an exchange transaction. It is the initial contract between parties.

First Party: When there are two or more deeds transferred, parties are designated to be a first or second party. A first party may be the one that pays out boot, or the property with greatest value, or the one requiring the greatest amount of detail in setting up the escrow instructions.

Probate: The formal judicial proceeding to prove or confirm the validity of a will, to collect the assets of the estate and to pay debts and taxes with the remainder to pass to those designated as heirs.

Second Party: The one designated by escrow to distinguish from the first party.

Sold to the State: A tax collector book transaction to initiate the beginning of a redemption period at the end of which title does pass to the state.

Tax-Free Exchange: An exchange where capital gains tax is deferred until the property is later disposed of in a taxable exchange.

Trade-Ins: An agreement by a developer or new home builder to accept from a buyer a designated property as part of the purchase price of another property.

Valuation Form: A form used to calculate the exchange of properties to be sure the elements of the exchange balance out and are understood by the escrow officer before instructions are prepared.

XIX. CHAPTER QUIZ

1. The main reason for exchanging real property is to defer:

    a. property taxes.
    b. income taxes.
    c. probate.
    d. nothing.

2. When there is an exchange, there usually is:

    a. one deed.
    c. four deeds.
    b. two deeds.
    d. none of the above.

3. When "A" exchanges houses with "B", the usual term for "A" and "B" is:

    a. first party.
    c. both a and b.
    b. second party.
    d. neither a nor b.

4. Real property is technically "sold to the state" after not receiving:

    a. one property tax installments.
    b. two property tax installments.
    c. three property tax installments.
    d. four property tax installments.

5. The main purpose of probate for the decedent's estate is to:

    a. gather assets.
    b. pay debts.
    c. pay taxes.
    d. all of the above.

6. Exchange escrow instructions, like most other escrow instructions, contain:

    a. general provisions in the back.
    b. blanks in the back.
    c. a special design in the back.
    d. all of the above.

7. Adjustments (prorations) in cost are usually fixed at the date:
   - a. escrow opens.
   - b. instructions are signed.
   - c. escrow closes.
   - d. none of the above.

8. A check-list:
   - a. lists charges.
   - b. reduces errors.
   - c. has check marks.
   - d. all of the above.

9. The last step in the exchange escrow process is:
   - a. proration.
   - b. closing.
   - c. to type checks.
   - d. store escrow file.

10. Giving numbers to the parties to the escrow, how many escrow numbers are NORMALLY used in an exchange?
   - a. One
   - b. Two
   - c. Three
   - d. None of the above

ANSWERS: 1. b; 2. c; 3. c; 4. b; 5. d; 6. a; 7. c; 8. d; 9. d; 10. b

Processing the Exchange Escrow

I. The Progress and Settlement Sheets

As you worked to complete the escrow instructions, it would have been a good idea to start filling in your **escrow progress sheet** (**Figure 12-1**).

With a little imagination, the normal sales progress sheet can be adequately adapted to serve for an exchange escrow such as this one.

Just be sure to keep it up date as items are handed into escrow. Once again we must stress that **this form be kept current as the escrow progresses**.

The settlement sheet should also be developed at this time (**Figure 12-2**). The one we are using is specifically designed for an exchange transaction. It should, by this time, contain all the needed details of this escrow as we now know them.

Firstly, we have the deposit of funds by the first party. As we have indicated here, Hornbussel has only given you the promised $2,000.00. The other $3,000.00 and the rest of his fees and charges will have to be paid in later. Still, all the known fees and charges are noted. The rest will be added as escrow proceeds and their amounts are specified.

CHAPTER OUTLINE

Figure 12-1

PROGRESS SHEET

	REQUIRED		ORDERED		RECEIVED	
SELLER'S ESCROW INSTRUCTIONS	✓					
BUYER'S ESCROW INSTRUCTIONS	✓					
AMENDMENTS						
AMENDMENTS						
STATEMENT OF IDENTITY - BUYER-SELLER						
COMMISSION ORDER						
GRANT DEED						
TRUST DEED & NOTE						
PRELIMINARY REPORT						
APPROVAL OF CONDITION OF TITLE						
OTHER DOCUMENTS:						
1.						
2.						
DEMANDS - BENEFICIARY STATEMENTS:						
1st LIEN						
2nd LIEN						
RECONVEYANCE						
RENT STATEMENT						
INSURANCE POLICY						
TERMITE REPORT						
TERMITE COMPLETION						
CONTINGENCIES						
1.						
2.						
9/A						
LOAN APPROVAL						
LOAN PROCEEDS						
BALANCE OF FUNDS						
1. BUYER'S						
2. SELLER'S						
3. AGENT'S						

MISCELLANEOUS

SETTLEMENT REQUIREMENTS

REC'D.   SENT

1. DELAYED RECON.
2. POLICY
3. FEES
4. FIRE INSURANCE
5. MONEY DUE

Started by Debbi

DATE OPENED ....

BROKER ... W. HUBER ......

NAMES Richard Hornbussell/Pedro Gonzales ......

TITLE No. ....

ESCROW No. 243279 / 243280

DATE ....

Figure 12-2

TITLE/ESCROW SETTLEMENT SHEET – EXCHANGE

TITLE/ESCROW SETTLEMENT SHEET
EXCHANGE

☒ ESTIMATED STATEMENT	☐ FINAL STATEMENT	DATE 7-12-XX	E.O./T.O. NAME YOUR NAME	ESCROW NO. 243279 / ESCROW NO. 243280

PROPERTY DESCRIPTION/ADDRESS: 2120 Carson, Street, Los Angeles — FIRST PARTY: Richard Hornbussel — ADDRESS

PROPERTY DESCRIPTION/ADDRESS: 1918 Maine Road, San Francisco — SECOND PARTY: Pedro Gonzales — ADDRESS

	DEBIT	CREDIT	DESCRIPTION	DEBIT	CREDIT	
P R O P E R T Y B E I N G C O N V E Y E D		55 000 00	EXCHANGE VALUE–FIRST PARTIES PROPERTY	55 000 00		**P R O P E R T Y B E I N G A C Q U I R E D**
			DEPOSIT TO:			
			DEPOSITS RETAINED BY:			
			EXISTING LOAN BALANCE			
			EXISTING LOAN TRUST FUNDS			
			EXISTING LOAN – TRANSFER FEE			
	XXX XX		**P R O R A T E** TAXES $ FR TO		XXX XX	
			INSURANCE $ FR TO			
			INTEREST $ FR TO			
			RENT $ FR TO			
			ASSMNT. INT. $ FR TO			
			RENT DEPOSIT			
P R O P E R T Y B E I N G A C Q U I R E D	136 000 00		EXCHANGE VALUE–SECOND PARTIES PROPERTY		136 000 00	**P R O P E R T Y B E I N G C O N V E Y E D**
			DEPOSIT TO:			
			DEPOSITS RETAINED BY:			
		76 000 00	EXISTING LOAN BALANCE (adj. to exact fig.)	76 000 00		
			EXISTING LOAN TRUST FUNDS			
			EXISTING LOAN – TRANSFER FEE			
		XXX XX	**P R O R A T E** TAXES $ FR TO	XXX XX		
			INSURANCE $ FR TO			
			INTEREST $ FR TO			
			RENT $ FR TO			
			ASSMNT. INT. $ FR TO			
		300 00	RENT DEPOSIT	300 00		
N E W L O A N (S)			NEW LOAN WITH			**N E W L O A N (S)**
			L O A N C H A R G E S FHA MTG. $ INS. RESERVE $			
			TAX RES. $ RECON. FEE $			
			CR. REPORTS $ TAX SERVICE $			
			LOAN FEE $ APPRAISAL FEE $			
			INTEREST $			
			INT @ FR TO $			
			TOTAL OF ABOVE			
			INSURANCE			
L O A N P A Y O F F S			PAY OFF LOAN TO			**L O A N P A Y O F F S**
			PRINCIPAL $			
			INTEREST $			
			INT. @ FR TO $			
			PREPAYMENT PENALTY $			
			RECON. FEE $			
			$			
			LESS LOAN TRUST FUND DEPOSITS $(			
			TOTAL OF ABOVE			
	142 00		TITLE INSURANCE $55000 ☒Owners ☐JP ☐STR 142 00			
			PREMIUM FOR $ ☐Loan ☐Alta			
			TITLE INSURANCE $36000 ☒Owners ☐JP ☐STR 214 50	214 50		
			PREMIUM FOR $ ☐Loan ☐Alta			
			IND 110.5	XXX XX		
	108 50		ESCROW FEE	217 00	108 50	
			RECONVEYANCE FEE			
			RECORDING			
M I S C.			NOTARY FEE			**M I S C.**
	5 00		DOCUMENT PREP.	10 00	5 00	
	18 15		TRANSFER TAX CO. $ CITY $	18 15		
			TRANSFER TAX CO. $ CITY $			
			TOTAL			
			TAX COLLECTOR			
	3 300 00		COMMISSION			
				8 160 00		
			CHECK TO:			
			◀— BALANCE DUE COMPANY FROM —▶			
			TOTALS			

Just as with the progress sheet, the settlement sheet must be kept up to date at all times.

Keeping it current in the early stages will doubtless save much valuable time later during the demanding final stages of the escrow. Remember to make settlement entries **in pencil**. These will inevitably change. Don't worry about erasures. It is meant to be a worksheet not a work of art. All that matters is that it be complete and up to date. So long as you, perhaps a secretary or coworker, and anyone who might have need to take over the escrow for you can understand it, it is well drawn.

II. Title Orders

Let's return to the progress sheet (Figure 12-1). The best next step for you would be to order the title reports. The truth is this is all you can do at this point while you wait for others to carry the ball.

So let's proceed and arrange the title orders for the two properties. Once again, you may recall, it is a term of the escrow instructions that both title orders are recorded concurrently. In ordering your reports, inform the title companies in both counties of this requirement. They should also be given the **title order number** for the order involving the other property in the transaction. (See **Figure 12-3**).

Gonzales, you will remember, already initiated a title order on his own. He contacted Confidential Title and Trust of San Francisco and they assigned him order number 5209. You should contact your title officer in Los Angeles and set up your order by telephone for the first property. After he has opened the order and assigned it a number, you can send written instructions to the San Francisco company regarding the second property, which they are already examining. You should also formalize the Los Angeles title order in writing, as we do here. The statements of information and deed should be sent on to your title officer to help speed the processing along.

III. Filing

At this point all you can do is wait. You have ordered title reports on the two properties. All other matters must await actions to be taken by someone else. The best thing you can do is file the escrow papers carefully away in such a manner that they will be easily accessible as they are needed later.

Here are a few suggestions for maintaining the separate files in your office. This is an important problem because, if you are doing your job as an escrow agent, you might easily be dealing with a hundred or so escrows at any given time. Each working day you are receiving funds and important documents. Principals, brokers, lenders, and title

Figure 12-3

ORDER (1)

DATE ___7/13/XX___   **ORDER**   TITLE OFFICER _____

Please enter ☐   ORDER NO ___5209___
THIS CONFIRMS ☐ } order for policy or policies of title insurance as checked below:
CLTA OWNER'S/LENDER'S   Standard Coverage Form . . . . . ☐ with liability in the amount of . . . . $ 136,000.00
CLTA JOINT PROTECTION   Standard Coverage Form . . . . . ☐ with liability in the amount of . . . . $ _____
ALTA LENDER'S   American Land Title Association Form   ☐ with liability in the amount of . . . . $ _____
CLTA INDORSEMENT   110.5   ☒
→ IF ALTA POLICY IS REQUESTED   ☐ SINGLE RESIDENCE ☐ MULTIPLE RESIDENCE ☐ COMMERCIAL
   THIS INFORMATION WILL EXPEDITE YOUR REPORT →   ☐ STREET ADDRESS _____

The property to be covered is described as

        Lots 23 and 24 of SUMMER VIEW TRACT
        City and County of San Francisco, @20/28 of Maps

Present Owner's Name ___Pedro Gonzales and Angela Gonzales, his wife as joint tenants___
We Enclose the Following: (amount to be
Deed from ___Gonzales___   To ___Hornbussel___   DTTS furnished later
Deed from _____   To _____   DTTS _____
Deed of Trust by _____   Amount $ _____
Deed of Trust by _____   Amount $ _____
Recon _____   Item _____ of your report dated _____
Note _____ Deed of Trust _____ Request for Recon _____ Item _____ of your report dated _____
Miscellaneous ___(Documents to term. jttncy & modification of T/D will follow)___
Statements of Information _____ Buyer ___1st pty Hornbussel___ Seller ___2nd pty Gonzales___
Other _____

Upon Further Authorization you will record all instruments without collection when you can issue said form of Policy showing
Title vested in ___Richard Hornbussel, a single man___

Free from Encumbrances except 1. ___All___   General and special Taxes for fiscal year 20 XX to 20 XX
        2. Covenants, conditions, restrictions, and easements of record, if any.

        3. Deed of trust of record for $100,000 in favor of Premiere Financial Co.

Additional Instructions   This order was originally opened by Pedro Gonzales for the purpose
of terminating the joint tenancy with Angela Gonzales. We will pay all charges
which have been incurred to date, as well as those resulting from this order.
This order to be recorded concurrently with Confidential Title & Trust of Los
Angeles, Order No. 1066.
G.Gairn, TO.
Send ___3___ copies of report to ___undersigned___   Customer Name ___Your Escrow Company___

_____   Street ___111 N. Business Street___
Street _____
City _____ Zip _____   City ___Anytown___   Zip ___94321___
Order Tax Service _____ Type _____ Years
Please Forward (check items requested, if any.)   By ___Your Name___
☐ _____ copies of covenants, conditions and restrictions.
☒ ___3___ copies of plat map.   Telephone _____
☒ Amount of ___XX-XX___ taxes for proration purposes
This order   Escrow No. ___243280___   Loan No. _____
Return to _____

ORDER (2)

DATE **7/13/XX**   **ORDER**   TITLE OFFICER **G. Gairn**

ORDER NO. **1066**

Please enter ☐
THIS CONFIRMS ☒ } order for policy or policies of title insurance as checked below:

CLTA OWNER'S/LENDER'S   Standard Coverage Form   ☒ with liability in the amount of .... $ **55,000**
CLTA JOINT PROTECTION   Standard Coverage Form   ☐ with liability in the amount of .... $
ALTA LENDER'S   American Land Title Association Form   ☐ with liability in the amount of .... $
CLTA INDORSEMENT .... ☐
  → IF ALTA POLICY IS REQUESTED   ☐ SINGLE RESIDENCE ☐ MULTIPLE RESIDENCE ☐ COMMERCIAL
    THIS INFORMATION WILL EXPEDITE YOUR REPORT → ☐ STREET ADDRESS

The property to be covered is described as

     The S 100' of the NE 1/4 of the SE 1/4 of
     the NW 1/4 of Sec 55 Twp 9N Range 20 W SBM

Present Owner's Name **Matilda Hornbussel (deceased)**
We Enclose the Following:
Deed from **Hornbussel**   To **Gonzales**   D.T.T.S **18.15**
Deed from   To   D.T.T.S
Deed of Trust by   Amount $
Deed of Trust by   Amount $
Recon   Item   of your report dated
Note   Deed of Trust   Request for Recon   Item   of your report dated
Miscellaneous **Decree of distribution in estate of Matilda Hornbussle will follow**
Statements of Information   Buyer **1st pty Hornbussel** Seller **2nd pty Gonzales**
Other:

Upon Further Authorization you will record all instruments without collection when you can issue said form of Policy showing
Title vested in **Pedro Gonzales, a widower**

Free from Encumbrances except: 1   **All**   General and special Taxes for fiscal year 20 **XX** to 20 **XX**
   2   **CC&R and easements of record, if any.**

Additional Instructions: **This order is to be recorded concurrently with**
Confidential Title and Trust of San Francisco, Order No. 5209

Send **3** copies of report to **undersigned**   Customer Name **Your Escrow Company**

Street **111 N. Business Street**

Street
City   Zip   City **Anytown**   Zip **94321**
Order Tax Service   Type   Years   By **Your Name**
Please Forward (check items requested, if any.)
☐ 1.   copies of covenants, conditions and restrictions   Telephone
☒ 2.   copies of plat map
☒ 3. Amount of **XX-XX** taxes for proration purposes
This Order   Escrow No. **243279**   Loan No.
Referred By

officers are phoning in hourly with specific inquiries regarding these numerous pending transactions.

You must nave a comprehensive indexing system that will allow you to store and quickly locate specific files.

Even with the proliferation of computer use in information storage, a good filing system is still essential. After all, computers still cannot store the original documents, which you must keep on hand, in the same way a good indexing system can.

A. INDEXING

Every escrow file is numbered and stored numerically in your filing cabinet. But generally you must locate a file based not upon the escrow number but upon the names of the principals involved. To accomplish this we recommend an alphabetical cross-index system that can be set up any number of ways.

You can put this information on a computer. You type in the name and obtain the escrow file number. Many companies, though, still rely on the traditional escrow index books. These books are really just loose-leaf finders with alphabetized tab dividers. New pages are readily added as needed.

Each escrow can be included twice, once under the name of the buyer and once under the name of the seller. In the case of an exchange such as the Hornbussel/ Gonzales transaction, Hornbussel is listed as the first party and Gonzales is listed as the second.

NAME	S/B	NAME	S/B	ESCROW #
Holden, Joe & Irene	S	Hamilton, Carol	B	480310
Hornbussel, Richard	1st	Gonzales, Pedro	2nd	243279/80

If you prefer, index cards work as well, If not better, than the loose-leaf notebook. Two separate cards can be filled in as each transaction is recorded and filed. One of these is for the seller, the other is for the buyer. Each contains the file number under which the escrow file is being stored, the same information shown to be used with the notebook system.

The file cards are more flexible in some respects. They contain more space than the loose-leaf column so more handy information can be included. The opening and closing dates of the escrow are good to note. (There is often room for this even with the notebook system.) The name of the broker and the commission might be useful. The fact is, your own practice and experience will tell you what to include on your index card or notebook page. You may want to remove files or transfer them to an inactive status after a few years. The file card system is obviously a bit better suited for this also.

B. A TICKLER SYSTEM

A necessary practice is the creation of a "tickler" or review system.

While not necessarily a filing or indexing system, this approach will prove essential to you in completing the processing of your existent escrow files.

The principle is simple. You are dealing with a number of escrows at once. The situation is such that you are dependent upon the arrival of certain documents at certain times so that you can keep things moving ahead. In the exchange transaction we are examining here, you are now awaiting a pest control report, the beneficiary statement, two title reports, a decree of distribution and numerous other documents from various sources. Imagine that you have more than one hundred such escrows pending!

As you might imagine, it is not uncommon for documents of this sort to get lost in the mails or bogged down somewhere in the jumbled maze of office interaction. Perhaps someone drops the ball and doesn't even bother to provide a promised piece of paper. You might be waiting for something that may never arrive. There is no sense in delaying an escrow in this manner. Still, no one person could store all such diverse elements in their head and remember to coax and search when they don't arrive on time. A tickler system will fill this need.

The purpose of such a system is to minimize the risk of something being forgotten in the shuffle by reminding you to check each file periodically to see that important elements are attended to.

There are any number of ways a tickler file can be set up. One approach is to note escrow file numbers on your desk calendar on days when items need to be double-check. Another is to set up a separate index card system listing the various events of the escrow and the dates on which they should occur. A good approach is to affix color-coded plastic tabs to all your files. Each day you double-check a different color, several files at a time. In this way every file is systematically reviewed weekly and any potential delays can be discovered and acted upon.

IV. Processing

In the last chapter we saw the escrow instructions completed and signed. The parties have executed their respective deeds. Title insurance has been ordered. From this point on the processing of this exchange escrow proceeds in much the same fashion as if it were two separate sale's escrows.

There are still peculiarities to deal with, however, but the same could be said of any so-called "normal" escrow because, as you have probably come to realize, there is no such thing as a "normal'" escrow.

No two escrows are alike. Every transaction involves different people and different parcels and each presents unique challenges.

In this transaction, we have hit upon several areas not previously discussed at length in this book. We still have the tax sale to pay off and the need to establish title through a decree of distribution on the Hornbussel property (property number one). The Gonzales parcel (property number two) has a lien from a sewer bond against it and there is still the matter of the joint tenancy with the late Angela Gonzales, which must be legally terminated. You must also arrange for concurrent recording of the documents of transfer in Los Angeles and San Francisco counties and settle accounts for both parties to the exchange. We will cover each of these items and try to plot a logical sequence of events leading to the successful closing of this escrow.

A. SECOND PROPERTY TITLE REPORT

As expected, the title report for the second property comes in first. You will recall, Pedro Gonzales had already ordered a title report to be used in terminating the joint tenancy he held with his deceased wife. He placed this title order on their property before getting involved in the exchange transaction. This report arrives on your desk on July 17, several days before the report on the first property can be expected. (See **Figure 12-4**.)

Of course, your first move is to note receipt of the report on the escrow progress sheet for this transaction. You ordered three copies from Confidential Title, one for each of the principals and one for your escrow file. You check this copy over and make any notes on it which might prove helpful later.

1. Exceptions to Title

You double-check the vesting and property description against the escrow instructions. Everything matches up. The report goes on to enumerate the exceptions and exclusions to title.

Number one is the current taxes, as indicated in your instructions. Number two is the sewer bond. Gonzales wants you to pay off this bond in full. This term was included in the instructions. Confidential has included the amount owed if you pay off the bond in full before November 30. As you expect to close escrow before August 30, this should be no problem. However, one never knows. It would be a good idea to <u>underline this date</u> and keep it in mind later if, for some reason, escrow is unreasonably late in closing.

Figure 12-4

SECOND PROPERTY TITLE REPORT (1)

CONFIDENTIAL OF SAN FRANCISCO

YOUR ESCROW COMPANY   Our No. SF-5209-RN
111 N. BUSINESS STREET
ANYTOWN, CA 94321   Your No. 243280

In response to the above referenced application for a policy of title Insurance, Confidential Insurance and Trust Company hereby reports that it is prepared to issue, or cause to be issued, as of the date hereof, a California Land Title Association Standard Coverage form Policy of Title Insurance describing the land and the estate or interest therein hereinafter set forth, insuring against loss which may be sustained by reason of any defect, lien or encumbrance not shown or referred to as an Exception below or not excluded from coverage pursuant to the printed Schedules, Conditions and Stipulations of said policy form.

This report (and any supplemments or amendments thereto) is issued solely for the purpose of facilitating the issuance of a policy of title Insurance and no liability is assumed hereby. If it is desired that liability be assumed prior to the issuance of a policy of title insurance, a Binder or Commitment should be requested.

Dated as of ___July 14_____ , 20XX , at 7:30 a.m. _John Hatem_____
                                                         Title Department
The estate or Interest In the land hereinafter described or referred to covered by this Report is a fee.

Title to said estate or interest at the date hereof is vested in:

PEDRO GONZALES AND ANGELA GONZALES, HUSBAND AND WIFE, AS JOINT TENANTS

At the date hereof exceptions to coverage in addition to the printed exceptions and exclusions contained in said policy form would be as follows:

1. 20XX-XX taxes, a lien not yet payable.

2. Bond #310, Series 12, issued October 2. 20XX , Original amount
    $1,805.02, payable in 10 annual installments beginning July 2,
    20XX. All amounts payable July 2, 19XX have been paid. Unpaid
    balance $722.00. Amount to pay in full prior to November 30,
    20XX , $743.66.

SECOND PROPERTY TITLE REPORT (2)

Page 2

3. Covenants, conditions, and restrictions set forth in the Declaration executed by Summer View Corporation, recorded June 12, 20XX, as instrument No. M-9941, in Book 41968, at page 26 of Official Records, which provides among other things that a violation thereof shall not defeat or render invalid the lien of any mortgage or deed of trust made in good faith and for value.

    Restrictions, if any, based upon race, color, relligion or national origin are deleted.

4. A deed of trust to secure an indebtedness of the amount stated herein and any other amounts payable under the terms thereof

    DATED   :   June 17, 20XX
    AMOUNT   : $100,000.00
    TRUSTOR   :   Pedro Gonzales and Angela Gonzales
    TRUSTEE   :   Premiere Holding Company
    BENEFICIARY   :   Premiere Financial Company
                        A California Company
    RECORDED   :   June 20, 20XX, in Book 46603, Page 290, Official Records
    INSTRUMENT NO.: P-75424

5. The requirements that the death of Angela Gonales, one of the grantees in the deed dated May 25, 20XX, executed by Pat Cirelli and Mary Cirelle, husband and wife, in favor of Pedro Gonzales and Angela Gonzales, husband and wife, as Joint Tenants, recorded as Instrument No. P-3279 on June 20, 20XX, in Book R-09921, page 480, Official Records, be established of record.

6. Any Lien for inheritance tax payable to the State of California by reason of the death of Angela Gonzales, former owner in Joint Tenancy with Pedro Gonzales.

NOTE: Amount of 2nd installment 20XX-XX taxes for proration purposes, $725.00.

DESCRIPTION OF THE LAND REFERRED TO HEREIN:

    All of the real property situated in the City and County of San Francisco, State of California, described as follows:

    Lots 23 and 24 of Summer View Tract, City and County of San Francisco, State of California, as per map recorded April 30, 1989, in Book 20 of Maps, Page 28, in the office of the Recorder of the City and County of San Francisco, State of California.

Exception number three consists of the covenants, conditions, and restrictions. These were written out as part of the printed form in the escrow instructions. Things look pretty standard here. They should present no particular difficulty.

Note, once again, the clearly stated deletion of restrictions based upon race, color, religion, and national origin.

Exception four is Gonzales's trust deed from Premiere Financial Company. All of the information given matches up with what Pedro Gonzales told you. You should probably make a note on the report that you will need a modification and assumption agreement for the transfer of this loan to Hornbussel. You will probably do nothing else regarding this exception until you receive the beneficiary's statement outlining the current balance and status of the debt.

Number five requires that the death of Angela Gonzales be officially added to the record in order to terminate the current joint tenancy status of the second property. In exception six, the report indicates the possibility that an inheritance tax may be due because of her death. Gonzales already knows that he must clear these two matters up before the transfer will be possible. His attorney, Sam Black, will provide you with the documents needed to eliminate these two exceptions. A note to this effect at this point in the report might be a good idea. How you will terminate the joint tenancy and clear the inheritance tax will be discussed further after Black has sent you the necessary documents.

B. FIRST PROPERTY TITLE REPORT

On July 18, you receive the other title report, the one for the first property (see **Figure 12-5**). Just as with the report on the second property, you must note the receipt of this report on the progress sheet for this escrow and check each item against your instructions and other notes to make sure there are no discrepancies.

The vesting of this property is of particular interest. As you will recall, Hornbussel informed you that he would have to acquire title to this property from the estate of his deceased mother. The report confirms this as it shows title to be held by "the heirs or devisees of Matilda Hornbussel, deceased." You can now anticipate being given the necessary court decree from Hornbussel's attorney to vest title in Richard Hornbussel.

1. Exceptions to Title

There are three exceptions to title in this case and all of them are covered by the escrow instructions. The tax sale will require a little extra concern, but the general tax lien and the public utilities easement are both pretty standard.

Figure 12-5

FIRST PROPERTY TITLE REPORT (1)

CONFIDENTIAL OF LOS ANGELES

TO: YOUR ESCROW COMPANY
     111 N. BUSINESS STREET
     ANYTOWN, CALFIORNIA 94321

YOUR NO.: 243279
OUR NO.: 946747

IN RESPONSE TO THE ABOVE REFERENCED APPLICATION FOR A POLICY OF TITLE INSURANCE, TITLE INSURANCE AND TRUST COMPANY REPORTS THAT IT IS PREPARED TO ISSUE, OR CAUSE TO BE ISSUED, AS OF THE DATE HEREOF, A CALIFORNIA LAND TITLE ASSOCIATION STANDARD COVERAGE FROM POLICY OF TITLE INSURANCE DESCRIBING THE LAND AND THE ESTATE OR INTEREST THEREIN HEREINAFTER SET FORTH, INSURING AGAINST LOSS WHICH MAY BE SUSTAINED BY REASON OF ANY DEFECT, LIEN OR ENCUMBRANCE NOT SHOWN OR REFERRED TO AS AN EXCEPTION BELOW OR NOT EXCLUDED FROM COVERAGE PURSUANT TO THE PRINTED SCHEDULES, CONDITIONS AND STIPULATIONS OF SAID POLICY FORM.

THIS REPORT (AND ANY SUPPLEMENTS OR AMENDMENTS THERETO) IS ISSUED SOLELY FOR THE PURPOSE OF FACILITATING THE ISSUANCE OF A POLICY OF TITLE INSURANCE AND NO LIABILITY IS ASSUMED HEREBY. IF IT IS DESIRED THAT LIABILITY BE ASSUMED PRIOR TO THE ISSUANCE OF A POLICY OF TITLE INSURANCE, A BINDER OR COMMITMENT SHOULD BE REQUESTED.

DATED AT 7:30 A.M. AS OF JULY 16, 20XX

TITLE OFFICER: G. GAVIN

TITLE TO SAID ESTATE OR INTEREST AT THE DATE HEREOF IS VESTED IN:

THE HEIRS OR DEVISEES OF MATILDA HORNBUSSEL, DECEASED, SUBJECT TO ADMINISTRATION IN THE ESTATE OF SAID DECEDENT; RICHARD HORNBUSSEL BEING THE DULY APPOINTED, QUALIFIED, AND ACTING EXECUTOR, SUPERIOR COURT, LOS ANGELES COUNTY, CASE NO. 818420, PROBATE.

THE ESTATE OR INTEREST IN THE LAND HEREINAFTER DESCRIBED OR REFERRED TO COVERED BY THIS REPORT IS: A FEE.

FIRST PROPERTY TITLE REPORT (2)

CONFIDENTIAL OF LOS ANGELES

AT THE DATE HEREOF EXCEPTIONS TO COVERAGE IN ADDITION TO THE PRINTED EXCEPTIONS AND EXCLUSIONS CONTAINED IN SAID POLICY FORM WOULD BE AS FOLLOWS:

1.   GENERAL AND SPECIAL COUNTY AND CITY TAXES FOR THE FISCAL YEAR 20XX-20XX, A LIEN NOT YET PAYABLE.

AMOUNT OF SECOND INSTALLMENT TAXES FOR PRORATION, $430.00.

2.   A SALE TO THE STATE OF CALIFORNIA FOR GENERAL AND SPECIAL TAXES AND SUBSEQUENT DELINQUENCIES FOR THE
FISCAL YEAR   :   20XX - 20XX
TAXING AUTHORITY   :   LOS ANGELES COUNTY TAX COLLECTOR
ORIGINAL AMOUNT   : $430.00
AMOUNT TO PAY PRIOR TO: JULY 31, 20XX, $444.30

3.   AN EASEMENT AFFECTING THE PORTION OF SAID LAND AND FOR THE PURPOSES STATED HEREIN, AND INCIDENTAL PURPOSES,
IN FAVOR OF: TELEPHONE COMPANY OF THE USA
FOR   : PUBLIC UTILITIES
RECORDED : IN BOOK 87620 PAGE 240, OFFICIAL RECORDS
AFFECTS   : THE REAR 16 FEET

DESCRIPTION:

THE SOUTH 100 FEET OF THE NORTHEAST QUARTER OF THE SOUTHEAST QUARTER OF THE NORTHWEST QUARTER OF SECTION 55, TOWNSHIP 9 NORTH, RANGE 20 WEST, SAN BERNARDINO MERIDIAN, IN THE COUNTY OF LOS ANGELES, STATE OF CALIFORNIA.

XX/XX, 3 COPIES, PLATS ENCL.

It will be your job, under authorization from the first party, to pay off the tax sale. The total amount owed to redeem the property is listed as $444.30. You will note, however, that this amount only applies up until a July 31 deadline. For each month after that in which the taxes remain unpaid, additional penalty charges will accrue, You should, therefore, highlight that date in your copy of the report and note it elsewhere, as it is rather unlikely that escrow will be closing a month earlier than the August 30 deadline. You will have to obtain more up-to-date figures later so that you can pay the full amount and properly close escrow without incurring an escrow loss.

2. Structural Pest Control Report

On the first of August you receive another document into escrow. It is a pest control inspection report from the Residential Exterminator Company (see **Figure 12-6**). Hornbussel, you will recall, agreed to furnish such a report to show that the first property is free of wood destroying pests or organisms. He further promised that if any infestation or damage were found, he would have the situation corrected at his own expense.

The first page of the report shows that the exterminator company found the structure to be infested with subterranean termites and fungus. A list outlines the nature of the problems while a diagram of the house indicates the various trouble-spots. Structural damage has been discovered and the exterminators estimate a cost of $2,850.00 to repair it.

This estimate is given at the bottom of the second page under a detailed explanation of all recommended repairs. Included in this is the cost of the inspection and report. If the parties opt not to have the work done or go to another company for the repairs, Residential Exterminator company is entitled to their inspection fee of $50.

This discovery of pest control damage at the Hornbussel property brings on several important questions. Have both of the parties seen this report? Do they really want the repair work done as indicated in your instructions or will they come to some other arrangement? Will escrow be handling the charges for the repair work or will it be handled on the outside, if at all? No matter what the answers to these questions will be, you are obliged to proceed cautiously. A great deal of work is indicated and the $2,850.00 is no small expense. You must get the agreement and approval of both parties before any more can be done to resolve this matter.

V. Supplemental Escrow Instructions

You learn from Hornbussel that both he and Gonzales have received copies of the report and that everything is okay on both ends. They do not wish to delay the close of escrow, however, while awaiting completion of the required repairs. Hornbussel, instead, will

Figure 12-6

STRUCTURAL PEST CONTROL REPORT (1)

STANDARD STRUCTURAL PEST CONTROL INSPECTION REPORT
(WOOD-DESTROYING PESTS OR ORGANISMS)
This is an inspection report only - not a Notice of Completion.

ADDRESS OF PROPERTY INSPECTED	BLDG. NO. 2120	STREET Carson Street	CITY Los Angeles CO. CODE	DATE OF INSPECTION 7-25-XX

RESIDENTIAL EXTERMINATOR CO.
564 W. Ninth Street
Los Angeles, CA   90012

Affix stamp here on Board copy only
↓ **A LICENSED PEST CONTROL** ↓
OPERATOR IS AN EXPERT IN
HIS FIELD. ANY QUESTIONS
RELATIVE TO THIS REPORT
SHOULD BE REFERRED TO HIM.

FIRM LICENSE NO. 1492   CO. REPORT NO.   STAMP NO.   1066 R

Inspection Ordered by (Name and Address) Richard Hornbussel, 1551 Sunset Ave., Los Angeles, CA
Report Sent to (Name and Address) _Confidential Title Insurance & Trust Co., Escrow 243279_
Owner's Name and Address   same as above
Name and Address of a Party in Interest
Original Report ☒   Supplemental Report ☐   Limited Report ☐   Reinspection Report ☐   No. of Pages: 2

YES	CODE	SEE DIAGRAM BELOW	YES	CODE	SEE DIAGRAM BELOW	YES	CODE	SEE DIAGRAM BELOW	YES	CODE	SEE DIAGRAM BELOW
X	S	Subterranean Termites		B	Beetles-Other Wood Pests		Z	Dampwood Termites		EM	Excessive Moisture Condition
	K	Dry-Wood Termites	X	FG	Faulty Grade Levels		SL	Shower Leaks		IA	Inaccessible Areas
X	F	Fungus or Dry Rot		EC	Earth-wood Contacts	X	CD	Cellulose Debris		FI	Further Inspection Recom.

1. SUBSTRUCTURE AREA (soil conditions, accessibility, etc.)   See 1 below
2. Was Stall Shower water tested?   none   Did floor coverings indicate leaks?
3. FOUNDATIONS (Type, Relation to Grade, etc.)   See 3 below
4. PORCHES . . . STEPS . . . PATIOS   See 4 below
5. VENTILATION (Amount, Relation to Grade, etc.)   Adequate
6. ABUTMENTS . . . Stucco walls, columns, arches, etc.   See 6 below
7. ATTIC SPACES (accessibility, insulation, etc.)   No infestation found
8. GARAGES (Type, accessibility, etc.)   Attached finished interior walls
9. OTHER   See 9 below

DIAGRAM AND EXPLANATION OF FINDINGS (This report is limited to structure or structures shown on diagram.)

General Description _One-story single residence. Stucco frame, tile roof. Interior furnished,_

but unoccupied at time of inspection. Inspection Tag Posted (location)
Other Inspection Tags

Inspected by _Rich & Larry_   License No. _1840 and 4128_ Signature *John Bacooni*

YOU ARE ENTITLED TO OBTAIN COPIES OF ALL REPORTS AND COMPLETION NOTICES ON THIS PROPERTY FILED WITH THE BOARD DURING THE PRECEDING TWO YEARS UPON PAYMENT OF A $2.00 SEARCH FEE TO: STRUCTURAL PEST CONTROL BOARD, 1430 HOWE AVE., SACRAMENTO, CA. 95825.

STRUCTURAL PEST CONTROL REPORT (2)

SECOND PAGE OF STANDARD INSPECTION REPORT OF THE PROPERTY LOCATED AT:

Address of
Property
Inspected

<u>2120</u>   <u>Carson Street</u>   <u>Los Angeles, CA</u>
Bldg. No.   Street   City

<u>1066 R</u>   July 25, 20XX
Stamp No.   Date of Inspection   Co. Report No.
                                           (If any)

1. <u>SUBSTRUCTURE</u> – light amount debris, subtermite tubes in subsoil.

    Rec. A – Remove all scrapwood and cellulose debris from the under-
           area and haul away from premises.

    Rec. B – Treat under-area with toxic solution for extermination of
           subtermites, using not less than 5 gallons per each 100 sq.ft.

3. <u>FOUNDATION</u> – Faulty grade foundation and subtermites entering.

Rec. – Install concrete curbing as indicated.

4. <u>PORCHES</u> – Subtermited entering from walkway indicated, west side,
           fungus damage under carriage steps and landing.

Rec. – Drill and treat soil below at walkway.

6. <u>ABUTMENT</u> – Subtermites damaged beams over stucco-covered columns
             in front of garage.

Rec. A – Remove and replace overhead beams.

Rec. B – Install raised masonry bases at 4 stucco columns and drill and
          treat at interior columns.

9. <u>OTHER</u> – Fungus-infected rear door noted.

Rec. – Remove and replace door.

Cost of items 1AB, 3, 4, 6AB, & 9: $2,850.00

We enclose out bill for $50.00 to cover this inspection, which will be
waived if we perform work.

One year guarantee on work completed by this company.

be debited the $2,850.00 in escrow and the money will be credited to Gonzales account. Gonzales will then have the option of proceeding with the repairs at his own expense or simply keeping the money. You are authorized to pay the $50 fee for the inspection and report and to charge this amount to Hornbussel.

All of this is fine except that it requires you to draw up a supplemental escrow instructions outlining the changes requested for the official approval of both parties. If you look at the form, you can see that everything is laid out clearly and concisely (see **Figure 12-7**).

VI. Decree of Death

Another of the interesting particulars in this transaction is the problem of the joint tenancy that must be terminated in order to free Pedro Gonzales to transfer the second property. This is listed as exception number five on the title report.

The fact of Angela Gonzales's death must be established of record for title insurance purposes. One way of doing this is to obtain a decree through a court proceeding. This decree establishes the fact of the joint tenant's death and terminates the joint tenancy when recorded. This is the route taken by Gonzales (see **Figure 12-8**).

On August 10, Sam Black, Pedro Gonzales' attorney, delivers to you this decree in accordance with Gonzales' instructions. As you can see, in addition to officially establishing the death of Gonzales's wife and joint tenant, this court decree indicates that no inheritance tax is due on her estate. It finishes up with a legal description of the property.

A federal inheritance tax referee was appointed by the court to appraise the Gonzales property and render a report. In this case, he or she found there to be no inheritance tax due. A certificate was issued indicating this officially and the petition went to a hearing to obtain the decree. If he or she had found that taxes were owed, the court would determine the amount. Only when the tax was settled would the decree of death be issued by the court. A certified copy of the decree is then recorded.

A. AFFIDAVIT – DEATH OF JOINT TENANT

Another method of terminating the joint tenancy of a deceased joint tenant is through an affidavit. An Affidavit—Death of Joint Tenant is recorded (see **Figure 12-9**). To this is attached a certified copy of the death certificate and an inheritance tax release. Although joint tenancy simplifies a number of things in holding title to the property, as you can see, it does not eliminate the possibility of federal estate or state inheritance taxes (there are no state inheritance taxes in California). These must be considered and, if owed, paid.

Figure 12-7

SUPPLEMENTAL ESCROW INSTRUCTIONS

SUPPLEMENTAL

ESCROW INSTRUCTIONS

Escrow No.   243279

Date   August 1, 20XX

Reference is made to the exchange escrow instructions dated July 12, 20XX in this escrow.

Said instructions are hereby modified and/or supplemented in the following particulars only:

Both parties have received a copy of the termite inspection report of the Residential Exterminator Co. dated July 25, 20XX, pertaining to the first property. The matter is to be resolved in the following manner:

    1.   Upon closing of escrow, you will charge the first party's account to the sum of $50, which you will pay to Residential Exterminator Co. as its inspection fee.

    2.   You will charge to first party's account the sum of $2,850.00 and credit that amount to second party's account.

You are not to be concerned with the completion of any of the corrective work recommended in the above inspection report. Second party accepts the $2,850.00 credit and waives the completion of the termite inspection work.

                                       Richard Hornbussel

                                       Pedro Gonzales

Figure 12-8

DECREE OF DEATH

SUPERIOR COURT OF CALIFORNIA
COUNTY OF SAN FRANCISCO

Decree establishing fact of death of)   No. 91028 Probate
)
ANGELA GONZALES   )

   The verified petition of Pedro Gonzales, by Sam Black, his attorney, to establish the fact of death of Angela Gonzales, deceased,
joint tenant in the above entitled proceeding, in certain property,
coming on regularly to be heard on August 8, 19XX, in Department B,
the Honorable Herb Patterson, Judge presiding, the Court, after examining the petition and hearing the evidence, and finding that all
notices of said hearing have been duly given as required by law, and
that the facts alleged in said petition are true, and that the inheritance tax appraiser's Certificate of No Tax is on file herein, grants
said petition as follows:

   It is Ordered, Adjudged, and Decreed that said Angela Gonzales
died on March 28, 20XX.

   The property owned by Pedro Gonzales and decedent, as joint tenants, is described as follows:

   Lots 23 and 24 of SUMMER VIEW TRACT, in the City and
   County of San Francisco, State of California, as per
   map recorded in Book 20, page 28 of Maps in the office
   of the county recorder of said county.

Dated: August 8, 20XX

                                   Herb Patterson
                                   _____
                                   Judge of the Superior Court

THIS INSTRUMENT IS A CORRECT COPY OF THE
ORIGINAL ON FILE IN THIS OFFICE.

ATTEST *August 8*   20 XX

         B. F. BECK
COUNTY CLERK AND CLERK OF THE SUPERIOR
COURT OF THE STATE OF CALIFORNIA IN AND
FOR THE COUNTY OF SAN FRANCISCO.

BY *P. Olds*   DEPUTY

Figure 12-9

AFFIDAVIT – DEATH OF JOINT TENANT

RECORDING REQUESTED BY

AFTER RECORDING MAIL TO

SPACE ABOVE THIS LINE FOR RECORDER'S USE

AFFIDAVIT — DEATH OF JOINT TENANT

State of California,

County of __San Francisco__ } ss.

__Pedro Gonzales__, of legal age, being first duly sworn, deposes and says:

That __Angela Gonzales__, the decedent mentioned in the attached certified copy of Certificate of Death, is the same person as __Angela Gonzales__

named as one of the parties in that certain __grant deed__ dated __May 15__, 20 __XX__,

executed by __Pat Cirelli and Mary Cirelli, husband and wife__

to __Pedro Gonzales and Angela Gonzales__

as joint tenants, recorded as Instrument No. __P-3279__ on __June 20__, 20 __XX__, in Book __R-09921__ Page __480__, of __)fficial__ Records of __San Francisco__ County, California, covering the following described property situated in the said County, State of California:

Lots 23 and 24 of SUMMER VIEW TRACT as per map
recorded in Book 20, page 28 of Maps in the
office of the county recorder of said county.

That the value of all real and personal property owned by said decedent at date of death, including the full value of the property above described, did not then exceed the sum of $ __136,000.00__

Pedro Gonzales
/S/ Pedro Gonzales

Subscribed and Sworn to before me

this __8th__ day of __July__, 20 __XX__

Barbara McNulty (Sign)
Notary Public Commissioned for said County and State
/S/ Barbara McNulty

OFFICIAL SEAL
BARBARA McNULTY
NOTARY PUBLIC--CALIFORNIA
PRINCIPAL OFFICE IN
SAN FRANCISCO COUNTY
My Commission Expires July 15, 19XX

1024-OFC-74

VII. Estate Taxes

The federal estate tax is a tax imposed by the federal government upon the right to dispose of property upon death.

It is computed based upon the net value of the estate, without regard for the number or relationship of the heirs involved. If the gross value of the estate exceeds a certain limit, then a federal estate tax must be filed. This limit is constantly being readjusted to keep up with the economy. The current ceiling should be obtainable by contacting the tax board in your area. The point here is that the tax is computed based upon the net property value as provided by law.

The federal estate tax becomes a lien on real property immediately upon death. No recording is necessary. The lien continues for ten years after the death of the property owner.

The tax laws are a very fluid thing. There have been reforms and changes back and forth in recent years. Be sure to keep current on what is required from the estates to your escrow, as any information we give you here is likely to be out-of-date almost as soon as it is written.

VIII. Decree of Distribution

When a person dies, their property passes to their heirs or devisees only after it has been administered according to probate law.

The first property, as you may recall from the vesting of the title report, is still in the name of Matilda Hornbussel, Richard's deceased mother. Before he can deed it to Gonzales, he must establish title in his own name. Richard is entitled to the property according to the terms of Matilda's estate but the official vesting of title has yet to be changed (see **Figure 12-10**).

The law allows people to pass on property after death with the use of a will or, more officially, a last will and testament.

If there is no will the estate passes to heirs under statutory intestate succession. These heirs are determined according to familial relationships as subject to the laws current at the time of death. Inheritance laws are rather complicated and constantly subject to changes and revision so it would be rather pointless to detail them here. A probate proceeding is generally required before the heirs or devisees can gain marketable title to the property of the deceased.

Figure 12-10

DECREE OF DISTRIBUTION

```
 1                    SUPERIOR COURT OF CALIFORNIA
 2                       COUNTY OF LOS ANGELES
 3
 4    IN THE MATTER OF THE ESTATE )    No.   466200
 5            OF                   )
 6    MATILDA HORNBUSSEL           )    ORDER SETTLING FINAL ACCOUNT AND
 7                  DECEASED  )    DECREE OF DISTRIBUTION UNDER WILL
 8
 9        The petition of RICHARD HORNBUSSEL, as Executor of the Will of MATILDA
10    HORNBUSSEL, deceased, for order settling final account and decree of distri-
11    bution under will, STEPHEN TISCHLER appearing as attorney for said petitioner,
12    coming on regularly to be heard this 3rd day of August, 20XX    , the Court, after
13    examining the petition and hearing the evidence, finds that due notice of the
14    hearing of such petition has been given as required by law; that notice to cre-
15    ditors has been duly given as required by law, that all the allegations of said
16    petition are true, that all inheritance taxes and all personal property taxes
17    due and payable by said estate have been paid, and that said account should be
18    settled and distribution ordered as prayed for:
19        It is therefore ordered, adjudged, and decreed by the Court that notice
20    to creditors has been duly given as required by law, and that said RICHARD
21    HORNBUSSEL has in his possession belonging to said estate, after deducting
22    credits to which he is entitled, a balance of $61,290.00, of which $6,040.00
23    is in cash, and the remainder consists of the property hereinafter described
24    at the appraised value; that said account be allowed and settled accordingly;
25    that out of the residue of cash in his hands said executor pay $2,730.00 hereby
26    allowed as Attorney's fees and retain $2,570.00 as commission allowed by law
27    for his services; that the following described property be and the same hereby
28    is distributed in the following manner:
29        The South 100 feet of the Northeast quarter of the Southeast
30        quarter of the Northwest quarter of Section 55, Township 9
31        North, Range 20 West, SBM, County of Los Angeles, State of
32        California.
33
34        TO:  RICHARD HORNBUSSEL, a single man.
35
36    and that all other property of said estate, whether described herein or not,
37    be and the same hereby is distributed as follows:
38
39        TO:  RICHARD HORNBUSSEL, a single man.
40
41    Dated August 3, 20XX
42
43
44                                          John T. Murphy
45                                   _____
                                     Judge of the Superior Court
46
47    THIS INSTRUMENT IS A CORRECT COPY OF THE
48    ORIGINAL ON FILE IN THIS OFFICE.
49
50    ATTEST   August 3              20 XX
51          ABNER SMITH
52
53    COUNTY CLERK AND CLERK OF THE SUPERIOR
54    COURT OF THE STATE OF CALIFORNIA IN AND
55    FOR THE COUNTY OF PROPERTY

      BY                              DEPUTY
```

IX. Probate

In probate, all the assets of the deceased person's estate are gathered and tabulated. Any debts or taxes that may be owed are paid off. The balance of the estate is then distributed.

One of the main functions of escrow is to determine who the heir is to be.

Probate proceeds in a series of steps:

1. The heirs, devisees, and legatees are notified.
2. A representative, called either an executor (executrix if female) or administrator (administratrix if female) is named by the probate court.

An "executor" is a representative named in the will. An "administrator" is appointed by the court if the property owner dies intestate (without a will).

3. Public notice must be published in a newspaper of general circulation to notify creditors that the decedent's estate is being distributed.
4. An inventory of all property to the estate is made and everything is appraised, listing the value for tax purposes.
5. All outstanding debts and taxes are then paid.
6. A Decree of Distribution is entered. This decree names the persons who, in the opinion of the court, are entitled to the property of the estate and it lists exactly what portion or share each distributee takes.
7. The decree is recorded with the county recorder's office in the county where the real property involved is located.

Once the decree of distribution is recorded, it establishes marketable title for the distributees.

There is no need for a deed from the executor or administrator. The decree itself is evidence of property ownership.

In the matter of the Hornbussel estate, it takes until August 13 before you receive a certified copy of the necessary decree. In all cases it is called an Order Settling Final Account and Decree of Distribution under Will. Richard Hornbussel now has a good evidence of marketable title.

X. Trust Deed Documents

A letter from Premiere Financial arrives on August 15 (see **Figure 12-11**). Enclosed with it is the beneficiary's statement and the assumption agreement, along with the required modifications, so that Hornbussel can take over Gonzales's loan (Figures 12-12 and 12-13).

Different lenders have different procedures for the assumption and modification of a trust deed and note.

In this instance, for example, Premiere has already executed the agreement and requests that you make sure the two principals execute it also. More often you will find that lenders want the two parties to sign the papers first, before they are sent back to the company for the signatures of the loan officers. In this case Premiere has instructed you to have the agreement recorded and insured by an indorsement to be attached to the ALTA title insurance policy. Other lenders will not want the agreement recorded or insured at all.

Policies will differ, and your job as an escrow officer is to follow the lender's instructions so long as they do not conflict and remain within the scope of the escrow instructions received from your principals.

In this case there seems to be no difficulty whatsoever. The instructions in the cover letter correspond precisely with those in your escrow instructions. You won't need any further authorization from your principals. Be sure to note the assumption charges, however. These will be figured into your final settlement of the escrow accounts.

A. BENEFICIARY'S STATEMENT

The present unpaid balance on the loan is $75,462.15—quite close to the $76,000.00 Gonzales estimated. The escrow instructions provide that "In the event said statement shows the unpaid principal balance to be more or less that $76,000.00, you are to adjust the difference in cash." (See **Figure 12-12**.) The $537.85 difference will have to be adjusted on the final settlement sheet.

B. ASSUMPTION AGREEMENT

The assumption agreement very clearly expresses the original circumstances of the Gonzales loan and states all the new modifications, completely conforming with the terms of the escrow instructions (see **Figure 12-13**). The wording in the instructions establishes that execution of this assumption agreement constitutes approval of all its terms and conditions. In this way the contingency is fully satisfied.

Figure 12-11

LENDER'S COVER LETTER

PREMIERE FINANCIAL COMPANY

August 12, 20XX

Your Escrow Company
111 N. Business Street
Anytown, California 94321

Attention: Your Name

RE: Escrow 243280
Gentlemen: Loan No. 04-1849

We hand you herewith the following:

1. Modification of trust deed and promissory note executed in triplicate by Premiere Financial Company, modifying deed of trust recorded in Book 46603, page 290, Official Records.

2. Beneficiary's statement covering above deed of trust.

3. ALTA Lender's Policy #14469 of Confidential Title Insurance and Trust Co.

You are instructed and authorized to use the foregoing documents and cause the modification agreement to be recorded in San Francisco County provided:

1. You hold for our account:

    A. An assumption fee of $754.62, being 1 % of the unpaid principal owing on the note herein referred to.

    B. A fee of $50 to cover our processing costs and beneficiary's statement.

2. You can obtain a CLTA 110.5 Indorsement insuring said modification, to be attached to the above mentioned ALTA policy.

Upon receipt of said indorsement of ALTA policy, we will cause the note to be properly endorsed to reflect the terms of the modification. Please instruct the San Francisco recorder to mail the recorded modification to the attention of the undersigned.

Sincerely,

Stephen Carrasco

Steven Carrasco
Vice President

Figure 12-12

BENEFICIARY'S STATEMENT

PREMIERE
FINANCIAL
COMPANY | **BENEFICIARY'S STATEMENT**

Your Company ....

Your Street Address...................

Your City and State...................

Escrow No. 123462 ....

Loan No. ..04-1849 ....

Date ...... August 12, 20XX ....

This is to certify that **AMERICAN FINANCIAL COMPANY** is the legal holder of that certain promissory note described as follows:

Original Amount of note $ 100,000.00 ....

Date of note ....June 17, 20XX ....

Date payment due ....1st day each month ...

Interest rate ....12%..............

Monthly payments

Principal and interest $. 1,277.77, or more

Taxes and insurance $. --...............

Total payment ..... $. 1,277.77..........

Delinquency charge: 10% of any installment not paid within 10 days of due date.

Note provides for ... 6.... months interest bonus in event of prepayment.

Deed of Trust securing note, recorded .. June 20, 20XX ... in Book .. 46603 ... Page ... 290 ...

LOAN STATUS	Original Statement	First Amendment
Unpaid balance	$.. 75,462.15 ...	$.............
Interest paid to	August 1, 20XX ..	....
Impounds held by us	$. ------...	$.............
Total delinquency	$. ------...	$.............
This delinquency includes payment due	....	....
Next payment due	September 1, 20XX	....

We hold the following fire insurance policies:

Policy No. and Company	Amount	Expiration	Premium	Agent
62131 Quality Insurance Co.	$136,000	9/22/XX	$280 (3 yrs)	Wm. Birney & Co.

COMMENTS: UNDER NO CIRCUMSTANCES WILL WE ACCEPT TRANSFER OF THIS LOAN UNLESS ALL LOAN PAYMENTS, TAXES, AND ASSESSMENTS ARE CURRENT AT THE TIME YOUR ESCROW IS CLOSED. IN THE EVENT OF A SALE OR CONVEYANCE OF THE SUBJECT PROPERTY OR OF ANY INTEREST THEREIN, we have the option under the terms of our deed of trust to declare all sums secured thereby immediately due and payable unless the Trustors obtain our written consent to such sale or conveyance.

After the CLOSE of your escrow, send the insurance assignments to us. Fire insurance policies may not be substituted without our approval. In the event of such substitution, there is a $5.00 insurance substitution fee on each substituted policy.

IF THIS LOAN IS DELINQUENT OR IN FORECLOSURE we will commence or continue with foreclosure proceedings or put this loan into foreclosure until such time it is reinstated or paid in full if the reinstatement period has expired. ANY INSTALLMENTS BECOMING DUE ARE TO BE PAID ON THE DUE DATES OR LATE CHARGES WILL BE ADDED. If any installment becomes due or is subsequently paid, the computations above set forth are subject to change, and it will be your responsibility to obtain all information relative thereto.

..... *Kathy Enger* ....
Loan Service Department

Figure 12-13

ASSUMPTION AGREEMENT (1)

MOFIFICATION OF TRUST DEED AND PROMISSORY NOTE

AND ASSUMPTION AGREEMENT

This agreement made this 12th day of August, 20XX between PEDRO GONZALES, an unmarried man, hereinafter called Trustor, RICHARD HORNBUSSEL, a single man, hereinafter called Assumptionor, and PREMIERE FINANCIAL COMPANY, a California Corporation, hereinafter called Beneficiary.

WITNESSETH:

That WHEREAS, heretofore, on the 17th day of June, 20XX, Trustor and Angela Gonzales, husband and wife, did make, execute, and deliver to Beneficiary that certain promissory note in the original amount of $100,000.00, payable in installments of $1,277.77, or more, on the first day of each calendar month, including interest at 12% per annum, commencing on the first day of August, 20XX and continuing until principal and interest have been paid, which promissory note is secured by a deed of trust recorded June 20, 20XX in Book 46603, page 290, of official records in the office of the county recorder of San Francisco County describing the following property:

  Lots 23 and 24 of SUMMER VIEW TRACT, in the City
  and County of San Francisco, State of California,
  as per map recorded in Book 20, page 28 of Maps
  in the office of the county recorder of said county.

WHEREAS, the payments of principal and interest on said promissory note are presently current, with all amounts due and owing to September 1, 20XX having been paid, with the unpaid principal balance being $75,462.15;

WHEREAS, said deed of trust contains the following provision: Should the property described in this deed of trust be sold and conveyed by the maker hereof prior to the maturity of the note secured hereby, the whole sum of principal and interest shall become immediately due and payable at the option of the holder of said note;

WHEREAS, ANGELA GONZALES did die on March 28, 20XX, as evidenced by Decree Establishing Death entered August 8, 20XX in Case No. 91028 Probate, San Francisco Superior Court;

WHEREAS, Trustor desires to sell said property and Assumptionor desires to purchase said property;

ASSUMPTION AGREEMENT (2)

NOW, THEREFORE, in consideration of the premises and other valuable consideration, receipt of which is acknowledged, the parties do hereby agree:

1. Beneficiary consents to the sale of the property to Richard Hornbussel and waives the due-on-sale provision of the deed of trust for the purpose of this transaction only.

2. The terms of said promissory note are modified as follows:

   A. Interest on the unpaid principal balance owing shall be at the rate of 12% per annum.

   B. Principal and interest shall be payable in installments of $1,391.44, or more, on the first day of each calendar month commencing on September 1, 20XX and continuing until said principal and interest have been paid.

3. Assumptionor assumes and agrees to pay the unpaid balance of principal and interest on said promissory note as so modified.

4. Beneficiary consents and agrees to the assumption of said promissory note, as so modified, by Assumtionor.

5. Beneficiary releases Trustor of all further personal liability as the maker of said promissory note and trustor of said deed of trust.

IN WITNESS WHEREOF, the parties have executed this instrument.

_____
Pedro Gonzales

_____
Richard Hornbussel

PREMIERE FINANCIAL COMPANY,
a California Corporation

by _____*Bob Pearce*_____
Vice President

by _____*Julia Bigsby*_____
Assistant Secretary

(ACKNOWLEDGEMENTS)
(OF ALL THREE)
(PARTIES)

Record the arrival of these documents on your progress sheet and include all the important figures and adjustments on the settlement sheet. We are now ready to finish up the processing of this exchange transaction escrow.

XI. Final Processing Items

The next thing that arrives is Hornbussel's fire insurance policy. Enter this on your progress sheet. You now have all the documents needed to close this escrow. There are still, however, a number of things that need to be done before you can record the property transfer:

1. The supplemental escrow instructions must be signed by both parties.
2. The trust deed assumption and modification agreement must be signed by both parties.
3. The signed agreement and the two decrees must be sent to the title company for recording.

These signatures can be obtained any number of ways. You could invite the parties back to your office. You could mail them out with an envelope for return postage. You could arrange with the brokers involved to gather the signatures on your behalf, There is nothing unique about this exchange transaction in this respect. The point is, all of these things are easily accomplished in a week or two and you find yourself one step closer to closing with about a week left before the 60-day deadline.

XII. Settling the First Party

Hornbussel now needs to bring in the additional funds to balance out his escrow account. He already paid in $2,000.00, but owes another $3,000.00 in boot to balance his equity in the first property with Gonzales's equity in the second property. Late in the processing he instructed you to credit Gonzales with $2,850.00 to cover the cost of repairs for termite and fungus damage. He also owes escrow the $50 termite report fee. These, too, must be debited to his account.

Reviewing your settlement sheet (see **Figure 12-14**), you see that you will need sufficient funds to pay the tax sale on the Los Angeles property, the assumption charges and fee on the loan for the San Francisco property and the broker's commission owed for the sale of the first property. These plus his share of taxes, title and escrow charges must all be paid into escrow by Hornbussel.

By this time you should have no trouble estimating the necessary funds for closing. The procedure in this case is much the same as in the other escrow examples we have explored.

Figure 12-14

TITLE/ESCROW SETTLEMENT SHEET

TITLE/ESCROW SETTLEMENT SHEET
EXCHANGE

☐ ESTIMATED STATEMENT	☒ FINAL STATEMENT	DATE 8/24/XX	E.O./T.O. NAME YOUR NAME	ESCROW NO. 243279 ESCROW NO. 243280

PROPERTY DESCRIPTION/ADDRESS
2120 Carson Street, Los Angeles

PROPERTY DESCRIPTION/ADDRESS
1019 Maine Road, San Francisco

FIRST PARTY
Richard Hornbussel

SECOND PARTY
Pedro Gonzales

ADDRESS

ADDRESS

	DEBIT	CREDIT	DESCRIPTION	DEBIT	CREDIT	
P R O P E R T Y B E I N G C O N V E Y E D		55 000 00	EXCHANGE VALUE—FIRST PARTIES PROPERTY	55 000 00		**P R O P E R T Y B E I N G A C Q U I R E D**
		2 000 00	DEPOSIT TO: Escrow			
			DEPOSITS RETAINED BY:			
			EXISTING LOAN BALANCE			
			EXISTING LOAN TRUST FUNDS			
			EXISTING LOAN – TRANSFER FEE			
	2 850 00		Adjustment for Termite Work		2 850 00	
	64 50		P TAXES $215 ea inst FR 7/1 TO 8/25		64 50	
		60 86	R INSURANCE $ FR TO	60 86		
			O INTEREST $ FR TO			
			R RENT $ FR TO			
			A ASSMNT. INT. $ FR TO			
			T RENT DEPOSIT			
P R O P E R T Y B E I N G A C Q U I R E D	136 000 00		EXCHANGE VALUE—SECOND PARTIES PROPERTY		136 000 00	**P R O P E R T Y B E I N G C O N V E Y E D**
			DEPOSIT TO:			
			DEPOSITS RETAINED BY:			
		75 462 15	EXISTING LOAN BALANCE	75 462 15		
			EXISTING LOAN TRUST FUNDS			
	804 62		EXISTING LOAN – TRANSFER FEE Assumption fee			
	1 319 44		Sept. 1 Loan pmt.			
		108 75	P TAXES $362.50ea i FR 7/1 TO 8/25	108 75		
	84 51		R INSURANCE $ 192 FR 1/25 TO 2/18/51		84 27	
		67 44	O INTEREST $ 12% FR 8/1 TO 8/25	67 44		
		399 96	R RENT $ FR TO	399 96		
			A ASSMNT. INT. $ FR TO			
		300 00	T RENT DEPOSIT	300 00		
			NEW LOAN WITH:			
N E W L O A N (S)			L FHA MTG. $ INS. RESERVE $			**N E W L O A N (S)**
			O TAX RES $ RECON FEE $			
			A CR REPORTS $ TAX SERVICE $			
			N LOAN FEE $ APPRAISAL FEE $			
			C INTEREST $ $			
			A INT @ FR TO $			
			R TOTAL OF ABOVE			
			INSURANCE			
L O A N P A Y O F F S			PAY OFF LOAN TO			**L O A N P A Y O F F S**
			PRINCIPAL $			
			INTEREST $			
			INT @ FR TO $			
			PREPAYMENT PENALTY $			
			RECON FEE $			
			$			
			LESS LOAN TRUST FUND DEPOSITS $			
			TOTAL OF ABOVE			
M I S C	142 00		TITLE INSURANCE $ 55000 ☒Owners ☐JP ☐STR 142 00			**M I S C**
			PREMIUM FOR $ ☐Loan ☐Alta			
			TITLE INSURANCE $ 136000 ☒Owners ☐JP ☐STR 214 50	214 50		
			PREMIUM FOR $ ☐Loan ☐Alta			
	64 35		IND 110.5			
	108 50		ESCROW FEE	217 00	108 50	
			RECONVEYANCE FEE			
	11 00		RECORDING Dd Dec Dist Assump Agr 11 00			
			Deed Term. J. T.	6 00	6 00	
			NOTARY FEE			
	5 00		DOCUMENT PREP.	10 00	5 00	
	18 15		TRANSFER TAX CO. $ 18.15 CITY $	18 15		
			TRANSFER TAX CO. $ 24.20 CITY $	24 20	24 20	
			TOTAL			
	448 60		TAX COLLECTOR Tax Sale (to 8/31)			
			Bond	743 66		
	3 300 00		COMMISSION			
				8 160 00		
			CHECK TO:			
	50 00		Termite Insp. Fee			
					1 662 25	
		11 871 51	BALANCE DUE COMPANY FROM			
	145 270 67	145 270 67	**TOTALS**	140 661 02	140 661 02	

All of these various adjustments prorations, expenses, fees, and commissions are noted on the final settlement sheet.

By the time everything is added in, the balance due from Hornbussel is $11,871.51, quite a bit more than $3,000.00. Of course, to allow a margin for error, it would probably be wise to call for a total of $12,000.00. When escrow is successfully closed, you can refund him the difference ($128.49). Hornbussel delivers a certified check for this amount on August 25.

XIII. Settling the Second Party

If you take a look at Gonzales' side of the settlement sheet, you will see that his charges, fees, and adjustments add up to $140,661.02. You will recall that he is responsible for a share of the taxes, title and escrow expenses, as well as the sewer bond and a number of other items resulting in a debit to his account.

In this case, these debits are somewhat more than the amount of funds in his account, $138,998.77. You will need a check for $1,662.25 from Gonzales in order to balance out his account and close the escrow. You telephone him and he sends $1,700.00 immediately. You will refund the $37.75 difference after closing.

XIV. Closing

Today is August 26. Everything is ready so that escrow may be closed tomorrow. You need to make it official.

You must authorize Confidential Title, both in Los Angeles and San Francisco, to record the documents that they now hold. This is under the condition, of course, that they are able to comply with your earlier instructions and will issue all the needed title policies, including the CLTA 110.5 Indorsement, which the lender required as a condition of assignment for the trust deed. This business is conducted exactly as you would in a normal sale situation except that, once again, you must make certain that the documents are recorded concurrently in both counties.

All this can be achieved any number of ways according to your preference, your company's policies, and the amount of time you have before deadline. You could, for example, write to each county location of the title company instructing them to record on a specified date, making sure to record concurrently with the branch in the other county. A telephone call, text message, fax, or e-mail serves almost as well as a letter (although it should certainly be followed up with something in writing). In this case a phone call is probably more advisable because of the time factor.

Perhaps the best approach of all would be to telephone the title company's inter-county service representative and instruct him or her to coordinate the concurrent recording. If you were not aware that this person existed, you should become so. Most good title companies have one and they can be a very good friend to you in your escrow duties. These representatives can help out by expediting the movement of documents across the state, speeding your access to information and, as needed here, helping with the recording of documents in other counties as well as seeing to it that you receive the proper information regarding recording fees.

XV. After Closing

Even after the escrow is closed your work is hardly done, as you well know. All charges must be reviewed and verified. You must complete the final settlement and disburse checks to the parties owed money from the escrow. The principals, in this case, are both owed refunds. You must send these off along with the escrow closing statements.

Transfer the fire insurance policies (or new policies) officially to the respective new owners. And, when the title insurance policies arrive, they too must be mailed off to each of your principals. You have seen all of these matters before with reference to other escrow samples. Review these procedures now, if you wish.

XVI. Final Comment

We have now completed our discussion of the real property exchange escrow. We have gone through this procedure step by step, from taking the escrow, through processing, up to the closing and beyond. The sample we have created here is, perhaps, not the most difficult exchange transaction imaginable. It is, however, entirely adequate to show the fundamental peculiarities of this kind of escrow operation. Exchanges are frequently more complex than this but the basic concepts remain the same.

XVII. CHAPTER SUMMARY

When the escrow has started, a PROGRESS SHEET should be used to keep track of the items ordered and received. The FILES as set up by escrow will keep the various documents safe and organized as they are needed. INDEXING is an office procedure that allows the escrow to quickly locate specific files. If a TICKLER SYSTEM is used, it will remind the escrow of important dates to avoid missing deadlines.

In a title report, there will be EXCEPTIONS TO TITLE which exclude or limit coverage in those areas listed.

During the escrow, one may have to deal directly with an EXECUTOR or ADMINISTRATOR. They are representatives of the probated will and the court that oversees the estate. The court will order a DECREE OF DISTRIBUTION when it has decided the heirs that will receive their portion of the estate.

In a title policy there may be INDORSEMENTS which are notations that modify or change the contents of the title policy.

An INHERITANCE TAX REFEREE will inventory all property to an estate and then lists the value for tax purposes. An AFFIDAVIT is a sworn witnessed statement that attests to the truth or accuracy of a statement.

The ESTATE TAX is the federal tax imposed on the right to dispose of property upon the death of someone and will be computed on the net value of the estate. INHERITANCE TAX due, if any, is the state imposed tax on heirs for their right to inherit property. (California has no state inheritance tax.)

XVIII. TERMS

Administrator/Administratrix: The persons appointed by the court to settle the estate of a person who had died intestate.

Affidavit: A sworn statement by an affiant stating under oath before a witness that the facts contained in the affidavit are true and correct.

Decree of Distribution: A court ordered decree that names the persons that are entitled to the property of the estate listing what portion is given to each heir.

Estate Tax: Federal tax imposed on the right to dispose of property upon death computed on the net value of the estate.

Exceptions to Title: When used in the title report, it refers to items specifically excluded from coverage under a title insurance policy.

Executor/Executrix: The persons appointed by a testator to carry out the directions and requests in their last will and testament.

Files: The method of keeping escrow papers carefully saved and accessible as they are needed later.

Indexing: An office procedure that allows one to store and quickly locate specific files when needed usually by an alphabetical cross index system.

Indorsement: A notation added to an instrument, as a title policy, after its execution that is made to change or clarify the document's contents.

Inheritance Tax: A state "estate" tax imposed on heirs for their right to inherit property.

Inheritance Tax Referee: The pubic official appointed to inventory all property to the estate and listing the value for tax purposes.

Progress Sheet: A printed checkoff form used in escrow to keep track of the items that are required to be ordered and when they are received.

Tickler System: A review system that reminds the escrow officer to check each file periodically to see that important matters are attended to. It may involve a desk calendar, or affixing color coded tabs to each file.

XIX. CHAPTER QUIZ

1. A progress sheet shows:
    a. dates.
    b. check marks.
    c. dollar amounts.
    d. none of the above.

2. If a settlement sheet has entries in pencil, it is really a:
    a. working settlement sheet.
    b. final settlement sheet.
    c. both a and b.
    d. neither a nor b.

3. When typing an exchange escrow "title order," information to the title company should:
    a. always be given.
    b. never be given.
    c. both a and b.
    d. neither a nor b.

4. Indexing is the process of identifying escrows according to:
    a. numbers.
    b. dates.
    c. both a and b.
    d. neither a nor b.

5. An index system using a hard copy that is easy to insert and remove is:
    a. a computer.
    b. a card file.
    c. loose-leaf binder.
    d. none of the above.

6. A common exception(s) or exclusion(s) to title insurance policies are:
    a. current taxes.
    b. sewer bonds.
    c. C C& Rs.
    d. all of the above.

7. Supplemental escrow instructions are used to:
    a. change instructions.
    b. add instructions.
    c. delete instructions.
    d. any of the above.

8. To settle the estate of the deceased, probate requires:
    a. decree of distribution.
    b. decree of real estate.
    c. both a and b.
    d. neither a nor b.

9. The last step in probate is:
    a. inform heirs.
    b. funeral.
    c. record decree.
    d. none of the above.

10. After closing, the escrow officer:
    a. completes final statement.
    b. disburses checks.
    c. transfers fire insurance.
    d. all of the above.

ANSWERS: 1. b; 2. a; 3. a; 4. a; 5. b; 6. d; 7. d; 8. a; 9. c; 10. d

Note and Trust Deed Escrow Sample

I. The Sale of a Loan

Often, buyers will take back a second deed of trust and a promissory note as part of the negotiated sale of their property.

The buyer owes the seller money with the property as security (note and trust deed). Most first and second trust deeds of this type call for monthly payments from the buyer.

The financial objectives of people constantly change. Many times the seller who holds the trust deed who receives the payments would later prefer a large amount of cash all at once, so he or she may decide to sell the buyer's note and trust deed to obtain a lump sum of cash.

II. When Less Than Fee Title is Conveyed

Up to this point in the book all of the escrow transactions we have discussed have involved owners selling the fee title to a parcel of real property. It is also possible for an owner to sell personal property interests in real property. In this example we will illustrate how an interest (less than the fee title) is conveyed; a promissory note secured by a deed of trust will be sold and this sale will be handled through escrow.

CHAPTER OUTLINE

There are many reasons for transactions of this type. A purchaser may not have sufficient cash to equal the equity held by the property owner. A owner wishing to keep the sale alive will take back a purchase money note and deed of trust as part of the consideration. If the owner needs cash, he or see can then sell the trust deed to a third party.

As another example, a third party lender who makes a loan to an owner to be secured by a trust deed, either a first trust deed or even a second or third, may later decide to sell the trust deed.

> *The financial objectives of investors shift constantly. When cash is needed, the sale of trust deeds and notes is a viable option.*

There are a number of investors in today's market who deal exclusively in this type of investment.

The escrow officer will find this type of escrow transaction relatively simple. However, there are several different procedures, new documents and instruments we have not encountered before. You will also become familiar with new points of law. All of these will be discussed in this chapter.

An introduction of the parties and aspects of the transaction are the first order of business. This is how the information is presented to you on June 10, 20XX.

III. Information About This Sample

On April 20 of this year, Mr. and Mrs. Todd Slavkin sold their home in Indio to Mr. and Mrs. Paul Montgomery. The sales price of the property was $45,000. The Montgomerys paid $5,000 of this amount down and borrowed $35,000 of the balance from Industrial Bank, secured by a first trust deed on the property. The Slavkins accepted a $5,000 note from the Montgomerys for the remainder of the purchase price. A second trust deed on the property secures this note.

The Slavkins want to raise some cash to purchase another parcel of land. Selling this note and second trust deed is a viable option to obtain the needed cash. The real estate broker they're using for the purchase of the new property deals occasionally with an investor named Leigh Bennet. Bennet's main business is the purchase of such trust deeds. She offers to purchase the note and trust deed. The Slavkins negotiate a reasonable discount with Bennet and an agreement is struck.

IV. Opening Escrow

The promissory note and the trust deed securing it will be transferred in this transaction. Both must end up in the hands of the purchaser at the close of escrow. The transfer of

the note is simple—an indorsement on the document itself will accomplish the task. An Assignment of Trust Deed, which will be recorded at the County Recorder's Office to make it a matter of public record, will be required to transfer the interest under the trust deed.

Your first duty is to take a good, hard look at the trust deed and note the Slavkins hand you. Examine the trust deed to be sure that the payees on the note are also named as beneficiaries in the trust deed. Make sure that the trust deed was properly recorded.

Next, check the note to see that it has been signed by the maker and that it is easily identifiable as the note secured by this particular deed of trust. Are there are any other endorsements written on the back side of the note?

The beneficiary is asked to bring the title insurance policy covering the deed of trust being sold. Mr. Slavkin presents a CLTA Joint Protection Policy issued at the time of the purchase of the property by the Montgomerys. The Slavkins are insured as beneficiaries under the second trust deed and the Montgomerys as owners of the real property by the policy. You will find the information contained in the policy important when filling out the escrow instructions. When a new policy is obtained for Bennet, the purchaser, this policy will be needed.

A. INSTRUCTIONS FOR SALE OF TRUST DEED AND NOTE

Even a fairly simple escrow procedure such as this one still requires a great deal of clearly stated information taken in the proper form.

Lets start taking the escrow instructions for this transaction from the parties. Though it may not seem designed for this use, the escrow memo form (**Figure 13-1**) can be adapted for use in gathering all the proper information. Why use a form in a transaction where it is not ideally suited? We've found that sticking as close as possible to a systematic procedure with each escrow helps speed the preparation of the escrow instructions.

Actually, you'll find that many of the details will be similar to those encountered in previous escrows examined in this book. There will be, however, unique features and new elements peculiar to the sale of a trust deed and note transaction. The memo form can be adapted to aid in dealing with these unique features. The reassignment of spaces in the memo that are not needed for this type of transaction will be necessary. The route that we will take in filling in the memo is not meant as any standard method. You will want to practice preparing your own memo, in your own way and your own language.

Remember: The gathering of all needed information quickly and clearly, so that it can be transcribed later into formal escrow instructions, is the key here.

Figure 13-1

ESCROW MEMO

SALE ~~LOAN~~ ~~EXCHANGE~~ of a trust deed and note

TIME LIMIT June 25, 20XX

CASH THROUGH ESCROW NOW $ 4,248.72

LATER $_____

~~CASH OUTSIDE~~ plus interest (to the

MTG. TRUST DEED close of escrow) on the unpaid balance

CASH OUTSIDE OF ESCROW $_____

TOTAL CONSIDERATION $ 4,248.72

FIRST PARTY Todd Slavkin and Elisa Slavkin

ADDRESS 1315 Mesa St

Indio, Ca 94201

(Riverside County)

SECOND PARTY Leigh Bennet

ADDRESS 197 Stoner Street

Bakersfield, Ca 93302

ISSUE: (CLTA) ~~owners, loan, alta, leasehold~~ 104A Endorsement FOR $ 4,720.80

(Insure 2nd party and attach indorsement to policy)

ON Lot 88 Tract 4470 in the city of Indio, Riverside County

56/2 book of maps # 71506, dated April 20, 20XX.

VEST IN Paul Montgomery and Jill Montgomery, as shown in said policy

SUBJECT TO: all GENERAL AND SPECIAL TAX 20 XX 20 XX; ~~bonds and assessments~~

COVENANTS, CONDITIONS, RESTRICTIONS, AND EASEMENTS OF RECORD Shown as exception #2 and #3

in the policy

~~MORTGAGE~~ TRUST DEED (OF RECORD) exception #4 in the policy FORM EXECUTED BY

TO SECURE A NOTE FOR $ 35,000 PAYABLE IN INSTALLMENTS TO Industrial Bank 846 Hill St, L.A.

loan number 144-01

AT_____ WITH INTEREST FROM_____ ON UNPAID PRINCIPAL AT_____ % PER ANNUM (PAYABLE_____).

PRINCIPAL (AND INTEREST) PAYABLE IN INSTALMENTS OF $_____ OR MORE ON THE_____ DAY OF EACH_____ MONTH

BEGINNING_____ MATURITY DATE_____ PREPAYMENT PRIVILEGE_____

PRESENT UNPAID BALANCE $ obtain beneficiary's statement not to exceed $34,330 with no delinquency

~~MORTGAGE~~ TRUST DEED (OF RECORD) exception #5 in the policy FORM EXECUTED BY

TO SECURE A NOTE FOR $ 5,000 ~~PAYABLE IN INSTALLMENTS TO~~ note to be endorsed by Todd Slavkin and Elisa Slavkin as shown below:

AT_____ WITH INTEREST FROM_____ ON UNPAID PRINCIPAL AT_____ % PER ANNUM (PAYABLE_____).

PRINCIPAL (AND INTEREST) PAYABLE IN INSTALLMENTS OF $_____ OR MORE ON THE_____ DAY OF EACH_____ MONTH

BEGINNING_____ MATURITY DATE_____ PREPAYMENT PRIVILEGE_____

PRESENT UNPAID BALANCE $ "Pay to the order of Leigh Bennet, without recourse"

~~FIRE INS. AS OF~~ attach 2nd loss payable

BASIS clause to existing fire insurance

~~INSURANCE AS OF~~ prepare and record

~~INTEREST AS OF~~ Req for N/D

BASIS to be

RENTS AS OF executed by Bennet

BASIS_____

WATER STOCK & SEC'Y STATEMENT_____

P CHARGES PAID BY Seller

A TRANSFER TAX $_____ TAX SERVICE_____

Y COMM. $_____ TO_____

M ADDRESS_____ BROKER No_____

E TAXES_____ TAX SALES_____ ASSESSMENTS_____

N PAY THE FOLLOWING AT CLOSE OF ESCROW_____

T _____

S ESCROW OPENED AND CHARGES GUARANTEED BY_____

WE DRAW Assignment and Request for Notice

REMARKS Obtain offset statement from Paul Montgomery 1019 Louise St, Indio 94201

showing unpaid principal balance to be $4,720.80,

with interest at 13%, paid up to 6-1-XX

Let's take it item per item.

1. What is the Type of Transaction?

Sale of trust deed and note.

2. What Consideration Will Be Paid?

The "consideration" is not the unpaid balance. It is the price the purchaser is paying for the note.

Here, as in almost all cases, the amount paid will be less than the actual balance due on the note. This is true because the purchaser negotiates a discount price based upon the speculation risk involved in such a purchase. Entirely legal and reasonable, this kind of discount provides a fair margin of profit for the purchaser.

The market value of a second trust deed is usually less than its face value.

For purchasers to obtain a sufficient return on their investment, or for other reasons, they will only buy such loans if they can do so at a discounted price. The amount of the discount is negotiated between the parties. The law makes no provisions for the amount of profit or discount that may be requested in the purchase and sale of trust deeds and notes. Just as in buying a home, the actual market value is based upon the amount an informed buyer is willing to pay and a seller is willing to accept.

B. FACTORS THAT AFFECT THE PRICE OF A NOTE

There are a number of factors, both extrinsic and intrinsic, which influence the salability of such a note and, indirectly, the purchase price.

For example, let's look at the economy. The status of the money market at a given point in time and the availability and cost of money will undoubtedly play an important role in setting market value of a trust deed and note. Look at the rate of interest the note bears and the term of the loan. Are they current and reasonable? How valuable is the security? What type of property is it and where is it located? What priority is the deed of trust over other liens or encumbrances against the property? Is it a first, a second, a third ...?

What about the seasoning of the loan—Have the borrowers been making their payments and are they on time? These are all important factors that influence the marketability of loan papers.

These factors are mentioned as a point of information only.

In general practice, most parties will have determined the purchase price of the trust deed and note to everyone's satisfaction long before arriving at your desk.

This might be stated as an exact sum of money, or it might be a principal sum plus accrued interest to a specified date, most often the close of escrow. This transaction involves the latter circumstances. So the sum of the consideration will be subject to adjustment during escrow. You will be responsible for this adjustment.

C. DISCOUNTING THE PRICE OF A NOTE

So the sellers, Todd and Elisa Slavkin, inform you that the amount Leigh Bennet will pay for the note and trust deed is the unpaid balance of the principal, less a 10% discount, together with interest on the unpaid balance up to close of escrow. Mr. Slavkin discloses that the present unpaid balance totals $4,720.80 and that the note is current. The last payment was made on June 1 of this year. Interest is paid up until that date. Miss Bennet has agreed to pay all of the consideration in cash through escrow.

The purchase price is arrived at by taking the amount of the balance and subtracting 10%. You should come up with the figure $4,248.72, the correct purchase price. Even though there will be an adjustment based upon interest, you should show this figure as the consideration listed on your memo sheet.

D. TIME LIMIT FOR THE CLOSE OF ESCROW

The time limit for the close of the escrow is decided upon by agreement of the parties.

Your only concern is that there be allowed enough time for completion of the escrow. Fifteen days should be enough time for this type of transaction. Today is June 10. Escrow will close by the 25th.

E. PARTIES TO THE TRANSACTION

At this time you have no information regarding any prior transfer of the note, so the first parties should be listed as Todd Slavkin and Elisa Slavkin, the payees named in the note. The second party is the purchaser, Leigh Bennet. She is a single woman, acquiring title to the note and trust deed in her own name alone.

F. TITLE INSURANCE

Title insurance protection will normally be required by persons buying notes secured by a trust deed on real property in California.

It is normal to presume that the persons who deliver the note and trust deed to an escrow holder are indeed the owners of these instruments, but there is always the possibility that the documents are stolen or lost.

There are certain things that might affect the note owner's ability to transfer his or her ownership. He or she might be declared an incompetent person, have a federal tax lien on all his or her accounts or be judged against in a bankruptcy proceeding. Real property taxes can also be a problem. These taxes may become due subsequent to the date of recording of the trust deed, but they are still prior liens. Escrow does not protect against such matters, making title insurance a necessity.

Assignee title insurance can usually be obtained by attaching an indorsement, issued by the title company, to the policy that insured the trust deed. The issuance of a new policy that insures the assignee or buyer of the note is another way to go.

A trust deed insured by a title policy will often have any assignment of the trust deed insured by indorsement.

The assignment of the trust deed must be recorded and the title company will do a title search before issuing an indorsement. The liability assumed by the indorsement will generally have to be limited to the amount of unpaid principal of the note if the assignment indorsement is to insure both owner and lender. Several types of indorsements are available to ensure such assignments (Discussed below).

A policy of title insurance issued in favor of the assignee is the only option when the trust deed has not been insured.

Sometimes an assignee will request that the assignment be insured in the form of a new policy, though the trust deed may have previously been insured by indorsement. With either situation, this insurance may be provided by a CLTA Standard Loan Policy or by an ALTA Extended Coverage Loan Policy, depending upon how much coverage an assignee requires.

With this transaction, Mr. and Mrs. Slavkin (sellers) handed you their policy—the trust deed was previously insured. Your job now will be to determine what type of insurance Leigh Bennet (assignee) requires. Will she require an entirely new policy or an indorsement? A CLTA or ALTA policy? If insurance is by an indorsement, what form of coverage is to be provided? Ms. Bennet chooses a CLTA 104A Indorsement that will be attached to the existing policy insuring the loan. (See **Figure 13-2**.)

G. DIFFERENT INDORSEMENTS

Persons in the business of buying trust deeds are usually familiar with the different types of title insurance policies available. They know the type of coverage required and will so inform you. You will be required, with other purchasers, to explain the forms of indorsement available and what coverages are afforded by them.

You, as an escrow officer in this field, must be familiar with the basic types of indorsements so that you can communicate with the knowledgeable customer.

With the less experienced purchaser, you will be able to help him or her understand what type of title protection is available. With this in mind, let's briefly discuss the available indorsements and the main features and relative cost of each one. We will start with Ms. Bennet's request, the CLTA 104A indorsement.

1. CLTA Form 104A

The *CLTA FORM 104A INDORSEMENT is designed for use with standard coverage policies when the beneficial (lender's) interest in the insured deed of trust has been assigned.* In this case, the assignee requests insurance provided in the indorsement instead of having an assignee's policy issued.

The title company will have to determine that the party attempting to sell the note is the owner of the note before issuing this indorsement. The insurance coverage given by this indorsement requires the title company to search the tax, bond and assessment records, and the company's property index and general index.

All matters that affect the validity of the assignment, the competency of the assignor or any liens on the beneficial interest must be considered and shown in the indorsement, or cleared by the parties or their representatives. If requested by the parties, and for an additional fee, the indorsement may include the present vesting of the title to the land secured by the trust deed. **Recording of all assignments of the beneficial interest will be required by the title company**.

2. CLTA Form 104

CLTA Form 104 indorsement coverage is comparable to CLTA Form 104A coverage. The *FORM 104 INDORSEMENT is designed for use with ALTA loan policies when the beneficial (lender's) interest in the insured deed of trust has been assigned.* In this case, the assignee requests insurance provided in the indorsement instead of having an ALTA form of assignee's policy issued.

3. CLTA Form 104.1

CLTA FORM 104.1 INDORSEMENT is designed for use with ALTA or Standard Coverage policies when the beneficial interest in the insured deed of trust has been assigned. The assignee requests the limited guarantee as provided in the indorsement. By including it in some or all of the CLTA Form 104A coverages, expanded coverage (for an additional fee) in the CLTA Form 104.1 indorsement may be given if so requested by the parties.

Figure 13-2

POLICY OF TITLE INSURANCE (1)

POLICY No. 1- 9026138

Confidential Title Insurance
and Trust Company

POLICY OF TITLE INSURANCE

SUBJECT TO SCHEDULE B AND THE CONDITIONS AND STIPULATIONS HEREOF, CONFIDENTIAL TITLE INSURANCE AND TRUST COMPANY, a California corporation, herein called the Company, insures the insured, as of Date of Policy shown in Schedule A, against loss or damage, not exceeding the amount of insurance stated in Schedule A, and costs, attorneys' fees and expenses which the Company may become obligated to pay hereunder, sustained or incurred by said insured by reason of:

1. Title to the estate or interest described in Schedule A being vested other than as stated therein;

2. Any defect in or lien or encumbrance on such title;

3. Unmarketability of such title; or

4. Any lack of the ordinary right of an abutting owner for access to at least one physically open street or highway if the land, in fact, abuts upon one or more such streets or highways;

   and in addition, as to an insured lender only;

5. Invalidity of the lien of the insured mortgage upon said estate or interest except to the extent that such invalidity, or claim thereof, arises out of the transaction evidenced by the insured mortgage and is based upon

   a. usury, or
   b. any consumer credit protection or truth in lending law;

6. Priotity of any lien or encumbrance over the lien of the insured mortgage, said mortgage being shown in Schedule B in the order of its priority; or

7. Invalidity of any assignment of the insured mortgage, provided such assignment is shown in Schedule B.

Title Insurance and Trust Company

by

President

362

POLICY OF TITLE INSURANCE (2)

(CONDITIONS AND STIPULATIONS Continued and Concluded From Reverse Side of This Page)

8. Reduction of Insurance; Termination of Liability

All payments under this policy, except payment made for costs, attorneys' fees and expenses, shall reduce the amount of the insurance pro tanto; provided, however, if the owner of the indebtedness secured by the insured mortgage is an insured hereunder, then such payments, prior to the acquisition of title to said estate or interest as provided in paragraph 2(a) of these Conditions and Stipulations, shall not reduce pro tanto the amount of the insurance afforded hereunder as to any such insured, except to the extent that such payments reduce the amount of the indebtedness secured by such mortgage.

Payment in full by any person or voluntary satisfaction or release of the insured mortgage shall terminate all liability of the Company to an insured owner of the indebtedness secured by the insured mortgage, except as provided in paragraph 2(a) hereof.

9. Liability Noncumulative

It is expressly understood that the amount of insurance under this policy as to the insured owner of the estate or interest covered by this policy, shall be reduced by any amount the Company may pay under any policy insuring (a) a mortgage shown or referred to in Schedule B hereof which is a lien on the estate or interest covered by this policy, or (b) a mortgage hereafter executed by an insured which is a charge or lien on the estate or interest described or referred to in Schedule A, and the amount so paid shall be deemed a payment under this policy. The Company shall have the option to apply to the payment of any such mortgage any amount that otherwise would be payable hereunder to the insured owner of the estate or interest covered by this policy and the amount so paid shall be deemed a payment under this policy to said insured owner.

The provisions of this paragraph 9 shall not apply to an owner of the indebtedness secured by the insured mortgage, unless such insured acquires title to said estate or interest in satisfaction of said indebtedness or any part thereof.

10. Subrogation Upon Payment or Settlement

Whenever the Company shall have paid or settled a claim under this policy, all right of subrogation shall vest in the Company unaffected by any act of the insured claimant, except that the owner of the indebtedness secured by the insured mortgage may release or substitute the personal liability of any debtor or guarantor, or extend or otherwise modify the terms of payment, or release a portion of the estate or interest from the lien of the insured mortgage, or release any collateral security for the indebtedness, provided such act occurs prior to receipt by such insured of notice of any claim of title or interest adverse to the title to the estate or interest or the priority of the lien of the insured mortgage and does not result in any loss of priority of the lien of the insured mortgage. The Company shall be subrogated to and be entitled to all rights and remedies which such insured claimant would have had against any person or property in respect to such claim had this policy not been issued, and the Company is hereby authorized and empowered to sue, compromise or settle in its name or in the name of the insured to the full extent of the loss sustained by the Company. If requested by the Company, the insured shall execute any and all documents to evidence the within subrogation. If the payment does not cover the loss of such insured claimant, the Company shall be subrogated to such rights and remedies in the proportion which said payment bears to the amount of said loss, but such subrogation shall be in subordination to an insured mortgage. If loss should result from any act of such insured claimant, such act shall not void this policy, but the Company, in that event, shall as to such insured claimant be required to pay only that part of any losses insured against hereunder which shall exceed the amount, if any, lost to the Company by reason of the impairment of the right of subrogation.

11. Liability Limited to this Policy

This instrument together with all endorsements and other instruments, if any, attached hereto by the Company is the entire policy and contract between the insured and the Company. Any claim of loss or damage, whether or not based on negligence, and which arises out of the status of the lien of the insured mortgage or of the title to the estate or interest covered hereby, or any action asserting such claim, shall be restricted to the provisions and Conditions and Stipulations of this policy.

No amendment of or endorsement to this policy can be made except by writing endorsed hereon or attached hereto signed by either the President, a Vice President, the Secretary, an Assistant Secretary, or validating officer or authorized signatory of the Company.

No payment shall be made without producing this policy for endorsement of such payment unless the policy be lost or destroyed, in which case proof of such loss or destruction shall be furnished to the satisfaction of the Company.

12. Notices, Where Sent

All notices required to be given the Company and any statement in writing required to be furnished the Company shall be addressed to it at the office which issued this policy or to its Home Office, 6300 Wilshire Boulevard, P.O. Box 92792, Los Angeles, California 90009.

13. THE PREMIUM SPECIFIED IN SCHEDULE A IS THE ENTIRE CHARGE FOR TITLE SEARCH, TITLE EXAMINATION AND TITLE INSURANCE.

CONFIDENTIAL
TITLE INSURANCE
AND TRUST COMPANY

Policy of Title Insurance

POLICY OF TITLE INSURANCE (3)

Schedule A

No.	Date of Policy:
9026138	April 20, 20XX; 9:00 a.m.

Amount of Insurance:	Premium
$ 45,000.00	$ 330.50

1. Name of Insured

>   Paul Montgomery and Jill Montgomery, Todd Slavkin and Elisa Slavkin

2. The estate or interest referred to herein is at Date of Policy vested in

>   Paul Montgomery and Jill Montgomery, husband and wife as Joint Tenants

3. The estate or interest in the land described in Schedule C and which is covered by this policy is a fee.

POLICY OF TITLE INSURANCE (4)

This policy does not insure against loss or damage, nor against costs, attorneys' fees or expenses, any or all of which arise by reason of the following:

Part I

All matters set forth in paragraphs numbered 1(one) to 11(eleven) inclusive on the inside cover sheet of this policy under the heading of Schedule B Part I.

Part II

1. GENERAL AND SPECIAL COUNTY AND CITY TAXES FOR THE FISCAL YEAR 20XX-20XX, A LIEN NOT YET PAYABLE.

2. AN EASEMENT AFFECTING THE PORTION OF SAID LAND AND FOR THE PURPOSES STATED HEREIN, AND INCIDENTAL PURPOSES,

IN FAVOR OF	:	AMERICAN BUILDERS
FOR	:	POLE LINES AND CONDUITS
RECORDED	:	IN BOOK 11721 PAGE 82, OFFICIAL RECORDS
AFFECTS	:	THE SOUTH 8 FEET.

3. COVENANTS, CONDITIONS, AND RESTRICTIONS IN THE ABOVE RECORDED INSTRUMENT WHICH PROVIDE THAT A VIOLATION THEREOF SHALL NOT DEFEAT OR RENDER INVALID THE LIEN OF ANY MORTGAGE OR DEED OF TRUST MADE IN GOOD FAITH AND FOR VALUE.

4. A DEED OF TRUST TO SECURE AN INDEBTEDNESS OF THE AMOUNT STATED HEREIN AND ANY OTHER AMOUNTS PAYABLE UNDER THE TERMS THEREOF

DATED	:	April 18, 20XX
AMOUNT	:	$35,000.00
TRUSTOR	:	PAUL MONTGOMERY AND JILL MONTGOMERY, HUSBAND AND WIFE
TRUSTEE	:	CALIFORNIA INDUSTRIAL CORPORATION, A CORPORATION
BENEFICIARY	:	INDUSTRIAL BANK, A CORPORATION
RECORDED	:	April 20, 20XX , IN BOOK 6822 PAGE 93, OFFICIAL RECORDS
INSTRUMENT NO.	:	9623

5. A DEED OF TRUST TO SECURE AN INDEBTEDNESS OF THE AMOUNT STATED HEREIN AND ANY OTHER AMOUNTS PAYABLE UNDER THE TERMS THEREOF

DATED	:	April 10, 20XX
AMOUNT	:	$5,000.00
TRUSTOR	:	PAUL MONTGOMERY AND JILL MONTGOMERY, HUSBAND AND WIFE
TRUSTEE	:	CONFIDENTIAL TITLE INSURANCE AND TRUST COMPANY, A CORPORATION
BENEFICIARY	:	TODD SLAVKIN ELISA SLAVKIN, HUSBAND AND WIFE AS JOINT TENANTS
RECORDED	:	April 20, 20XX AS INSTRUMENT NO. 9624

POLICY OF TITLE INSURANCE (5)

Schedule C

The land referred to herein is described as follows:

Lot 88 of Tract No. 4470, in the City of Indio, Riverside County, State of California, as per map recorded in Book 56 Page 2 of maps, in the office of the county recorder of said county.

INDORSEMENT (1)

Fee $ 46.15

I N D O R S E M E N T

ATTACHED TO POLICY NO. 71506

ISSUED BY

CONFIDENTIAL TITLE INSURANCE AND TRUST COMPANY

The Company assures   Leigh Bennet

(a) That by a valid assignment or assignments the beneficial interest under the mortgage referred to in paragraph   5   of Part II of Schedule B has been transferred to said Assured;

(b) That there are no subsisting tax or assessment liens which are prior to said martgage, except:
> General and Special County and City Taxes for the Fiscal Year 20XX-XX, a lien not yet payable.

(c) That there are no matters shown by the Public Records affecting the valldity or priority of the lien of said mortgage, other than those shown in said policy, except:
> None

(d) That there are no United States Tax Llens or bankruptcy proceedings affecting the title to said estate or interest shown by the Public Records, other than those shown in said policy, except:
> None

The Company hereby insures said Assured against any loss of principal, interest or other sums secured by said mortgage, which said Assured shall sustain in the event that the assurances herein shall prove to be incorrect.

The total liability of the Company under said policy and any indorsements therein shall not exceed, in the aggregate, the face amount of said policy and costs which the Company is obligated under the conditions and stipulations thereof to pay.

This Indorsement is made a part of said policy and is subject to the schedules, conditions and stipulations therein, except as modified by the provisions hereof.

This Indorsement is not to be construed as insuring the title to said estate or interest as of any later date than the date of said policy, except as herein expressly provided as to the subject matter hereof.

Dated   June 22, 20XX at 9:00 a.m.

CONFIDENTIAL TITLE AND TRUST COMPANY

By   *Robert Jones*   Secretary

367

INDORSEMENT (2)

Fee $ 26.40

INDORSEMENT

ATTACHED TO POLICY NO. 71506

ISSUED BY

CONFIDENTIAL TITLE INSURANCE AND TRUST COMPANY

The Company assures   LEIGH BENNET

(a) That by a valid assignment or assignments the beneficial interest under the mortgage referred to in paragraph   5   of Schedule   B   has been transferred to said Assured;

(b) That no reconveyance, either full or partial, of said mortgage, or any modification or subordination thereof, appears of record.

(c) THAT THERE ARE NO SUBSISTING TAX OR ASSESSMENT LIENS WHICH ARE PRIOR TO SAID MORTGAGE, EXCEPT, GENERAL AND SPECIAL COUNTY AND CITY TAXES FOR THE FISCAL YEAR 20XX-XX , A LIEN NOT YET PAYABLE.

The Company hereby insures said Assured against loss which said Assured shall sustain in the event that the assurance herein shall prove to be incorrect.

The total liability of the Company under said policy and any indorsements therein shall not exceed, in the aggregate, the face amount of said policy and costs which the Company is obligated under the conditions and stipulations thereof to pay.

This indorsement is made a part of said policy and is subject to the schedules, conditions and stipulations therein, except as modified by the provisions hereof.

This indorsement is not to be construed as insuring the title to said estate or interest as of any later date than the date of said policy, except as herein expressly provided as to the subject matter hereof.

Dated   June 22, 20XX at 9:00 a.m.

CONFIDENTIAL TITLE AND TRUST COMPANY

By

Corporate Seal

SECRETARY

INDORSEMENT (3)

Fee $ 61.25

INDORSEMENT

ATTACHED TO POLICY NO. 71506

ISSUED BY

CONFIDENTIAL TITLE INSURANCE AND TRUST COMPANY

The Company assures Leigh Bennet

    (a) That by a valid assignment or assignments the beneficial interest under the mortgage referred to in Schedule A has been transferred to said Assured;

    (b) That there are no subsisting tax or assessment liens which are prior to said mortgage, except:

        General and Special County and City Taxes for the Fiscal Year 20XX-XX, a lien not yet payable.

    (c) That there are no matters affecting the validity or priority of the lien of said mortgage, other than those shown in said policy, except:

        None

    (d) That there are no United States Tax Liens or bankruptcy proceedings affecting the title to said estate or interest shown by the Public Records, other than those shown in said policy, except:

        None

The Company hereby insures said Assured against any loss which said Assured shall sustain in the event that the assurances herein shall prove to be incorrect.

    The total liability of the Company under said policy and any indorsements therein shall not exceed, in the aggregate, the face amount of said policy and costs which the Company is obligated under the conditions and stipulations thereof to pay.

    This indorsement is made a part of said policy and is subject to the schedules, conditions and stipulations therein, except as modified by the provisions hereof.

    This indorsement is not to be construed as insuring the title to said estate or interest as of any later date than the date of said policy, except as herein expressly provided as to the subject matter hereof.

Dated June 22, 20XX at 9:00 a.m.

CONFIDENTIAL TITLE AND TRUST COMPANY

By   *Robert Jones*   Secretary

Title company charges for each type of indorsement will differ depending on the type of title search and extent of coverages requested.

The charge for the CLTA 104 indorsement would be higher than that for the 104A, due to the extended coverage insurance afforded by the policy and indorsement. The limited insurance of the 104.1 indorsement makes it the least expensive.

The parties will make the decision as to the type and form of title insurance to be obtained.

If requested, your responsibility will be to provide them with any information that will aid them in making a decision. There is, of course, a substantial difference in the available insurance. You are not expected to be an expert on the subject.

Remember: You can always consult management or your title officer for assistance should the discussion reach beyond your working knowledge.

H. TITLE POLICY AGREEMENT

As discussed earlier, title insurance in our example is to be obtained through an indorsement affixed to the existing policy of title insurance. When drawing the escrow instructions, you can incorporate the description, vesting and encumbrances as shown in that policy. On the memo sheet, add the words "as shown in the policy" to the vesting, and show the excepted number of the encumbrances (easements, CC&Rs, and the trust deeds) as they appear in the policy. This may help dispense with any need to discuss the encumbrances that are to be approved. Also, it will save time in writing up the various items.

The Slavkins (sellers) will need to provide you with the address of the beneficiary of the first trust deed, the loan number and the unpaid balance of this loan, insofar as they have this information. The lender will provide you with a beneficiary's statement. If you have their address and loan number at this time it will expedite ordering and obtaining this statement. You will also show the unpaid balance of this loan, as submitted by the seller, in your escrow instructions.

I. BENEFICIARY'S STATEMENT

You are already familiar with the nature of a beneficiary's statement (see **Figure 13-3**). You will verify the information regarding the first trust deed through the beneficiary's statement. The sellers already provided you with an approximate amount of the unpaid balance of this loan. A formal beneficiary's statement from the lender will verify these figures and show that there is no payment delinquency of principal or interest.

Figure 13-3

BENEFICIARY'S STATEMENT

CONFIDENTIAL TITLE INSURANCE AND TRUST

BENEFICIARY'S STATEMENT OF LOAN CONDITION	DATE June 8, 20XX
Paul Montgomery	LOAN NO.
1326 Mesa Street	BORROWER: Montgomery
Indio, CA 94201	ESCROW NO. 1066

An escrow has been opened with this Company concerning the real property briefly described as follows: Lot 88 of Tract 4470, City of Indio, Riverside County, State of California, as per map recorded in Book 56, page 2, of Maps.

The Company is advised that you hold a note and deed of trust on said land as security for a loan made to Paul Montgomery and Jill Montgomery

Said deed of trust, in the original amount of $ 5,000.00 was recorded on April 20, 20XX In Book/Reel 6822 Page/Image 93 Recorders Instrument No. 9624 Official Records of _____ County, California

[X] The escrow involves a sale of said ~~XXXXXXX~~ note and deed of trust

with ~~XXX~~ the deed of trust to remain of record.

[ ] The escrow involves a new obligation secured by a note and deed of trust in the principal amount of $_____ that will be recorded junior to yours. No change of ownership of the title to the land is contemplated.

The principals have requested the Company to ask you to complete the statements below and transmit this form to the Company. Include in your transmittal any (1) water stock that you hold with your loan.

The attached copy of this form is for your records.

Thank you in advance for your co-operation.

CONFIDENTIAL TITLE INSURANCE AND TRUST COMPANY

By Your Name

Date June 14, 20XX

To: CONFIDENTIAL TITLE AND TRUST COMPANY

I am the legal holder of that certain promissory note dated April 10, 20XX and secured by a deed of trust recorded April 20, 20XX In Book/Reel 6822 Page/Image 93 Recorders Instrument No. 9624 Official Records of Riverside County, California

The unpaid principal of said note, including advances, is $ 4720.80 . Interest at the rate of 13 % per annum, payable ~~XXXXXXXXXXXXXXXXXXX~~ (monthly) is paid to June 1 , 20 XX

Principal and interest is payable in mo. installments of $ 126.46 (or more) on the first day of each and every monthly and continue until the ~~XXXXXXXXXXXXXXXXXXXXXXXXXX~~ first of April, 20XX

The payment due June 1 has been made and the next payment is due July 2

The balance is due and payable on April 1, 20XX

There are no agreements altering the terms of said note except None

The property covered by the above loan is insured as follows: Coverage_____ ; Premium paid (1yr.) $_____ (3 yrs.) $_____ ; Effective date_____ ; Policy No._____ ; Issued by_____ ; Agent_____

Enclosed is certificate No._____ for_____ shares of the_____ Water Company.

Please have the necessary changes made to reflect any change of ownership of the title to the land. You shall return such papers to me after completion of the escrow.

I make this statement for the benefit of Confidential Title Insurance and Trust Company, the seller and purchaser of the subject property, and/or the beneficiary of the new deed of trust.

Paul Montgomery
Paul Montgomery

BENEFICIARY'S ADDRESS AND TELEPHONE NO.	
NAME	
ADDRESS	
CITY, STATE, ZIP CODE	TEL. NO.

371

J. TRANSFERRING THE NOTE

How will the note be transferred? Since this is actually the evidence of the obligation, the note must bear evidence of the transfer of its ownership. A note's ownership can be transferred in a number of ways. *The payees could sign their names on the back of the note, just as a check is endorsed. Though simple, this is an adequate form of endorsement to transfer ownership. This is known as an* **ENDORSEMENT IN BLANK**. Another method will require additional language. *The buyer may prefer to have the note specifically endorsed in his or her favor. This form is known as a* **SPECIAL ENDORSEMENT**.The following is an acceptable way to word this:

"Pay to the order of _____("With recourse" or "without recourse", as the case may be)

Principal balance $ _____

Interest paid to_____

(signatures)   (_____

                   (_____

We will not discuss all of the forms of endorsement here. You should, however, be familiar with the procedure and not confuse it with the "indorsement" of a title insurance policy. Right now, we will examine this particular form and especially the words "with recourse."

A note may be transferred "with recourse" or "without recourse."

A **WITH RECOURSE TRANSFER** *means the seller of the note guarantees the payment of the note should the payor fail to make the payments. A transfer* **WITHOUT RECOURSE** *relieves the seller of being held accountable for nonpayment.* The intention of the parties must be reflected in the endorsement. It is helpful to show the unpaid balance of the note and the date to which the interest has been paid in the endorsement. This will eliminate any misunderstandings the parties may have regarding these items.

You, as escrow holder, will neither suggest which endorsement will be shown on the note, nor discuss the relative merits or shortcomings of any particular endorsement.

The rights of the parties may be affected by the particular language you may use and, more importantly, the endorsement to be used is something they must determine.

Under the **Negotiable Instruments Law**, the language used in the endorsement of the note could have a direct bearing on the rights of the parties. A practice in some areas is to use a form of recital which reads in part:

"... I,_____, do hereby transfer and assign to_____, the within note, together with all rights accrued or to accrue ... "

This is an example of a transfer by assignment rather than by negotiation. By using such language, the purchaser of the note becomes an "assignee" instead of a "holder in due course."

Under the provisions of the Negotiable Instruments Law, a "holder in due course" will obtain benefits that may not be available to an assignee.

As can be seen, care must be exercised in preparing the words of transfer so that the wishes of the parties are fulfilled.

Bennet responds to your inquiry by stating that the note is to be endorsed to her "without recourse," and that the endorsement is to show that the unpaid balance of the note is $4,720.80, with interest paid until June 1. This is acceptable to the Slavkins, who request you to type the endorsement on the note for their signatures as sellers of the note and trust deed. Make the appropriate notation on your memo sheet, being certain to show the exact language of the endorsement as it will appear in the escrow instructions.

A further study of endorsements and negotiable instruments, in general, will be helpful knowledge for the escrow officer. However, your only direct concern here is with the appropriate type of endorsement to be used in this escrow that will correctly reflect the wishes and intentions of the parties.

K. ASSIGNMENT OF THE DEED OF TRUST

A transfer of the indebtedness (the note) carries with it the rights of the parties to the security (the trust deed). The beneficial interest in the deed of trust, in most circumstances, is also formally transferred. This is accomplished by the use of a separate instrument called the "Assignment of Deed of Trust" (See **Figure 13-3**).

One reason for this practice is that, when properly executed (signed and acknowledged), the assignment is recorded and the change of ownership of the trust deed is established on the record. Establishing such ownership is important.

Title insurance policy and endorsement coverage rely to a considerable extent on the record.

Also, the title company will require that the assignment be recorded before the assignee will be insured.

Figure 13-4

ASSIGNMENT OF DEED OF TRUST

RECORDING REQUESTED BY

AND WHEN RECORDED MAIL TO

Name Leigh Bennet
Street Address 197 Stoner Street
City & State Bakersfield, CA 93302

————————— SPACE ABOVE THIS LINE FOR RECORDER'S USE —————————

Assignment of Deed of Trust

For Value Received, the undersigned hereby grants, assigns and transfer to **Leigh Bennet, a single woman**

all beneficial interest under that certain Deed of Trust dated **April 10, 20XX**
executed by **Paul Montgomery and Jill Montgomery**

to **Confidential Title and Trust Company** Trustee,
and recorded as Instrument No **9624** on **April 20, 20XX** in Book Reel **6822**
Page Image **93** of Official Records in the County Recorder's office of **Riverside** County,
California. describing land therein as

        Lot 88, Tract 4470, City of Indio, Riverside County,
        State of California, as per map recorded in Book 56,
        page 2 of Maps.

Together with the note or notes therein described or referred to. the money due and to become due thereon with
interest, and all rights accrued or to accrue under said Deed of Trust
Dated **June 10, 20XX**

                                    /S/ Todd Slavkin

                                    /S/ Elisa Slavkin

FOR CORPORATE ACKNOWLEDGEMENT

STATE OF CALIFORNIA
COUNTY OF _____ } SS
On _____ before me. the undersigned, a Notary Public in and for said State, personally appeared
_____ known to me to be the _____ President, and
_____ known to me to be _____ Secretary of the Corporation that
executed the within Instrument known to me to be the persons who executed the within Instrument on behalf of the Corporation
therein named, and acknowledged to me that such Corporation executed the within Instrument pursuant to its by-laws or a resolution
of its board of directors.
WITNESS my hand and official seal. Signature _____

FOR INDIVIDUAL ACKNOWLEDGEMENT

STATE OF CALIFORNIA
COUNTY OF **Los Angeles** } SS
On **June 10, 20XX** before me. the undersigned, a Notary Public in and for said State,
personally appeared **Todd Slavkin and Elisa Slakin**
_____ known to me to be the person **S** whose name **S are** subscribed to the within
instrument and acknowledged that **they** executed the same
WITNESS my hand and official seal. Signature _____

                                    Mary Payne

FOR PARTNERSHIP ACKNOWLEDGEMENT

STATE OF CALIFORNIA
COUNTY OF _____ } SS
On _____ before me. the under-
signed. a Notary Public in and for said State, personally appeared
_____
_____ known to me
to be _____ of the partners of the partnership that
executed the within instrument, and acknowledged to me that such
partnership executed the same
WITNESS my hand and official seal

Signature _____

OFFICIAL SEAL
MARY PAYNE
NOTARY PUBLIC-CALIFORNIA
LOS ANGELES COUNTY
My Commission Expires _____

(This area for official notarial seal)

Title Order No. _____ Escrow or Loan No. **1066**

There are numerous printed forms of assignments of trust deed available. The one illustrated in Figure 13-4 is typical.

The information required to complete the Assignment of Trust Deed form is taken from the trust deed.

Your escrow instructions must contain provisions for the execution and recording of this assignment. Make sure the appropriate entry is made on your memo sheet.

L. OWNER'S OFFSET STATEMENT

The Slavkins gave Bennet certain information concerning the obligation during negotiations for the sale of the trust deed and note. They informed her of the unpaid balance of principal due on the note ($4,720.80) and the date when the last payment was made (June 1). They also informed her that the note is current with no delinquencies. Paul and Jill Montgomery, the present property owners, will verify this information. Bennet will ask you to obtain an "Owner's Offset Statement" from them.

We can adapt a form designed for another purpose. This one is in reality a beneficiary's statement. We use it to obtain the same type of information, but from an owner rather than a beneficiary. It is referred to as an Owner's Offset Statement when used for this purpose.

"Offset" refers to a counterclaim against the beneficiary based on a dispute as to the amount or terms of the obligation.

Let's say the Montgomery's discovered some material defect in the house after the previous sale escrow had closed. They could claim misrepresentation or fraud, and attempt to "offset" the amount of damage claimed against the amount of their obligation expressed in the note. Such claims are rare, and usually the information obtained from the property owners will confirm the information supplied by the seller of the note. A smart investor, though, will require that the offset statement be obtained.

A property owner often does not understand the purpose of the offset statement. He or she may have no interest in whether the beneficiary sells the note and will not submit the form, completed or otherwise. It is important to point this out to the sellers of the note and give them the option of going to the owners for the needed signatures. They should at least phone the Montgomerys and advise them of the pending escrow, the purpose of the offset statement, and that it is being mailed to them for their signatures.

If you are requested to mail the statement to the owners for signatures, fill it out as completely as possible. Be sure to use the unpaid balance of the note and not the purchase price. A courteous letter of explanation and a stamped return envelope will

show your professionalism and help assure its prompt return. Any delay in the return of this statement might hold up the close of escrow.

The escrow instructions in this type of transaction must always contain an instruction regarding the offset statement. When the note purchaser does not want to call for such a statement, the instructions must show that no offset statement will be obtained.

M. REQUEST FOR NOTICE OF DEFAULT

A smart investor will make certain that payments of the note under the first trust deed are up to date before completing the purchase of a junior or subordinate trust deed. Such an investor will also check to make sure there are no delinquencies. The beneficiary's statement you order from the bank will be the source of this information. The recordation of a Request for Notice (**Figure 13-5**) will prevent the possibility of a future foreclosure of the first trust deed without the investor's knowledge.

Here are the steps which occur when a deed of trust is in default:

1. A default occurs in a trust deed.
2. Beneficiary (lender) requests that the property be sold by the trustee at a trustee's sale.
3. A notice of default is executed by the trustee or beneficiary and recorded in the office of the county recorder in the county where the property is located.

The recordation discloses that the trust deed is in default. It is part of the public record that the property will be sold unless the default is cured. The purchaser at the sale would acquire title to the property free of the second trust deed. The second trust deed holder would probably lose their investment.

Miss Bennet, to protect her money, cannot be expected to check the recorder's records each month to see if such a notice of default has been recorded. She should record a Request for Notice of Default pursuant to the provisions of Section 2924b of the Civil Code. When a Request for Notice of Default has been recorded, the person requesting such notice is entitled, within a prescribed time, to receive a copy of the notice of default and a copy of the notice of sale.

Figure 13-5

REQUEST FOR NOTICE

RECORDING REQUESTED BY

AND WHEN RECORDED MAIL TO

Name Leigh Bennet
Street Address 195 Stoner Street
City & State Bakersfield, CA 93302

SPACE ABOVE THIS LINE FOR RECORDER'S USE

Request for Notice

UNDER SECTION 2924b CIVIL CODE

In accordance with Section 2924b, Civil Code, request is hereby made that a copy of any Notice of Default and a copy of any Notice of Sale under the Deed of Trust recorded as Instrument No. **9624** on **April 20 20 XX** in Book **6822** page **93**, Official Records of **Riverside** County, California, and describing land therein as

Lot 88, Tract 4470, City of Indio, Riverside County, State of California, as per map recorded in Book 56, page 2 of Maps.

Executed by **Paul Montgomery and Jill Montgomery** as Trustor, in which **Industrial Bank** is named as Beneficiary, and **California Industrial Corporation** as Trustee, be mailed to **Leigh Bennet** at **197 Stoner Street**
Number and Street
Bakersfield, California 93302 Dated **June 10, 20XX**
City and State

Leigh Bennet

FOR CORPORATE ACKNOWLEDGEMENT

STATE OF CALIFORNIA
COUNTY OF _____ } SS

FOR INDIVIDUAL ACKNOWLEDGEMENT

STATE OF CALIFORNIA
COUNTY OF **Los Angeles** } SS
On **June 19, 20XX** before me, the undersigned, a Notary Public in and for said State, personally appeared **Leigh Bennet** known to me to be the person whose name **is** subscribed to the within instrument and acknowledged that **she** executed the same
WITNESS my hand and official seal. Signature **Mary Payne**

FOR PARTNERSHIP ACKNOWLEDGEMENT

STATE OF CALIFORNIA
COUNTY OF _____ } SS

OFFICIAL SEAL
MARY PAYNE
NOTARY PUBLIC - CALIFORNIA
LOS ANGELES COUNTY

Title Order No. _____ Escrow or Loan No. **1066**

V. CHAPTER SUMMARY

An escrow will be involved with negotiable instruments that require ENDORSEMENT as a means of transferring title. The ASSIGNMENT of a negotiable instrument, such as a promissory note, is the formal transfer of rights from one person to another. Usually when promissory notes are assigned, there will be a DISCOUNT which is the difference between face value and cash value.

If it is a SEASONED note, it means that there has been a good payment history by a borrower.

When notes are transferred, the buyer will choose between various title policies. They include CLTA FORM 104A, CLTA FORM 104 and CLTA 104.1. The escrow officer should explain the different coverages to the buyers of the note so they know what coverages are included.

Negotiable instruments are negotiated by endorsements. They may be BLANK and may be with RECOURSE or WITHOUT RECOURSE. A HOLDER IN DUE COURSE is a person receiving a negotiable instrument in good faith and for value without knowledge of any defect or delinquency. The ASSIGNOR is transferring the rights and the ASSIGNEE receives those rights.

An OFFSET STATEMENT states the balance due on an existing loan and is often requested in junior financing. The NOTICE OF DEFAULT is the beginning step in the foreclosure of a trust deed.

VI. TERMS

Assignee: One who receives the rights to a contract

Assignment: In promissory notes, it is the transfer of the rights, title, and interest in the document of one person (assignor) to another (assignee).

Assignor: One who transfers rights to a contract.

Blank Endorsement: Payees sign their names on the back of the note the same as they would endorse a check.

CLTA Form 104: Used with ALTA loan policies when the lender's interest has been assigned.

CLTA Form 104A: The purchaser of the note is assured that the person selling the note is the true competent owner; no bankruptcy or unpaid taxes.

CLTA Form 104.1: Limits coverage to putting the assignee in the shoes of the assignor. Normally no examination is made for bankruptcy, taxes, assessments etc.

Discount: To sell at a reduced value; the difference between face value and cash value.

Endorsements: In negotiable instruments, the means of transferring title such as a promissory note by signing the owner's name on the reverse side of the document.

Holder in Due Course: A person who in good faith and for value accepts a negotiable instrument on the face is valid.

Notice of Default: The public filing of a delinquent loan that gives legal notice of a pending foreclosure.

Offset Statement: Statement by a lender as to the balance due on existing loans.

Recourse: An instrument where the holder or endorsee may take legal action against the endorser in the event of default.

Seasoned Loan: Refers to a loan paid by a borrower who has a stable and consistent loan history of payments. It indicates that the loan is not a new one and would be a better purchase risk.

Without Recourse: Prevents legal action against the endorser.

VII. CHAPTER QUIZ

1. Most first and second trust deeds require:

    a. monthly payments.
    b. interest only payments.
    c. principal only payments.
    d. none of the above.

2. One problem with taking a note and trust deed is that the seller may:

    a. later need cash.
    c. have to take the property back.
    b. die.
    d. none of the above.

3. Which of the following is a personal property interest in real property?

    a. A grant deed
    b. A quit claim deed
    c. A trust deed
    d. All of the above

4. Who usually buys trust deeds?

    a. Buyers
    b. Brokers
    c. Third parties
    d. None of the above

5. Of the following, who usually sells trust deeds?

    a. Buyers
    b. Lenders
    c. Minors
    d. Brokers

6. The sale of a note and trust deeds starts with:

    a. escrow memo in escrow.
    b. escrow instructions in escrow.
    c. title insurance in escrow.
    d. writing checks in escrow.

7. The price of a note and trust deed will almost always NOT be:

    a. the balance due.
    b. less than the balance due.
    c. double the balance due.
    d. none of the above.

8. Questions about the title insurance cost and coverage can best be handled by the:
   a. broker.
   b. title insurance officer.
   c. escrow agent.
   d. any of the above.

9. The step(s) that occur when a deed of trust is in default are:
   a. default occurs.
   b. request trustee to sell.
   c. file notice of default.
   d. all of the above.

10. A "request for notice" alerts a person to a:
    a. lease.
    b. default.
    c. normal sale.
    d. any of the above.

ANSWERS: 1. a; 2. a; 3. c; 4. c; 5. b; 6. a; 7. c; 8. b; 9. d; 10. b

Processing the Note and Trust Deed Escrow

I. Completing The Escrow Instructions

You will have to choose the particular form that you think will best serve the needs of this transaction before starting to prepare the escrow instructions. Many escrow and title companies develop their own computer-printed escrow instruction forms designed specifically for note and trust deed escrows.

There are certain advantages to using these specialized forms instead of standard escrow instruction forms. First, the form itself becomes a checklist to assist in making certain that all details of the transaction are properly reflected in the instructions. The instruction form, rather than a memo sheet, can be used to take the instructions. Secondly, the specific instruction form makes preparation easy, since it consists for the most part in transferring the appropriate information to the form.

Many escrow offices follow the practice of using one general computer-printed form of escrow instructions for all types of escrows.

A general form is usually designed for sale escrows, but with a few adjustments, it can be adapted for use in almost any type of escrow.

CHAPTER OUTLINE

These multi-use forms will have to be prepared paragraph by paragraph. Although this procedure may require more time, and frequently requires some modification of the printed language of the form and insertion of additional clauses, it does allow the escrow officer the advantage of expressing each party's desires in greater detail. Our simple note and trust deed transfer does not require such a form. However, it can be of considerable importance when handling complex procedures.

Your office procedures will determine the form of instructions you choose.

However, it doesn't hurt for you to be familiar with all types of forms available. You should be able to prepare acceptable instructions using any form. We have included, for your comparison and study, two such forms filled in with the details of this transaction.

As you can see, the first set of instructions (**Figure 14-1**) is the same type used and illustrated in the exchange escrow from the previous chapters. The second, however, is a different type of form (see **Figure 14-2**). This one has been specifically designed for use in an escrow involving the sale of a trust deed and note, and shows the exact same instructions in an entirely different way. Which of the two do you prefer? Since you are already familiar with the first form, we will focus our attention on this second form.

II. Altering a Standard Escrow Instructions Form

With a normal sale escrow, this form of instructions will usually provide for the delivery of funds when certain documents, such as a grant deed, have been obtained and when a policy of title insurance can be issued. With our escrow, however, the instructions (Figure 14-2) are modified to provide for the delivery of funds upon the condition that the specified CLTA indorsement for an assignment of note and trust deed is issued by Confidential Title.

Instructions relating to obtaining the various required documents, such as the note, trust deed, and assignment forms, will be found in subsequent paragraphs within the body of the instructions.

Since no new title policy is being issued, the instructions refer to the description, vesting, and exceptions to title, such as taxes, CC&Rs, easements, and the first and second trust deeds as they are shown in the existing policy to which the indorsement will be attached.

A. TITLE INSURANCE INDORSEMENT

In this paragraph we define the coverages to be provided by the CLTA indorsement required by the purchaser. Note the provisions regarding the taxes. If the existing title policy had been written during a previous year, title might be subject to the taxes for

Figure 14-1

ESCROW INSTRUCTIONS - BUYERS (1)

ESCROW INSTRUCTIONS

ESCROW NO. 1066

SELLERS ☐   BUYERS ☒   BORROWERS ☐   DATE 6/10/XX

To: YOUR COMPANY

On or before   6/25/XX   I/we will   hand you the sum of $4,248.72
and interest as provided for below.

Which you will deliver when you obtain for my/our account an assignment of deed of trust
executed by Todd Slavkin and Elisa Slavkin assigning the beneficial interest
under said second trust deed to the undersigned, Leigh Bennet, a single woman

and when you can issue your CLTA 104 A indorsement to your   policy of title
Insurance #9026138 dated April 20, 19XX covering real property described as:

   Lot 88 of Tract 4470, in the city of Indio, Riverside County, California,
   as per map recorded in Book 56, page 2 of Maps, records of said county

showing title vested in   Paul Montgomery and Jill Montgomery, husband and wife as
   joint tenants

SUBJECT ONLY TO: All   taxes for the fiscal year 20XX - 20 XX
Covenants, conditions, restrictions, and easements of record; and deeds of trust all as shown
as exceptions 1, 2, 3, 4, and 5 of said policy #9026138

The CLTA Indorsement 104A called for above will insure Leigh Bennet as assignee under
the deed of trust shown as exception #5 of said policy and will show: that there are
no subsisting tax or assessment liens prior to said second trust deed 20XX-XX taxes;
that there are no matters shown by the public records affecting the validity or priority
of the lien of said trust deed other than shown above; that there are no U.S. tax liens
or bankruptcy proceedings affecting the title of said estate or interest shown by the
public records.

****

At the close of escrow, you are to deliver to the undersigned, Leigh Bennet, the
promissory note for $5,000 endorsed as shown below, and second trust deed securing
said note.

Said note shall be endorsed as follows:

    Pay to the order of Leigh Bennet without recourse,
    Principal Balance $4,720.80
    Interest paid to 6/1/XX

_____   _____
Todd Slavkin   Elisa Slavkin
                  ****

Continued on Page 2

ESCROW INSTRUCTIONS - BUYERS (2)

ESCROW INSTRUCTIONS

ESCROW NO. 1066

SELLERS ☐   BUYERS ☒   BORROWERS ☐   DATE   6/10/XX

Prepare for my execution a Request for Notice relating to the first trust deed, which Request is to be recorded as an accomodation.

Obtain offset statement from Paul Montgomery, 1019 Louise Street, Indio, California 94202; principal is $4,720.80 with interest at 13% per annum, paid to 6/1/XX.

Obtain beneficiary's statement from the holders of the note secured by the first trust deed, Industrial Bank, indicating that the note is current with no delinquencies of principal or interest, and that the unpaid balance of principal does not exceed $34,330.00.

Obtain a memorandum copy of the existing fire insurance policy, covering the premises known as 1019 Louise Street, Indio, California, in the amount of $40,000.00 with second loss payable clause in favor of Leigh Bennet. The policy is held by Industrial Bank.

Upon close of escrow, you are authorized to deduct from my/our account the following:

I pay no expenses in connection with this transaction except you will charge me and credit the seller of the note with the interest accruing from the last payment, as disclosed by the owner's offset statement, to the date of close of this escrow, which shall be the date on which the Assignment of Trust Deed is recorded.

The GENERAL PROVISIONS printed on the reverse side of this page of these instructions are by reference thereto incorporated herein and made a part hereof and have been read and are hereby approved by the undersigned.

Time is of the essence of these instructions. If this escrow is not in condition to close by the "time limit date" of June 25, 20 XX , and demand for cancellation is received by you from any principal to this escrow after said date, you shall act in accordance with Paragraph 7 of the General Provisions printed on the reverse side hereof. If no demand for cancellation is made, you will proceed to close when the principals have complied with the escrow instructions.

Any amendments of or supplements to any instructions affecting this escrow must be in writing. I will hand you any funds and instruments required to complete this escrow.

All documents, balances and statements due the undersigned are to be mailed to the address shown below.

Signature _____   Address _197 Stoner Street___   Telephone _(805) 663-2792_
　　　　Leigh Bennet   Bakersfield, CA

Signature _____   Address _____   Telephone _____

ESCROW INSTRUCTIONS - SELLERS

ESCROW INSTRUCTIONS
SELLERS

ESCROW NO. 1066

DATE   6/10/XX

To: YOUR COMPANY

I/we have read and approve the Instructions of   Leigh Bennet   dated 6/10/XX

On or before   6/25/XX   I/we will hand you   a note for $5,000.00 containing
endorsement, trust deed securing said note, assignment of trust deed, together
with other documents, all as called for in the foregoing instructions.

                                                                with 104A indorsement
which you will deliver when you can issue the policy of title insurance called for therein/and when you
obtain for my/our account:

Hold for my account the sum of $4,248.72 plus interest as specified in the foregoing
instructions.

I/we pay all costs and charges in connection with this escrow.

The GENERAL PROVISIONS printed on the reverse side of this page of these instructions are by reference
thereto incorporated herein and made a part hereof and have been read and are hereby approved by the
undersigned.
     Time is of the essence of these instructions. If this escrow is not in condition to close by the
"time limit date" of June 25, 20XX   , and demand for cancellation is received by you from any principal
to this escrow after said date, you shall act in accordance with Paragraph 7 of the General Provisions
printed on the reverse side hereof. If no demand for cancellation is made, you will proceed to close when
the principals have complied with the escrow instructions.

Any amendments of or supplements to any instructions affecting this escrow must be in writing. I will hand
you any funds and instruments required to complete this escrow.

All documents, balances and statements due the undersigned are to be mailed to the address shown below.

Signature ___✔_____ Address _1313 Mesa Street_____ Telephone (619) 743-2552
          Todd Slavkin   Indio, California 94201

Signature ___✔_____ Address____Same_____ Telephone _Same_____
          Elisa Slavkin

ESCROW INSTRUCTIONS - GENERAL PROVISIONS (1)

GENERAL PROVISIONS

1. Deposit of Funds

All funds received in this escrow shall be deposited with other escrow funds in a general account or accounts of Title Insurance and Trust Company, with any state or national bank, and may be transferred to any other such general escrow account or accounts. All disbursements shall be made by check of Title Insurance and Trust Company.

Any commitment made in writing to Title Insurance and Trust Company by a bank, trust company, insurance company, or savings and loan association to deliver its check or funds into this escrow may, in the sole discretion of Title Insurance and Trust Company, be treated as the equivalent of a deposit in this escrow of the amount thereof.

2. Prorations and Adjustments

All prorations and/or adjustments called for in this escrow are to be made on the basis of a thirty (30) day month unless otherwise instructed in writing.

The phrase "close of escrow" (COE or CE) as used in this escrow means the date on which documents are recorded and relates only to proration and/or adjustments unless otherwise specified.

3. Recordation of Instruments

Recordation of any instruments delivered through this escrow, if necessary or proper for the issuance of the policy of title insurance called for, is authorized.

4. Authorization to Furnish Copies

You are authorized to furnish copies of these instructions, supplements, amendments, or notices of cancellation and closing statements in this escrow, to the real estate broker(s) and lender(s) named in this escrow.

5. Authorization to Execute Assignment of Hazard Insurance Policies

You are to execute, on behalf of the principals hereto, form assignments of interest in any insurance policy (other than title insurance) called for in this escrow; forward assignment and policy to the agent requesting that insurer consent to such transfer and/or attach a loss clause and/or such other indorsements as may be required; and, forward such policy(s) to the principals entitled thereto.

6. Personal Property Taxes

No examination or insurance as to the amount or payment of personal property taxes is required unless specifically requested.

ESCROW INSTRUCTIONS - GENERAL PROVISIONS (2)

7. Right of Cancellation

Any principal instructing you to cancel this escrow shall file notice of cancellation in your office, in writing. You shall within two (2) working days thereafter mail, by certified mail, one copy of such notice to each of the other principals at the addresses stated in this escrow. Unless written objection to cancellation is filed in your office by a principal within ten (10) days after date of such mailing, you are authorized to comply with such notice and demand payment of your cancellation charges as provided in this agreement. If written objection is filed, you are authorized to hold all money and instruments in this escrow and take no further action until otherwise directed, either by the principals' mutual written instructions, or final order of a court of competent jurisdiction.

The principals hereto expressly agree that you, as escrow holder, have the absolute right at your election to file an action in interpleader requiring the principals to answer and litigate their several claims and rights among themselves and you are authorized to deposit with the clerk of the court all documents and funds held in this escrow. In the event such action is filed, the principals jointly and severally agree to pay your cancellation charges and costs, expenses and reasonable attorney's fees which you are required to expend or incur in such interpleader action, the amount thereof to be fixed and judgment therefor to be rendered by the court. Upon the filing of such action, you shall thereupon be fully released and discharged from all obligations to further perform any duties or obligations otherwise imposed by the terms of this escrow.

8. Termination of Agency Obligation

If there is no action taken on this escrow within six (6) months after the "time limit date" as set forth in the escrow instructions or written extension thereof, your agency obligation shall terminate at your option and all documents, monies or other items held by you shall be returned to the parties depositing same.

In the event of cancellation of this escrow, whether it be at the request of any of the principals or otherwise, the fees and charges due Title Insurance and Trust Company, including expenditures incurred and/or authorized shall be borne equally by the parties hereto (unless otherwise agreed to specifically).

9. Conflicting Instructions

Upon receipt of any conflicting instructions other than cancellation instructions, you are no longer obligated to take any further action in connection with this escrow until further consistent instructions are received from the principals to this escrow except as provided in Paragraph 7 of these General Provisions.

Figure 14-2

ESCROW INSTRUCTIONS (1)

ESCROW INSTRUCTIONS
for Assignment of Trust Deed

To: YOUR COMPANY

Escrow No. 1066
Date ... June 10, 20XX
Escrow Officer. Your Name

I will hand you $ 4,248.72, which you are to use on or before June 25 20 XX, provided you hold for me the following:

1. DEED OF TRUST recorded April 20, 20 XX in Book 6822, page 93, Official Records of Riverside County, covering the following property.

   Lot 88 of Tract No. 4470, city of Indio, Riverside County, California as per map recorded in Book 56, page 2 of Maps, records of said county.

2. PROMISSORY NOTE secured by the above deed of trust, in the original amount of $ 5,000.00 executed by Paul Montgomery and Jill Montgomery, dated April 20, 20 XX, which note shall be endorsed without recourse as follows:

   Pay to the order of Leigh Bennet without recourse Principal balance of $4,720.80. Interest paid to 6/1/XX.

   _____   _____
   Todd Slavkin   Elisa Slavkin

3. ASSIGNMENT OF TRUST DEED executed by Todd Slavkin & Elisa Slavkin assigning the beneficial interest under said trust deed to Leigh Bennet, which assignment you shall have recorded in the county in which the property is located.

4. TITLE INSURANCE, either:

   A. CLTA 104A Indorsement to be attached to existing CLTA Policy of Title Insurance No. 9026138 dated April 20, 20 XX, issued by Confidential Title Insurance & Trust Co. insuring said deed of trust as of the date of said policy and subject to all matters contained in said policy which the undersigned hereby acknowledges he has examined and does hereby approve.

      (not cover any examination of taxes)
      Said indorsement is to (show only taxes for fiscal year 20 XX 20 XX and ....)

ESCROW INSTRUCTIONS (2)

   (CLTA Standard)
  B. (ALTA Extended) Coverage Policy of Title Insurance with liability
   of $ ...., insuring said deed of trust as of the date of
   recordation of the assignment being delivered herein, subject only
   to ....taxes for the fiscal year 20XX-XX , covenants,
   conditions, restrictions, and easements of record.......................
   ....

       (New)
5. FIRE INSURANCE (Memorandum of existing) Fire Insurance Policy in the amount
  of at least $.40,000.00.covering premises known as.1019.Louise.St..
  ..Indio,.CA..............with.second.... loss payable clause attached.

6. OWNER'S OFFSET STATEMENT from payors of above note, showing unpaid principal
  balance of said note to be $.4,720.80.... with interest at.13...% to be paid
  to .6/1/XX..............
  PRORATE INTEREST to date of recording of assignment of trust deed.

7. BENEFICIARY'S STATEMENT from.Industrial.Bank........., holder of.first....
  trust deed showing no delinquencies in principal or interest with an unpaid
  balance of principal not exceeding $.34,330.00.........

8. REQUEST FOR NOTICE under Section 2924B, California Civil Code, which you are
  to prepare for my execution to be recorded as an accommodation.

I do not pay for title, escrow, or other fees in connection with this escrow.

If the conditions of this escrow have not been complied with at the time provided
herein, you are nevertheless to complete the same as soon as the conditions (except
as to time) have been complied with, unless I shall have made written demand upon you
for the return of money and for instruments deposited by me. Time is hereby declared
to be the essence thereof. In the event this escrow shall not be in a condition to
be closed by the date provided herein, the party who then shall have fully complied
with his instructions may, in writing, demand the return of his money and/or
instructions.

The undersigned agree that in consideration of your acceptance of the within escrow
you shall not be liable for the failure of any of the conditions hereof caused by the
exercise of your discretion in any particular manner, except gross negligence or
willful misconduct.

Should any controversy arise between parties hereto, or any other person, you shall
not be liable to take any action of any kind but may withhold all moneys, securities,
documents, or other things herein deposited until such controversy shall be determined by agreement of the parties, or proper legal process.

It is understood that the fees hereunder agreed to be paid for your services are for
ordinary and usual services only, and should there be any extraordinary or unusual
services rendered by you hereunder, the undersigned agrees to pay you a reasonable
compensation for such extraordinary or unusual services, together with any costs and

If possible, now is a good time to obtain all documents, money, and instructions from the principals that are necessary to comply with the terms of the escrow. After these items have been obtained, avoid calling upon them for anything further unless absolutely necessary.

Bothering your client with last minute details is a nuisance, not to mention that it provides an opening for a principal to possibly change his or her mind.

If the beneficiary's statement and the owner's offset statement are not delayed, and the statements confirm the information given to you by the seller, the seller has done everything usually required of him or her. Now you want to be certain that the purchaser does the same.

B. THE BUYER'S DEPOSIT OF FUNDS

The report of title will ordinarily be in your hands within a very few days. Now is the time to ask the buyer to deposit the money. Be prepared to furnish a quick estimate of the amount to be deposited.

The sellers have agreed to pay all of the escrow charges. You will need to obtain from Bennet only the principal amount that she is to pay for the note and trust deed ($4,248.72), plus the interest accrued on the note. You will have to calculate this latter amount. Your escrow instructions provide that this is to be computed from June 1 to the date of close of escrow. While the escrow may close earlier, for this preliminary estimate you can assume a closing date of June 20. Calculate the daily interest based upon 19 days (June 20 - June 1) and prorate the amount owed. This will give you a figure of $26.80, the amount of interest which will have accrued.

Adding this amount to the $4,248.72 gives you a total of $4,275.52. To be on the safe side, round this figure off and ask Bennet for a deposit of $4,300. This will allow for a few extra days' interest in the event the closing of the escrow should be delayed for any reason. Any excess money will be returned to Bennet from your escrow company.

IV. Ordering The Title Insurance

In this type of transaction, your instructions to the title company are best expressed using a letter instead of the title order form. We have included such a letter for you to study (see **Figure 14-3**).

You will enclose the title policy and all documents to be recorded. Give precise instructions regarding the insurance coverage your parties require. The title company will often want to examine the note to verify that it has been properly transferred. Another option is to accept a statement from you, as is the case in the letter, that you have the note in your

Figure 14-3

INSTRUCTIONS TO THE TITLE COMPANY

Y O U R   C O M P A N Y

June 10, 20 XX

Re: New Order
Escrow No. 1066
Attention:_____

To: Confidential Title Insurance Company

Gentlemen:

Enclosed are:

1. TI Policy #9026138 dated 4/20/XX.

2. Assignment of trust deed shown as exception #5
   in said policy executed by Todd Slavkin and
   wife to Leigh Bennet.

3. Request for Notice of Default executed by Leigh
   Bennet, referring to the trust deed shown as
   exception #4 in said policy.

We have in our possession the note secured by the trust deed
being assigned with a present unpaid balance of $4,720.80.
This note has been endorsed by Todd Slavkin and Elisa Slavkin
to Leigh Bennet, and will be sent to you for examination upon
your request.

Please make the necessary examination of title preparatory to
issuing your CLTA 104A Indorsement insuring Leigh Bennet as
assignee upon recording of the above assignment. Your indorsement is to show the trust deed being assigned to be subject
only to 20 XX-XX taxes and exceptions 2, 3, and 4 of said policy.

Notify the undersigned whether you can comply, but do not record
until further authorized.

YOUR COMPANY

_____
Your Name

possession and it has been properly endorsed. If the note is sent to the title company, use the title company's messenger service or send it by registered or certified mail with a return receipt requested. A lost note will obviously create serious problems.

Title companies in the larger counties have special departments to handle the issuance of indorsements. In other counties your title officer will handle the order. If at all possible, determine in advance the name of the person or department handling this special type of title work so that your letter is properly directed.

V. Closing the Note and Trust Deed Escrow

It is the afternoon of June 19. It appears you will be ready to close by tomorrow morning. The information shown in the received beneficiary's statement and owner's offset statement coincides with the information furnished by the sellers of the note. The title company reports that it can comply with your instructions. The steps in closing this escrow are similar to the procedures you have followed in previous practice escrows.

A. SETTLEMENT SHEET

Completing the settlement sheet is usually the first step in the closing process. This will ascertain that you have sufficient funds to close.

The settlement sheet for this transaction is shown, dated for a June 20 closing.

Your work is simplified because you included the progress and settlement sheets (see **Figures 14-4** and **14-5**) in your file at the time the escrow first opened and kept them current. Recheck your work to make certain you haven't overlooked any charges, a document to be drawn or any requirements of the parties. You verified the price of the CLTA 104A indorsement as being $30.00. Don't overlook the bank's charge of $20.00 for issuing the beneficiary's statement.

You can estimate recording charges for the assignment and request for notice. These amounts will be verified when you receive the title company's charges. You will have to re-compute the interest to be charged on the loan based on the new recording date. As a final check, enter and total the disbursement items to be sure that your settlement balances.

B. RECORDING PROCEDURE

Follow your customary procedure in authorizing the recording of the documents. This can be accomplished by a telephone call confirmed by written directions to the title company, With the recording verified, you are ready to complete the final steps in closing the escrow.

Figure 14-4

PROGRESS SHEET

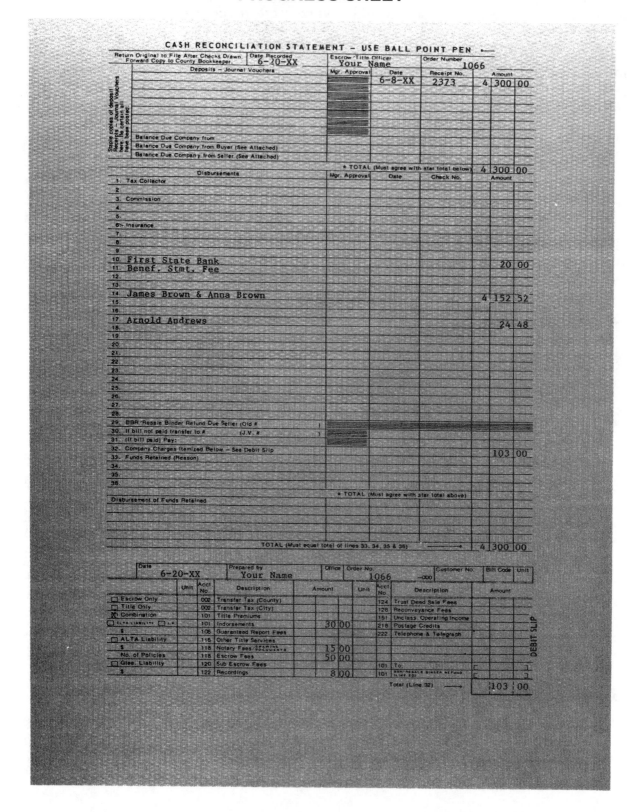

Figure 14-5

SETTLEMENT SHEET

TITLE/ESCROW SETTLEMENT SHEET
EXCHANGE

		ESCROW NO. 1066
☐ ESTIMATED STATEMENT ☒ FINAL STATEMENT	DATE 6-20-XX	E.O./T.O. NAME Your Name	ESCROW NO.

PROPERTY DESCRIPTION/ADDRESS — PROPERTY DESCRIPTION/ADDRESS

FIRST PARTY Todd Slavkin & Elisa Slavkin
ADDRESS 1313 Mesa St., Indio, CA

SECOND PARTY Leigh Bennet
ADDRESS 197 Stoner St., Bakersfield, CA

	DEBIT	CREDIT	DESCRIPTION	DEBIT	CREDIT
		4 248 72	EXCHANGE VALUE—FIRST PARTIES PROPERTY	4 248 72	
			DEPOSIT TO: Escrow		4 300 00
			DEPOSITS RETAINED BY:		
			EXISTING LOAN BALANCE		
			EXISTING LOAN TRUST FUNDS		
	20 00		EXISTING LOAN – XXXXXXXX Benef. Stmt. Fee		
			TAXES $ FR TO		
			INSURANCE $ FR TO		
		26 80	INTEREST $ FR 6-1 TO 6-20	26 80	
			RENT $ FR TO		
			ASSMNT. INT. $ FR TO		
			RENT DEPOSIT		
			EXCHANGE VALUE—SECOND PARTIES PROPERTY		
			DEPOSIT TO:		
			DEPOSITS RETAINED BY		
			EXISTING LOAN BALANCE		
			EXISTING LOAN TRUST FUNDS		
			EXISTING LOAN – TRANSFER FEE		
			TAXES $ FR TO		
			INSURANCE $ FR TO		
			INTEREST $ FR TO		
			RENT $ FR TO		
			ASSMNT. INT $ FR TO		
			RENT DEPOSIT		
			NEW LOAN WITH:		
			FHA MTG $ INS. RESERVE $		
			TAX RES. $ RECON. FEE $		
			CR. REPORTS $ TAX SERVICE $		
			LOAN FEE $ APPRAISAL FEE $		
			INTEREST $ $		
			INT @ FR TO $		
			TOTAL OF ABOVE		
			INSURANCE		
			PAY OFF LOAN TO		
			PRINCIPAL $		
			INTEREST $		
			INT @ FR TO $		
			PREPAYMENT PENALTY $		
			RECON. FEE $		
			$		
			LESS LOAN TRUST FUND DEPOSITS $		
			TOTAL OF ABOVE		
			TITLE INSURANCE $ ☐Owner ☐JP ☐STR		
			PREMIUM FOR $ ☐Loan ☐Alta		
			TITLE INSURANCE $ ☐Owner ☐JP ☐STR		
			PREMIUM FOR $ ☐Loan ☐Alta		
	30 00		IND 104.A	30 00	
	50 00		ESCROW FEE	50 00	
			RECONVEYANCE FEE		
	8 00		RECORDING Assgt. & Req./Not.	8 00	
			NOTARY FEE		
	15 00		DOCUMENT PREP Req./Not. & Assgt.	15 00	
			TRANSFER TAX CO. $ CITY $		
			TRANSFER TAX CO. $ CITY $		
			TOTAL	103 00	
			TAX COLLECTOR		
			COMMISSION		
	4 152 52		CHECK TO:	24 48	
			BALANCE DUE COMPANY FROM		
	4 275 52	4 275 52	TOTALS	4 300 00	4 300 00

Make up the closing statements and have the checks drawn and mailed. The promissory note must be delivered to Bennet. She may request that the note and the check for the balance of funds be delivered to her in your office. If not, as always, send them registered or certified mail, return receipt requested.

Send the fire insurance policy to the agent. You will need to obtain a memorandum of the policy for the assignee, with the second "mortgage clause" changed in his favor. Also request a waiver of the interest of Todd Slavkin and his wife. The original fire policy must be returned to the bank. You can instruct the agent to send it to the bank directly after all the necessary changes nave been made.

You should now make one last check of the escrow file to be certain that nothing has been left undone. You have now successfully completed another escrow. Mark your file "closed" and send it to the place where your closed files are stored.

VI. A Note and Trust Deed Are Negotiable Instruments

You will find this type of transaction to usually quite simple, more so than it may appear from this detailed discussion. Very little information is required from your parties, most of it is available from the existing title policy and the note and trust deed. The most important consideration is the use of the proper title insurance indorsement forms and the adaptation of the escrow instruction forms to fit the customer's requirements. Before leaving this subject, there are a few points we will discuss.

In discussing the transfer of the note, reference was made to the effect the negotiable instruments law might have on the rights of the parties.

Promissory notes secured by deeds of trust are customarily in the form of negotiable instruments and, as such, will fall under the California Uniform Commercial Code.

The most important consideration in this type of transaction is the use of the proper title insurance indorsement forms and the adaptation of the escrow instruction forms to fit the customer's requirements.

This law governs the method of transfer of the instrument and the rights of subsequent holders of the obligation. As an escrow officer, then, you will want to be acquainted with this law. We will touch only briefly on the subject of negotiable instruments here. The serious student of escrows will find a business law course on negotiable instruments (or "notes and trust deeds," as it is popularly called) extremely valuable.

VII. Negotiable Instruments Law

The negotiable instruments law is the oldest of the "uniform laws."

A **UNIFORM LAW** *set forth in the Uniform Commercial Code is one all or most of the states adopt as the law on a particular subject, so as to achieve substantial uniformity of law throughout the country.*

Essentially, a **NEGOTIABLE INSTRUMENT** *is a written promise or order to pay money.* Negotiable instruments may take the form of a check, a draft, a bill of exchange or a promissory note. Section 3104 (1) of the Uniform Commercial Code defines a negotiable instrument as "a written, signed, unconditional promise or order to pay a sum certain in money to order or to bearer, on demand or at a definite time." To be a negotiable instrument, the instrument must meet all of these formal requirements. The following are examples of language sufficient to create a negotiable instrument.

"On demand, I promise to pay to the order of John Doe $1,000;"

or

"On or before July 4, 20XX, I promise to pay to John Doe or order $1,000;"

or

"I promise to pay to bearer on demand the sum of $1,000."

A note that reads "On demand, I promise to pay John Doe $1,000" would not be a negotiable instrument because it is payable only to a designated person and not "to order" or "to bearer". This type of a note would be a "nonnegotiable instrument". This type of note can still be transferred. Both negotiable and nonnegotiable instruments may be transferred to third parties. The difference will be in the rights acquired by subsequent holders.

A. PERSONAL DEFENSES

Negotiability is the capacity to transfer the ownership of an instrument free of certain "personal defenses" of the maker of the instrument.

These defenses include such matters as failure of consideration or misrepresentation as to the area of the property.

Suppose that sellers of an improved parcel of land misrepresent the age or condition of the improvements to induce the purchasers to buy the property. The purchasers would have a cause of action for damages or other appropriate relief against the seller. All or a portion of any purchase money trust deed taken back by the seller as part of the consideration might be ordered canceled by the court to offset the possible loss to the purchasers.

Under the negotiable instruments law, if the seller sells a negotiable note, the purchaser of such note is given a favored status.

In other words, the buyer of the real property will still be obligated to pay the purchaser of the note the full amount due, and he or she will have to seek out the original seller for relief from damages.

A purchaser of a nonnegotiable instrument acquires no such favored status. Such a purchaser becomes merely an "assignee" of the payee, gaining no greater rights than those held by the assignor. What happens here is that the assignee is subject to the same defenses that can be used against the original payee, and the assignee will be left to look to his assignor for any damages that might be incurred as a result of the assertion of any such defenses.

B. HOLDER IN DUE COURSE

For a subsequent holder of a negotiable instrument to be entitled to this specially protected position, he or she must attain the status of what the law calls a "holder in due course." He or she must purchase the instrument in good faith, for value, and is without notice that it is overdue or that there are defenses to it. The transferee achieves the status of a holder in due course by having the transfer of the instrument negotiated, which means a delivery of the instrument with the necessary endorsement.

Delivery is the means by which a note made payable to "bearer" is transferred.

With a note made payable to the order of a named payee, that person will "order" the maker to pay the transferee. He or she does this by endorsement. Such an endorsement must be "written by or on behalf of the holder on the instrument or on a paper so firmly affixed to the instrument as to become part of it."

C. ENDORSEMENTS

There are various types of endorsements, including the following:

BLANK, where the holder signs his or her name on the back of the note.

SPECIAL, where the holder writes "Pay to the order of (named transferee)" and signs.

RESTRICTIVE, where the holder restricts future negotiation, for example, he or she writes "Pay to the order of State Bank, for deposit only" and then signs.

QUALIFIED, where the holder adds the words "without recourse" to what would otherwise be a simple blank or special endorsement. This means that if the maker refuses to pay, the endorser is not liable for the amount. However, by negotiating a note by simple delivery, or by endorsing the instrument, the endorser still warrants that:

The instrument is genuine;

He or she, the transferor, holds a good title to the instrument;

All prior parties had capacity to contract; and

He or she has no knowledge of any fact that would impair the validity of the instrument or render it valueless.

The endorser would have to add the words "without warranties" or some equivalent language to avoid the foregoing warranties.

The question of warranties does not arise in most cases. The problem is usually one of ability to pay. If the maker doesn't pay the holder when the note is due because he or she has no money, the holder cannot look to the qualified endorser for payment. The endorser is liable to subsequent holders who are unable to collect from a defaulting maker when dealing with the ordinary unqualified endorsement. In order to assert their rights, such holders must present the instrument properly for payment and must give the endorser due notice of dishonor.

D. REAL DEFENSES

As noted above, such a purchase is acquired free of "personal defenses." However, real defenses are good even against a holder in due course.

Real defenses include such matters as forgery and alteration.

If your name is forged on a negotiable instrument as its apparent maker, the note cannot be enforced against you. It is simply not your instrument. If such an instrument is altered, i.e., raised from $100 to $1000, it can be enforced against you only to the extent of its original amount, that is, only in the amount of $50.

Protection against these defenses is provided either in the policy of title insurance, or the indorsement attached to such a policy, insuring the assignment of the trust deed.

The Uniform Commercial Code states that words of assignment or disclaimer accompanying an endorsement do not affect its character as an endorsement.

Such words are usually added by laymen to indicate formally that the instrument is conveyed.

Although the law sets specific requirements for negotiability, the inclusion of other provisions is permitted that does not destroy negotiability. For instance, the negotiability of a promissory note is not adversely affected by the fact that it is secured by a mortgage or deed of trust.

Similarly, the negotiability of the note would not be affected by the inclusion of clauses that add attorney's fees or court costs in the event of litigation.

The negotiability of the note would not be affected by the inclusion of clauses that add attorney's fees or court costs in the event of litigation.

As can be seen, the question of endorsements can be quite complex. What should be the role of the escrow holder in obtaining the necessary signatures for transferring such a note? The escrow holder should have the parties state the form they want to use and make certain that the language relating to this is typed in specific terms on the note and reflected in the escrow instructions. The escrow officer should recommend consulting their attorney if the parties are in doubt as to the best way to accomplish their purpose.

Impending problems that might develop from the use of incomplete or inconsistent language by the parties can be more reasonably recognized by an escrow officer who is knowledgeable on the subject of negotiable instruments.

VIII. Usury Law

Generally speaking, California law does not restrict the amount of discount that may be exacted in the purchase and sale of a trust deed and note.

Marketability factors control this discount. It is a matter of agreement between the seller and buyer of the note. A usury law violation may result if, by means of deception, the original maker (trustor) is obligated to bear the discount.

Suppose that in negotiating for the sale of the property to the Montgomerys, the Slavkins did not want to accept a $5,000 purchase money second trust deed, knowing that they would be forced to offer a discount to sell it. The Montgomerys could agree to execute a note in an amount large enough to give the Montgomerys $5,000 after discount. Also, the Montgomerys might arrange to find a buyer to purchase the note through the same escrow. Although actually usurious, an agreement between the buyer and seller with regard to the amount of the note could be concealed from you in this manner.

As a matter of policy, most escrow offices will not handle an escrow involving a trust deed note being sold at a discount concurrent with its execution. When confronted with a request to handle such an escrow, discuss the problem with your management before accepting the instructions.

IX. Collateral

You will have a second concern besides your principle concern of seeing that the form of the endorsement on the note conforms to the instructions of the parties. You will want to be sure that the transfer of ownership of the note is intended to be unconditional and absolute, and not collateral.

A "collateral assignment" creates security for the performance of an obligation.

The holder of such a note might borrow money from a bank or other lending institution, pledging the note as security for that loan. He or she would execute a collateral assignment of the note in favor of the bank and deliver the note and trust deed to the bank. The bank would only hold the collateral assignment until he or she has paid back the borrowed money. After this obligation has been discharged, the collateral assignment would no longer be effective as an assignment.

Collateral assignments can be handled in an escrow. In such cases, however, the escrow instructions must contain appropriate language to reflect the nature of the transaction. The title company must also be informed of the fact that a collateral assignment exists. Another and different form of indorsement (CLTA 104.4) is used to insure such a collateral assignment.

X. CHAPTER SUMMARY

The standard items in an escrow are called GENERAL PROVISIONS and include items such as deposits, prorations, recording, and taxes. If there is an ACCOMMODATION, the escrow is providing an additional service to the parties usually without additional charges by escrow.

NEGOTIABLE INSTRUMENTS allow documents to circulate as money to encourage their use and are granted special legal protections. The UNIFORM COMMERCIAL CODE specifies the rules for their negotiation.

If it is a DEMAND INSTRUMENT, the holder may request payment upon presentation and proper notice. PERSONAL DEFENSES refer to the payor's defenses against a holder while the REAL DEFENSES are the payor's defenses against a holder in due course.

A SPECIAL ENDORSEMENT states the person to whom the instrument is payable while a RESTRICTIVE one prevents further negotiation. If it is QUALIFIED, it means there is a limit in the liability.

USURY is the charging of excessive and illegal amounts of interest. When there is a COLLATERAL ASSIGNMENT, the property is pledged and will be returned to the owner upon satisfying the conditions or liens.

XI. TERMS

Accommodation: The act of providing a service usually without cost when preparing documents for a client.

Blank Endorsement: Where the holder simply signs his name on the back of the instrument.

California Uniform Commercial Code: Uniform codes of law relating to commercial transactions. The law covers sales contracts, personal property and commercial paper.

Collateral Assignment: The creation of security or lien for the performance of an obligation. An example is a pledge of personal property which is returned to the owner upon satisfying the lien.

Demand Instrument: A financial instrument that permits the holder to call for proceeds upon notice to the payor.

General Provisions: The provisions of an escrow that involve the main standard items for most transactions. May include deposits, prorations, recording, and taxes.

Holder In Due Course: A good faith purchaser of a negotiable instrument who gives value and without notice of any defect in the instrument or wrongdoing in connection with it.

Negotiable Instruments: Any instrument transferable by endorsement or delivery. Examples are promissory notes, checks, drafts that are allowed to circulate as money does.

Personal Defenses: Refers to those refusals to pay on the negotiable instrument that are valid against a holder but not a holder in due course. Examples include failure of consideration and misrepresentation.

Qualified Endorsement: An endorsement that limits liability in the event of a refusal to pay by the maker.

Real Defenses: Those defenses are valid against a holder in due course. Sometimes called universal defenses and may include matters as forgery and alteration of the instrument.

Restrictive Endorsement: An endorsement that prevents further negotiation.

Special Endorsement: An endorsement that specifies the person to whom or to whose order the instrument is payable.

Usury: Charging of interest in excess of that permitted by law.

XII. CHAPTER QUIZ

1. When selling a note and deed of trust, what also may happen to the note?

    a. Assign the note
    b. Send the note
    c. Destroy the note
    d. Cancel the note

2. Notice of default lets the holder of the second trust deed know if the borrower defaults on the:

    a. first trust deed.
    b. grant deed.
    c. quit claim deed.
    d. all of the above.

3. Statements from lenders could be called beneficiary or:

    a. the statement.
    b. offset statement.
    c. income statement.
    d. no statement.

4. Adjustments (proration) of interest in an escrow may vary from transaction to transaction depending on the:

    a. financial instruction.
    b. escrow instructions.
    c. real estate broker.
    d. none of the above.

5. The normal first step in any escrow closing is to be sure that:

    a. the settlement balances.
    b. there are sufficient funds.
    c. all checks are written.
    d. all of the above.

6. When it is time to ask the buyer for funds, be prepared to:

    a. request cash only.
    b. estimate amount.
    c. seek a banker's advice.
    d. none of the above.

7. When ordering title insurance in a complicated transaction, it is best to use:
    a. a pre-printed form.
    b. a hand-written note.
    c. a typed letter.
    d. none of the above.

8. "Your Company" is usually the name of:
    a. a real estate company.
    b. your firm.
    c. a title company.
    d. an escrow company.

9. Which of the following is sufficient to create a negotiable instrument?
    a. "On demand"
    b. "On or before"
    c. "I promise to pay to bearer"
    d. All of the above

10. Which is a personal defense of a negotiable instrument?
    a. Misrepresentation
    b. A valid contract
    c. A bad day
    d. None of the above

ANSWERS: 1. a; 2. a; 3. b; 4. b; 5. b; 6. c; 7. b; 8. b; 9. c; 10. a

JUSTICE

S ANGELES COUNTY COU

Laws, Regulations, and Sale of a Business

I. Laws and Codes

In California, the real estate industry leads the nation in voluntary and required ethic conduct from its salespeople. This chapter is designed to state and clarify all required ethical laws and voluntary ethical codes of real estate trade associations. The following is the sequence in which the material is presented.

A. STATE CODES (CALIFORNIA)

1. Section 10176 (Licensees)
2. Section 10177 (Non-Licensees)

B. STATE AND FEDERAL LAWS

1. Fair Employment and Housing Act (California)
2. Unruh Civil Rights Act (California)
3. Fair Housing Act (Federal)
4. Housing Financial Discrimination Act (Federal)
5. Blind and Physically Disabled (California)
6. Equal Housing Lender

CHAPTER OUTLINE

C. VOLUNTARY ASSOCIATIONS

1. Realtors® Code of Ethics
2. Realtists Code of Ethics

Business and Professions Code 10176
(Real Estate Licensee Acting As Licensee)

Grounds for Revocation or Suspension

Misrepresentation - 10176(a)

The licensee must disclose to his or her principal all material facts that the principal should know. Failure to do so or lying is cause for disciplinary action. A great majority of the complaints received by the commissioner allege misrepresentation on the part of the broker or his or her salespeople.

False Promise - 10176(b)

A false promise is a false statement about what the promisor is going to do in the future. Many times a false promise is proved by showing the promise was impossible to perform and that the person making the promise knew it was impossible.

(continued)

Business and Professions Code 10176
(Real Estate Licensee <u>Acting</u> As Licensee)

Grounds for Revocation or Suspension

Continued and Flagrant Misrepresentation by Agents - 10176(c)

This section gives the commissioner the right to discipline a licensee for a continued and flagrant course of misrepresentation or making of false promises through real estate agents or salespeople.

Divided Agency - 10176(d)

This section requires a licensee to inform all of his or her principals if he or she is acting as an agent for more than one party in a transaction.

Commingling - 10176(e)

Commingling occurs when a broker has mixed the funds of his or her principals with his or her own money. A broker should keep all funds separate.

Definite Termination Date - 10176(f)

A specified termination date in writing is required for all exclusive listing transactions.

Secret Profit - 10176(g)

Secret profit cases usually arise when the broker makes a low offer, usually through a "dummy" purchaser, when he or she already has a higher offer from another buyer. The difference is the secret profit.

Listing Option - 10176(h)

This section requires a licensee, when he or she has used a form which is both an option and a listing, to obtain the written consent of his or her principal approving the amount of such profit before the licensee may exercise the option. This does not apply where a licensee is using an option only.

Dishonest Dealing - 10176(i)

Dishonest dealing is a catch-all section used when the acts of the person required a license but he or she did not have a license.

(continued)

Signatures of Prospective Purchasers - 10176(j)

Brokers must obtain a written (business opportunities) authorization to sell from an owner before securing the signature of a prospective purchaser to the agreement. This section strikes at what was once a common practice in some areas in the sale of business opportunities, where the prospective purchaser was forced to deal with the broker who furnished him or her the listing.

Business and Professions Code 10177
(R.E. Licensee <u>Not Necessarily Acting</u> as a Licensee)

Grounds for Revocation or Suspension

Obtaining License by Fraud - Section 10177(a)

This section gives the Commissioner the power to take action against a licensee for misstatements of fact in an application for a license and in those instances where licenses have been procured by fraud, misrepresentation, or deceit.

Convictions - Section 10177(b)

This section permits proceedings against a licensee after a criminal conviction for either a felony or a misdemeanor which involves moral turpitude (anything contrary to justice, honesty, modesty, or good morals).

False Advertising - Section 10177(c)

This section makes licensees who are parties to false advertising subject to disciplinary action. The ban extends to subdivision sales as well general property sales.

Violations of Other Sections - Section 10177(d)

This section gives the Department authority to proceed against the licensee for violation of any of the other sections of the Real Estate Law, the regulations of the commissioner, and the subdivision laws.

Misuse of Trade Name - Section 10177(e)

Only active members of the national association or local associations of real estate boards are permitted to use the term "Realtor®." This term belongs exclusively to such members, and no licensee may advertise or hold himself or herself out as a "Realtor®" without proper entitlement.

(continued)

Business and Professions Code 10177
(R.E. Licensee <u>Not Necessarily Acting</u> as a Licensee)

Grounds for Revocation or Suspension

Conduct Warranting Denial - Section 10177(f)

This is a general section of the Real Estate Law and almost any act involving crime or dishonesty will fall within it. An essential requirement for the issuance of a license is that the applicant be honest, truthful, and of good reputation.

Negligence or Incompetence - Section 10177(g)

Demonstrated negligence or incompetence, while acting as a licensee, is just cause for disciplinary action. The department proceeds in those cases where the licensee is so careless or unqualified that to allow him or her to handle a transaction would endanger the interests of his or her clients or customers.

Supervision of Salespersons - Section 10177(h)

A broker is subject to disciplinary action if he or she fails to exercise reasonable supervision over the activities of his or her salespersons.

Violating Government Trust - Section 10177(i)

Prescribes disciplinary liability for using government employment to violate the confidential nature of records thereby made available.

Other Dishonest Conduct - Section 10177(j)

Specifies that any other conduct which constitutes fraud or dishonest dealing may subject the one involved to license suspension or revocation.

Restricted License Violation - Section 10177(k)

Makes violation of the terms, conditions, restrictions, and limitations contained in any order granting a restricted license grounds for disciplinary action.

Inducement of Panic Selling (Blockbusting) - Section 10177(l)

It is a cause for disciplinary action to solicit or induce a sale, lease, or the listing for sale or lease, of residential property on the grounds of loss of value because of entry into the neighborhood of a person or persons of another race, color, religion, ancestry, or national origin.

(continued)

Violation of Franchise Investment Law - Section 10177(m)

Violates any of the provisions of the Franchise Investment Law or any regulations of the Corporations Commissioner pertaining thereto.

Violation of Securities Law - Section 10177(n)

Violates any of the provisions of the Corporations Code or any regulations the Commissioner of Corporations relating to securities as specified.

Violation of Securities Law - Section 10177(o)

Failure to disclose to buyer the nature and extent of ownership interest licensee has in property in which the licensee is an agent for the buyer. Also, failure to disclose ownership on the part of licensee's relative or special acquaintance in which licensee has ownership interest.

Violated Article 6 (commencing with Section 10237) - Section 10177(p)

If a corporation real estate broker has not done any of the foregoing acts, either directly or through its employees, agents, officers, directors, or persons owning or controlling 10 percent or more of the corporation's stock, the Commissioner may not deny the issuance of a real estate license to, or suspend or revoke the real estate license of, the corporation, provided that any offending officer, director, or stockholder, who has done any of the foregoing acts individually and not on behalf of the corporation, has been completely disassociated from any affiliation or ownership in the corporation.

II. California Fair Employment and Housing Act

(Sections 35700 - 35745 of the Health and Safety Code)

The California Fair Employment and Housing Act has many ramifications applying to the owners of residential property, to real estate brokers and salespeople, and to other agents and financial institutions. The *CALIFORNIA FAIR HOUSING ACT comprises sections 35700 through 35745 of the California Health and Safety Code, which is based on the policy that race discrimination is a threat to the health and safety of those who suffer under it.*

The code sections were amended to clearly forbid discrimination, by any means, based upon race, color, national origin, religion, sex, familial status, and handicap. It outlaws such discrimination in the sale, rental, lease or financing of all housing and sets up clear-cut guidelines for preventing and remedying violations.

For example, if a landlord is found to violate this law with respect to a prospective tenant being unjustly turned away, the landlord can be forced to go through with the rental. If the original desired unit is no longer available, the discriminated party is entitled to the next vacancy or to a like rental if one is available. If none of these compensations can be arranged, the landlord can be liable for up to $1,000 in damages.

III. Unruh Civil Rights Act
(Sections 51 - 52 of the California Civil Code)

The Unruh Civil Rights Act amended the California Civil Code to read (in part):

> "All persons within the jurisdiction of this state are free and equal, and no matter what their race, color, religion, ancestry or national origin, they are entitled to the full and equal accommodations, advantages, facilities, privileges, or services in all business establishments of every kind whatsoever..."

The validity of this act has been tested. It has been held repeatedly to apply with regard to real estate transactions. Thus, real estate brokers who unlawfully discriminate on the grounds of race or color are in violation of the law. Any violator is liable, for each offense, for the actual money damages plus $250 of additional penalty awarded to the person denied their rights.

IV. Fair Housing Act
(Title VIII - IX of the U.S. Civil Rights Act of 1968)

The Federal Civil Rights Act of 1968 (also known as the Fair Housing or Open Housing Law) had the following effect:

1. The Unruh and Rumford Acts remain in effect, and what discrimination those two do not prohibit Federal law now does. THERE ARE NO EXCEPTIONS.

2. No person may refuse to sell, lease, or rent to another because of race or color, and no real estate licensee may do so, regardless of his seller's directions. If asked to do so, the salesman must refuse to accept the listing.

3. No real estate board or multiple listing service may deny membership or participation because of race, color, religion, or national origin, or discriminate against a person in terms or conditions or membership.

As part of the Civil Rights Act of 1968, a fair housing poster (**Figure 15-1**) must be displayed at all real brokerage offices and subdivision model homes. This poster must also be displayed at any financial institution or mortgage lender who makes loans to the general public.

Figure 15-1

Equal Housing Lender

**We Do Business In Accordance With The
Federal Fair Housing Law**

**(Title VIII of the Civil Rights Act of 1968,
as Amended by the Housing and Community
Development Act of 1974)**

**IT IS ILLEGAL TO DISCRIMINATE AGAINST ANY PERSON
BECAUSE OF RACE, COLOR, NATIONAL ORIGIN, RELIGION,
SEX, FAMILIAL STATUS (including children under the age of 18
living with parents or legal custodians, pregnant women, and
people securing custody of children under the age of 18),
and HANDICAP, TO:**

■ Deny a loan for the purpose of purchasing, constructing, improving, repairing or maintaining a dwelling or

■ Discriminate in fixing of the amount, interest rate, duration, application procedures or other terms or conditions of such a loan.

**IF YOU BELIEVE YOU HAVE BEEN DISCRIMINATED
AGAINST, YOU MAY SEND A COMPLAINT TO:**

**U.S. DEPARTMENT OF HOUSING AND URBAN DEVELOPMENT
Assistant Secretary for Fair Housing and Equal Opportunity
Washington, D.C. 20410**

or call your local HUD Area or Insuring Office.

DISCRIMINATION IN HOUSING AND EMPLOYMENT

In California the Department of Fair Employment and Housing enforces the California state laws which prohibit discrimination in Housing, Public Accomodations, and employment . It also accepts and investigates complaints alleging violations of the Ralph Civil Rights Act, which prohibits hate violence or threats of hate violence.

The Department of Fair Employment and Housing administers these laws in several ways:

1. Investigates harassment and discrimination complaints;
2. Assists individuals in complaints to resolve disputes;
3. Pursues violations of the law to public hearing; and
4. Educates citizens about the laws prohibiting discrimination through literature, seminars, conferences, and round tables.

REMEDIES

If there is not a voluntary settlement, the case may be heard by the Fair Employment and Housing Commission for public hearing or possible prosecution. Remedies may include one or more of the following:

1. Housing or employment may be awarded.
2. Compensation, back pay, or promotion.
3. Specific actions to avoid future discrimination.
4. Fines or damages.

HOUSING AND EMPLOYMENT DISCRIMINATION

It shall be illegal to discriminate unlawfully in the renting, leasing, and selling of housing based on any of the following:

1. Race	7. Handicap
2. Color	8. Age
3. National Origin	9. Medical Condtion
4. Religion	10. Denial of Pregnancy Disability Leave
5. Sex	11. Refusal of Family Care Leave
6. Familial Status	12. Retaliation for reporting patient abuse in tax-supported institutions.

(continued)

It shall be illegal to discriminate illegally in the following business activities:

1. Advertisements
2. Mortgage lending and insurance
3. Application and selection processes
4. Terms, conditions, and privileges of occupancy, including freedom from harassment
5. Public and private land use practices including the existence of restrictive covenants

It shall be illegal to discriminate illegally in accomodations and services in the following areas:

1. Hotels and Motels
2. Non-profit Organizations
3. Restaurants
4. Theaters
5. Hospitals
6. Barber and Beauty Shops
7. Housing Accomodations
8. Local Government and Public Agencies
9. Retail Establishments

HATE VIOLENCE

It is against the law for any person to threaten or commit acts of violence against a person or property based on race, color, religion, ancestry, national origin, age, disability, sex, sexual orientation, political affiliation or position in a labor dispute.

RESTRICTIVE COVENANTS

The Fair Employment and Housing Act expressly prohibits the existence of a restrictive covenant that makes housing opportunities unavailable based on race, color, religion, sex, familial status, marital status, disability, national origin, or ancestry. In conjunction with this prohibition, county recorders, title insurance companies, escrow companies, real estate brokers, or associations that provide declarations, governing documents, or deeds to any person are required to place a cover page over the document, or a stamp on the first page of the document, stating that any restrictive covenant contained in the document violates state and federal fair housing laws and is void.

V. Housing Financial Discrimination Act (Redlining)

The Housing Financial Discrimination Act of 1977 (Sections 35800-35833 of the Health and Safety Code) changed the California Health and Safety Code to include a ban on "redlining." *REDLINING is the practice of financial institutions denying loans or varying the terms of loans because of the location of the property*. Under the Housing Financial Discrimination Act this practice is now against the law.

VI. Blind and Physically Disabled

Sections 54-55.1 of the California Civil Code states that:

> "Blind persons, visually handicapped persons, and other physically disabled persons shall have the same right as the able-bodied to the full and free use of the streets, highways, sidewalks, walkways, public buildings, public facilities, medical facilities (including hospitals, clinics, and physicians' offices), and other public places."

These are the terms of the opening section of the California Civil Code passage referring to the rights of the blind and handicapped.

Under this law, a landlord may not refuse to rent to a person because they are handicapped. In fact, even if the owner has a "no pets" policy, blind persons must be allowed their guide dogs, signal dogs, or service dogs.

Any person interfering with the rights of a blind or disabled person may be found liable, for each offense, for the actual money damages and any amount as may be determined by a jury or court sitting, and not more than three times the damages amount, but no less than $1,000 and attorney fees.

VII. National Association of Realtors® (NAR) Code of Ethics

The National Association of Realtors® (NAR) Code of Ethics is presented on the following pages.

Code of Ethics and Standards of Practice of the National Association of REALTORS® Effective January 1, 2002

Where the word REALTORS® is used in this Code and Preamble, it shall be deemed to include REALTOR-ASSOCIATE®s.

While the Code of Ethics establishes obligations that may be higher than those mandated by law, in any instance where the Code of Ethics and the law conflict, the obligations of the law must take precedence.

Preamble...

Under all is the land. Upon its wise utilization and widely allocated ownership depend the survival and growth of free institutions and of our civilization. REALTORS® should recognize that the interests of the nation and its citizens require the highest and best use of the land and the widest distribution of land ownership. They require the creation of adequate housing, the building of functioning cities, the development of productive industries and farms, and the preservation of a healthful environment.

Such interests impose obligations beyond those of ordinary commerce. They impose grave social responsibility and a patriotic duty to which REALTORS® should dedicate themselves, and for which they should be diligent in preparing themselves. REALTORS®, therefore, are zealous to maintain and improve the standards of their calling and share with their fellow REALTORS® a common responsibility for its integrity and honor.

In recognition and appreciation of their obligations to clients, customers, the public, and each other, REALTORS® continuously strive to become and remain informed on issues affecting real estate and, as knowledgeable professionals, they willingly share the fruit of their experience and study with others. They identify and take steps, through enforcement of this Code of Ethics and by assisting appropriate regulatory bodies, to eliminate practices which may damage the public or which might discredit or bring dishonor to the real estate profession. REALTORS® having direct personal knowledge of conduct that may violate the Code of Ethics involving misappropriation of client or customer funds or property, willful discrimination, or fraud resulting in substantial economic harm, bring such matters to the attention of the appropriate Board or Association of REALTORS®. (Amended 1/00)

Realizing that cooperation with other real estate professionals promotes the best interests of those who utilize their services, REALTORS® urge exclusive representation of clients; do not attempt to gain any unfair advantage over their competitors; and they refrain from making unsolicited comments about other practitioners. In instances where their opinion is sought, or where REALTORS® believe that comment is necessary, their opinion is offered in an objective, professional manner, uninfluenced by any personal motivation or potential advantage or gain.

The term REALTORS® has come to connote competency, fairness, and high integrity resulting from adherence to a lofty ideal of moral conduct in business relations. No inducement of profit and no instruction from clients ever can justify departure from this ideal.

In the interpretation of this obligation, REALTORS® can take no safer guide than that which has been handed down through the centuries, embodied in the Golden Rule, "Whatsoever ye would that others should do to you, do ye even so to them."

Accepting this standard as their own, REALTORS® pledge to observe its spirit in all of their activities and to conduct their business in accordance with the tenets set forth below.

Duties to Clients and Customers
Article 1

When representing a buyer, seller, landlord, tenant, or other client as an agent, REALTORS® pledge themselves to protect and promote the interests of their client. This obligation to the client is primary, but it does not relieve REALTORS® of their obligation to treat all parties honestly. When serving a buyer, seller, landlord, tenant or other party in a non-agency capacity, REALTORS® remain obligated to treat all parties honestly. (Amended 1/01)

Standard of Practice 1-1

REALTORS®, when acting as principals in a real estate transaction, remain obligated by the duties imposed by the Code of Ethics. (Amended 1/93)

Standard of Practice 1-2

The duties the Code of Ethics imposes are applicable whether REALTORS® are acting as agents or in legally recognized non-agency capacities except that any duty imposed exclusively on agents by law or regulation shall not be imposed by this Code of Ethics on REALTORS® acting in non-agency capacities. As used in this Code of Ethics, "client" means the person(s) or entity(ies) with whom a REALTOR® or a REALTOR®'s firm has an agency or legally recognized non-agency relationship; "customer" means a party to a real estate transaction who receives information, services, or benefits but has no contractual relationship with the REALTOR® or the REALTOR®'s firm; "agent" means a real estate licensee (including brokers and sales associates) acting in an agency relationship as defined by state law or regulation; and "broker" means a real estate licensee (including brokers and sales associates) acting as an agent or in a legally recognized non-agency capacity. (Adopted 1/95, Amended 1/99)

Standard of Practice 1-3

REALTORS®, in attempting to secure a listing, shall not deliberately mislead the owner as to market value.

Standard of Practice 1-4

REALTORS®, when seeking to become a buyer/tenant representative, shall not mislead buyers or tenants as to savings or other benefits that might be realized through use of the REALTOR®'s services. (Amended 1/93)

Standard of Practice 1-5

REALTORS® may represent the seller/landlord and buyer/tenant in the same transaction only after full disclosure to and with informed consent of both parties. (Adopted 1/93)

Standard of Practice 1-6

REALTORS® shall submit offers and counter-offers objectively and as quickly as possible. (Adopted 1/93, Amended 1/95)

NATIONAL ASSOCIATION OF REALTORS®

The Voice for Real Estate®

www.realtor.org/realtororg.nsf/pages/narcode
DRE Code of Ethics

Standard of Practice 1-7

When acting as listing brokers, REALTORS® shall continue to submit to the seller/landlord all offers and counter-offers until closing or execution of a lease unless the seller/landlord has waived this obligation in writing. REALTORS® shall not be obligated to continue to market the property after an offer has been accepted by the seller/landlord. REALTORS® shall recommend that sellers/landlords obtain the advice of legal counsel prior to acceptance of a subsequent offer except where the acceptance is contingent on the termination of the pre-existing purchase contract or lease. (Amended 1/93)

Standard of Practice 1-8

REALTORS® acting as agents or brokers of buyers/tenants shall submit to buyers/tenants all offers and counter-offers until acceptance but have no obligation to continue to show properties to their clients after an offer has been accepted unless otherwise agreed in writing. REALTORS® acting as agents or brokers of buyers/tenants shall recommend that buyers/tenants obtain the advice of legal counsel if there is a question as to whether a pre-existing contract has been terminated. (Adopted 1/93, Amended 1/99)

Standard of Practice 1-9

The obligation of REALTORS® to preserve confidential information (as defined by state law) provided by their clients in the course of any agency relationship or non-agency relationship recognized by law continues after termination of agency relationships or any non-agency relationships recognized by law. REALTORS® shall not knowingly, during or following the termination of professional relationships with their clients: 1) reveal confidential information of clients; or 2) use confidential information of clients to the disadvantage of clients; or 3) use confidential information of clients for the REALTOR®'s advantage or the advantage of third parties unless: a) clients consent after full disclosure; or b) REALTORS® are required by court order; or c) it is the intention of a client to commit a crime and the information is necessary to prevent the crime; or d) it is necessary to defend a REALTOR® or the REALTOR®'s employees or associates against an accusation of wrongful conduct. Information concerning latent material defects is not considered confidential information under this Code of Ethics. (Adopted 1/93, Amended 1/01)

Standard of Practice 1-10

REALTORS® shall, consistent with the terms and conditions of their real estate licensure and their property management agreement, competently manage the property of clients with due regard for the rights, safety and health of tenants and others lawfully on the premises. (Adopted 1/95, Amended 1/00)

Standard of Practice 1-11

REALTORS® who are employed to maintain or manage a client's property shall exercise due diligence and make reasonable efforts to protect it against reasonably foreseeable contingencies and losses. (Adopted 1/95)

Standard of Practice 1-12

When entering into listing contracts, REALTORS® must advise sellers/landlords of: 1) the REALTOR®'s general company policies regarding cooperation with and compensation to subagents, buyer/tenant/agents and/or brokers acting in legally recognized non-agency capacities; 2) the fact that buyer/tenant agents or brokers, even if compensated by listing brokers, or by sellers/landlords may represent the interests of buyers/tenants; and 3) any potential for listing brokers to act as disclosed dual agents, e.g. buyer/tenant agents. (Adopted 1/93, Renumbered 1/98, Amended 1/99)

Standard of Practice 1-13

When entering into buyer/tenant agreements, REALTORS® must advise potential clients of: 1) the REALTOR®'s general company policies regarding cooperation and compensation; and 2) any potential for the buyer/tenant representative to act as a disclosed dual agent, e.g. listing broker, subagent, landlord's agent, etc. (Adopted 1/93, Renumbered 1/98, Amended 1/99)

Standard of Practice 1-14

Fees for preparing appraisals or other valuations shall not be contingent upon the amount of the appraisal or valuation. (Adopted 1/02)

Article 2

REALTORS® shall avoid exaggeration, misrepresentation, or concealment of pertinent facts relating to the property or the transaction. REALTORS® shall not, however, be obligated to discover latent defects in the property, to advise on matters outside the scope of their real estate license, or to disclose facts which are confidential under the scope of agency or non-agency relationships as defined by state law. (Amended 1/00)

Standard of Practice 2-1

REALTORS® shall only be obligated to discover and disclose adverse factors reasonably apparent to someone with expertise in those areas required by their real estate licensing authority. Article 2 does not impose upon the REALTOR® the obligation of expertise in other professional or technical disciplines. (Amended 1/96)

Standard of Practice 2-2

(Renumbered as Standard of Practice 1-12 1/98)

Standard of Practice 2-3

(Renumbered as Standard of Practice 1-13 1/98)

Standard of Practice 2-4

REALTORS® shall not be parties to the naming of a false consideration in any document, unless it be the naming of an obviously nominal consideration.

Standard of Practice 2-5

Factors defined as "non-material" by law or regulation or which are expressly referenced in law or regulation as not being subject to disclosure are considered not "pertinent" for purposes of Article 2. (Adopted 1/93)

Article 3

REALTORS® shall cooperate with other brokers except when cooperation is not in the client's best interest. The obligation to cooperate does not include the obligation to share commissions, fees, or to otherwise compensate another broker. (Amended 1/95)

Standard of Practice 3-1

REALTORS®, acting as exclusive agents or brokers of sellers/landlords, establish the terms and conditions of offers to cooperate. Unless expressly indicated in offers to cooperate, cooperating brokers may not assume that the offer of cooperation includes an offer of compensation. Terms of compensation, if any, shall be ascertained by cooperating brokers before beginning efforts to accept the offer of cooperation. (Amended 1/99)

Standard of Practice 3-2

REALTORS® shall, with respect to offers of compensation to another REALTOR®, timely communicate any change of compensation for cooperative services to the other REALTOR® prior to the time such REALTOR® produces an offer to purchase/lease the property. (Amended 1/94)

Standard of Practice 3-3

Standard of Practice 3-2 does not preclude the listing broker and cooperating broker from entering into an agreement to change cooperative compensation. (Adopted 1/94)

Standard of Practice 3-4

REALTORS®, acting as listing brokers, have an affirmative obligation to disclose the existence of dual or variable rate commission arrangements (i.e., listings where one amount of commission is payable if the listing broker's firm is the procuring cause of sale/lease and a different amount of commission is payable if the sale/lease results through the efforts of the seller/landlord or a cooperating broker). The listing broker shall, as soon as practical, disclose the existence of such arrangements to potential cooperating brokers and shall, in response to inquiries from cooperating brokers, disclose the differential that would result in a cooperative transaction or in a sale/lease that results through the efforts of the seller/landlord. If the cooperating broker is a buyer/tenant representative, the buyer/tenant representative must disclose such information to their client before the client makes an offer to purchase or lease. (Amended 1/02)

Standard of Practice 3-5

It is the obligation of subagents to promptly disclose all pertinent facts to the principal's agent prior to as well as after a purchase or lease agreement is executed. (Amended 1/93)

Standard of Practice 3-6

REALTORS® shall disclose the existence of an accepted offer to any broker seeking cooperation. (Adopted 5/86)

Standard of Practice 3-7

When seeking information from another REALTOR® concerning property under a management or listing agreement, REALTORS® shall disclose their REALTOR® status and whether their interest is personal or on behalf of a client and, if on behalf of a client, their representational status. (Amended 1/95)

Standard of Practice 3-8

REALTORS® shall not misrepresent the availability of access to show or inspect a listed property. (Amended 11/87)

Article 4

REALTORS® shall not acquire an interest in or buy or present offers from themselves, any member of their immediate families, their firms or any member thereof, or any entities in which they have any ownership interest, any real property without making their true position known to the owner or the owner's agent or broker. In selling property they own, or in which they have any interest, REALTORS® shall reveal their ownership or interest in writing to the purchaser or the purchaser's representative. (Amended 1/00)

Standard of Practice 4-1

For the protection of all parties, the disclosures required by Article 4 shall be in writing and provided by REALTORS® prior to the signing of any contract. (Adopted 2/86)

Article 5

REALTORS® shall not undertake to provide professional services concerning a property or its value where they have a present or contemplated interest unless such interest is specifically disclosed to all affected parties.

Article 6

REALTORS® shall not accept any commission, rebate, or profit on expenditures made for their client, without the client's knowledge and consent. When recommending real estate products or services (e.g., homeowner's insurance, warranty programs, mortgage financing, title insurance, etc.), REALTORS® shall disclose to the client or customer to whom the recommendation is made any financial benefits or fees, other than real estate referral fees, the REALTOR® or REALTOR®'s firm may receive as a direct result of such recommendation. (Amended 1/99)

Standard of Practice 6-1

REALTORS® shall not recommend or suggest to a client or a customer the use of services of another organization or business entity in which they have a direct interest without disclosing such interest at the time of the recommendation or suggestion. (Amended 5/88)

Article 7

In a transaction, REALTORS® shall not accept compensation from more than one party, even if permitted by law, without disclosure to all parties and the informed consent of the REALTOR®'s client or clients. (Amended 1/93)

Article 8

REALTORS® shall keep in a special account in an appropriate financial institution, separated from their own funds, monies coming into their possession in trust for other persons, such as escrows, trust funds, clients' monies, and other like items.

Article 9

REALTORS®, for the protection of all parties, shall assure whenever possible that agreements shall be in writing, and shall be in clear and understandable language expressing the specific terms, conditions, obligations and commitments of the parties. A copy of each agreement shall be furnished to each party upon their signing or initialing. (Amended 1/95)

Standard of Practice 9-1

For the protection of all parties, REALTORS® shall use reasonable care to ensure that documents pertaining to the purchase, sale, or lease of real estate are kept current through the use of written extensions or amendments. (Amended 1/93)

Duties to the Public

Article 10

REALTORS® shall not deny equal professional services to any person for reasons of race, color, religion, sex, handicap, familial status, or national origin. REALTORS® shall not be parties to any plan or agreement to discriminate against a person or persons on the basis of race, color, religion, sex, handicap, familial status, or national origin. (Amended 1/90) REALTORS®, in their real estate employment practices, shall not discriminate against any person or persons on the basis of race, color, religion, sex, handicap, familial status, or national origin. (Amended 1/00)

Standard of Practice 10-1

REALTORS® shall not volunteer information regarding the racial, religious or ethnic composition of any neighborhood and shall not engage in any activity which may result in panic selling. REALTORS® shall not print, display or circulate any statement or advertisement with respect to the selling or renting of a property that indicates any preference, limitations or discrimination based on race, color, religion, sex, handicap, familial status, or national origin. (Adopted 1/94)

Standard of Practice 10-2

As used in Article 10 "real estate employment practices" relates to employees and independent contractors providing real-estate related services and the administrative and clerical staff directly supporting those individuals. (Adopted 1/00)

Article 11

The services which REALTORS® provide to their clients and customers shall conform to the standards of practice and competence which are reasonably expected in the specific real estate disciplines in which they engage; specifically, residential real estate brokerage, real property management, commercial and industrial real estate brokerage, real estate appraisal, real estate counseling, real estate syndication, real estate auction, and international real estate.

REALTORS® shall not undertake to provide specialized professional services concerning a type of property or service that is outside their field of competence unless they engage the assistance of one who is competent on such types of property or service, or unless the facts are fully disclosed to the client. Any persons engaged to provide such assistance shall be so identified to the client and their contribution to the assignment should be set forth. (Amended 1/95)

Standard of Practice 11-1

When REALTORS® prepare opinions of real property value or price, other than in pursuit of a listing or to assist a potential purchaser in formulating a purchase offer, such opinions shall include the following: 1) identification of the subject property 2) date prepared 3) defined value or price 4) limiting conditions, including statements of purpose(s) and intended user(s) 5) any present or contemplated interest, including the possibility of representing the seller/landlord or buyers/tenants 6) basis for the opinion, including applicable market data 7) if the opinion is not an appraisal, a statement to that effect. (Amended 1/01)

Standard of Practice 11-2

The obligations of the Code of Ethics in respect of real estate disciplines other than appraisal shall be interpreted and applied in accordance with the standards of competence and practice which clients and the public reasonably require to protect their rights and interests considering the complexity of the transaction, the availability of expert assistance, and, where the REALTOR® is an agent or subagent, the obligations of a fiduciary. (Adopted 1/95)

Standard of Practice 11-3

When REALTORS® provide consultive services to clients which involve advice or counsel for a fee (not a commission), such advice shall be rendered in an objective manner and the fee shall not be contingent on the substance of the advice or counsel given. If brokerage or transaction services are to be provided in addition to consultive services, a separate compensation may be paid with prior agreement between the client and REALTOR®. (Adopted 1/96)

Standard of Practice 11-4

The competency required by Article 11 relates to services contracted for between REALTORS® and their clients or customers; the duties expressly imposed by the Code of Ethics; and the duties imposed by law or regulation. (Adopted 1/02)

Article 12

REALTORS® shall be careful at all times to present a true picture in their advertising and representations to the public. REALTORS® shall also ensure that their professional status (e.g., broker, appraiser, property manager, etc.) or status as REALTORS® is clearly identifiable in any such advertising. (Amended 1/93)

Standard of Practice 12-1

REALTORS® may use the term "free" and similar terms in their advertising and in other representations provided that all terms governing availability of the offered product or service are clearly disclosed at the same time. (Amended 1/97)

Standard of Practice 12-2

REALTORS® may represent their services as "free" or without cost even if they expect to receive compensation from a source other than their client provided that the potential for the REALTOR® to obtain a benefit from a third party is clearly disclosed at the same time. (Amended 1/97)

Standard of Practice 12-3

The offering of premiums, prizes, merchandise discounts or other inducements to list, sell, purchase, or lease is not, in itself, unethical even if receipt of the benefit is contingent on listing, selling, purchasing, or leasing through the REALTOR® making the offer. However, REALTORS® must exercise care and candor in any such advertising or other public or private representations so that any party interested in receiving or otherwise benefiting from the REALTOR®'s offer will have clear, thorough, advance understanding of all the terms and conditions of the offer. The offering of any inducements to do business is subject to the limitations and restrictions of state law and the ethical obligations established by any applicable Standard of Practice. (Amended 1/95)

Standard of Practice 12-4

REALTORS® shall not offer for sale/lease or advertise property without authority. When acting as listing brokers or as subagents, REALTORS® shall not quote a price different from that agreed upon with the seller/landlord. (Amended 1/93)

Standard of Practice 12-5

REALTORS® shall not advertise nor permit any person employed by or affiliated with them to advertise listed property without disclosing the name of the firm. (Adopted 11/86)

Standard of Practice 12-6

REALTORS®, when advertising unlisted real property for sale/lease in which they have an ownership interest, shall disclose their status as both owners/landlords and as REALTORS® or real estate licensees. (Amended 1/93)

Standard of Practice 12-7

Only REALTORS® who participated in the transaction as the listing broker or cooperating broker (selling broker) may claim to have "sold" the property. Prior to closing, a cooperating broker may post a "sold" sign only with the consent of the listing broker. (Amended 1/96)

Article 13

REALTORS® shall not engage in activities that constitute the unauthorized practice of law and shall recommend that legal counsel be obtained when the interest of any party to the transaction requires it.

Article 14

If charged with unethical practice or asked to present evidence or to cooperate in any other way, in any professional standards proceeding or investigation, REALTORS® shall place all pertinent facts before the proper tribunals of the Member Board or affiliated institute, society, or council in which membership is held and shall take no action to disrupt or obstruct such processes. (Amended 1/99)

Standard of Practice 14-1

REALTORS® shall not be subject to disciplinary proceedings in more than one Board of REALTORS® or affiliated institute, society or council in which they hold membership with respect to alleged violations of the Code of Ethics relating to the same transaction or event. (Amended 1/95)

Standard of Practice 14-2

REALTORS® shall not make any unauthorized disclosure or dissemination of the allegations, findings, or decision developed in connection with an ethics hearing or appeal or in connection with an arbitration hearing or procedural review. (Amended 1/92)

Standard of Practice 14-3

REALTORS® shall not obstruct the Board's investigative or professional standards proceedings by instituting or threatening to institute actions for libel, slander or defamation against any party to a professional standards proceeding or their witnesses based on the filing of an arbitration request, an ethics complaint, or testimony given before any tribunal. (Adopted 11/87, Amended 1/99)

Standard of Practice 14-4

REALTORS® shall not intentionally impede the Board's investigative or disciplinary proceedings by filing multiple ethics complaints based on the same event or transaction. (Adopted 11/88)

Duties to REALTORS®

Article 15

REALTORS® shall not knowingly or recklessly make false or misleading statements about competitors, their businesses, or their business practices. (Amended 1/92)

Standard of Practice 15-1

REALTORS® shall not knowingly or recklessly file false or unfounded ethics complaints. (Adopted 1/00)

Article 16

REALTORS® shall not engage in any practice or take any action inconsistent with the agency or other exclusive relationship recognized by law that other REALTORS® have with clients. (Amended 1/98)

Standard of Practice 16-1

Article 16 is not intended to prohibit aggressive or innovative business practices which are otherwise ethical and does not prohibit disagreements with other REALTORS® involving commission, fees, compensation or other forms of payment or expenses. (Adopted 1/93, Amended 1/95)

Standard of Practice 16-2

Article 16 does not preclude REALTORS® from making general announcements to prospective clients describing their services and the terms of their availability even though some recipients may have entered into agency agreements or other exclusive relationships with another REALTOR®. A general telephone canvass, general mailing or distribution addressed to all prospective clients in a given geographical area or in a given profession, business, club, or organization, or other classification or group is deemed "general" for purposes of this standard. (Amended 1/98)

Article 16 is intended to recognize as unethical two basic types of solicitations:

First, telephone or personal solicitations of property owners who have been identified by a real estate sign, multiple listing compilation, or other information service as having exclusively listed their property with another REALTOR®; and Second, mail or other forms of written solicitations of prospective clients whose properties are exclusively listed with another REALTOR® when such solicitations are not part of a general mailing but are directed specifically to property owners identified through compilations of current listings, "for sale" or "for rent" signs, or other sources of information required by Article 3 and Multiple Listing Service rules to be made available to other REALTORS® under offers of subagency or cooperation. (Amended 1/93)

Standard of Practice 16-3

Article 16 does not preclude REALTORS® from contacting the client of another broker for the purpose of offering to provide, or entering into a contract to provide, a different type of real estate service unrelated to the type of service currently being provided (e.g., property management as opposed to brokerage). However, information received through a Multiple Listing Service or any other offer of cooperation may not be used to target clients of other REALTORS® to whom such offers to provide services may be made. (Amended 1/93)

Standard of Practice 16-4

REALTORS® shall not solicit a listing which is currently listed exclusively with another broker. However, if the listing broker, when asked by the REALTOR®, refuses to disclose the expiration date and nature of such listing; i.e., an exclusive right to sell, an exclusive agency, open listing, or other form of contractual agreement between the listing broker and the client, the REALTOR® may contact the owner to secure such information and may discuss the terms upon which the REALTOR® might take a future listing or, alternatively, may take a listing to become effective upon expiration of any existing exclusive listing. (Amended 1/94)

Standard of Practice 16-5

REALTORS® shall not solicit buyer/tenant agreements from buyers/tenants who are subject to exclusive buyer/tenant agreements. However, if asked by a REALTOR®, the broker refuses to disclose the expiration date of the exclusive buyer/tenant agreement, the REALTOR® may contact the buyer/tenant to secure such information and may discuss the terms upon which the REALTOR® might enter into a future buyer/tenant agreement or, alternatively, may enter into a buyer/tenant agreement to become effective upon the expiration of any existing exclusive buyer/tenant agreement. (Adopted 1/94, Amended 1/98)

Standard of Practice 16-6

When REALTORS® are contacted by the client of another REALTOR® regarding the creation of an exclusive relationship to provide the same type of service, and REALTORS® have not directly or indirectly initiated such discussions, they may discuss the terms upon which they might enter into a future agreement or, alternatively, may enter into an agreement which becomes effective upon expiration of any existing exclusive agreement. (Amended 1/98)

Standard of Practice 16-7

The fact that a client has retained a REALTOR® as an agent or in another exclusive relationship in one or more past transactions does not preclude other REALTORS® from seeking such former client's future business. (Amended 1/98)

Standard of Practice 16-8

The fact that an exclusive agreement has been entered into with a REALTOR® shall not preclude or inhibit any other REALTOR® from entering into a similar agreement after the expiration of the prior agreement. (Amended 1/98)

Standard of Practice 16-9

REALTORS®, prior to entering into an agency agreement or other exclusive relationship, have an affirmative obligation to make reasonable efforts to determine whether the client is subject to a current, valid exclusive agreement to provide the same type of real estate service. (Amended 1/98)

Standard of Practice 16-10

REALTORS®, acting as agents of, or in another relationship with, buyers or tenants, shall disclose that relationship to the seller/landlord's agent or broker at first contact and shall provide written confirmation of that disclosure to the seller/landlord's agent or broker not later than execution of a purchase agreement or lease. (Amended 1/98)

Standard of Practice 16-11

On unlisted property, REALTORS® acting as buyer/ tenant agents or brokers shall disclose that relationship to the seller/landlord at first contact for that client and shall provide written confirmation of such disclosure to the seller/landlord not later than execution of any purchase or lease agreement.

REALTORS® shall make any request for anticipated compensation from the seller/landlord at first contact. (Amended 1/98)

Standard of Practice 16-12

REALTORS®, acting as agents or brokers of sellers/ landlords or as subagents of listing brokers, shall disclose that relationship to buyers/tenants as soon as practicable and shall provide written confirmation of such disclosure to buyers/tenants not later than execution of any purchase or lease agreement. (Amended 1/98)

Standard of Practice 16-13

All dealings concerning property exclusively listed, or with buyer/tenants who are subject to an exclusive agreement shall be carried on with the client's agent or broker, and not with the client, except with the consent of the client's agent or broker or except where such dealings are initiated by the client. (Adopted 1/93, Amended 1/98)

Standard of Practice 16-14

REALTORS® are free to enter into contractual relationships or to negotiate with sellers/landlords, buyers/tenants or others who are not subject to an exclusive agreement but shall not knowingly obligate them to pay more than one commission except with their informed consent. (Amended 1/98)

Standard of Practice 16-15

In cooperative transactions REALTORS® shall compensate cooperating REALTORS® (principal brokers) and shall not compensate nor offer to compensate, directly or indirectly, any of the sales licensees employed by or affiliated with other REALTORS® without the prior express knowledge and consent of the cooperating broker.

Standard of Practice 16-16

REALTORS®, acting as subagents or buyer/tenant agents or brokers, shall not use the terms of an offer to purchase/lease to attempt to modify the listing broker's offer of compensation to subagents or buyer's agents or brokers nor make the submission of an executed offer to purchase/lease contingent on the listing broker's agreement to modify the offer of compensation. (Amended 1/98)

Standard of Practice 16-17

REALTORS® acting as subagents or as buyer/tenant agents or brokers, shall not attempt to extend a listing broker's offer of cooperation and/or compensation to other brokers without the consent of the listing broker. (Amended 1/98)

Standard of Practice 16-18

REALTORS® shall not use information obtained from listing brokers through offers to cooperate made through multiple listing services or through other offers of cooperation to refer listing brokers' clients to other brokers or to create buyer/ tenant relationships with listing brokers' clients, unless such use is authorized by listing brokers. (Amended 1/02)

Standard of Practice 16-19

Signs giving notice of property for sale, rent, lease, or exchange shall not be placed on property without consent of the seller/landlord. (Amended 1/93)

Standard of Practice 16-20

REALTORS®, prior to or after terminating their relationship with their current firm, shall not induce clients of their current firm to cancel exclusive contractual agreements between the client and that firm. This does not preclude REALTORS® (principals) from establishing agreements with their associated licensees governing assignability of exclusive agreements. (Adopted 1/98)

Article 17

In the event of contractual disputes or specific non-contractual disputes as defined in Standard of Practice 17-4 between REALTORS® (principals) associated with different firms, arising out of their relationship as REALTORS®, the REALTORS® shall submit the dispute to arbitration in accordance with the regulations of their Board or Boards rather than litigate the matter.

In the event clients of REALTORS® wish to arbitrate contractual disputes arising out of real estate transactions, REALTORS® shall arbitrate those disputes in accordance with the regulations of their Board, provided the clients agree to be bound by the decision. The obligation to participate in arbitration contemplated by this Article includes the obligation of REALTORS® (principals) to cause their firms to arbitrate and be bound by any award. (Amended 1/01)

Standard of Practice 17-1

The filing of litigation and refusal to withdraw from it by REALTORS® in an arbitrable matter constitutes a refusal to arbitrate. (Adopted 2/86)

Standard of Practice 17-2

Article 17 does not require REALTORS® to arbitrate in those circumstances when all parties to the dispute advise the Board in writing that they choose not to arbitrate before the Board. (Amended 1/93)

Standard of Practice 17-3

REALTORS®, when acting solely as principals in a real estate transaction, are not obligated to arbitrate disputes with other REALTORS® absent a specific written agreement to the contrary. (Adopted 1/96)

Standard of Practice 17-4

Specific non-contractual disputes that are subject to arbitration pursuant to Article 17 are:

1) Where a listing broker has compensated a cooperating broker and another cooperating broker subsequently claims to be the procuring cause of the sale or lease. In such cases the complainant may name the first cooperating broker as respondent and arbitration may proceed without the listing broker being named as a respondent. Alternatively, if the complaint is brought against the listing broker, the listing broker may name the first cooperating broker as a third-party respondent. In either instance the decision of the hearing panel as to procuring cause shall be conclusive with respect to all current or subsequent claims of the parties for compensation arising out of the underlying cooperative transaction. (Adopted 1/97)

2) Where a buyer or tenant representative is compensated by the seller or landlord, and not by the listing broker, and the listing broker, as a result, reduces the commission owed by the seller or landlord and, subsequent to such actions, another cooperating broker claims to be the procuring cause of sale or lease. In such cases the complainant may name the first cooperating broker as respondent and arbitration may proceed without the listing broker being named as a respondent. Alternatively, if the complaint is brought against the listing broker, the listing broker may name the first cooperating broker as a third-party respondent. In either instance the decision of the hearing panel as to procuring cause shall be conclusive with respect to all current or subsequent claims of the parties for compensation arising out of the underlying cooperative transaction. (Adopted 1/97)

3) Where a buyer or tenant representative is compensated by the buyer or tenant and, as a result, the listing broker reduces the commission owed by the seller or landlord and, subsequent to such actions, another cooperating broker claims to be the procuring cause of sale or lease. In such cases the complainant may name the first cooperating broker as respondent and arbitration may proceed without the listing broker being named as a respondent. Alternatively, if the complaint is brought against the listing broker, the listing broker may name the first cooperating broker as a third-party respondent. In either instance the decision of the hearing panel as to procuring cause shall be conclusive with respect to all current or subsequent claims of the parties for compensation arising out of the underlying cooperative transaction. (Adopted 1/97)

4) Where two or more listing brokers claim entitlement to compensation pursuant to open listings with a seller or landlord who agrees to participate in arbitration (or who requests arbitration) and who agrees to be bound by the decision. In cases where one of the listing brokers has been compensated by the seller or landlord, the other listing broker, as complainant, may name the first listing broker as respondent and arbitration may proceed between the brokers. (Adopted 1/97)

The Code of Ethics was adopted in 1913. Amended at the Annual Convention in 1924, 1928, 1950, 1951, 1952, 1955, 1956, 1961, 1962, 1974, 1982, 1986, 1987, 1989, 1990, 1991, 1992, 1993, 1994, 1995, 1996, 1997, 1998, 1999, 2000, and 2001.

Explanatory Notes

The reader should be aware of the following policies which have been approved by the Board of Directors of the National Association:

In filing a charge of an alleged violation of the Code of Ethics by a REALTOR®, the charge must read as an alleged violation of one or more Articles of the Code. Standards of Practice may be cited in support of the charge.

The Standards of Practice serve to clarify the ethical obligations imposed by the various Articles and supplement, and do not substitute for, the Case Interpretations in Interpretations of the Code of Ethics.

Modifications to existing Standards of Practice and additional new Standards of Practice are approved from time to time. Readers are cautioned to ensure that the most recent publications are utilized.

VIII. National Association of Real Estate Brokers (NAREB) - Code of Ethics

A. PART I. RELATIONS TO THE PUBLIC

1. A REALTIST IS NEVER RELIEVED OF THE RESPONSIBILITY TO OBSERVE FULLY THIS CODE OF ETHICS.

2. A REALTIST SHOULD NEVER BE INSTRUMENTAL IN ESTABLISHING, REENFORCING OR EXTENDING LEASED OR DEED RESTRICTIONS THAT LIMIT THE USE AND/OR OCCUPANCY OF REAL PROPERTY TO ANY RACIAL, RELIGIOUS OR NATIONAL ORIGIN GROUPS.

3. THE REALTIST REALIZES THAT IT IS HIS (OR HER) DUTY TO PROTECT THE PUBLIC AGAINST ANY MISREPRESENTATIONS, UNETHICAL PRACTICES OR FRAUD IN HIS (OR HER) REAL ESTATE PRACTICES, AND THAT HE (OR SHE) OFFER ALL PROPERTIES ON HIS (OR HER) LISTING SOLELY ON MERIT AND WITHOUT EXAGGERATION, CONCEALMENT, DECEPTION OR MISLEADING INFORMATION.

A REALTIST SHOULD ALWAYS AVOID OFFERING A PROPERTY WITHOUT (A) WRITTEN AUTHORIZATION OF THE OWNER OR A PERSON ACTING IN HIS (OR HER) BEHALF BY POWER OF ATTORNEY, (B) FULLY INFORMING HIMSELF (OR HERSELF) OF THE PERTINENT FACTS CONCERNING THE PROPERTY, AND (C) ADVISING HIS CLIENT TO SECURE ADVICE OF COUNSEL AS TO THE LEGALITY OF INSTRUMENTS BEFORE RECEIVING OR CONVEYING TITLE OR POSSESSION OF REAL PROPERTY, LAWS, PROPOSED LEGISLATION AND PUBLIC POLICY RELATIVE TO THE USE AND/OR OCCUPANCY OF THE PROPERTY.

5. THE REALTIST SHOULD ALWAYS OFFER THE PROPERTY AT THE PRICE THE OWNER HAS AGREED TO ACCEPT, BUT NEVER GREATER.

6. THE REALTIST SHOULD ALWAYS INFORM ALL PARTIES OF HIS (OR HER) OWN POSITION IN THE TRANSACTION AND SHOULD NOT DEMAND OR ACCEPT A COMMISSION FROM BOTH PARTIES, EXCEPT WITH THE KNOWLEDGE AND CONSENT IN WRITING AND SIGNED BY ALL PARTIES.

7. THE REALTIST SHOULD BE DILIGENT IN PREVENTING PROPERTY UNDER HIS MANAGEMENT FROM BEING USED FOR IMMORAL OR ILLEGAL PURPOSES.

8. THE REALTIST REALIZES THAT ALL CONTRACTS AND AGREEMENTS FOR THE OWNERSHIP, USE AND/OR OCCUPANCY OF REAL PROPERTIES SHOULD BE IN WRITING AND SIGNED BY ALL PARTIES, OR THEIR LAWFULLY AUTHORIZED AGENTS.

9. THE REALTIST SHOULD DISCLOSE THE FACT, IF HE (OR SHE) IS PURCHASING A PROPERTY TO THE ACCOUNT OF HIS (OR HER) CLIENT AND IF HE (OR SHE) HAS A PERSONAL INTEREST IN THE OWNERSHIP.

B. PROFESSIONAL RELATIONS

1. THE REALTIST SHOULD ALWAYS BE LOYAL TO HIS LOCAL BOARD OR REAL ESTATE BROKERS AND ACTIVE IN ITS WORK.

   THE FELLOWSHIP OF HIS (OR HER) ASSOCIATES AND THE MUTUAL SHARING OF EXPERIENCES ARE ALWAYS ASSETS TO HIS OWN BUSINESS.

2. THE REALTIST SHOULD SO CONDUCT HIS (OR HER) BUSINESS AS TO AVOID CONTROVERSIES WITH HIS (OR HER) FELLOW REALTISTS. CONTROVERSIES BETWEEN REALTISTS, WHO ARE MEMBERS OF THE SAME LOCAL BOARD OF REAL ESTATE BROKERS, SHOULD BE SUBMITTED IN WRITING FOR ARBITRATION IN ACCORDANCE WITH THE REGULATIONS OF HIS OR HER REAL ESTATE BOARD AND NOT IN AN ACTION AT LAW. THE DECISION IN SUCH ARBITRATION SHOULD BE ACCEPTED AS FINAL AND BINDING.

3. CONTROVERSIES BETWEEN REALTIST WHO ARE NOT MEMBERS OF THE SAME LOCAL BOARD SHOULD BE SUBMITTED FOR ARBITRATION TO AN ARBITRATION BOARD CONSISTING OF ONE ARBITRATOR CHOSEN BY EACH REALTIST FROM THE BOARD OF REAL ESTATE

BROKERS TO WHICH HE (OR SHE) BELONGS AND ONE OTHER MEMBER, OR A SUFFICIENT NUMBER OF MEMBERS TO MAKE AN ODD NUMBER, SELECTED BY THE ARBITRATORS THUS CHOSEN.

ALL EMPLOYMENT ARRANGEMENTS BETWEEN BROKER AND SALESPERSON SHOULD BE REDUCED TO WRITING AND SIGNED BY BOTH PARTIES. IT IS PARTICULARLY IMPORTANT TO SPECIFY RIGHTS OF PARTIES, IN THE EVENT OF TERMINATION OF EMPLOYMENT. ALL LISTINGS ACQUIRED BY A SALESPERSON DURING HIS (OR HER) TENURE OF EMPLOYMENT WITH THE BROKER, SHALL BE THE EXCLUSIVE PROPERTY OR RIGHT OF THE EMPLOYING BROKER AFTER SUCH TERMINATION.

5. A REALTIST SHOULD NEVER PUBLICLY CRITICIZE A FELLOW REALTIST; HE (OR SHE) SHOULD NEVER EXPRESS AN OPINION OF A TRANSACTION UNLESS REQUESTED TO DO SO BY ONE OF THE PRINCIPALS AND HIS (OR HER) OPINION THEN SHOULD BE RENDERED IN ACCORDANCE WITH STRICT PROFESSIONAL COURTESY AND INTEGRITY.

6. A REALTIST SHOULD NEVER SEEK INFORMATION ABOUT FELLOW REALTISTS' TRANSACTIONS TO USE FOR THE PURPOSE OF CLOSING THE TRANSACTION HIMSELF (OR HERSELF) OR DIVERTING THE CLIENT TO ANOTHER PROPERTY.

7. WHEN A COOPERATING REALTIST ACCEPTS A LISTING FROM ANOTHER BROKER, THE AGENCY OF THE BROKER WHO OFFERS THE LISTING SHOULD BE RESPECTED UNTIL IT HAS EXPIRED AND THE PROPERTY HAS COME TO THE ATTENTION OF THE COOPERATING REALTIST FROM A DIFFERENT SOURCE, OR UNTIL THE OWNER, WITHOUT SOLICITATION, OFFERS TO LIST WITH THE COOPERATING REALTIST: FURTHERMORE, SUCH A LISTING SHOULD NOT BE PASSED ON TO A THIRD BROKER WITHOUT THE CONSENT OF THE LISTING BROKER.

8. NEGOTIATIONS CONCERNING PROPERTY WHICH IS LISTED WITH ONE REALTIST EXCLUSIVELY SHOULD BE CARRIED ON WITH THE LISTING BROKER, NOT WITH THE OWNER.

THE REALTIST IS FREE TO NEGOTIATE FEES IN THE LEASE, SALE OR EXCHANGE OF REAL ESTATE. FEES SHOULD BE BASED ON REASONABLE COMPENSATION FOR SERVICES TO BE RENDERED TO THE CLIENT. THE REALTIST SHOULD REFRAIN FROM MAKING ANY VESTIGE OF UNFAIR COMPETITION OR MAKING FEE STRUCTURES AND/OR THE ADVERTISING THEREOF IN SUCH A MANNER AS TO BE DEMEANING TO THE REAL ESTATE PROFESSION.

10. A REALTIST SHOULD NOT SOLICIT THE SERVICES OF ANY EMPLOYEE IN THE ORGANIZATION OF A FELLOW REALTIST WITHOUT THE WRITTEN CONSENT OF THE EMPLOYER.

11. SIGNS SHOULD NEVER BE PLACED ON ANY PROPERTY BY A REALTIST WITHOUT THE WRITTEN CONSENT OF THE OWNER.

C. ARTICLE I - NAME

THE NAME OF THE ORGANIZATION SHALL BE:

NATIONAL ASSOCIATION OF REAL ESTATE BROKERS,
INCORPORATED.

D. ARTICLE II - PURPOSES

THE PURPOSES OF THE NATIONAL ASSOCIATION SHALL BE:

1. Section 1

TO UNITE THOSE ENGAGED IN THE RECOGNIZED BRANCHES OF THE REAL ESTATE BUSINESS, INCLUDING BROKERAGE, MANAGEMENT. MORTGAGE FINANCING APPRAISING, LAND DEVELOPMENT AND HOME BUILDING. AND ALLIED FIELD IN THE UNITED STATES OF AMERICA AND CANADA, FOR THE PURPOSE OF EXERTING EFFECTIVELY A COMBINED INFLUENCE UPON MATTERS AFFECTING REAL ESTATE INTERESTS:

2. Section 2

TO ENABLE ITS MEMBERS TO TRANSACT THEIR BUSINESS TO BETTER ADVANTAGE THAN HERETOFORE, BY THE ADOPTION OF SUCH RULES AND REGULATIONS AS THEY MAY DEEM PROPER:

3. Section 3

TO PROMOTE AND MAINTAIN HIGH STANDARDS OF CONDUCT IN THE TRANSACTION OF THE REAL ESTATE BUSINESS:

4. Section 4

TO FORMULATE AND ENFORCE A CODE OF ETHICS FOR THE MEMBERS OF THE NATIONAL ASSOCIATION OF REAL ESTATE BROKERS, INCORPORATED:

5. Section 5

TO LICENSE ITS MEMBERS THE RIGHT TO USE THE TERM OR SYMBOL "REALTIST" WHICH IS HEREBY DEFINED AS DESIGNATING A PERSON ENGAGED IN THE REAL ESTATE BUSINESS WHO IS A BOARD MEMBER OR INDIVIDUAL MEMBER OF THE NATIONAL ASSOCIATION OF REAL ESTATE BROKERS, INCORPORATED. IS SUBJECT TO ITS RULES AND REGULATIONS, OBSERVES ITS STANDARDS OF CONDUCT, AND IS ENTITLED TO ITS BENEFITS: AND

6. Section 6

TO PROTECT THE PUBLIC AGAINST UNETHICAL, IMPROPER OR FRAUDULENT PRACTICES BY THE AFFIXING OF THE TERM OR SYMBOL "REALTIST" TO ADVERTISING MATTER, STATIONERY, SIGNBOARDS, STOCK CERTIFICATED, BONDS, MORTGAGES, AND OTHER INSTRUMENTS OR OTHER MATERIAL USED BY OR IN CONNECTION WITH THE REAL ESTATE BUSINESS, AND TO EDUCATE THE GENERAL PUBLIC TO DEAL ONLY WITH THOSE PERSONS WHO HAVE AGREED TO OBSERVE THE STANDARDS MAINTAINED BY THE NATIONAL ASSOCIATION OF REAL ESTATE BROKERS, INCORPORATED.

E. ARTICLE III - MEMBERSHIP

1. Section 1

(A) THE MEMBERS OF THE NATIONAL ASSOCIATION OF REAL ESTATE BROKERS, INCORPORATED, SHALL CONSIST OF SEVEN (7) CLASSES:

1. MEMBER BOARDS
2. LOCAL BOARD MEMBERS
3. ASSOCIATE MEMBERS
4. INDIVIDUAL MEMBERS
5. ALLIED MEMBERS
6. HONORARY MEMBERS

1. MEMBER BOARDS SHALL CONSIST OF LOCAL BOARDS OF REAL ESTATE BROKERS WHICH SHALL INCLUDE CITY, COUNTY, OR INTER-COUNTY BOARDS AND STATE ASSOCIATIONS OF REAL ESTATE BROKERS.

2. LOCAL BOARD MEMBERS SHALL BE PERSONS WHO ARE CERTIFIED BY A LOCAL BOARD AS ELIGIBLE FOR MEMBERSHIP IN THE NATIONAL ASSOCIATION OF REAL ESTATE BROKERS, INCORPORATED.

IX. Small Business Opportunities

As a broker, you may wish to engage in a variety of activities that complement your basic real estate brokerage operation. Not only can each activity supplement income from real estate sales, but they can also provide you with additional sources of prospects. The satisfied client who has bought or sold a business through you, for instance, may become a buyer or seller of a home or income-producing property. Also, you can ask the client for referrals.

A client may purchase a security interest, such as a trust deed note, through the same broker whom he or she considers a financial adviser. A client may seek your counsel on hazard insurance for his or her property. Notary services are a convenience for your daily operations and can provide an additional source of income and prospects. Exchanging and broker specialization are other activities, for which no specialized license is required.

You should be aware of the value of informing all your clients about other services offered by your company, such as property management.

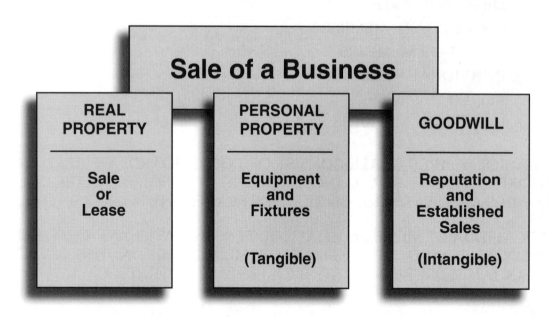

X. Selling a Business

Section 10030 of the Real Estate Law defines a *BUSINESS OPPORTUNITY as a "sale or lease of the business and goodwill of an existing business enterprise or opportunity."* Since this transaction consists of the sale of personal property, the rules and laws governing the transfer of chattels (personal property) apply. Usually the transaction involves very few assets and is comparatively small in size. Examples of this kind of business opportunity are drug stores, service stations, cocktail bars, restaurants, auto parts stores, floral shops, bakeries, garages, photo stores, hardware stores, beauty shops, delicatessens, dress shops, laundromats, liquor stores, dry cleaning establishments, and others. The principal assets that are transferred in these sales are stock-in-trade or inventory, fixtures, equipment, and **GOODWILL**, *defined as the expectation of continued public patronage.* Real property seldom is involved in the transaction; instead, the existing lease, or leasehold interest, is normally transferred to the purchaser.

A. LISTING AGREEMENT

In the first step, an agency is created by securing a listing on the business, just as in real estate.

B. UNIFORM COMMERCIAL CODE (UCC)

The **UNIFORM COMMERCIAL CODE (UCC)** *is a body of law adopted throughout the United States that standardizes a number of practices commonly found in commerce and business.*

Article 6 covers the subject of bulk transfers. It stipulates that whenever there is a sale or transfer in bulk, and not in the ordinary course of the transferor's business, certain requirements must be met in order to protect creditors of the business being transferred.

In real estate talk, the expression "bulk transfer" means the same thing as a business opportunity—an extraordinary sale of more than half of a seller's inventory and equipment.

Most entrepreneurs, who wish to grow in their businesses, borrow money for working capital to purchase inventory, to buy or lease equipment, and so on. The creditors who have played a part in the growth of the business must be protected when the owner transfers the business to another. Merchants can easily commit commercial fraud, leaving the creditors holding the bag. This type of fraud can take two forms: the owner-debtor could sell his or her stock in trade to anyone for any price, pocket the proceeds, and then disappear, leaving creditors unpaid; or the merchant owing debts might sell his or her stock to a friend for less than it's worth and pay his or her creditors less than what's owed them, hoping to come back into the business surreptitiously in the future. The requirements imposed under Article 6 of the UCC mitigate against such fraudulent practices.

Whenever a bulk sale or transfer is made, the transferee must give public notice to the transferor's creditors by recording a Notice to Creditors of Bulk Sale (Figure 15-2) at least twelve days before the bulk transfer is consummated.

Moreover, the notice to creditors must be delivered to the county tax collector before the transfer is to be consummated. This procedure must be followed in the office of

Figure 15-2

NOTICE TO CREDITORS OF BULK SALE

RECORDING REQUESTED BY AND
WHEN RECORDED, MAIL TO

ESCROW NO.   SPACE ABOVE THIS LINE FOR RECORDER USE

NOTICE TO CREDITORS OF BULK SALE
(Notice pursuant to UCC Sec. 6105)

NOTICE IS HEREBY GIVEN that a bulk sale is about to be made.
The name(s) and business address of the seller are:

Doing business as:

All other business name(s) and address(es) used by the seller(s) within the past three years, as stated by the seller(s), are:
(if none, so state):

The location in California of the chief executive office of the seller is:

The name(s) and business address of the buyer(s) are:

The assets being sold are generally described as:

and are located at:

The bulk sale is intended to be consummated at the office of:

                                          and the anticipated sale date is _____

The bulk sale _____ subject to California Uniform Commercial Code Section 6106.2.
                 is/is not

                    [If the sale is subject to Sec. 6106.2, the following information must be provided.]

The name and address of the person with whom claims may be filed is:

                              and the last day for filing claims by any creditor shall be _____
                              which is the business day before the anticipated sale date specified above.

                              _____
                              _____
                              _____
                              _____
                                              Buyer(s)
                                                        MET-LGL 1024

the county recorder in which the property is located. In addition, at least twelve days before the bulk transfer, the notice of its intended sale must be published, at least once, in a newspaper of general circulation in the judicial district in which the property is located.

Accurate completion of the **Notice to Creditors of Bulk Sale** form assures that the specific requirements of the UCC are met. These requirements include:

1. information that a bulk transfer is to be made;
2. location and general description of the property to be transferred;
3. the name and business address of the transferor, and all other names and addresses used by him within the previous three years, so far as is known to the intended transferee; and
4. the place and date on or after which the bulk transfer is to be consummated.

Noncompliance with the notice requirements renders the transfer fraudulent and void against those creditors of the transferor whose claims are based on credit transactions prior to the bulk transfer. With compliance, on the other hand, the creditors' recourse is against sellers only, not against the business or buyers.

C. SECURITY AGREEMENT AND FINANCING STATEMENT

Under **Article 9** of the Uniform Commercial Code, titled "Secured Transactions; Sales of Accounts, Contract Rights and Chattel Paper," a filing system is established as additional protection for creditors and for purchasers. It regulates security transactions in personal property, replacing a variety of previously used security instruments (conditional sales contracts, chattel mortgages, trust receipts, assignment of accounts receivable) with a uniform and comprehensive Security Agreement and Financing Statement. The *SECURITY AGREEMENT AND FINANCING STATEMENT shows the debtor's name and address (cosigners and trade names would be included); the secured party's name and address (assignee); description and nature of the property used as collateral; and other items.* (The Financing Statement is shown in **Figure 15-3**.)

Although the **Financing Statement** is subject to a Security Agreement, only the former is **filed with the Secretary of State** in California. Since California is a leader in the volume of credit transactions secured by personal property (and the Security Agreement may run many pages), to require the filing of the agreement would create a massive space and storage problem. Only the brief, one-page Financing Statement, executed in quadruplicate is required on file. Moreover, security transactions which involve consumer goods—personal, family, or household purchases—do not have to be filed. That leaves commercial transactions, the subject that you, as a broker, will be concerned with in the sale of a business opportunity.

Figure 15-3

UCC FINANCING STATEMENT

UCC FINANCING STATEMENT
FOLLOW INSTRUCTIONS (front and back) CAREFULLY

A. NAME & PHONE OF CONTACT AT FILER [optional]

B. SEND ACKNOWLEDGMENT TO: (Name and Address)

THE ABOVE SPACE IS FOR FILING OFFICE USE ONLY

1. DEBTOR'S EXACT FULL LEGAL NAME - insert only <u>one</u> debtor name (1a or 1b) - do not abbreviate or combine names

1a. ORGANIZATION'S NAME			
OR 1b. INDIVIDUAL'S LAST NAME	FIRST NAME	MIDDLE NAME	SUFFIX
1c. MAILING ADDRESS	CITY	STATE · POSTAL CODE	COUNTRY

1d TAX ID #· SSN OR FIN	ADD'L INFO RE ORGANIZATION DEBTOR	1e. TYPE OF ORGANIZATION	1f. JURISDICTION OF ORGANIZATION	1g. ORGANIZATIONAL ID #, if any
				☐ NONE

2. ADDITIONAL DEBTOR'S EXACT FULL LEGAL NAME - insert only <u>one</u> debtor name (2a or 2b) - do not abbreviate or combine names

2a. ORGANIZATION'S NAME			
OR 2b. INDIVIDUAL'S LAST NAME	FIRST NAME	MIDDLE NAME	SUFFIX
2c. MAILING ADDRESS	CITY	STATE · POSTAL CODE	COUNTRY

2d. TAX ID #: SSN OR EIN	ADD'L INFO RE ORGANIZATION DEBTOR	2e. TYPE OF ORGANIZATION	2f. JURISDICTION OF ORGANIZATION	2g. ORGANIZATIONAL ID #, if any
				☐ NONE

3. SECURED PARTY'S NAME (or NAME of TOTAL ASSIGNEE of ASSIGNOR S/P) - insert only <u>one</u> secured party name (3a or 3b)

3a. ORGANIZATION'S NAME			
OR 3b. INDIVIDUAL'S LAST NAME	FIRST NAME	MIDDLE NAME	SUFFIX
3c. MAILING ADDRESS	CITY	STATE · POSTAL CODE	COUNTRY

4. This FINANCING STATEMENT covers the following collateral:

5. ALTERNATIVE DESIGNATION [if applicable]:	☐ LESSEE/LESSOR	☐ CONSIGNEE/CONSIGNOR	☐ BAILEE/BAILOR	☐ SELLER/BUYER	☐ AG. LIEN	☐ NON-UCC FILING

6. ☐ This FINANCING STATEMENT is to be filed [for record] (or recorded) in the REAL ESTATE RECORDS.   Attach Addendum   [if applicable] | 7. Check to REQUEST SEARCH REPORT(S) on Debtor(s) [ADDITIONAL FEE]   [optional] | ☐ All Debtors | ☐ Debtor 1 | ☐ Debtor 2

8. OPTIONAL FILER REFERENCE DATA

FILING OFFICE COPY — NATIONAL UCC FINANCING STATEMENT (FORM UCC1) (REV. 07/29/98)

The purposes for filing a Financing Statement with the state are similar to those for recording real property interests with the county—to protect innocent purchasers and encumbrancers for value.

ENCUMBRANCERS are those who have an interest in the property by virtue of having placed a lien on the property, acquired an easement against the property, imposed restrictions against it, or acquired any other interest which might be said to encumber the subject property. Just as local records establish priorities for lien claimants on real estate matters, state records establish priorities for claimants on debts secured by personal property. Thus, if a financing statement is not filed, subsequent purchasers without actual knowledge take that property free of the prior security interest, that is, they would not be liable for the pre-existing debt.

By taking advantage of the UCC filing provisions, secured parties protect their interests against those of subsequent purchasers.

In any transaction handled by an escrow agent, the transferee must deposit with the escrow the full amount of purchase price or consideration. No funds can be drawn from escrow prior to the actual closing and completion of the escrow for payment of any commission, fee, or other consideration as compensation for a service that is contingent upon the performance of any act, condition, or instruction set forth in the escrow.

Not all escrow companies handle the sale of business opportunities.

D. SALES AND USE TAXES

Whenever a merchant engages in a business where sales of personal property at retail are made, he or she must secure a seller's permit from the State Board of Equalization.

The sale of a business opportunity is also subject to sales tax. Taxes are payable on the tangible personal property items only, and not on goodwill, patents, closes in action (a personal right not reduced to possession, but recoverable by court suit), and other intangibles. Thus, when a Business Opportunity (BO) is sold, sales tax must be charged on the furniture, trade fixtures, and equipment that are transferred. Until these taxes are paid, together with sales and use taxes owed by the seller to the state Board of Equalization, that agency will not issue its *CERTIFICATE OF PAYMENT OF SALES AND USE TAX. The issuance of this certificate releases the buyer from liability for the seller's unpaid sales and use taxes.* Without it, buyers will find themselves responsible for their payment, popularly referred to as successor's liability.

To guard against the possibility of unpaid taxes, the escrow agent is required to withhold from the purchase price a sufficient amount to cover any liability.

Similar withholdings of funds are also applicable to certain other state agencies to which contributions are due, such as unemployment taxes and disability insurance premiums owed the state Employment Development Department (EDD). Through such safeguards, the transferee is able to acquire the business free of taxes that are otherwise due and payable, and that might not be discovered until months after the close of escrow. This concept is just like the bulk transfer notice under Article 6 of the UCC.

By filing and publishing the required notices of intent to sell, the buyer takes the business free of unfiled claims, and creditors who fail to file claims must look solely to the seller for payment.

As for taxation, the sovereign powers of the state are affected, and the successor to the business will still be liable until released.

E. BILL OF SALE

The **BILL OF SALE** *serves the same function in the transfer of personal property as the grant deed does for real property.*

F. ASSIGNMENT OF LEASE

Because few BOs transfer the underlying fee title to the land and improvements, one of the major reasons why businesses sell for comparatively less (in contrast to real property) is that only the personal property is being purchased, accompanied by an assignment of the lessee's interest in the realty.

Obviously, a going concern is not as valuable without continued operation from a given location, particularly if a major reason for its success is its location. Many factors account for goodwill, not the least of which is the value of the location. Therefore, it may be critical that the business continue from the same site under the new owner. Securing a lease assignment from the transferor, along with consent to such assignment from the lessor, is the only way to insure goodwill.

You should make sure that the business lease is assignable.

After all the foregoing have been met, prorations are made for insurance, rents, taxes, licenses, receivables, loan payments, and other applicable items; closing statements are prepared and delivered along with the fully executed documents to the respective parties, and escrow is closed.

XI. Valuation of Business Opportunities

You should learn how to determine the value of a business—before you embark on your first listing. There is no magic formula to calculate the value of a BO, any more than there is for the valuation of real property. However, there are some guidelines to follow, though generalities apply to BOs less reliably than they do to realty. More variables are involved, especially in pegging a true appraisal on the leasehold.

A business opportunity may have one value to the lessor, but an altogether different value to the lessee.

Many differences of opinion inevitably exist because of the varying degrees of knowledge and skill of the appraisers and the approaches they utilize. When the business is large and involved, advise your seller to bear the expense of having it appraised by a trained specialist.

There are tables that show rules of thumb as price guides, but these tables do not include inventory value, age, appearance and usefulness of the furnishings, fixtures, equipment, the exterior and interior physical appearance of the improvements, specific location, and terms and conditions of the lease. For example, new furniture and fixtures depreciate half of their value as they are used. After a few years of service, they're not worth much more than a third of the original cost. If they're not used in the operation of the business, but rather are sold on the open market, they bring hardly more than 15 percent of cost. Equipment is somewhat more stable, and value depends on age, utility, and condition. The value of used or rebuilt equipment can best be determined by wholesale equipment suppliers.

As might be expected, the value of goodwill is the most difficult to measure.

In establishing valuation for this intangible asset, consideration is given to the length of time the business has been in existence, location, customer traffic, vehicle count, adaptability to change (if desired), present and future competition, continued use of a well-established and respected business name, the quality of service and dependability, provision for a noncompetition clause included in the sale, customer habits, personalities and abilities of key personnel who will remain, and a variety of other factors.

You should visit an establishment on different days and at various times to determine business activities.

Based upon collection of data over many years, guidelines have been established to compute the value of a particular business. These guidelines may be said to be *NET MULTIPLIERS, that is, the amount that a business would sell for, based upon the multiplication of its annual net income by some standardized number, or multiplier. GROSS MULTIPLIERS are commonly used in valuations of income-producing real estate; multipliers are also applied to the annual net income of businesses.* These multipliers are based on the annual net prior to allowance for depreciation, owner's salary or withdrawals, and interest. In the table *Guidelines for Selling a Business,* only general guides are set up and figures must be adjusted

for these factors. For instance, if an auto parts store has net annual earnings of $50,000, it should sell for from 100 percent to 150 percent of that income.

As the broker, you must be careful to obtain an accurate breakdown of income and expenses, as well as a correct count of the stock in trade. Assisting the transferor in the physical inventory may avoid misunderstandings.

Much more can be said about business opportunities. Only the limitations of space preclude discussion of the use of options occasionally employed in BO transactions; procedures for bulk transfers at public auction; the detailed provisions of the California Sales and Use Tax Law; the Alcoholic Beverage Control Act; lease analysis; and analysis of financial statements, especially the balance sheet and profit and loss statement.

Any agent who hopes to deal in business opportunities would be wise to take at least a basic course in accounting.

XII. Tax Consequences on the Sale of Business Opportunities

The tax implications and applications in the sale of businesses differ from those in the sale of real property. The method of allocation of the various business assets has tax consequences to both seller/transferor and buyer/transferee.

A covenant not to compete is valid in California. Under the terms of a **COVENANT NOT TO COMPETE**, *the seller agrees that he or she will not open a competing business for a period of time within a specified geographical area.* The amount paid for the covenant not to compete is ordinary income to the seller and is a deductible item to the buyer over the period of the covenant, that is, the buyer amortizes or spreads out that portion of the price that is allocated to the covenant.

The amount paid for leasehold improvements is deductible by the buyer over the remaining term of the lease. It is a capital transaction to the seller, with long- or short-term capital gain consequences dependent upon the holding period.

The amount paid for goodwill is not deductible by the buyer and is a capital item to the seller.

Amounts paid for fixtures and equipment are depreciable by the buyer and subject to special tax treatment to the seller, which goes beyond the scope of this discussion. Finally, inventory is generally priced at the seller's cost and does not have any immediate tax consequence to the buyers.

XIII. Alcoholic Beverage Control Act

The *CALIFORNIA DEPARTMENT OF ALCOHOLIC BEVERAGE CONTROL (ABC) is charged with administration and enforcement of the Alcoholic Beverage Control Act, which regulates the issuance of liquor licenses* (See **Figure 15-4**).

As a broker negotiating the sale of a business involving the sale and distribution of alcoholic beverages, you should be familiar with the legal controls and procedures for transfer of the liquor license or permit. In addition to federal statutes, many laws govern the manufacture, sale, and possession of alcoholic beverages in California. A detailed discussion of the subject is not essential for our purposes, but the reader who is interested in pursuing the matter is advised to consult the DRE Reference Book to obtain more information. Among the topics in this volume are the requirements for obtaining and transferring a license, classifications of liquor licenses, filing and escrow procedures, original and renewal license fees, limitations on use, and excerpts from the Alcoholic Beverage Control Act.

XIV. Ancillary Activities and Specialty Roles

Inevitably, as a broker, you will be engaged in many activities which complement that of your main concern, general brokerage. A review of some of these activities follows.

A. REAL PROPERTY SECURITIES DEALER (RPSD)

Closely associated with loan brokerage is the activity of the real property securities dealer, who is regulated under Chapter 3, Article 6 of the Real Estate Law.

The essential difference between the real property securities dealer and the real property loan broker is that the loan broker is dealing with new loans in the primary mortgage (or money) market, while the *REAL PROPERTY SECURITIES DEALER (RPSD) is engaged in the secondary market, in addition to a host of activities that come under the definition of real property securities.*

The statutes that regulate this area of real estate activity cover bulk transactions in trust deeds, real property sales contracts and investment plans dealing with them.

To secure endorsement as a real property securities dealer, you must first have a real estate broker license.

A real property securities dealer is defined as "any person, acting as principal or agent, who engages in the business of: (A) Selling real property securities to the public..." These are defined by Section 10237.1, subdivision (a) of the Business and Professions Code as investment contracts made in connection with the sale of a secured promissory

Figure 15-4

ALCOHOLIC BEVERAGE CONTROL
(ABC)

Any California real estate licensee who is interested in negotiating business opportunity transactions should be familiar with the legal controls on the transfer of licenses for the sale of alcoholic beverages.

The Department of Alcoholic Beverage Control (ABC) administers the Alcoholic Beverage Control Act and issues all licenses there under.

Alcoholic beverage licenses are issued to qualified adults, partnerships, fiduciaries, and corporations for use at a particular premises, which also has to be approved by the ABC. The ABC may refuse to issue a license to any person who has a criminal record or has violated the ABC Act. The premises may be disapproved for various reasons, including over concentration of alcoholic beverage licenses in the area, the creation of a police problem, or the proximity to a school, playground, or church.

With the sale of a business opportunity involving a liquor license, you cannot automatically assume that the ABC will permit the transfer. An escrow is legally required and no consideration may be paid out before the license and the sale of the business is approved. Each application and transfer is subject to protest by local officials and private parties within 30 days of the posted notice of intention to sell alcoholic beverages.

New licenses for bars (on-sale) and liquor stores (off-sale) are usually obtained through a lottery type system in each county. The maximum sales price for a new license is $6,000, but after a period of five years from the date of the original issuance, this restriction is lifted for resale, and the purchase price is usually considerably more.

DEPARTMENT OF ALCOHOLIC BEVERAGE CONTROL
1901 BROADWAY
SACRAMENTO, CALIFORNIA

 www.abc.ca.gov
(Alcoholic Beverage Control)

note, or a property sales contract, wherein the dealer or his principal expresses or implies agreement to any kind of guarantee, payment, or repurchase of such investment contracts. The dealer might, for instance, guarantee the note or contract against loss or nonpayment of either principal or interest, guarantee a specific yield or return on the note or contract, agree to assume one or more payments in order to protect the security, or even to repurchase the note or contract.

The Real Estate Law continues the definition:

"(b) Offering to accept or accepting funds for continual reinvestment in real property securities, or from placement in an account, plan, or program whereby the dealer implies that a return will be derived from a specific real property sales contract or promissory note secured directly or collaterally by a lien on real property which is not specifically stated to be based upon the contractual payments thereon."

The statute adds, however, that the phrase "sale to the public" is interpreted as excluding sales to corporations; pension, retirement or similar trust funds; to institutional lending agencies; or to real estate brokers, attorneys, or licensed general building contractors.

A generalized definition of real property securities as set forth in Section 10237.1 holds them to be deeds of trust sold under an investment contract where the dealer guarantees the deed of trust in any one of several ways, or makes advances to or on behalf of the investor. Also included in the definition is the sale of one of a series of promotional notes or sales contracts. Promotional, as used here, refers to a note secured by a trust deed on unimproved real property in a subdivision; or a note executed after construction of an improvement on the property, but before the first sale; or executed as a means of financing the first purchase of property so improved, and which is subordinate to another trust deed, such as a purchase money second deed of trust on a new house in a subdivision.

Before selling real property securities to the public, the broker must obtain a permit from the Real Estate Commissioner.

This permit may be for selling existing securities, or the permit may authorize the applicant to acquire and sell securities under a proposed plan or program. In the latter case, the permit is obtained prior to the acquisition of the securities. Before issuing a permit, the Commissioner evaluates the application to determine whether the proposed plan and sale are equitable.

All advertising material that will be used must be filed with the Commissioner ten days prior to its use. No dealer shall use any advertising material after receiving notice in writing that such material contains any false or misleading statement or omits necessary information to make the statement complete and accurate.

A Real Property Security Statement must be furnished to the purchaser of a real property security.

This disclosure statement is to the real property securities dealer and his client what the Broker's Loan Statement is to the loan broker and his client. Both statements are designed to protect the investing public by prescribing disclosures of certain pertinent data. In certain situations (described in Sections 10239 et seq. of the Business and Professions Code), the Real Estate Commissioner is empowered to take possession of the records, business, and assets of the real property securities dealer and, when necessary, liquidate these assets in the interest of investors.

B. NOTARY PUBLIC SERVICES

A very significant part of every real estate transaction is the acknowledgement of a variety of documents used in the sale and purchase of real property. As you should be aware, such an *ACKNOWLEDGEMENT is a formal declaration before a duly authorized officer, by a person executing an instrument (that is, a formal document) that such execution is his or her act and deed.* Its purpose is to entitle the document to be recorded so as to impart constructive notice of its contents, and, in most cases, to entitle the instrument to be used as evidence of its existence and validity. Often such notarial service is performed for a nominal fee by a broker who is also a notary. Those who do not charge for such services perform them as an accommodation to the transaction.

Additional benefits from obtaining a notary commission may be monetary in nature, but the principal benefits are the conveniences for the broker and his or her clients— being a notary expedites real estate and business opportunity transactions. Indeed, a substantial number of the over 100,000 notaries public in this state are real estate licensees, most of whom presumably went through the expense and effort to obtain the appointment in order to better service their clientele. All documents, before recorded, must first be acknowledged before a notary public or qualified public officer.

As a notary public, you can notarize your clients' documents, but many successful brokers rely on assistants to take care of this detail.

XV. Property Management Activities

As with the insurance aspects, the managing of properties for others is a natural adjunct to your general practice as a broker. Usually this is done on the basis of a percentage of gross rentals or for a flat fee. You are guided by the same principle here: as agent for the owner, you are obligated to obtain the most competitive prices for your client when, for example, purchasing supplies and equipment for the property.

FREQUENTLY ASKED QUESTIONS REGARDING NOTARY PUBLIC

1. What is a Notary Public?

The California Secretary of State is authorized to appoint and commission notaries public to administer oaths, to attest and certify documents by their signature and official seal.

2. How do I obtain a Notary Public commission?

Applicants must be 18 years of age, be a legal California resident, satisfactorily complete a written examination prescribed by the Secretary of State's Office, and clear a background check.

3. What Educational seminars and materials are available to assist in preparing for the exam?

California is one of the few states whose notaries must pass a written examination in order to become a notary public. The most indispensable resource is The Notary Public Handbook. It contains all the laws and will answer the questions to pass the examination. Seminars are available in the state to provide an active learning environment.

4. Must I post a bond?

Yes, applicants will be required to file a bond in the county clerk of the local county in the amount of $10,000 and first-time applicants must be fingerprinted.

5. What records will I be required to maintain?

The notary must keep a sequential journal containing specific information as (1) date, time, and type of offical act; (2) Character of instrument acknowledged; (3) Signature of each person acknowledged; (4) Nature of information used to verify the identity; and (5) fee charged if any.

6. What is the responsibility of the Notary Public?

There is considerable responsibility including having satisfactory proof on the oath or affirmation of a credible witness known to him and that the fact the individual who is described and who executed the instrument. Both the bond surety and the notary are liable for any misconduct or negligence.

XVI. Escrow Activities

Under the Real Estate Law, an individual cannot be licensed as an escrow company; however, a broker may act as an escrow agent in those transactions in which he or she represents the buyer or seller or both.

Remember: Only the seller and buyer may select the escrow they wish to use.

Any real estate licensee who acts as an escrow agent (or escrow holder) must maintain all escrow funds in a trust account subject to inspection by the Real Estate Commissioner, and keep proper records.

Licensed escrow companies are prohibited by law from paying referral fees to anyone except a regular employee of the company. This prohibits the giving of commissions to real estate brokers and other outsiders for sending business to a particular escrow company. Such fees include gifts of merchandise or other things of value. Further, no commission payments can be made prior to actual closing and completion of the escrow.

Escrow companies are prohibited by law from soliciting or accepting escrow instructions or amended or supplemental instructions containing any blank to be filled in after the signing or initialing of the instructions, amendments or supplemental instructions.

They may not permit any person to make any addition to, deletion from, or alteration of an escrow instruction or amended or supplemental escrow instruction unless it is signed or initialed by all persons who had signed or initialed the original instructions or amendments thereto. Escrow companies are charged by law with delivering, at the time of execution, copies of any escrow instruction or amended or supplemental instruction to all parties executing it. However, escrow instructions, being confidential, may not be disclosed to non-parties. Limited disclosure to parties is permissible where the instructions form a part of the contract to which the person desiring disclosure has become a party.

The escrow holder is the agent for both the buyer and seller.

When the conditions are performed, the escrow holder usually becomes the agent of each of the parties, that is, of the grantor to deliver the deed and of the grantee to pay over the purchase money. The agency, however, is considered a limited one, and the only obligations to be fulfilled by the escrow holder are those set forth in the instructions.

XVII. Loan Brokerage Activities

To compliment their business activities, an increasing number of real estate brokers are getting involved in the field of financing.

In playing the role of a negotiator, as the broker, you have considerable influence on the size of the down payment and balance of payment due the seller. As explained in an earlier chapter, the seller, instead of waiting for the buyer to obtain institutional financing, may accept a purchase money mortgage or trust deed and finance the buyer personally. If the purchaser has little cash, the seller may be willing to take a second trust deed behind the loan of an outside financing agency. In cases where the seller desires the full purchase price in cash, a buyer must be found with ample down payment funds of his or her own, possibly with an assist of a new loan on the property, if it is free and clear, or a buyer willing to assume an existing obligation acceptable to the existing lenders.

The volume of loan applications originating in your real estate office may become so great that you may wish to set up a loan division or subsidiary mortgage company and become a loan representative or agent of an insurance company, or a commercial or savings bank, usually situated in other locales. A loan representative or mortgage company can bring idle money to an area where it is in demand, thus aiding in creating a fluid market for loanable funds on a long-term basis. Also, you may wish to lend your own funds or funds of large private investors who prefer this form of investment to bonds and stocks.

In the normal course of your brokerage operation, you may perform only the single function of aiding the purchaser in making application for a loan from a financial institution. However, if so inclined, you may go a step further and become a representative, agent, or correspondent for a mortgage lending institution.

XVIII. Syndication

Another area opening up to licensees on a very broad scale is syndication. Here, you have an opportunity to capitalize on the marketing and financing of real estate. Opportunities for syndication abound because of the increasing demand for land, population influx, relatively small outlays required of investors, and the solution which the syndication vehicle provides for the problem of tight money.

A "Syndicate" is an association formed to operate an investment business. It can be a corporation, partnership, or trust.

Readers who may want to specialize in the exciting field of syndication should plan to attend specialized seminars on this subject.

XIX. Brokerage Opportunities in Probate Sales

An executor possessing a power of sale under the terms of a will may sell directly or through one or more brokers.

If you are the broker, but don't have such power of sale, or you're a court-appointed administrator, you may also seek offers, providing you publish a legal notice advising that the property is to be sold on specified terms and conditions, and that offers from interested parties are invited.

Information concerning a sale is usually obtained from the attorney handling the estate or from a bank or trust company that is acting as executor or administrator. When the public administrator is in charge of the administration of an estate, inquiry is directed to that office.

Written offers to purchase must conform to statutory requirements and to the rules of the local superior court governing probate sales.

They must be for at least 90 percent of the inheritance tax appraisal value and should conform to the terms stated in any public notice. The personal representative may accept an offer, subject to court confirmation. The court sets the matter for a hearing and, at that time, anyone may bid more in open court, provided he or she increases the offer by at least 10 percent of the first $10,000, and 5 percent of the remaining portion of the original bid price. At the discretion of the court, the bidding may proceed on lesser raises, until the court declares a bid to be the highest and best obtainable, and thereby confirms the sale to the successful bidder.

If you are the broker representing a bidder, you should attend the confirmation hearing and should be familiar with local court rules governing advance bidding, deposits required, and other matters. Normal escrow procedures are used to consummate the transaction, under terms and conditions approved by court.

Of course, as the broker, you should have a written agreement with the personal representative for payment of compensation. Commissions (5%) paid to participating brokers are governed by statute, and discretion is vested in the court as to distribution. **Generally, if more than one bid is made, half the commission goes to the broker representing the original bidder on the original amount, and the balance goes to the broker whose bidder submitted the higher bid, based on the higher amount.**

If the successful bidder is not produced by a bona fide agent, then the agent holding the contract is allowed a full commission on the amount of the original bid.

A. MECHANICS OF THE PROBATE SALE

Figure 15-5 is the CAR Probate Listing Agreement form that may be used to accomplish the marketing of probate property.

1. Right to Sell

The full and correct name of the decedent is inserted here, along with the agent's. The description of the property or properties (since more than one property may be involved) follows.

2. Term

An exclusive right to sell for a period not in excess of 90 days may be entered if, prior to the execution of the agreement, the executor or administrator of the estate has obtained court permission.

XX. State of California Sales Opportunities

Occasionally, the state has real property for disposal, such as excess land acquired for easements that is no longer needed. The Department of Finance may authorize employment of a broker to effect sales when, after proper advertising, bids offered for such properties do not equal the appraised value.

A. BOARD OF EDUCATION REAL ESTATE SALES

The Education Code provides that the governing body of any school district may pay a commission to a broker who procures a buyer for real estate sold by the board.

The sealed bid must be accompanied by the name of the broker to whom the compensation is to be paid, and by a statement of the rate or amount of the commission. In the event of an oral overbid submitted through another broker, half the commission based on the highest written bid is payable to the submitting broker, and the balance is paid to the broker who procured the purchaser to whom the sale is confirmed.

B. CALTRANS

Under the Airspace Development Program, licensees are permitted to negotiate airspace leases through the California Division of Highways, and receive commissions for such services.

1. Background

California law prescribes that airspace multiple-use parcels are in the state's right of way and can be over, under, or adjacent to a state highway.

Figure 15-5

PROBATE LISTING AGREEMENT (1)

CALIFORNIA ASSOCIATION OF REALTORS®

PROBATE LISTING AGREEMENT
Under Authority of the Probate Code
(C.A.R. Form PL, Revised 10/99)

1. **EXCLUSIVE RIGHT TO SELL:** _____,
the court-appointed representative of the ☐ estate, ☐ conservatorship or ☐ guardianship identified by Superior Court case name as_____, case # _____ ("Seller"),
hereby employs and grants _____ ("Broker") the exclusive and irrevocable right, commencing on (date) _____ and expiring at 11:59 P.M. on (date) _____ ("Listing Period") (not to exceed 90 days), to sell or exchange the real property in the City of _____, County of _____, California, described as follows: _____
_____ ("Property").

2. **COURT CONFIRMATION** of any sale ☐ **is required** (limited authority), ☐ **may not be required** (full authority).

3. **TERMS OF SALE:**
   A. **LIST PRICE:** The listing price shall be _____
   _____ ($_____).
   B. **PERSONAL PROPERTY:** The following items of personal property are included in the above price: _____
   _____
   _____
   C. **ADDITIONAL TERMS:** _____
   _____
   _____

4. **MULTIPLE LISTING SERVICE:** Information about this listing ☐ **will**, ☐ **will not**, be provided to a multiple listing service ("MLS") of Broker's selection and all terms of the transaction will be provided to the MLS for publication, dissemination and use by persons and entities on terms approved by the MLS. Seller authorizes Broker to comply with all applicable MLS rules.

5. **TITLE:** Seller warrants that title to the Property is as follows: _____
   _____

6. **COMPENSATION TO BROKER:**
   Notice: The amount or rate of real estate commissions is not fixed by law. They are set by each Broker individually and may be negotiable between Seller and Broker. (Local court rules may establish maximum permissible amounts.)
   A. Seller agrees to pay to Broker from the proceeds of the sale, as compensation for services, irrespective of agency relationships, and subject to California Probate Code, or an amount determined by the court, either ☐ _____ percent of the sales price, **OR** ☐ $_____, **AND** _____ if Broker, cooperating broker, Seller, or any other person, produces a buyer who purchases the Property on the above price and terms or any other terms and conditions acceptable to Seller during the Listing Period or any extension.
   B. Broker is authorized to cooperate with other brokers, and divide with other brokers the above compensation in any manner acceptable to Broker, or as allowed or determined by the Court.
   C. Seller warrants that Seller has no obligation to pay compensation to any other Broker regarding the transfer of the Property except: _____.
   If the Property is sold to anyone listed above during the time Seller is obligated to compensate another broker: **(a)** Broker is not entitled to compensation under this Agreement; and **(b)** Broker is not obligated to represent Seller with respect to such transaction.

Buyer's Initials (_____)(_____)
Seller's Initials (_____)(_____)

Reviewed by _____ Date _____

EQUAL HOUSING OPPORTUNITY

PROBATE LISTING AGREEMENT (PL PAGE 1 OF 2)

PROBATE LISTING AGREEMENT (2)

Property Address: _____ Date: _____

7. **BROKER'S AND SELLER'S DUTIES:** Broker agrees to exercise reasonable effort and due diligence to achieve the purposes of this Agreement, and is authorized to advertise and market the Property in any medium selected by Broker. Seller agrees to consider offers presented by Broker, and to act in good faith toward accomplishing the sale of the Property. Seller further agrees, regardless of responsibility, to indemnify, defend and hold Broker harmless from all claims, disputes, litigation, judgments and attorney's fees arising from any incorrect information supplied by Seller, whether contained in any document, omitted therefrom, or otherwise, or from any material facts which Seller knows but fails to disclose.

8. **AGENCY RELATIONSHIPS:** Broker shall act as the agent for Seller in any resulting transaction. Depending upon the circumstances, it may be necessary or appropriate for Broker to act as an agent for both Seller and buyer, exchange party, or one or more additional parties ("Buyer"). Broker shall, as soon as practicable, disclose to Seller any election to act as a dual agent representing both Seller and Buyer. If a Buyer is procured directly by Broker or an associate licensee in Broker's firm, Seller hereby consents to Broker acting as a dual agent for Seller and such Buyer. In the event of an exchange, Seller hereby consents to Broker collecting compensation from additional parties for services rendered, provided there is disclosure to all parties of such agency and compensation. Seller understands that Broker may have or obtain listings on other properties, and that potential buyers may consider, make offers on, or purchase through Broker, property the same as or similar to Seller's Property. Seller consents to Broker's representation of sellers and buyers of other properties before, during, and after the expiration of this Agreement.

9. **DEPOSIT:** Broker is authorized to accept and hold on Seller's behalf a deposit to be applied toward the sales price.

10. **LOCKBOX:**

   A. A lockbox is designed to hold a key to the Property to permit access to the Property by Broker, cooperating brokers, MLS participants, their authorized licensees and representatives, and accompanied prospective buyers.

   B. Broker, cooperating brokers, MLS and Associations/Boards of REALTORS® are **not** insurers against theft, loss, vandalism or damage attributed to the use of a lockbox. Seller is advised to verify the existence of, or obtain, appropriate insurance through Seller's own insurance broker.

   C. (If checked:) ☐ Seller authorizes Broker to install a lockbox. If Seller does not occupy the Property, Seller shall be responsible for obtaining occupant(s)' written permission for use of a lockbox.

11. **SIGN:** (If checked:) ☐ Seller authorizes Broker to install a FOR SALE/SOLD sign on the Property.

12. **EQUAL HOUSING OPPORTUNITY:** The Property is offered in compliance with federal, state, and local anti-discrimination laws.

13. **ADDITIONAL TERMS:** _____
   ☑ Probate Advisory (C.A.R. Form PAL) _____
   _____
   _____
   _____
   _____

14. **ENTIRE CONTRACT:** All prior discussions, negotiations, and agreements between the parties concerning the subject matter of this Agreement are superseded by this Agreement, which constitutes the entire contract and a complete and exclusive expression of their agreement, and may not be contradicted by evidence of any prior agreement or contemporaneous oral agreement. This Agreement and any supplement, addendum, or modification, including any photocopy or facsimile, may be executed in counterparts.

Seller warrants that Seller has the authority to execute this agreement.
Seller acknowledges that Seller has read and understands this Agreement, and has received a copy.

Date _____ at _____, California   Date _____ at _____, California

By _____   By _____

Court-Appointed Representative(s) of _____

Address _____   Address _____

City, State, Zip _____   City, State, Zip _____

Phone/Fax/Email _____   Phone/Fax/Email _____

Real Estate Broker (Firm) _____   By (Agent) _____ Date _____

Address _____   Phone _____

City _____ State _____ Zip _____   Fax/Email _____

THIS FORM HAS BEEN APPROVED BY THE CALIFORNIA ASSOCIATION OF REALTORS® (C.A.R.). NO REPRESENTATION IS MADE AS TO THE LEGAL VALIDITY OR ADEQUACY OF ANY PROVISION IN ANY SPECIFIC TRANSACTION. A REAL ESTATE BROKER IS THE PERSON QUALIFIED TO ADVISE ON REAL ESTATE TRANSACTIONS. IF YOU DESIRE LEGAL OR TAX ADVICE, CONSULT AN APPROPRIATE PROFESSIONAL.

This form is available for use by the entire real estate industry. It is not intended to identify the user as a REALTOR®. REALTOR® is a registered collective membership mark which may be used only by members of the NATIONAL ASSOCIATION OF REALTORS® who subscribe to its Code of Ethics.

Published and Distributed by:
REAL ESTATE BUSINESS SERVICES, INC.
a subsidiary of the California Association of REALTORS®
525 South Virgil Avenue, Los Angeles, California 90020

SURE TRAC
The System for Success®
PL REVISED 10/99 (PAGE 2 OF 2)

Reviewed by _____ Date _____

EQUAL HOUSING OPPORTUNITY

PROBATE LISTING AGREEMENT (PL PAGE 2 OF 2)

www.caltrans.ca.gov/hq/row

The state has entered into an active program to lease many sites for long-term development proposals for such uses as parking facilities, warehouses, office buildings, and stores. The uses for airspace are virtually unlimited. Rather than being a drain on tax monies for maintenance and upkeep, the properties should return money to the taxpayer in the form of local real estate, sales, and business taxes. This is intended to ease the burden of local taxes as well as bring a return to the state.

2. Procedure

Each State Highway District Office has an inventory of available airspace sites for the broker to review. Once you secure a specific potential tenant for a specific airspace site, you will sign a Broker's Commission Agreement that obligates the state to pay a commission, under prescribed conditions, based upon a schedule made a part of the agreement. The commission is paid when the lease is consummated and the state begins receiving payment.

If you are interested in entering the program, you should contact the Division of Highways, Right of Way Department, Airspace Development, at one of the eleven district offices located throughout the state.

C. SUBDIVISION SALES OPPORTUNITIES

1. Intrastate Sales

The division and subsequent sale of real property are governed by the Subdivision Map Act and the Subdivided Lands Act.

Under these two laws, the regulation of new subdivisions is administered by the Real Estate Commissioner's office, and the county or municipal authorities responsible for review of new maps proposing the division of land for development or sale.

Property may be divided in several manners, such as a record of survey or parcel maps. The most common division of property is through the use of a subdivision map.

The subdivision engineer usually processes the map through the various agencies for such matters as public schools, public utility availability, public roads, environmental impact reports, and involvement with the coastal commission, if required. This is merely a brief description of a complex process. The basic objective is to create a map where the yet-to-be completed lot improvements are in conformance with the general plan, and the proposed densities can be adequately served by available resources, or resources to be created as part of the project. A good example is the requirement that the subdivider provide a catch basin to alleviate water runoff during heavy rains.

Some brokerages specialize in the sale of new properties, which could fall in the following areas:

1. Home and condominium sales
2. Improved lot sales for custom construction
3. Sale and lease of industrial properties
4. Sale and lease of commercial properties
5. Time share sales

New Construction. In conjunction with improved lot sales, normally a buyer has the intent to improve the lot. In order to properly serve your client, you should be familiar with construction lenders in your area, their underwriting criteria, and their willingness to cooperate with brokers. As previously mentioned, loan placement is another commission opportunity to be explored.

2. Interstate Sales

As a California licensee, you also have the privilege to sell real estate to purchasers outside the state. With such opportunities also come responsibilities.

Because of the massive scale of land promotions and abuses, Congress passed the *INTERSTATE LAND SALES FULL DISCLOSURE ACT. With certain exceptions, an offering for sale or lease of a subdivision of 25 lots or more through interstate commerce or by mail requires a permit from the Department of Housing and Urban Development. This permit is called a **PROPERTY REPORT**.*

A developer who has already complied with the state Subdivided Lands Act (California Real Estate Law) is required only to file a copy of the subdivision questionnaire with the Department of Real Estate, together with supporting documents and an abbreviated statement. Once submitted, the filing becomes effective immediately, instead of the 30-day wait in most other states. The prospective purchaser receives both the state **Public Report** and the federal **State Property Report Disclaimers**. Both are designed to protect purchasers by requiring full disclosure of all material facts that affect the subdivision. However, both reports contain disclaimers, stating in so many words that the agency has not passed upon the accuracy or adequacy of the report, or any of the advertising material.

A provision of the federal statute is that, with a contract for purchase or lease of a lot in a subdivision of this type, the purchaser has a right of rescission within a limited period. *In California, this type of remote subdivision is known as a **LAND PROJECT**.*

D. REAL ESTATE INVESTMENT COUNSELOR

For the real estate broker who has considerable experience and superior education, there is another specialized field of real estate activity. The *REAL ESTATE INVESTMENT COUNSELOR is the broker's broker or consultant, doing for other brokers what those brokers cannot do for themselves, until their own knowledge and experience is of such magnitude as to qualify them for similar status.*

Though you must be careful not to practice law without a license, the real estate counselor resembles the attorney: your only product is advice, for which you are paid a fee, whether or not the advice is taken. You will be concerned with diversified problems in the broad field of real estate involving all segments of the business. Your functions encompass analysis, interpretation, and recommendations. You will often be used by business firms which have become involved in real estate investing for profitable diversification, inflation hedge, tax advantages, and other benefits. The scope of such activities is reducible to four principal areas, namely:

1. firms that have organized real estate divisions or subsidiaries;
2. companies that have bought or merged with existing real estate firms;
3. companies that, by accident rather than design, got into real estate by involving themselves in buying and selling homes as a service for transferred employees;
4. corporations desiring the benefits of real estate investment without the concerns of staffing a department or acquiring an existing real estate firm.

As a consultant, you may wish to specialize in a limited area of real estate. You may choose subdividing land and assessment procedures, work primarily with retail leases, or confine your activities to mobile home parks or motels. Questions of land utilization—to buy, sell, rent or exchange, remodel or demolish, and many others—will confront you as a counselor. Accordingly, your background must cover not only a narrow and technical field for appraising or subdividing, but also at least a working knowledge of all fields of real estate. To counsel wisely and assist in making intelligent decisions based upon a number of possible alternatives, you should understand estate planning principles, and the advantages and disadvantages of the stock and bond market. You should also have a firm grasp of life insurance, and possess a wealth of knowledge in the fields of general business, law, income taxation, valuation, financing, economics, and research.

1. Investment Planning and Counseling

If you're a broker who expects to build up a following in the field of real estate investments, you will need to do more than the typical agent. To pick up repeat business, you will have to earn the respect and trust of the client. This trust can come only after you have gained a thorough knowledge and understanding of the client's total financial and family picture. A confidential file should be maintained for each client. By integrating all the data and information about the client, you're in a better position to render superior service. It goes without saying that education in this field is a must.

Investment planning may be thought of as the integration of a number of steps, starting with a thorough analysis of the client's investment requirements—income, appreciation, retirement, estate buildup, resale or exchange, tax shelter, diversification, leverage liquidity, funding of children's education years hence, or any combination of these. Conferring with the client's attorney, accountant, or business advisor is advisable somewhere along the way.

Researching and selecting properties to meet the objectives of the client is the second step. When a decision to buy a particular property is made, you will negotiate its acquisition, followed by title search and escrow. Management of the property is the next step, in order to safeguard the investment, to minimize expenses, and to maximize profits. You must be cognizant of change, along every step of the way, offering suggestions and making recommendations as the circumstances warrant.

XXI. Manufactured Housing and the Licensee

Although no longer referred to as "mobile homes," manufactured homes are what the original name implies, homes that can be moved. Like a vehicle, the *MANUFACTURED HOME is built on a steel chassis and equipped with wheels so that it can be pulled by truck from the factory to a dealer's lot and then to a site in a park or on private land. To be classed as a mobile home, a vehicle must be at least 8 feet wide and at least 32 feet long.*

Each manufactured home unit is called a **SINGLEWIDE**; *two or more manufactured home units together form a* **MULTISECTIONAL**. The multisectionals account for about one-third of all total manufactured home sales.

A manufactured home can be built in a matter of hours in factories that are models of modern assembly line technology. This technology allows manufacturers to control quality, improve product, reduce waste, and drastically cut labor costs.

A. MOBILE HOME PARKS

The mobile home park is an established form of residential development in California. These parks range from attractive, well-kept subdivisions with numerous amenities to the old, rundown parks that give this type of development a bad image.

Traditionally, spaces in mobile home parks have been rented, but with the high cost of traditional housing, the trend toward ownership continues unabated. It is very likely that the evolving interest in meeting the demand for decent, relatively low-cost housing will see an increasing number of developments planned to accommodate factory-built housing or mobile homes.

The majority of mobile home parks cater to retired and semi-retired residents, but greater attention is being devoted to the growing number of first-time buyers, unmarrieds, and singles. For "empty-nesters" who suddenly find themselves in a house which has become too large or too expensive to maintain, a mobile home park might provide a good alternative to condominium or apartment living.

Like all residential subdivisions, maps for own-your-own-lot mobile home parks are filed with the Department of Real Estate, but city and county governments control the development of the parks through zoning laws.

Some counties, for example, do not permit own-your-own mobile home parks, while they may permit rental spaces.

B. OPPORTUNITIES

The manufactured housing industry represents to the licensee a source of additional revenue that for the most part has been ignored. Is the manufactured home buyer a bona fide prospect? Can the manufactured home be sold as real estate? Do zoning regulations restrict sales? What about depreciation, financing, sales, and service?

C. MOBILE HOME DEALER VS. REAL ESTATE BROKER

New manufactured homes cannot be sold by real estate licensees.

Real estate licensees are not allowed to act as agents in the sale of mobile homes that can be used as vehicles on the highway. To mitigate against such practice, licensees are not even permitted to maintain any place of business where two or more mobile homes are displayed and offered for sale by such person, unless the broker is also licensed as a vehicle dealer pursuant to the California Vehicle Code.

D. MARKETING

California specifically regulates manufactured home sales with a statute outlining rules and regulations permitting real estate brokers to sell the units.

Brokers may sell manufactured homes that have been registered with the Department of Motor Vehicles for at least one year and are greater than 8 feet in width and 40 feet in length.

Manufactured homes create greater title problems than ordinary real estate transactions. Before listing such property, you should demand and receive the owner's registration papers indicating the true owner and outstanding loans, if any.

The future of the manufactured home industry is tied to the industry's ability to get the real estate profession to realize that in manufactured home development lies an opportunity for great profit. The manufactured home industry is a natural business for licensees in both sales and resales.

E. LISTING MANUFACTURED HOMES

CAR's Manufactured Home Listing Agreement (for Real and Personal Property) is a form that may be used in the listing of manufactured homes (see **Figure 15-6**). In listing such properties, you must ascertain park rules to be sure you are not violating restrictions imposed by the park owners. Determination of ownership is vital at this stage, notwithstanding the owner's warranty to that effect in paragraph 2(e) of the listing form. As a licensee, you are liable for disciplinary action and criminal action if you knowingly participate in acquiring or disposing of a stolen mobile home. Further, you must be sure that the manufactured homes comply with the Department of Housing insignia and that no alterations have been done without complying with DOH regulations or local ordinances.

Where the purchase price includes manufactured home and lot, separate the transaction into two components: the manufactured home may be treated as the sale of a vehicle, unless it is taxed as real property because it rests on a permanent foundation; the land would, in any case, be treated as the sale of real property. If the manufactured home is located on a site other than an established park, you must check to determine that the installation is in accordance with local codes and zoning ordinances. Finally, anyone listing manufactured homes should fill in the agreement accurately and completely, leaving nothing to chance or possible disagreement.

Figure 15-6
MANUFACTURED HOME LISTING AGREEMENT (1)

CALIFORNIA ASSOCIATION OF REALTORS®

MANUFACTURED HOME LISTING AGREEMENT
FOR REAL AND PERSONAL PROPERTY
(C.A.R. Form MHL, Revised 10/99)

1. **EXCLUSIVE RIGHT TO SELL:** _____ ("Seller") hereby employs and grants
_____ ("Broker") the exclusive and irrevocable right, commencing on
(date) _____ and expiring at 11:59 P.M. on (date) _____ ("Listing Period"), to sell or exchange
the Manufactured Home Situated In _____, County Of _____,
California, described as _____, and as further described below, ("Property").

2. **TYPE OF MANUFACTURED HOME:** (Check box below which applies: A(1), A(2) or B. Check ONLY one.):
    A. **PERSONAL PROPERTY MANUFACTURED HOME**
       (1) ☐ **A Manufactured Home On Leased Or Rented Land** (complete paragraph 2A(3)).
           Space Number _____ Park Name _____

OR   (2) ☐ **A Manufactured Home To Be Sold With Real Property** (complete paragraph 2A(3)) described as _____
           _____
           PURCHASE PRICE ALLOCATED AS FOLLOWS: Manufactured Home $_____ Land $_____
           (3) **ADDITIONAL DESCRIPTION:** (For personal property manufactured home only)
           Manufacturer's Name _____ Model _____ Date Of Manufacture_____ Date Of First Sale _____
           Property is: ☐ On Local Property Tax Roll, ☐ Department of Housing and Community Development ("HCD") registered
           (Use Tax Applies).
           Approximate Width _____ Approximate Length _____ (Without Hitch) Expando Size _____
           HCD/HUD License/Decal Number _____
           SERIAL NUMBERS: 1. _____   2. _____   3. _____
           Label/Insignia: 1. _____   2. _____   3. _____

OR B. ☐ **A REAL PROPERTY MANUFACTURED HOME** (A real property manufactured mobile home is one that meets the following
       requirements: **(1)** a building permit is obtained from local authorities pursuant to Health and Safety Code §18551, **(2)** the
       manufactured home is affixed to a foundation pursuant to Health & Safety Code §18551, **(3)** a certificate of occupancy is issued
       by local authorities, and **(4)** there is recordation with the local authorities of a form pursuant to Health and Safety Code §18551.)

3. **TERMS OF SALE:**
    A. **LIST PRICE:** The listing price shall be _____ ($ _____).
    B. **PERSONAL PROPERTY:** The following items of personal property (exclusive of the Property) are included in the above
       price: _____
       _____
    C. **ADDITIONAL TERMS:** _____
       _____
       _____

4. **MULTIPLE LISTING SERVICE:** Information about this listing ☐ will, ☐ will not, be provided to a multiple listing service ("MLS")
   of Broker's selection and all terms of the transaction, including, if applicable, financing will be provided to the MLS for publication,
   dissemination and use by persons and entities on terms approved by the MLS. Seller authorizes Broker to comply with all applicable
   MLS rules.

5. **TITLE AND COMPLIANCE WITH MANUFACTURED HOME LAWS:**
    A. Seller warrants that Seller and no other persons have title to the Property, except as follows: _____
       _____
    B. Seller agrees Property shall be free of liens and encumbrances, recorded, filed, registered or known to Seller.
    C. Seller agrees that **(1)** evidence of title to the manufactured home, if personal property, shall be in the form of a duly endorsed,
       dated and delivered Certificate of Ownership; and **(2)** Seller shall deliver the current Registration Certificate of Title as required
       by law.
    D. Seller represents that Property, if personal property, is either: **(1)** Located within an established mobilehome park as defined in
       California Health and Safety Code §18214, and that advertising or offering it for sale is not contrary to any provision of any
       contract between Seller and mobilehome park ownership; OR **(2)** That Property is located pursuant to a local zoning ordinance
       or permit on a lot where its presence has been authorized or its continued presence and such use would be authorized for a
       total and uninterrupted period of at least one year.
    E. If applicable, Seller agrees to deliver as soon as possible to Broker, for submission to buyer, a copy of Seller's lease or rental
       agreement and all current park and/or Homeowners' Association rules and regulations, and to inform Broker of any changes to
       either during the Listing Period.

Buyer's Initials (_____)(_____)
Seller's Initials (_____)(_____)

Reviewed by _____ Date _____

EQUAL HOUSING OPPORTUNITY

MHL REVISED 10/99 (PAGE 1 OF 3) Print Date

MANUFACTURED HOME LISTING AGREEMENT (MHL PAGE 1 OF 3)

MANUFACTURED HOME LISTING AGREEMENT (2)

Property Address: _____ Date: _____

6. **COMPENSATION TO BROKER:**
   Notice: The amount or rate of real estate commissions is not fixed by law. They are set by each Broker individually and may be negotiable between Seller and Broker.
   A. Seller agrees to pay to Broker as compensation for services irrespective of agency relationship(s), either ☐ _____ percent of the listing price (or if a sales contract is entered into, of the sales price), or ☐ $ _____, AND _____ as follows:
      (1) If Broker, Seller, cooperating broker, or any other person, produces a buyer(s) who offers to purchase the Property on the above price and terms, or on any price and terms acceptable to Seller during the Listing Period, or any extension;
      (2) If within _____ calendar days after expiration of the Listing Period or any extension, the Property is sold, conveyed, leased, or otherwise transferred to anyone with whom Broker or a cooperating broker has had negotiations, provided that Broker gives Seller, prior to or within **5 calendar days** after expiration of the Listing Period or any extension, a written notice with the name(s) of the prospective purchaser(s);
      (3) If, without Broker's prior written consent, the Property is withdrawn from sale, conveyed, leased, rented, otherwise transferred, or made unmarketable by a voluntary act of Seller during the Listing Period, or any extension.
   B. If completion of the sale is prevented by a party to the transaction other than Seller, then compensation due under paragraph 6A shall be payable only if and when Seller collects damages by suit, settlement, or otherwise, and then in an amount equal to the lesser of one-half of the damages recovered or the above compensation, after first deducting title and escrow expenses and the expenses of collection, if any.
   C. In addition, Seller agrees to pay: _____
   D. Broker is authorized to cooperate with other brokers and, provided the Property is or includes a personal property manufactured home, with HCD licensed dealers, and divide with other brokers and dealers the above compensation in any manner acceptable to Broker.
   E. Seller hereby irrevocably assigns to Broker the above compensation from Seller's funds and proceeds in escrow.
   F. Seller warrants that Seller has no obligation to pay compensation to any other broker or dealer regarding the transfer of the Property, except: _____
      If the Property is sold to anyone listed above during the time Seller is obligated to compensate another broker or dealer; (a) Broker is not entitled to compensation under this Agreement; and (b) Broker is not obligated to represent Seller with respect to such transaction.

7. **BROKER'S AND SELLER'S DUTIES:** Broker agrees to exercise reasonable effort and due diligence to achieve the purposes of this Agreement, and is authorized to advertise and market the Property in any medium selected by Broker. Seller agrees to consider offers presented by Broker, and to act in good faith toward accomplishing the sale of the Property. Seller further agrees, regardless of responsibility, to indemnify, defend and hold Broker harmless from all claims, disputes, litigation, judgments and attorney's fees arising from any incorrect information supplied by Seller, whether contained in any document, omitted therefrom, or otherwise, or from any material facts which Seller knows but fails to disclose.

8. **AGENCY RELATIONSHIPS:** Broker shall act as the agent for Seller in any resulting transaction. Depending upon the circumstances, it may be necessary or appropriate for Broker to act as an agent for both Seller and buyer, exchange party, or one or more additional parties ("Buyer"). Broker shall, as soon as practicable, disclose to Seller any election to act as a dual agent representing both Seller and Buyer. If a Buyer is procured directly by Broker or an associate licensee in Broker's firm, Seller hereby consents to Broker acting as a dual agent for Seller and such Buyer. In the event of an exchange, Seller hereby consents to Broker collecting compensation from additional parties for services rendered, provided there is disclosure to all parties of such agency and compensation.
   Seller understands that Broker may have or obtain listings on other properties, and that potential buyers may consider, make offers on, or purchase through Broker, property the same as or similar to Seller's Property. Seller consents to Broker's representation of sellers and buyers of other properties before, during, and after the expiration of this Agreement.

9. **DEPOSIT:** Broker is authorized to accept and hold on Seller's behalf a deposit to be applied toward the sales price.

10. **LOCKBOX:**
    A. A lockbox is designed to hold a key to the Property to permit access to the Property by Broker, cooperating brokers, MLS participants, their authorized licensees and representatives, and accompanied prospective buyers.
    B. Broker, cooperating brokers, MLS and Associations/Boards of REALTORS® are not insurers against theft, loss, vandalism, or damage attributed to the use of a lockbox. Seller is advised to verify the existence of, or obtain, appropriate insurance through Seller's own insurance broker.
    C. ☐ (If checked:) Seller authorizes Broker to install a lockbox. If Seller does not occupy the Property, Seller shall be responsible for obtaining occupant(s)' written permission for use of a lockbox.

11. **SIGN:** ☐ (If checked:) Seller authorizes Broker to install a FOR SALE/SOLD sign on the Property.

12. **DISPUTE RESOLUTION:**
    A. **MEDIATION:** Seller and Broker agree to mediate any dispute or claim arising between them out of this Agreement, or any resulting transaction, before resorting to arbitration or court action, subject to paragraph 12C below. Mediation fees, if any, shall be divided equally among the parties involved. If any party commences an action based on a dispute or claim to which this paragraph applies, without first attempting to resolve the matter through mediation, then that party shall not be entitled to recover attorney's fees, even if they would otherwise be available to that party in any such action. THIS MEDIATION PROVISION APPLIES WHETHER OR NOT THE ARBITRATION PROVISION IS INITIALED.

Buyer's Initials (_____)(_____)
Seller's Initials (_____)(_____)

Copyright © 1999, CALIFORNIA ASSOCIATION OF REALTORS®, INC.
MHL REVISED 10/99 (PAGE 2 OF 3)

Reviewed by _____ Date _____

MANUFACTURED HOME LISTING AGREEMENT (MHL PAGE 2 OF 3)

MANUFACTURED HOME LISTING AGREEMENT (3)

Property Address: _____ Date: _____

B. ARBITRATION OF DISPUTES: Seller and Broker agree that any dispute or claim in Law or equity arising between them regarding the obligation to pay compensation under this Agreement, which is not settled through mediation, shall be decided by neutral, binding arbitration, subject to paragraph 12C below. The arbitrator shall be a retired judge or justice, or an attorney with at least five years of residential real estate experience, unless the parties mutually agree to a different arbitrator, who shall render an award in accordance with substantive California Law. In all other respects, the arbitration shall be conducted in accordance with Part III, Title 9 of the California Code of Civil Procedure. Judgment upon the award of the arbitrator(s) may be entered in any court having jurisdiction. The parties shall have the right to discovery in accordance with Code of Civil Procedure §1283.05.

"NOTICE: BY INITIALING IN THE SPACE BELOW YOU ARE AGREEING TO HAVE ANY DISPUTE ARISING OUT OF THE MATTERS INCLUDED IN THE 'ARBITRATION OF DISPUTES' PROVISION DECIDED BY NEUTRAL ARBITRATION AS PROVIDED BY CALIFORNIA LAW AND YOU ARE GIVING UP ANY RIGHTS YOU MIGHT POSSESS TO HAVE THE DISPUTE LITIGATED IN A COURT OR JURY TRIAL. BY INITIALING IN THE SPACE BELOW YOU ARE GIVING UP YOUR JUDICIAL RIGHTS TO DISCOVERY AND APPEAL, UNLESS THOSE RIGHTS ARE SPECIFICALLY INCLUDED IN THE 'ARBITRATION OF DISPUTES' PROVISION. IF YOU REFUSE TO SUBMIT TO ARBITRATION AFTER AGREEING TO THIS PROVISION, YOU MAY BE COMPELLED TO ARBITRATE UNDER THE AUTHORITY OF THE CALIFORNIA CODE OF CIVIL PROCEDURE. YOUR AGREEMENT TO THIS ARBITRATION PROVISION IS VOLUNTARY."

"WE HAVE READ AND UNDERSTAND THE FOREGOING AND AGREE TO SUBMIT DISPUTES ARISING OUT OF THE MATTERS INCLUDED IN THE 'ARBITRATION OF DISPUTES' PROVISION TO NEUTRAL ARBITRATION." Seller's Initials _____/_____ Broker's Initials _____/_____

C. EXCLUSIONS FROM MEDIATION AND ARBITRATION: The following matters are excluded from Mediation and Arbitration hereunder: (a) A judicial or non-judicial foreclosure or other action or proceeding to enforce a deed of trust, mortgage, or installment land sale contract as defined in Civil Code §2985; (b) An unlawful detainer action; (c) The filing or enforcement of a mechanic's lien; (d) Any matter which is within the jurisdiction of a probate, small claims, or bankruptcy court; and (e) An action for bodily injury or wrongful death, or for latent or patent defects to which Code of Civil Procedure §337.1 or §337.15 applies. The filing of a court action to enable the recording of a notice of pending action, for order of attachment, receivership, injunction, or other provisional remedies, shall not constitute a violation of the mediation and arbitration provisions.

13. EQUAL HOUSING OPPORTUNITY: The Property is sold in compliance with federal, state, and local anti-discrimination Laws.

14. ATTORNEY'S FEES: In any action, proceeding, or arbitration between Seller and Broker regarding the obligation to pay compensation under this Agreement, the prevailing Seller or Broker shall be entitled to reasonable attorney's fees and costs, except as provided in paragraph 12A.

15. ADDITIONAL TERMS: _____
_____
_____

16. ENTIRE CONTRACT: All prior discussions, negotiations, and agreements between the parties concerning the subject matter of this Agreement are superseded by this Agreement, which constitutes the entire contract and a complete and exclusive expression of their agreement, and may not be contradicted by evidence of any prior agreement or contemporaneous oral agreement. This Agreement and any supplement, addendum, or modification, including any photocopy or facsimile, may be executed in counterparts.

Seller warrants that Seller is the owner of the Property or has the authority to execute this contract. Seller acknowledges that Seller has read and understands this Agreement, and has received a copy.

Seller _____ Date _____
Address/City/State/Zip _____
Phone _____ Fax _____ E-mail _____

Seller _____ Date _____
Address/City/State/Zip _____
Phone _____ Fax _____ E-mail _____

Real Estate Broker (Firm Name) _____
By (Agent) _____ Date _____
Address/City/State/Zip _____
Phone _____ Fax _____ E-mail _____

SURE TRAC — The System for Success®

MHL REVISED 10/99 (PAGE 3 OF 3)

Reviewed by _____ Date _____

EQUAL HOUSING OPPORTUNITY

MANUFACTURED HOME LISTING AGREEMENT (MHL PAGE 3 OF 3)

F. SELLING MANUFACTURED HOMES

You owe your buyers duties beyond that of the sale of conventional housing. You must provide prospective park residents with information concerning the lot and available utilities. You must ascertain ownership of manufactured homes and other items in compliance with park rules and regulations, and they must explain the conditions contained in the lease, the state law, and the policies, rules and regulations of the park owners and resident association, if any. The purchase should be made subject to buyer and park owner agreeing on future occupancy. If the manufactured home is to be moved, you must be certain that the moving will conform to DMV requirements. Since manufactured home moving is expensive, it would be wise to counsel the buyer on costs and to make the purchase subject to approval by the buyer of expenses, DMV requirements, and anything else of a material nature.

1. Buyer Profile

Who is the typical manufactured home buyer? According to Manufactured Housing Industry statistics, more than 12 million persons live in mobile homes. Of this figure, 43 percent are 34 years of age and younger; 26 percent are between the age of 35 and 54; and 31 percent are 55 years of age and older. Nearly 75 percent are married and have an average family size of 2.3 persons.

2. Financing

Twenty-five percent of all manufactured home buyers pay cash for their units; the remaining 75 percent make large down payments. Only a small percentage are financed as real estate, and most units go on the books of commercial banks that are active installment lenders.

Financing opportunities in the manufactured housing field are becoming more attractive to mortgage banks because more manufactured homes are dealt with as real estate and financed by the familiar deed of trust.

One stimulus to manufactured home financing is federal legislation that authorizes savings banks to finance new manufactured home purchases, creates an FHA insurance guaranty program for manufactured home loans, and makes manufactured homes eligible for VA-guaranteed loans.

XXII. CHAPTER SUMMARY

In this chapter, you are introduced to a BUSINESS OPPORTUNITY Escrow which is the sale and lease of an existing business. A CHATTEL is personal property and will be transferred along with leases on the real property.

Escrow is to be concerned with the proper procedure of this transfer as it is fraudulent not to notify affected parties as creditors and taxing agencies. A BULK TRANSFER is any conveyance not in the ordinary course of the business where a substantial amount of materials, supplies or inventory is transferred. A FICTITIOUS NAME is filed by the new owner when a name is used other than his or her actual name.

It will be a FINANCING STATEMENT that is file to perfect a creditor's security in personal property.

In the transfer of mobile or manufactured housing, the DEPARTMENT OF HOUSING AND COMMUNITY DEVELOPMENT is responsible for recording ownership. There are various locations throughout the state where these agencies are located.

SUBDIVISIONS are the breaking up of land into parcels for immediate or future development. Escrow and title companies assist in this process by complying with state regulations. Any escrow company that does subdivisions should be acquainted with the SUBDIVISION MAP ACT and the SUBDIVIDED LANDS ACT.

A BUSINESS OPPORTUNITY (BO) is the sale or lease of a business (inventory, fixtures, and equipment), as well as the goodwill of the existing business. GOODWILL is the expectation of continued public patronage. Also known as a BULK TRANSFER, the sale of a business is covered by the Uniform Commercial Code (UCC). A NOTICE TO CREDITORS OF BULK SALE must be given to a seller's creditors at least 12 days before the sale is consummated.

To protect buyers and creditors (encumbrancers), a SECURITY AGREEMENT AND FINANCING STATEMENT is also required for commercial transactions, although only the Financing Statement must be filed with the Secretary of State. The State Board of Equalization issues a CERTIFICATE OF PAYMENT OF SALES AND USE TAX to release the buyer from liability for the seller's unpaid sales and use tax.

As a sale of a business opportunity is considered the transfer of personal property, a BILL OF SALE is used, which serves the same function as a grant deed for real property.

NET MULTIPLIERS and GROSS MULTIPLIERS are commonly used as guidelines to compute the value of a business.

A seller who agrees not to open a competing business for a period of time within a specific geographical area has entered into a COVENANT NOT TO COMPETE.

The issuance of liquor licenses is regulated by the CALIFORNIA DEPARTMENT OF ALCOHOLIC BEVERAGE CONTROL (ABC).

REAL PROPERTY SECURITY DEALERS (RSPDs) are involved in the secondary mortgage (or money) market, and must have a broker's license as well as a permit issued by the Real Estate Commissioner.

In order to be recorded and give constructive notice, most real estate transaction documents require ACKNOWLEDGEMENT before a licensed NOTARY PUBLIC. Many brokers (or their assistants) acquire this assignation as a way to expedite and make transactions more convenient for clients.

In addition to notarial services, many brokers offer their clients PROPERTY MANAGEMENT and ESCROW services. An individual cannot be licensed as an escrow company in California, but a broker may act as an escrow agent when he or she represents the buyer or seller or both. Licensees acting as escrow agents must keep proper records and maintain all escrow funds in a trust accounts subject to inspection by the Real Estate Commissioner.

Brokers can supplement their brokerage activities by lending their own money, or money of investors, as well as acting as representatives, agents, or correspondents for mortgage lending institutions. They can also organize or join a syndication, whereby funds are pooled by investors to purchase real estate.

Yet another avenue for business expansion is the marketing and sales of probate property (court-ordered sale of a deceased person's property or properties).

The DEPARTMENT OF FINANCE may authorize a broker to earn a commission on the sale of state-owned property, including sales by the Board of Education. The California Division of Highways (Caltrans) permits licensees to negotiate the leasing of airspace under the Airspace Development Program.

Within California (intrastate), the SUBDIVISION MAP ACT and the SUBDIVIDED LANDS ACT govern the division and subsequent sale of real property. The Real Estate Commissioner's office (and responsible county or municipal authorities) administer new subdivision regulations. Subdivision maps are the most commonly used method of property division.

When selling or leasing a subdivision of 25 lots or more (LAND PROJECT) through interstate commerce or by mail, a PROPERTY REPORT permit must be obtained.

from the DEPARTMENT OF HOUSING AND URBAN DEVELOPMENT (HUD). Potential buyers receive a (state) PUBLIC REPORT and (federal) STATE PROPERTY REPORT DISCLAIMERS.

Superior knowledge is required for a broker involved in investment planning and counseling. Investment planning involves: 1) analyzing a client's investment requirements; 2) researching and selecting appropriate properties; 3) negotiating the purchase followed by title search and escrow; and 4) property management details.

Finally, brokers may sell MANUFACTURED (MOBILE) HOMES that have been registered with the Department of Motor Vehicles (DMV) for at least one year, and are greater than 8 feet wide and 40 feet long. A MANUFACTURED HOME LISTING AGREEMENT (for real and personal property) form is used for these types of sales. Brokers cannot sell mobile homes that can be used as vehicles on the highway, unless they are licensed vehicle dealers. Spaces in mobile home parks are no longer only available to rent, and ownership is on the rise. As residential subdivisions, these parks file subdivision maps with the DRE, although city and county zoning laws control their development.

XXIII. TERMS

Acknowledgement: A formal declaration before a duly authorized officer, by a person executing an instrument (that is, a formal document) that such execution is his or her act and deed.

Bill of Sale: Serves the same function in the transfer of personal property as the grant deed does for real property.

Bulk Transfer: Any business transfer not in the ordinary course of the transferor's business, of a substantial part of the materials, supplies, merchandise, equipment, or other inventory of an enterprise.

Business Opportunity: The sale and lease of the business and good will of an existing business enterprise opportunity.

California Department of Alcoholic Beverage Control (ABC): Charged with administration and enforcement of the Alcoholic Beverage Control Act, which regulates the issuance of liquor licenses.

Certificate of Payment of Sales and Use Tax: The issuance of this certificate releases the buyer from liability for the seller's unpaid sales and use taxes.

Chattel: An item of personal property

Covenant Not to Compete: The seller agrees that he or she will not open a competing business for a period of time within a specified geographical area.

Department of Housing and Community Development: The California agency responsible for recording ownership of and security interest in a manufactured home, mobilehome, commerical coach, floating home, or truck camper.

Encumbrancers: Those who have an interest in the property by virtue of having placed a lien on the property, acquired an easement against the property, imposed restrictions against it, or acquired any other interest which might be said to encumber the subject property.

Fictitious Business Name: A business name other than that of the person under whom the business is registered.

Financing Statement: A brief document filed to "perfect" or establish a creditor's security interest in personal property.

Goodwill: The expectation of continued public patronage.

Gross Multipliers: Commonly used in valuations of income-producing real estate; multipliers are also applied to the annual net income of businesses.

Interstate Land Sales Full Disclosure Act: With certain exceptions, an offering for sale or lease of a subdivision of 25 lots or more through interstate commerce or by mail requires a permit from the Department of Housing and Urban Development. This permit is called a **Property Report**.

Land Project: In California, a remote subdivision.

Manufactured Home: Built on a steel chassis and equipped with wheels so that it can be pulled by truck from the factory to a dealer's lot and then to a site in a park or on private land. To be classed as a mobile home, a vehicle must be at least 8 feet wide and at least 32 feet long. Each manufactured home unit is called a **Singlewide**; two or more manufactured home units together form a **Multisectional**.

Net Multipliers: The amount that a business would sell for, based upon the multiplication of its annual net income by some standardized number, or multiplier.

Real Estate Investment Counselor: The broker's broker or consultant, doing for other brokers what those brokers cannot do for themselves, until their own knowledge and experience is of such magnitude as to qualify them for similar status.

Real Property Securities Dealer (RPSD): Engaged in the secondary market, in addition to a host of activities that come under the definition of real property securities.

Security Agreement and Financing Statement: Shows the debtor's name and address (cosigners and trade names would be included); the secured party's name and address (assignee); description and nature of the property used as collateral; and other items.

Subdivided Lands Act: State law that grants the Real Estate Commissioner authority to administer necessary regulations to protect purchasers from fraud, misrepresentation, or deceit in the initial sale of subdivided property.

Subdivision Map Act: State law that allow local government direct control over the types of subdivision ordinances and control over the projects and improvements to be installed.

Syndicate: An association formed to operate an investment business. It can be a corporation, partnership, or trust.

Uniform Commercial Code (UCC): A body of law adopted throughout the United States that standardizes a number of practices commonly found in commerce and business.

XXIV. CHAPTER QUIZ

1. Which of the following is a civil rights law?

    a. Rumford Act

    b. Unruh Act

    c. Fair Housing Act

    d. All of the above

2. Which section of the Civil Code deals with "False Promise"?

    a. 10176(a)

    b. 10176(b)

    c. 10176(c)

    d. 10176(d)

3. The California Fair Employment and Housing Act has many ramifications that apply to:

    a. real estate brokers.

    b. salespeople.

    c. owners of residential property.

    d. all of the above.

4. The Federal Civil Rights Act of 1968 deals with:

    a. jurisdiction.

    b. disclaimers.

    c. discrimination.

    d. job security.

5. It is unlawful to threaten or commit acts of violence against a person or property based on:

    a. race.

    b. color.

    c. religion.

    d. all of the above.

6. Examples of a business opportunity include all of the following, except:

    a. drugstores.

    b. service stations.

    c. residential apartments.

    d. beauty shops.

7. A body of law adopted throughout the United States that standardizes a number of practices commonly found in commerce and business is known as the:

    a. Uniform Conduct Code.
    b. Uniform Commercial Code.
    c. Uniform Code of Commerce.
    d. Uniform Class of Creditors.

8. All exclusive listings must have:

    a. a definite termination date.
    b. at least 8 pages.
    c. at least 2 pages.
    d. a cash advance.

9. Which of the following items would not be included in a bill of sale transferring title to a retail merchandising business?

    a. Inventory of stock
    b. Assignment of lease
    c. The trade name
    d. List of fixtures and equipment

10. A real estate syndicate can be a:

    a. corporation.
    b. partnership.
    c. trust.
    d. all of the above.

ANSWERS: 1. d; 2. b; 3. d; 4. c; 5. d; 6. c; 7. b; 8. a; 9. b; 10. d

Glossary of Terms

A

ALTA Title Policy (American Land Title Association): A type of title insurance policy issued by title insurance companies which expands the risks normally insured against under the standard type policy to include unrecorded mechanic's liens; unrecorded physical easements; facts a physical survey would show; water and mineral rights; and rights of parties in possession, such as tenants and buyers under unrecorded instruments.

ALTA Owner's Policy (Standard Form B-1962, as amended 1969): An owner's extended coverage policy that provides buyers or owners the same protection the ALTA policy gives to lenders.

Abatement of Nuisance: Extinction or termination of a nuisance.

Absolute Fee Simple Title: Absolute or fee simple title is one that is absolute and unqualified. It is the best title one can have.

Abstract of Judgment: A condensation of the essential provisions of a court judgment.

Abstract of Title: A summary or digest of the conveyances, transfers, and any other facts relied on as evidence of title, together with any other elements of record which may impair the title.

Abstraction: A method of valuing land. The indicated value of the improvement is deducted from the sale price.

Acceleration Clause: Clause in trust deed or mortgage giving lender right to call all sums owing him or her to be immediately due and payable upon the happening of a certain event.

Acceptance: When the seller's or agent's principal agrees to the terms of the agreement of sale and approves the negotiation on the part of the agent and acknowledges receipt of the deposit in subscribing to the agreement of sale, that act is termed an acceptance.

Access Right: The right of an owner to have ingress and egress to and from his or her property.

Accommodation: The act of providing a service usually without cost preparing documents for a client.

Accretion: An addition to land from natural causes as, for example, from gradual action of the ocean or river waters.

Accrued Depreciation: The difference between the cost of replacement new as of the date of the appraisal and the present appraised value.

Accrued Items of Expense: Those incurred expenses which are not yet payable. The seller's accrued expenses are credited to the purchaser in a closing statement.

Acknowledgment: A formal declaration before a duly authorized officer by a person who has executed an instrument that such execution is his or her act and deed.

Acoustical Tile: Blocks of fiber, mineral or metal, with small holes or rough-textured surface to absorb sound, used as covering for interior walls and ceilings.

Acquisition: The act or process by which a person procures property.

Acre: A measure of land equalling 160 square rods, or 4,840 square yards, or 43,560 square feet, or a tract about 208.71 feet square.

Adjusting Interest: The calculation of how much interest is due usually based on the number of days interest is earned or will be prepaid.

Adjustments: A means by which characteristics of a residential property are regulated by dollar amount or percentage to conform to similar characteristics of another residential property.

Affiant: A person who has made an affidavit.

Administrator/Administratrix: The persons appointed by the court to settle the estate of a person who had died intestate.

Administrator/Executor Deed: A deed given as a result of transfer of decedent's property.

Ad Valorem: A Latin phrase meaning, "according to value." Usually used in connection with real estate taxation.

Advance: Transfer of funds from a lender to a borrower in advance on a loan.

Advance Commitment: The institutional investor's prior agreement to provide long-term financing upon completion of construction.

Advance Fee: A fee paid in advance of any services rendered. Specifically that unethical practice of obtaining a fee in advance for the advertising of property or businesses for sale, with no obligation to obtain a buyer, by persons representing themselves as real estate licensees, or representatives of licensed real estate firms.

Adverse Possession: The open and notorious possession and occupancy under an evident claim or right, in denial or opposition to the title of another claimant.

Affidavit: A statement or declaration reduced to writing sworn to or affirmed before some officer who has authority to administer an oath or affirmation.

Affidavit of Title: A statement in writing, made under oath by seller or grantor, acknowledged before a Notary Public in which the affiant identifies himself or herself and his or her marital status certifying that since the examination of title on the contract date there are no judgments, bankruptcies or divorces, or unrecorded deeds, contracts, unpaid repairs or improvements or defects of title known to him or her and that he or she is in possession of the property.

Affirm: To confirm, to aver, to ratify, to verify.

AFLB: Accredited Farm and Land Broker.

Agency: The relationship between principal and agent which arises out of a contract, either expressed or implied, written or oral, wherein the agent is employed by the principal to do certain acts dealing with a third party.

Agent: One who represents another from whom he or she has derived authority.

Agreement of Sale: A written agreement or contract between seller and purchaser in which they reach a meeting of minds on the terms and conditions of the sale.

Air Rights: The rights in real property to use the air space above the surface of the land.

Alienation: The transferring of property to another; the transfer of property and possession of lands, or other things, from one person to another.

Allodial Tenure: A real property ownership system where ownership may be complete except for those rights held by government. Allodial is in contrast to feudal tenure.

Alluvium: Soil deposited by accretion. Increase of earth on a shore or bank of a river.

Amendment to Instructions: A change to either correct or alter or add to the escrow instructions to avoid any conflict in the instructions.

Amenities: Satisfaction of enjoyable living to be derived from a home; conditions of agreeable living or a beneficial influence arising from the location or improvements.

American Escrow Association: A group of title and escrow representatives that meet to further goals in education and professionalism for the escrow industry as a whole.

American Institute of Real Estate Appraisers: A trade association of real estate appraisers.

AMO: Accredited Management Organization.

Amortization: The liquidation of a financial obligation on an installment basis; also, recovery: over a period, of cost or value.

Amortized Loan: A loan that is completely paid off, interest and principal, by a series of regular payments that are equal or nearly equal. Also called a **Level Payments Loan**.

Annuity: A series of assured equal or nearly equal payments to be made over a period of time or it may be a lump sum payment to be made in the future. The installment payments due to the landlord under a lease is an Annuity. So are the installment payments due to a lender. In real estate finance we are most concerned with the first definition.

Anticipation, Principle of: Affirms that value is created by anticipated benefits to be derived in the future.

Appraisal: An estimate and opinion of value; a conclusion resulting from the analysis of facts.

Appraiser: One qualified by education, training and experience who is hired to estimate the value of real and personal property based on experience, judgment, facts, and use of formal appraisal processes.

Appropriation of: A legal term including the act or acts involved in the taking and reducing to personal possession of water occurring in a stream or other body of water, and if applying such water to beneficial uses or purposes.

Approval Recital: A stamped or typed statement when signed by a buyer or seller indicates acceptance or approval of the document.

Appurtenance: Something annexed to another thing which may be transferred incident to it. That which belongs to another thing, as a barn, dwelling, garage, or orchard is incident to the land to which it is attached.

Architectural Style: Generally the appearance and character of a building's design and construction.

ASA: American Society of Appraisers.

Assessed Valuation: A valuation placed upon property by a public officer or board, as a basis for taxation.

Assessed Value: Value placed on property as a basis for taxation.

Assessment: The valuation of property for the purpose of levying a tax or the amount of the tax levied.

Assessor: The official who has the responsibility of determining assessed values.

Assignment: A transfer or making over to another of the whole of any property, real or personal, in possession or in action, or of any estate or right therein.

Assignment of Rents: An agreement in the deed of trust that grants the right to the lender to collect rents even though title is held by the trustor.

Assignor: One who assigns or transfers property.

Assigns; Assignees: Those to whom property shall have been transferred.

Assumed: The written act of agreeing to be personally liable for the terms and conditions of an existing loan thereby relieving the previous borrower of that liability.

Assumption Agreement: An undertaking or adoption of a debt or obligation primarily resting upon another person.

Assumption Fee: A lender's charge for changing over and processing new records for a new owner who is assuming an existing loan.

Assumption of Mortgage: The taking of title to property by a grantee, wherein he assumes liability for payment of an existing note secured by a mortgage or deed of trust against the property; becoming a co-guarantor for the payment of a mortgage or deed of trust note.

Attachment: Seizure of property by court order, usually done to have it available in event a judgment is obtained in a pending suit.

Attest: To affirm to be true or genuine; an official act establishing authenticity.

Attorney in Fact: One who is authorized to perform certain acts for another under a power of attorney; power of attorney may be limited to a specific act or acts, or be general.

Avulsion: The sudden tearing away or removal of land by action of water flowing over or through it.

Axial Growth: City growth which occurs along main transportation routes. Usually takes the form of star-shaped extensions outward from the center.

B

Backfill: The replacement of excavated earth into a hole or against a structure.

Balloon Payment: Where the final installment payment on a note is greater than the preceding installment payments and it pays the note in full, such final installment is termed a balloon payment.

Bargain and Sale Deed: Any deed that recites a consideration and purports to convey the real estate; a bargain and sale deed with a covenant against the grantor's acts is one in which the grantor warrants that he or she has done nothing to harm or cloud the title.

Baseboard: A board placed against the wall around a room next to the floor.

Base and Meridian: Imaginary lines used by surveyors to find and describe the location of private or public lands.

Base Molding: Molding used at top of baseboard.

Base Shoe: Molding used at junction of baseboard and floor. Commonly called a carpet strip.

Batten: Narrow strips of wood or metal used to cover joints, interiorly or exteriorly; also used for decorative effect.

Beam: A structural member transversely supporting a load.

Bearing Wall or Partition: A wall or partition supporting, any vertical load in addition to its own weight.

Bench Marks: A location indicated on a durable marker by surveyors.

Beneficiary: (1) One entitled to the benefit of a trust; (2) One who receives profit from an estate, the title of which is vested in a trustee; (3) The lender on the security of a note and deed of trust.

Beneficiary's Statement: A statement of the unpaid balance of a loan and the condition of the indebtedness, as it relates to a deed of trust transaction.

Bequeath: To give or hand down by will; to leave by will.

Bequest: That which is given by the terms of a will.

Betterment: An improvement upon property which increases the property value and is considered as a capital asset or distinguished from repairs or replacements where the original character or cost is unchanged.

Bill of Sale: A written instrument given to pass title of personal property from vendor to the vendee.

Binder: An agreement to consider a down payment for the purchase of real estate as evidence of good faith on the part of the purchaser. Also, a notation of coverage on an insurance policy, issued by art agent, and given to the insured prior to issuing of the policy.

Blacktop: Asphalt paving used in streets and driveways.

Blank Endorsement: Payees sign their names on the back of the note the same as they would endorse a check.

Blanket Mortgage: A single mortgage which covers more than one piece of real estate.

Blighted Area: A declining area in which real property values are seriously affected by destructive economic forces, such as encroaching inharmonious property usages, infiltration of lower social and economic classes of inhabitants, and/or rapidly depreciating buildings.

Board foot: A unit of measurement of lumber; one foot wide, one foot long, one inch thick; 144 cubic inches.

Bona Fide: In good faith, without fraud.

Bond: An obligation under seal. A real estate bond is a written obligation issued on security of a mortgage or trust deed.

Boot: Money or other property that is considered "not like-kind" which is given to make up any difference in value or equity between exchanged property.

Bracing: Framing lumber nailed at an angle in order to provide rigidity.

Breach: The breaking of a law, or failure of duty, either by omission or commission.

Breezeway: A covered porch or passage, open on two sides, connecting house and garage or two parts of the house.

Bridging: Small wood or metal pieces used to brace floor joists.

Broker: A person employed by another, to carry on any of the activities listed in the license law definition of a broker, for a fee.

B.T.U.: British thermal unit. The quantity of heat required to raise the temperature of one pound of water one degree Fahrenheit.

Building Code; A systematic regulation of construction of buildings within a municipality established by ordinance or law.

Building Line: A line set by law a certain distance from a street line in front of which an owner cannot build on his lot. (A setback line.)

Building, Market Value of: The sum of money which the presence of that structure adds to or subtracts from the value of the land it occupies. Land valued on the basis of highest and best use.

Building Paper: A heavy waterproofed paper used as sheathing in wall or roof construction as a protection against air passage and moisture.

Built-In: Cabinets or similar features built as part of the house.

Bulk Transfer: Any business transfer not in the ordinary course of the transferor's business, of a substantial part of the materials, supplies, merchandise, equipment, or other inventory of an enterprise.

Bundle of Rights: Beneficial interests or rights.

Business Opportunity: The sale and lease of the business and good will of an existing business enterprise opportunity.

Buyer Credit: An increase to the buyer's side as deposit, loans, and prorations.

Buyer Debit: A charge against the buyer's side as in the purchase price and other expenses.

C

CBD: Central Business District.

CCIM: Certified Commercial Investment Member.

CC&Rs: Abbreviation for covenants, conditions, and restrictions.

CLTA: California Land Title Association title policy that covers owners, lenders, and leaseholds in various ways.

CLTA Form 104: Used with ALTA loan policies when the lender's interest has been assigned.

CLTA Form 104A: The purchaser of the note is assured that the person selling the note is the true competent owner; no bankruptcy or unpaid taxes.

CLTA Form 104.1: Limits coverage to putting the assignee in the shoes of the assignor. Normally no examination is made for bankruptcy, taxes, assessments etc.

CLTA Owner's Standard Policy: The usual policy issued to a owner that protects against matters of record and certain off record hazards.

CPM (Certified Property Manager): A designation of the Institute of Real Estate Management.

California Department of Alcoholic Beverage Control (ABC): Charged with administration and enforcement of the Alcoholic Beverage Control Act, which regulates the issuance of liquor licenses.

California Escrow Association (CEA): An association dedicated to the professionalism of escrow personnel through education and legislation.

Cancellation: Specific agreement by parties to cancel or terminate a contract or escrow.

Capable Parties: Principals must legally be able to enter into a contract.

Capital Assets: Assets of a permanent nature used in the production of an income, such as: land, buildings, machinery, and equipment, etc. Under income tax law, it is usually distinguishable from "inventory" which comprises assets held for sale to customers in ordinary course of the taxpayers' trade or business.

Capital Gain: Income from a sale of an asset rather than from the general business activity. Capital gains are generally taxed at a lower rate than ordinary income.

Capitalization: In appraising, determining value of property by considering net income and percentage of reasonable return on the investment. Thus, the value of an income property is determined by dividing *annual net income* by the *Capitalization Rate.*

Capitalization Rate: The rate of interest which is considered a reasonable return on the investment, and used in the process of determining value based upon net income. It may also be described as the yield rate that is necessary to attract the money of the average investor to a particular kind of investment. In the case of land improvements which depreciate to this yield rate is added a factor to take into consideration the annual amortization factor necessary to recapture the initial investment in improvements. This amortization factor can be determined in various ways: (1) straight-line depreciation method, (2) Inwood Tables, and (3) Hoskold Tables. (To explore this subject in greater depth, the student should refer to current real estate appraisal texts.)

Casement Window: Frames of wood or metal, which swing outward.

Cash Flow: The net income generated by a property before depreciation and other non cash expenses.

Cashier's Check: A check drawn by a bank upon itself and payable on demand. It is considered by escrow to be "good" funds in preference to a personal check.

Caveat Emptor: "Let the buyer beware." The buyer must examine the goods or property and buy at his or her own risk.

Center of Influence: One, who, by nature of his or her relationships, is in a position to sway others.

Certificate of Completion: Given by the pest control operator after the work ordered by the customer has been done.

Certificate of Compliance: Issued by a governmental authority indicating that the owner has completed the requirements mandated by the government.

Certificate of Payment of Sales and Use Tax: The issuance of this certificate releases the buyer from liability for the seller's unpaid sales and use taxes.

Certificate of Reasonable Value (CRV): The federal Veterans Administration appraisal commitment of property value.

Certificate of Taxes Due: A written statement or guaranty of the condition of the taxes on a certain property, made by the County Treasurer of the county wherein the property is located. Any loss resulting **to any person** from an error in a tax certificate shall be paid by the county which such treasurer represents.

Certified Copy: A copy of a document, such as a deed, signed by the person having possession of the original and declaring it to be a true copy.

Chain: A unit of measurement used by surveyors. A chain consists of 100 links equal to 66 feet.

Chain of Title: A history of conveyances and encumbrances affecting the title from the time the original patent was granted, or as far back as records are available.

Change, Principle of: Holds that it is the future, not the past, which is of prime importance in estimating value.

Characteristics: Distinguishing features of a (residential) property.

Charges Check list: A separate sheet not part of escrow where the escrow considers all the charges to the escrow to minimize the chances of forgetting any items.

Chattel Mortgage: A claim on personal property (instead of real property) used to secure or guarantee a promissory note. (See definition *of A Security Agreement* and *Security Interest.)*

Chattel Real: An estate related to real estate, such as a lease on real property.

Chattels: Goods or every species of property movable or immovable which are not real property.

Circuit Breaker: An electrical device which automatically interrupts an electric circuit when an overload occurs; may be used instead of a fuse to protect each circuit and can be reset.

Clapboard: Boards usually thicker at one edge used for siding.

Closing Statement: An accounting of funds made to the buyer and seller separately. Required by law to be made at the completion of every real estate transaction.

Cloud on the Title: Any conditions revealed by a title search which affect the title to property; usually relatively unimportant items but which cannot be removed without a quitclaim deed or court action.

Collar Beam: A beam that connects the pairs of opposite roof rafters above the attic floor.

Collateral: This is the property subject to the security interest. (See definition of *Security Interest*.)

Collateral Assignment: The creation of security or lien for the performance of an obligation. An example is a pledge of personal property which is returned to the owner upon satisfying the lien.

Collateral Security: A separate obligation attached to contract to guarantee its performance; the transfer of property or of other contracts, or valuables, to insure the performance of a principal agreement.

Collusion: An agreement between two or more persons to defraud another of his rights by the forms of law, or to obtain an object forbidden by law.

Color of Title: That which appears to be good title but which is not title in fact.

Combed Plywood: A grooved building material used primarily for interior finish.

Commercial Acre: A term applied to the remainder of an acre of newly subdivided land after the area devoted to streets, sidewalks and curbs, etc., has been deducted from the acre.

Commercial Paper: Bills of exchange used in commercial trade.

Commission: An agent's compensation for performing the duties of his agency; in real estate practice, a percentage of the selling price of property, percentage of rentals, etc.

Commission Instructions: An order signed by parties to the escrow that authorizes and instructs to pay commissions as stated through escrow.

Commitment: A pledge or a promise or firm agreement.

Common Law: The body of law that grew from customs and practices developed and used in England "Since the memory of man runneth not to the contrary."

Community: A part of a metropolitan area that has a number of neighborhoods that have a tendency toward common interests and problems.

Community Property: Property accumulated through joint efforts of husband and wife living together.

Compaction: Whenever extra soil is added to a lot to fill in low places or to raise the level of the lot, the added soil is often too loose and soft to sustain the weight of the buildings. Therefore, it is necessary to compact the added soil so that it will carry the weight of buildings without the danger of their tilting, settling or cracking.

Comparable Sales: Sales which have similar characteristics as the subject property and are used for analysis in the appraisal process.

Competent: Legally qualified.

Competition, Principle of: Holds that profits tend to breed competition and excess profits tend to breed ruinous competition.

Component: One of the features making up the whole property.

Compound Interest: Interest paid on original principal and also on the accrued and unpaid interest which has accumulated.

Conclusion: The final estimate of value, realized from facts, data, experience and judgment.

Condemnation: The act of taking private property for public use by a political subdivision; declaration that a structure is unfit for use.

Condition: A qualification of an estate granted which can be imposed only in conveyances. They are classified as *conditions precedent* and *conditions subsequent.*

Condition Precedent: A condition that requires certain action or the happening of a specified event before the estate granted can take effect. Example: most installment real estate sale contracts state all payments shall be made at the time specified before the buyer may demand transfer of title.

Condition Subsequent: When there is a condition subsequent in a deed, the title vests immediately in the grantee, but upon breach of the condition the grantor has the power to terminate the estate if he or she wishes to do so. Example: A condition in the deed prohibiting the grantee from using the premises as a liquor store.

Conditional Commitment: A commitment of a definite loan amount for some future unknown purchaser of satisfactory credit standing.

Conditional Sales Contract: A contract for the sale of property stating that delivery is to be made to the buyer, title to remain vested in the seller until the conditions of the contract have been fulfilled. (See definition of *Security Interest.*)

Condominium: A system of individual fee ownership of units in a multi-family structure, combined with joint ownership of common areas of the structure and the land. (Sometimes referred to as a vertical subdivision.)

Conduit: Usually a metal pipe in which electrical wiring is installed.

Confession of Judgment: An entry of judgment upon the debtor's voluntary admission or confession.

Confirmation of Sale: A court approval of the sale of property by an executor, administrator, guardian or conservator.

Confiscation: The seizing of property without compensation.

Conformity, Principle of: Holds that the maximum of value is realized when a reasonable degree of homogeneity of improvements is present.

Conservation: The process of utilizing resources in such a manner which minimizes their depletion.

Consideration: Anything of value given to induce entering into a contract; it may be money, personal services, or even love and affection.

Constant: The percentage which, when applied directly to the face value of a debt, develops the annual amount of money necessary to pay a specified net rate of interest on the reducing balance and to liquidate the debt in a specified time period. For example, a 6% loan with a 20 year amortization has a constant of approximately 8.5%. Thus, a $10,000 loan amortized over 20 years requires an annual payment of approximately $850.00.

Construction Loans: Loans made for the construction of homes or commercial buildings. Usually funds are disbursed to the contractor/builder during construction and after periodic inspections. Disbursements are based on an agreement between borrower and lender.

Constructive Eviction: Breach of a covenant of warranty or quiet enjoyment, e.g., the inability of a lessee to obtain possession because of a paramount defect in title, or a condition making occupancy hazardous.

Constructive Notice: Notice given by the public records.

Consummate Dower: A widow's dower interest which, after the death of her husband, is complete or may be completed and become an interest in real estate.

Contour: The surface configuration of land.

Contract: An agreement, either written or oral, to do or not to do certain things.

Contribution, Principle of: Holds that maximum real property values are achieved when the improvements on the site produce the highest (net) return commensurate with the investment.

Consumer Goods: These are goods used or bought for use primarily for personal, family or household purposes.

Conventional Mortgage: A mortgage securing a loan made by investors without governmental underwriting, i.e., which is not F.H.A. insured or G.I. guaranteed.

Conversion: Change from one character or use to another.

Conveyance: This has two meanings. One meaning refers to the process of transferring title to property from one person to another. In this sense it is used as a verb. The other meaning refers to the document used to effect the transfer of title (usually some kind of deed). In this last sense, it is used a noun.

Cooperative Ownership: A form of apartment ownership. Ownership of shares in a cooperative venture which entitles the owner to use, rent, or sell a specific apartment unit. The corporation usually reserves the right to approve certain actions such as a sale or improvement.

Corner Influence Table: A statistical table that may be used to estimate the added value of a corner lot.

Corporation: A group or body of persons established and treated by law as an individual or unit with rights and liabilities or both, distinct and apart from those of the persons composing it. A corporation is a creature of law having certain powers and duties of a natural person. Being created by law it may continue for any length of time the law prescribes.

Corporeal Rights: Possessory rights in real property.

Correction Lines: A system for compensating inaccuracies in the Government Rectangular Survey System due to the curvature of the earth. Every fourth township line, 24 mile intervals, is used as a correction line on which the intervals between the north and south range lines are re-measured and corrected to a full 6 miles.

Correlate the Findings: Interpret the data and value estimates to bring them together to a final conclusion of value.

Correlation: To bring the indicated values developed by the three approaches into mutual relationship with each other.

Cost: A historical record of past expenditures, or an amount which would be given in exchange for other things.

Cost Approach: One of three methods in the appraisal process. An analysis in which a value estimate of a property is derived by estimating the replacement cost of the improvements, deducting therefrom the estimated accrued depreciation, then adding the market value of the land.

Counter Flashing: Flashing used on chimneys at the roof line to cover shingle flashing and to prevent moisture entry.

Covenant: Agreements written into deeds and other instruments promising performance or nonperformance of certain acts or stipulating certain uses or non uses of the property.

Covenant Not to Compete: The seller agrees that he or she will not open a competing business for a period of time within a specified geographical area.

Crawl Hole: Exterior or interior opening permitting access underneath building, as required by building codes.

CRB: Certified Residential Broker.

CRE: Counselor of Real Estate. Members of American Society of Real Estate Counselors.

Cubage: The number or product resulting by multiplying the width of a thing by its height and by its depth or length.

Curable Depreciation: Items of physical deterioration and functional obsolescence which are customarily repaired or replaced by a prudent property owner.

Curtail Schedule: A listing of the amounts by which the principal sum of an obligation is to be reduced by partial payments and of the dates when each payment will become payable.

Curtesy: The right which a husband has in a wife's estate at her death.

D

Damages: The indemnity recoverable by a person who has sustained an injury, either in his or her person, property, or relative rights, through the act or default of another.

Data Plant: An appraiser's file of information on real estate.

Debenture: Bonds issued without security.

Debtor: This is the party who "owns" the property which is subject to the Security Interest. Previously he was known as the *mortgagor* or the *pledger,* etc.

Deciduous Trees: Lose their leaves in the autumn and winter.

Deck: Usually an open porch on the roof of a ground or lower floor, porch or wing.

Declaration of Abandonment: The termination of a previously recorded Declaration of Homestead that will terminate the homestead when recorded.

Decree of Distribution: A court ordered decree that names the persons that are entitled to the property of the estate listing what portion is given to each heir.

Decree of Foreclosure: Decree by a court in the completion of foreclosure of a mortgage, contract, or lien.

Dedication: An appropriation of land by its owner for some public use accepted for such use by authorized public officials on behalf of the public.

Deed: Written instrument which, when properly executed and delivered, conveys title.

Deed of Trust: Creates a lien on real property securing it for repayment of a financial obligation or the performance of some other condition.

Deed Restrictions: This is a limitation in the deed to a property that dictates certain uses that may or may not be made of the property.

Default: Failure to fulfill a duty or promise or to discharge an obligation; omission or failure to perform any act.

Defeasance Clause: The clause in a mortgage that gives the mortgagor the right to redeem his or her property upon the payment of his or her obligations to the mortgagee.

Defeasible Fee: Sometimes called a base fee or qualified fee; a fee simple absolute interest in land that is capable of being defeated or terminated upon the happening of a specified event.

Deferred Maintenance: Existing but unfulfilled requirements for repairs and rehabilitation.

Deferred Payment Options: The privilege of deferring income payments to take advantage of the tax statutes.

Deficiency Judgment: A judgment given when the security pledge for a loan does not satisfy the debt upon its default.

Demand: From a beneficiary, it sets forth exactly how much is needed to pay of the existing loan balance.

Demand Instrument: A financial instrument that permits the holder to call for proceeds upon notice to the payor.

Department of Housing and Community Development: The California agency responsible for recording ownership of and security interest in a manufactured home, mobilehome, commercial coach, floating home, or truck camper.

Deposit: Money received from the buyer used as partial payment towards the down payment and demonstrating good faith.

Depreciation: Loss of value in real property brought about by age, physical deterioration or functional or economic obsolescence. Broadly, a loss in value from any cause.

Depth Table: A statistical table that may be used to estimate the value of the added depth of a lot.

Desist and Refrain Order: An order directing a person to desist and refrain from committing an act in violation of the real estate law.

Deterioration: Impairment of condition. One of the causes of depreciation and reflecting the loss in value brought about by wear and tear, disintegration, use in service, and the action of the elements.

Devisee: One who receives a bequest made by will.

Devisor: One who bequeaths by will.

Directional Growth: The location or direction toward which the residential sections of a city are destined or determined to grow.

Discount: An amount deducted in advance from the principal before the borrower is given the use of the principal (see point(s)).

Disintermediation: The relatively sudden withdrawal of substantial sums of money savers have deposited with savings and loan associations, commercial banks, and mutual savings banks. This term can also be considered to include life insurance policy purchasers borrowing against the value of their policies. The essence of this phenomenon is financial intermediaries losing within a short period of time billions of dollars as owners of funds held by those institutional lenders exercise their prerogative of taking them out of the hands of these financial institutions.

Disposable Income: The after-tax income a household receives to spend on personal consumption.

Dispossess: To deprive one of the use of real estate.

Documentary Transfer Tax: A state enabling act allowing a county to adopt a documentary transfer tax to apply on all transfer of real property located in the county. Notice of payment is entered on face of the deed or on a separate paper filed with the deed.

Dominant Tenement: The owner of property whose property gains the benefit of the easement.

Donee: A person to whom a gift is made.

Donor: A person who makes a gift.

Dower: The right which a wife has in her husband's estate at his death.

Drawing Fee: Charges made in escrow for preparation of documents as the deed, deed of trust note, etc.

Dry Rot: A fungus which affects damp or wet wood.

Dry Wood Termites: Termites that migrate from tree and wood structures to roof areas.

Due on Sale: Permits the lender to require the owner pay the entire mortgage debt in the event title is transferred. It is the same as an alienation clause.

Duress: Unlawful constraint exercised upon a person whereby he is forced to do some act against his will.

E

Earnest Money: Down payment made by a purchaser of real estate as evidence of good faith.

Easement: Created by grant or agreement for a specific purpose, an easement is the right, privilege or interest which one party has in land of another. (Example: right of way.)

Easement Appurtenant: An easement created to benefit the owner of adjacent land.

Eaves: The lower part of a roof projecting over the wall.

Ecology: The relationship between organisms and their environment.

Economic Life: The period over which a property will yield a return on the investment, over and above the economic or ground rent due to land.

Economic Obsolescence: A loss in value due to factors away from the subject property but adversely affecting the value of the subject property.

Economic Rent: The reasonable rental expectancy if the property were available for renting at the time of its valuation.

Effective Age of Improvement: The number of years of age that is indicated by the condition of the structure.

Effective Date of Value: The specific day the conclusion of value applies.

Effective Interest Rate: The percentage of interest that is actually being paid by the borrower for the use of the money.

Eminent Domain: The right of the government to acquire property for necessary public or quasi-public use by condemnation; the owner must be fairly compensated. The right of the government to do this and the right of the private citizen to get paid is spelled out in the 5th Amendment to the United States Constitution.

Encroachment: Trespass, the building of a structure or construction of any improvements, partly or wholly on the property of another.

Encumbrance: Anything which affects or limits the fee simple title to property, such as mortgages, easements or restrictions of any kind. Liens are special encumbrances which make the property security for the payment of a debt or obligation, such as mortgages and taxes.

Encumbrancers: Those who have an interest in the property by virtue of having placed a lien on the property, acquired an easement against the property, imposed restrictions against it, or acquired any other interest which might be said to encumber the subject property.

Endorsements: In negotiable instruments, the means of transferring title such as a promissory note by signing the owner's name on the reverse side of the document.

Equity: The interest or value which an owner has in real estate over and above the liens against it; branch of remedial justice by and through which relief is afforded to suitors in courts of equity.

Equity of Redemption: The right to redeem property during the fore-closure period, such as a mortgagor's right to redeem within a year after foreclosure sale.

Erosion: The wearing away of land by the action of water, wind or glacial ice.

Escalation: The right reserved by the lender to increase the amount of the payments and/or interest upon the happening of a certain event.

Escalator Clause: A clause in a contract providing for the upward or downward adjustment of certain items to cover specified contingencies.

Escheat: The reverting of property to the State when heirs capable of inheriting are lacking.

Escrow: The deposit of instruments and funds with instructions to a third neutral party to carry out the provisions of an agreement or contract; when everything is deposited to enable carrying out the instructions, it is called a complete or perfect escrow.

Escrow Check List: A pre-printed sheet used for keeping track of an escrow's status or progress.

Escrow Fee: The fee normally split by buyer and seller for the services of the escrow company.

Escrow File: A desk file that contains the documents and preprinted sheets relevant to a specific escrow.

Escrow Institute: An organization of independent escrow companies.

Escrow Instructions: A writing signed by buyer and seller that details the procedures necessary to close a transaction and directs the escrow agent how to proceed.

Escrow Memo/Order: Record of the transaction details taken at the initial interview of the parties to an escrow.

Escrow Recapitulation: A printed summary form of the details in the exchange that appears in the instructions.

Escrow Settlement Sheet: Called Estimated Charges Sheet; the accounting report for escrow where all funds are accounted for and all fees and charges are listed.

Estate: As applied to the real estate practice, the term signifies the quantity of interest, share, right, equity, of which riches or fortune may consist, in real property. The degree, quantity, nature, and ex-tent of interest which a person has in real property.

Estate of Inheritance: An estate which may descend to heirs. All freehold estates are estates of inheritance, except estates for life.

Estate for Life: A freehold estate, not of inheritance, but which is held by the tenant for his own life or the life or lives of one or more other persons, or for an indefinite period which may endure for the life or lives of persons in being and beyond the period of life.

Estate from Period-to-Period: An interest in land where there is no definite termination date but the rental period is fixed at a certain sum per week, month, or year. Also called a periodic tenancy.

Estate at Sufferance: An estate arising when the tenant wrongfully holds over after the expiration of his term. The landlord has the choice of evicting the tenant as a trespasser or accepting such tenant for a similar term and under the conditions of the tenant's previous holding. Also called a tenancy at sufferance.

Estate of Will: The occupation of lands and tenements by a tenant for an indefinite period, terminable by one or both parties.

Estate for Years: An interest in lands by virtue of a contract for the possession of them for a definite and limited period of time. A lease may be said to be an estate for years.

Estate Tax: Federal tax imposed on the right to dispose of property upon death computed on the net value of the estate.

Estimate: To form a preliminary opinion of value.

Estimated Remaining Life: The period of time (years) it takes for the improvements to become valueless.

Estoppel: A doctrine which bars one from asserting rights which are inconsistent with a previous position or representation.

Ethics: That branch of moral science, idealism, justness, and fairness, which treats of the duties which a member of a profession or craft owes to the public, to his or her clients or patron, and to his or her professional brethren or members.

Eviction: Dispossession by process of law. The act of depriving a per-son of the possession of lands, in pursuance of the judgment of a court.

Exceptions to Title: When used in the title report, it refers to items specifically excluded from coverage under a title insurance policy.

Exchange: A real estate transaction where one property is traded for another.

Exchange Agreement: A type of deposit receipt prepared by a broker to become a binding agreement in an exchange transaction. It is the initial contract between parties.

Exclusive Agency Listing: A written instrument giving one agent the right to sell property for a specified time but reserving the right of the owner to sell the property himself or herself without the payment of a commission.

Exclusive Right to Sell Listing: A written agreement between owner and agent giving agent the right to collect a commission if the property is sold by anyone during the term of his or her agreement.

Execute: To complete, to make, to perform, to do, to follow out; to execute a deed, to make a deed, including especially signing, sealing, and delivery; to execute a contract is to perform the contract, to follow out to the end, to complete.

Executor/Executrix: The persons appointed by a testator to carry out the directions and requests in their last will and testament.

Expansible House: Home designed for further expansion and additions in the future.

Expansion Joint: A bituminous fiber strip used to separate units of concrete to prevent cracking due to expansion as a result of temperature changes.

Expenses: Certain items which may appear on a closing statement in connection with a real estate sale.

Extended Policy: Additional protection at added cost that protects against risks limited in the standard policy.

F

Facade: Front of a building.

Farmers Home Administration: An agency of the Department of Agriculture. Primary responsibility is to provide financial assistance for farmers and others living in rural areas where financing is not available on reasonable terms from private sources.

Fair Market Value: This is the amount of money that would be paid for a property offered on the open market for a reasonable period of time with both buyer and seller knowing all the uses to which the property could be put and with neither party being under pressure to buy or sell.

Federal Deposit Insurance Corporation (FDIC): Agency of the federal government which insures deposits at commercial banks and savings banks.

Federal Home Loan Bank (FHLB): A district bank of the Federal Home Loan Bank system that lends only to member savings and loan associations.

Federal Home Loan Bank Board (FHLBB): The administrative agency that charters federal savings and loan associations and exercises regulatory authority over the FHLB system.

Federal Housing Administration: (FHA) An agency of the federal government that insures mortgage loans.

Federal National Mortgage Association (FNMA): "Fanny Mae" a quasi-public agency being converted into a private corporation whose primary function is to buy and sell FHA and VA mortgages in the secondary market.

Federal Reserve Regulation Z: Also known as Truth in Lending with a purpose of insuring borrower' are given disclosure of the cost of credit.

Fee: An estate of inheritance in real property.

Fee Simple: In modern estates, the terms "Fee" and "Fee Simple" are substantially synonymous. The term "Fee" is of Old English derivation. "Fee Simple Absolute" is an estate in real property, by which the owner has the greatest power over the title which it is possible to have, being an absolute estate. In modern use, it expressly establishes the title of real property in the owner, without limitation or *end. He or she may dispose of it by sale, or trade or will, as he or she chooses.*

Feudal Tenure: A real property ownership system where ownership rests with a sovereign who, in turn, may grant lesser interests in return for service or loyalty. In contrast to allodial tenure.

Feuds: Grants of land.

Fictitious Business Name: A business name other than that of the person under whom the business is registered.

Fictitious Deed of Trust: After recording, any provision of a fictitious mortgage or trust deed may be incorporated by reference to another trust deed affecting real property in the same county.

Fidelity Bond: A security posted for the discharge of an obligation of personal services.

Fiduciary: A person in a position of trust and confidence, as between principal and broker; broker as fiduciary owes certain loyalty which cannot be breached under the rules of agency.

Files: The method of keeping escrow papers carefully saved and accessible as they are needed later.

Filtering Down: The process of making housing available to successively lower income groups.

Final Escrow Settlement: A detailed cash accounting of a real estate transaction prepared by escrow. Shows all cash received, all charges and credits made and all cash paid out in the transaction.

Financial Intermediary: Financial institutions such as commercial banks, savings and loan associations, mutual savings banks and life insurance companies which receive relatively small sums of money from the public and invest them in the form of large sums. A considerable portion of these funds are loaned on real estate.

Financing Statement: This is the instrument which is filed in order to give public notice of the security interest and thereby protect the interest of the secured parties in the collateral. See definitions of *Security Interest and Secured Party.*

Finish Floor: Finish floor strips are applied over wood joists, deadening felt and diagonal subflooring before finish floor is installed; finish floor is the final covering on the floor: wood, linoleum, cork, tile, or carpet.

Fire Insurance: Property insurance required when escrow closes covering losses due to fire, and other specific perils.

Fire Stop: A solid, tight closure of a concealed space, placed to prevent the spread of fire and smoke through such a space.

First Mortgage: A legal document pledging collateral for a loan (see "mortgage") that has first priority over all other claims against the property except taxes and bonded indebtedness.

First Party: When there are two or more deeds transferred, parties are designated to be a first or second party. A first party may be the one that pays out boot, or the property with greatest value, or the one requiring the greatest amount of detail in setting up the escrow instructions.

Fiscal Controls: Federal tax revenue and expenditure policies used to control the level of economic activity.

Fixity of Location: The physical characteristic of real estate that subjects it to the influence of its surroundings.

Fixtures: Appurtenances attached to the land or improvements, which usually cannot be removed without agreement as they become real property; examples: plumbing fixtures, store fixtures built into the property, etc.

Flashing: Sheet metal or other material used to protect a building from seepage of water.

Footing: The base or bottom of a foundation wall, pier, or column.

Foreclosure: Procedure whereby property pledged as security for a debt is sold to pay the debt in event of default in payments or terms.

Forfeiture: Loss of money or anything of value, due to failure to perform.

Foundation: The supporting portion of a structure below the first floor construction, or below grade, including the footings.

Franchise: A specified privilege awarded by a government or business firm which awards an exclusive dealership.

Fraud: The intentional and successful employment of any cunning, deception, collusion, or artifice, used to circumvent, cheat or deceive another person, whereby that person acts upon it to the loss of his or her property and to his or her legal injury.

Freehold: An estate of indeterminable duration, e.g., fee simple or life estate.

Frontage: Land bordering a street.

Front Foot: Property measurement for sale or valuation purposes; the property measures by the front foot on its street line—each front foot extending the depth of the lot.

Front Money: The minimum amount of money necessary to initiate a real estate venture.

Frostline: The depth of frost penetration in the soil. Varies in different parts of the country. Footings should be placed below this depth to prevent movement.

Full Reconveyance: The instrument which discharges the debt and ends the borrower and lender relationship.

Full Release of Mortgage: The formal release of a mortgage lien when the lender is satisfied to complete the release.

Functional Obsolescence: A loss of value due to adverse factors from within the structure which affect the utility of the structure.

Furring: Strips of wood or metal applied to a wall or other surface to even it, to form an air space, or to give the wall an **appearance** of greater thickness.

Future Benefits: The anticipated benefits the present owner will receive from his property in the future.

G

Gable Roof: A pitched roof with sloping sides.

Gambrel Roof: A curb roof, having a steep lower slope with a flatter upper slope above.

General Lien: A lien on all the property of a debtor.

General Provisions: The provisions of an escrow that involve the main standard items for most transactions. May include deposits, prorations, recording, and taxes.

Gift Deed: A deed for which the consideration is love and affection and where there is no material consideration.

Girder: A large beam used to support beams, joists and partitions.

Grade: Ground level at the foundation.

Goodwill: The expectation of continued public patronage.

Graduated Lease: Lease which provides for a varying rental rate, often based upon future determination; sometimes rent is based upon result of periodical appraisals; used largely in long-term leases.

Grant: A technical term made use of in deeds of conveyance of lands to import a transfer.

Grant Deed: A deed in which "grant" is used as the word of conveyance. The grantor warrants that he has not already conveyed to any other person, and that the estate conveyed is free from encumbrances done, made or suffered by the grantor or any person claiming under him, including taxes, assessments, and other liens.

Grantee: The purchaser; a person to whom a grant is made.

Grantor: Seller of property; one who signs a deed. GRI: Graduate, Realtors Institute.

Grid: A chart used in rating the borrower risk, property, and the neighborhood.

Gross Income: Total income from property before any expenses are deducted.

Gross Multipliers: Commonly used in valuations of income-producing real estate; multipliers are also applied to the annual net income of businesses.

Gross National Product (GNP): The total value of all goods and services produced in a economy during a given period of time.

Gross Rate: A method of collecting interest by adding total interest to the principal of the loan at the outset of the term.

Gross Rent Multiplier: A figure which, times the gross income of a property, produces art estimate of value of the property.

Ground Lease: An agreement for the use of the land only, sometimes secured by improvements placed on the land by the user.

Ground Rent: Earnings of improved property credited to earnings of the ground itself after allowance is made for earnings of improvements; often termed economic rent.

Guarantee of Title: Title company assurances about the title to real property however no title policy is issued.

H-I

Habendum Clause: The "to have and to hold" clause in a deed.

Header: A beam placed perpendicular to joists and to which joists are nailed in framing for chimney, stairway, or other opening.

Highest and Best Use: An appraisal phrase meaning that use which at the time of an appraisal is most likely to produce the greatest net return to the land and/or buildings over a given period of time; that use which will produce the greatest amount of amenities or profit. This is the starting point for appraisal.

Hip Roof: A pitched roof with sloping sides and ends.

Holder in Due Course: One who has taken a note, check or bill of exchange in due course: (1) Before it was overdue; In good faith and for value; Without knowledge that it has been previously dishonored without notice of any defect at the time it was negotiated to him.

Holdover Tenant: Tenant who remains in possession of leased property after the expiration of the lease term.

Homestead: A home upon which the owner or owners have recorded a Declaration of Homestead, as provided by Statutes in some states; protects home against judgments up to specified amounts.

HUD Statement: A required loan statement by the Housing and Urban Development allocating the appropriate charges and credits.

Hundred Percent Location: A city retail business location which is considered the best available for attracting business.

Hypothecate: To give a thing as security without the necessity of giving up possession of it.

Impounds: A trust-type account established by lenders for the accumulation of funds to meet taxes, FHA mortgage insurance premiums, and/or future insurance policy premiums required to protect their security. Impounds are usually collected with the note payment.

Inchoate Right of Dower: A wife's interest in the real estate of her husband during his life which upon his death may become a dower interest.

Income Approach: One of the three methods in the appraisal process; an analysis in which the estimated gross income from the subject residence is used as a basis for estimating value along with gross rent multipliers derived.

Incompetent: One who is mentally incompetent, incapable; person who, though not insane, is by reason of old age, disease, weakness of mind, or any other cause, unable, unassisted, to properly manage and take care of himself/herself or his/her property and by reason thereof would be likely to be deceived or imposed upon by artful or designing persons.

Incorporeal Rights: Non possessory rights in real estate.

Increment: An increase. Most frequently used to refer to the increase of value of land that accompanies population growth and increasing wealth in the community. The term unearned increment is used in this connection since values are supposed to have increased without effort on the part of the owner.

Indemnity: An agreement to reimburse or compensate someone for a loss.

Indenture: A formal written instrument made between two or more persons in different interests.

Independent Escrow Agent: An escrow company licensed by the California Department of Corporations.

Indexing: An office procedure that allows one to store and quickly locate specific files when needed usually by an alphabetical cross index system.

Indirect Lighting: The light is reflected from the ceiling or other object external to the fixture.

Indorsement: The act of signing one's name on the back of a check or note, with or without further qualification.

Inheritance Tax: A state "estate" tax imposed on heirs for their right to inherit property.

Inheritance Tax Referee: The pubic official appointed to inventory all property to the estate and listing the value for tax purposes.

Injunction: A writ or order issued under the seal of a court to restrain one or more parties to a suit or proceeding from doing an act which is deemed to be inequitable or unjust in regard to the rights of some other party or parties in the suit or proceeding.

Input: Data, information, etc., that is fed into a computer or other system.

Installment Contract: Purchase of real estate wherein the purchase price is paid in installments over a long period of time, title is retained by seller, upon default the payments are forfeited. Also known as a land contract.

Installment Note: A note which provides that payments of a certain sum or amount be paid on the dates specified in the instrument.

Installment Note – Interest Extra: Interest payments are at interval times and the remaining amount plus interest owing comes due at a specified date.

Installment Reporting: A method of reporting capital gains by installments for successive tax years to minimize the impact of the totality of the capital gains tax in the year of the sale.

Instrument: A written legal document; created to effect the rights of the parties.

Interest: The charge in dollars for the use of money for a period of time. In a sense, the "rent" paid for the use of money.

Interest Rate: The percentage of a sum of money charged for its use.

Interim Binder: Written agreement by a title company to issue a title policy at a later date. It is not a title policy and will normally have a time limit to be issued.

Interim Loan: A short-term loan until long-term financing is available.

Interpleader: A legal proceeding whereby escrow deposits with the court funds and papers to be properly distributed.

Interspousal Deed: A deed executed between married couples to transfer or otherwise correct title.

Intestate: A person who dies having made no will, or one which is defective in form in which case his or her estate descends to his or her heirs at law or next of kin.

Interstate Land Sales Full Disclosure Act: With certain exceptions, an offering for sale or lease of a subdivision of 25 lots or more through interstate commerce or by mail requires a permit from the Department of Housing and Urban Development. This permit is called a **Property Report**.

Involuntary Lien: A lien imposed against property without consent of an owner; example: taxes, special assessments, federal income tax liens, etc.

Irrevocable: Incapable of being recalled or revoked; unchangeable.

Irrigation Districts: Quasi-political districts created under special laws to provide for water services to property owners in the district; an operation governed to a great extent by law.

J

Jalousie: A slatted blind or shutter, like a venetian blind but used on the exterior to protect against rain as well as to control sunlight.

Jamb: The side post or lining of a doorway, window or other opening.

Joint: The space between the adjacent surfaces of two components joined and held together by nails, glue, cement, mortar, etc.

Joint Note: A note signed by two or more persons who have equal liability for payment.

Joint Tenancy: Joint ownership by two or more persons with right of survivorship; all joint tenants own equal interest and have equal rights in the property.

Joint Venture: Two or more individuals or firms joining together on a single project as partners.

Joist: One of a series of parallel beams to which the boards of a floor and ceiling laths are nailed, and supported in turn by larger beams, girders, or bearing walls.

Judgment: The final determination of a court of competent jurisdiction of a matter presented to it; money judgments provide for the payment of claims presented to the court, or are awarded as damages, etc.

Judgment Lien: A legal claim on all of the property of a judgment debtor which enables the judgment creditor to have the property sold for payment of the amount of the judgment.

Junior Mortgage: A mortgage second in lien to a previous mortgage.

Jurisdiction: The authority by which judicial officers take cognizance of and decide causes; the power to hear and determine a cause; the right and power which a judicial officer has to enter upon the inquiry.

L

Laches: Delay or negligence in asserting one's legal rights.

Land and Improvement Loan: A loan obtained by the builder-developer for the purchase of land and to cover expenses for subdividing.

Land Contract: A contract ordinarily used in connection with the sale of property in cases where the seller does not wish to convey title until all or a certain part of the purchase price is paid by the buyer; often used when property is sold on small down payment.

Landlord: One who rents his or her property to another.

Land Project: In California, a remote subdivision.

Late Charge: An added charge to a borrower for failure to pay a regular installment when it is due.

Later Date Order: The commitment for an owner's title insurance policy issued by a title insurance company which covers the seller's title as of the date of the contract. When the sale closes the purchaser orders the title company to record the deed to purchaser and bring down their examination to cover this later date so as to show purchaser as owner of the property.

Land Patent/Grant: An original conveyance from the government to a private owner.

Lateral Support: The support which the soil of an adjoining owner gives to his or her neighbors' land.

Lath: A building material of wood, metal, gypsum, or insulating board fastened to the frame of a building to act as a plaster base.

Lawful Nature: Subject matter of an escrow must able to be legally bought or sold.

Lease: A contract between owner and tenant, setting forth conditions upon which tenant may occupy and use the property, and the term of the occupancy.

Leasehold Estate: A tenant's right to occupy real estate during the term of the lease. This is a personal property interest.

Legal Description: A description recognized by law; a description by which property can be definitely located by reference to government surveys or approved recorded maps.

Lessee: One who contracts to rent property under a lease contract. Lessor: An owner who enters into a lease with a tenant.

Lessor: An owner who enters into a lease with a tenant.

Level-Payment Mortgage: A loan on real estate that is paid off by making a series of equal (or nearly equal) regular payments. Part of the payment is usually interest on the loan and part of it reduces the amount of the unpaid balance of the loan. Also sometimes called an "amortized mortgage."

Lien: A form of encumbrance which usually makes property security for the payment of a debt or discharge of an obligation. Example: judgments, taxes, mortgages, deeds of trust, etc.

Life Estate: An estate or interest in real property which is held for the duration of the life of some certain person.

Limited Partnership: A partnership composed of some partners whose contribution and liability are limited.

Lintel: A horizontal board that supports the load over an opening such as a door or window.

Liquidated Damages: A sum agreed upon by the parties to be full damages if a certain event occurs.

Lis Pendens: Suit pending, usually recorded so as to give constructive notice of pending litigation.

Listing: An employment contract between principal and agent authorizing the agent to perform services for the principal involving the Tatter's property; listing contracts are entered into for the purpose of securing persons to buy, lease or rent property. Employment of an agent by a prospective purchaser or lessee to locate property for purchase or lease may be considered a listing.

Loan Administration: Also called loan servicing. Mortgage bankers not only originate loans, but also "service" them from origination to maturity of the loan.

Loan Application: The loan application is a source of information on which the lender bases his or her decision to make the loan, defines the terms of the loan contract; gives the name of the borrower, place of employment, salary, bank accounts, and credit references;

and, describes the real estate that is to be mortgaged. It also stipulates the amount of loan being applied for, and repayment terms.

Loan Closing: When all conditions have been met, the loan officer authorizes the recording of the trust deed or mortgage. The dispersal procedure of funds is similar to the closing of a real estate sales escrow. The borrower can expect to receive less than the amount of the loan, as title, recording, service, and other fees may be withheld, or he or she can expect to deposit the cost of these items into the loan escrow. This process is sometimes called "funding" the loan.

Loan Commitment: Lender's contractual commitment to a loan based on the appraisal and underwriting.

Loan-Value Ratio: The percentage of a property's value that a lender can or may loan to a borrower. For example, if the ratio is 80% this means that a lender may loan 80% of the property's appraised value to a borrower.

Long Form: A recital of all of the terms and conditions related to a deed of trust with its general provisions.

Lost Instrument Bond: In the event of lost instruments, an insurance bond may be issued to serve as indemnity in the event of a claim.

Louver: An opening with a series of horizontal slats set at an angle to permit ventilation without admitting rain, sunlight, or vision.

M

MAI: Member of the Appraisal Institute. Designates a person who is a member of the American Institute of Real Estate Appraisers of the National Association of Realtors®.

Manufactured Home: Built on a steel chassis and equipped with wheels so that it can be pulled by truck from the factory to a dealer's lot and then to a site in a park or on private land. To be classed as a mobile home, a vehicle must be at least 8 feet wide and at least 32 feet long. Each manufactured home unit is called a **Singlewide**; two or more manufactured home units together form a **Multisectional**.

Margin of **Security:** The difference between the amount of the mortgage loan(s) and the appraised value of the property.

Marginal Land: Land which barely pays the cost of working or using.

Market Data Approach: One of the three methods in the appraisal process. A means of comparing similar type residential properties, which have recently sold, to the subject property.

Market Price: The price paid regardless of pressures, motives or intelligence.

Market Value: (1) The price at which a willing seller would sell and a willing buyer would buy, neither being under abnormal pressure; (2) as defined by the courts, is the highest price estimated in terms of money which a property will bring if exposed for sale

in the open market allowing a reasonable time to find a purchaser with knowledge of property's use and capabilities for use.

Marketable Title: Merchantable title; title free and clear of objectionable liens or encumbrances.

Material Fact: A fact is material if it is one which the agent should realize would be likely to affect the judgment of the principal in giving his consent to the agent to enter into the particular transaction on the specified terms.

Mechanics' Lien: A lien created by statute which exists against real property in favor of persons who have performed work or furnished materials for the improvement of the real estate.

Memoranda of Agreement: Items asked for by the principals that escrow cannot attend are listed under a separate memoranda of agreement. A heading stating that the escrow is not to be concerned will be included.

Memory Bank: Data and information held in storage in the computer.

Meridians: Imaginary north-south lines which intersect base lines to form a starting point for the measurement of land.

Metes and Bounds: A term used in describing the boundary lines of land, setting forth all the boundary lines together with their terminal points and angles.

Mile: 5,280 feet.

Mineral Rights: Rights to subsurface land and profits; usually passes to the new owner unless reserved to a previous grantor.

Minor: All persons under 18 years of age.

Misplaced Improvements: Improvements on land which do not conform to the most profitable use of the site.

Modular: A building composed of modules constructed on an assembly line in a factory. Usually, the modules are self-contained.

Moldings: Usually patterned strips used to provide ornamental variation of outline or contour, such as cornices, bases, window and door jambs.

Monetary Controls: Federal Reserve tools for regulating the availability of money and credit to influence the level of economic activity.

Monument: A fixed object and point established by surveyors to establish land locations.

Moratorium: The temporary suspension, usually by statute, of the enforcement of liability for debt.

Mortgage: An instrument recognized by law by which property is hypothecated to secure the payment of a debt or obligation; procedure for foreclosure in event of default is established by statute.

Mortgage Contracts with Warrants: Warrants make the mortgage more attractive to the lender by providing both the greater security that goes with a mortgage, and the opportunity of a greater return through the right to buy either stock in the borrower's company or a portion of the income property itself.

Mortgage Guaranty Insurance: Insurance against financial loss available to mortgage lenders from Mortgage Guaranty Insurance Corporation, a private company organized in 1956.

Mortgagee: One to whom a mortgagor gives a mortgage to secure a loan or performance of an obligation, a lender. (See definition of *Secured Party.*)

Mortgagor: One who gives a mortgage on his property to secure a loan or assure performance of an obligation; a borrower. (See definition of *Debtor.*)

Multiple Listing: A listing, usually an exclusive right to sell, taken by a member of an organization composed of real estate brokers, with the provisions that all members will have the opportunity to find an interested client; a cooperative listing.

Mutual Consent: In a contract it is the meeting of the minds with a proper offer and acceptance.

Mutual Water Company: A water company organized by or for water users in a given district with the object of securing an ample water supply at a reasonable rate; stock is issued to users.

N

NAREB: National Association of Real Estate Brokers.

NAR: National Association of Realtors®.

Narrative Appraisal: A summary of all factual materials, techniques and appraisal methods used by the appraiser in setting forth his value conclusion.

Negotiable: Capable of being negotiated; assignable or transferable in the ordinary course of business.

Negotiable Instruments: Any instrument transferable by endorsement or delivery. Examples are promissory notes, checks, drafts that are allowed to circulate as money does.

Net Listing: A listing which provides that the agent may retain as compensation for his services all sums received over and above a net price to the owner.

Net Multipliers: The amount that a business would sell for, based upon the multiplication of its annual net income by some standardized number, or multiplier.

Nominal Interest Rates: The percentage of interest that is stated in loan documents.

Notary Public: An appointed officer with authority to take the acknowledgment of persons executing documents, to sign the certificate and affix his or her seal.

Note: A signed written instrument acknowledging a debt and promising payment.

Notice: Actual knowledge acquired by being present at the occurrence.

Notice of Default: The public filing of a delinquent loan that gives legal notice of a pending foreclosure.

Notice of Nonresponsibility: A notice provided by law designed to relieve a property owner from responsibility for the cost of work done on the property or materials furnished therefor; notice must be verified, recorded and posted.

Notice of Work Completed/Not Completed: A report that states any termite work completed or not completed on specific property.

Notice to Quit: A notice to a tenant to vacate rented property.

O

Obsolescence: Loss in value due to reduced desirability and usefulness of a structure because its design and construction become obsolete; loss because of becoming old-fashioned and not in keeping with modern needs, with consequent loss in income.

Offset Statement: Statement by owner of property or owner of lien against property, setting forth the present status of liens against said property.

Open-End Mortgage: A mortgage containing a clause which permits the mortgagor to borrow additional money after the loan has been reduced, without rewriting the mortgage.

Open Housing Law: Congress passed a law in April 1968 which prohibits discrimination in the sale of real estate because of race, color, or religion of buyers.

Open Listing: An authorization given by a property owner to a real estate agent wherein said agent is given the non exclusive rights to secure a purchaser; open listings may be given to any number of agents without liability to compensate any except the one who first secures a buyer ready, willing and able to meet the terms of the listing, or secures the acceptance by the seller of a satisfactory offer.

Opinion of title: An attorney's evaluation of the condition of the title to a parcel of land after his examination of the abstract of title to the land.

Option: A right given for a consideration to purchase or lease a property upon specified terms within a specified time.

Oral Contract: A verbal agreement; one which is not reduced to writing.

Orientation: Placing a house on its lot with regard to its exposure to the rays of the sun, prevailing winds, privacy from the street and protection from outside noises.

Overhang: The part of the roof extending beyond the walls, to shade buildings and cover walks.

Over Improvement: An improvement which is not the highest and best use for the site on which it is placed by reason of excess size or cost.

P

Parquet Floor: Hardwood flooring laid in squares or patterns.

Participation: In addition to base interest on mortgage loans on income properties, a small percentage of gross income is required, sometimes predicated on certain conditions being fulfilled, such as minimum occupancy or a percentage of net income after expenses, debt service and taxes.

Partition Action: Court proceedings by which co-owners seek to sever their joint ownership.

Partnership: A decision of the California Supreme Court has defined a partnership in the following terms: " A partnership as between partners themselves may be defined to be a contract of two or more persons to unite their property, labor or skill, or some of them, in prosecution of some joint or lawful business, and to share the profits in certain proportions."

Party Wall: A wall erected on the line between two adjoining properties, which are under different ownership, for the use of both properties.

Par Value: Market value, nominal value.

Patent: Conveyance of title to government land.

Penalty: An extra payment or charge required of the borrower for deviating from the terms of the original loan agreement. Usually levied for being late in making regular payment or for paying off the loan before it is due.

Penny: The term, as applied to nails, serves as a measure of nail length and is abbreviated by the letter "d."

Percentage Lease: Lease on the property, the rental for which is determined by amount of business dome by the lessee; usually a percentage of gross receipts from the business with provision for a minimum rental.

Perimeter Heating: Baseboard heating, or any system in which the heat registers are located along the outside walls of a room, especially under the windows.

Personal Defenses: Refers to those refusals to pay on the negotiable instrument that are valid against a holder but not a holder in due course. Examples include failure of consideration and misrepresentation.

Personal Property: Any property which is not real property.

Pest Control Inspection Report: A report from a licensed operator showing a range of pests that damage and destroy wood.

Physical Deterioration: Impairment of condition. Loss in value brought about by wear and tear, disintegration, use and actions of the elements.

Pier: A column of masonry, usually rectangular in horizontal cross section, used to support other structural members.

Pitch: The incline or rise of a roof.

Planned Unit Development (PUD): A land use design which provides intensive utilization of the land through a combination of private and common areas with pre-arranged sharing of responsibilities for the common areas.

Plate: A horizontal board placed on a wall or supported on posts or studs to carry the trusses of a roof or rafters directly; a shoe, or base member as of a partition or other frame; a small flat board placed on or in a wall to support girders, rafters, etc.

Plat Map: The public record of maps of subdivided land showing the division of the land into blocks, lots, and parcels indicating the dimensions of various parcels.

Pledge: The depositing of personal property by a debtor with a creditor as security for a debt or engagement.

Pledgee: One who is given a pledge or a security. (See definition of *Secured Party.*)

Pledgor: One who offers a pledge or gives security. (See definition of *debtor.*)

Plottage Increment: The appreciation in unit value created by joining smaller ownerships into one large single ownership.

Plywood: Laminated wood made up in panels; several thicknesses of wood glued together with grain at different angles for strength.

Points: Under FHA-insured or VA-guaranteed loans, discounts or points paid to lenders are, in effect, prepaid interest, and are used by lenders to adjust the effective interest rate so that it is equal to or nearly equal to the prevailing market rate (the rate charged on conventional loans). The discounts are absorbed by the sellers and a point is one percent of the loan amount. On FHA-insured and VA-guaranteed loans, buyers may be charged only one percent "service charge." This restriction does not apply to conventional loans. Under conventional loans the charge for making a loan at most institutions is usually called a "loan fee," "service charge," "commitment fee," or may be referred to as "points to the buyer."

Police Power: The right of the State to enact laws and enforce them for the order, safety, health, morals and general welfare of the public.

Power of Attorney: An instrument authorizing a person to act as the agent of the person granting it, and a general power authorizing the agent to act generally in behalf of the principal. A special power limits the agent to a particular or specific act as: a landowner may grant an agent special power of attorney to convey a single and specific parcel of property. Under the provisions of a general power of attorney, the agent having the power may convey any or all property of the principal granting the general power of attorney.

Prefabricated House: A house manufactured and sometimes partly assembled, before delivery to building site.

Preliminary Report of Title: A report that is issued before a title insurance policy generally at the time an escrow is opened.

Prepaid Items of Expense: Prorations of prepaid items of expense which are credited to the seller in the closing statement.

Prepayment: Provision made for loan payments to be larger than those specified in the note.

Prepayment Penalty: Penalty for the payment of a mortgage or trust deed note before it actually becomes due if the note does not provide for prepayment.

Present Value: The lump sum value today of an annuity. A $100 bill to be paid to someone in *one year is* worth *less* than if it were a $100 bill to be paid to someone *today.* This is due to several things, one of which is that the money has *time value. How* much the $100 bill to be paid in one year is worth today will depend on the interest rate that seems proper for the particular circumstances. For example, if 6% is the appropriate rate, the $100 to be paid one year from now would be worth $94.34 today.

Presumption: A rule of law that courts and judges shall draw a particular inference from a particular fact, or from particular evidence, unless and until the truth of such inference is disproved.

Prima Facie: Presumptive on its face.

Principal: This term is used to mean either the employer of an agent or the amount of money borrowed or the amount of the loan.

Principal Note: The promissory note which is secured by the mortgage or trust deed.

Privity: Mutual relationship to the same rights of property, contractual relationship.

Probate: The formal judicial proceeding to prove or confirm the validity of a will, to collect the assets of the estate and to pay debts and taxes with the remainder to pass to those designated as heirs.

Procuring Cause: That cause originating from series of events that, without break in continuity, results in the prime object of an agent's employment producing a final buyer.

Progression, Principle of: The worth of a lesser valued residence tends to be enhanced by association with many higher valued residences in the same area.

Progress Sheet: A printed checkoff form used in escrow to keep track of the items that are required to be ordered and when they are received.

Promissory Note: Following a loan commitment from the lender, the borrower signs a note, promising to repay the loan under stipulated terms. The promissory note establishes personal liability for its repayment.

Property: The rights of ownership. The right to use, possess, enjoy, and dispose of a thing in every legal way and to exclude everyone else from interfering with these rights. Property is generally classified into two groups, personal property and real property.

Property Taxes: Tax levied against real property by local agencies and municipalities. They are levied for the general support of government.

Proper Writing: Refers to the requirements of law that states certain contracts must be in writing to be enforceable.

Proration: Adjustments of interest, taxes, and insurance, etc., on a pro-rata basis as of the closing date. Fire insurance is normally paid for three years in advance. If a property is sold during this time, the seller wants a refund on that portion of the advance payment that has not been used at the time the title to the property is transferred. For example, if the property is sold two years later, he will want to receive 113 of the advance premium that was paid.

Proration of Taxes: To divide or prorate the taxes equally or proportionately to time of use.

Proximate Cause: That cause of an event is that which, in a natural and continuous sequence unbroken by any new cause, produced that event, and without which the event would not have happened. Also, the procuring cause.

Public Trustee: The county public official whose office has been created by statute, to whom title to real property, in certain states, e.g., Colorado, is conveyed by Trust Deed for the use and benefit of the beneficiary, who usually is the lender.

Public Utility Easement: An easement that gives utility companies the right to construct and maintain pipes and power lines through property.

Purchase and Installment Saleback: Involves purchase of the property upon completion of construction and immediate saleback on a long-term installment contract.

Purchase of Land, Leaseback and Leasehold Mortgages: An arrangement whereby land is purchased by the lender and leased back to the developer with a mortgage negotiated on the resulting leasehold of the income property constructed. The lender receives an annual ground rent, plus a percentage of income from the property.

Purchase and Leaseback: Involves, the purchase of property subject to an existing mortgage and immediate leaseback.

Purchase Money Deed of Trust: A deed of trust given as part of the purchase price.

Purchase Money Mortgage or Trust Deed: A trust deed or mortgage given as part or all of the purchase consideration for property. In some states the purchase money mortgage or trust deed loan can be made by a seller who extends credit to the buyer of property or by a third party lender (typically a financial institution) that makes a loan to the buyer of real property for a portion of the purchase price to be paid for the property. (In many states there are legal limitations upon mortgagees and trust deed beneficiaries collecting deficiency judgments against the purchase money borrower after the collateral hypothecated under such security instruments has been sold through the foreclosure process. Generally no deficiency judgment is allowed if the collateral property under the mortgage or trust deed is residential property of four units or less with the debtor occupying the property as a place of residence.)

Q-R

Qualified Endorsement: An endorsement that limits liability in the event of a refusal to pay by the maker.

Quantity Survey: A highly technical process in arriving at cost estimate of new construction, and sometimes referred to in the building trade as the *price take-off* method. It involves a detailed estimate of the quantities of raw material lumber, plaster, brick, cement, etc. used, as well as the current price of the material and installation costs. These factors are all added together to arrive at the cost of a structure. It is usually used by contractors and experienced estimators.

Quarter Round: A molding that presents a profile of a quarter circle.

Quiet Enjoyment: Right of an owner to the use of the property without interference of possession.

Quiet Title: A court action brought to establish title; to remove a cloud on the title.

Quitclaim Deed: A deed to relinquish any interest in property which the grantor may have.

Radiant Heating: A method of heating, usually consisting of coils or pipes placed in the floor, wall, or ceiling.

Rafter: One of a series of boards of a roof designed to support roof loads. The rafters of a flat roof are sometimes called *roof joists.*

Range: A strip of land six miles wide determined by a government survey, running in a north-south direction.

Ratification: The adoption or approval of an act performed on behalf of a person without previous authorization.

Real Defenses: Those defenses are valid against a holder in due course. Sometimes called universal defenses and may include matters as forgery and alteration of the instrument.

Real Estate Board: An organization whose members consist primarily of real estate brokers and salesmen.

Real Estate Investment Counselor: The broker's broker or consultant, doing for other brokers what those brokers cannot do for themselves, until their own knowledge and experience is of such magnitude as to qualify them for similar status.

Real Estate Licensees: A licensee by the Department of Real Estate capable of representing buyers or sellers in a real estate transaction.

Real Estate Settlement Procedures Act: A federal disclosure law effective June 20, 1975, requiring new procedures and forms for settlements (closing costs) involving federally related loans.

Real Estate Trust: A special arrangement under Federal and State law whereby investors may pool funds for investments in real estate and mortgages and yet escape corporation taxes.

Real Property: Land and those things affixed to it.

Real Property Securities Dealer (RPSD): Engaged in the secondary market, in addition to a host of activities that come under the definition of real property securities.

Realtist: A real estate broker holding active membership in a real estate board affiliated with the National Association of Real Estate Brokers.

Realtor®: A real estate broker holding active membership in a real estate board affiliated with the National Association of Realtors®.

Recapture: The rate of interest necessary to provide for the return of an investment. Not to be confused with interest rate, which is a rate of interest on an investment.

Reconveyance: The transfer of the title of land from one person to the immediate preceding owner. This particular instrument of transfer is commonly used when the performance or debt is satisfied under the terms of a deed of trust, when the trustee conveys the title he or she has held on condition back to the owner.

Recording: The process of placing a document on file with a designated public official for everyone to **see.** This public official is usually a county officer known as the *County Recorder*. He or she designates the fact that a document has been given to him or her by placing his or her stamp upon it indicating the time of day and the date when it was officially placed on file. Documents filed with the Recorder are considered to be placed on open notice to the general public of that county. Claims against property usually are given a priority on the basis of the time and the date *they* are recorded with the most preferred claim status going to the earliest one recorded and the next claim going to the next earliest one recorded, and so on. This type of notice is called "constructive notice" or "legal notice."

Recording Fee: Required by the County Recorder for recording deeds, etc. The fee will vary by county.

Recourse: An instrument where the holder or endorsee may take legal action against the endorser in the event of default.

Redemption: Buying back one's property after a judicial sale.

Refinancing: The paying-off of an existing obligation and assuming **a** new obligation in its place.

Reformation: An action to correct a mistake in a deed or other document.

Rehabilitation: The restoration of a property to satisfactory condition without drastically changing the plan, form or style of architecture.

Release Clause: This is a stipulation that upon the payment of a specific sum of money to the holder of a trust deed or mortgage, the lien of the instrument as to a specific described lot or area shall be removed from the blanket lien on the whole area involved.

Release Deed: An instrument executed by the mortgagee or the trustee reconveying to the mortgagor the real estate which secured the mortgage loan after the debt has been paid in full. Upon recording it cancels the mortgage lien created when the mortgage or trust deed was recorded.

Remainder: An estate which takes effect after the termination of the prior estate, such as a life estate.

Remainder Depreciation: The possible loss in value of an improvement which will occur in the future.

Rental Agreement: Agreement between landlord and tenant specifying the terms and conditions of the residential agreement.

Rent Statement: Prepared by the owner that shows the status of tenants and the amounts of rent paid to certain dates.

Replacement Cost: The cost to replace the structure with one having utility equivalent to that being appraised, but constructed with modern materials, and according to current standards, design and layout.

Report: Refers to a structural pest control report that lists all the damage seen, its location in the structure, and the planned method of treatment with the cost.

Reproduction Costs: The cost of replacing the subject improvement with one that is the exact replica, having the same quality of workmanship, design, and layout.

Request for Full Reconveyance: Written to the trustee of record requesting that the trustee execute the reconveyance.

Request for Notice: When recorded, a trustee in a foreclosure is required to notify all persons requesting notice if a notice of default is recorded on a specific property.

Rescission of Contract: The abrogation or annulling of contract; the revocation or repealing of contract by mutual consent by parties to the contract, or for cause by either party to the contract.

Reservation: A right retained by a grantor in conveying property.

RESPA: Real Estate Settlement Procedures Act.

Restriction: The term as used relating to real property means the owner of real property is restricted or prohibited from doing certain things relating to the property, or using the property for certain purposes. Property restrictions fall into two general classifications — public and private. Zoning ordinances are examples of the former type. Restrictions may be created by private owners, typically by appropriate clauses in deeds, or in agreements, or in general plans of en-tire subdivisions. Usually they assume the form of a covenant, or

promise to do or not to do a certain thing. They cover a multitude of matters including use for residential or business purposes, e.g. houses in tract must cost more than $25,000 etc.

Restrictive Endorsement: An endorsement that prevents further negotiation.

Retrospective Value: The value of the property as of a previous date.

Reversion: The right to future possession or enjoyment by the person, or his or her heirs, creating the preceding estate.

Reversionary Interest: The interest which a person has in lands or other property, upon the termination of the preceding estate.

Ridge: The horizontal line at the junction of the top edges of two sloping roof surfaces. The rafters at both slopes are nailed at the ridge.

Ridge Board: The board placed on edge at the ridge of the roof to support the upper ends of the rafters; also called roof tree, ridge piece, ridge plate or ridgepole.

Right of Survivorship: Right to acquire the interests of a deceased joint owner; distinguishing feature of a joint tenancy.

Right of Way: A privilege operating as an easement upon land, whereby the owner does by grant, or by agreement, give to another the right to pass over his or her land, to construct a roadway, or use as a roadway, a specific part of his or her land, or the right to construct through and over his or her land, telephone, telegraph, or electric power lines, or the right to place underground water mains, gas mains, or sewer mains.

Riparian Rights: The right of a landowner to water on, under, or adjacent to his or her land.

Riser: The upright board at the back of each step of a stairway. In heating, a riser is a duct slanted upward to carry hot air from the furnace to the room above.

Risk Analysis: A study made, usually by a lender, of the various factors that might affect the repayment of a loan.

Risk Rating: A process used by the lender to decide on the soundness of making a loan and to reduce all the various factors affecting the repayment of the loan to a qualified rating of some kind.

Roman Brick: Thin brick of slimmer proportions than standard building brick.

S

Sales Contract: A contract by which buyer and seller agree to terms of a sale.

Sale Escrow Memo Sheet: A memo sheet when completed will contain all the information necessary to start an escrow.

Sale-Leaseback: A situation where the owner of a piece of property wishes to sell the property and retain occupancy by leasing it from the buyer.

Sandwich Lease: A leasehold interest which lies between the primary lease and the operating lease.

Sash: Wood or metal frames containing one or more window panes.

Satisfaction: Discharge of mortgage or trust deed lien from the records upon payment of the evidenced debt.

Satisfaction of Judgment: A legal document when filed with the record will release a previous judgment lien.

Satisfaction Piece: An instrument for recording and acknowledging payment of an indebtedness secured by a mortgage.

Schedule A: Part of the preliminary title report that is reserved for the identification of the recorded owner and the property in question.

Schedule B: Part of the preliminary title report that shows the encumbrances of record.

Scribing: Fitting woodwork to an irregular surface.

Seal: An impression made to attest the execution of an instrument.

Seasoned Loan: Refers to a loan paid by a borrower who has a stable and consistent loan history of payments. It indicates that the loan is not a new one and would be a better purchase risk.

Secondary Financing: A loan secured by a second mortgage or trust deed on real property. These can be third, fourth, fifth, sixth … on and on ad infinitum.

Second Party: The one designated by escrow to distinguish from the first party.

Second Trust Deed: A junior trust deed to other loans having priority.

Secured Party: This is the party having the security interest. Thus the *mortgagee*, the *conditional seller*, the *pledgee*, etc., are all now referred to as the secured party.

Security Agreement and Financing Statement: Shows the debtor's name and address (cosigners and trade names would be included); the secured party's name and address (assignee); description and nature of the property used as collateral; and other items.

Security Interest: A term designating the interest of the creditor in the property of the debtor in all types of credit transactions. It thus re-places such terms as the following: *chattel mortgage; pledge; trust receipt; chattel trust; equipment trust; conditional sale; inventory lien;* etc.

Section: Section of land is established by government survey and contains 640 acres.

Seizin: Possession of real estate by one entitled thereto.

Seller Credit: An increase to the sellers side such as sales price and other increases as prorations.

Seller Debit: An offset or charge against the seller's credits.

Separate Property: Property owned by a husband or wife which is not community property; property acquired by either spouse prior to marriage or by gift or devise after marriage.

Septic Tank: An underground tank in which sewage from the house is reduced to liquid by bacterial action and drained off.

Servicing: Supervising and administering a loan after it has been made. This involves such things as: collecting the payments, keeping accounting records, computing the interest and principal, foreclosure of defaulted loans, and so on.

Servient Tenement: The owner of land whose property is subject to an easement for the benefit of adjoining land.

Set-Back Ordinance: An ordinance prohibiting the erection of a building or structure between the curb and the setback line.

Settlement Sheet: Also called a closing statement or adjustment sheet. The statement shows how all closing and adjustment costs plus prepaid and unpaid expenses are allocated between buyer and seller. Separate closing statements are prepared for the buyer showing credits, charges and the balance due at closing; for the seller it shows credits, charges and the proceeds they will receive at closing.

Severalty: Ownership by one person or corporation.

Shake: A hand-split shingle, usually edge grained.

Sheathing: Structural covering usually boards, plywood, or wallboards, placed over exterior studding or rafters of a house.

Sheriff's Deed: Deed given by court order in connection with sale of property to satisfy a judgment.

Shopping Center, Regional: A large shopping center with 250,000 to 1,000,000 square feet of store area, serving 200,000 or more people.

Short Form: A recordable document such as a trust deed that simply recites the fact that a contract has been made between the parties covering certain described property.

Sill: The lowest part of the frame of a house, resting on the foundation and supporting the uprights of the frame. The board or metal forming the lower side of an opening, as a door sill, window sill, etc.

Sinking Fund: Fund set aside from the income from property which, with accrued interest, will eventually pay for replacement of the improvements.

SIR: Society of Industrial Realtors.

Soil Pipe: Pipe carrying waste out from the house to the main sewer line.

Sold to the State: A tax collector book transaction to initiate the beginning of a redemption period at the end of which title does pass to the state.

Sole or Sole Plate: A member, usually a 2 by 4, on which wall and partition studs rest.

Span: The distance between structural supports such as walls, columns, piers, beams, girders, and trusses.

Special Assessment: Legal charge against real estate by a public authority to pay cost of public improvements such as: street lights, sidewalks, street improvements, etc.

Special Endorsement: An endorsement that specifies the person to whom or to whose order the instrument is payable.

Special Warranty Deed: A deed in which the grantor warrants or guarantees the title only against defects arising during his ownership of the property and not against defects existing before the time of his ownership.

Specific Liens: Liens which attach to only a certain specific parcel of land or piece of property.

Specific Performance: An action to compel performance of an agreement, e.g., sale of land.

S.R.A.: Designates a person who is a member of the Society of Real Estate Appraisers.

SREA: Society of Real Estate Appraisers.

Stakeholder: Refers to the role of an escrow holder.

Standard Depth: Generally the most typical lot depth in the neighborhood.

Standard Notice of Work Completed and Not Completed: The written report of the pest control operator with a clearance of work completed or not completed together with the statement of charges.

Standard Provisions: Standard escrow provisions usually on the reverse side which are part of the contract. They state who will pay for what and gives escrow directions as to the accepted procedure for implementing the items.

Standby Commitment: The mortgage banker frequently protects a builder by a "standby" agreement, under which he or she agrees to make mortgage loans at an agreed price for many months in the future. The builder deposits a "standby fee" with the mortgage banker for this service. Frequently, the mortgage banker protects himself or herself by securing a "standby" from a long-term investor for the same period of time, paying a fee for this privilege.

Statement of Information: A confidential form prepared for the title and escrow company to insure against mistaken identity.

Status: Refers to the legal character or condition of how a person holds title, i.e., Married, Single, etc.

Statute of Frauds: State law which provides that certain contracts must be in writing in order to be enforceable at law. Examples: real property lease for more than one year; agent's authorization to sell real estate.

Statutory Warranty Deed: A short form warranty deed which warrants by inference that the seller is the undisputed owner and has the right to convey the property and that he or she will defend the title if necessary. This type of deed protects the purchaser in that the conveyor covenants to defend all claims against the property. If he or she fails to do so, the new owner can defend said claims and sue the former owner.

Straight-Line Depreciation: Definite sum set aside annually from income to pay cost of replacing improvements, without reference to interest it earns.

Straight Note: Written so that the entire sum of principal and interest come due and payable on a specified date usually in a lump sum.

String, Stringer: A timber or other support for cross members. In stairs, the support on which the stair treads rest.

Studs or Studding: Vertical supporting timbers in the walls and partitions.

Subdivided Lands Act: State law that grants the Real Estate Commissioner authority to administer necessary regulations to protect purchasers from fraud, misrepresentation, or deceit in the initial sale of subdivided property.

Subdivision Map Act: State law that allow local government direct control over the types of subdivision ordinances and control over the projects and improvements to be installed.

Subject to Mortgage: When a grantee takes a title to real property subject to mortgage, he or she is not responsible to the holder of the promissory note for the payment of any portion of the amount due. The most that he or she can lose in the event of a foreclosure is his or her equity in the property. See also "assumption of mortgage" in this section. In neither case is the original maker of the note released from his or her responsibility.

Sublease: A lease given by a lessee.

Subordinate: To make subject to, or junior to.

Subordination Clause: Clause in a junior or a second lien permitting retention of priority for prior liens. A subordination clause may also be used in a first deed of trust permitting it to be subordinated to subsequent liens as, for example, the liens of construction loans.

Subpoena: A process to cause a witness to appear and give testimony.

Subrogation: The substitution of another person in place of the creditor, to whose rights he or she succeeds in relation to the debt. The doctrine is used very often where one person agrees to at and surety for the performance of a contract by another person.

Substitution, Principle of: Affirms that the maximum value of a property tends to be set by the cost of acquiring an equally desirable and valuable substitute property, assuming no costly delay is encountered in making the substitution.

Subterranean Termites: A specific breed of termites which breed in the ground and tunnel to nearby to eat.

Sufficient Consideration: Contractual requirement that value must be exchanged for value.

Sum-of-the-Years Digits: An accelerated depreciation method.

Supplement to Instructions: When there is limited space to list all items in an escrow, a supplement is prepared (not an amendment) as an extra page that does not modify the original instruction.

Supply and Demand, Principle of: Affirms that price or value varies directly, but not necessarily proportionally with demand, and inversely, but not necessarily proportionately with supply.

Surety: One who guarantees the performance of another: Guarantor.

Surplus Productivity, Principle of: Affirms that the net income that remains after the proper costs of labor, organization and capital have been paid, which surplus is imputable to the land and tends to fix the value thereof.

Survey: The process by which a parcel of land is measured and its area is ascertained.

Syndicate: A partnership organized for participation in a real estate venture. Partners may be limited or unlimited in their liability.

T

Take-Out Loan: The loan arranged by the owner or builder developer for a buyer. The construction loan made for construction of the improvements is usually paid from the proceeds of this loan.

Tax Deed: A deed that conveys title sold by a governmental agency for nonpayment of taxes.

Tax-Free Exchange: Income property exchanged on an even basis for other income property which does not have to pay a capital gain tax at the time.

Tax Sale: Sale of property after a period of nonpayment of taxes.

Tenancy in Common: Ownership by two or more persons who hold undivided interest, without right of survivorship; interests need not be equal.

Tenants by the Entireties: Under certain state laws, ownership of property acquired by a husband and wife during marriage which is jointly owned. Upon death of one spouse, it becomes the property of the survivor.

Tentative Map: The Subdivision Map Act requires subdividers to submit initially a tentative map of their tract to the local planning commission for study. The approval or disapproval of the planning commission is noted on the map. Thereafter a final

map of the tract embodying any changes requested by the planning commission is required to be filed with the planning commission.

Tenure in Land: The mode or manner by which an estate in lands is held.

Termites: Ant-like insects which feed on wood.

Termite Shield: A shield, usually of non corrodible metal, placed on top of the foundation wall or around pipes to prevent passage of termites.

Testator: One who leaves a will in force at his death.

Threshold: A strip of wood or metal beveled on each edge and used above the finished floor under outside doors.

Tickler System: A review system that reminds the escrow officer to check each file periodically to see that important matters are attended to. It may involve a desk calendar, or affixing color coded tabs to each file.

Tiers: A row of townships extending east and west.

Time Is the Essence: One of the essential requirements to forming of a binding contract; contemplates a punctual performance.

Title: Evidence that owner of land is in lawful possession thereof, an instrument evidencing such ownership.

Title Insurance: Insurance written by a title company to protect property owner against loss if title is imperfect.

Title Order: A request to the title officer to begin preparation of the Preliminary Report of Title.

Title Report: A report which discloses condition of the title, made by a title company preliminary to issuance of title insurance.

Title Theory: Mortgage arrangement whereby title to mortgaged real property vests in the lender.

Topography: Nature of the surface of land; topography may be level, rolling, mountainous.

Torrens Title: System of title records provided by state law (no longer used in California).

Tort: A wrongful act; wrong, injury; violation of a legal right.

Township: A territorial subdivision six miles long, six miles wide and containing 36 sections, each one mile square.

Trade Fixtures: Articles of personal property annexed to real property, but which are necessary to the carrying on of a trade and are removable by the owner.

Trade-In: An increasingly popular method of guaranteeing an owner a minimum amount of cash on sale of his or her present property to permit him or her to purchase another. If the property is not sold within a specified time at the listed price, the broker agrees to arrange financing to purchase the property at an agreed-upon discount.

Treads: Horizontal boards of a stairway.

Trim: The finish materials in a building, such as moldings, applied around openings (window trim, door trim) or at the floor and ceiling (baseboard, cornice, picture molding).

Trust Account: An account separate and apart and physically segregated from broker's own funds, in which broker is required by law to deposit all funds collected for clients.

Trust Deed: Just as with a mortgage, this is a legal document by which a borrower pledges certain real property or collateral as guarantee for the repayment of a loan. However, it differs from the mortgage in a number of important respects. For example, instead of there being two parties to the transaction, there are three. There is the borrower who gives the trust deed and who is called the trustor. There is the third, neutral party (just as there is with an escrow) who receives the trust deed and who is called the trustee. And, finally, there is the lender who is called the beneficiary since he or she is the one who benefits from the pledge arrangement in that in the event of a default the trustee can sell the property and transfer the money obtained at the sale to him or her as payment of the debt.

Trustee: One who holds property in trust for another to secure the performance of an obligation.

Trustee Deed: A deed given at a foreclosure sale. Not to be confused with a trust deed.

Trustor: One who deeds his or her property to a trustee to be held as security until he or she has performed his or her obligation to a lender under terms of a deed of trust.

U

Under Improvement: An improvement which, because of its deficiency in size or cost, is not the highest and best use of the site.

Underwriting: The technical analysis by a lender to determine the borrower's ability to repay a contemplated loan.

Undue Influence: Taking any fraudulent or unfair advantage of another's weakness of mind, or distress or necessity.

Unearned Increment: An increase in value of real estate due to no effort on the part of the owner; often due to increase in population.

Uniform Commercial Code (UCC): Establishes a unified and comprehensive scheme for regulation of security transactions in personal property, superseding the existing statutes on chattel mortgages, conditional sales, trust receipts, assignment of accounts receivable and others in this field.

Unit-In-Place Method: The cost of erecting a building by estimating the cost of each component part, i.e. foundations, floors, walls, windows, ceilings, roofs, etc. (including labor and overhead).

Urban Property: City property; closely settled property.

U.S. Government Survey: One of three legal description methods that rely on principal meridian and base lines that survey designated areas into checkerboard squares.

Usury: On a loan, claiming a rate of interest greater than that permitted by law.

Utilities: Refers to services rendered by public utility companies, such as: water, gas, electricity, telephone.

Utility: The ability to give satisfaction and/or excite desire for possession.

V

Valid: Having force, or binding force; legally sufficient and authorized by law.

Valley: The internal angle formed by the junction of two sloping sides of a roof.

Valuation: Estimated worth or price. Estimation. The act of valuing by appraisal.

Valuation Form: A form used to calculate the exchange of properties to be sure the elements of the exchange balance out and are understood by the escrow officer before instructions are prepared.

Vendee: A purchaser; buyer.

Vendor: A seller; one who disposes of a thing in consideration of money.

Veneer: Thin sheets of wood.

Vent: A pipe installed to provide a flow of air to or from a drainage system or to provide a circulation of air within such system to protect trap seals from siphonage and back pressure.

Verification: Sworn statement before a duly qualified officer to correctness of contents of an instrument.

Vested: Bestowed upon someone; secured by someone, such as a title to property.

Void: To have no force or effect; that which is unenforceable.

Voidable: That which is capable of being adjudged void, but is not void unless action is taken to make it so.

Voluntary Lien: A lien placed on property with consent of, or as a result of, the voluntary act of the owner.

W-Z

Wainscoting: Wood lining of an interior wall; lower section of a wall when finished differently from the upper part.

Waive: To relinquish, or abandon; to forego a right to enforce or require anything.

Warranty Deed: A deed used to convey real property which contains warranties of title and quiet possession, and the grantor thus agrees to defend the premises against the lawful claims of third persons. It is commonly used in many states but in others the grant deed has supplanted it due to the modern practice of securing title insurance policies which have reduced the importance of express and implied warranty in deeds.

Waste: The destruction, or material alteration of, or injury to premises by a tenant for life or years.

Water Stock Certificate: Evidence of water stock issued to an owner of real property that entitles them to use of water. It is considered to be appurtenant to the property therefore transfers with the land.

Water Table: Distance from surface of ground to a depth at which natural groundwater is found.

Without Recourse: Prevents legal action against the endorser.

Wrap-Around Mortgage: Involves the borrower entering into a second mortgage. This arrangement represents the means by which he can add to his development without refinancing the first mortgage at substantially higher current rates.

Yield: The interest earned by an investor on his investment (or bank on the money it has lent). Also called *Return.*

Yield Rate: The yield expressed as a percentage of the total investment. Also called *Rate of Return.*

Zone: The area set off by the proper authorities for specific use; subject to certain restrictions or restraints.

Zoning: Act of city or county authorities specifying type of use to which property may be put in specific areas.

Index

Textbooks From Educational Textbook Company

Order Department

Sometimes our textbooks are hard to find!

If your bookstore does not carry our textbooks, send us a check or money order and we'll mail them to you with our 30-day money back guarantee.

Other Great Books from Educational Textbook Company:

California Real Estate Principles, 10th ed. (2nd Printing), by Huber. . . . . $65.00 _____
How To Pass The Real Estate Exam (850 Exam Questions), by Huber. . . . . $50.00 _____
California Real Estate Law, by Huber & Tyler. . . . . $50.00 _____
Real Estate Finance, by Huber & Messick. . . . . $50.00 _____
Real Estate Economics, by Huber, Messick, & Pivar. . . . . $50.00 _____
Real Estate Appraisal, by Huber, Messick, & Pivar. . . . . $50.00 _____
Mortgage Loan Brokering, by Huber & Pivar. . . . . $50.00 _____
Property Management, by Huber & Pivar. . . . . $50.00 _____
Escrow I: An Introduction, 3rd ed., by Huber & Newton. . . . . $50.00 _____
California Real Estate Practice, by Huber & Lyons. . . . . $50.00 _____
Real Estate Computer Applications, by Grogan & Huber. . . . . $50.00 _____
Homeowner's Association Management, by Huber & Tyler. . . . . $50.00 _____
California Business Law, by Huber, Owens, & Tyler. . . . . $65.00 _____
Hubie's Power Prep CD – 100 Questions - Vol. 1, by Huber. . . . . $50.00 _____

Subtotal _____
Add shipping and handling @ $5.00 per book _____
Add California sales tax @ 8.25% _____
TOTAL _____

Allow 2-3 weeks for delivery

Name: _____

Address: _____

City, State, Zip: _____

Phone: _____

Check or money order: Educational Textbook Company, P.O. Box 3597, Covina, CA 91722

For faster results, order by credit card from the Glendale Community College Bookstore:
1-818-240-1000 x3024
1-818-242-1561 (Direct)
Check us out at: www.etcbooks.com